TENTH EDITION

DEVIANT BEHAVIOR

☑ P9-CQO-137

ERICH GOODE

Emeritus, State University of New York at Stony Brook

PEARSON

Boston   Columbus   Indianapolis   New York   San Francisco   Upper Saddle River
Amsterdam   Cape Town   Dubai   London   Madrid   Milan   Munich   Paris   Montréal   Toronto
Delhi   Mexico City   São Paulo   Sydney   Hong Kong   Seoul   Singapore   Taipei   Tokyo

Editor in Chief: Ashley Dodge
Publisher: Nancy Roberts
Editorial Assistant: Molly White
Marketing Coordinator: Jessica Warren
Managing Editor: Denise Forlow
Program Manager: Mayda Bosco
Senior Operations Supervisor: Mary Fischer
Operations Specialist: Diane Peirano
Art Director: Jayne Conte
Cover Designer: Bruce Kenselaar
Cover Image: Shutterstock/mlkcorp
Director of Digital Media: Brian Hyland
Digital Media Project Manager: Tina Gagliostro
Full-Service Project Management and Composition: Sudip Sinha, PreMediaGlobal, Inc.
Printer/Binder: RR Donnelley/STP Crawford GT 31
Cover Printer: RR Donnelley/STP Crawford GT 31
Text Font: Times 10/11

Credits and acknowledgments borrowed from other sources and reproduced, with permission, in this textbook appear on appropriate page within the text or in the credit section beginning on page 350.

Copyright © 2015, 2011, 2008 by Pearson Education, Inc. All rights reserved. Printed in the United States of America. This publication is protected by Copyright and permission should be obtained from the publisher prior to any prohibited reproduction, storage in a retrieval system, or transmission in any form or by any means, electronic, mechanical, photocopying, recording, or likewise. To obtain permission(s) to use material from this work, please submit a written request to Pearson Education, Inc., Permissions Department, One Lake Street, Upper Saddle River, New Jersey 07458 or you may fax your request to 201-236-3290.

Many of the designations by manufacturers and seller to distinguish their products are claimed as trademarks. Where those designations appear in this book, and the publisher was aware of a trademark claim, the designations have been printed in initial caps or all caps.

Library of Congress Cataloging-in-Publication Data

Goode, Erich.
   Deviant behavior / Erich Goode, Stony Brook University. — Tenth Edition.
      pages cm
   Includes bibliographical references and index.
   ISBN-13: 978-0-205-89966-1
   ISBN-10: 0-205-89966-8
   1. Deviant behavior.   2. Criminal behavior.   I. Title.
   HM811.G66 2014
   302.5'42—dc23

                                                    2013049605

10 9 8 7 6 5 4 3 2 1

ISBN 10:   0-205-89966-8
ISBN 13: 978-0-205-89966-1

Brief Contents

Contents

Preface

In Brooklyn and Albany, a member of the New York State assembly makes unwanted sexual advances toward several female members of his staff; they file grievances against him, and are paid more than $100,000 to keep quiet about the incidents. In a small, quaint community on the coast of Maine, a grand jury indicts a twenty-nine-year-old woman for engaging in prostitution out of her fitness studio and secretly videotaping sessions with her clients. At Cambridge, Harvard University officials accuse 125 students with cheating on an exam. The Dean of Students at the University of Montana alleges that four football players gang-raped a female student. Several weeks later, officials fire the Grizzly coach, and after four months, Missoula prosecutors charge the quarterback with having "intercourse without consent" with the woman. Across America, gay teenagers are teased, taunted, even beaten, because of their effeminacy and sexual orientation. In rural, conservative school districts around the country, parents, teachers, board members, and administrators vehemently disagree about teaching of evolution in the public school curriculum. Nationwide, businesses shut down and go bankrupt, putting millions out of work, generating foreclosures, the loss of homes, poverty, and in some cases, homelessness—along with shame, humiliation, disgrace, and blame.

These are human interest stories, and they became media stories as well—but they also convey a sociological message. They tell us about accusations and imputations of wrongdoing; they tell us about transgressions, alleged or actualized, and about reactions by aggrieved parties or their supporters, and counter-reactions by accused parties. In short, they tell us about deviance.

The sociology of deviance is based on a concept that offers us a perspective, a point of view that rearranges our conception of taken-for-granted phenomena. Chances are that you, the reader, think about what you and others do, and who you and others are, in a certain way. But if you think sociologically about these things, you may have to put aside your preconceptions and substitute them for more fruitful ways of interpreting the social world. Most of us hold a distorted notion of what "deviance" is, and who the "deviant" is. In contrast, this book aims to offer a testament to how productive and perceptive the sociological view of deviance is.

The sociology of deviance reveals political processes at work. Referring to an act as an instance of sociological deviance argues that its negative quality is interpreted by persons who condemn it. More specifically, calling or treating behavior or beliefs *as* wrongful or deviant, is a political act. Evangelical Christians regard homosexuality as sinful, deviant—an orientation they feel they ought to condemn. The sociologist does not necessarily agree (or disagree) with the judgment, but takes note of it; the assertion that it *is* sinful is a sociological fact, and denouncing and punishing homosexuals, homosexuality, and homosexual acts has sociological consequences. Contending factions in various states struggle over the harmfulness and morality of and self-indulgence in marijuana use so that they can retain, or repeal, the laws outlawing the drug's possession and sale. Liberals and conservatives debate the virtue, iniquitousness, acceptability, or moral neutrality of abortion, birth control, pornography, gay marriage, capital punishment, acts that violate the law, the teaching of evolution versus creationism and intelligent design, atheism, obesity, and feminism. A major role of politics is designating what is good and bad and mobilizing the political and economic wherewithal to enforce that designation. Do the rich deserve their wealth? Should the poor be blamed for their poverty? Who is responsible for the financial crisis? What should be done about racism and discrimination, environmental protection, global warming, taxes, government spending, the deficit, the debt? About housing the homeless? How the mentally disordered ought to be treated? What about the obese? Is it okay to be fat? All of these are political and ideological questions; they are prompted by, and have implications for, the political order, and enforcing one or another interpretation of right and wrong is enacted as a consequence of the wielding of power, which is what politics are all about. And all such interpretations, in one way or another, address the question of what, and who, is deviant, whose version of wrong and right should be taken seriously, regarded as mainstream and hegemonic, and supported by the government, the educational system, the media. Should the deviant be socially and politically marginalized? Do we have the right to be fearful of people who are different from ourselves? Do we have the obligation to protect ourselves from those who are? Deviance is fraught with politics, and in neglecting this fundamental verity, the sociologist would be derelict in attempting to understand how the social world works.

This edition of *Deviant Behavior* offers an up-to-date discussion of behavior, conditions, and characteristics that are regarded as unacceptable, undesirable, and unwanted by members of certain social circles—those circles including the population at large, members of the criminal justice system, officials at the upper reaches of a given institution or organization, conservatives or liberals, evangelical Christians and atheists, the educated and the uneducated, residents of a single community and residents of many, rural dwellers urbanites, drinkers and teetolers. These social circles or collectivities may cohere for the lifetime of their members, and even those of their descendants, or they may exist simply by virtue of their attitudes on a given issue, only to vaporize for a different issue, assembling and reassembling as issues arise. Societies are made up of webs of varying strengths, some of which float off into the breeze almost day-by-day and are replaced with other equally flimsy and evanescent strands, others so strong they hold the social structure together for centuries.

The first edition of *Deviant Behavior* was published in 1978; this is the volume's tenth edition. During the interim, a great many changes have taken place—across the globe, in the society at large, in the field of sociology and the subfield of the sociology of deviance—and in the author's thinking. Public tolerance and even acceptance of many activities and views once regarded as seriously unacceptable and unconventional has increased, including gay sex, gay marriage, racial and gender equality, interracial marriage, the use of marijuana—in fact, acceptance and tolerance of a wide swath of activities that were once condemned has grown. Many of mainstream feminism's fundamental insights have become widely accepted, and the full participation of women in the marketplace is taken for granted; the feminist assault against pornography has virtually evaporated, and porn is freely available on the Internet in a flood that is literally unprecedented in human history. In September 1989, drug abuse was named by two-thirds of the respondents in a *New York Times*/CBS public opinion poll as the nation's number one social problem; after that, the issue virtually disappeared into the ozone (Oreskes, 1990). Today, the major problem is the economy—jobs, unemployment, the debt burden; politicians hardly ever mention the drug problem, and if they do, voters do not respond to its siren song. After 2001, a new deviant emerged on the landscape: the militant Muslim terrorist. After the 1990s, fear of crime receded as the crime rate declined. Racial prejudices and conflicts have likewise declined, though the intertwining of race and poverty remains. And, in the field of the sociology of deviance, publishers have put out dozens of texts, and most have fallen by the wayside, gone out of print. As for deviance texts, behaviors that past deviance texts once prominently featured—for instance, premarital sex, homosexuality, abortion, contraception, and pornography—have receded in importance, or heinousness, and have all but disappeared from their pages.

Three fundamental principles anchor the discussions throughout this book.

First, I emphasize that "deviance" is a morally neutral term; it *describes* and *analyzes* moral judgments but it does not share in them. Sociologists who use the term stress that its meaning pivots on the judgment of audiences, not the inherent wrongful or untoward nature of the behavior, condition, or characteristics themselves. Whenever critics of this sociological approach to deviance argue that we sociologists intend pathology or inherent wrongfulness when we use the term, they commit the fallacy of reification, or "misplaced concreteness"—that is, when the meaning of a term in one context is rigidly applied to all contexts. As it has been used in the past, as it is popularly used, and as it is used in clinical psychology and in psychiatry, "deviance" indicates a form of pathology or disorder. In contrast, in the field of sociology, it conveys no such meaning whatsoever. To sociologists, deviance means behavior, beliefs, conditions, or characteristics that violate a norm among the members of certain social circles, and tend to attract censure, condemnation, or punishment. The notion that the *use* of the term, "deviance," with reference to categories of behavior and of humanity that or who are widely disparaged *stigmatizes* them has become a tired cliché that should have been retired long ago. If these critics want us to use a different term, they should suggest one; either they haven't or those that they have suggested do not even remotely convey the conceptual territory we explore.

Second, throughout this volume, I stress the fact that definitions of deviance are relativistic and *poly-contextual*, multi-situational. By this I mean that what's considered wrongful and nonnormative is dependent on the audience who reacts to it, and varies as well from one context or situation to another. There is, in other words, a *horizontal* element to what's deviant. For example, as we cast our gaze around American society, we notice small circles of vegans who consider meat-eating wrongful, the violation of a sacred pact humans have with nature to protect our fellow animal creatures. Though they comprise a tiny minority of the population, vegans consider meat-eating *deviant*; many of them look upon human carnivores with an emotion that borders on disgust and disdain. But if we look across the map, we see that in Texas and Nebraska, the vegan is very likely to court a label of unconventionality, eccentricity, oddness in the extreme. Definitions of deviant need not be dominant, enshrined into law, or the ruling of the majority; deviance is only deviant *within* a particular context, *to* a particular audience. Of course, one possible audience could be the society at large; there's a *vertical* dimension to deviance as well as a horizontal one. Hegemony is not a necessary definitional component of the sociologist's definition of deviance. An act, belief, or trait may be deviance in one context and conventional in another. Hence, the argument that if definitions of deviance are not applied everywhere, throughout the entire society, at all times, it is invalid, false; in an increasingly post-modern society, such a definition proves bogus and nonsensical. Most

sociologists of deviance regard both the horizontal (from one context to another) and the vertical (for the society as a whole) perspectives relevant to judgments of deviance.

And third, I also emphasize that, though deviance entails normative violations, it is not, necessarily or by definition *willful* or intentional behavior; in fact, it may not be manifested in behavior at all. Ned Polsky argued that people who are not *morally* stigmatized should be excluded from the conceptualization of deviance—for instance, the unusually ugly—because they possess conditions or characteristics that are *not their fault* (1998, pp. 202–203). This is clearly wrong, and it is based on a blatantly non-sociological presumption. The fact is possessors of traits that are "not the individual's fault" *are* judged to be morally stigmatizing; their relations with others who do not possess these traits tend to become strained, awkward, and they themselves are pitied, scorned, derided, humiliated—in a word, considered *deviants*. Is this fair? Of course not! Is it common practice? Yes, it is. Correspondingly, in the sixth edition of this book (2001), I added a chapter on physical characteristics as deviant, and have retained it since then. In this edition, I have added two other chapters that discuss characteristics that are "not the individual's fault" but that likewise often attract scorn from specific audiences—race and ethnicity, which determine what Erving Goffman referred to as "tribal stigma" (1963, pp. 4–5), and poverty, which, in certain quarters, *is* considered the "fault" of the poor and which attracts what David Matza refers to as "disrepute" (1966a, 1971). Certain audiences who deride minority ethnicities and the poor "blame the victim" (Ryan, 1976), insisting that African Americans, Jews, or the very poor, are somehow responsible for their plight, and that the behavior of members of certain racial and ethnic categories, or the poverty-stricken, reflects that fact. Yes, members of the audiences who make such judgments are mistaken, racist, biased, and decidedly unfair. But under certain circumstances, these prejudiced audiences have the power to *deviantize* members of racial and ethnic categories, at least, in certain social circles, within specific contexts, and, at times, these audiences have enshrined their judgments into law. Unfair, indeed—but it points to a reality nonetheless, and one that we, as *observers* of our unfair society, have to investigate and learn about. Even unfair and mistaken judgments can become a reality that we need to study. In this edition, I have eliminated the chapter on research methods and refocused the chapter on organizational behavior to concentrate entirely on white collar and corporate crime.

In addition to the updates I've made to this edition, I have added and deleted a substantial amount of material. All of the accounts except one are new to this edition, and I solicited or gathered all of them. I consolidated the two former chapters on criminal behavior and violence, and consolidated the two on alcohol abuse and illicit drug use. The two chapters I added represent a substantial innovation with regard to the conventional content of the deviance text. The chapter on poverty and disrepute elaborates an idea which sociologist David Matza introduced decades ago (1966a, 1966b, 1971) that, with one exception (Ankleu, 1991), textbook authors have not incorporated into their discussions of deviance. The chapter on race and ethnicity examines Erving Goffman's "tribal stigma" (1963, pp. 4–5)— again, the attribution of a form of disrepute that sociologists have undeservedly excluded from the deviance curriculum. I believe that Matza, on poverty, and Goffman, on race and ethnicity, make extremely strong cases for introducing these novel topics into the general discourse on deviance. In suggesting these changes, I do not wish to court getting labeled as a crank or a curmudgeon, nor do I want to isolate myself from the sociological mainstream. These proposals may be ignored as an eccentricity; they may not be widely adopted, and it's even possible that instructors will find their inclusion disconcerting. But as I see it, their exclusion has been caused not by conceptual or analytic considerations, but has come about as the result of a narrow and hidebound way of thinking, the persistence of a mythology based on political correctness, and outright inertia. I suggest that embracing these topics strengthens the sociology of deviance, advances a broader conceptualization of the field, and offers a more focused analytic vision to our investigation. To me, it makes sense.

I owe a debt of gratitude to numerous friends, acquaintances, colleagues, or facilitators in helping me gather and assemble the material offered in this volume. Elizabeth Crane at SAMHSA

(Substance Abuse and Mental Health Services Administration) helped me make sense of the Drug Abuse Warning Network (DAWN) data. Dicy Painter and James Colliver at SAMHSA did the same for me for the National Survey on Drug Use and Health's statistics, as did Patti Meyer of Monitoring the Future. These researchers' assistance was generous and helpful, and for that I am grateful. People who helped me get in touch with persons who could provide the accounts that appear at the end of the chapters include my brother, Andrew Goode, Linda Silber, at Union College in Barbourville, KY, and Sandra McCoombs, at the Maryland Fund for Excellence and Alumni Membership. Persons who agreed to conduct interviews with me, who conducted interviews with others and provided them to me, or provide accounts of their, or others', activities include Henry Mesias, Sally Sternglanz, Danny Goode, and Michelle Birdsong. I am likewise grateful to the anonymous interviewees and authors of the accounts, who took the time to talk to me, or contributed written narratives of their lives and risked exposure, and allowed me to publish their stories here. I'd also like to thank Britny Kinneberg of Old Dominion University for catching a small but crucial mistake and Charles Gray, her instructor, for bringing it to my attention; Nachman Ben-Yehuda for reading and commenting on portions of this manuscript; and Barbara Weinstein for her wisdom and insight.

For their thorough reviews of the ninth edition, I'd like to thank Nicolas Simon of Eastern Connecticut State University; Scott Dolan of SUNY Albany; and Carlos Zeisel of Hesser College.

Additionally, I'd like to thank Waveland Press for permitting me to use several paragraphs from *Deviance in Everyday Life* (2002) in Chapter 3 of this book. I am thankful to McGraw-Hill Publishing for allowing me to adapt four paragraphs that appear here in Chapter 4, which were originally published *Drugs in American Society* (2012); I gratefully acknowledge the use of this material. I'd also like to thank Temple University Press for allowing me to adapt three paragraphs from *Justifiable Conduct: Self-Vindication in Memoir* (published 2013), which appear here.

Erich Goode
Greenwich Village, New York City

Introduction
What Is Deviance?

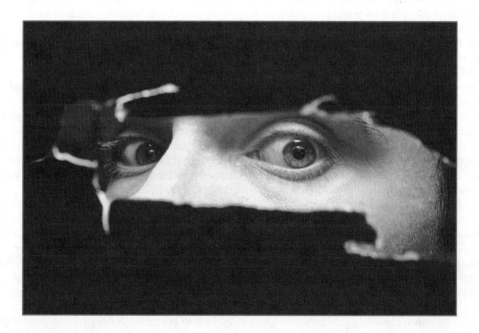

Learning Objectives:

After reading this chapter, you will be able to:

- discuss deviance in everyday life;
- understand the sociology of deviance as a non-pejorative;
- recognize societal and situational deviance;
- recount the ABCs of deviance;
- understand deviant behavior;

- discuss deviant attitudes and beliefs;
- understand the role physical characteristics play in the discussion of deviance;
- discuss what role relativism plays in deviance;
- compare and contrast essentialism and constructionism in terms of deviance;
- discuss the concept of positive deviance.

Tracy Thorne-Begland, a former naval officer and fighter pilot, appears on ABC's *Nightline* and discloses that he was—and still is—gay. Dishonorably discharged from the military because of its "don't ask, don't tell" rule, he fought the ruling, and lost. In 2012, after completing a law degree, he became a prosecutor in Richmond, VA, and then stepped forward as a candidate for district court judge. The Family Foundation opposes his nomination, and in May of that year, the Republican-dominated Virginia House of Delegates votes to deny him the judgeship. His opponents claim that, as a homosexual, he cannot be "impartial," and worse, he'll become engaged in "activism." Gays in public office and legal positions are "notorious" for "homosexual activism" (Tavernise, 2012, pp. A15, A16). In short, Mr. Thorne-Begland's outspoken opponents—anti-gays all—brand him a *deviant*.

In Chapel Hill, NC, as John Edwards walks toward the courthouse steps, he is mobbed by reporters and onlookers pressing to get close to him. Edwards, a onetime Democratic U.S. senator (1998–2004), representing the state of North Carolina, was the vice-presidential running mate of John Kerry in 2004 and a failed presidential candidate in 2008. But in 2011, a North Carolina grand jury indicts Edwards for misappropriating campaign funds to cover up an extra-marital affair he had carried on while running for office, at a time when his wife was suffering from breast cancer, an affliction to which she succumbed in 2010. The deception deepens: Edwards impregnated his paramour, Rielle Hunter, she bore a child, and he convinced a "loyal campaign aide," Andrew Young, to claim paternity of the child. Prosecution argues that Edwards had paid his mistress to keep quiet about the affair and the child in order to sidestep train-wrecking his presidential bid. In his defense, Edwards claims he paid the hush money to keep his ailing wife from finding out—a personal matter, not an illegal political conspiracy. If convicted, he faces the possibility of spending the next three decades of his life in prison (Severson, 2012). But guilty or not, John Edwards discredits himself—deeply disappointing his donors, destroying his political career, dishonoring his personal life, and bringing shame to his family. Although months later he is acquitted in criminal court—judged not guilty on one count while the

judge declares a mistrial on the others—his shenanigans cast a shadow on everything he had done before. The public exposure of his misdeeds seriously *deviantizes* former senator John Edwards.

Joey Paulk was riding in a Humvee in Afghanistan when it hit a land mine and exploded. He regained consciousness twenty feet from the vehicle, on fire. Weeks later, waking up from a coma in a San Antonio military hospital, Joey looked at his hands and realized that he had no fingers. While shuffling down a hallway, he forced himself to look in the mirror. His face was mutilated—melted and scarred beyond recognition. After months of skin grafts and further operations to permit him to open his mouth enough to eat a hamburger, give definition to his chin, and align his eyelid and lower lip, he was able to say to himself, "From a distance, you can't tell I was injured." He's had to learn how to do things for himself, but he can now drive, send texts, use zippers, and hold a drink at a party. But children have gawked at him and drunks have taunted him, and he feels self-conscious about his hands. "I'm just doing what I'm doing to survive," he says (Dao, 2012). Surely at this point Joey must be wondering, "What's going to become of me? Will I be able to live a normal life? Will uninjured, unblemished people stigmatize me? Will more drunks taunt me, more children gawk at me? Will I get treated like a cripple, be isolated, cut off from conventional social relations? Will I ever get married and have children?"

Beginning in the early 2000s, representatives of Wal-Mart de Mexico began making bribes—"envelopes of cash," eventually totaling millions of dollars—to local government officials ("facilitators") to obtain permits and favorable contracts to open stores in Mexico. They concealed these practices from the hierarchy at headquarters in the United States and, when Sergio Cicero Zapata, then a top executive at the firm, reported the malfeasances to the top brass at the subsidiary, only the most superficial investigation was conducted; for years, the matter was shelved. In 2004, Zapata resigned from the firm, and then, eight years later, talked to *The New York Times* about his allegations. Bribes, he said, helped the company grow quickly—faster than the competition. "They got zoning maps changed. They made environmental objections vanish. Permits that typically took months to process magically materialized in days." What the company was buying, he said, "was time" (Barstow, 2012, p. 8). Over the course of the following year, the firm attracted legal attention and public hostility for multiple additional offenses, including purchasing its goods from factories that imperiled the safety of its employees—in one of them, in Bangladesh, over 100 workers died in a possibly preventable fire—and operated under sweatshop conditions. When the corporation's chief executive appeared before a meeting of a foreign relations council, he was met by the jeers of a "raucous crowd of protesters" (Greenhouse and Yardley, 2012, p. A1).

In New York, outside a courtroom, a pimp announces that he and his lawyers will "stage-manage" his trial to increase the box office appeal of a movie about his life that's in the works (Buettner, 2012). In New York, a newscaster is fired for making stereotypical and derogatory remarks about Muslims (Stelter, 2010). In Washington, at a time when nationwide rates of violence continue to decline, the FBI announces a nationwide rise in the murder of police officers (Schmidt and Goldstein, 2012). Across the country, the use of food stamps continues to rise as its stigma fades (DeParle and Gebeloff, 2009). Again, in Washington, researchers announce that as racial differences in test reading scores have declined, differences between students from high-income and low-income families have increased (Tavernise, 2011).

These events, tales, narratives, and human dramas are the stuff of life. They are about real people who engage in real activities and suffer real—whether deserved or undeserved—reactions from others. They indicate that certain members of society regard or are likely to regard what the protagonists did, said, or are as negatively valued, undesirable, unacceptable in some way. Many sociologists who contemplate their behavior believe that the way these people react indicate the existence, relevance, and the importance of the phenomenon they refer to as "deviance."

DEVIANCE IN EVERYDAY LIFE

Just about everyone has done *something* that someone else frowns upon; just about everyone believes something that certain others don't like,

holds attitudes of which somebody disapproves, or possesses physical or ethnic characteristics that touch off disdain or hostility or denigration in this, that, or some other social circle, "audience," or person. Perhaps we've stolen something, or told a lie, or gossiped about another person in an especially unflattering manner. Maybe more than once we've gotten drunk, or high, or driven too fast, or recklessly, or gone through a red light without bothering to stop. Have we ever worn clothes someone else thought were out of style, offensive, or ugly? Have we ever belched at the dinner table, broken wind, or picked our nose in public? Have we ever cut class or failed to read an assignment? Do we like a television program someone else finds stupid and boring? Didn't we once date someone our parents and friends didn't like? Maybe our religious beliefs and practices don't agree with those of the members of another theological group, organization, sect, or denomination. Perhaps we're a liberal, or a conservative, or somewhere in the middle—*someone* doesn't approve of those views. Some among us are prejudiced, or racist, or anti-Semitic, or xenophobic—on principle, they don't like foreigners—or rabidly anti-French, or hostile to Japanese people, or against any and all Arabs or Muslims, regardless of what they're like as individuals.

Humans are evaluative creatures. However warranted or unwarranted, we make judgments about the behavior, beliefs, or appearance or characteristics of others. Each and every one of us does the same thing—all of us evaluate others, although in somewhat different ways. Societies everywhere have rules or *norms* governing what we may and may not do, how we should and shouldn't think, what we should and should not believe, even how we should and shouldn't look, and those norms are so detailed and complex, and so dependent on the views of different audiences or social circles of evaluators, that what *everyone* does, believes, and is, is looked on negatively by *someone*—indeed, in all likelihood, by *lots* of other people. Believers in God look down on atheists; atheists think believers in God are misguided and mistaken. Fundamentalist Christians oppose the beliefs of fundamentalist Muslims, and vice versa. Liberals disapprove of and oppose the views of conservatives; to conservatives, the feeling is mutual. Many college campuses are divided into mutually exclusive ethnic and racial enclaves; in student unions, often, the whites sit together in their own area and African Americans in theirs. Jocks and druggies, brains and preppies, Greeks, geeks, hippies—the number of ways that what we believe, or do, or are, is judged negatively by others is almost infinite.

There are four necessary ingredients for deviance to take place or exist: one, a rule or *norm*; two, someone who violates (or is thought to violate) that norm; three, an audience, someone who judges the normative violation to be wrong; and four, a likelihood of a negative reaction—criticism, condemnation, censure, stigma, disapproval, punishment, and the like—*by* that audience. To qualify as deviance, it isn't even necessary to violate a norm that's serious, like the Ten Commandments. Norms are everywhere, and they vary in seriousness, and different social circles believe in and profess different norms. In other words, "deviance" is a matter of degree, a continuum or a *spectrum*, from trivial to extremely serious, and it is relative as to audience. "I've never done anything seriously wrong," we might tell ourselves. "There's nothing deviant about me!" we add. But "wrong" according to *whose* standards? And "deviant" in what *sense*? And to what degree? We might feel that our belief in God is a good thing, but, as we saw, an atheist is likely to disagree. Chances are, we think our political position is reasonable; many of our fellow citizens will disagree, finding our politics foolish and wrongheaded. Our friends are probably in sync with us with respect to lifestyle and taste in clothing, but unbeknownst to us, behind our backs, there are others who make fun of us because of the way we dress and act. The point is, nearly everything about every one of us—both the reader and the author of this book included—is a potential source of criticism, condemnation, or censure, in *some* social circles, from the point of view of *some* observers.

The point is, deviance is not a simple quality resting with a given action, belief, or trait inherent in, intrinsic to, or indwelling within them. An act, for example, is not regarded as deviant everywhere and at all times (though some acts are *more widely* condemned than others are). What makes a given act deviant is the way it is seen, regarded, judged, evaluated, and the way that others—audiences—treat the person who engages in that act. Deviance is that which is reacted to

negatively, in a socially rejecting fashion, within certain social settings. Acts, beliefs, and traits are deviant *to* certain persons or audiences or *in* certain social circles. What *defines* deviance is the actual or potential *reaction* that actions, beliefs, and traits generate or are likely to generate in audiences. It is this negative reaction that defines or *constitutes* a given act, belief, or trait *as* deviant. Without that reaction, actual or potential, we do not have a case of deviance on our hands. When that reaction takes place, or is expressed in an interview or a questionnaire, sociologists refer to whatever touches off that reaction as deviant—*to* the person or the members of a particular collectivity who react to it in a negative fashion.

Humans create and enforce rules. But we also *violate* some of society's rules; the tendency to do as we please, against the norms, is inherently disobedient. We park in "No Parking" zones; behind their backs, we make fun of bosses, parents, and professors; we smoke when and where we're not supposed to; speed to get where we're going; perhaps occasionally have sex with the wrong partner. Not one of us is passive, obeying all rules like a robot, programmed to follow society's commands. The human animal is active, creative, and irrepressible. All societies generate a multitude of rules and their violations, likewise, are multitudinous. In fact, the more numerous and detailed the rules, the more opportunities there are for normative violations.

Virtually no one abides by *all* rules *all* the time. Indeed, this is a literal impossibility, since some of these rules contradict one another. None of these rules are considered valid by everyone in any society. As we saw, there is in every society on Earth—in some far more than in others—a certain degree of variation in notions of right and wrong from one person to another, one group or category to another, one subculture to another. Especially in a large, complex, urban, multicultural, multiethnic, multinational society such as the United States, this variation is considerable—indeed, immense. This means that almost any action, belief, or characteristic we could think of is approved in some social circles and condemned in others. Almost inevitably, we deviate from *someone's* rules simply by acting, believing, or being, since it is impossible to conform to all the rules that prevail. We'll get to the "but" part of our equation momentarily.

THE SOCIOLOGY OF DEVIANCE AS NON-PEJORATIVE

When sociologists say that something is deviant in a certain social circle or a society, do we conclude that it *should* be condemned? Of course not! Every one of us has our own views, and those views may agree or disagree with the audiences whose reactions we are looking at. Does this mean that when we use the term "deviant" *as a form of sociological analysis* we seek to denigrate, put down, or humiliate anyone to whom the term applies? Absolutely not! Again, we may *agree* or *disagree* with the judgment, but if we observe it, it hits us like a pie in the face. We would be *foolish* and *ignorant* to pretend that it doesn't exist. We are taking note of how members of particular social collectivities regard or treat certain individuals. Saying that a president's approval rating is high, or low, does not mean that we approve, or disapprove, of that president. What it means is that we take note of public opinion. When we say that many people in American society look down upon prostitutes, political radicals, criminals, and atheists and regard them as deviants, this does not mean that the observer necessarily agrees with that judgment. It means that, as sociologists, we recognize that certain negative consequences are likely to result from announcing to a cross-section of American society that one is a prostitute, a radical, a criminal, or an atheist. These reactions, taken as a whole, constitute a social fact, and we would be foolish to pretend that they don't exist. In other words, when sociologists use the terms "deviance" and "deviant," they use them in an absolutely *non-pejorative* fashion. This means that they are descriptive terms that apply to what others think and how they are likely to react. You may hate a particular movie, but if it is number one at the box office, you can still say it is a "popular" movie—because it *is*. You could be an atheist and still say that atheism is deviant to many Americans. *Even if you don't agree with that judgment*, it is materially real in that it has consequences, and as sociologists, we must acknowledge the existence of those attitudes and consequences.

In short, deviance is an analytic category: It applies to all spheres and areas of human life; it is a trans-historical, cross-cultural concept. The dynamics of deviance have taken place throughout recorded history and in every known society, anywhere humans have interacted with one another. Everywhere, people are evaluated on the basis of what they do, what they believe, and who they are—and they are thus reacted to accordingly. Deviance takes place during a basketball game, during your professor's office hours, during "happy hour" in the local bar, during final exams, in department stores, on the street, in the church, synagogue, and mosque, and within the bosom of the family. Deviance-defining processes take place everywhere and anywhere people engage in behavior, hold and express beliefs, and possess traits that others regard as unacceptable. Normative violations, and reactions to normative violations, occur everywhere. They exist and have existed in all societies everywhere and throughout human history. They are a central and foundational social process. Although the term has been used derogatively in popular parlance and in psychiatric evaluations, "deviance" does *not* refer to immorality or psychopathology; *sociologically*, it means one thing and one thing only: the violation of social norms that can result in punishment, condemnation, or ridicule. As such, it is a descriptive, not a pejorative term.

SOCIETAL AND SITUATIONAL DEVIANCE

So far, it seems I've been arguing that *anything* can be deviant. If a collectivity of people—a group, a social circle, a segment of the population, any assemblage of people, really—regard something as offensive, by our definition, it is deviant. This is technically true, but it's only half true. There's a really big "*but*" attached to this generalization. There are two sides to judgments of deviance. One is its vertical or *hierarchical* side, the side that says people with more power (or the majority of a society) get to say what's deviant because they influence the climate of opinion and have more influence in the political and legislative realms. This differential influence is a sociological fact—not a matter of opinion or an expression of moral bias. The other side to judgments of deviance is its horizontal or "grassroots" or "mosaic" side, the side that says deviance can be anything that *any* collectivity says it is, no matter how little power they have. In other words, according to Kenneth Plummer (1979, pp. 97–99), we must make a distinction between *societal* and *situational* deviance.

Societal deviance is composed of those actions and conditions that are widely recognized, in advance and in general, to be deviant. There is a high degree of consensus on the identification of certain categories of deviance. In this sense, rape, robbery, corporate theft, terrorism, and transvestism are deviant because they are regarded as reprehensible *to* the majority of the members of this society. These are examples of "high consensus" deviance, in that a substantial proportion of the population disapproves of them. In most social circles, if evidence revealed that someone engaged in one of them, such a revelation would cause negative reactions from most members of these circles. Even though specific individuals enacting or representing specific instances of these general categories may not be punished in specific situations, *in general*, the members of this society see them as serious normative violations. Certain acts, beliefs, and traits are deviant *society-wide* because they are condemned, both in practice and in principle, by the majority, or by the most powerful members of the society. "Societal" judgments of deviance represent the *hierarchical* side of deviance.

On the other hand, *situational deviance* does not possess a general or society-wide quality, but manifests itself in actual, concrete social gatherings, circles, or settings. We can locate two different types of situational deviance: one that violates the norms dictating what one may and may not do *within a certain social or physical setting* and one that violates the norms *within certain social circles or groups*. The type of situational deviance that is dependent on *setting* is fairly simple to understand and illustrate. You may take your clothes off in your bedroom but not in public, in the street. You may shout and cheer at a basketball game, but not at a Quaker wake. Boxers punch one another at will, but outside of the ring, trying to knock someone out is usually illegal, and could result in your being arrested. Killing the enemy within the context of warfare is condoned, encouraged, and legal; under most other circumstances, civilians who kill during peacetime commit murder. In these cases, the norms condemning certain behaviors apply *only within specific contexts* and

not others; the behavior that these norms condemn is *situationally*, not *societally*, deviant.

The social definition of deviance also varies by the group or collectivity or social circle within which behavior is enacted, beliefs are expressed, or traits are known about. For instance, in certain cities or communities in the United States (Greenwich Village in New York, for instance, or San Francisco generally), homosexuality is accepted by the majority; hence, *in* such cities or communities, homosexuality *is not deviant*. But in the country *as a whole*, the majority still disapproves of it, although that disapproval is declining over time. Sexual abstinence is the norm among Roman Catholic priests and nuns; sexual activity, and particularly sex with multiple partners, is frowned upon—a violation of the rules governing the sexual behavior of Catholic functionaries. Among *haredi* or ultra-Orthodox Jews, reporting certain crimes to the police results in social isolation, censure, chastisement, punishment. In the general population, *not* reporting to the police may itself be a crime, and is generally disapproved of. Again, the behavior that is condemned is seen as wrong only *among certain social circles in the society*—not in the society as a whole.

The distinction between "societal" deviance (acts, beliefs, and traits that are considered bad or wrong in a society generally) and "situational" deviance (acts, beliefs, and traits that are considered bad or wrong specifically *within* a particular group, social circle, setting, or context) casts doubt on the cliché, "Everything is deviant." It is true that "everything is deviant"—to *someone*—but that is not a very useful statement, since, societally, certain things (murdering an infant in its crib) stand a *much* higher likelihood of being condemned than others do (chewing bubble gum). Understanding the dynamics of deviance *demands* that we make the distinction between societal and situational deviance. It also frees us from making the equally silly, meaningless, and indefensible statement that unless complete consensus exists about the rules, there's no such thing as deviance (Sumner, 1994). What's important here is that *deviance is a matter of degree*. Some acts are highly *likely* to attract condemnation and censure, while others are extremely *unlikely* to do so—or likely only *in* certain settings or *among* certain collectivities.

Looking at deviance from a vertical (or hierarchical) perspective raises the question of the *dominance* of one category or society over another. That is, even though different groups, categories, social circles, and societies hold different views of what's deviant, some of them are more powerful, influential, and numerous than others. In addition to looking at variation from one setting to another, we also have to look at which categories or groups wield the power to influence definitions of right and wrong in other categories, or in general. Social scientists say that a dominant belief or institution is *hegemonic*: It holds sway over beliefs held or institutions supported by less powerful social groupings in the society. The vertical conception of deviance is obviously compatible with the societal definition of deviance; it defines the *hegemonic* view of what's deviant *as* deviant, that is, what the majority or the most influential segments of the society regard as deviant. Acts, beliefs, and conditions that are societally deviant are those that are regarded as wrong nearly everywhere in a given society. Most of the time, they can be regarded as *high-consensus* deviance: There is widespread agreement as to their deviant character.

In contrast, the "horizontal" or "grassroots" property of deviance refers to the fact that a given act, belief, or trait represents a normative violation in *one* group, category, or society, but is conformist in *another*. This quality of deviance allows us to see society, or different societies, as a kind of "mosaic" or a loose assemblage of separate and independent collectivities of people who do not influence one another. Here, we have a jumble of side-by-side audiences evaluating behavior, beliefs, and traits only within their own category, independent of what's going on in other categories. Enacting certain behavior, holding a certain belief, possessing a certain characteristic makes someone a conformist in one setting and a deviant in another. Such a view does not examine the impact of these settings, groups, or societies on one another. Clearly, the horizontal approach to deviance is compatible with the situational definition of deviance. Acts, beliefs, and conditions that are situationally, but not societally, deviant may be regarded as *low-consensus* deviance, in that public opinion is *divided* about their deviant status. What fetches condemnation in one social circle produces indifference or even praise in another.

THE ABCs OF DEVIANCE

To recapitulate: Sociologists refer to behavior, beliefs, or characteristics that violate, or depart or deviate from, a basic norm, and that are likely to generate negative reactions in persons who observe or hear about that norm violation, as *social deviance* or simply "deviance." Many courses and books on the subject (including the book you are reading at this very moment), as well as the major academic journals in the field, bear the title "deviant behavior." This isn't exactly accurate. "Deviant behavior" is a handy term that sociologists of deviance use to refer to the field. The field might better be referred to as "social deviance," but unfortunately, we are stuck with the handy term because it's easily recalled. But the field isn't *only* about deviant *behavior*. It's about deviant behavior—and a great deal more. It's also about deviant attitudes or beliefs, and about deviant traits or characteristics—in short, anything and everything that results in interpersonal or institutional rejection or punishment. Adler and Adler (2009, p. 13) use the term, the "ABCs of deviance—*Attitudes*, *Behavior*, and *Conditions*." "Attitudes" refer to unpopular, unconventional beliefs that may or may not manifest themselves in overt actions. "Behavior" is made up of any overt action (which includes the failure to act) that is likely to attract condemnation, hostility, or punishment. And "conditions" include physical characteristics or traits that, likewise, make someone a target of an audience's disapproval, avoidance, derision, or other types of negative social reactions. In short, to the sociologist, deviance encompasses all three of the "ABCs"—attitudes, behavior, and conditions. Let's look at each one in turn.

DEVIANT BEHAVIOR

Most people who encounter the study of social deviance imagine that the field is entirely and exclusively about *behavior* that is regarded as unacceptable and likely to generate negative reactions. It is true that *most* forms of deviance we're likely to think of, as well as most of those that tend to be punished, are behavioral in nature. The vast majority of people, when asked to provide examples of deviance, offer types of *behavior*. In addition, thumbing through deviance textbooks and anthologies tells us that most of the forms of deviance their authors discuss are, again, behavioral. In short, non-normative *behavior* is an element of most people's stereotype of what's deviant.

It *is* true that *much* of what we evaluate one another on the basis of is what we *do*. "Actions speak louder than words," we say—and most of the time, to most of us, they do. A man says he loves his wife—and he may in fact love her very much—but if he is out every night having affairs with other women, his behavior is likely to be weighed very heavily in his wife's assessment of him as a decent husband, not his protestations of love. A woman says she believes that cocaine is a harmful drug, that no one should or can play around with it, but if she uses it regularly, no one is likely to take what she claims her beliefs are very seriously. In other words, *even if we actually do believe something*, our behavior is weighed more heavily than our beliefs. We'll come back to the ideas of sociologist Erving Goffman (1922–1982) throughout this book because some of his ideas remain important, relevant, and insightful for students and researchers in the field of deviance. His book *Stigma* (1963) is a classic. The fact is, as Goffman says, most of us see behavior we regard as deviant as indicating "blemishes of individual character" (1963, p. 4). A dishonest character is revealed or manifested mainly by dishonest *behavior;* a weak will and an inability to resist temptation are revealed by drug abuse, alcoholism, adultery, gambling, and so on. To repeat, while deviant *behavior* is a major type of social deviance, it is not the only type. In this book, we intend to look at several others as well.

DEVIANT ATTITUDES AND BELIEFS

Is simply expressing an unpopular belief a form of deviance? Of course it is! Behavior is not solely or exclusively a set of physical or mechanical motions. When someone expresses a point of view, it is not simply the physical act of talking or writing that counts but the content of *what* that person says, the *worldview* that those words express and what that worldview *means* to the people listening to or reading them. Holding unconventional, unorthodox, unpopular—or deviant—beliefs may be regarded as *cognitive deviance*. This category includes religious, political, and scientific beliefs that are regarded as unacceptable. The negative reactions toward the people who hold such beliefs are very similar to those that would be touched off by the discovery of participation in behavior that is regarded as unacceptable. Note that *expressing favorable attitudes toward deviant behavior* represents a type of cognitive deviance or a deviant belief system. If one *engages* in adultery and, at the same time, *tells others* that adultery is acceptable and desirable, one has both engaged in deviant behavior and expressed a deviant belief. Not everyone who violates behavioral norms believes that the deviant acts in which they engage *should* be practiced. As St. Augustine wisely said, "no thief will submit to being robbed by another" (400/1963, p. 45). Most murderers and robbers not only do not want to be murdered or robbed, they realize that a society that freely allows them cannot long endure; they justify their enactment of these crimes by citing special circumstance. *In contrast*, homosexuals, marijuana smokers, atheists, evolutionists and creationists, transsexuals, the eccentric and the mildly unconventional, conservatives in liberal communities, liberals in conservative communities, drinkers in "dry" counties, abstainers in a drinking environment—virtually none believe their behavior is wrong, all want *their* behavior to be acceptable to parties that currently deviantize them, and all want to be left alone to be themselves. (Of course, some want to impose their views on others as well.) And when they express such beliefs, they may be tagged as *cognitive* deviants.

It is possible that, in the history of the world, holders of unacceptable beliefs have been attacked, criticized, condemned, arrested, even persecuted (in a word, *deviantized*) almost as often and almost as severely as enactors of unacceptable behavior (Perrin, 2007). Consider, for example, the Spanish Inquisition (1480–1834), during which thousands of "heretics" were executed for their beliefs (or supposed beliefs); the Crusades, the attempt by Christians during the eleventh to the fourteenth centuries to wrest Jerusalem from "unbelievers," that is, Muslims; the current Islamic *jihad*, in which its recently assassinated architect, Osama bin Laden, targeted "Crusaders," that is, Christians, as well as Jews;

and, in ancient times, the execution of Christians who refused to worship the Roman emperor as a god. These are the expression of beliefs held by certain people that others considered wrong—evil, heretical, blasphemous, and deviant. Clearly, the expression of one's beliefs *has been regarded*, and is *still* regarded, as deviant.

Could a self-proclaimed atheist be elected president of the United States? It is unlikely; a substantial proportion of Americans would vote against such a candidate, simply because of his or her atheistic views, and in a close election, every vote counts. In the eyes of many mainstream and conventional citizens of the United States, godlessness is considered very close to immorality. Hence, for much of the American population, not believing in God remains a deviant belief.

One absolutely crucial point in any examination of cognitive deviance: Certain beliefs are *not* deviant simply because they are wrong. They are deviant because they violate the norms of a given society, or an institution, or members of a social circle within a society, and, as a result, they are likely to elicit negative reactions. When we see these negative reactions, we know we have a case of deviance on our hands. Hence, cognitive deviance is a major type of deviance.

You, the reader, believe that racism is bad; so do I. But to the sociologist, racism is not deviant *because* it is bad, immoral, or wrong in some abstract sense. The expression of racist views—even in the absence of racist behavior—is deviant in certain sectors of this society because it offends many, most, or certain members of this society; it is also all-too-often translated into racist *behavior*. Before the Civil War, if a white southerner were to argue for the abolition of slavery *in* the South, *among* slaveowners and other whites, that view, and the person who expressed it, would have been regarded as *deviant*. Again, *not* because it was wrong—everyone today agrees that it was the correct position—but because it was considered deviant *to* Southern whites generally, and *to* slave owners specifically. Once again, "deviant" does not mean "wrong"; it means "offensive to audiences *in* certain social circles, likely to elicit negative reactions by members in those collectivities."

Nearly all biologists and geologists believe that creationism is scientifically and factually wrong. But to the sociologist, creationism is not deviant because it is scientifically wrong. Indeed, belief in *evolution* is deviant as well—*to* fundamentalist Christians and Muslims and Orthodox Jews. The reason we know that certain beliefs are deviant is that their expression violates the norms that prevail in certain social groups, thereby generating negative reactions among the members of those groups. This is what we *mean* by deviant.

Likewise, it is not clear that atheism is "wrong" or "right" in some abstract sense. Indeed, most scientists and philosophers believe that the factual matter of theism or atheism can't be empirically tested. What *makes* atheism deviant is that it violates a norm of theism, or a belief in God, held by roughly 90 percent of the American public. In many social contexts, atheists are not treated the same way that believers are; they are, in those contexts, looked down upon, vilified, and condemned. According to a Pew Global Attitude Survey (taken in 2011), a majority of the American public (53%) believes that "it is necessary to believe in God to be moral," a clear statement that atheism is not only deviant, but immoral as well. In contrast, in Western Europe, this is a minority view, ranging from 39 percent in Germany to only 10 percent in Sweden.

It turns out many beliefs thought to be false have been demonstrated to be true (Ben-Yehuda, 1985, pp. 106–167), and the scientists who held them then were ostracized just as much as those scientists who hold beliefs we now regard as false. In other words, *some* deviant beliefs may be correct! In the 1850s, the physician Ignaz Semmelweis (1818–1865) discovered that the patients of doctors who delivered babies after washing their hands had lower rates of maternal mortality than doctors whose hands were dirty. He was ridiculed for his theory and hounded out of the medical profession, eventually being driven to insanity and suicide. Semmelweis's discovery was not accepted until the 1890s, but, although scientifically *true*, for nearly half a century, his belief was *deviant*. Likewise, Louis Pasteur's germ theory, Alfred Wegener's theory of continental drift, Karl Jansky's and Grote Reber's theory of radio waves, and Copernicus's and Galileo's heliocentric theory of the solar system were rejected and ridiculed by the powers that be in their day, yet all of them later became accepted as fact (Ben-Yehuda, 1985, pp. 123–135).

PHYSICAL CHARACTERISTICS

What about physical traits or characteristics? Can someone be regarded as deviant as a result of possessing certain undesirable, involuntarily acquired physical characteristics—such as being extremely ugly, short, obese, disabled, or deformed? Ask yourself: Is a disabled person treated the same way as the rest of us? Do many "abled" persons socially avoid or shun the disabled? Do some of them tease, humiliate, joke about, stereotype, or make fun of the handicapped? Do they pity or scorn them? Is a great deal of social interaction between persons with a "normal" appearance and one who is disfigured, strained, awkward, distant, and difficult? Haven't obese children often become an object of taunts, ridicule, harassment, and condemnation? Aren't the possessors of certain undesirable physical characteristics excluded from full social participation? (These are rhetorical questions, of course. The writer or speaker uses them to convince an audience of a certain point of view. You, the reader, should be wary of such devices.) Hence, if we mean by "deviant" the fact that persons with certain physical traits are often treated in a condescending, pitying, scornful, and rejecting fashion, the answer is, *of course* possessing unconventional, unacceptable physical traits is deviant! If the disabled are more likely to receive negative social reactions than the abled, then sociologically, we may regard them as deviant.

Is this fair? Of course not! Most people with an undesirable physical trait have not done anything wrong to acquire it. Hence, it is unfair for others to reject or otherwise treat them negatively. But notice: It is not the *sociologist* who is being unfair here, or who is rejecting the possessors of these traits. Rather, it is the social *audience* the sociologist takes note of, that is, the majority, or a sector of the society, that rejects such people and, hence, treats them unfairly. Sociologists of deviance aren't rejecting the disabled; they are merely observing that many abled members of the society do that. It doesn't matter whether behavior, beliefs, or physical characteristics are freely chosen or thrust upon us. Again, if they result in social rejection of some kind, they are deviant, and may qualify their enactors, believers, or possessors as deviants. The fairness or justice of this rejection is a separate matter. We'll be looking at physical characteristics in a later chapter.

The fact that physical characteristics represent a major form of deviance points us to a distinction that has been a fixture in the field of sociology for practically its entire existence: that between *achieved* and *ascribed* statuses (Adler and Adler, 2009, p. 13). Some social statuses are "achieved" (although they may have been *assisted* by certain inborn characteristics). Being a college graduate is something that has to be accomplished: One has to *do* something—such as have a high school record good enough to be admitted, enroll in courses, study to pass the courses one takes, complete all the graduation requirements—to graduate from college. But being born into a rich family or a poor one; a black, white, Asian, or Latino one; or one in which one's parents are themselves college graduates or high school dropouts—these are *ascribed* statuses. They are not achieved, but are thrust upon the infant at birth. There is nothing a child can do to achieve or choose his or her family or parents.

As with statuses in general, so it is with deviant statuses: They may be achieved or ascribed. Being a drug addict is a result of making certain choices in life: to use drugs or not, to use to the point that one's life becomes consumed by drugs or not. Clearly, being a drug addict is an *achieved* status. In contrast, being a dwarf or an albino is ascribed. One is born with certain characteristics or traits that are *evaluated* in a certain fashion by the society in which one lives. It is these evaluations, and the reactions that embody them, that determine whether or not a given ascribed characteristic is deviant. To the extent that these evaluations and reactions are negative, derisive, rejecting, or hostile, we have an instance of deviance on our hands. Is this fair? Once again: Of course not. But the sociologist would be foolish and ignorant to pretend that these negative evaluations and reactions *do not exist* and *do not have an important impact on people's lives*. In fact, it is *only* when we understand them—their basis, their dynamics, and their consequences—that we can face and deal with society's many injustices.

TRIBAL STIGMA: LABELING RACE AND ETHNICITY

Erving Goffman pinpointed a type of stigma he referred to as "tribal stigma of race, religion, and nation" (1963, p. 4). A team of sociologists (Disha, Cavendish, and King, 2011) has found that, in the months following the attack on the World Trade Center on September 11, 2001, in the United States, hate crimes targeting Arabs and Muslims increased dramatically. A 2012 poll conducted in Canada revealed that a majority of Canadians (52%) said that they "distrust" Muslims; among French Canadians, only 30 percent said that they trust Muslims (*Huffington Post*, March 26, 2012). In the United States, a *Time* magazine poll indicated that a majority of Americans (61%) opposed the building of a mosque two blocks from Ground Zero, the site of the 9/11 attack; seven in ten (70%) said that it would be an "insult" to the victims of 9/11. Over a quarter (28%) was opposed to a Muslim sitting on the Supreme Court, and a third (33%) said that Muslims should be barred from running for President (Altman, 2010).

Throughout recorded history, members of one ethnic group have stigmatized, "deviantized," or "demonized" members of another simply because of the category to which they belonged. Any exploration of deviance must take a look at Goffman's "tribal stigma of race, nation, and religion." It is a form of deviance that *automatically* discredits someone for belonging to a racial, national, ethnic, and religious category of humanity. It is every bit as important as deviance that is determined by behavior or beliefs.

RELATIVITY

Another absolutely crucial point: The sociology of deviance is *relativistic*. The concept of relativity has been grossly misunderstood. Some people think that accepting relativity means that we have no right to make our own moral judgments. This is completely false. Accepting relativity as a fact does not take away our right to make moral judgments. Relativity says: Judgments of what is good and bad vary from society to society, and this variation plays a role in influencing whether certain actors are condemned, depending on where they live. We have the right to our own judgments about good and bad, but if we are studying deviance, we have to pay attention to how such judgments vary through time and space. How *we*—how I, the author, how you, the reader, how *any* observer—feel about or react to an act, a belief, or a condition is *completely separate* from how *others* feel and act toward it. We may *despise* the injustice an act inflicts on its victims, or the injustice that punishing or condoning an act entails, but as sociologists of deviance we *cannot* permit ourselves to be so ignorant that we fail to recognize that the behavior *is* enacted, punished, or tolerated in certain places or at certain times.

In my view, accepting relativism poses no ethical "dilemma," as some have argued (Henshel, 1990, p. 14). It does not advocate a "hands-off" policy toward practices we consider evil. It simply says that what we consider evil may be seen as good *to others*—that is a fact we have to face—and before we attack that evil, we have to understand how others come to view it as good and come to practice it. Relativism simply says that our personal view of things may be irrelevant to how beliefs are actually put into practice and what their reception is in a given context. Hang onto your own moral precepts, relativity says, but make sure you are fully aware that *others* may not share yours, and that *their* moral precepts may guide them to do things *you* consider immoral.

In addition, the relativist approach emphasizes variations in judgments of deviance from one group, subculture, social circle, or individual to another *within the same society*. For instance, some social circles approve of marijuana use, while others condemn it. Some individuals condemn homosexuality while, increasingly, others do not. We will *almost always* be able to locate certain circles of individuals who tolerate or accept forms of behavior that are widely or more typically condemned within a given society. Some of these circles are, of course, practitioners of deviance themselves. But others are made up of individuals who, although they do not practice the behavior in question, do not condemn those who do, either.

Variations in definitions of deviance over *historical time* are at least as important as variations from one society to another. In 1993, the then-senator representing New York state, Daniel Patrick Moynihan, argued that deviance has been redefined over time to the point where a great deal of crime and other harmful behavior that once generated stigma, condemnation, even arrest, is now tolerated and normalized, its enactors exempt from punishment. The mentally ill have been released onto the street, no longer held behind the walls of mental institutions. Unwed mothers no longer bear the burden of social stigma. And levels of crime once considered alarming are now regarded as acceptable, tolerable—business as usual. Defenders of the old standards of decency are powerless to halt this process of "defining deviancy down," Moynihan argues.

In response, social and political commentator Charles Krauthammer (1993) asserted that, true, some forms of deviance have been defined "down," but a parallel and equally important process is taking place as well: "defining deviancy up." Behaviors that once were tolerated have become targets of harsh condemnation. Just as what is regarded as deviant has become normal, "once innocent behavior now stands condemned as deviant" (p. 20). Entirely new areas of behavior, such as date rape and politically incorrect speech, have been located and condemned, Krauthammer argued. And old areas, such as child abuse, have been "amplified," often to the point where groundless accusations are assumed to be true. While two out of three instances of ordinary street crime are never reported, "two out of three reported cases of child abuse are never shown to have occurred" (p. 21). Over-reporting of child abuse, Krauthammer claims, results from "a massive search to find cases." Where they cannot be found, they must be invented (p. 22). Date rape, Krauthammer claims, is so broadly defined as to encompass any and all sexual intercourse. In some social circles, he argues, the distinction between violence and consensual sex has been erased (p. 24). And the right to hold notions that differ from the mainstream has been taken away, Krauthammer claims. "Thought crimes" and "speech codes" have replaced differences of opinion and their expression.

It is possible that both Moynihan and Krauthammer have overstated their cases. Both were catastrophically wrong about the direction that crime was to take in the United States after the early 1990s. Both believed that the disintegration of the traditional family—more specifically, the increase in families without a father—would lead to significantly higher crime rates. Fatherless families have increased—as Moynihan argued was happening—but correspondingly, the crime rate in the United States has actually declined since the 1990s, according to both multiple victimization surveys sponsored by the federal government and The Uniform Crime Reports, a year-by-year tabulation of arrests conducted by the Federal Bureau of Investigation (FBI). Hence, we are led to ask: If the intact father-and-mother family is so important to insulating children against crime, how is it possible that fatherless families increased, yet the crime rate declined? In any case, Moynihan's and Krauthammer's point should be clear: Definitions of right and wrong vary over time. What is defined as wrong at one time may be tolerated in another; what is accepted during one era may be condemned in another. But they do not necessarily go in a single direction—down or up. It's probably easier to point to instances of deviance being defined down, where acts once condemned are now tolerated, but try smoking in class, at work, or any other "smoke-free" setting, and see how others react. Chances are, they won't ignore or tolerate it.

In sum, relativity applies across societies and from one collectivity to another, as well as up and down through the corridors of time. In order to understand deviance, just as we must be relativistic from one society and social circle to another, we must also be relativistic from one time period to another. While for some behaviors consensus in judgments of wrongdoing may be widespread, as students of deviance, we find the variation just as significant. The concept of relativity will continue to appear throughout this book. It is one of the basic building blocks of the sociology of deviance.

DEVIANCE: ESSENTIALISM VERSUS CONSTRUCTIONISM

So far, we've learned that "deviance" is that which violates the norms of a society, or a segment of the society, and is likely to call forth punishment, condemnation, or censure of the norm violator. Deviance can be *anything* the observers or "audiences" in a particular collectivity don't like and react against. In the next two chapters, I'd like to take a step further and suggest that the study of deviance is fundamentally two independent but interlocking enterprises. When sociologists look at normative violations and censure of the violator, they think along two tracks and investigate two separate types of questions. In other words, they are up to two entirely different endeavors.

When we think of deviance, the question we should ask ourselves is this: *What is to be explained?* And deviance is explained or addressed through the lens of two very different perspectives toward reality. Sociologists refer to these two perspectives as *essentialism* and *constructionism*. We can regard these two approaches as "master visions." They might seem contradictory but in fact they complement one another; they are two halves of the same coin.

Essentialism sees deviance as a specific, concrete phenomenon in the material world, such like oxygen, gravity, a volcano, or a snapping turtle. It does not have to be defined to be real, it just *is*; it's *there* for any and all to observe. In effect, its reality is in the material world, not in our minds. According to the essentialistic view, the reality of deviance is taken for granted, indisputable, apparent and obvious to all observers, an objective fact. And *because* deviance is objective or real, we are led to the inevitable question: "Why?" In other words, essentialism implies *positivism*, the belief that we can answer a question scientifically, with empirical or observable data. "Why do some people engage in deviance, hold deviant beliefs, and possess deviant physical characteristics?" The answer to the "What is to be explained?" question is that it is the *deviant behavior, beliefs, or conditions themselves* that must be explained. What causes these things to happen or exist is the sociologist's guiding concern. The ruling questions the positivist is likely to ask are, What kind of person would do such things? What social arrangements or factors encourage such behavior? Why is the crime rate so much higher in some societies or countries than in others? What *kinds of people* violate the norms of their society? For instance, why are men so much more likely to engage in most forms of deviance than women? The young

versus the old? Urban dwellers as opposed to people living in small towns? Which categories in the population are more likely to engage in violence? Who uses and abuses psychoactive substances and why? What causes some young people to engage in sex at an early age? What factors or variables encourage, cause, or influence white collar crime? These are the sorts of questions positivists who study deviance and crime ask, and they center around the guiding question: *Why do they do it?* (The positivistic approach to deviance usually studies deviant behavior, rarely deviant beliefs, and almost never deviance conditions.) Once sociologists decide that something is objectively real, as scientists, it is their mission to explain its occurrence.

In contrast, the approach sociologists call *constructionism* or *social constructionism* answers the "What is to be explained?" question by saying that it is *thinking about* and *reacting to* rule violators that is crucial. This approach argues that it is the *rules*, the *norms*, the *reactions to*, the *cultural representations of* certain behavior, beliefs, or conditions that need to be looked at and illuminated. In other words, constructionism is curious about how and why something comes to be *regarded as* or *judged to be* deviant in the first place, what is *thought, made of, said about*, and *done about* it. How are phenomena generally, and deviant phenomena specifically, *conceptualized, defined, represented, reacted to*, and *dealt with*? How do certain actions *come to be regarded* as "crime," "prostitution," "treachery," or "incest"? How are certain beliefs conceptualized *as* "heresy," "blasphemy," "godlessness," "disloyalty," "ignorance"? Why are certain physical characteristics even *noticed* in the first place? Are the disabled stigmatized? Are they integrated into the mainstream or "abled" society? Are the obese treated and reacted to differently in different societies? Why is a specific behavior, belief, or trait condemned in one society but not in another? Why does atheism cause the nonbeliever to be burned at the stake in one place, during one historical era, and ignored or tolerated elsewhere, at another time? Do the members of a society think of corporate crime as "real" crime? What does the treatment of the mentally disordered tell us about how they are viewed by the society at large? How do the media report news about drug abuse? What do the members of a society *do* to someone who engages in a given behavior, holds a particular belief, bears a specific trait? In turn, how is the person who is designated as a deviant *react to*, *handle*, and *deal with* the deviant designation, the label, the stigma? The constructionist is more interested in issues that have to do with thinking, talking, writing about, narrating, or reacting to such actions than in why deviant behavior, beliefs, or traits take place, occur, or exist in the first place. To the constructionist, deviant behavior, beliefs, and traits "exist"—*as a social category*—because they are conceptualized in a certain way. The constructionist does not take the "deviance" of an act, a belief, a condition, for granted; instead, it is *how something is regarded and dealt with* that must be explained, not the occurrence of the behavior, the beliefs, or the conditions. Chapters 2 and 3 will discuss these two radically different approaches to deviance.

POSITIVE DEVIANCE?

Controversy nurtures innovation. Without disagreement there can be no change—cognitive, intellectual, behavioral, social, or otherwise. Disciplines and fields of study need to be enriched with new ideas and novel concepts that stir up opposition, conflict, and dispute—otherwise these fields will become stale, lifeless, irrelevant, and insignificant. Some scholars believe that for the sociology of deviance, "positive deviance" is just such a concept.

In 1964, Leslie Wilkins published a book entitled *Social Deviance*, which depicted a bell-shaped curve diagram (p. 45) that delineated the distribution of the degree to which hypothetical acts conform to norms. In the middle, at the hump of the bell curve, most acts conform to a given norm; on the left tail of the curve, there are those acts that are regarded as wrong, sinful, or seriously criminal; those that occupy the right tail of the bell curve are those that are very positive or saintly acts. Wilkins pointed out that the more seriously deviant an act is, the rarer it is, and the more saintly an act, likewise, the rarer it is, so both tails trail off gradually, becoming rarer and rarer, eventually approaching zero. Wilkins's idea of rare acts that have a beneficial effect seems to have been adopted in the area of social reform;

it refers to "how unlikely innovators solve the world's toughest problems" (Pascale, Sternin, and Sternin, 2010). As used in the field of casework with vulnerable, at-risk children, it refers to more positive or more favorable outcomes than expected (Robinson and Fields, 1983; Marsh et al., 2004). More generally, it alerts us to the fact that "in every community there are certain individuals or groups whose uncommon behaviors and strategies enable them to find better solutions to problems than their peers," according to the Positive Deviance Initiative Web site. The Positive Deviance Initiative is used in a variety of programs to solve community problems, including childhood malnutrition and traffic deaths and accidents in Vietnam, neonatal deaths and illness throughout the Third World, girl trafficking in Indonesia, female genital mutilation in Egypt, educational dropout among primary school children in Argentina, and reintegrating previously abducted girl soldiers in Uganda. This is the most popular meaning of "positive deviance," which googling is most likely to turn up.

In sociology, the term has a very different meaning. A dozen years after Wilkins's book, Posner (1976) endorsed the positive deviance notion by discussing "the stigma of excellence," or "being just right." Since the 1970s, numerous scholars have discussed, analyzed, ruminated about, interpreted and reinterpreted, illuminated, and in one way or another made use of the positive deviance concept (Norland, Hepworth, and Monette, 1976; Dodge, 1985; Heckert, 1989; Ben-Yehuda, 1990; Jones, 1998; Irwin, 2003; West, 2003). In this context, positive deviance refers to a specific type of putatively wrongful, non-normative, and supposedly scandalous, harmful, and/or socially unacceptable behavior, beliefs, or conditions (examples: crime, white collar offenses, delinquency, incest, illicit drug abuse, obesity, political radicalism)—not the usual, run-of-the-mill deviance, but a special type. But *what* type?

A few examples that scholars and researchers have used to illustrate positive deviance include wilderness survivalism (Harrison, 2008), "random acts of kindness" (Jones, 1998), "overconformity to the sports ethic" (Hughes and Coakley, 1991), French impressionism (Heckert, 1989), tattoo collecting (Irwin, 2003)—along with weight lifting, body building, running, giftedness, engaging in safe sex practices, terrorism, running sweatshops, the civil rights movement, and just about anything and everything that *some* audiences consider good while others consider not so good; or acts that have some positive features or consequences and some negative ones; or can be looked at both positively and negatively; or have positive consequences even though they are widely considered bad; or have negative consequences even though they are generally considered good. Winning in sports is good, but maybe "winning at all cost" is deviant. Innovating in art is good—just look at the French impressionists. But if your art is *too* innovative, you alienate conventional audiences and artists, and that's deviant. Going out into the wilderness is good; you get all that fresh air, exercise, build your body to peak condition, get away from urban society's contamination. But what about its dangers and risks? Isn't there a fanatical, "edgework" side to the enterprise? That's where the deviance comes in. Whenever there's an activity with both a positive and a negative side to it, or whenever something is judged as positive by one group and negative by other—that's positive deviance.

The fact is this "positive deviance" exercise can be multiplied endlessly; all you need is a brain, the eyes to see what's going on in the society around you, and not worry too much about conceptual or theoretical consistency. Some fanciful possible candidates for positive deviants include the following—and the sorts of things that they do constitute examples of positive deviance: successful prostitutes and pimps; an insane but revered charismatic religious leader—Rasputin perhaps; a serial rapist who is admired by his buddies; a serial arsonist who brings his community together; antiheroes; social or populist bandits and "primitive rebels"—Frank and Jesse James, Billy the Kid, Butch Cassidy, John Dillinger, "Pretty Boy" Floyd, Bonnie Parker and Clyde Barrow, Guiliano, the Sicilian bandit-hero, Lampião, the Brazilian bandit-hero, Jesus, Mohammed; a white collar swindler who contributes millions to charity; Bernard Madoff, who stole from the fairly rich and bought nice things for his family; getting high on illicit drugs. The list is endless (Stebbins, 2011, pp. 28–29). Why end there?

Some scholars (Sagarin, 1985)—as I do—consider the positive deviance concept oxymoronic, a contradiction in terms. It seems to be used in such a variety of different and inconsistent ways that the inconsistency itself provides the possibility of the "positiveness" in "positive deviance." I've located at least nine different meanings of the concept: (1) overconformity, or following the norms too closely (Posner, 1976); (2) extraordinary or unusually superior behavior, resulting in reward (Wilkins, 1964; Dodge, 1985; Heckert, 1989; Ben-Yehuda, 1990); (3) too much of a good thing, the possession of an extraordinary abundance of a positive value, resulting in condemnation (Posner, 1976); (4) normative flexibility, bending the rules (Harman, 1985; Ben-Yehuda, 1990); (5) societal functionality of something that some regard as negative (Harman, 1985; Ben-Yehuda, 1990); (6) social change (Ben-Yehuda, 1990); (7) individuals and actions once designated as deviant that become acceptable or rewarded later on, and vice versa (Heckert, 1989; Ben-Yehuda, 1990); (8) acts or traits that are regarded as deviant in one context or social circle that are acceptable or praiseworthy elsewhere (Ben-Yehuda, 1990); anti-heroes, that is, criminals and deviants who are admired (Heckert, 1989). In short, anyone who is untroubled by conceptual slippage, inconsistency, and sloppiness can play in this sand box and attract an interested audience. If an act is *only* celebrated, that is viewed positively by *any and all* relevant audiences and social circles, it is indeed self-contradictory or oxymoronic. If it is an act that some audiences view positively and others negatively, or if an act, once condemned, is celebrated and praised at a later point in time, some supporters of the concept have referred to it as "positive deviance," but this merely emphasizes the relativity of deviance, as we've emphasized all along. This simply makes it a run-of-the-mill, everyday, meat-and-potatoes instance of deviance—nothing special. If a widely condemned action has unintended consequences that some social collectivities praise, celebrate, consider positive, this is an example of what Durkheim (1938/1958) and Erikson (1966) referred to when discussing the "functions" of deviance—we've known that for a century. This is pretty much true of deviance in general. If a customarily regarded "good" action or trait (an Olympic gold medal, or great beauty) generates envious reactions among certain individuals or audiences, then indeed, this highlights the dual nature of deviance; it is not self-contradictory to call this a form of "positive deviance." In short, "positive deviance" is a jumble of different kinds of actions, with different sorts of qualities, some of which are self-contradictory, while others can pass conceptual muster—but all in all, focus on the concept seems to be making a mountain out of a molehill.

SUMMARY

Humans evaluate one another according to a number of criteria, including beliefs, behavior, and physical traits. If, according to the judgment of a given audience doing the evaluation, someone holds the "wrong" attitudes, engages in the "wrong" behavior, or possesses the "wrong" traits or characteristics, he or she will be looked down upon, treated in a negative, punishing, condemnatory fashion. Sociologists refer to beliefs, behavior, or traits that violate or depart or deviate from a basic norm or rule held by a collectivity of people, and are likely to generate negative reactions among the members of that collectivity who observe or hear about that norm violation, as *social deviance* or simply *deviance*.

There are four necessary ingredients for deviance to occur: One, a rule or a norm; two, someone who violates or is thought to violate that norm; three, an "audience" who judges the violation; and four, the likelihood of negative reactions from this audience. What *defines* or *constitutes* deviance are the actual or potential negative reactions that certain acts, beliefs, or traits are likely to elicit.

Defining deviance is not a mere matter of departing from just *anyone's* norms, however. The sociologist is interested in the likelihood that a given normative departure will result in punishment, condemnation, and stigma. Hence, we must focus on the *number* and the *power* of the people who define a given act, belief, and trait as "wrong." The greater the number and the power of the people who regard something as wrong, the greater the likelihood that its believers, enactors, and possessors will be punished, condemned, or stigmatized—and hence, the more deviant that something is.

The distinction between *societal* and *situational* deviance is crucial here for understanding the *likelihood* of attracting condemnation, censure, punishment, scorn, and stigma. Societal deviance includes acts, beliefs, and conditions that are widely condemned pretty much throughout the society—in a phrase, "high-consensus" deviance. Looking at deviance as a societal or society-wide phenomenon adopts a "vertical" perspective: It sees judgments of right and wrong as being hierarchical in nature. Some judgments have more influence than others. In contrast, "situational" deviance is whatever attracts condemnation, censure, punishment, scorn, and stigma specifically in *particular* settings, groups, or social circles. This view of deviance looks "horizontally" or "across" the society and accepts the idea that different groups, circles, and categories have different judgments of right and wrong and hence, different notions of deviance. "Situational" deviance is usually "low-consensus" deviance since there is a low level of agreement throughout the society that such acts, beliefs, and traits are deviant.

Contrary to the stereotype, deviance includes more than behavior. Sociologists refer to the ABCs of deviance—*attitudes, behavior*, and *conditions*. True, behavior constitutes a major form of deviance, but so do beliefs and physical traits or conditions. Throughout history, people are judged to be normative violators for their beliefs almost as often, and almost as severely, as for their behavior. And judgments of physical appearance, likewise, are sharply judgmental, pervasive, and deeply determinative of society's rewards and punishments. In addition, racial, ethnic, religious, and "tribal" distinctions play a major role in judgments of deviance; Erving Goffman analyzes such distinctions in his delineation of sources of stigma. I refer to tribal stigma as collective deviance. Some members of certain ethnic groups stigmatize *every* member of one or more other groups, regardless of what any given individual has done to deserve it. Ethnicity is a quality that is passed through lineage or parentage and qualitatively different from one's own behavior. Please note that Goffman's "blemishes of individual character" stigma encompass the Adlers's attitudes ("treacherous and rigid beliefs") *and* behavior ("addiction, alcoholism, homosexuality, unemployment, suicidal attempts, and radical political behavior"). Even though both typologies entail three types of deviance of stigma, they overlap imperfectly. The Adlers's typology does not discuss tribal stigma.

Deviance is a coat of many colors; it assumes myriad forms, varieties, and shapes. Deviance is a conceptual category that cuts through a diversity of acts, beliefs, and traits. Hence, it might seem that, on the surface, phenomena that sociologists refer to as deviant share very little in common. But the very fact that the concept points to such diversity is what gives it its power. The concept of deviance highlights or illuminates features of social life that we might not otherwise have noticed. In the struggle to attain respectability, members of one category may resent being categorized with a less respectable category. For instance, self-avowed homosexual spokespersons feel the term "deviance" "taints" them and their behavior. This is an example of what philosophers called the "fallacy of reification," that is, identifying the part with the whole. "Deviance" represents only one dimension, and *in some ways*, homosexuals and murderers *do* share important characteristics, that is, their behavior and their identity are discredited in the eyes of much of the public. When I ask these spokespersons, "Are homosexuals discriminated against and looked down upon by most Americans?" their answer is an immediate, "Of course!" My reply is, "That's exactly what I'm taking about!" In a similar vein, adultery, using cocaine, prostitution, being an atheist, and being autistic are also deviant.

Several criteria are used by the uninformed observer to define deviance: absolute criteria, mental disorder, statistical departures from the norm, and harm to individuals and to the society. These are false criteria, naïve definitions of deviance. Sociologically, deviance is not defined by absolute criteria, mental disorder, unusualness, or harm. Indeed, many absolute definitions of wrongness or deviance have been proposed, but everyone has his or her own such definition, and none of them have anything to do with how the majority reacts to certain behavior, beliefs, or conditions. Most "deviants" are mentally normal, so clearly, mental disorder is separate and independent from deviance. Unusual behavior, beliefs, and conditions are not always deviant, and common ones are not always conventional. And lots of harmless acts are deviant, while many harmful ones are conventional. Clearly, these four definitions of deviance are misleading and naïve; sociologically, they are dead-ends. Immorality,

mental disorder, dysfunction, and abnormality, a statistical departure from the norm, and harm are *invalid* definitions of deviance; even though any of them *could be* defined as deviant, not one of them defines deviance in general.

To the sociologist, deviance is *relative, contextual, contingent*, and *probabilistic*.

Saying that deviance is "relative" means that members of different societies and social circles, as well as periods of historical eras, define good and bad, true and false, in different ways, and reward or punish different behaviors, beliefs, and physical characteristics. We may not agree with these judgments, but the fact that they exist and determine reactions and interactions is an indisputable fact.

Saying that deviance is "contextual" means that people's definition of wrongdoing depends on the physical or social situation or *context* within which behavior takes place, beliefs are expressed, or characteristics appear. Nudity is acceptable in certain locales but not others; the taking of human life is tolerated in warfare but not under normal circumstances; a delinquent boy can express academic knowledge and interest to his teacher, with no one else around, but not among members of his gang; acting slightly drunk or tipsy may be encouraged and approved at a raucous party, but it is unacceptable in the classroom, at a board meeting, or in a house of worship. The same behavior, in the same society, at the same historical era, is not always judged in the same way under all circumstances: *Context* matters.

Saying that deviance is "contingent" means that whether someone is punished, rewarded, or ignored for engaging in an act, expressing a belief, or possessing a given trait, is *dependent* on a variety of factors *independent* of the act, belief, or trait itself. One of these factors is *who the person is*. Usually, high status insulates the deviant actor from the consequences of deviance, but usually, scandal that engulfs a politician causes him (and most politicians who get caught up in scandal are men) to lose his position.

Saying that deviance is "probabilistic" means that condemnation and punishment do not inevitably follow discovery. We could draw a spectrum or continuum from acts, beliefs, and conditions that are *extremely likely* to draw negative reactions at one end, over to those that are unlikely. To each act, expression of belief, and physical condition, we can attach a certain *likelihood* of censure and punishment upon discovery. Picture a white supremacist with a Swastika tattooed on his bald head, screaming out racist slogans at a church, synagogue, mosque, university, mainstream political gathering, or school. Most of us would say the likelihood is extremely high that he would be socially shunned, censured, or condemned in these groups; indeed, that likelihood is very high. On the other hand, lots of acts, beliefs, and conditions are very *unlikely* to result in seriously negative reactions among most audiences: birdwatching, wearing glasses, driving an old car, eating beef tongue, reading poetry, growing pansies, listening to Muzak, keeping an iguana for a pet, believing that Pluto is a planet, being an inch or two taller or shorter than the norm. It's important to recognize that deviance is a *continuum* that stretches from whatever others find *extremely* offensive all the way over to the norm—which most others regard as not at all offensive.

Some behaviors are so widely condemned that they have been condemned pretty much everywhere; with them, there is virtually no "relativity" at all. No society on Earth accepts the unprovoked killing of an in-group member; robbery (the "Robin Hood" syndrome notwithstanding), rape, and serious or aggravated assault very rarely result in widespread tolerance or approval. On the other hand, many behaviors, beliefs, and traits vary enormously over time and cultural space with respect to the degree to which members of societies are condemned for committing, believing in, and possessing them. Affirming atheism during the Spanish Inquisition typically resulted in torture and execution; today, the disbeliever meets mild but not savage disapproval. At one time, in some places, teaching evolution was illegal and deviant; today, evolution is taught in every nonreligious high school, college, and university in the country. As late as the 1960s, the distribution of hard-core pornography was a crime, and was prosecuted; today, graphic hard-core porn depicting almost every conceivable sex act is available, in almost unlimited quantity, to anyone with access to the Internet. These changes tell us that the study of deviance is about setting, enforcing, and violating rules as well as the degree to which rules vary or remain the same over time and from one society to another. Some rules apply pretty much everywhere (though the punishment of the perpetrator does vary). With others, the sociologist's job is to understand and explain the variation. This book accepts the challenge of that task.

Sociologists adopt one of two radically different approaches to deviance: essentialism and constructionism. Essentialism argues that deviance exists objectively and hence, its occurrence, rate, and distribution can be explained scientifically. In other words, essentialism implies and even demands scientific positivism. In contrast, constructionism argues that what's deviant is a subjectively arrived-at phenomenon, dependent on time and place, society and culture, observer and enactor. What's most important about deviance is how different audiences regard behavior, beliefs, and conditions, both conceptually and evaluatively. What something "is," and whether it is good, bad, or neutral, are outcomes of judgments of social actors within specific contexts. Behavior, beliefs, and conditions exist, *as deviance*, only as a result of the actions and reactions of audiences.

Some scholars believe that "positive deviance" provides some conceptual and theoretical purchase. Others believe that the notion is sloppy, flabby, imprecise, and an intellectual dead-end. The controversy, they believe, comes down to a matter of semantics; *what something means* can never be resolved by fiat or as a result of empirical verification or refutation. Either you're comfortable with using a concept that is internally contradictory or you're not. If that concept proves to have theoretical pay-off, then it's worth using it; if it doesn't, it's not. Perhaps time will tell, perhaps not.

Account: What Is Sexual Harassment? Is It Deviant?

In 2012, five women who formerly worked for the office of Brooklyn state Assemblyman Vito Lopez, talked to The New York Times *about having been sexually harassed in the politician's office; two had already spoken to representatives of the state assembly's Ethics Committee about the matter, and the committee substantiated their claims, sending Mr. Lopez a letter of reprimand, stripping him of his committee chairmanship, and barring interns under the age of twenty-one from working in his office. The Assemblyman, these women alleged, used crude language and jokes, made unwanted sexual advances toward them, asked them to wear more provocative dress—shorter skirts, no bra, higher heels, blouses that would enable the Assemblyman to peek down their cleavage— and asked them to accompany him on overnight trips. The Assemblyman paid special attention to the women he referred to as the "well endowed." One of the complainants added, "Vito doesn't hire ugly girls," indicating that looks rather than ability determined the politician's hiring practices. Even more surprising, in June of 2012, Sheldon Silver, the state assembly's speaker, authorized a payment of $103,000 to settle prior allegations from two other women for the same violations—money that was paid out of New York taxpayers' pockets; later, Silver paid out an additional $32,000, which was private not state money. Mr. Lopez vigorously denied having engaged in any form of sexual harassment (Dolnick and Hakim, 2012).*

How do women determine that they are on the receiving end of an act of sexual harassment? How do the representatives of the relevant agencies decide that the act of sexual harassment has been inflicted upon the complainant? Howard Becker (1963, pp. 155–162) wrote about "rule enforcers," who define a particular action as wrongful and attempt to sanction the rule violator. The men who make unwanted sexual advances and/or create a hostile work environment for women by engaging in sexual harassment are engaging in deviant behavior; if rule enforcers determine that harassment has taken place, a representative of the university may admonish violators and ask them to desist from their objectionable behavior. If they continue violating the rules spelling out harassment, the university may take sterner, more formal punishments. The interviewee, Sarah Sternglanz (whose nickname is "Sally"), who has a PhD in psychology, has handled sexual harassment cases in the affirmative action office of a large state university. She spells out wrongful, actionable deviant behavior, and illustrates those acts that fall into a gray or acceptable area that are not wrongful or deviant and should not be punished or condemned—of which, Dr. Sternglanz says, the latter cases are never or hardly ever reported. Here, I am the interviewer.*

ERICH: How would you define sexual harassment?

SALLY: Making unwelcome sexual advances and/or creating a hostile work environment based on sexual status. It can be sexist without a specifically sexual component. I'd estimate that the unwelcome sexual advances category makes up half of our cases and the hostile work environment category makes up the other half. It's very rare that a trivial case or something borderline is reported to us. When we get a report it's a matter of explaining it to the person who's doing it and getting them to stop doing it. The complainant rarely wants a person fired, they want the person to stop doing it. Usually, before they come to us, they've complained to the person and the person doesn't stop. Often, there's a power differential. Here's an example, a real case that happened and was reported to us. A professor likes to tell dirty jokes to a secretary and she becomes flustered. She complains directly to him and he actually stops telling the jokes directly to her, but he does it in front of her desk and he tells his chums where she can hear. She told us she

(Continued)

Account: What Is Sexual Harassment? Is It Deviant? Continued

used to feel sick every morning before coming to work. She filed a grievance with us and he agreed that what she said happened actually did happen, but he felt he should be able to do that. He was a full professor and she was only a secretary. The crucial factor is how the victim feels about it. Unless the complainant is really off the wall. For some courses, talking about sex is appropriate. A sex education course, for instance. Or sex in literature: You may have to discuss the works of the Marquis de Sade. For some courses, certain kinds of touching are appropriate. Teaching someone the correct fingering on a violin, for instance. Teaching the forward roll in gym. These things should be done in the least invasive way possible, but they have to be done. But there are marginal cases. What if the theater department decides to put on *O! Calcutta!*? [A play in which the actors take off their clothes on stage.] Should a student be forced to appear in it? Where do we draw the line between appropriate and gratuitous sex? There are times when a professor drags in sex gratuitously. Here's something that happened and was reported to us. A social sciences instructor was talking about the relationship between a hypothesis and a fact. "So, Ms. Jones," he said in front of the class, standing in front of her, "how would you test the hypothesis that I am the world's best lover?" She crouched down in her seat and turned a bright red. By doing this, he created a hostile learning environment for her. Which he realized immediately when we explained this to him.

ERICH: Did she report this incident to your office?

SALLY: No. Two other students in her class did. She became upset about it, they were her friends, and they wanted to make sure the professor didn't do it again. In fact, he was aware that it was a problem as soon as he said it. He said, "I was waiting for you to call." A majority of sexual harassers [that are reported to our office] are repeat offenders. Most people

don't report a case of one-time offenders. They make a slip once and realize their mistake and they don't do it again. Most of our students are pretty sophisticated. They don't get upset about nude pictures or the occasional remark about sex. In fact, I think they put up with too much.

ERICH: What about sexual advances? Do they mainly involve faculty or graduate instructors and TAs [teaching assistants]?

SALLY: A majority are faculty. Let me give you the worst case scenario. A faculty member came up behind a secretary and unzipped his fly and took out his penis and put it on her shoulder. Here's another one. A faculty member told a secretary, "That's a pretty dress. It makes you look really beautiful. It's getting me really excited. Here, let me show you," and he put her hand on his crotch.

ERICH: How many cases do you get that are unwanted sexual advances?

SALLY: During the three years I worked in that office, we got ten cases a year where I had to do investigation. We also got a lot of little cases which didn't involve investigation, maybe two times as many [as the ones that did]. The complainant wanted to know whether what happened was sexual harassment and usually I'd say, yes, that probably is a case of sexual harassment, I'd have to investigate it, do you want me to investigate? And they'd say, no, I just wanted to know. What the victim almost always wants is to get the harasser to stop. "I just want to be left alone to do my job in peace" is the refrain we hear over and over again. They don't want the harasser drawn and quartered. One professor was constantly making lewd remarks. I'd love to see you in a see-through blouse, tell me what you and your boyfriend do in bed, things like that. One professor got really physical with his students. He was a major contender for a very big prize. He was extremely devoted to his research area and he had no life outside his research, and so he was socially incompetent. He didn't segue from talking about his research to talking about sex. We had a four-hour session involving the dean, his chair, my boss, and so on. He refused to understand that other people were upset about what he was doing. "But I love so-and-so," he'd say. "But she doesn't love you," we'd tell him. After we talked to him, another student came in and reported yet another incident. All these students wanted to work with him. This one told us that she was very careful not to see him for dinner, only lunch, never to see him in a situation in which he could come on to her. I wanted to work with him, she said, I never reported his advances, I wanted to keep working with him, I didn't want to be singled out. So I told him, she said, about the dinner, you remember, I'm married, and he said, yes, yes, I know. But he tried to get me into bed anyway, she told us. And so we called him. We said, wait a minute, I thought you agreed that you wouldn't do this sort of thing any more. My former boss asked him, did you think we were being reasonable in telling you that you had to stop? He agreed that we were being reasonable. But still you did it, she told him. That was it for him.

ERICH: What do you mean, "That was it for him"?

SALLY: The university had the option to renew his contract or not renew and we [the university] chose not to renew. It was made very clear to him why. He was gone.

ERICH: At [the university], over the past five to ten years, has there been any change in the number of cases of sexual harassment?

SALLY: I would like to think that at [the university] there are fewer cases of sexual harassment today than in the past. My guess is, less than 1 percent of the [male] faculty are doing things that would be classified as sexual harassment. Maybe we put the fear of God into them or we got rid of people who did that sort of thing. Maybe they took early retirement. We cleaned house to some extent. Maybe hearing an official training or generating publicity makes departments aware that we are taking this seriously. Cases of tenured faculty took place.

ERICH: What's your theory of why sexual harassment takes place?

SALLY: I could get all "feminist theory" about why it takes place [which would be an explanation] that's about power. But personally, as for me, I'd say it's people who are selfish, bully-type people who don't seem to care about the fact that they're making other people miserable. The behavior is appalling. They're doing things their mother told them not to do. Why should we have laws telling [what] people should be doing in the first place? There's also gender roles, the power structure, that sort of thing. Most of the cases we see involve disparities in power. But some of the cases, the really serious cases, involve psychiatric problems. I mean, I fail to see why we have to tell people to do what ordinary common decency tells them to do in the first place. I just don't get it, I really don't.

QUESTIONS

Awareness of the existence and wrongfulness of sexual harassment arose during the feminist upsurge in the 1970s. It was an era in which what was taken-for-granted behavior—that women in the workforce should tolerate unwanted sexual advances, crude sexual comments and jokes, comments about their anatomy—became defined as deviant. Catherine MacKinnon's book, *The Sexual Harassment of Working Women: A Case of Sex Discrimination* (1979) was unquestionably the most influential publication in generating social change; in effect, she and her ideological colleagues were, in Howard Becker's phrase (1963, pp. 147–152), "rule creators."

Actions that were common in the past have become uncommon today—but they still happen, as we see in the introduction to this account and in the cases Dr. Sternglanz adjudicates. Is sexual harassment an instance of "defining deviancy up" (Krauthammer, 1993)? Have we gone too far in condemning and punishing harmless flirtation and kidding around, as some critics say? Or is a

(Continued)

Account: What Is Sexual Harassment? Is It Deviant?   Continued

workplace free of sexual harassment an entirely laudable objective? When Howard Becker wrote about deviance in the 1960s, do you think he could have imagined that, in their actions, "rule creators" and "rule enforcers" would have been advancing a liberal or progressive cause, and reactionaries and conservatives would have been opposing such rules and their enforcement? Do you think that sexual harassment cases result in too many cases of false accusations? Or do you think that women who lodge such complaints are highly likely to have a legitimate complaint? In the case of the allegations made against Kings County Assemblyman Lopez, does the multiple confirmation by more than a half-dozen women who say essentially the same thing indicate that they have a just grievance? Do the specific cases Dr. Sternglanz mentions sound like sexual harassment to you?

Explaining Deviant Behavior

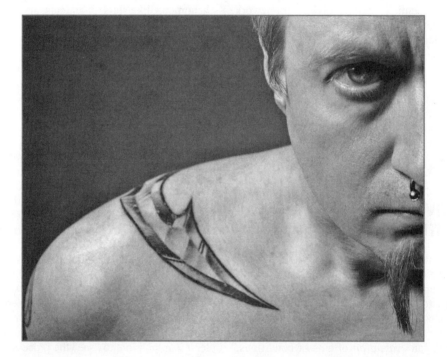

Learning Objectives:

After reading this chapter, you will be able to:

- compare and contrast positivism and essentialism with relation to deviance;
- answer the question "Deviant behavior: why do they do it?";
- understand biological theories of crime and deviance;
- discuss free will, rational calculation, and routine activities theory;
- discuss social disorganization as a concept as well as the Chicago School;
- recognize anomie and strain theory;
- understand differential association and learning theory;
- understand social control theory;
- examine self-control theory as a general theory of crime.

The sociology of deviance is made up of two distinct but interlocking enterprises—essentialism and constructionism. Essentialism sees deviance as objectively real and hence, scientifically explicable. In contrast, constructionism argues that the most crucial feature of deviance is the fact that rules, judgments of wrongdoing, and assigning offenders to deviant categories, are made by specific audiences in specific contexts and hence, have no reality apart from such judgments. Essentialism *implies* positivism, or the scientific effort to explain, in a cause-and-effect fashion, *why* people engage in deviant behavior. Here, we'll focus on the perspectives that make use of the essentialist and positivistic framework. "Explaining" deviance in a positivistic fashion entails attempting to answer the "Why do they do it?" question. In a very real sense, these two enterprises—essentialism and constructionism—are disparate and incommensurable; the framework of each approaches the phenomenon from radically different angles. Essentialism regards the deviant *act* as the primary concern; constructionism regards the process by which the act is judged and reacted to *as* deviant (Wright, 1984, pp. 188, 189, 190).

POSITIVISM AND ESSENTIALISM

Even the most positivistic of criminologists and sociologists of deviance recognize that *all* forms of crime and deviance are socially constructed according to laws and rules; hence, they are relativistic and socially constructed. Gwynn Nettler states that crime, and by extension deviance, represents "an *evaluation* of acts or conditions." Definitions of crime and deviance rest on moral judgments and consequently, "*there is no essence of criminality* [or deviance] to be observed in an act or situation" (1984, p. 1). But—and this is a big "but"—all positivists believe, and *must* believe, in order for their enterprise to be legitimate, that an objective common core or common thread holds deviance and crime together; otherwise there would be nothing to explain. No positivist believes that deviance and crime are "just" a matter of social convention or construction, possessing no objective or concrete quality in

common. To put the matter another way, positivists are *more likely to stress* the essential, indwelling characteristics common to all phenomena called "deviance" and "crime." In contrast, constructionists are more likely to stress the process by which certain things come to be regarded and judged *as* crime and deviance.

What is positivism in the social sciences? *It is the application of the scientific* method to the study of *human behavior*. The practitioners of positivism maintain that sociology and criminology are not radically different from the natural sciences. They believe that deviance and crime can be studied in much the same way that natural phenomena, like stars, chemicals, and ocean tides can be studied—of course, making the necessary adjustments in research methods, predictability, and agency.

Positivism is based on three fundamental assumptions, one, *empiricism*, two, *objectivism*, three, *determinism*.

Empiricism

Positivism assumes that the material world is real and that the scientist can know the world through the five senses; in other words, the positivist is an *empiricist*. Empiricism is the belief that seeing, feeling, hearing, tasting, and smelling convey information that gives the observer sense impressions of the way things are. Often, these senses must be aided by instruments (such as a microscope, a telescope, or an oscilloscope). In addition, many things can never be directly observed, such as historical and geological events that happened in the past; hence, reasoning about them entails inferring from the data available to the scientist. For example, it is impossible to "see" the process of macroevolution take place, so biologists and geologists infer its existence by means of fossil and DNA evidence. Recent "cutting edge" cosmology—studies of the universe by astronomers—often transcends immediate observation. The physicist and astronomer theorize about or have to infer, but cannot directly observe, quarks, the Higgs boson, mesons, alternate universes, and black holes—the last of these, stars whose gravitational field is so dense that light cannot escape from them.

The guiding principle of the empiricist is, "I trust my senses to tell me what's true," and it is the guiding principle of all positivists. Positivists believe that if phenomena are not directly—or indirectly—observable through the information provided by the five senses and cannot be integrated into existing or conceivable theoretical and conceptual perspectives, questions asked and issues raised are not scientifically meaningful. Not necessarily wrong, just nonscientific: outside the scientific framework. Hence, the question of whether a given work of art, poetry, form of behavior, belief, or political regime is "good" or "bad," or whether or not a painting or a musical composition is "beautiful," or whether or not God exists, are considered *non-empirical*, and hence, nonscientific, questions. And the positivistic enterprise is amoral; matters of good and evil are analytically separate from matters of empirical truth or falsity.

The fact that certain things cannot be directly observed by the scientist is especially crucial for the sociologist and the criminologist because *most* human behavior cannot be seen at the moment it is enacted. Instead, social scientists must infer what happened through a variety of *indirect* indicators, including the answers to questions about the behavior of subjects, informants, and interviewees. Researchers have developed a variety of methods to determine the validity of answers to questions about behavior, and some of them get very close to the reality they are attempting to describe. Some research methods *do* entail direct observation—participant observation as well as field and laboratory experiments, for instance. But *most* social science research methods rely on indirect indicators, and here, the researcher must be skeptical, clever, and resourceful.

Objectivism

The second assumption of positivism, objectivism, means that phenomena in the material world are *objectively real* and possess certain objective or internally consistent characteristics that distinguish them from other phenomena. In line with our interests, the social scientist can distinguish deviant behavior from conventional, conforming behavior. In other words, the many forms of deviant behavior share a *common thread, a differentiating trait* that distinguishes them from conventional, conforming, legal behavior. Positivists

reject the notion that definitions of right or wrong are really as relative as constructionist sociologists of deviance argue. Public perceptions of right and wrong do not vary much across societal lines; there *is* a "common core" from society to society to what's regarded as deviant (Newman, 1976). A few observers have mistakenly argued that that "common core" is *harm:* Behavior that is harmful to society, they say, is highly likely to be defined as wrongdoing; hence, the central assumption of deviance researchers—relativism—is incorrect, and consequently, "deviance is dead" (Costello, 2006). Others seek different qualities, but explanations cannot exist without *something* that ties together the phenomena they attempt to explain. *All* positivists know that deviance and crime are socially constructed, but they must minimize their "artificial" quality to account for them *as a form of behavior.*

The same thing applies to crime. As we saw, while positivistic criminologists will warn that there is no "essence," no common core, to criminal behavior (Nettler, 1984, pp. 1, 16), most will nonetheless regard correlations between this phenomenon, this entity, this phenomenon or *thing*—crime—and key sociological characteristics, as extremely important. If crime were not a real "thing" or phenomenon in the material or behavioral world, they say, then how could it possibly manifest statistical relationships with key variables such as race, socioeconomic status, gender, and residence? Crime is not a simple product of the process of social construction, they say. There *is* a material reality to crime above and beyond social and legal definitions. Crime is much more than a mere social construction; there is an identifiable behavior core (or "essence") to criminal behavior. If labels were not at least minimally internally consistent, there would be no point in studying them as an analytic category; they would have no coherence and possess nothing in common except their label.

For instance, are definitions of mental illness arbitrary? Is a person who is labeled mentally ill in one society considered sane in another? Is there a common thread in mental disorder? Or is the term *nothing but* a label applied by psychiatrists, or by the general public? Does the principle of relativity apply to conditions that are commonly referred to as mental disorder, as some claim (Curra, 2000, pp. 169–185)? Is the enterprise of psychiatry little more than an updated version of "witchcraft," as other observers have argued (Turner and Edgley, 1983)? Positivists say no. Mental disorder is an identifiable "thing" or condition in the world and not the mere imposition of a socially constructed definition (Spitzer, 1975). Says Gwynn Nettler, an outspoken advocate of the positivistic position in the study of deviance and crime: "Some people are more crazy than others; we can tell the difference and calling lunacy a name does not cause it" (Nettler, 1974, p. 894).

Determinism

The third assumption positivists make is determinism. They ask: What *causes* the deviant behavior, beliefs, or conditions? For centuries, the question, *why do they do it?* has been asked about persons who stray beyond society's moral or legal boundaries. What is it that influences some people to violate society's norms—the Ten Commandments, for example—while the rest of us do not? Or, taking the question to a structural, society-wide, or categorical level, what is it about certain societies or categories of people that leads to higher rates of deviance among their ranks than other societies or other categories? Do specific social *conditions* (such as anomie) encourage deviance? Do other conditions, such as societal integration, inhibit it? These sorts of questions ask for an explanation of deviance as a certain type of action or behavior.

Scientists seek *naturalistic* explanations, that is, they stress the cause-and-effect relationships that they can discover in the material world. They avoid spiritual, supernatural, or paranormal explanations for causality. In contrast, for instance, parapsychologists claim that they have empirical evidence that shows the mind can influence the workings of the material world. Most scientists reject parapsychology as a scientific discipline because its practitioners leave out of the picture the *mechanism* by which this influence takes place, that is, the question of precisely *how* the mind influences the workings of the material world. Most scientists don't accept parapsychology as a natural science discipline because it doesn't fit in with a materialistic or scientific framework. The same is true of the so-called

theory of "intelligent design," which argues that evolution produced living species, including humans, as a result of "designs" by an intelligent entity, presumably God. Most scientists reject intelligent design as non-empirical because it cannot be integrated into a naturalistic or materialistic framework of how the world works.

Positivist theories of deviance and crime look for cause-and-effect *explanations* for non-normative acts and beliefs. The assumption that the world works in a cause-and-effect fashion is referred to as *determinism*. And an explanation for a general class of phenomena or events is called a *theory*. The positivist assumes that the phenomena and events of the world do not take place at random, by accident; there is a *reason* for their patterning. A theory addresses the question: Why are things the way they are? This means that we must seek the reasons for the regularities we observe. When we discover that men are more likely to violate society's norms than women, we want to find out *why* this is so. Urbanization increases rates of drug abuse: Again, *why?* Conditions or factors such as gender and urbanism *cause* or *influence* specific forms of behavior, deviance included. It is the scientist's job to locate the dynamics of the cause-and-effect sequences that exist in the world.

Some positivistic approaches are *individualistic* (or "micro") in that they focus on the characteristics of categories of individuals who violate norms or break the law. They argue that deviants share a trait or characteristic in common—which non-deviants lack—that can be isolated, which will help provide an explanation for deviance. Other positivistic approaches are more *structural* (or "macro"). They look at the "big picture" and argue that certain *deviance-inducing conditions* share a common thread that can be discovered, which will lead to an explanation of deviance—such as urbanism, anomie, society-wide income distributions, and so on. Whether individually or structurally produced, deviance results from certain factors in a cause-and-effect fashion, which can be discovered and explicated by the scientifically inclined sociologist.

Positivists seek broad, general, even universal explanations. This means that scientists are not satisfied with explanations of specific, particular, or unique events. The goal of every scientist is to explain as many observations in the material world as possible. This means that they all look for *patterns* or *regularities* in the material world. When criminologists study criminal violence in one delinquent gang, they are looking for patterns of criminal violence in *all* delinquent gangs, for gangs *in general*. To the positivist, a case study of one prostitute is meaningful only insofar as it sheds light on *all* prostitutes, or the institution of prostitution *as a whole*. Positivists are not interested in particulars or specifics for their own sake. They want to know how and to what extent these particulars fall into recognizable *patterns* that will enable scientists to make generalizations about how the world as a whole works.

DEVIANT BEHAVIOR: WHY DO THEY DO IT?

The earliest theories of wrongdoing, what we now call deviance, typically concentrated on the question: *Why do they do it?* Why adultery, murder, witchcraft, thievery, disobedience to authority, insanity? And why deviant beliefs—atheism, unbelief, blasphemy, heresy? And since undesirable *physical characteristics* were thought to be a consequence or product of evil deeds or thoughts, people in the past asked questions such as: Why are some of us afflicted with the curse of leprosy? What causes birth defects? Why are some women "barren," or childless? What causes blindness, albinism, curvature of the spine, dwarfism, extreme ugliness, as well as any manner of undesirable traits? In short, members of societies in the past attempted to explain the deviant "ABCs"—actions, beliefs, and conditions (Adler and Adler, 2009, p. 13).

Although from today's vantage point, the explanations that were devised in earlier times were inadequate or fallacious, they all centered on an effort to account for anomalous, undesirable differentness that needed explaining. They cannot be referred to as "positivistic" theories because they lacked the essential ingredients of scientific theories: They were not *empirical*—they could not be falsified by observable evidence of any kind. And they were not theoretical; they did not offer a satisfying, materialistic or scientific cause-and-effect account of how certain behavior, belief, or traits came to be. However

crude from today's vantage point, past theories of wrongdoing *did* ask "*Why do they do it?*" This question has ancient roots.

Historically, the oldest explanation for deviant behavior was *demonic possession*. For many thousands of years, evil spirits, including the devil, were thought to cause men and women to engage in socially unacceptable behavior. A half-million years ago, Stone Age humans drilled holes into the skulls of individuals who engaged in wrongdoing of some kind—who, today, would be recognized as being mentally ill—so that evil spirits could escape. The ancient Hebrews, Egyptians, Greeks, and Romans performed rites of exorcism to cast out demonic beings dwelling in the body and soul of transgressors. During the Renaissance in Europe (roughly, the early 1400s to the early 1600s), hundreds of thousands of women and men were burned at the stake for "consorting" with the devil and engaging in wicked deeds. For millennia, humanity used demonic possession to explain untoward phenomena, and today, peoples in some parts of the world still accept this explanation.

BIOLOGICAL THEORIES OF CRIME AND DEVIANCE

For the most part, biological theories of crime and deviance have had an unsuccessful and undistinguished career among sociologists. The Italian physician Cesare Lombroso (1835–1909) put forth the claim that someone who is "born criminal" possesses "atavisms" or primitive evolutionary characteristics that produced violent, savage, apelike tendencies in humans. Charles Goring (1913), a medical officer in various English prisons, claimed to have discovered that criminals are "markedly" physically inferior to noncriminals—mainly, shorter and less heavy. In his well-known formulation, he declared that "physique selects crime." Ernest Hooton, a physical anthropologist, argued that criminals possessed low, sloping foreheads, high nasal bridges, thin lips, and compressed jaws. As a group, he declared, criminals "represent an aggregate of . . . biologically inferior individuals" (1939, p. 309). William H. Sheldon, a psychologist (1949), claimed that mesomorphs, or youths who have an athletic body build, are more likely to commit street crime than endomorphs (soft, pear-shaped individuals) or ectomorphs (thin, angular people). All of these theories are now considered invalid, trivial, and distracting. Moreover, sociologists began realizing, biological theories of crime seemed to stigmatize segments of the population for being physically different from the majority.

In the mid-sixties, a team of geneticists (Jacobs et al., 1965) published a brief paper claiming that they had discovered that men with an "extra Y" chromosome possessed exaggeratedly male features (they called them "super males") who were tall, big-boned, not very bright—and criminally-inclined. For over a decade, researchers conducted a substantial number of studies which located the same genetic variant coupled with the same deviant tendencies; for this period, for some observers, genetics seemed to be the key that unlocked the mystery of violent and wayward behavior. But eventually, epidemiological studies that examined real-world behavior found no differences in criminal behavior between extra-Y males and males without this supposed genetic aberration. By the 1980s, the "extra Y" theory was dropped by researchers (Kolata, 2012).

Beginning with the 1990s, however, biological and genetic factors made a comeback in the study of crime and deviance. In 1993, a team of geneticists published an influential article in *Science* magazine which reported on a Dutch family whose males were "affected by borderline mental retardation and abnormal behavior, which included impulsive aggression, arson, attempted rape, and exhibitionism" (Brunner et al., 1993). All of the men in this family who possessed a "deficiency of enzymatic activity" had a "disturbed regulation of impulsive aggression"; none of the males who did not possess this trait were violent (p. 578). Again, later epidemiological research revealed that men *outside of this particular family* who possessed this trait were no more violent than those who lacked it. In other words, the finding was not generalizable. Still, today, most researchers agree that a genetic predisposition to alcoholism, depression, schizophrenia, ADHD, aggression, anger, obesity, and impulsivity or a lack of self-control—all of which are linked to untoward behavior—is more than a mere possibility (Fishbein, 2002; Ball, 2011); in all likelihood, genetic markers will be found for

some or many of them. Genetic factors alone do not "cause" deviant or criminal behavior. Instead, such an outcome is a combination of genetic factors and environmental "triggers," such as stress, child abuse, an absence of a loving, caring parent, and various kinds of deprivation. Unfortunately, the research required to definitively establish these relationships is at least a generation away. "It is almost inconceivable that there is a common genetic factor" in all deviant, criminal, and violent behavior, says Robert C. Green, a geneticist and neurologist at Harvard. But, adds J.H. Pate Skene, a neurobiologist at Duke, "I think doing researchers on outliers, people at the end of a spectrum on something of concern like violent behavior, is certainly a good thing" (Kolata, 2012, p. D6). Nailing down the role of biological and genetic factors in the genesis of crime and deviance inevitably necessitates invoking the cliché, "more research is needed."

One of the more sophisticated and elegant statements of the position that biological mechanisms cause deviant and criminal behavior comes from David Eagleman, a neuroscientist (2011). He makes a more convincing argument that neurological forces cause unconventional, untoward, risky, deviant behavior than any previous medical figure, but his thesis does not always distinguish between the extreme acts he uses to make his case and the generic categories that social scientists delineate as "crime" and "deviance." He offers the case of Charles Whitman, a man who murdered thirteen people, shooting most of them with a rifle from the tower of the University of Texas library. Whitman's autopsy revealed a tumor "the diameter of a nickel" which "compromised" the frontal lobes of the brain, causing him to become "disinhibited" and engage in "startling behaviors" (2011, p. 114). Was Whitmore responsible for his behavior? If he had not been shot by the police, would he have been charged with a crime, prosecuted in court, and imprisoned or executed? Eagleman suggests that therapy would have been more appropriate. Genes govern neurological activity. Eagleman tells his readers that there is a "carrier of a particular set of genes" who commit violent crime four times more than those who lack the gene; "three times as likely to commit robbery, five times as likely to be arrested for murder, and thirteen times as likely to be arrested for a sexual offense." The vast majority of convicts carry the gene, and 98 percent of death-row inmates carry it. These statistics alone, Eagleman tells us, indicate that biological drives have a major impact on our untoward, wrongful behavior. *We're* not "steering the boat of our behavior," he says, our "inaccessible microscopic history" is (p. 115). Who are these carriers of these dangerous genes? They're called males.

Eagleman's clever trick alerts us to the dangers and the limitations of his reasoning. Charles Whitman's brain tumor almost certainly influenced him to lose all inhibitions on the murder of his fellow humans, but does this case offer a ready applicability to the regularities we see in variations in behavior from one society to another? Do men suffer five times, or thirteen times, or fifty times, more from this medical defect than women? Do African Americans, who engaged in murder (and are victims of murder) at five times the rate of whites, five times more likely to carry this tumor in their brains than whites? This conclusion is unlikely and implausible. As we'll see, in some societies, the criminal homicide rate is below 1 per 100,000 in the population per year; in others, it is over 80 per 100,000. Dr. Eagleman is not suggesting that brain irregularities among the populations living in the high-homicide countries are more than eighty times more common than those in the low-homicide countries. Consider periods of mass murder in countries such as Germany, Russia, China, Rwanda, and Cambodia; Eagleman does not claim that such episodes can be explained by malfunctions of the brain. In the United States between the 1990s and the early 2000s, the crime rate plummeted by 30 to 60 percent, depending on the crime. Did a decline in brain malfunction cause this decline? Surely not. But the point is not to argue that biological—genetic and neurological—factors do not play a rule in certain violent or other untoward or unconventional behaviors. Certainly they do. What's important is to stress that social, cultural, and historical factors play a role, conceptually independent of biological factors, and under certain circumstances, transcend them. How a brain irregularity produces a killer such as Charles Whitman is mediated by culture; with the same condition, others differently situated in the society would not have committed—and do not commit—such a crime. The fact that

males possess an extra y gene is one of many factors leading to higher crime rates; social scientists would say that the roles men and women play in society influences their respective crime rates far more. As Eagleman says we need both genes and environment to give us a full picture. But here, in this book, I emphasize the sociological dimension and put biological factors on the back burner.

FREE WILL, RATIONAL CALCULATION, AND ROUTINE ACTIVITIES THEORY

By the 1700s, intellectuals had abandoned the idea of the intervention of the devil and other evil, diabolical spirits to explain worldly phenomena and, instead, concentrated on material or worldly forces. Rather than being seen as a result of seduction by demons, the violations of rules, norms, and laws were thought to be caused by *free will*—a rational calculation of pleasure versus pain. The "free will" or "classical" school of criminology was the first sophisticated and academically respectable perspective or theory of criminal or deviant behavior. This theory argued that individuals choose among a number of alternative courses of action according to benefits they believe will accrue to them. This model sees people—criminals included—as free, rational, and hedonistic. Actions that bring pleasure are likely to be enacted and continued; those that are painful will be abandoned. Or so eighteenth century rationalists believed. The way to ensure conformity to society's norms and laws is to apprehend and punish offenders with celerity (or certainty), swiftness, and with just sufficient severity to make the pain following a violation greater than the pleasure the actor derives from it. The celerity, swiftness, and severity of punishment will deter crime, these theorists argued.

The classical school made several assumptions we now recognize as false. We see that people are not completely rational in their behavior; they engage in deviance and crime for several reasons aside from pursuing pleasure and avoiding pain. And what is pleasurable to one person may be painful to another, and vice versa. Moreover, most of the time when a rule or a law is violated, the offender is not caught, thereby nullifying one of the theory's major underpinnings—celerity or certainty—making the offender's calculation of pleasure and pain more complicated than these early thinkers imagined. Overall, as it was originally formulated, the classical school of criminology held a faulty model of human behavior.

The most often cited and discussed of all the contemporary free will or rationality theories is referred to as *routine activities theory* (Cohen and Felson, 1979; Clarke and Felson, 1993). Routine activities theory argues that criminal behavior will take place when and where there is a conjunction of three elements or factors: *the motivated offender*, a *suitable target*, and the *absence of a capable guardian*. The most remarkable feature of this theory is that it makes a radical break with positivistic theory in that it dispenses with criminal motivation. The "motivated offender" is very much in the background, a given—simply *assumed* by the theory. There's no need to invoke background factors, routine activities theory argues, because there will always be an abundant supply of people who are motivated to break the law, if that action is profitable to them. It is not *criminality* that we need to explain, but the criminal *act*. Criminal behavior, the theory argues, is a *purposive* and *rational* means of attaining an end—usually, acquiring money more efficiently than by any other method. People tend to act according to the utility that the outcome of their actions has for them, this theory argues. If homeowners leave a house unoccupied and a door unlocked, the motivated offender is more likely to burglarize that house than if it were occupied, the doors were locked, burglar alarms were installed, and a large guard dog were inside. Many—no doubt most—people will not burglarize the house because their utility is not maximized by the burglary, but still, the likelihood that they will be caught and punished, and that they will not be able to steal anything of value to them, is increased by an occupied house, and it is decreased if unoccupied.

This theory focuses mainly on *the immediate situational and environmental factors in explaining the commission and distribution of crime*—and by extension, a great deal of deviant behavior as well (Tillyer, 2011). A "suitable target" could be

money, property, even the opportunity to engage in a certain activity that might be deemed desirable by a motivated offender. And the "absence of a capable guardian" would refer to the fact that formal or informal agents of social control are not operative in a particular situation. Hence, for instance, if a potential rapist were to encounter a woman, alone, in a physical setting in which she could be threatened or overpowered, the likelihood that a rape will take place is greater than if she were accompanied. To the extent that corporate behavior is not monitored by or accountable to government or any other social control agencies, then corporate crime is more likely to take place than if these control systems are operative. The theory would predict that motivated users are more likely to consume illicit drugs if their access to them were greater than is currently the case; in the absence of video cameras, store guards, and the prying eye of sales clerks, customers are more likely to engage in shoplifting than they otherwise would; and students are more likely to cheat on exams if watchful professors, teaching assistants, and honest fellow students were absent. In other words, many more of us would engage in non-normative—or *deviant*—behavior if "capable guardians" were not watching over us and able to sanction our potential wrongdoing than if they were.

Rationalistic theories do not so much attempt to explain deviance and crime as take the "motivated offender" for granted and focus on the conditions that bring him or her out of the woodwork. Although rationality certainly enters into the crime and deviance equation, the fact that jails, prisons, and reform schools are full of young and not-so-young men (and women) who committed crimes impulsively, without planning, and got caught as a consequence, indicates that at the very least their calculation of whether one or more capable guardians were in the picture is flawed. By itself, the free will factor alone does not constitute a complete explanation. People who engage in deviance and crime do not represent a cross-section of society; they are not simply people who conducted an erroneous calculation of the likelihood of getting caught. The fact is *most* individuals who commit crimes to make money could have earned more, in the long run, by working at a low-paying drudge job. Clearly, some other explanation is necessary; apparently, the thrill, excitement, and self-righteousness that much criminal behavior entails is at least as powerfully motivating as the rational acquisition of money or the engaging in self-evidently satisfying acts (Katz, 1988).

At the same time—even for "irrational" actors who seek more than a concrete goal such as money—opportunity is *related* to the enactment of deviance. For *all* actors and *all* activities, the greater the perceived payoff and the lower the perceived likelihood of apprehension and punishment, the greater the likelihood that deviance will be enacted.

SOCIAL DISORGANIZATION AND THE CHICAGO SCHOOL

Just after World War I, a school of thought emerged out of research that was conducted in the city of Chicago by professors and graduate students at the University of Chicago. This school came to view the factors that explained deviance and crime as being located not in the person or the individual but in the social structure. The Chicago School argued that *entire neighborhoods* had become so disorganized that merely living in them hugely increased the likelihood of engaging in certain forms of deviant behavior. As cities grew, their residents increasingly came into contact with strangers. This encouraged impersonality, social distance, and a decline in social harmony. People no longer shared the same values or cared about how others felt about them and what they did. As a city grows, its residents' sense of community declines. And as social disorganization in a given neighborhood or community increases, deviant behavior increases along with it (Park, 1926; Shaw and MacKay, 1942). Clearly, social disorganization theorists situate their theory at the *community* level; it is a structural, not an individual explanation.

Not all neighborhoods are equally disorganized, however; therefore, rates of deviance and crime vary from one area, neighborhood, and community to another. Certain neighborhoods of a city inadvertently encourage nonconforming behavior while others do not. Why? What is it about certain neighborhoods that make them more hospitable than others to delinquency, crime, and deviant behavior? Social disorganization theorists locate the mechanism influencing nonconforming behavior in *land values*. Dwelling units in neighborhoods with low rental and property value are regarded as undesirable and unattractive to live in. Hence, such dwelling units tend to attract residents with two characteristics.

First, they are geographically unstable. Proponents of the Chicago School referred to such neighborhoods as *zones of transition*. Residents of these areas invest little emotionally in the neighborhood, and move out as soon as they can. And second, such residents are socially, racially, and ethnically heterogeneous; hence, they do not cohere into a unified and organized community. Residents who do not sink roots into the community in which they live do not care about its fate or what happens in them. Residents who are very different from one another do not care about the evaluations that others make of their behavior.

Socially disorganized neighborhoods are unable to develop "strong formal and informal linkages" among their residents; hence residents find it difficult to "regulate the behavior of their fellow neighbors" and exercise the kind of social control that would discourage delinquency, crime, and deviant behavior (Bursik and Grasmick, 1993, pp. x, 7). In short, Chicago sociologists insisted that deviance varies systematically by physical and geographical *location*. Where somebody is located residentially determines the likelihood of that person committing deviant and criminal acts.

The most important factor in the social disorganization school is very closely related to one of routine activity's key explanatory variables: the absence of a capable guardian. Social disorganization is the "macro" equivalent of the many "micro" factors that do or do not guard a "suitable target." It is *entire neighborhoods* that have lost the ability, the will, or the power to monitor and sanction behavior their residents consider untoward and non-normative. When drug dealers move into an abandoned building, the community does not root them out—or lacks the clout with the police department to have them displaced. Prostitutes are permitted to patrol the streets, harass residents, and engage in sex in cars, alleyways, or hallways without local interference. Junkies shoot up on front stoops, homeless men urinate in hallways, burglars routinely rip off apartments and clean out their contents—and little or nothing is done to stop them. For the criminal and the deviant, a socially disorganized neighborhood is their playground. Clearly, such a community is the "absence of a capable guardian" writ large. More recent research has indicated that *independent of economic disadvantage and residential instability*, neighborhoods that exercise collective efficacy—social cohesion among neighbors and residents' willingness to intervene on behalf of the common good—is related to lower rates of violence (Sampson, Raudenbush, and Earls, 1997).

A qualification: The school's generalizations don't apply to many of the forms of deviance we'll be examining. For instance, does it explain homosexuality? Of course not; in fact, with homosexuality, in many ways, the causal process works in a fashion that is precisely the *opposite* of that which social disorganization theory would predict. That is, in many large cities of the world, a substantial number of homosexuals gravitate *to* certain neighborhoods whose residents are less likely to harass them than those which they left. Thus, here, in a sense, the dependent and independent variables are reversed. White collar corporate crime receives no illumination whatsoever from social disorganization theory. In fact, it is in the more affluent and *least* disorganized communities that the corporate offender is most likely to live! And while the most virulent forms of drug abuse and addiction can almost certainly be accounted for by a revamped version of social disorganization theory—that is, one that takes into account power and external political and economic factors—the more casual, recreational forms of drug use that were so common from the 1970s on remain unexplained by the Chicago School's approach.

The social disorganization school, with its emphasis on social disorganization, had its heyday between the two world wars, roughly from 1920 to 1940. By the end of World War II, it was widely regarded as obsolete. In 1987, a sociologist claimed that the social disorganization school "has been soundly dismissed" (Unnever, 1987, p. 845).

In the late 1980s and early 1990s, the social disorganization school made a comeback; a substantial volume of contemporary research and writing on deviance is making use of the Chicago school's approach, concepts, and theories. Although it will never regain its former dominant status in the field, social disorganization theory is experiencing a renaissance. However, to reenergize this approach, some theoretical reformulations were necessary.

What the early social disorganization theorists did not entirely grasp was the dimension of power and its relevance for their analysis. They never figured out how important decisions made at the top of the power structure impacted on the life of the community. Decisions made by the powerful can divide communities in two by approving the construction of a highway, or the destruction of small-unit housing and building a huge housing project, or the creation of a shopping mall. These dramatic disruptions of community life reflect the exercise of power. The fact is the fate of communities and the behavior of their residents are tied to political and economic realities. Contemporary theorists are looking at deviance, crime, and other phenomena in part through the lens of the social disorganization perspective; social disorganization is being revived, but with a sharper, tougher, power-oriented edge. The idea of community control of deviance is being given a political thrust, which it did not have in the 1930s (Feagin and Parker, 1990; Currie, 1993).

A major contribution of the social disorganization or Chicago school, however, was *empathy*: It asked readers to imagine that deviants, delinquents, and criminals were people much like themselves (Pfohl, 1994, p. 209). Since it located the cause of deviance not in individual characteristics but in neighborhood dislocation, the social disorganization school forced us all to realize that, in the shifting tide and fortune of an evolving society, we, too, could have been caught up in the process of ecological transition. Deviants are the way they are as a result of the fact that they are "disproportionally exposed to the disruptive forces of rapid social change" (p. 209). If the rest of us were to be exposed to the same forces, we could have ended up doing or being the same thing. This insight enables persons not living in such neighborhoods, and not caught up in a life of crime, to understand the plight of those who are.

ANOMIE AND STRAIN THEORY

Anomie theory was born in 1938 with the publication of Robert Merton's article, "Social Structure and Anomie" (1938). Influenced by the nineteenth-century study *Suicide* by French sociologist Émile Durkheim, Merton was struck by the insight that deviant behavior could be caused by a disturbance in the social order, which Durkheim called *anomie*. Major social changes generate *disruptions* in the traditional social order, resulting in a state of anomie, followed by a form of deviance—suicide (1897/1951) (Durkheim, 1951).

After reading Durkheim, Merton agreed that states of anomie influenced the frequency of deviant behavior. He argued that anomie must vary from one society to another and from one group or category in the same society; consequently, rates of deviant behavior must also vary correspondingly. Merton reasoned that "*social structures exert a definite pressure upon certain persons in the society to engage in non-conforming rather than conforming conduct*" (1957, p. 132). Certain pressures, he concluded, could produce very *unconventional* behavior from very *conventional* origins and motives. Anomie theory is also referred to as *strain* theory, because it hypothesizes that a certain kind of strain, or pressure, produces deviant behavior.

In fashioning his argument, Merton completely reconceptualized anomie. To Durkheim, anomie was a disruption of the social order. It was characterized by a state of normlessness, where norms no longer grip the populace or hold them in check. It is the social order that restrains our behavior and our desires and keeps us from engaging in deviant behavior. The norms keep deviance in check and an *absence* of the norms—anomie—results in deviance. When periods of anomie prevail, the populace is no longer guided by culturally approved appetites. Unlimited greed is the rule; human desires run rampant. People no longer have any guidelines as to what is permissible and what is not, what is possible and what is not. Their lust for anything imaginable is unleashed.

Merton's reformulation retains Durkheim's notion of "insatiable desires," but rather than being located in human nature, they were the products of culture and socialization. Merton saw crime as representing a "normal reaction, by normal persons, to abnormal conditions" (1938, p. 672; Brezina, 2011, p. 99). In Merton's view, deviance results not from a *too weak* hold of society's norms on actors, as Durkheim's did, but, in a sense, a *too-strong* hold—that is, from actors *following* society's norms. In addition, Merton's conception of anomie is far more specific than Durkheim's. Merton conceptualizes anomie as a disjunction between *culturally defined goals* and *structurally available opportunities*. Culturally defined goals are "held out as legitimate objectives for all or for diversely located members of the society" (1957, p. 132). These goals, Merton claims, are widely shared; more or less everyone in society wishes to attain them. Merton holds Durkheim's view that anomie is instrumental in unleashing greedy behavior—behavior that is directed at attaining goals which, under different circumstances, would not be sought. Still, behind both Durkheim's and Merton's conceptions of anomie is a loud and vehement voice clamoring, "I want! I want!" For Durkheim, what unleashed this voice is a *disruption* of the social order. But for Merton, *it is the social order itself* that releases this voice. Our culture actually *creates* our greedy desires. And it is the gap or *lack of congruence* between the cultural order (that says we must become materially successful) and the social and economic order (which won't give us what we have been socialized to want and expect) that causes deviant behavior.

What are Merton's culturally defined goals? In Western society, including the United States, they are, of course, primarily monetary and material success. "Making it," within the scope of the American Dream, means being affluent—rich, if possible. Everyone in this society is bombarded on all sides by messages to succeed. And success, for the most part, means only one thing: being able to buy the best that money can buy. This is an almost universal American value, a basic goal toward which nearly everyone aspires and by which nearly everyone is evaluated.

Every society places certain limitations on how to achieve culturally defined goals. While nearly everyone in our society may value wealth, it is a separate question as to how we are permitted to acquire that wealth. Some societies place a heavy emphasis on attaining a given goal but remain fairly tolerant about just *how* one goes about attaining it. Here we have a case of "winning at any cost." Merton maintains that we have such a situation in contemporary America. Contemporary culture "continues to be characterized by a heavy emphasis on wealth as a basic symbol of success, without a corresponding emphasis on the legitimate avenues on which to march toward this goal" (1957, p. 139). We have an acquisitive society, in which "considerations of technical expediency" rule supreme. It is less important just *how* one makes it; the important thing, above all, is *making it*.

In contemporary America, we have a conflict between the *culture* (what people are taught to aspire to) and the *social and economic structure* (the opportunities they have to succeed). We have, in other words, a *malintegrated* society. The available material resources cannot possibly satisfy our culturally generated desire. While the aspirations of the population are unlimited, our actual chances of success are quite limited. This creates pressure to commit deviance. "It is only when a system of cultural values extols [or praises], virtually above all else, certain *common* success-goals *for the population at large* while the social structure rigorously restricts or completely closes access to approved modes of reaching these goals *for a considerable part of that same population*, that deviant behavior ensures on a large scale" (Merton, 1957, p. 134). "It is . . . my central hypothesis," Merton wrote, "that aberrant behavior may be regarded sociologically as a symptom of disassociation between culturally prescribed aspirations and socially structured avenues for realizing these aspirations" (1957, p. 134). By itself, an ambitious monetary goal for the population will not produce a high rate of crime; by itself, the lack of opportunities to achieve that goal, likewise, does not produce a great deal of crime. It is their *combination* or *conjunction* that imparts American society with a high predatory crime rate, at least among Western societies.

It should be noted that anomie theory is based on very nearly the *opposite* explanatory factor from that offered by the routine activities and social disorganization theories. Anomie theory tries to explain the *motives* for non-normative behavior. It is based on the notion that the desire for material success must be *socialized into us* for deviance to take place. In other words, we need to be given a "push" to deviate. Without the desire to become—and the expectation of becoming—materially successful, our failure to succeed would not produce the necessary deviant "adaptations." In contrast, routine activities and social disorganization theories do *not* assume that we need to be "pushed" into deviance. Instead, these theories assume that some offenders will always be in sufficient supply to take advantage of the absence of social control by deviating from the rules or laws. What some of us lack is opportunity. In short, anomie theory assumes that it is *dev*iant behavior that needs to be explained, while routine activities and social disorganization theories assume that deviance and crime don't need to be explained; instead, it is the *monitoring and sanctioning of illicit behavior* that need to be explained. Everyone would deviate if given a sufficiently golden opportunity, but some social conditions offer that opportunity while others do not. For the latter, the absence of social control explains deviant behavior.

Another important point: Merton's theory is "macro" in scope, that is, it looks at differences between and among *large social units* such as entire societies in explaining and predicting deviant behavior. The theory does *not* focus on individual or "micro" differences in levels of anomie and hence, deviant behavior. Merton's theory, for instance, would argue that American society is more anomic than, for example, Portuguese society, since expectations of high levels of material success tend to be much more the rule in the United States. Because of this, the theory would predict that America's rates of *deviant* behavior would be correspondingly higher. The theory does *not* explain why one person in the same society deviates while another does not.

Merton drew up a typology of different responses to goal attainment and legitimate versus illegitimate means of attaining these goals. People subject to these conflicting pressures adapt to or react to them in different ways. What types of deviance should we predict for success-hungry Americans?

Conformity, or the *conformist* mode of adaptation, accepts both cultural values of success and the institutionalized, legitimate, or conventional means for reaching these goals. The conformist strives for material success and chooses law-abiding ways of achieving success. This mode of adaptation is not of interest to the student of deviance except as a negative case since it is not characterized by violations of the norms. It is in the typology simply for the purpose of comparing it with various forms of deviance. Becoming an accountant, a physician, a lawyer, and striving for material success by becoming successful in one's profession—becoming affluent through a legal, legitimate profession, performed in a law-abiding, respectable fashion—is an example of the most common mode of adaptation: *conformity*. Conformity is not, in any case, deviance.

The mode of adaptation Merton called *innovation* involves accepting the goal of success but choosing to achieve it in an illegal, illegitimate, or deviant fashion. This adaptation is clearly the most interesting of all modes to Merton; he devoted more space to describing it than all the others put together. An innovative mode of adaptation to the pressures of American culture and society would encompass most types of money-making criminal activities; for example, white collar crime, embezzlement, pick-pocketing, running a confidence game, bank robbery, burglary, prostitution, and pimping. Innovators want success but they attempt to achieve it by seeking a deviant or criminal route.

In contrast, *ritualism* entails "the abandoning or scaling down of the lofty cultural goals of great pecuniary success and rapid social mobility," but "almost compulsively" following the conventional or "institutionalized norms" (1957, pp. 149–150). The ritualist plays it safe, plays by the book, doesn't take chances. Ritualism as an adaptation to American society's heavy emphasis on success is a kind of *partial* withdrawal—an abandonment of the goal of success, but a *retention* of the *form* of doing things properly, following all the rules to the letter. In many ways, ritualism is a kind of *overconformity*. A petty bureaucrat, who insists that all rules and regulations be followed in every detail but ignores the fact that such a narrow interpretation of doing things fails to achieve the desire goal, would exemplify this mode of adaptation. Hence, the *purpose* of bureaucratic institutions—presumably, to serve the public—has been *subverted* by a rigid adherence to the rules.

Retreatism is a rejection of both goals and institutionalized means. It is a total cop-out, a "retreat" from the things that society values most. The retreatist gives up both the goal of success and any and all avenues of achieving it. Retreatists are "true aliens." In this category Merton places "some of the adaptive activities of psychotics, autists, pariahs, outcasts, vagrants, vagabonds, tramps, chronic drunkards, and drug addicts" (1957, p. 153). Retreatism is brought on by repeated failure, which causes severe personal conflict and a withdrawal from valuing success and any possible routes to attain it. Merton feels that this mode of adaptation is the least frequently resorted to of those discussed so far.

Rebellion "involves a genuine transvaluation." It is an attempt to deal with the dominant goals and means by overthrowing them altogether. While the retreatist merely rejects them and puts nothing in their place, the rebel renounces prevailing values and goals, and legitimate avenues to achieve them, and introduces an alternative social, political, and economic structure, one in which the current stresses and strains presumably would not exist: a new, unconventional, or deviant goal (for instance, a classless society) achieved by a new, unconventional, or deviant way of achieving it—launching a violent revolution dedicated to the overthrow of the existing political and economic order. Merton devotes the least attention to this mode.

The anomie theory of Robert K. Merton exerted an enormous impact on the field of the sociology of deviance for decades after its initial publication in 1938. In fact, half a century after its publication, it was measurably the most cited work ever written by a sociologist. (Recently, depending on the year, others have supplanted it.) Along with the attention it has received, anomie theory has also attracted considerable criticism.

Does anomie theory suffer from a middle-class bias? Some critics argue that it suffers from the same middle-class bias that skewed all earlier theories of deviance: It made the assumption that lower- and working-class people commit acts of crime and deviance *in general* significantly more frequently than is true of the members of the middle class. Today, most observers readily admit that "street" crime is committed more often by individuals at or toward the bottom of the class structure than is true of those at or near the top. Yet—and here is where the problem enters—there are many criminal and deviant actions that are equally likely, or even more likely, to be engaged in by the more affluent, prestigious, well-educated, and powerful members of society. Although official police statistics on who commits crimes show that crime is a predominantly lower-class phenomenon, it is now clear that the specific crimes that upper-middle-class people commit are those that are far less likely to result in police scrutiny and action—specifically arrest—and court action, specifically prosecution and imprisonment, than is true of lower- and working-class individuals. This is especially the case for white collar and corporate crimes, the crimes of the rich and the powerful, which, its critics argue, anomie theory does not address.

Is anomie theory relevant to all forms of deviance? At one point, Merton claims that anomie theory "is designed to account for some, not all, forms of deviant behavior, customarily described as criminal or delinquent" (1957, p. 178). Yet in other places, he makes a case for anomie being the major cause of deviance in general. Deviance, he says, "is a symptom of disassociation between culturally prescribed aspirations and socially structured avenues for realizing these aspirations" (p. 134). Again, Merton writes, "It is *only* when" goals and means are disjunctive, "*deviant behavior ensues on a large scale*" (p. 146; my emphasis). Though Merton "is vague as to which behavior is covered by this explanation and which is not" (Clinard, 1964, p. 19), he clearly believes that *rates* of deviance vary by degree of anomie. Consequently, though some forms of deviance may be exempt from the theory (Merton never explains which ones are, however), deviance *in general* is supposedly explained by it.

Although the malintegration between means and goals that characterizes contemporary American society will typically put pressure on many members to engage in certain forms of deviance, *most forms of deviant behavior will not be produced by the pressure of such malintegration.* Merton's theory is not an explanation of deviant behavior in general, as he claims, but a delineation of some of the possible outcomes of a certain kind of strain induced by specific social and economic factors. The anomie approach turns out to be largely *irrelevant* to *most* forms of deviant behavior. Activities such as *non-addicting* recreational

drug use, assault, criminal homicide, petty gambling, adultery, homosexuality, child molestation, the consumption of pornography, holding unconventional beliefs, and homosexuality, and so on, *are completely unexplained by anomie theory*.

In the 1950s and 1960s, anomie theory was the most frequently used theoretical tradition in the study of deviance and crime (Cole, 1975). But by the early 1970s, the anomie perspective underwent a sharp decline in influence, and from the mid-1970s and the mid-1980s, it seemed as if it would disappear from the field altogether, tossed onto the "dustbin of history." In 1978, in a detailed appraisal of theories of deviance, crime, and delinquency, Ruth Kornhauser stated: "Strain models are disconfirmed" (p. 253). She advised that sociologists seeking an explanation of delinquency, crime, and deviance forget anomie theory and turn their attention elsewhere.

But, as with social disorganization theory, some time in the late 1980s to the early 1990s, anomie theory experienced a renaissance. As with the social disorganization framework, anomie or strain theory will never recapture its former glory as the field's preeminent approach to the study of deviance. However, judging by a recent rebirth in research and writing adopting the theory as a lens with which to examine deviant phenomena, it remains as vital as ever (Adler and Laufer, 1995; Messner and Rosenfeld, 1997).

According to the *Social Science Citation Index*, which lists articles that refer to or cite a particular work, Merton's "Social Structure and Anomie," which appeared nearly seven decades ago, is actually cited more frequently today, in the 2000s, than it was in the 1970s and 1980s. It has helped countless researchers illuminate dozens of deviant, delinquent, and criminal activities. For instance, one recent research endeavor that has made use of anomie theory is the study of drug dealing. Bourgois (1995, p. 326, 2003) argues that drug dealers should be accorded "their rightful place within the mainstream of American society. These deviant actors are," he states, "made in America. . . . Highly motivated, ambitious inner-city youths have been attracted to the rapidly expanding, multibillion-dollar drug economy . . . precisely because they believe in Horatio Alger's version of the American Dream." Again, Merton's theory continues to be relevant. Duneier (1999, pp. 60–62, 364) describes

Merton's retreatism adaptation, which he refers as "The 'Fuck It!' Mentality." This takes place when a homeless person has given up on both goals and means. It is, he explains, a pervasive state of resignation that affects "most major aspects of his life," when he "becomes indifferent to behavior that he once thought of as basic, such as sleeping in a bed or defecating in a toilet" (p. 61). It is, in Merton's "brilliant scheme" (Duneier's term), "an extreme form of retreatism" (p. 61), the end point along a continuum of an "I don't care" attitude. Clearly, in the sociology of deviance and crime, Merton's anomie theory remains influential. It is not likely to go away any time soon.

DIFFERENTIAL ASSOCIATION AND LEARNING THEORY

In 1939, a major theory of deviance was propounded for the first time (Sutherland, 1939). It was called the theory of *differential association*, and it has become one of a small number of important perspectives in the field. Sutherland set for himself two somewhat different but overlapping tasks. The first was to explain what he referred to as *differential group organization*: why crime rates vary among different groups of people, why a criminal tradition was endemic in certain social circles. The second task was to explain why some individuals engage in crime more than other individuals. Unfortunately, Sutherland did not develop his ideas on differential group organization in detail.

The first and most fundamental proposition of the theory of differential association states that criminal behavior, and by extension, deviance as well, is *learned*. This proposition was directed against biological theories that assert that crime is caused by genetic, metabolic, or anatomical defects, and against the view that criminal behavior is hit upon accidentally or through independent invention. Hardly anyone, Sutherland asserted, stumbles upon or dreams up a way to break the law; this must be passed on from one person to another in a genuine learning process. The theory of differential association also opposed the view that mental illness or an abnormal, pathological

personality is a major causal factor in the commission of criminal behavior. Rather, Sutherland argued, crime is learned in a straightforward, essentially normal fashion, no different from the way in which members of American society learn to speak English or brush their teeth.

A second proposition of the theory of differential association is that criminal behavior, and, again, by extension, deviance as well, must be learned through face-to-face interaction between people who are close or intimate with one another. People are not persuaded to engage in criminal behavior as a result of reading a book or a newspaper, seeing a movie, or (today, as opposed to 1939) watching television. Criminal knowledge, skills, sentiments, values, traditions, and motives are all passed down as a result of *interpersonal*—not impersonal—means. Two major factors that intensify this process are *priority* and *intensity*. The earlier in one's life one is exposed to attitudes and values ("definitions") favorable to committing crimes, the greater the likelihood that one will in fact commit crime. And the closer and more intimate the friends, relatives, and acquaintances who endorse committing crime, likewise, the more swayed one will be to break the law.

Sutherland's theory argued that people who engage in criminal behavior *differentially associate* with individuals who endorse violations of the law. Notice that the theory does not say that one needs to associate with actual criminals to break the law oneself—only that one should be more heavily exposed to *definitions* favorable to criminal actions. One can be exposed to law-abiding definitions emanating from criminals and criminal definitions emanating from law-abiding individuals (though, of course, it usually works the other way around). Still, as most of us know, "actions speak louder than words," and one wonders how much more of an impact the example of criminal actions has than criminal words.

Sutherland's theory of differential association holds that a person becomes delinquent or criminal because of an excess of definitions favorable to the violation of the law over definitions unfavorable to the violation of the law. The key to this process is the *ratio* between definitions favorable to the violation of the law to definitions that are unfavorable. When favorable definitions exceed unfavorable ones, an individual will turn to crime.

The theory of differential association has been criticized for being vague and untestable. Later efforts to refine and operationalize the theory have not been entirely successful in rescuing it from imprecision. Exactly how would a researcher measure this ratio of favorable to unfavorable definitions of violations of the law? And exactly how could "favorable" and "unfavorable" be indicated or measured? Even one of the theory's staunchest defenders admits that Sutherland's formulation of the differential association process "is not precise enough to stimulate rigorous empirical test" (Cressey, 1960, p. 57). Some conceptualizations of learning theory attempt to address these and other objections by incorporating additional factors and variables into the framework (Burgess and Akers, 1966; Akers, 1998). In so doing, they depart radically from Sutherland's original formulation and become eclectic rather than instances of learning theory.

Much crime is, indeed, learned in intimate social settings. However, it seems at least as overly ambitious to assume that all criminal behavior is learned in a straightforward fashion as it is to assume that all noncriminal behavior is learned. Many actions, criminal and noncriminal alike, are invented anew by individuals in similar situations. All behavior is not learned, at least not directly. Much of it, deviant or otherwise, may be devised in relative isolation. There is a great deal of independent invention of certain forms of deviance, delinquency, and crime. The human mind is, after all, almost infinitely creative. The idea to do something, and its eventual enactment, almost always have a cultural or learning *foundation*, but it was not necessarily learned in detail. One can, either by oneself or in the company of an equally untutored individual, "put the pieces together." One can enact certain behaviors *in the absence of learning those behaviors themselves*; learning may take one to a certain point, after which creativity and imagination take over. Any learning theory that requires that one learn positive values *about the precise behavior itself* must therefore be incomplete and deficient. Any learning theory that includes all the other factors that go into human behavior, such as biological drives, the pleasure principle, and so on, is likely to be so vague as to be a tautology—true by definition.

Many criminal activities do not fit the differential association model at all: check forgery (Lemert, 1972, pp. 150–182), embezzlement (Cressey, 1953), child molestation (McCaghy, 1967, 1968), wartime black market violations (Clinard, 1952), certain crimes of passion (Katz, 1988), and crimes involving psychiatric compulsion (such as kleptomania). While, for many deviant and criminal activities, learning may assist their enactment, they do not cause them. Some observers (Gottfredson and Hirschi, 1990) have gone so far as to argue that one does not have to learn anything to enact deviant or criminal behavior; it is simply "doing what comes naturally." In addition, many forms of crime are not even approved of by a majority of the people who engage in them—such as child molestation and murder. Consequently, they could not be learned in anything like the fashion that Sutherland suggests. That is, one may learn *about* certain crimes but one hardly ever learns that they are activities or states one should emulate. In short, while it is true that much criminal behavior is learned, much of it is not. As a partial theory, differential association is valuable. As a complete or general theory, it is overly ambitious. "There can be little argument that social learning theory has come to be recognized as an important general theory of crime" and deviance (Jennings and Akers, 2011, p. 112). True enough, as far as it goes, though many enactors of untoward behavior do not valuatively approve of what they do, nor is learning the key factor that separates them from those who do not enact the behavior. Rather than a theory that explains all crime and deviance, differential association should be regarded as a concept that helps us to understand a particular process that some rule violators go through and some do not.

SOCIAL CONTROL THEORY

Control theory is a major paradigm in the fields of deviance behavior and criminology. Control theorists see their perspective as a critique of and a replacement for both anomie theory and the *subcultural* or learning approaches. While most theories ask, "Why do they do it?"—that is, what processes *encourage* deviant behavior—control theory turns the question around and asks, "Why *don't* they do it?" In other words, control theory assumes that engaging in deviance is not problematic, that, if *left to our own devices*, all of us would deviate from the rules of society. In fact, control theorists believe that deviance is *inherently attractive*. Under most circumstances, we are encouraged to break the rules; deviance-making processes are strong and obvious and commonsensical. Why *shouldn't* we lie and steal, if they are what gets us what we want? *Why not* hang out on street-corners and get drunk and throw bottles through windows—it's so much fun! This approach takes for granted the allure of deviance, crime, and delinquency. What has to be explained, control theorists argue, is why most people *don't* engage in deviance, why are they discouraged from engaging in delinquent behavior, why are they dissuaded or deterred from breaking the law and engaging in a life of crime. Practically all the other theories of wrongdoing argue that deviance, crime, and delinquency are *positively motivated*; control theories argue the opposite—that wrongdoing results from *weak restraints and controls* (Agnew, 2011, p. 114). Most of us do not engage in deviant or criminal acts because of strong bonds with or ties to conventional, mainstream social institutions. If these bonds are weak or broken, we will be released from society's rules and will be free to deviate. It is not so much deviants' ties to an unconventional group or subculture that attracts them to deviant behavior, but their *lack* of ties with the conforming, law-abiding culture; this frees them to engage in deviance (Reiss, 1951; Toby, 1957; Reckless, 1961; Briar and Piliavin, 1965; Hirschi, 1969). What causes deviant behavior, these theorists say, is the *ineffectiveness* or *absence* of social control (Inderbitzen, Bates, and Gainey, 2013, pp. 284–338).

Researchers find three distinctly different *types* of social control: *direct control*; *stake in conformity*; and *internal controls*, or beliefs regarding wrongdoing (Agnew, 2011, p. 115). These types help explain *individual differences* in rates of offending, as well as *group differences over the life course* (Sampson and Laub, 1992). Direct control refers to all those actions that agents take, and which act, to ensure that individuals refrain from engaging in deviance "out of fear that they will be caught and sanctioned" (p. 115). They include the cop on the corner, the parent hovering over his or her child, the teacher watching students taking an exam. However, individuals vary with respect to the *effectiveness* of sanctioning because they vary with respect to their *stake in conformity*. In short, some people have less to lose if they are caught and punished. Some such "stakes" include plans for college, accomplishments, emotional attachments to others, material possessions, reputation; they may be jeopardized by exposure as a thief, a cheat, a liar, a brawler, a substance abuser. Almost intuitively, it seems obvious that deviance is more likely among individuals who have little to lose if they are caught (p. 116). And lastly, social control may be internalized at a relatively early age. Children whose parents closely monitor and consistently sanction them tend to continue to believe that deviance is wrong and should not be committed; those whose parents are ineffective as agents of social control are more likely to be amoral toward offending and do not believe that deviant acts are wrong. For the most part, researchers have verified most propositions of social control theory (Agnew, 2006; Vold, Bernard, and Gerould, 2009), although, as with many such perspectives, the causal arrow isn't always clear.

Control theory would predict that, to the extent that a person has a *stake in conformity*, he or she will tend not to break the law and risk losing that stake; to the extent that a person lacks that stake in conformity, he or she will be willing to violate the law. Thus, jobs, especially satisfying, high-paying jobs, may act as something of a deterrent to crime. Attending college, likewise, represents a stake or investment that many students are not willing to risk losing. Being married and having a family, too, will discourage criminal behavior to the extent that arrest may undermine their stability. Everyone knows that *some* crime is committed by the employed, by college students, by married persons with a family. But control theory would predict that there are *major differences* in the crime rates of the employed versus the unemployed, college students versus their non-college age peers, and married parents versus the unmarried. To the extent that a society or a neighborhood is able to invest its citizens or residents with a stake worth protecting, it will have lower rates of crime; to the extent that it is unable to invest that stake in its citizens or residents, its crime rate will be correspondingly higher. Home ownership, for instance, can act as a deterrent to crime, as can organizational and community involvement. A society with many citizens who have nothing to lose is a society with a high crime rate.

Control theory does not state that individuals with strong ties to conventional society are absolutely *insulated* from deviance, that they will *never* engage in *any* deviant or criminal action, regardless of how mildly unconventional it is. It does, however, assert that both deviance and social control are matters of degree: The more attached we are to conventional society, the lower the likelihood of engaging in behavior that violates its values and norms. A strong bond to conventionality does not insulate us from mildly deviant behavior, but it does make it less likely.

The theory works a great deal better for some behaviors than others. Control theory sees many deviant, criminal, and delinquent activities as natural, recreational, and requiring no special explanation. But what about more seriously aggressive and violent behavior—such as murder, robbery, and rape? Are they part of the same constellation of acts that, if left to our own devices and in the absence of simple societal controls, we would naturally gravitate toward and engage in? It's difficult to envision that the same logic applies. In fact, there may be a very good reason why the vast majority of the research applying control theory has been self-report surveys of relatively minor delinquencies among youths: It works best for them. As we saw, such studies run into a serious roadblock. Hirschi's 1969 study found few class differences in rates of delinquency. There is a good reason why. The most important crimes, those that criminologists are most interested in (murder, robbery, and rape) tend to be relatively rare. The least important crimes are sufficiently common to make a self-report possible. The less common the behavior, the more difficult it is to study by means of self-report surveys, since so few of the sample will have engaged in them, especially within a recent time frame. Hence, control theorists are a bit like the drunk who is searching for his keys, not in the dark, where he lost them, but in the light, where he can see more clearly. In spite of this restriction, control theory represents one of the more powerful and insightful approaches we have to explain crime, deviance, and especially delinquency.

A GENERAL THEORY OF CRIME: SELF-CONTROL THEORY

In 1990, Michael Gottfredson and Travis Hirschi devised what they refer to as *a general theory of crime*, that is, force or fraud in pursuit of self-interest (p. 15). The field of criminology refers to it as self-control theory, and it shares with social control theory the idea that deviance is self-evident and inherently attractive. The authors claim that their theory applies to any and all crimes, regardless of type: white collar and corporate crime, embezzlement, murder, robbery, rape, the illegal sale of drugs, underage drinking, burglary, shoplifting—indeed, any and all illegal actions. In fact, in their view, their theory is even more general than that, since it is an explanation of actions that may not even be against the law or entail inflicting force or fraud against a victim. More properly, it is a general theory of deviance and includes, besides crime, a variety of self-indulgent actions (like smoking, getting high or drunk, and, one might suppose, even being a couch potato), and reckless behavior that has a high likelihood of resulting in accidents (such as driving dangerously fast or preferring a motorcycle to a car). Their theory, they say, stresses both the factors present in the immediate or "proximate" situation of the criminal action which determine or influence its *enactment* (which they refer to as "crime"), *and* those background or "distant" factors, which determine or influence the *tendency* or *propensity* to commit crime (which they term *criminality*).

The origin of crime, Gottfredson and Hirschi say, is *low self-control* which, in turn, results from inadequate, ineffective, and inconsistent socialization by parents early in childhood. Parents who raise delinquent and criminal offspring lack affection for them, fail to monitor their behavior, fail to recognize when they are committing deviant acts, and fail to control wrongdoing. What makes crime especially attractive to people who lack self-control? We can characterize criminal acts, Gottfredson and Hirschi say, by the fact that they provide *immediate* and *easy* or *simple* gratification of desires (p. 89). "They provide money without work, sex without courtship, revenge without court delays" (p. 89). People who lack self-control "tend to lack diligence, tenacity, or persistence in a course of action" (p. 89). In addition, criminal acts are *"exciting, risky, or thrilling"*; crime provides, in the typical case, *"few or meager long-term benefits"*; it requires *"little skill or planning"*; and often results in *"pain or discomfort for the victim"* (p. 89; the emphasis is theirs). As a result of the last of these characteristics, people with low self-control and hence, frequent enactors of criminal behavior, tend to be "self-centered, indifferent, or insensitive to the suffering and needs of others" (p. 89), although they may also "discover the immediate and easy rewards of charm and generosity" (p. 90).

Since crime entails "the pursuit of immediate pleasure," it follows that "people lacking in self-control will also tend to pursue immediate pleasures that are *not* criminal: they will tend to smoke, drink, use drugs, gamble, have children out of wedlock, and engage in illicit sex" (p. 90). Some crimes entail not so much pleasure but an attempt at relief from irritation or discomfort, such as physically abusing a crying child or beating up an annoying stranger in a bar. People with low self-control have little tolerance for frustration and little skill at dealing with difficult circumstances verbally or by applying complex, difficult-to-master solutions. "In short, people who lack self-control will tend to be impulsive, insensitive, physical (as opposed to mental), risk-taking, short-sighted, and nonverbal, and they will therefore tend to engage in criminal and analogous acts" (p. 90).

Their general theory of crime, Gottfredson and Hirschi argue, is both consistent with the facts of criminal behavior and contradicts the bulk of mainstream criminological theories. The authors are not modest either about the reach of their theory or its devastating implications for competing explanations. They insist that their general theory of crime *cannot* be reconciled with other theories; instead, they insist, it must of necessity *annihilate* them. In fact, Gottfredson and Hirschi abandon even Hirschi's own social control theory (discussed earlier), formulated some forty years ago. The *social* controls that Hirschi saw previously as central, he and his coauthor now view as secondary to the *internal* controls they argue are developed in childhood. They reject life circumstances such as marriage, employment, and home ownership—so crucial to control theory—as having

little or no independent impact on crime. After all, how can someone with low self-control maintain a marriage, keep a job, or buy a house? They lack emotional and psychic wherewithal—the self-control—to do what has to be done in order even to be *subject* to external or social controls. It is self-control that determines social control, not the other way around, Hirschi and Gottfredson argue.

The problem with the theories of crime that are now dominant in criminology, Gottfredson and Hirschi claim, is that they are inconsistent with the evidence.

Strain or anomie theory "predicts that offenders will have high long-term aspirations and low long-term expectations," but that turns out to be false; "people committing criminal acts tend to have lower aspirations than others," while, among offenders, "expectations for future success tend to be unrealistically high" (p. 162). In anomie theory, crime is a long-term, indirect solution to current life circumstances, whereas, in reality, Gottfredson and Hirschi say, crime is an impulsive act which provides short-term, usually skimpy rewards. Criminals lack the skills, diligence, and persistence necessary for the deviant "adaptations" spelled out by Merton. Strain does not explain the incidence or rate of criminal behavior as a whole, since most of it is petty, impulsive, and immediate.

Likewise, the many varieties of learning theory should be rejected as being inconsistent with the facts, Gottfredson and Hirschi argue. All such theories make the assumption that deviants engage in deviance as a result of a positive learning experience, that is, *they learn the value* of engaging in deviance and crime. In fact, one does *not* learn to engage in crime, since no learning is required. Criminal acts are simple, commonsensical, immediate, concrete, and result in immediate gratification. Neither the motivation nor the skill to commit them are problematic; everybody has such motivation and skill. What causes such behavior is not the *presence* of something—learning—but the *absence* of something—self-control. Learning theories simply fail utterly and completely to explain criminal, deviant, and delinquent behavior, Gottfredson and Hirschi argue.

More generally, they reject the idea that crime is *social* behavior (in fact, it is more accurate to refer to it as *asocial* in nature), that it is *learned* behavior ("when in fact no learning is required"), that the tendency to commit it can be an *inherited* trait (when it is clearly acquired, through childhood experiences), that it is *economic* behavior (when, in fact, "it is uneconomical behavior outside the labor force"). They reject all other explanations of criminal behavior except their own (p. 75); only a lack of self-control is truly consistent with the facts of crime. Gottfredson and Hirschi contemptuously reject any effort to integrate their own theory with the explanations they so roundly destroyed.

With two exceptions. Not all persons who exhibit low self-control commit crime; low self-control merely *predisposes* someone to commit crime. What determines which persons who are predisposed to commit crime will actually do so? In a word, opportunity. Hence, any explanation that focuses on the *patterning* and *distribution* of criminal opportunities—although incomplete—is consistent with the facts, Gottfredson and Hirschi argue. Their approach is an attempt to revitalize classical, free will, or rational choice theory, mentioned early in this chapter, as half the crime equation. The contemporary version of the classic approach to crime, referred to as opportunity theory, the routine activity approach, or rational choice theory, argues that crime can take place to the extent that a *motivated offender* has access to a "suitable target" (such as money and valuables) which lacks a "capable guardian." Routine activity theorists emphasize the factors of *proxim*ity, *accessibility*, and *reward* (Hough, 1987). They *assume* or *take for granted* a motivated offender—the criminal—since there will always be an abundant supply of them to go around; instead, they focus on the necessary preconditions for the commission of the crime. The assumption that crime is the most rational means to acquire property is abandoned, however, since Gottfredson and Hirschi argue that most crimes do not net the offender much in the way of goods or cash. Nonetheless, they say, opportunity is a crucial element in the crime equation. (Not in *criminality*, or the individual *propensity* to commit crime, but in *crime*, in the likelihood that criminal *actions* will take place.) While incomplete, Gottfredson and Hirschi say, a theory which focuses on opportunity is consistent with self-control theory. Moreover, they say, both are necessary for a complete explanation of criminal behavior (1987, 1990).

In addition, they argue, social disorganization theory is both consistent with classical theory and consistent with the facts of crime; the inability of a community to monitor the behavior of its residents complements, and is similar to, parallel parental incompetence (1990). As we saw, social disorganization theory is a form of control theory "writ large."

As might be expected, self-control theory has met with mixed reactions. Strain theorists argue that social strain and anomie are indeed significant causal precursors to criminal behavior. For instance, the aggressiveness and anger that many criminals exhibit when committing their crimes is far more than a lack of self-restraint; only strain theory explains it, they say (Agnew, 1995). Some learning theorists argue that a lack of self-control is a basic component or element of the deviant learning process (Akers, 1991)—hence, they say, learning theory *subsumes*, or swallows up, self-control theory. Certainly the reductionistic, mechanistic, either-or logic Gottfredson and Hirschi display in their theorizing has led some observers to believe that they may have missed crucial subtleties in characterizing and explaining human behavior (Lynch and Groves, 1995, pp. 372–378). One critic takes Gottfredson and Hirschi to task for selectively reading the data, focusing on those that seem to confirm their theory and ignoring those that would damage it (Polk, 1991). Gottfredson and Hirschi's theory clearly applies much more to the antisocial personality disorder (Black, 1999) than to deviance in general. It is too early to assess the validity of self-control theory in anything like a definitive fashion. Chances are, contrary to its claims, bits and pieces of it will be incorporated into mainstream criminology and deviance theory, while its global, overall—and perhaps overblown—critiques of rival theories will be taken far less seriously. It is likely that Gottfredson and Hirschi have not offered a "general theory" of crime and deviance, but a plausible account of bits and pieces of the phenomenon they purport to explain (Goode, 2008).

SUMMARY

Whenever some members of a society engage in what others regard as wrongdoing, the latter wonder why the former do it. Explanations for violating society's rules are as ancient as human existence. Historically, the most ancient of such explanations was demonic possession—the influence of the devil or evil spirits.

By the 1700s, intellectuals and the educated sectors of Western society no longer believed that evil spirits caused people to violate the norms or the law. The eighteenth century in Europe was referred to as the *Age of Reason*. Hence, it makes sense that it was in this era that an explanation for crime arose that focused on humans as reasonable and rational actors, exercising their free will and guided by the pursuit of pleasure and the avoidance of pain. The contemporary version of a rationalistic explanation of normative violations is referred to as *routine activities theory*. It stresses that crime and deviance take place to the extent that a motivated offender and a suitable target (something desirable and worth committing a crime for) are present, and a suitable guardian is lacking.

During the 1920s, sociologists came to see the community rather than the individual as the source of norm violations. Some neighborhoods are unstable by virtue of their undesirability. As a result, residents are relatively poor, heterogeneous (and hence, often strangers to one another), and do not sink roots into the community but frequently move out. In such neighborhoods, wrongdoing is common, since residents cannot or do not monitor or control normative and legal violations. In sum, deviance varies systematically by neighborhood or ecological location. The social disorganization school was the dominant perspective in academic sociology between the 1920s and the 1940s. After World War II, it suffered a serious decline in importance and influence. Although it never regained its former glory, roughly by 1990, the social disorganization school experienced a dramatic renaissance. Today, numerous researchers are conducting studies that are guided or inspired by the social disorganization perspective.

Anomie theory is distinctive by virtue of the fact that it had its origin (except for the work of Émile Durkheim, who had something different in mind) in a single article by a single sociologist: Robert K. Merton's "Social Structure and Anomie," published in 1938. Merton argued that, in the United States, deviance was a product of a disjunction or contradiction between the culture, whose norms urged material and financial

success for all members of society, and the social and economic structure, which granted high levels of success only to some. This condition produces a state of stress or *anomie*. As a result of failing in the traditional sectors of society, those who are left behind are forced into one of an array of deviant "adaptations." During the 1950s and 1960s, the anomie perspective was the most often-used approach in the study of deviance. But in the 1970s, the theory underwent a sharp decline in influence. However—as with several other perspectives in this field—anomie theory experienced a strong rebirth, beginning roughly in 1990. Today, once again, it is the focus of vigorous commentary and research.

Learning theories encompass a variety of perspectives which center on the idea that deviance, delinquency, and crime are learned in a fairly straightforward fashion. By being isolated from mainstream society and its definition of deviance and integrated into unconventional groups, some members of society learn deviant values, beliefs, and norms and thus, engage in deviant behavior. The most prominent of learning theories is differential association, devised by Edwin Sutherland in 1939. Learning theory, as with all other perspectives, has been attacked, defended, amended, and added to.

Social control theory takes strong issue with both anomie and learning theory. Deviants do not have to be stressed into committing deviance, nor does anyone have to learn to engage in deviant behavior. Indeed, what requires explaining, say the social control theorists, is conformity. Deviant behavior is readily understandable, commonsensical, and inherently appealing. Left to their own devices, everyone would deviate from the norms: It's easier, more fun, and more effective in obtaining what is regarded as desired than is true of conformity. The important question is not, why do we commit deviance? Instead it is, why *don't* we commit deviance? The factor or variable that social control theorists have isolated as the explanation is that people engage in conventional behavior to the extent that they are involved with and attached to conventional others, activities, and beliefs. To the extent that we have an investment or stake in conventionality, we will engage in conformity or conventional behavior. To the extent that we don't, we will engage in deviance.

In 1990, Gottfredson and Hirschi articulated the version of the control theory of deviance, self-control theory, that they called "a general theory of crime." It is based on several tenets of control theory (as well as classic, free will, or rationalistic theory), but it breaks with it in its lack of stress on *current* conventional attachments. People violate norms and the law because they lack self-control; they tend to be insensitive, self-centered, impulsive, and relatively unintelligent; they lack a long-range perspective, can't deal with frustration, and require immediate gratification. And they lack self-control because they were subject to inadequate, inconsistent, and ineffective socialization by their parents or other caregivers. Self-control theory is one of the few perspectives whose advocates argue that all other perspectives (except for rational choice and social disorganization) are completely incompatible with the facts of crime. Its advocates set out to destroy all now-dominant approaches to deviance and crime. As might be expected, self-control theory has met with a mixed reception.

Today, no single perspective or approach is dominant in the study of deviance. Moreover, contrary to what its advocates claim, the theories I discussed in this chapter are not, for the most part, contradictory or mutually exclusive; each of them contains a grain of truth, that is, represent valid explanations for some aspects of deviance and crime but not others. And, as we can see, all the approaches discussed in this chapter are concerned entirely with *an explanation of deviant behavior*. In this sense, they are all positivistic or "scientific" in their general approach. In the next chapter, we'll look at theories that are engaged in a very different task, in a sense, looking at the opposite side of the deviance coin. Instead of attempting to explain why deviant behavior is enacted, for the most part, they ask about the generation and the nature and operation of *definitions* of deviance and the exercise of *social control*. Instead of asking why deviance is enacted, they wonder about why definitions of deviance are *conceptualized*, *defined*, and *applied* or *enforced* in a certain way, and how and why certain behaviors, traits, and persons are caught up in the web of punishment, condemnation, and stigmatization. No examination of deviance is complete without an investigation of the nature, social roots, and the exercise of social control.

Before we proceed to the next chapter, however, I must issue a most emphatic warning. The perspectives we are about to examine are largely focused on how society or segments of society *define* and *deal with* deviance and deviants. Theories or perspectives that focus on social control constitute the *constructionist* approach to deviance. Unfortunately, two of the theories we looked at in this chapter share names that are very similar to this social control emphasis—"social control" theory and "self-control" theory. I must emphasize that they are *not* theories of social control in the sense that I'll be using the term in Chapter 3—that is, they are not constructionist in their approach. The social control and self-control theories are *etiological*, *explanatory*, *causal*, or *positivist* theories of deviance. They ask: "*Why do some persons engage in deviant behavior?*" Or, to be a bit more precise, some also ask, "Why do some people *not* engage in deviant behavior?" To repeat, they attempt to account for the behavior itself, *not* why it is defined in a certain way or why it is condemned. Proponents of these theories do not examine social control as problematic, that is, as the subject to be investigated. They do *not* ask "*Why social control?*" Don't be confused by the similarity in their names. Their approaches are completely different; they share little else with the perspectives discussed in this chapter *aside from* their names.

Account: Stealing Computers

This interview was conducted by Henry Mesias, who is a graduate of the University of Maryland.

JASON: Whether I try or not, I try to do my own thing and it always ends up pissing people off or getting me into trouble. Let me give you an example. There was this one group of friends that would literally kick my ass every single day in the gym locker room. It literally never stopped until I flipped out, grabbed one of them by the neck, held him about three inches off the ground and choked him against the wall until the gym teacher came down into the locker room and stopped me. And this was after these guys were slamming me into walls, throwing me into folding chairs, and cutting open my knee to the point where I had to have stitches. I really snapped and went totally ape on someone. Quite possibly I could have killed him if somebody hadn't intervened. I mean, it seemed in my life that there was no one there for me. Parents are [supposed to be] there to help you, teachers are [supposed to be] there to help. And when I said anything, when I needed help, they'd just go, "Hey, there's nothing we can do." And at that point, you realize you're on your own. If you don't do anything to help yourself, nobody is going to be there for you, so I just kinda went from there.

HENRY: You never had any help from your parents or anything?

JASON: Oh, definitely not. When they wouldn't get me basic computer programs to help me progress, I had to start acquiring them on my own, like stealing software and stuff like that. At one point, I found out how to pilot accounts [that a particular bank sponsors]. I figured out how to generate credit card numbers via algorithms. You could find bank extensions that would not be verified by [the bank]. So for example when you look at the first four digits of your credit card, that's a specific bank code, that specifies [a particular commercial bank]. A particular bank that comes out of a particular area code had to have that exact number. And I found out that an extension for a particular credit card that [the bank] didn't verify the expiration date of, they didn't verify the check sums, and they didn't verify the address on the card. So you could create an account online, you spend as much time as you want, and at the end of the month, the account gets deleted. They bill it, nobody pays the bill, and they realize they've lost that money. I found bank codes like that for about two and a half years until they started enacting measures to block it. When my parents found out, they told me that this was stealing, I can't do that, that's totally wrong. I told them that they had been pirating satellite and cable television and stuff like that—what's the difference? "We're your parents, that's the difference," was their reply. That kind of attitude is what I've gotten from my parents my whole life, it was like they were saying they could do things that were wrong and I couldn't, it's not the same. It was easy for me to draw parallels between what I was doing and what other people were doing.

HENRY: So you didn't really have any kind of remorse or guilt for stealing accounts or any kind of software?

JASON: Not at all.

HENRY: How old were you at the time?

JACOB: I was 14. At the time, they were gearing this product for older people, they weren't targeting it for 14-year-olds. So if they are not going to target it towards you, why should you feel any sort of obligation, remorse, or pity towards them for not compensating them for something they are not targeting at you?

HENRY: Did you steal for a specific purpose or did you do it just for fun?

JACOB: Well, I didn't steal anything physical until I had been in college for a couple of semesters and I ended up homeless. Until that point it was never a theft of goods, it was only a theft of services. You know, it was like software, online services, music, stuff like that.

HENRY: But you didn't just do it for fun. It was all software that you needed. Or did you do it for other people?

(Continued)

Account: Stealing Computers   Continued

JASON: When people needed things, I would do my best to find them because it was always like a puzzle. It was like a game. You had a wealth of information at your fingertips and there's a single needle in that haystack that you need to find. And the odds are stacked even more against you because it's something you're not supposed to be able to find because it's not supposed to exist in the place you're looking for it in. So it's no different from doing puzzle games. It's a game you're constantly working at and become better at, and you're almost becoming a librarian of information. And after a while you hone your skills on pirating software so that at a certain point, somebody says, "I can't find information on X," and you've developed this strategy of going at the problem that cuts down your time looking for it, especially in the kind of information you're looking for on the Internet. It's certainly come in handy, not that I don't pirate software as much because I've found routes to do it and ways that I've satisfied myself are legal.

HENRY: So you're saying at first your experience with pirating software was a challenge, then it grew to more of a need to gain information?

JASON: Exactly. I mean, it go to a point where you're tracking software you don't even have any intention of using. As soon as you find it, you're satisfied and you delete it. At that point, you haven't even stolen anything—it was just you finding it. It was digging through 30,000 pages of information and finding that one you were looking for, then burning it because you didn't really need it, it was a puzzle you needed to solve.

HENRY: That made you move from stealing software to stealing physical items you could grasp like products in stores, stuff like that?

JASON: Originally it was a necessity. My parents kicked me out of the house because they figured that things I did for recreation, like being in a band, having a girlfriend, and working part-time in a computer store, were all things that they didn't want me to do because they wanted me to work full-time on school. They figured college was the only route to becoming a productive member of society and that I had to put forty hours a week towards schoolwork. They figured I had to quit my part-time job, quit the band, leave my girlfriend—and none of this was optional. "My way or the highway" was what they told me. I had been succeeding in school and managed to save up some money on the side, which my parents pissed away, then told me they couldn't afford to send me to school, that I'd have to take out student loans and go into debt. So one night I emailed my teachers and told them I was leaving town for a personal emergency, could I take the finals via email, and at two in the morning, it was raining, it was a Thursday night, and I hopped on my bike, rode ten miles to the train station, waited two hours for a 5 AM train to DC, caught a ride down to Florida, stayed there for a couple of weeks, came back to this area, slept on couches for a while with people here, and ended up living in the warehouse my band was practicing in. I had a hundred dollars to my name, I lived in a warehouse in Baltimore, I didn't have a residence to receive mail or even could use to apply for a job or anything like that. I didn't even have enough money to rent an apartment. I was perfectly capable of sustaining myself, only not within the normal confines of what people would think of when they do that sort of thing. It was like me seeking out alternative ways of doing things that I had developed earlier when working on the computer. So I found food in dumpsters because people throw away so much food that it becomes easy to live off of donuts, bread, produce sealed in plastic bags that grocery stores toss out because they are two days past the expiration date. So I found food that way. If my clothes became messed up and unwearable, I'd go into a department store that is buying clothes exported from Asia made by exploited labor and there's a thousand percent markup, and I'd take stuff like that—nobody's getting hurt. The store's screwing people fifteen thousand miles away and now I'm going to screw the store for exploiting these people and get what I need. That's how it started—taking dumpster food, stealing clothes, shoes, and a backpack to carry them in. Mainly it was clothes.

HENRY: Mostly just necessities?

JASON: Yeah. I mean, when you're living outside, under bridges, you don't have the ability to wash your clothes, so they wear out and you have to replace them more often.

HENRY: You justified all this as payback to large corporations that were stealing from the Third World?

JASON: Exactly.

HENRY: Did it become a challenge, the way it was with the software?

JASON: That's exactly what it became. The security measures that are in all these different stores, are a joke. The tags they put on a pair of jeans, if you take thirty seconds and have half an idea of how the material is knit, you can take the tag off without damaging the product. So you grab three pairs, roll to the dressing room, pull the tags off, wear the jeans under your clothes, roll back out with a different pair, hand that one to the cashier, and just roll out. Nothing happens to you. It became so simple and second nature that the ease of it took away the adrenaline rush or thrill that came with stealing.

HENRY: How far did you take your theft? I mean, OK, you stole software and clothes, but did you steal TVs, cameras, stuff like that?

JACOB: Well, I never took anything from individuals directly—that's somebody working for it, and they lose personally from the theft. Big corporations are hiding profits, working shell games with third party organizations, that sort of thing, entities that only exist on paper. At one point, I went back to visit my parents, and I sat there with all these bills that had piled up for me defaulting on my student loans. I had given my library card to help out a public community radio station, so I even had fines from the library that totaled three or four hundred dollars, which really pissed me off. So one night, around midnight, I burglarized the radio station, which is located in the school, grabbed two monitors, put them on two chairs, and began wheeling them down the hallway. I was thinking about how this radio station had treated me, and that the teachers at the school were not doing their fucking

jobs, and I decided to go for the gold and see how much I could steal before I got caught. At that point I expected to get caught. There's all this shit just sitting there, it's just gonna take one person to notice. So I loaded up eight computers and ten monitors, a printer that weighed a hundred and fifty pounds, a separate printer, two keyboards that you can hook up to computers to make music, some digital recording gear, a whole binder full of CD software—like, a whole computer lab. And I wheeled it all to the exit. I walked out of the building, walked a half-mile down the road where I had parked a pick-up truck, pulled the truck up to the exit, backed it up, opened the tailgate, and began packing the shit into the bed of the truck. That took me about half an hour. I closed the gate on the truck, put down the door over the cap, and began driving toward the warehouse I lived in at the time. While I was driving, I began rehearsing what I would say to a cop that stopped me. What do cops stop you for? I began rehearsing all the possibilities. I wasn't going to speed or drive recklessly, the truck was in good shape, the headlights worked, I even set cruise control on 65. I got to the warehouse, spent the next hour stacking the stuff on the floor of the warehouse. Meanwhile, I'm coming down from the adrenaline rush I was going through. Then I drive to a gas station, gassed up, got some donuts for breakfast, drove to my parents' house, and let the dogs outside. My mom woke up because the dogs started barking. "What were you doing up so early?" my mom asked. "Oh, I was just letting the dogs out." I never got questioned. And three months after that, still nothing happened The police had no leads. I was finally caught on this when one of my friends at a nearby university needed a computer really bad, and I gave him one I had stolen, and he had a really big mouth and told all these people about it, so a private investigator heard about it and so he went to my friend flashing a badge and got my friend to admit to all kinds of shit, so the police arrested me. If it hadn't been for my generosity I would have gotten away with it. During the trial I was asked how many people were doing this with me. They could not believe that I was the only

(Continued)

Account: Stealing Computers   Continued

one doing it. They couldn't believe the security at school was so terrible. That it would take one person four hours to load a whole computer lab full of stuff and no one noticed anything. And the police claimed more was stolen than what I took. Somebody must have seen an opportunity after I rolled through there and took more stuff. Or maybe the school used the theft to collect more insurance. Or maybe a teacher took more stuff and never felt like giving it back. Looking back on it, I realize that I have to abide by the social contract that everyone under the law has to obey, and what I did was wrong. But when I think about how the school fucked me over and how brazenly everyone at the school works the system to their advantage, and how the school tried to profit from the theft—I mean, they got everything back, and I still had to pay them approximately $25,000 in restitution and damages. I mean, there was nothing really damaged. Looking back on it, it's hard for me to have any remorse because, yes, I victimized them, but they victimized me. Tit for tat. I'm not going to feel bad here. I can understand that this is something I shouldn't do in the future, as much for my own well-being as anything else. I don't want to have to spend a month and a half in jail waiting for someone to bail me out. I don't want to go on trial, I don't want to be on probation for five years, I don't want to owe the state $25,000, I don't want to be shut out of normal jobs, even after I've completed the probation and restitution. If you apply for a job at the state university, you'll notice that they ask a question, "Have you ever been charged with a crime?" They can find justification enough to deny you admission. So I have very little remorse for what I did because I am going to have to pay for it for the rest of my life. The insurance company is sucking blood out of everyone in order to make a profit. You're paying a company to hope that you don't have your stuff taken, and the chance is, it won't be, but it's this paranoia that is created that forces you to pay. So the school is gonna pay for it—more power to them—and it's good that they got something back on it.

HENRY: So, you saw it as just another aspect of people screwing one another over?

JASON: Exactly. That's the way things work.

HENRY: Have you committed any sorts of crimes like this since then? I mean, you said you pretty much abstained from it, but were there any exceptions?

JASON: Well, initially, when I had first gotten out of jail, I was homeless, I didn't even have access to the warehouse I had been living in earlier. My friends ostracized me, I was left with not a single cent to my name. I had to go back to stealing clothes and other stuff to get by. But other than the bare necessities, no, I haven't stolen anything since then.

QUESTIONS

Does Jason's explanation for why he stole the computer equipment from the school correspond with any of the theories spelled out in this chapter? Do you find Jason's explanation plausible? Would other potential "audiences" be convinced by his justification for his illegal action? Was he unjustly or too-severely punished? Or do you find his deviance-neutralizing devices self-serving? Are they accurate or valid? Do they give the observer, the sociologist, the researcher insight to the etiology or cause of crime and deviance in general? Jason implies that the conditions for theft are constant and unchanging, but in real life, the crime rate goes up and down. During the 1990s and into the first two decades of the 2000s, the crime rate continues to decline; how does that address Jason's explanation of why people commit criminal behavior? The usual factors that observers use to explain crime—materialism, an aggressively acquisitive ethic, competition, exploitation, poverty, inequality, frustrated ambition, and so on—haven't substantially changed, but the crime rate continues to decrease. Which theory summarized in this chapter do you think has the most traction in explaining and illuminating why deviance, crime, and delinquency take place?

Constructing Deviance

Learning Objectives:

After reading this chapter, you will be able to:

- see the link between deviance and social control;
- understand the difference between formal and informal social control;
- discuss perspectives that focus on defining deviance;
- examine labeling or interactionist theory;
- recognize conflict theory;
- discuss feminism in relation to deviance;
- talk about controlology or the new sociology of social control.

In contrast to explanatory theories of deviance, constructionist approaches begin with the issue of *how wrongdoing is constructed*. Why are rules made in the first place? Who makes the rules? Why are *certain kinds* of rules made? Are enactors of *certain kinds of illegal behavior* and members of *certain social categories* more likely to be apprehended and punished? And are some more likely to be subject to *harsher* social control than others? Secondly, constructionist perspectives address the matter of what *consequences* rule-making and rule enforcement have. Does social control entrench the labeled person more deeply into the role of "a" deviant? Is the punishment of *certain kinds of people* more likely to lead to stigma, reinforcing the very behavior it is presumably designed to eliminate? Thirdly, constructionists consider the issue of etiology, but it is less central to their concerns, and they are likely to select *powerlessness* and *marginality* as one of the major causes of engaging in deviance and crime. While labeling theorists argue that any analysis of deviance has to begin with how wrongdoing is conceived and conceptualized, *in the typical case*, the person who is designated as deviant *did* do something, and there are *reasons* why this is so. While conflict theorists focus on differentials in power in the genesis of the law and its passage and enforcement—laws tend to be enacted by the powerful against the powerless—likewise, typically, society is so constituted that the very behavior that is legislated and enforced as *wrong* tends to be enacted by the powerless. And while feminist argue that in a patriarchal society, normative violations are stacked against women, certain acts of deviance *really are* engaged in more by women, and women's roles help explain why. Hence, the question becomes, "Are the poor, marginal, powerless, and stigmatized more likely to commit acts society defines as deviant and criminal than the more affluent, prominent, dominant, and prestigious members?"

Constructionism focuses on the creation of social categories, the imputation of deviance to those categories, why certain rules exist, how they work, what their consequences are, what the dynamics of enforcement are, and why certain behaviors tend to be enacted more by the powerless and politically and socially marginal. Constructionists do not *begin* with the "Why do they do it?" question; instead, the causes of deviant behavior, beliefs, and conditions they focus on are very much in the background. How members of society think and talk about and react to behavior, beliefs, and conditions they regard as unacceptable becomes the central focus. In short, the constructionist looks at *how deviance is defined, conceptualized, and represented*, and how those definitions, conceptualizations, and representations are *enacted*, and with what *consequences* (Best, 2011; Grattet, 2011a; Conyers, 2011; Interbitzen, Bates, and Gainey, 2013, pp. 339–484).

The social constructionist approach permits inquiry into *false accusations*; it is far from irrelevant, though it is atypical, that the accused person didn't "do it." Why were hundreds of thousands of women persecuted in Renaissance Europe for witchcraft? The positivist sociologist is powerless to ask this question because, in all likelihood, the women accused of witchcraft *didn't* engage in the crimes of which they were accused. In contrast, the constructionist is very comfortable about asking why the witch-craze arose (Ben-Yehuda, 1980, 1985, pp. 23–73) and why mainly women were accused and punished for a nonexistent crime. The fact that the crime didn't exist is crucial for the positivist, because you can't offer an explanation for the enactment of a behavior in which somebody didn't engage. To the sociologists looking only at the causes of behavior, the witches didn't engage in deviance because they didn't *do* anything to attract the condemnation. In contrast, the constructionist asks about the enterprise of persecution and condemnation, which is to some degree *independent* of the enactment of the behavior of which deviants are accused. In other words, constructionists are interested both in how rules arise and to whom they are applied—whether justly or unjustly—*and* whether and to what extent deviant behavior is more likely to be enacted by persons at the bottom of the socioeconomic hierarchy.

To the social constructionist, the distinctions between voluntary behavior, beliefs, and involuntary conditions are secondary. What counts is how people who are seen as violating the law are *thought of* and *treated* in a particular society. Are blind people more likely to be socially accepted by the sighted today as compared with centuries past? Does acceptance or rejection of blind people vary from one society to another? Does acceptance or rejection vary in the same society at the same time by social category or group? How do blind people regard their condition? How do they relate to the sighted? Do they interact mainly with one another or do they integrate into the world of the sighted? We can ask similar questions about a variety of social conditions, including obesity, dwarfism, albinism, physical disfigurement or disability, and extreme ugliness. To the constructionist, the fact that the conditions are involuntary is not the issue; that persons in such categories are treated in a certain fashion *is* the issue. For instance, the Greeks and other ancient peoples abandoned deformed children to the elements to die, believing that a stigma adhered to such imperfect creatures; in some societies, adulterers and presumed adulterers have been stoned to death, so serious is the stigma of the sin of adultery. Both the condition, physical deformity, and the voluntary behavior, adultery, are deviant in that they generate stigma and punishment. Irrespective of what caused them, from a constructionist perspective, both are, or have been regarded as, deviant.

These separate but interlocking intellectual enterprises—the study of causes and the study of the social construction of deviance—are not contradictory but independent of one another, yet complementary. On the one hand, there are reasons why some people violate society's rules and why some societies experience more deviance than others, and these reasons can be discovered and explained. But these norms are also created and enforced as a result of systematic, identifiable sociological processes. While the sociological positivist takes the norms and their enforcement *as if* they were a given, they are every bit a social product and every bit in need of an explanation as deviant behavior itself.

DEVIANCE AND SOCIAL CONTROL

Sociologists define social control as *efforts to construct and ensure conformity to a norm.* Every time people do something to induce someone to engage in behavior they believe is right, they are engaged in social control; every time they discourage someone from doing something they consider wrong, likewise, they are engaging in social control. When

a mother yanks her child's hand out of the cookie jar, she is exercising social control. When a police officer arrests a burglar for breaking and entering an apartment, that officer is engaging in social control. When a professor gives a grade of zero to a student caught cheating on an exam, he or she is practicing social control. When legislators enact a bill into law, they exercise social control. Social control includes "all of the processes by which people define and respond to deviant behavior" (Black, 1984, p. xi). Social control is both formal and informal, both governmental and interpersonal, both internal as well as external (Interbitzen, Bates, and Gainey, 2013, pp. 486–558).

To the constructionist who studies deviance, social control is a central—perhaps *the* central—concept. Now and throughout human history, all societies everywhere have set and enforced norms—rules about what their members should and should not do. We encounter norms everywhere. As we cast our gaze up and down the annals of time, among the world's many nations and societies, we notice that, though rules and norms differ, and likewise so do the nature and severity of the punishments for violating them, nonetheless, *rules and norms themselves are universal.* All societies set rules; some members of all societies violate some of those rules; and all societies attempt to enforce these rules by punishing or otherwise controlling those violators. There is not now and there has never been any country, society, or collectivity where "anything goes." If any such once existed, it could not long survive, for protectionist rules are the cornerstone of human survival.

But "deviance" is *not* simply the violation of norms and rules; it is the dynamic between their violation and their enforcement—what context they are violated in, who violates them, who is offended by their violation, and how severe their violation is thought to be. A "norm" is simply a rule that calls for proper behavior, a kind of blueprint for action. Implied in a norm is the expectation that violators are punished or sanctioned when they violate it. Some norms apply in specific contexts, settings, or situations. For instance, one must *not* laugh at a funeral, but one is *expected* to laugh at a comedy routine. (If it's funny.) The injunction against laughing is specific to certain settings, and the expectation of laughter, likewise, applies to specific settings.

Other norms apply to the behavior of members of certain groups or collectivities but not others. Members of a tough street gang are expected to meet the challenge of an insult, a taunt, a shove, with verbal and physical aggression. The failure to do so would result in chastisement from other gang members. However, if the faculty members at a university or the medical staff of a hospital were to respond as aggressively to a perceived verbal insult, it is their behavior that would be condemned. Such a response would be regarded as undignified, unprofessional, unacceptable—in a word, deviant.

Still other norms apply across the board, that is, to everyone in a given society. For instance, no one is permitted to kill a baby in its crib simply because its crying is annoying. There is no person in any society who is exempt from that norm, and there exists practically no situation or context when such behavior is allowed.

Regardless of whether a given norm applies to all situations or only some, to certain people or all of them, the fact is, *everyone, everywhere* is subject to *certain* norms. Being human means being subject to the norms of the groups to which one belongs and the society in which one lives. But some people are "more equal" than others, and the normative violations of some of us may be ignored or underplayed, while others will be more severely punished. Those who are favored are able to get away with a great many more sins than those who are disadvantaged—occasionally, even murder! Yes, the constructionist sociologist insists, life isn't fair, but that's the way it is! Perhaps some of these inequities can be corrected, but in every society that has ever existed, absolute equality has never existed; perhaps it never will.

As we saw, some minimal level of punishment for wrongdoing is necessary to ensure a minimal level of social order. At some point, the lack of norms in a given society would result in a state of collapse into a "war of all against all," in which life would be, in the words of seventeenth-century English philosopher Thomas Hobbes, author of *Leviathan*, "solitary, poor, nasty, brutish, and short." The central question for the functionalist sociologist is, given the natural human tendency to be selfish: *How is social order possible?* If there were no rules and we were permitted to obtain anything by any conceivable effective means—rape, murder, robbery, assault—then

how is it possible for societies to survive and even prosper? Why *don't* we collapse into a state of chaos, disorder, and disintegration? For the functionalists, a partial answer to this question is that *social control*, through both learning the acceptable norms and punishing unacceptable and rewarding acceptable behavior, operates to ensure a society's survival. The Sixth Commandment, "Thou shalt not murder" (*not* "kill," since the ancient Hebrews *did* kill a substantial number of their enemies—for instance, in warfare), is an obvious example of such a norm.

Actually, it is surprising how *few* norms are designed to condemn, punish, or protect a society or its members from injurious or predatory actions, such as murder, rape, robbery, or serious assault. Most norms attempt to discourage behavior that neither directly harms anyone nor threatens society with chaos and disintegration. Most norms are intended to make a statement about what is considered—by some, many, or most members of a society—to be right, good, and proper. They embody certain principles of moral correctness—separate and independent of what they do for society's physical survival. Norms such as the Sixth Commandment are in the minority of rules that members of a society learn and, for the most part, abide by. No one would be injured nor would society be threatened with disintegration if some of us were to wear our clothes backwards, speak every word twice, or eat steak by grabbing it with our hands and tearing at it with our teeth. But if any of us were to engage in these acts, others would greet us with disapproval, condemnation, and derision. Clearly, protecting society from actions that are so harmful as to threaten our and society's survival is not the sole purpose for the norms or the punishment of their violators. There is implicit in norms and their enforcement a version of moral correctness, an ethos, a way of life that is *an end in itself*. We are expected to do certain things because they are *right*, because *that's the way things are done*. Even if deviant behavior causes no overt physical harm, social controllers insist that the social and moral order and a decent way of life must be protected from subversion and aberration.

As I said, there are several distinctly different varieties of social control. *Internal* social control operates through the process of *socialization*, by learning and adopting the norms of society or a particular group or collectivity within society. All people are socialized by identifiable *agents*. The family is, of course, the earliest agent of socialization, one of whose primary functions is attempting to internalize into children the norms of society in which they live. If the family fails to do so, children are more likely to engage in behavior regarded by society as deviant. Later on, schools, peers, and the mass media represent influential agents of socialization. Much of their socialization also represents efforts at internal social control. When the norms of society are accepted as valid, they can be said to be *internalized*. When internalization is successful, persons feel guilty if they were to engage in the behavior society or their collectivity considers wrong. If they refuse to do so, it is in part as a consequence of the fact that the relevant norm was successfully internalized. We do not kill or assault people who make us angry simply because we will be punished for doing so, but in large part because we have come to accept that murder and assault are wrong.

Socialization is only one weapon in society's arsenal of social control. When conventional socialization operates effectively, it acts as an *internal* form of social control. But in one way or another, society is usually only partly successful in instilling its version of the norms into us. There are always some people—for the most important norms, the minority—who don't accept the legitimacy of the norms. Moreover, even people who are usually conformist and law-abiding will find situations that call for exceptions to a rule or norm. (If we are faced with an especially tempting reward, or potentially deadly harm, many of us reevaluate our rigid adherence to the norm.) The fact is, most of us are incompletely and to some degree partly *unsuccessfully* socialized. As a consequence, another form of social control is necessary; society moves to exercise *external* social control. A great deal of social control is coercive and repressive; it relies on punishment and force. Many of us wish to violate society's norms, to move "outside the lines." When we do so, certain agents of social control may detect our behavior and use some sort of punishment, coercion, or *external* social control to attempt to bring us back into line. Though rewards also make up a form of external social control, usually, we are not rewarded for things we are expected to do, we are simply not punished.

Most sociologists of deviance focus on external social control rather than internal. External social control is made up of the system of rewards and punishments that persons, parties, and agents use to induce others to conform to a norm. Rewards and punishments are referred to as *sanctions*. Obviously, a positive sanction is a reward and a negative sanction is a punishment. Slapping, screaming at, ignoring, snubbing, ridiculing, insulting, taunting, gossiping about, humiliating, frowning at, denouncing, reprimanding, berating, criticizing, nagging, arresting, "dissing," mocking, stigmatizing, showing contempt toward, acting in a condescending fashion toward, laughing at, booing, jeering—these and a host of others are negative reactions to someone, in the estimation of a particular audience, whose behavior, beliefs, and physical traits fail to measure up. They are all *negative* and *external* forms of social control. And social control is the very foundation stone of the sociologist's definition of deviance. *Deviance is that which calls forth efforts at social control.*

FORMAL AND INFORMAL SOCIAL CONTROL

Sociologists distinguish between *formal* and *informal* social control. In-between, we find what might be referred to as "semiformal" social control.

"Informal" social control takes place in interpersonal interaction between and among people who are acting on their own, in an unofficial capacity. As we saw, reactions such as a frown or a smile, criticism or praise, shunning or being warm toward someone, are ways we have of exercising *informal* social control. They act to remind someone that their behavior upsets or annoys us. Since most people seek the approval of others whom they care about, they tend to adjust their behavior to avoid the disapproval of significant others by discontinuing the offensive behavior or at least hiding it from public view.

However, in large, complex societies, especially with a substantial volume of contact between and among strangers, informal social control is usually no longer sufficient to bring about conformity to the norms. In such societies, it becomes easy to ignore the disapproval of others if you do not care enough about them to be concerned about how they feel about you. So, *formal* social control becomes necessary. "Formal social control" is made up of efforts to bring about conformity to the law by agents of the criminal justice system: the police, the courts, and jails and prisons. In principle, agents of formal social control act not as individuals with their own personal feelings about whether behavior is wrong or right, but as occupants of specific statuses in a specific bureaucratic organization, that is, the criminal justice system. The sanctions they apply to wrongdoers flow from their offices or positions, not from their personal relationship with the rule-violator. It is the job or function of such agents to act, when transgressions occur, to bring about conformity to the formal code, that is, the law. Both formal and informal social control may operate at the same time. A drug dealer may simultaneously be arrested by the police *and* shunned by his neighbors. A child molester may serve a 10-year sentence for his crime and, after he is released, be shunned and humiliated by members of the community in which he lives.

Somewhere in between informal social control, which is based on personal and interpersonal reactions between and among interacting parties, and the formal social control of the criminal justice system—the police, the courts, and the correctional institutions—we find "semiformal" social control. Here we have a huge territory of noncriminal, non-penal bureaucratic social control, administered by the government, which attempts to deal with the troublesome behavior of persons under their authority. If a person's behavior becomes extremely troublesome to others, an array of agencies, bureaucracies, and organizations may step in to handle or control that person, to punish or bring him or her into line with the rules. In other words, persons deemed difficult or problematic by members of a community come under "the purview of professional controllers" (Hawkins and Tiedeman, 1975, p. 111). These "professional controllers" do not have the power of arrest or incarceration but they can make recommendations to agents of the criminal justice system that may have bearing on arrest and incarceration. Such agents include social workers, psychiatrists, truant officers, and representatives, functionaries, and officers of mental hospitals,

civil courts, the Internal Revenue Service and other official tax agencies, social welfare offices, unemployment offices, departments of motor vehicles, and the educational system.

Some sociologists of deviance equate "social control" with formal and semiformal social control. They ignore the private, informal, interpersonal reactions to behavior and beliefs by individuals as a means of keeping people in line with the rules and norms of society (Cohen, 1985; Horwitz, 1990). The reason is that such a focus is consistent with their theory that social control is centralized and repressive (Meier, 1982). On the other hand, if you broaden your conception of social control to include informal social control as well, you have to recognize the fact that interpersonal relations are messy, untidy, less likely to conform to a pattern, far less centralized and far less subject to elite control. These "social control" thinkers (Foucault, 1979; Cohen, 1985; Lowman, Menzies, and Palys, 1987; Scull, 1988) equate state or state-like control, assuming that state control, much like an octopus, reaches out and grabs people who are administered by agencies and organizations spread throughout society.

But contrary to such "social control" theorists, *most of the time* that social control is exercised, it is informal. Most of the time that deviant behavior is sanctioned, the actor is punished or condemned interpersonally, by individuals, not formally by representatives of a bureaucratic organization. Informal social control is the "meat and potatoes," the "nuts and bolts" of the labeling process. Relatively speaking, formal social control tends to be much less common and more fitfully applied. The vast majority of rule-breaking behavior—such as making unwanted sexual passes at parties, breaking wind at the dinner table, insulting one's peers—is *ignored* by the apparatus of formal and semiformal social control. Informal social control is the foundation of social life.

PERSPECTIVES THAT FOCUS ON DEFINING DEVIANCE

The constructionist approaches include labeling or interactionist theory, conflict theory, feminist theory, and contrology or the "new" sociology of social control. As with all perspectives, constructionists deal mainly with behavior rather than beliefs and conditions. But *unlike* the essentialist, causal, and positivistic perspectives we looked at in Chapter 2, constructionists— especially labeling and feminist approaches—look at beliefs and conditions *in addition to* behavior.

Labeling or *interactionist* theory or school focuses on rule-making and, especially, *reactions to* rule-breaking (Becker, 1963; Lofland, 1969; Schur, 1971). This school shifts attention away from the circumstances that produced the deviant act to "the important role of social definitions and negative sanctions" as well as "what happens to people *after* they have been singled out, identified, and defined as deviants" (Traub and Little, 1999, pp. 375, 376).

Conflict theory deals with the question of making the rules, especially the criminal law. Why is certain behavior outlawed? And why is other, often even more damaging behavior, *not* outlawed? Conflict theory focuses its attention on the role of powerful groups and classes in the formation and enforcement of the criminal law. The powerful are able to ensure that laws favorable to their own interests and detrimental to the interests of other, less powerful groups and classes, are passed and enforced (Turk, 1969; Quinney, 1970).

Feminist theory is a variety of conflict theory focusing specifically on the role of sex and gender in deviance and crime: How do men express and maintain their dominance by defining and enforcing certain actions as deviant and criminal? Why does patriarchy exist, whose functions does it serve, and what impact does it have on deviance and social control? (Schur, 1984; Daly and Chesney-Lind, 1988).

Controlology or the "new" sociology of social control is a perspective that grew out of the work of the French philosopher Michel Foucault. It argues that social control is not only the central issue for the sociologist of deviance, but for the sociologist generally. Contemporary society has devised a system for the control of troublesome behavior that appears to be humane and scientific, but it is far more thoroughgoing, systematic, efficient, and *repressive* than older, seemingly more barbarous forms of control that entailed torture and public execution. "Knowledge is power," this approach asserts, and the powerful strata employ

scientific knowledge to control and manipulate the unruly, threatening masses (Foucault, 1979, 2003; Cohen, 1985).

LABELING OR INTERACTIONIST THEORY

In the 1960s, a small group of researchers produced a small body of work that exerted an enormous influence on the sociological approach to deviance; it came to be looked upon as a more or less unified perspective that is widely referred to as *labeling theory* (Schur, 1971). Labeling theory grew out of a more general perspective in sociology called *symbolic interactionism*. This approach is based on "three simple premises." First, people act on the basis of the *meaning* that things have for them. Second, this meaning grows out of *interaction* with others, especially intimate others. And third, meaning is continually modified by *interpretation* (Blumer, 1969, p. 2). These three principles—meaning, interaction, and interpretation—form the core of symbolic interactionism and likewise of labeling theory as well. People are not robots, interactionists argued; they are active and creative in how they see and act on things in the world. People are not simple "products" of their upbringing or socialization, or of their environment, but arrive at what they think, how they feel, and what they do through a dynamic, creative process. All behavior, deviance included, is an interactional product; its properties and impact cannot be known until we understand how it is defined, conceptualized, interpreted, apprehended, and evaluated—in short, what it *means* to participants and relevant observers alike. Labeling theory is not a separate theory but an application of symbolic interactionism to deviant phenomena.

The year 1938 marked the publication of a book written by Frank Tannenbaum, a professor of history and a Latin American specialist; it was entitled *Crime and the Community*. Tannenbaum argued that in a slum area, nearly all boys engage in a wide range of mischievous, sometimes illegal behavior—getting into fights, skipping school, stealing apples, throwing rocks at windows. These actions, perfectly normal and taken for granted by the boys themselves, are often regarded as deviant and criminal by the authorities—by teachers, the police, and the courts. In an effort to curtail this behavior, the police apprehend and punish some of these boys. If the boys persist in this behavior, they will be sent to reform school. However, punishment often has the ironic effect of escalating the seriousness of the deeds that these boys commit. Arrest and incarceration often results in the community regarding a boy as incorrigible—a budding criminal in the flesh. By being treated as a delinquent and forced to associate with slightly older and more experienced young criminals in reform schools, the troublemaker comes to see himself as a true delinquent. This escalates his deviant career, increasing the chance that he will go on to a life of crime. Note that Tannenbaum did *not* examine the social construction of the laws of juvenile delinquency; but he did examine the tendency for *working class boys* to be arrested and incarcerated, and the tendency of arrest and incarceration to *reinforce* and *entrench* delinquency among these boys.

About a dozen years later, Edwin Lemert published a textbook with the anachronistic title, *Social Pathology* (1951). Lemert distinguished between *primary* and *secondary* deviation. Primary deviation is simply the enactment of deviant behavior itself—any form of it. Lemert argued that primary deviation is *polygenetic* (1951, pp. 75–76, 1972, pp. 62–63)—caused by a wide range of factors. For instance, someone may drink heavily for a variety of reasons—the death of a loved one, a business failure, belonging to a group whose members call for heavy drinking, and so on. In fact, Lemert asserted, the original cause or causes of a particular form of deviance is not especially important. What counts is the social reaction *to* the behavior from others.

Secondary deviation occurs when the individual who enacts deviant behavior deals with the problems created by social reactions to his or her primary deviations (1951, p. 76). "The secondary deviant, as opposed to his [or her] actions, is a person whose life and identity are organized around the facts of deviance" (1972, p. 63). When someone is singled out, stigmatized, condemned, or isolated for engaging in deviant behavior, it becomes necessary to *deal with* and *manage* this social reaction in certain ways. One comes to see oneself in a certain way, defines oneself in different

terms, adopts different roles, associates with different individuals. Being stigmatized forces one to become a deviant—to engage in secondary deviation. "Secondary deviation" does not *necessarily* mean that labeling causes more frequent enactment of the behavior that generated the label, but it is more likely than the absence of labeling.

Lemert recognized that not all primary deviation results in punishment or condemnation; some communities or social circles display more "tolerance" for rule-breaking behavior than others (1951, pp. 57–58). When primary deviation results in punishment, however, the individuals engaging in it tend to be stigmatized, shunned, and socially isolated. They are forced into social groups or circles of other individuals who are also stigmatized. This isolation from mainstream, conventional society reinforces the individual's commitment to these unconventional, deviant groups and circles and the individual's commitment to the deviant behavior itself. Lemert pointed out that the media tend to "call attention" to an offender's minority status as a Latino or African American; their marginal and "economically unpropertied status . . . heightens their visibility as deviants" and reinforces the stereotype of certain ethnic groups as being "criminally inclined" (p. 52). As with Tannenbaum, Lemert did not explore the social construction of deviant behavior—in fact, the behaviors he discussed "covered the waterfront": blindness, speech defects, radicalism, prostitution, crime, alcoholism, and mental disorder. However, he did propose the notion that some members of society are more vulnerable to a designation of deviance than others, and he did stress the self-reinforcing nature of designations of deviance.

According to Becker (1973, pp. 177–208) and Kitsuse (1972, 1980), labeling theory is not so much an explanation for why certain individuals engage in deviant behavior as it is a perspective whose main insight tells us that the labeling process is crucial and cannot be ignored. Labeling "theory" is an orientation, the delineation of a "useful set of problems" centered on the origins and consequences of labeling (Plummer, 1979, pp. 88, 90). The interactionist approach shifts attention away from the traditional question of "Why do they do it?" to a focus on how and why judgments of deviance come to be made and what their consequences are. Why are certain acts condemned at one time and in one place but toler-ated at another time, in another place? Why does one person do something and get away "scot-free," while another does the same thing and is severely punished for it? What happens when someone is caught violating a rule and is stig-matized for it? What consequences does labeling have for stigmatization? What is the difference between enacting rule-breaking behavior which does not result in getting caught, and enacting that same behavior and being publicly denounced for it? These are some of the major issues labeling theorists have been concerned with.

In many ways, labeling theory is a model or quintessential example of the constructionist approach. It addresses issues such as the creation of deviant categories, the social construction of moral meanings and definitions, social and cul-tural relativity, the how and why of social control, the politics of deviance, the criminalization of behavior, and the role of contingency in the labe-ling process. Together, these issues constitute the foundation stone of constructionism. It's impor-tant to emphasize a couple of points in advance to ensure that the reader does not become entan-gled in bogus issues that misguided critics have raised. First, though the interactionist approach emphasizes that being labeled as *having engaged in* deviant behavior and being labeled as *a* devi-ant are contingent on factors such as marginal-ity and powerlessness, the approach insists that *deviance labeling is not random with respect to rule-violations.* Some critics leave the reader with the feeling that for "radical" constructionists, an individuals' behavior is "deemed irrelevant to the labeling process" (Gove, 1975a, 1980; Grattet, 2011a). "One sometimes gets the impression from reading this literature that people go about mind-ing their own business, and then—"wham"—bad society comes along with a stigmatized label" (Akers, 1968, p. 463). And second, some critics aver, labelists argue that *once someone is forced into the role of deviant*, one "has little choice but to be deviant" (p. 463). Both assumptions are false. Labeling theorists do not make either of these assumptions. They do *focus on* the con-tingencies of labeling and the reinforcement of the labeling process, but this is very different from saying labeling is random and its impact is permanent.

The concerns of labeling theory center on audiences, *labeling and stigma*, *reflexivity*, the inner world of deviance, and *the "stickiness" of labels* and *the self-fulfilling prophecy.*

Audiences

An audience is an individual or any number of individuals who observe and evaluate an act, a condition, or an individual. An audience could be one's friends, relatives, or neighbors, cowork-ers, the police, teachers, a psychiatrist, bystand-ers or observers—even oneself, for you can be an observer and an evaluator of your own behavior or condition (Becker, 1963, p. 31). *Audiences* deter-mine whether something or someone is deviant: no audience, no labeling, therefore, no deviance. However, an audience need not *directly* view an act, condition, or person; audiences can witness behavior or conditions "indirectly," that is, they can hear or be told about someone's behavior or condition, or they can simply have a negative or condemnatory attitude toward a class or category of behavior: "The critical variable in the study of deviance . . . is the social audience rather than the individual actor, since it is the audience which eventually determines whether or not any episode of behavior *or any class of episodes* is labeled deviant" (Erikson, 1964, p. 11; my emphasis). In other words, audiences can evaluate *categories* of deviance and stand ready to condemn them, even before they have actually witnessed specific, con-crete cases of these categories. As we've seen in Chapter 1, audiences are absolutely central in the sociological definition of deviance. Whether an act, a belief, or a trait is deviant or not depends on the audience who does or would evaluate and react to the actor, the believer, or the possessor accordingly. Without specifying real-life audi-ences, the question of an act's, a belief's, or a trait's deviance is meaningless. Audiences include society at large, official agents of social control, and the significant others of the actor, such as inti-mates. These audiences may or may not evaluate or react to the actor's behavior in the same way.

Labeling and Stigma

The key elements in "becoming" deviant are labe-ling and stigma. The processes of labeling and stigmatizing are done by a relevant audience. The audience is relevant according to the circumstances or context. Gang members can label the behavior of a follow member of the gang—for instance, the refusal to fight—as deviant *within the gang context*; the police can label an action of a gang member, for instance, fighting, as deviant, wrong, or illegal by arresting or harassing him. Each audience or person can label each action, belief, or condition of each person as deviant—but the weight or *consequences* of that labeling process vary according to the audience and the context.

The labeling or stigmatization process entails two steps. First, an audience labels an *activity* (or belief or condition) deviant, and second, it labels a specific *individual* as *a* deviant. In these two labeling processes, if no audience labels something or someone deviant, *no deviance exists*. An act, belief, condition, or person cannot be deviant *in the abstract*, that is, without reference to how an audience does or would label it. Something or someone must be defined as such by the members of a society or a group *as* deviant—it must be *labeled* as reprehensible or wrong. Likewise, a person cannot be regarded as a deviant until this labeling process takes place. An act, belief, or condition need not be *actually* or *concretely* labeled to be regarded as deviant, however, but it is deviant if it belongs to a category of similar actions, beliefs, or conditions. In other words, *we already know* that the public regards shooting the proprietor of a store and taking the contents of that store's cash register as deviant. Even if the robber gets away with the crime, we know that *if known about*, it would be regarded as deviant in society at large—that is, it is an instance of "societal deviance."

Labeling involves attaching a *stigmatizing* definition to an activity, a belief, or a condition. Stigma is a stain, a sign of reproach or social undesirability, an indication to the world that one has been singled out as a shameful, morally discredited human being. Someone who has been stigmatized is a "marked" person; he or she has a "spoiled identity." A stigmatized person is one who has been labeled a deviant. Once someone has been so discredited, relations with conventional, respectable others become difficult, strained, problematic. In other words, "being caught and branded as a deviant has important consequences for one's further participation and self-image. . . . Committing the improper act and

being publicly caught at it places [the individual] in a new status. He [or she] has been revealed as a different kind of person from the kind he [or she] was supposed to be. He [or she] is labeled a 'fairy,' 'dope fiend,' 'nut,' or 'lunatic,' and treated accordingly" (Becker, 1963, pp. 31, 32).

So crucial is this labeling process that, in some respects, it does not necessarily matter whether or not someone who has been stigmatized has actually engaged in the behavior of which he or she is accused. As we saw, according to the logic of labeling theory, *falsely accused* deviants—if the accusation sticks—are still deviants (Becker, 1963, p. 20). In many important respects, they resemble individuals who really *do* commit acts that violate the rules. For example, women and men burned at the stake for the crime of witchcraft in the fifteenth and sixteenth centuries were deviants in the eyes of the authorities and the community (Ben-Yehuda, 1980), even though they clearly did not engage in a pact with the devil. Two individuals, one who engaged in a deviant act and the second of whom is falsely accused, will share important experiences and characteristics, *by virtue of the labeling process alone*, even though they are poles apart with respect to having committed the behavior of which they were accused. While their lives are unlikely to be *identical* simply because both are seen by the community as deviants, the similarities they share are likely to be revealing. Is this fair? Of course not! Is this the way the world works? Of course it is.

Reflexivity

Reflexivity means looking at ourselves in part through the eyes of others. It is what is widely referred to, although too mechanistically, as the "looking-glass self." Labeling theory is based on a seemingly simple but fundamental observation: "We see ourselves through the eyes of others, and when others see us in a certain way, at least for long enough or sufficiently powerfully, their views are sure to have some effect" (Glassner, 1982, p. 71).

In other words, both direct *and* indirect, or concrete *and* symbolic labeling operate in the world of deviance (Warren and Johnson, 1972, pp. 76–77). "Indirect" or "symbolic" labeling is the awareness by a deviance enactor that his or her behavior is *saturated with public scorn*, his or her identity is potentially discreditable, that he or she *would be* stigmatized if discovered. People who violate norms have to deal with the probable and potential, as well as the actual and concrete, reactions of the respectable, conventional, law-abiding majority. All violators of major norms must at least ask themselves, "How would others react to me and my behavior?" If the answer is, "They will punish me," then the rule breaker must try to avoid detection, remain within deviant or minority circles, or be prepared to be punished, condemned, and stigmatized.

The Inner World of Deviance

One major endeavor of the labeling theorist is the attempt to understand the *inner world* of deviance. Interactionism stresses the ethnographic, anthropological, or participant observation research method: hanging around the individuals under study, observing them in their natural habitat, getting as close to the activity of interest as possible. This means attempting an understanding of the deviant world *as the deviant lives and understands it.* For instance, how do homosexuals see and define their behavior? What is their attitude about being gay? How do they experience being homosexual? How do they look upon the "straight" world? What is the construction of *their* moral meaning like? How do they define right and wrong with respect to sexuality? What does it feel like to be a member of a minority whose members are looked down upon by the straight majority? To know how the world of homosexuality is lived, it is necessary to enter that world and listen to and observe those who actually live it. Interactionists are *fascinated* by the details of the lives of individuals and groups defined as deviant. Interactionism emphasizes how *creative* and *diverse* reactions to being so defined are, how *incapable* powerful deviance-definers are in imposing their will and conceptions on deviants, how *active* deviants are in creating their own definitions and conceptions, and how truly *complex* the lives of deviants are.

The "Stickiness" of Labels and the Self-Fulfilling Prophecy

Labeling theorists argue that stigmatizing someone as a socially and morally undesirable character has important consequences for that person's further rule-breaking. Under certain circumstances, being labeled may intensify one's commitment to a deviant identity and contribute to further deviant behavior. Some conventional, law-abiding citizens believe, "once a deviant, always a deviant." Someone who has been stigmatized and labeled "is ushered into the deviant position by a decisive and often dramatic ceremony, yet is retired from it with hardly a word of public notice." As a result, the deviant is given "no proper license to resume a normal life in the community. Nothing has happened to cancel out the stigma imposed upon him" or her. The original judgment "is still in effect." The conforming members of a society tend to be "reluctant to accept the returning deviant on an entirely equal footing" (Erikson, 1964, pp. 16, 17).

Deviant labels tend to be "sticky." The community tends to stereotype someone as, above all and most importantly, a deviant. When someone is identified as a deviant, the community asks, "What kind of person would break such an important rule?" The answer that is given is "one who is different from the rest of us, who cannot or will not act as a moral being and therefore might break other important rules" (Becker, 1963, p. 34). Deviant labeling is widely regarded as a quality that is "in" the person, an attribute that is carried wherever he or she goes; therefore, it is permanent or at least long-lasting. Deviant behavior is said to be caused by an indwelling, essentialistic trait; it is not seen as accidental or trivial, but a fixture of the individual. Once a deviant label has been attached, it is difficult to shake. Ex-convicts find it difficult to find legitimate employment upon their release from prison; once psychiatrists make a diagnosis of mental illness, hardly any amount of contrary evidence can dislodge their faith in it; ex-mental patients are carefully scrutinized for odd, eccentric, or bizarre behavior.

Such stigmatizing tends to deny to deviants "the ordinary means of carrying on the routines of everyday life open to most people. Because of this denial, the deviant must of necessity develop illegitimate routines" (Becker, 1963, p. 35). As a consequence, the labeling process may actually increase the deviant's further commitment to deviant behavior. It may limit conventional options and opportunities, strengthen a deviant identity, and maximize participation in a deviant group. Labeling someone, thus, may become "a self-fulfilling prophecy" (Becker, 1963, p. 34) in that *someone becomes what he or she is accused of being*—even though that original accusation may have been false (Merton, 1948, 1957, pp. 421–436; Jones, 1977; Jones, 1986).

Labeling Theory Today

Labeling theory left two legacies to the contemporary study of deviance. The first was its constructionist vision. Other, earlier approaches were careful to point out that deviance and crime were a matter of violating rules, norms, and laws, which are socially constructed and vary somewhat historically and culturally. But labeling theory stressed and highlighted this point more forcefully. Indeed, it went further and emphasized that definitions of wrongdoing vary not only from society to society but from one *category* or *social context* to another. This remains a basic and crucial assumption in all sociological work on deviance. The second legacy of labeling theory, its "minor" mode (which, unfortunately, critics stress as its main point), is its argument about the causal mechanism of deviance: being labeled as a wrongdoing inevitably or usually leads to a strengthening of a deviant identity and hence, an escalation in the seriousness and frequency of deviant behavior. This argument is as often wrong as it is right; its lack of empirical verification should not negate the perspective's "major" mode or constructionist legacy.

Labeling theory's influence declined sharply since its heyday roughly from the mid-1960s to the mid-1970s. At that time, it was the most influential and most frequently cited perspective in the study of deviance. This was especially so among the field's younger scholars and researchers, who yearned for a fresh, unconventional, and radically different way of looking at deviance. The perspective was widely and vigorously attacked, and many of these criticisms stuck. Eventually, much of the field recognized and emphasized its flaws and moved on to other perspectives, or sharply modified or adapted interactionist or labeling insights. Today, no single approach or paradigm dominates the field in the way that the Chicago School did in the 1920s or labeling theory circa 1970. What we see today is diversity, fragmentation, and theoretical dissensus. While the practitioners of a variety of perspectives attacked labeling theory for its inadequacies, no single perspective has managed to succeed in attracting a majority following in the field. In spite of the criticisms, the labeling school left an legacy to the field that even its critics make use of, albeit, for the most part, implicitly. Today it is clear that while, as a total approach to deviance, labeling *theory* is incomplete, labeling *processes* take place in all deviance, and deserve a prominent place in its study.

By the 2000s, the insights of labeling theory became so taken-for-granted and densely interwoven into the conventional wisdom of criminology and the sociology of deviance that it provided a case of "obliteration by incorporation" (Merton, 1979; Goode, 2002, pp. 115–116). In other words, "the central strands of the perspective live on in cognate areas of inquiry" (Grattet, 2011a, p. 186). Ongoing research has demonstrated that the consequences of negative labeling tend to be long-lasting and often dire. Grattet's summary of this literature is most revealing (2011a, 2011b). Matsueda's study of troublesome boys revealed that parental definitions ("informal social control") often resulted in self-conceptions that increased the likelihood of these boys' further delinquencies (1992; Grattet, 2011b, p. 124). Work on mental disorder by Bruce Link and his associates "has also been a fertile area" for demonstrating the baleful impact of stigma and deviance labeling. Working with a "modified labeling theory," Link uncovered how mental illness processing agencies "perceptions of patient dangerousness" as well as their putting social distance between themselves and the patient are likely to make the condition more serious (Link et al., 1989). Sampson and Laub have advanced the hypothesis of "cumulative disadvantage," which refers to the consequences of repeating and increasing seriousness of involvement in criminal sanctioning over the life course (Grattet, 2011b, p. 124). Their contention is that there is only "one theoretical position in criminology that is inherently developmental in nature—labeling theory" (Sampson and Laub, 1997, p. 3). This cumulative disadvantage represents a kind of "snowballing effect" which increasingly "mortgages" the offender's future, especially when negative evaluations in the realms of school and employment further reduce their life chances. For instance, convicted felons face increasingly diffi-cult conditions for reintegrating into civil society, disenfranchising them and making the choice of further criminal activity increasingly attractive; negative labeling by work settings, marriage, and family dynamics all make desistance increasingly difficult (Petersilia, 2003; Uggen and Manza, 2006; Western, 2006). A criminal record has a powerful chilling effect on employment outcomes. Pager introduces the concept of "negative creden-tials" to stress this process; these are the "offi-cial markers that restrict access and opportunity rather than enabling them" (Pager, 2007, p. 32). As Grattet argues (2011a, 2011b), recent research powerfully argues for the ongoing influence of the labeling/interactionist tradition in the study of crime and deviance.

CONFLICT THEORY

Social scientists can be divided according to how much *consensus* versus *conflict* they see in contemporary society. Many of the early soci-ologists viewed the social order through the lens of the *functionalist* perspective (Parsons, 1951b; Merton, 1957). Even an early analy-sis of the "functions of social conflict" (Coser, 1956) adopted a functionalist view of conflict. Functionalism adopts a consensus paradigm: Harmony is the rule, and a disruption of that harmony calls for steps to reestablish peace and tranquility. The members of a society are social-ized to behave properly; most of them accept the central values and norms of their society and act accordingly; a few are improperly or inadequately socialized, or, for some reason, the components of the social system are improperly integrated; deviance ensues, disrupting the social order; the forces of equilibrium act to restore society to its former state of balance, harmony, and cohesion.

In contrast, conflict theorists do not believe that consensus, harmony, or cohesion prevail in contemporary society. They see groups with com-peting and clashing interests and values. They see struggles between and among categories, sectors, groups, and classes in society, with winners and losers resulting from the outcome of these strug-gles. Most social institutions, they argue, do not benefit society as a whole. Rather, they benefit

some groups *at the expense of* others. Conflict theorists envision the resources of society as being distributed according to a "zero sum game," that is, they are of a fixed size, and whatever is distrib-uted to one faction or category is taken away from another. For instance, they challenge the func-tionalists' analysis of stratification as benefiting society as a whole (Davis and Moore, 1945). In contrast, the conflict theorists argue, stratification benefits the rich and the powerful *at the expense of* the poor and the weak. Moreover, it is to the advantage of the rich and the powerful to have the disadvantaged *believe* that stratification is for the good of the entire society; that way, the disad-vantaged will be less likely to threaten the interests and privileges of the rich. Likewise, in contrast to the functional analysis of prostitution as ben-efitting society as a whole (Davis, 1937), conflict theorists argue that prostitution benefits the more powerful members of society—mainly men—who profit from society's patriarchal institutions.

The central focus of a conflict theory of crime and deviance is *the criminalization process*. Groups struggle to have their own definitions of right and wrong enacted into law. The key word here is *hegemony*, or dominance: Groups attempt to legitimate their own special interests and views and to discredit and nullify the influence of those of competing groups. Societies are made up of factions vying for dominance or hegemony, striv-ing to have their own views translated into law and public opinion. The conflict theorist sees a contin-ual battle or contest between and among compet-ing groups and categories in contemporary society, with the most powerful strata usually winning out.

Perhaps the most conflict-oriented of all the conflict theorists are the Marxists. (Of course, come the institutionalization of the socialist rev-olution, society's major conflicts will dissolve and harmony, peace, and equilibrium will pre-vail.) Their ideas are somewhat distinct and dif-ferent from the non-Marxist conflict theorists. For Marxist criminology, social class is the key explanatory concept. Crime is the outcome of eco-nomic disadvantage. The more harshly penalized the criminal behavior, the greater the likelihood that it will be disproportionally engaged in by persons at the bottom of the social class hierarchy. A Marxist approach would argue that the moti-vation for crime among the underclass or lower class is survival—"a means of economic subsistence" (White, 2011, p. 151). In contrast, for the working class, crime is a matter of supplementing an all-too-meager income. Richard Quinney, a leading Marxist criminologist of the 1980s—he later shifted to Buddhism, and then to a "peacemaking" position, based on "self-reflection of the individual to see how one can positively contribute to a peaceful community" (Conyers, 2011, p. 139)—distinguished between *crimes of domination*, which are committed by the capitalist class and their agents, and the state against the working class, and crimes of *accommodation and resistance*, such as robbery, murder, rape, sabotage, and protests, committed by the weak, poor, and powerless (Quinney, 1977). Since the 1980s, Marxism has plummeted in intellectual and theoretical influence—in the study of deviance, and more broadly, among sociologists, and, even more generally, among academics and intellectuals as a whole. This is unfortunate, since social class is a fundamental component of both the etiology and the control of crime and deviance, but the approach was done in by its all-too-sweeping, even apocalyptic, approach to human behavior.

The central issue for all conflict-oriented criminologists is the emergence and enforcement of norms, rules, and, especially, laws. How do laws get passed? Which groups manage to get their own special interests and views enacted into laws? Who profits by the passage of laws? Which laws are enforced, and which are passed but never enforced—and why? Why are certain activities regarded as deviant while others are regarded as conventional by the members of a given society? The answer provided by the conflict approach is that laws, rules, and norms grow out of a power struggle between and among interests groups, factions, and social classes. The most powerful group or groups in society are those that are successful in having their own views of right and wrong accepted by society as a whole and formulated into the criminal law. Likewise, the enforcement of the law represents the application of power against the powerless by the powerful.

Conflict theorists explicitly *reject* two commonly held views concerning the law. The first is the *consensus* view that the law is a "reflection of the social consciousness of a society," that laws make up a "barometer of the moral

and social thinking of a community" (Friedman, 1964, p. 143) and reflect "the will of the people." Instead, conflict theorists argue that public views on what is regarded as conventional or deviant, law-abiding or criminal, vary strikingly from group to group in a large, complex society. Even where consensus exists on a given issue as to what should be against the law, the conflict theorist asks *how* and *why* that consensus is achieved. For most issues, there is no majority consensus—only different views held by different social groups. The point of view held by the most powerful of these groups tends to be the one that becomes law.

The second widely held view that conflict theory rejects is that laws are passed and enforced to protect society as a whole, to protect all classes and groups more or less equally. The conflict theorist argues that laws do not protect the rights, interests, and well-being of the many, but the interests of the few. There is no such thing as "society as a whole," the conflict theorist would argue. Societies are broken up into segments, sectors, classes, groups, or categories that have very different interests. Very few laws have an equal impact on all segments of society equally. For instance, the earliest laws of vagrancy in England were passed to protect the interests of the wealthiest and most powerful members of English society—the landowners in the 1300s and the merchant class in the 1500s (Chambliss, 1964). In the 1400s, the courts interpreted the laws of theft in England as a means of protecting the property of merchants, the emerging powerful class at that time, a class the Crown needed to protect and curry favor with (Hall, 1952).

Conflict theorists do *not* see laws as an expression of a broad consensus or as an altruistic desire to protect a large number of the members of a society from objective, clear, and present danger. Rather, they are the embodiment of the beliefs, lifestyle, and/or economic interests of certain sectors of society. Thus, the law is a means of forcing one group's beliefs and way of life onto the rest of society. Laws are passed and enforced not because they protect society in general or because many people believe in their moral correctness but because they uphold the ideological or material interests of the most powerful sector of society. This serves to stop certain people from doing what others consider evil, undesirable, or unprofitable—or to make them do something that others consider good, desirable, or profitable. The passage of a law represents the triumph of a point of view or an ideology held by the members of a particular group, social category, or organization—even if that law is not enforced.

Conflict theorists also emphasize the role that power and status play in the enforcement process. Even for the same offense, apprehension is more likely to lead to more serious punishment if the law is upheld by the person who commands more power and a higher ranking in the socioeconomic status system; for juveniles, especially, this extends to the parents of offenders. The members of two juvenile gangs, the "Saints" and the "Roughnecks," were accorded very different treatment at the hands of local law enforcement. The "Saints," whose parents had respectable, relatively powerful upper-middle-class occupational positions, were treated far more leniently by law enforcement than the "Roughnecks," whose parents were lower and working class. None of the "Saints" had ever been arrested, while all of the "Roughnecks" had, and most of them, on numerous occasions; yet, their offenses, and the frequency with which they had been committed, were quite comparable (Chambliss, 1973). A tenet of the conflict perspective is that not only does the *law* define actions as illegal in conformity with the interests of the most powerful segments of society, but the *enforcement* of the law is also unequal in that, in any society, it reflects the distribution of power.

In addition to being interested in the passage and enforcement of criminal laws, conflict theorists also examine—although to a far lesser extent—the question of the *causes* of criminal behavior. These are the etiological concerns discussed in Chapter 2. What causes criminal behavior according to the conflict perspective? To be succinct about it, conflict theorists answer this question by pointing to the *nature of the society* we are focusing on and the classes or categories in them. Conflict theorists generally would argue that inequalities in power and income cause certain types of criminal behavior; Marxists, for instance, would say that *capitalist society is criminogenic*—that the exploitation of the working class by the capitalist class or ruling elite causes certain kinds of crime to take place, that is, "crimes of rebellion," expressions of the powerless—common crime, street crime, and political crimes.

The conflict theorist is careful to point out that the issue is not explaining criminal behavior as such, but explaining forms of behavior that have *a high likelihood of being defined as criminal*. What forms of behavior are these? The behavior of the poor and the powerless stand a higher likelihood of being defined as crimes, while the behavior of the rich and the powerful stand a considerably lower likelihood. Thus, the predatory actions that the poorer strata are more likely to commit (robbery, rape, and murder, for instance) are actions that tend to be criminalized and enforced, while the harmful, unethical corporate actions of the wealthier strata are not as likely to be defined as crimes, and, if they are, tend not to lead to arrest, and are not as often studied by the criminologist. Thus, when someone asks "What causes criminal behavior?" he or she almost invariably means, "What causes people to engage in a particular *type* of illegal behavior—namely, street crimes such as robbery, rape, and murder?"

FEMINISM

Until a generation or two ago, most Western intellectuals viewed the world through the perspective of *androcentrism*, *patriarchy*, and *sexism*. *Androcentrism* is a male-centered bias. It is the view that men are the center of the universe and women are at the periphery of the action. Women take on relevance only insofar as they relate to men and their activities. The androcentric bias in the study of deviance and crime began to be subject to criticism only in the late 1960s, and these critiques are having an impact on the way sociologists view the phenomenon of deviance. *Patriarchy* refers to a male-dominated power structure, and *sexism* to prejudice and discrimination against women. And it was *feminism* that launched this assault on androcentrism, patriarchy, and sexism.

There is no single universally agreed-upon definition of feminism. Indeed, a substantial array of *feminisms* have emerged that are "sometimes in sharp contrast with each other" (Tong, 2009; Bailey, 2011, p. 164). For example, radical cultural feminists have denounced prostitution and pornography as degrading to women and expressions of "patriarchal privilege," while radical libertarian feminists argue that women should be free to express their sexuality in any way they choose, including sex work; in fact, the very anti-pornography ordinances that radical cultural feminists fought to establish were repealed as a result of the political efforts of liberal feminists (Bailey, 2011, p. 167). Indeed, many feminists have a difficult time absorbing the very concept, "sex work," especially when female sex workers openly support the idea of engaging in a line of employment that feminist theory regards as inherently oppressive (Delacoste and Alexander, 1998). Still, we find some unity among the many varieties of feminism. Perhaps the definition that might win the broadest acceptance is this one: Feminism is the perspective that stresses that "women experience subordination on the basis of their sex" (Gelsthorpe and Morris, 1988, p. 224). Feminism argues that men and women are typically treated as *representatives* or *embodiments of sexual categories* and that men attempt to keep women subordinate to men. Feminists are concerned with uncovering the origins and functions of this unequal treatment and seek to bring about a more sexually equalitarian society. For feminists, the enemy is *patriarchy*—institutions of male dominance. Patriarchy—male domination—is responsible for the oppression of women, and hence, patriarchy must be analyzed, critiqued, and eliminated. Feminists often begin their analysis with an examination of how a given field has studied a phenomenon in the past, because past theories typically justified patriarchy. Such an analysis usually entails uncovering the sexist biases of more traditional approaches.

In 1968, Frances Heidensohn noted that the "deviance of women" was one area that has been "most notably ignored in [the] sociological literature." At first glance, she said, this seems understandable; after all, in comparison with men, women "have low rates of participation in deviant activities." Such a defense might seem to be a reasonable explanation for the field's concentration on men, Heidensohn writes, "but not the almost total *exclusion*" of studies on female deviance and crime (Heidensohn, 1968, pp. 160, 161, 162). The exceptions to this rule, she argues, show that women are not only virtually invisible in the field of criminology and deviance studies, but they hold a peculiar and skewed place in its literature

as well. Feminists argue that traditional analyses of women as enactors solely of deviant behavior that embodies their gender—which has usually meant prostitution and sexual delinquency (Cohen, 1955, pp. 44–48, 137–147; Heidensohn, 1968, pp. 166–168)—should be replaced with a more balanced approach.

The neglect of women in the field of criminology and deviance studies, feminists argue, is not only characteristic of the traditional approaches; it also marked the more contemporary perspectives, such as labeling or interactionist theory and radical or Marxist theory. Marcia Millman (1975) argues that, in much of the writings by labeling theorists, men appeared as interesting, adventurous deviants who lead exciting lives, while women were depicted as boring, conventional, nagging drudges who attempt to rein in the wilder side of the men in their lives. While labeling theorists depicted deviants with understanding and empathy, they almost always described *men* engaged in the behavior, while *women* played a passive, inhibitory role. It was not until the 1980s that the implications of labeling theory were fully spelled out for the involvement of women in deviance (Schur, 1984).

Critical, radical, or Marxist criminology, some have said, was no better in its analysis of women's role in deviance and crime than the more conventional perspectives. As one feminist analysis of criminological theory pointed out, there is *not one word* about women in Taylor, Walton, and Young's radical treatise on the "new" criminology, and Quinney, a major self-designated Marxist of the 1970s, "is all but blind to the distinctions between conditions of males and females in capitalist society." These authors "thoroughly scrutinize and criticize theoretical criminology, yet they never notice the limited applicability of these theories to women" (Leonard, 1982, p. 176). The sexism lurking in earlier writings can be illustrated by a male-centered aside made by Alvin Gouldner, critic of traditional sociology, especially functionalism, and author of a well-known critique of the interactionist approach to deviance (1968), who, in arguing that the sexual lives of sociologists may influence their work, remarks: "For example, it is my strong but undocumented impression that when some sociologists change their work interests, problems, or styles, they also change mistresses or wives" (1970, p. 57). Are all sociologists men? The answer to this question is obvious, and betrays Gouldner's androcentric bias.

We can summarize the depiction of women in writings on deviance prior to the 1960s and 1970s in three generalizations, which apply even today, although to a far lesser extent. The first is, as we saw, that women represented a minor theme in these writings. They were studied less, appeared less often as subjects of attention, remained marginal, secondary, almost invisible. The study of women and deviance suffers from "a problem of omission"; women have been "largely overlooked in the literature" (Millman, 1975, p. 265).

Second, as we saw, the study of deviance reflects an androcentric or "a male-biased view" (Millman, 1975, p. 265). Not only was the deviance of women less often studied, when it was, it was also nearly always *specialized* deviance; the deviance of men was deviance *in general*, the deviance of women was *women's* deviance. In a chapter entitled "The Criminality of Women," which appeared in a textbook that was eventually published in multiple editions, Walter Reckless (1950, p. 116) argued that the criminal behavior of women should not be considered "in the same order of phenomena as crime in general"— meaning the criminal behavior of men. Unlike men, women are deceitful (p. 122), kill by administering poison (p. 121), throw acid in the face of a victim, "usually an unfaithful lover" (p. 122), and are prone to "make false accusations of a sexual nature" (p. 123). In sum, the *forms* of deviance and crime women engage in are said to be very different from those that men commit. The three forms of deviance that have attracted attention from the field are shoplifting, mental illness, and prostitution. While women do play a majority role in the first of these, at least an equal role in the second, and the overwhelmingly dominant role in the last of them, they *do* commit a far wider range of deviant actions than these, their participation in deviance *has* been stereotyped in the literature, and men's deviance is *not* equivalent to deviance "in general," as some authors claim.

And third, until recently, the role of women *as victims* of crime and deviance was underplayed. This was especially the case with respect to rape, domestic assault, and sexual harassment. It was not until the 1970s, when feminist scholars began a systematic examination of the ways women are brutalized and exploited by men, that deviant and criminal actions such as rape (Brownmiller, 1975), wife battering (Martin, 1976), and sexual harassment (MacKinnon, 1979) found a significant place in the literature on deviance and crime, and the suffering inflicted on women at the hands of men given sufficient attention. In the 1980s, a number of radicals recognized that the question of women as victims of crime created "enormous theoretical problems for the radical paradigm in criminology" (Jones, MacLean, and Young, 1986, p. 3; Gelsthorpe and Morris, 1988, p. 233). Specifically, feminist research on female victims of crime has brought home to certain radicals "the limits of the romantic conception of crime and the criminal" (Matthews and Young, 1986, p. 2; Gelsthorpe and Morris, 1988, pp. 232–233). While it is true that men are significantly more likely to be the victims of crime than women, for some crimes (such as the three I just mentioned), the sex ratio is *overwhelmingly* in the other direction. Moreover, women suffer certain crimes *specifically* because of their powerless position relative to that of men. In short, women victims of crime have been "hidden from history" (Summers, 1981). As Bailey (2011) observes, a major accomplishment of feminism has been "to have crimes against women, such as intimate partner violence and sexual assault, treated as crimes worthy of systematic analysis when they heretofore had received scant attention" (p. 166; Burgess-Proctor, 2006; Chesney-Lind, 2006).

No approach that treats the behavior of less than half the population as if it were behavior in general can claim to be adequate or valid. The fields of criminology and deviance studies still have a long way to go before they fully incorporate the insights of feminism into the way they look at their subject matter. It is possible that feminism may have a more revolutionary impact on the field than that of any other perspective we've examined. Feminism forces us to think about sex biases and how they distort our views of deviance, crime, the law, and the criminal justice system. These biases are deep and pervasive. Confronting and overcoming them makes us better sociologists, criminologists, and students of deviance, and perhaps, more capable of changing society for the better.

CONTROLOLOGY OR THE NEW SOCIOLOGY OF SOCIAL CONTROL

All constructionist theorists of deviance are interested in the dynamics of social control. The perspective that gives social control a central place and views social control as almost exclusively oppressive, centralized, and state-sponsored, is referred to as "controlology" or the "new sociology of social control." Perhaps the most dramatic image of this school's perspective was captured by Stanley Cohen, one of controlology's central thinkers, in the following quote: "Imagine that the entrance to the deviancy control system is something like a gigantic fishing net. Strange and complex in its appearance and movements, the net is cast by an army of different fishermen and fisherwomen working all day and even into the night according to more or less known rules and routines, subject to more or less authority and control from above, knowing more or less what the other is doing. Society is the ocean—vast, troubled and full of uncharted currents, rocks, and other hazards. Deviants are the fish" (Cohen, 1985, pp. 41–42).

The spiritual father of the school of thought known as the new sociology of social control is Michel Foucault (pronounced "foo-COH"), a French philosopher. Foucault's ideas have been extremely influential; he may be the most frequently cited intellectual in the world. For the contrologist, the field of deviance is about a "struggle over whose rules prevail" (Marshall, Douglas, and McDonnell, 2007, p. 71). This emphasis has been the foundation stone of the field at least since Howard Becker's *Outsiders*, published in 1963.

In *Discipline and Punish* (1979), Foucault elaborated the idea of enlightened but repressive social control. The centerpiece of traditional social control was torture and execution. Its goal was the mutilation or destruction of the offender's (or supposed offender's) body. Traditional means of punishment were fitful and sporadic rather than continual and ongoing. Public confessions, torture, and execution created spectacle but, increasingly, they were ineffective. Eventually, crowds came not to be seized by the terror of the scaffold but instead began protesting the injustice of harsh punishment. In the end, public executions produced disorder and mob violence, not fear and compliance.

With the growing importance of portable property in the 1700s, the merchant class needed a stable, predictable means of protecting their investments from the predatory activities of the lower classes. The traditional means of punishment had to be replaced by a system of control that was more effective, certain, comprehensive, and which operated all the time. The traditional prison was used almost exclusively to detain suspected offenders before trial or execution. It was only in the second half of the eighteenth century that the modern prison became a location specifically for the incarceration and punishment of the offender. The new prison, Foucault believed, revealed the special character of the new age.

Jeremy Bentham (1748–1832), British philosopher, reformer, and utilitarian, came up with a plan for the modern prison. It was designed so that a small number of guards could observe a large number of inmates. He called this arrangement the *panopticon*. It was Foucault's belief that the central thrust in the history of Western society was the evolution away from traditional society where the many observe the few (as was true in spectacles such as execution) to modern society, where the few observe the many (as in the modern prison, with its panopticon). According to Foucault, Bentham's panopticon was typical, characteristic, or paradigmatic of modern society in general. The panoptic principle, Foucault believed, had become generalized and imitated throughout the entire society. We live, he said, in a society in which state and state-like agents are bent on observing and controlling its citizens in a wide range of contexts. In a sense, then, Foucault believed, modern society had become one gigantic, monstrous panopticon.

Foucault's argument is a more literary and philosophical formulation than a sociological one. To describe historical changes, Foucault uses clever analogies and metaphors that may or may not fit empirically. He takes *thought* and *discourse* as concretely realized behavior, as indicative of the way things are—in a sense, as even more "real" than actions. In fact, modern prisons are not even remotely like Bentham's panopticon. In real-life prisons, surveillance and control require a substantial ratio of guards to prisoners. As a general rule, Foucault takes consequences, including unintended consequences, as if they were a direct outcome of the motives of the powerful actors on the scene. He ignores all countervailing forces that operate to control the exercise of power. In his scheme, there is no political opposition (Garland, 1990, p. 167). He nearly always presents the control potential of the powers that be as the reality (p. 168). And, for all its claims to being a political understanding of modern society, *Discipline and Punish* presents a "strangely apolitical" analysis of the exercise of power (p. 170). There is no "motive to power"—only more power, more discipline, and more control. Why and for what purpose the power is wielded is never fully explained. Foucault writes as if a society without the exercise of power is possible; he seems to be against power per se (pp. 173–174). He never presents an alternative system, one that could operate through the humane, enlightened exercise of hegemonic government institutions. In fact, to Foucault, in the context of modern society, "humane" and "enlightened" mean only one thing: insidious attempts at greater and more effective control, that is to say, *repression.*

Foucault died in 1984, of AIDS, before the emergence of the drug "cocktails"—developed, ironically, by the very oppressively scientific, state-sponsored agencies he denounced—that could have prolonged his life. His ideas have become the inspiration for later generations of "contrololo-gists." These are the central points of this school.

First, *social control is problematic; it should not be taken for granted.* By that, controlologists mean it does not emerge "naturally" and spontaneously by the "invisible hand" of society but is "consciously fashioned by the visible hand of definable organizations, groups, and classes" (Scull, 1988, p. 686). We cannot assume, as the functionalists seemed to have done, that society will be wise enough to preserve institutions and practices that serve the whole in the best possible way by sanctioning what is harmful and encouraging what is beneficial. Social control, as it is practiced, is not a product of a broad, widely shared social "need" or the workings of basic "functional prerequisites," to use functionalist terminology. Instead, the controlologists say, social control is imposed by specific, and powerful, social entities, for their own benefit, and at the expense of those individuals and groups who are controlled.

Second, *social control is typically coercive, repressive, and far from benign.* Agents of social control typically try to make control seem benevolent, or at least enlightened, but this is a façade; control appears as a "velvet glove" rather than an "iron fist." Traditional criminologists have looked upon social control generally, and the criminal justice system specifically, as society's natural, inevitable, and beneficial means of self-protection against harmful behavior. As viewed by controlologists, social control takes on a more sinister coloration; its purpose: to repress and contain troublesome populations. Hence, the purpose of psychiatry is not to heal but to control; the purpose of the welfare system is not to provide a safety net for the poor but to control; the purpose of education is not to teach but to control; the purpose of the mass media is not to inform or entertain but to control—or rather, the mass media entertain *in order to* control. And when segments of the population under institutional control are perceived as no longer threatening, they are dumped out of the system (Scull, 1984).

Third, *social control is coterminous with state or state-like control.* The government is made up of a virtual alphabet soup of agencies of social control, including the DEA (the Drug Enforcement Agency), the ATF (Bureau of Alcohol, Tobacco, and Firearms), the FDA (Food and Drug Administration), NIDA (the National Institute on Drug Abuse), NIMH (the National Institute of Mental Health), the INS (the Immigration and Naturalization Service), all of which have one aim—to monitor and control the behavior of troublesome populations. In addition, a number of organizations, agencies, and institutions are performing the function of social control *on behalf of or in the service of* the state. These include private social welfare agencies, psychiatrists and psychiatric agencies, professional organizations such as the American Medical Association, hospitals, clinics, mental health organizations, treatment facilities, educational institutions, and so on. It is the contention of controlologists that state control is increasingly being assumed by civil society. Troublesome populations can now be controlled on a wide range of fronts by a wide range of agencies. The same clients are circulated and recirculated between and among them. Even institutions that would appear to have little or nothing to do with the control of deviance as such—such as the mass media—are involved in social control through shaping public opinion about deviants (Ericson, Baranek, and Chan, 1991).

Fourth, *the social control apparatus is unified and coherent.* The subsystems "fit together" into interrelated, functionally equivalent parts.

Interlocking agencies and overarching institutions that work together to control troublesome populations may be referred to as the phenomenon of *transcarceration* (Lowman, Menzies, and Palys, 1987)—institutions of incarceration and control that reach across institutional boundaries. Foucault refers to this "transcarceral" system as the "carceral archipelago" (1979, p. 298), a reference to Aleksander Solzhenetisyn's description of the Soviet prison camps, *The Gulag Archipelago* (1974). The carceral archipelago transported the punitive approach "from the penal institution to the entire social body" (Foucault, 1979, p. 298). Controlologists point to a "peno-juridical, mental health, welfare and tutelage complex" in which "power structures can be examined only by appreciating cross-institutional arrangements and dynamics" (Lowman, Menzies, and Palys, 1987, p. 9). In other words, more or less all the organized entities in society have become a massive network dedicated to the surveillance and punishment of deviance.

One must be impressed with the variety and range of people-processing institutions and agencies in modern society, many of them designed to deal with or handle the behavior of troublesome individuals and groups. No one can doubt that some of the functionaries who work for these agencies are often uncaring and insensitive. Especially in the inner cities, these agencies are overwhelmed with the sheer volume of clients, and the community is shortchanged. But most of these problems stem not from too much control but too few resources. Modern society is unprecedented in the number, variety, and near-ubiquitousness of organizations, agencies, and institutions that perform state-like functions, that operate in place of and on behalf of the government. Social control is certainly one of their functions; how could this not be true? If people who make use of their services engage in unruly, troublesome, disruptive behavior, representatives of these agencies will predictably attempt to control that behavior. In most cases, from the clients' perspective, that may not even be their main function. Such service and welfare service institutions are neither primarily nor exclusively agencies of social control. Clients themselves seek out the services of these organizations, institutions, and agencies and are more likely to see them as a shield to protect them than a net to catch them.

Controlology or the new sociology of social control is not interested in social control per se. It is interested in how the state and its allied organizations and institutions control, or attempt to control, deviant behavior. In fact, the perspective's advocates are not interested in deviant behavior per se, either; they are interested more or less exclusively in the populations whom the elites consider troublesome and against whom the elites take action. What this perspective turns out to be is an exaggerated caricature of labeling theory, but with social control equated with formal (or semiformal) social control. It turns out to be an extremely narrow view of both deviance and social control.

SUMMARY

The other side of the coin, the "flip side," so to speak, of the positivist or etiological quest ("Why do they do it?") is the focus on the structure and dynamics of *social control:* definitions of deviance, rules, and their enforcement. The rules and their enforcement cannot be assumed or taken for granted. A variety of perspectives has taken this side of the equation as problematic and worthy of study. Less concerned with etiology or the causes of deviance itself, labeling theory, control theory, feminism, and "controlology" have tried to understand why certain definitions of deviance emerge and why they are enforced.

The labeling or interactionist perspective had its roots in the work of two precursors, Frank Tannenbaum and Edwin Lemert, who shifted their attention away from the etiology or causes of deviance, crime, and delinquency to an examination of what implications punishment has on the deviators' identity and the enactment of their further deviance. The labeling theorists of the 1960s (who never approved of the title, "labeling theory," to apply to their approach, preferring instead the term, "the interactionist perspective") stressed the relativity of deviance from one time and place to another; the social construction of moral meanings and definitions; the inner or subjective world of the deviant; the impact of labeling and stigma on the person so labeled; the role of audiences in defining deviance; the role of contingencies, such as ancillary characteristics in influencing the labeling process; the reflexive or the "looking glass" self; the "stickiness" of labels;

and the self-fulfilling prophecy. Although a number of its insights have been incorporated into the mainstream of the field, the labeling approach to deviance nonetheless remains controversial.

Conflict theory overlaps with the labeling approach but contrasts with functionalism on a number of key points. Conflict theory sees struggles between and among classes and categories in society, with winners and losers resulting from the outcome of these struggles. Advocates of this perspective stress the fact that (contrary to functionalists) the interests of one faction or segment of society often conflict with or contradict those of another; what helps one may hurt another, and vice versa. For instance, the institution of prostitution may reinforce male power and help to oppress women; social stratification may be good for the rich and harmful to the poor. Classes attempt to establish dominance over others to maintain their interests. The criminal law, for example, may help to reinforce the rule of the ruling elite by exploiting the poorest segments of society.

Feminists hold that women are subordinated as a result of their sex; it is their intention to eliminate *androcentrism* (a male-centered bias), *patriarchy* (male supremacy), and *sexism* (prejudice and discrimination against women). Feminist sociologists argue that earlier researchers displayed male biases in neglecting the deviance and crime of women; they looked at the few crimes that they did examine in a distinctly skewed, biased fashion; and they neglected the victimization of women by male-initiated acts of deviance and crime. Moreover, feminists stress, the issue of the social control of female versus male deviance and crime is a neglected topic and should be examined.

Controlology or the "new sociology of social control," received its primary inspiration from the writings of the French philosopher Michel Foucault. This perspective centers on how psychiatric and medical expertise has been used to control "troublesome populations" in ways that are more enlightened and sophisticated than was true in the past. "Knowledge is power," Foucault said, and power translates into more repressive means of control (the "velvet glove") than the naked brutality that characterized law enforcement in past centuries (the "iron fist"). The major social control agencies in modern society have become woven into a huge net to monitor and control deviants, controlologists claim. Some critics argue that this perspective neglects informal social control and pretends that the more benign features of modern bureaucracies do not exist.

Account: Interview with a Medical Marijuana User and Supplier

I conducted this interview in 2012 with "Jimmy," an employee of the plant-supply business. Jimmy lives in California, which permits the growing, possession, transportation, dispensing, and use of marijuana for medical purposes. He is also a licensed provider of marijuana. Some observers (Dokoupil, 2012) believe that de jure or at least de facto legal marijuana distribution is the wave of the future, and hence, a wise business investment.

ERICH: Why don't you say a few things about how it all got started? When did you begin using marijuana and why?

JIMMY: For seventeen years now I've been using pretty darn near every day. I guess the thing that justifies it is that I don't drink as much as I used to—I used to drink quite a bit—so now,

I don't consider myself a substance abuser. I'm consuming a much less harmful substance than I used to. How it got started was, in my senior year of high school, I was on the wrestling team, and my wrestling buddies would party regularly, and I would go out with them, and I'd get drunk. Now, for me drinking had really bad associations but I'd do it anyway. My biological mom was a really bad alcoholic, and I'd feel bad about myself when I drank so much that I'd be out of control. Heavy drinking was sort of a negative lesson from my mom—I knew what getting drunk was like from her, and I knew I shouldn't be doing this, and I didn't want to be like her. She had a lot of problems with her drinking. She had three children—my siblings and me—with three different men. She basically prostituted herself— she was a "crack whore." She went to truck stops

(Continued)

Account: Interview with a Medical Marijuana User and Supplier   Continued

and picked up men. Once, my sister told me, she went cross-country, having sex with this trucker; I don't know if she was paid or not. When I was young, growing up, hearing my mom having sex in the next room with multiple partners was weird and unsettling. I once saw my mom stumble through a sliding glass door because she was too drunk to see the glass. Another time, she got drunk and angry and threw a TV off the balcony of our house. If my siblings and I got into an argument, she'd clear out the living room of furniture and told us we had to have an all-out, full-tilt fight, with hitting and slapping and hair-pulling. And she had zero parenting skills. When I was with her, I didn't have to shower or change my clothes or brush my teeth. She allowed my life to be a free-for-all. When I was five, she was drunk and she hit me—just because she didn't want me to wear the shirt I was wearing—and there was a bruise and a slap mark, the outline of a hand, on my face. Then, at school, my teachers saw my face and reported the incident to Social Services, so they put all three of us in an orphanage, then they began fostering us out to different families. Some of those families were really bad. I remember, once, being punished because I looked up in the sky and saw an airplane and I said, "That airplane's landing gear looks like a penis." I felt I was often humiliated and punished for no reason at all. By this time, my father had remarried and he found out about some of the suffering I was experiencing, so he took us out of the foster care system and he and his wife took me in, away from the chaotic life I was living. My sister went to live with her father, and my little brother ended up staying with my mother again. With my father and his wife, my life was more normal—I had to follow the formal rules of an ordinary family. But I was never completely free from my mother's influence because even then, we had to visit her every weekend.

ERICH: So what was your first experience with marijuana like?

JIMMY: One night, my wrestling team-mates and I went out and instead of booze, they offered me a hit on a bong. I took it, and all at once I felt such a feeling of calm and order. I loved it. It allowed me to develop a more logical way of doing things and thinking about things. Being high on marijuana seemed to me to be the opposite of the life I had lived with my mom—chaotic and painful and disorganized and out of control. I had developed anger management problems, my mind was racing all the time, I felt defensive, I thought everyone was out to get me, I had a chip on my shoulder, and I had diagnosed myself as bipolar—and suddenly I realized I could live a different way. Smoking gave me a completely different frame of mind, it slowed my mind down, made me think about how I could solve my problems. My life was completely transformed. I'd drink sometimes, but always knowing that alcohol could be the death of me. I came to realize that most people are good and decent people. Even today, when I have a disagreement with somebody, like my coworkers, initially, I think they're trying to take advantage of me, but then I go through what they're saying and I'm able to take their position and walk through the steps from A to B to C and see why they would see things their way and become more empathetic. And after smoking for a while, I eventually gravitated to more quality people. You might say I have kind of a love affair with pot.

ERICH: Would you say you're a recreational or a medical marijuana user?

JIMMY: In 2004, Prop 215 went into effect. So I began doing marijuana for the legal, medical aspect of it because I didn't want to get arrested. It also made drinking irrelevant. Before legal marijuana, I'd hang out with some really questionable people, people who were in the illicit drug trade. I actually got shot at. Now that it's legal, users don't have to resort to the underground to get their supply, and I don't have to hang out with the shady people I knew before.

ERICH: Where does the medical side of it come in? What's the nature of your ailment?

JIMMY: I really do have an ailment. My L3 and L4 [vertebra] are bulging and they caused me a great deal of pain. The doctors wanted to fuse my spine. Before, I needed cortisone shots and prescriptions for Vicodin and opiates. Opiates really scare me and marijuana has helped me to the point where I don't take so many pills, plus it got me motivated to stop taking pills altogether. There are times and places where I smoke, and times and places where I don't do it. Like, I would never smoke in front of my wife's grandparents—it would be disrespectful.

ERICH: How did you get a license to grow and own and dispense medical marijuana?

JIMMY: I brought my medication bottles into to the doctor's office and showed them to him and told him I didn't want to take all of these medications. It's a dog and pony show—there's really not much to it. This doctor said, OK, and then I said, I'm also a plant grower, I'd like to be a provider, and he said, OK, and I signed both documents, paid the fee, and that was it. The whole thing took about five minutes. What I like about my current situation is that now, it's all legal.

ERICH: Where do you get your supply?

JIMMY: I grow the plants with my two associates.

ERICH: How much do you consume, let's say, yearly?

JIMMY: If you smoke two grams a day, you have to have two pounds for your consumption. Each plant produces from one to six pounds of consumable pot per year.

ERICH: Do you grow certain kinds of plants according to their effects?

JIMMY: Today, there's so much science behind growing strains—hydroponics, fertilizer, soil, and so on. The *sativa* strain produces more of a "head" or psychoactive high, while *indica* produces more of a "body" effect, which, for me, is desirable. But some of my clients might go more for the "head" effects.

ERICH: What does the harvesting process entail?

JIMMY: When they're mature, I cut them down and hang them upside down in the garage with a humidifier. One of my partners bought a circular basket with blades that have grooves that turn at 17 rpm, and the grooves cut into the plant material and groom it. After about ten-twelve minutes, you take out the groomed material and it's ready to go. This is a process that used to take about eight hours. Recently, we groomed 56 pounds, a process that would have taken weeks. My partners and I deal with about three people to whom we dispense maybe twenty–twenty-five pounds. Being licensed providers, we want it to end up in the right hands.

QUESTIONS

Do you agree with Jimmy that in California, all legal bans on the distribution of marijuana will be lifted? Is legal marijuana the "wave of the future"? Is what Jimmy doing a form of deviance? Does it predict the future—will it become regarded as conventional within a decade or two? In California, Jimmy's medical use of marijuana and his marijuana supply business are legal—but what's legal or illegal is often a matter of interpretation. In California, suppliers who grow an enormous number of plants on enormous tracts of land, drive flashy sports cars, and own big, expensive boats, tend to attract the attention of authorities; hence, sellers say, it makes sense to keep their operations "below the radar screen." As a consequence, Jimmy is very unlikely to get busted. If you were in his position, would you take the risk, expand your operation, and earn more money? Or do you feel that Jimmy's medical rationale for using and cultivating marijuana is credible and convincing? How does the social construction of deviance apply to the medical use and the cultivation of marijuana in California, where it is legal? Is the law the only social construction here? How do you think the general public feels about the matter? Do you think that what Jimmy is doing is an activity whose time has come for California? Does it predict its own coming adoption for the rest of the country? Is it an indicator of social change of notions of right and wrong for our society? How would what Jimmy is doing be *socially constructed* by the various social sectors and by residents of different locales around the country? Another social construction of the legal status of marijuana supply, which is promulgated by the federal government, is that it is wrong, illegitimate—an illegal, criminal activity that should be shut down whenever politically feasible, and the purveyors fined and/or imprisoned. What do you think?

Appendix: SB 420 Guidelines

Proposition 215, the California Compassionate Use Act, was enacted by the voters, and took effects Nov. 6, 1996 as California Health & Safety Code 11362.5. The law makes it legal for patients and designated primary caregivers to possess and cultivate marijuana for their personal medical use given the recommendation of a California-licensed physician. SB 420, a legislative statute, went into effect on January 1, 2004, as California H&S 11362.7–83. This law broadens Prop. 215 to transportation and other offenses in certain circumstances, allows patients to form medical cultivation "collectives" or "cooperatives," and establishes a voluntary state ID card system run through county health departments. SB 420 also establishes guidelines or limits as to how much patients can possess and cultivate. Legal patients who stay within the guidelines are supposed to be protected from arrest.

How Much Can I Possess or Grow? Under Prop. 215, patients are entitled to whatever amount of marijuana is necessary for their personal medical use. However, patients are likely to be arrested if they exceed the SB 420 guidelines. SB 420 sets a baseline statewide guideline of 6 mature or 12 immature plants, and ½ pound (8 oz.) processed cannabis per patient. Individual cities and counties are allowed to enact higher, but not lower, than the state standard. Patients can be exempted from the limits if their physician explicitly states that they need more. In a state supreme court ruling, *People v. Kelly* (2010), the court held that patients can NOT be prosecuted simply for exceeding the SB 420 limits; however, they can be arrested and forced to defend themselves as having had an amount consistent with their personal medical needs.

What Offenses Are Covered? Prop. 215 explicitly covers marijuana possession and cultivation (H&SC 11357 and 11358) for personal medical use. Hashish and concentrated cannabis, including edibles (HSC 11357a) are also included. Transportation (HSC 11360) has also

been allowed by the courts. Within the context of a bona fide collective or caregiver relationship, SB 420 provides protection against charges for possession for sale (11359); transportation, sale, giving away, furnishing, etc.; providing or leasing a place for distribution of a controlled substance (11366.5, 11570).

Who May Cultivate under Prop. 215? Patients with a physician's recommendation and their primary caregivers, defined as, "The individual designated by the person exempted under this act who has consistently assumed responsibility for the housing, health, or safety of that person." According to a State Supreme Court decision, *People v. Mentch* (2008), caregivers must supply some other services to patients than just providing marijuana. As an alternative, SB 420 allows patients to grow together in non-profit "collectives" or cooperatives. Collectives may scale the SB 420 limits to the number of members, but large gardens are always suspect to law enforcement. In particular, grows over 100 plants risk five-year mandatory minimum sentences under federal law.

Can I Still Be Arrested or Raided? YES, unfortunately. There is nothing in Prop. 215 to compel police to accept a patient as being valid. Many legal patients have been raided for having dubious recommendation, for growing amounts that cops deem excessive, on account of neighbors' complaints, and other things. A major purpose of the state ID card system is to avoid undue arrests. Once patients have been charged, it is up to the courts to pass judgment on their medical claim. A landmark State Supreme Court decision, *People v. Mower*, holds that patients have the same right to marijuana as to any legally prescribed drug. Under Mower, patients who have been arrested can request dismissal of charges at a pre-trial hearing. If the defendant convinces the courts that the prosecution hasn't established probable cause that it wasn't for medical purposes, criminal charges are dismissed. If not, the patient goes on to trial, where the prosecution must prove "beyond a reasonable doubt" that the defendant is guilty. Those who have had their charges dropped may file to have their property returned and claim damages. In many cases, police raid patients and take their medicine without filing criminal charges. In order to reclaim their medicine, patients must then file a court suit on their own. For legal assistance in filing suit for lost medicine, contact Americans for Save Access. Under the U.S. controlled Substances Act, possession of any marijuana is a misdemeanor and cultivation is a felony. A Supreme Court ruling, *Gonzalez v. Raich* (June 2005), rejected a constitutional challenge by two patients who argued that their personal medical use cultivation should be exempt from federal law because it did not affect interstate commerce. Despite this, federal officials have stated that they will not go after individual patients, and the administration has pledged not to intrude on state laws.

Poverty and Disrepute

Learning Objectives:

After reading this chapter, you will be able to:

- discuss perspectives on stigma and poverty;
- understand poverty in the United States;
- answer the question "Is poverty a form of deviance?";
- discuss unemployment in the United States and ramifications of the unemployment rate;

- understand welfare and its relation to deviance;
- discuss the indignity of begging and how it is viewed;
- understand the issues surrounding homelessness;
- understand the relation of disease to deviance;
- discuss the intersection of race and poverty.

For roughly seven decades, sociologists rarely discussed poverty as a *form* of deviance—though they frequently considered it a major *cause* of deviant behavior. The reason may be political correctness: We don't want to be accused of "blaming the victim" (Ryan, 1976)—that is, stigmatizing the poor by attaching a demeaning "deviance" or a "deviant" label to them (Matza, 1966a, p. 289). But the fact is, the poor are *already* socially stigmatized, and, contrary to some critics (Wright, 1993), when sociologists point out that fact, they do not contribute to this stigma. Indeed, quite the reverse is true: A systematic analysis of the phenomenon may enable society to reduce it, while ignoring it may help sustain it.

As we've seen, Robert Merton (1938) based his well-known anomie perspective on the notion that members of the lower economic reaches of society are more likely than the middle classes to engage in *innovative* and *retreatist* forms of deviance. The "greatest pressure toward deviation," he stated, is "exerted upon the lower strata" (1957, p. 144). According to anomie theory, the "innovative" adaptation to economic failure spawns such deviant enterprises as burglary and robbery, prostitution and pimping, drug dealing, and engaging in organized crime. Many of society's "double failures"—persons who are unable to achieve either in conventional or in deviant economic activities—Merton argues, eventually sink or *retreat* into the morass of psychosis, autism, addiction, alcoholism, permanent poverty, homelessness, and, at the extreme end of the line, suicide. (We need not *endorse* anomie theory, but we do need to recognize that its position on poverty as a cause of deviant behavior is crystal clear.) Thus, Robert Merton *implies*, but does not explicitly state, that Western society's "aversion to failure" condemns the poor to the condition of deviancy, but the focus of his analysis is on the contention that poverty *breeds* a range of deviancies rather than the more radical formulation that it *is* a form of deviance, in and of itself. Had Merton recognized that poverty is *itself* a form of deviance, his innovation would have been more substantial and the field of the sociology of deviance would have taken on a more constructionist character.

In any case, virtually all explanatory theories of deviance, from social disorganization to self-control theory, have agreed with Merton's assumption that occupying the bottom stratum of the economic ladder causes untoward, non-normative, or criminal behavior. Karl Marx, along with Willem Bonger—one of Marx's most avid disciples—theorized that under capitalism, economic degradation, exclusion from economic achievement, and class divisions, likewise give rise to criminality, especially among the lumpen proletariat (Bonger, 1916). The first edition of Marshall Clinard's classic deviance text (1957) included a section entitled "Poverty and Deviant Behavior" (pp. 92–100) that reasoned that poverty acts as a breeding ground of delinquency, crime, alcoholism, prostitution, vice, and addiction. Moreover, sociologists of deviance generally explain that poverty reduces agency and increases the likelihood of marginality, thereby rendering individuals more vulnerable to the harmful impact of drug use, alcoholism, mental disorder, as well as the consequences of arrest, conviction, and imprisonment—in effect, making deviants *more deviant* (Room, 2005; Ahern, Stuber, and Galea, 2007).

Centering on the Australian context, Sharyn Roach Anleu's *Deviance, Conformity, and Control* (1991, 2006), offers an exception to the rule, discussing poverty both as a *cause* and a *form* of deviance. "A range of activities and characteristics not usually defined as crime or illness nevertheless gets labelled deviant," says Anleu, distinguishing the *conceptual* ambit of deviance, which encompasses poverty itself, from its *delineation*, as it is explicitly spelled out by mainstream sociologists. Examples of the reach of deviance into poverty, explicates Anleu, "include unemployment, homelessness, begging, being disabled, single-parenting and poverty generally." People who receive welfare, she states, are "subject to negative labelling or stigmatization." All of the negative terms the affluent apply to the poor, the unemployed, the homeless, and the beggar, as with all such stigmata, "act like magnets and attract other deviant labels." People who have secure, well-paying jobs and a comfortable place to live often assume "that unemployed people are more likely to consume illicit drugs and engage in acquisitive crime" and "that homeless people are more likely to be mentally ill than other segments of the community" (1991, p. 176). All of this is exactly right. Western society places a strong value on economic achievement, and many individuals stereotypically believe that a failure to live up to the norm of job success manifests an inability to live up to society's moral standards on a broad range of fronts. In a like fashion, David Harvey argues that poverty "carries with it a *moral stain* as vexing as material uncertainty itself." Perhaps the most clear-cut manifestation of the deviantization of persons living in poverty is that, according to Goffman, minorities are likewise *disqualified from full social and civic participation*—marginalized in their own society (1963, p. i; Harvey, 2007, p. 3589). Critics who argue that sociologists *contribute* to the stigma of the poor apparently deny that the poor are stigmatized at all—an obviously false assertion. But it is not the sociologist who stigmatizes them—it is the society as a whole; sociologists only *take note of* and *write about* that stigma. They would be incompetent sociologists if they did otherwise.

An earlier generation of sociologists considered poverty not merely a breeding ground but also a form of deviance. Decades of reformers dating from the late nineteenth until well into the twentieth century took for granted the moral degradation of the urban slums; they felt them to be locales for "illegitimacy, abandonment of children, drinking, gambling, violence, bad habits, idleness and disease." In other words, early do-gooders have "viewed the city slums as lacking social control and their residents as needing social reform" (Anleu, 2006, p. 195). For example, over 150 pages of James Ford's *Social Deviation* (1939, pp. 289–459) were devoted to poverty itself as a "deviation" from the norm of middle-class existence. In contrast to most contemporary approaches, Ford argued that middle-class behavior, along with middle-class norms, *constitute* normalcy; the obverse, lower-class existence, not only bred but *manifested* deviancy. The majority of Ford's book was devoted to a range of deviations from normalcy—including mental defects and disorders, visual disorders, hearing disorders, and alcoholism. He used pathology, abnormality, and illness metaphors to delineate his notion of social deviation. And the lynchpin was pathology. As Howard Becker said a quarter century later, earlier generations of sociologists often used "a model of deviance based essentially on the medical notions of health and disease" (1963, p. 4)—and in Ford's

time, the fields of social health, social work, social policy, and social welfare tip-toed on that fuzzy line between physical and psychiatric illness and the inherent abnormality that such departures from middle-class standards supposedly entailed.

Here, I would like to turn this equation on its head. That is, following the constructionist perspective, I reject the earlier essentialism of Ford and the disorganization theorists of deviance as pathology and lower-class existence as inherently deviant, but I retain the notion that poverty *has attracted a label* of deviance, that pathologists have used illness as a metaphor, and that, to many health professionals and much of the society at large, poverty is demonstrably associated with ill health. It is clear that deviancies *do* tend to cluster, members of the lower and working classes in Western society *are* more likely to engage in the classic deviancies, including and perhaps especially, the offenses the FBI classifies as the Index Crimes—murder, rape, robbery, aggravated assault, burglary, motor vehicle theft, and larceny-theft—and *are* more likely to attract a deviant label by authorities. And they are more likely to fall victim to ill health and an early demise. Moreover, I maintain, the maldistribution of income unarguably generates pathological conditions associated with living at the bottom of the economic barrel. According to data gathered and tabulated by the United Nations (UN) Development Programme, the per capita Gross Domestic Product (GDP) is substantially more inequitably distributed in the United States than almost any of the three-dozen wealthiest nations on the planet; in other words, the rich are richer and the poor are poorer in the United States than is true of practically any of the other countries with a comparably high average GDP. And the people at the bottom of the distribution ladder suffer from an absence of many of the good things of life—including physical and psychiatric health—that characteristically emanate from being affluent. Income distribution seems to be the key variable here. Clearly, in order to understand deviance, we have to understand how a society's poorly distributed income generates a substantial stratum of very poor people, what causes the United States—a country manifestly among the world's most affluent nations—to generate such a high rate of poverty, and what implications this fact has for our understanding of the sociology of deviance.

PERSPECTIVES ON STIGMA AND POVERTY

Poverty will probably always be with us, but the extent and depth of poverty varies from one society to another. The UN's figures indicate that the most equitably distributed economies are nations in Scandinavia (such as Denmark, Sweden, and Norway)—small, affluent, democratic, European countries. The *least* equitable economies are those in poor, Third World countries, mainly in Africa and Latin America, with tiny, very rich elites—for example, South Africa, Angola, Brazil, and Honduras. The distribution of the economy of the United States is somewhere in between these two extremes. At one time, the most equalitarian societies on Earth were small, nomadic hunting and gathering bands, all of whose members lacked very much in the way of physical possessions; hardly any such collectivities exist today.

Since antiquity, numerous philosophers and theologians have commented and speculated on poverty from a variety of perspectives. *Proverbs* (14:31) declared, "He who oppresses the poor shows contempt for his Maker, but whoever is kind to the needy honors God." In his *Politics,* Aristotle (384–322 B.C.E.) argued that "poverty is the parent of revolution and crime." In *Satires,* Juvenal (first to the second century C.E.) opined that "It is not easy for men to rise whose qualities are thwarted by poverty." More recent statements by theorists and social scientists have added depth and complexity to these ancient assertions. Some of the commentators whose observations bear most directly on the matter of poverty and disrepute, or stigma and deviance, include Thomas Robert Malthus (1766–1834), Max Weber (1864–1920), and our twenty-first century contemporaries, David Matza, Melvin Lerner, Amartya Sen, Diego Zavaleta Reyles, and Loïc Wacquant.

Thomas Robert Malthus. One of the earliest arguments charging the poor with a moral failing was laid out by Thomas Malthus, in his *An Essay on the Principle of Population*, published in 1798. Malthus contended that the population is theoretically capable of growing geometrically, but the resources needed to support that increase only arithmetically. At some point during this hypothetical growth, an expanding population will put a severe strain on available resources, making unemployment and starvation commonplace. As a consequence, checks on the population are necessary. The refusal of the lower classes to limit family size can be seen both as a moral failing and a cause of their poverty. They are "incorrigibles" and therefore we need not dispense charity to them; it would be best for the society, Malthus argued, for the profligate poor to starve to death and not burden the virtuous and abstemious with their superfluous, squanderous, and impecunious presence. Malthus saw the poor who bred more children than they could support as human feces that should be eliminated from the body. Malthus was one of the most venomous stigmatizers of the poor in the history of social thought. As it turns out, birth control and the "green revolution" made Malthus's argument increasingly irrelevant, at least in the more fully developed industrial societies with adequate welfare systems.

Max Weber. Some social theorists have looked at all sides of the stigma of poverty, that is, not only how the privileged view the disprivileged, how the privileged view their own good fortune, and how the poor view the distribution of wealth, specifically their own lack of it. Max Weber in particular argued that societies adapt religious beliefs to their own social and cultural needs. This applies especially to social class: The wealthy and privileged will be attracted to certain religious beliefs that reassure them that their wealth is deserved; the poor and less privileged will seek those sacred ideologies that promise them a glorious existence in the next life—in heaven itself. He calls this tendency *elective affinity*—the tendency of people located in specific social classes or strata to generate or gravitate toward religions, or aspects of religions, that resonate with demands and exigencies of their earthly existence (1946, pp. 62–63, 284–285). Hence, Weber explains, "classes with high social and economic privilege will . . . assign to religion the primary function of legitimating their own life pattern and situation in the world." There exists, he explained, the "psychological need for reassurance as to the legitimation or deservedness of [the source of] one's happiness, whether it involves political success, superior economic status, bodily health, success in the game of love, or anything else. What the privileged classes require of religion," Weber explained, "is this psychological reassurance of legitimacy" (1922/1963, p. 107). Less fortunate members of the society, such as the poor, the privileged reason, have been "visited by adversity" because they are not pleasing to God, or the gods, who look unfavorably upon them and punish them for their sins. In short, according to Max Weber, there is a nearly universal tendency for religions of the upper strata to develop a *theodicity* that *legitimates* the good fortune of the rich and privileged and the ill fortune of the poor, arguing that rich and poor alike *merit* their status in life. Social class is "tangible proof" of God's favor or disfavor (p. 114). The rich find these theological justifications compatible with their world view and adapt them to their everyday lives—even in their secular ideology, detached from their sacred origins. In short, the rich are attracted to a sacred ideology that says the poor are *responsible* for their own poverty—because they are unmotivated and lazy and deserve what they get, including a measure society's contempt.

David Matza.   American society is supposed to root for the little guy, cheer when people pick themselves up by their bootstraps and become successful, overcoming all odds to forge their place in a competitive society. But the fact is, though we all love Horatio Alger stories of triumphs over adversity, many of us look down upon those who are not able to overcome the odds and remain entrenched in the swamp of poverty; they must not have tried hard enough, many of us feel, they must have become overwhelmed by torpor, fecklessness, ineptitude—or sheer laziness. David Matza argued that sociologists have ignored the issue of the "disreputable poor" because they did not want to be charged with stigmatizing them; he decided to grapple with the issue. It was Matza who coined the phrase, "poverty and disrepute" (1966b, 1971). To understand the stigma of poverty, he contended, we need to picture three concentric circles. The larger, outer, wider circle encompasses all poor people in the society; not all are stigmatized, nor are all considered disreputable. The intermediary circle is considerably smaller, and includes those who are poor and have received government welfare assistance at some point in their lives. The smallest or inner circle represents poor people who are sporadically or permanently on some

sort of government assistance program, "and, additionally, suffer the special defects and stigma of demoralization" (1966b, p. 620). In a competitive, achievement-oriented society, *some* measure of disrepute adheres to *all* poor, even those "who are deemed deserving and morally above reproach. Poverty itself is slightly disreputable, and being on welfare somewhat more disreputable." But the "so-called hard core," the innermost circle, is located at the furthest point along this range of disrepute. These people possess the "major moral defects of demoralization and immorality" (p. 620). Poverty, Matza contended, is especially stigmatizing to the extent that certain persons remain unemployed or casually employed during periods of prosperity and full employment; the "disreputable or able-bodied poor" resist training, remain recalcitrant and, in effect, *refuse* to work in spite of the inducement of wages. They are the "hard-to-reach," the disaffiliated, representing very probably society's only "authentic outsiders," remaining at or on the margins of society as if by choice, continuing to be "disproportionately costly" to the rest of us, causing the majority of its social problems—crime and delinquency, imprisonment, mental illness, welfare, family desertion, separation, divorce, and so on. These are the lumpen proletariat of Karl Marx and Friedrich Engels, those workers who remain outside the work force, the downtrodden, the chronic paupers, the apathetic, the aimless drifters, the beggars and tramps, the "dregs," the "sediment," the least educated and least uneducable persons who "have no place in the class hierarchy," who are "content to live in filth and disorder with a bare subsistence," (Matza, 1966a, p. 292, 1971, pp. 624–636; Matza and Miller, 1976).

Impoverishment, said Matza, is not the same as "pauperization." The pauperized are not only poor but oppressed, degraded, and debased as well, while the impoverished are merely poor and have not yet become pauperized (1966a, p. 299). We penalize the poor for being poor; they have become inured and resigned to their poverty, having fallen into an impulsive, turbulent, immobilized, demoralized existence, all of which circularly contributes to their entrenchment in the pauperized class. Matza painted a bleak portrait of poverty and disrepute, making us believe that little can be done to improve the hapless, hopeless existence of the stigmatized, demoralized, pauperized poor. They are truly among society's deviants, he argued.

Melvin Lerner. The line of thinking that holds that people are responsible for their own condition, that the well-favored and well-off *deserve* their good fortune while the poor, the unfortunate, and the miserable deserve the hardship they suffer, is called the *belief in a just world* or the *just world hypothesis* (Lerner, 1980). Most researchers regard the belief in a just world as a "fundamental delusion," yet it is strongly held by much, perhaps most, of the population. It is a widely held cognitive bias that human behavior results in fair, appropriate, and equitable consequences. Ultimately, many feel, evil actions result in punishment and ignominy, and noble actions result in reward and admiration. "You reap what you sow," or "You get what's coming to you," or "You made your bed, now lie in it," are common refrains that support this biased view of retribution. Social psychologist Melvin Lerner has spent a career conducting research on the origin and dynamics of this widespread but fallacious belief, as well as the conditions under which it is more likely to be held, and those under which it is less likely (1980; Montada and Lerner, 1998). Early on in his career, Lerner was struck by the fact that when someone meets unfortunate circumstances, people often blame the victim, conjuring up a reasonable-sounding rationale for their derogation. Belief in a just world, Lerner discovered in his research, is crucial for people to maintain a sense of well-being. The reality that individuals and categories of people suffer for no reason at all, while others enjoy fabulous good fortune, again, without apparent cause, is too painful for most of us to sustain. We need an explanation for how things work that eases the jarring reality of irrationality, the randomness, even the seeming cruelty of fate, and the just world hypothesis serves that function for a major sector of the population. This bias accounts for stereotypes held about the poor, attributions for the causes of poverty, and why conservatives express less compassion and more scorn for the poor while liberals express more compassion and less scorn for them (Furnham and Gunter, 1984; Cozzarelli, Wilkinson, and Tagler, 2001). Taking the process a step further, persons who believe in the logic of a just world regard poverty as just desserts, the poor as deserving of their destitution and scorn they receive—and

hence, in effect, believe that they are, and deserve to be regarded as, deviants. Melvin Lerner lent social-psychological rigor to our understanding of why some among us stigmatize the poor.

Amartya Sen and Diego Zavaleta Reyles. To reiterate, there's a moral dimension to poverty. People who are poor are often excluded from mainstream society principally *by virtue of their poverty alone*, and typically feel disparaged and dishonored as a result. Adam Smith first enunciated this principle in his influential volume, *The Wealth of Nations*, which was extended by Sen and Reyles. Amartya Sen is an Indian economist internationally well-known for his work on reducing famine by improving food distribution. But he also developed the argument that the poor are unjustly stigmatized—and self-stigmatized—for their poverty (2000). Absolute deprivation, or extreme poverty, not only causes hunger, it likewise brings about "the inability to appear in public without shame" (Sen, 2000, pp. 4, 5). Being poor in a Third World village often entails the inability to purchase a pair of shoes or sandals or a shirt made of decent cloth and having to go about bare-footed or dressed in shabby clothes, which causes shame, humiliation and discomfort as a result of being stared at and commented on. Reyles expands on precisely this motif. Being at the bottom of the heap in a context of extreme inequality results in discrimination, social marginality, and exclusion, and contributes not only to the experience of poverty but also the *social ostracism* of the poor (Reyles, 2007, p. 407)—that is, their experience of being deviants in their own communities. In *The Voice of the Poor*, a study of attitudes and feelings toward poverty in sixty countries around the world, respondents cited "indignity, shame, and humiliation as painful components of their deprivation." The "stigma of poverty is a recurrent theme among the poor, with people often trying to conceal their poverty to avoid humiliation" (p. 407). The sense of humiliation and shame that poverty engenders results in a reduced freedom and agency, being unable to do what is considered customary for a functioning member of the community, having to accept charity or alms, experiencing painful encounters with officials, or belonging to sectors of the society "to which negative values are attached"—that is, stereotypes dictating that poverty "is associated with laziness, incompetence, or criminality" (p. 407)

Loïc Wacquant.   Loïc Wacquant draws what is probably the most dismal and pessimistic portrait of the growing convergence of poverty, disrepute, race, and marginality. His *Urban Outcasts* (2008) argues that advanced capitalism—he focuses specifically on France and the United States—has produced an *advanced marginality* which entails the physical removal of stigmatized populations, mainly the poverty-stricken and, in the United States, virtually all African Americans, who have become increasingly incorporated into a "penal state" in which the ghetto (a term Wacquant uses but doesn't like) and the prison are indistinguishable—elements in a "carceral continuum" (à la Foucault)—and "surplus" populations suffer "structural constraints" and the "vulnerable fractions of the urban proletariat" have become increasingly "spatially stigmatized," marginalized, and alienated (p. 286). The "dazzling growth of corporate benefits," says Wacquant, "go hand in hand with wage work" (p. 286). The state has cut the poor loose to fend for themselves, but retains its "public monopoly of systems of surveillance and sanction of deviancy" (p. 12). Wacquant's work on the expansion of the super-rich, the stigmatization and ghettoization of the urban poor and racial minorities, the "penalization of misery," and the hyper-surveillance of deviance sound a great deal like George Orwell's dystopic *1984*. To someone living in Paris, New York, or Chicago, the portrait he draws may seem exaggerated—the fact is, racial residential segregation is declining in the United States over time, albeit unevenly, rather than increasing (Glaeser and Vigdor, 2012)—but his image does capture what it must be like to live at the bottom economic stratum in one of the most affluent societies on Earth, and to feel marginalized, stigmatized, and deviantized by persons who are vastly better off.

POVERTY IN THE UNITED STATES

Economists have struggled to systematically define poverty at least as long ago as 1965, when Lyndon Johnson declared his "War on Poverty."

The federal government defines a household as living in poverty according to the household's income from all sources, number of people in the household, and the local consumer price index. In 2011, the poverty threshold for a one-person household was drawn at $11,484; for a two-person household, at $14,657; and for four people, at $23,021; and so on. By this designation, about 15 percent of the American population lives in poverty; clearly, there is some arbitrariness in these designations, and a different set of calculations would create a different set of figures. Technology, sanitation, and modern medicine have made it possible for the population in contemporary industrialized countries, including the poor, to live longer, healthier, and less physically debased lives. In most respects, on average, Americans are materially better off than residents of Third World nations, and better off today than they were a century or two ago. And yet poverty persists in the United States, as do *regions* and *categories* of poverty. In fact, surprisingly, as I'll explain shortly, among the seventeen most affluent countries on earth, the health of Americans, specifically the health of poor Americans, is the worst in the world.

The poorest five cities in America are former industrial "rust belt" municipalities. In 1950, Detroit was a prosperous, urban, industrial, unionized working-class community of over 1.8 million; in 2012, the city numbered only 575,000 souls, leaving behind a crumbling, hollowed-out shell of its former infrastructure. Detroit is now, declares *Time* magazine, a semi-abandoned "ghost town" in which more than a third of its residents (36%) live in poverty. (Keep in mind that different organizations and agencies define and measure income and poverty in slightly different ways and hence, get slightly different results; moreover, these results change year by year.) During the same period, Cleveland's population plummeted from over 900,000 to below 400,000, and a third of its residents (35%) are likewise currently classified as impoverished. During the past half century, these and hundreds of other deindustrialized cities lost millions of jobs and trillions of dollars in municipal and state revenues. A substantial percentage of the poorer residents who remain in the inner cities of these and other, similarly disadvantaged regions around the country, are virtually guaranteed a poverty-stricken existence and a life of economic want. A substantial level of unemployment seems ineradicable, as does the concentration of unemployment, under-employment, and sub-employment in specific sectors of the population, specifically among racial and ethnic minorities. Moreover, it is not only the nonworking or low-income wage-earners who are poor; their children are also impoverished. According to the U.S. Census figures, over half (54%) of Detroit's *children* live in poverty, as do Cleveland's (53%). A third to nearly half of the children living in two dozen of America's medium-to-large cities, from Cincinnati, Ohio (48%) to Corpus Christi, Texas (32%) are poverty-stricken. Today, the child poverty rate is higher than it has been in twenty years.

Rural poverty is even more extreme than its urban counterpart. According to the Census, the majority of the 100 communities in America with the lowest per capita incomes, where the most serious and persistent poverty is concentrated, are rural communities or "census designated places" (CDP), are too small and too poor to maintain a municipal government, nearly all of which have limited or non-existent economic opportunities, virtually no possibility for upward mobility, and a substantial lack of access to markets; more than half of these places are located in only two states—in Texas, nearly all of them in the Rio Grande Valley, and South Dakota, mostly on or near Indian reservations. Yet Texas also boasts two cities (Dallas and Houston) with large and immensely wealthy elites.

We see substantial state-by-state variation in income. Median household income in the most affluent state (Maryland, in 2011, at $68,876) is almost $30,000 higher than the earnings in the poorest state, Kentucky (at $39,956). As we saw, 15 percent of the American population meets the criteria of poverty, which also varies significantly by state, with Mississippi (23%) and Louisiana (22%) having the highest percentages, and Connecticut (8%) and New Hampshire (7%) with the lowest. All of the Southern states except for Virginia encompass a percentage of their resident poor that is higher than the national average, and all of the New England states have a lower-than-average percent of poor people.

The poverty of a state is related to its lack of education. This may be cause or consequence—

that is, poor states spend the least on public education, and hence, educate a lower percent of their population, or well-educated people are not attracted to states that have a high percentage of poor people, sensing that economic opportunity lies elsewhere. Or a lack of education may cause poverty, or poverty may cause already educated people to move out. In any case, the states with under 20 percent of twenty-five-year-olds who are college graduates (West Virginia, 17%; Arkansas, 19%; and Mississippi, 20%) are at or near the bottom of the state-by-state income ladder, while those whose numbers include over 35 percent with a bachelor's degree (Connecticut, 36%; Maryland, 36%; Colorado, 36%; and Massachusetts, 38%) are at or near the top. When we compare states with one another, education is very closely related to income; hence, poverty is clustered in much the same way that a lack of education is.

Poverty doesn't confine itself to pin-points on a map of rural America or to decaying neighborhoods in formerly industrialized cities. It is persistent even in areas where affluence is widespread. The percentage of poor people in a country is determined not only by its average income but also by how that nation's income is *distributed*. Income distribution is an "objective" indicator of the scale and spread of riches versus poverty. By knowing a nation's Gross Domestic Product (GDP) and how well its income is distributed, we can determine how many poor people live in it. The income earned by quintiles (or 20 percent layers) in the population is one way of expressing how income is distributed; in the United States in 2011, the top quintile (one-fifth of the population) earned *14 times* more than the bottom; in 1968, the ratio was 7.7 to one. In short, income inequality in the United States is substantially *growing*, and it has taken place under administrations of both parties. According to data gathered by the Brookings Institution, which sponsors research on public policy issues, in 2011, "tax units" at the tenth percentile of incomes earned $9,235; nearly all of the persons in this category are unarguably poor. The federal government's definition of poverty for a family of four is $17,029. The fiftieth percentile—the median income for tax units in the United States in 2011—was $42,327. And the income of the ninety-ninth percentile was just over half a million dollars—$506,553. But income tends to rise very steeply at the very top of the distribution ladder; at the 99.5th percentile, income stands at $815,868, and at the 99.9th percentile rung, it is $2,070,574. In 2012, the U.S. Census released a report on *family* income and poverty in the United States, particularly focusing on recent changes. The top *5 percent* of the population increased their share of the total income by 4.9 percent—from 21.3 percent to 22.3 percent, and the top quintile (20%) increased their share of total income by 1.6 percent (DeNavas-Walt, Proctor, and Smith, 2012, p. 10).

The Gini coefficient lends precision to income distribution. (Most economists believe that it makes the most sense to measure Ginis in *after tax* income distribution.) A low Gini is represented, not surprisingly, by a low number (closer to 0) while a high Gini is represented by a high (that is, a number closer to 1). The Kuznets Curve predicts that as countries undergo economic development, they first move from a low Gini (little inequality, as with tiny hunting and gather bands) to a high Gini (substantial inequality, as among the agrarian empires of ancient Rome and medieval Europe) to, once again, a low Gini (less inequality, as in modern urban democracies). As a general rule, incomes in economically developing countries, such as Mexico (a Gini of 0.476), Turkey (0.409), and Chile (0.494), are less equitably distributed than incomes in more fully developed nations, such as France (0.293), Germany (0.295), and Switzerland (0.303). In addition, as we saw, the Scandinavian countries (Norway, Sweden, Denmark, and Finland) have the most equally distributed incomes in the world (all with a Gini at about 0.250). And the United Kingdom (0.345) and the United States (0.380) have more equitably distributed incomes than the industrializing countries of the Second and Third World, but *less* than those of the more fully industrialized and post-industrialized First World countries of Western Europe. (Gini measures for income distribution vary year by year and according to how the relevant indicators are measured.) Among the thirty-four fully industrialized countries of the world, the United States ranks near the bottom (thirty-first) in how equitably its income is distributed—in other words, it is the, or one of the most, *in*equalitarian of the richest countries. In the United States, the richest stratums earn a huge slice of the total income earned, while the poor, a relatively small proportion of it.

Though America is also an affluent country, and its total Gross Domestic Product (GDP) is enormous—the highest in the world—among industrialized nations, its income is not well distributed. Hence, compared with countries such as Sweden, the Netherlands, and France, a substantially higher proportion of Americans live in poverty. Here's another statistic: In the United States, during 2010 (that is, from January 1, 2010 to December 31, 2010), *93 percent of the economic growth in income was monopolized by the richest 1 percent of society*. And another: adjusted for inflation, the 2011 per capita income was $1,000 *lower* than it was in 1968—$32,986 versus $33,880. Income inequality is great, it is growing, and incomes are stagnating—except for the very rich. In fact, income inequality today in the United States has not been as great has it has since the 1920s, which preceded the Great Crash and the Depression. The United States has a higher proportion of its children living in poverty (a fifth) than all but one of the richest countries in the world—and even more so than is true of Bulgaria, Greece, and Latvia (Stiglitz, 2013, p. 8SR). These generalizations apply more to the United States than to any other affluent nation on Earth, but they apply even more so to most of the poorer Third World countries. It is possible that the current global economic stagnation is a cause of increasing inequality—but it's also possible that the reverse is true. In any case—and more to our point—poverty is one outcome of extreme inequality, and, increasingly, poverty toward the very poor breeds contempt among the affluent.

IS POVERTY A FORM OF DEVIANCE?

Granted that poverty is widespread—but what's stigmatizing about poverty *per se*?

In *Human Nature and the Social Order* (1902), Charles Horton Cooley discussed the implications of what he called "the looking-glass self," which, as we know, refers to *reflexivity*—seeing oneself as others see one. When we interact socially with others, we tend to picture ourselves as we appear to others, assess the presumed evaluations of that image—whether they consist of praise or condemnation—and, if we want to please others, adjust our behavior accordingly, on the basis of what sort of reaction we'd like to entice. Thomas Scheff (2003) pinpointed shame as a component of a cluster of emotions causally linked in Cooley's formulation; shame comes in infinite gradations, from discomfort through embarrassment, to abject, long-term humiliation. Starrin (2002, p. 5) suggests that the feeling of shame "has the potential of being harmful when the individual is the subject of ridicule and insult." Here, I am suggesting that poverty often results in ridicule and insult and hence, shame, especially if it takes the form of unemployment and welfare (pp. 9–30), two frequent accompaniments of poverty. And such outcomes can not only cause behaviors we regard as deviant—they are, *themselves*, manifestations of deviance. Is stigmatizing the poor *fair*? Most sociologists do not believe it is fair, since they argue that poverty is largely the result of structural conditions over which the poor have no control. But many members of this society *do* believe it is fair and just, arguing that people are responsible for their economic condition in life and hence—although few would admit it—the poor can be *blamed* for being impoverished. Hence, sociologists recognize that many Americans *do* stigmatize the poor, and we have to bring that stigmatization into the human equation. And to the extent that stigma is a manifestation of deviance, living in poverty is *deviantizing*—it brings disrepute to the lives and character of the poor.

Here, how economists define poverty is less relevant than how the members of population—including the poor themselves—*regard* or *look upon* the poor. And whether the poor are responsible for their condition is less relevant than whether the poor are *thought* to be responsible for their condition. Martha Nussbaum (2004) argues that poverty is one of humanity's most stigmatizing conditions; the poor are treated as inferior to (and by) persons who are not poor. Exactly at what income level this treatment kicks in depends on the audience—who engages in making this judgment, as well as in what contexts the poor appear and the judgment occurs. Unemployment contributes to poverty, and unemployment is, to

a substantial degree, *itself* stigmatizing; being on welfare is a manifestation or indicator of poverty, and it is likewise stigmatizing. Hence, both are relevant to the topic of poverty.

The stigma of poverty is a class-based form of disrepute that is built into the hegemonic structure of stratification in American society. Under capitalism, this line of reasoning goes, intelligence and hard work breed success, and success is a sign of virtue; poverty implies failure, and failure is impious, a kind of vice—virtually a sin. Outside of (and even within) their own social circles, the poverty-stricken very often find their character impugned *because* of their poverty. But not all poor persons affirm their own inferior status in relation to the class structure. While being without money is nearly considered undesirable everywhere, many poor people do not consider themselves less worthy human beings by virtue of being poor; not all are *ashamed* of their poverty. But nearly everywhere they go, the poor are *reminded* of their inferior economic condition; not only does much of what they value cost money they do not have, most of the people whose company they value agree with the proposition that it's worse to be poor than affluent. Thus, though self-assumed shame is not a universal outcome of poverty, stigma is very nearly so; one may not agree that one *deserves* to be stigmatized, but many others do, and it is difficult to avoid these people and their influence.

Poverty, stigma, and a lack of education indicate powerlessness and marginality from the society's cultural centers. These characteristics reflect the inability to attain the sorts of achievements that anomie theory argues society inculcates into all of us to value and covet; hence, such a life-condition potentiates us for innovative forms of deviance and, failing that, retreatist adaptations. But in addition, most people in an achievement-oriented society look down on persons who have been unable to rise on the economic ladder, remaining mired in deep, stagnating, permanent poverty. They feel sorry for such people—although they are also moved by sentiments of compassion as well—and don't want to remain in their company for very long, or at all. "How can they live like that?" they are likely to exclaim if they see photographs of them, or see them from the highway, or hear or read about their condition. Most of us don't *want* to live like that, and shun people in our everyday lives who live in such conditions. Moreover, most of the people who live in extreme poverty share many of those same sentiments, but structural conditions, a lack of opportunity, a lack of education, disability, or old age have conspired to keep them in their place. The urban and rural poor live in places that others have abandoned, as has the economy, and many of those who leave avoid, snub, and disdain those who remain. In the larger picture, the extremely poor are—unfairly—stigmatized as deviants.

In 2001, National Public Radio (NPR) conducted a poll on the public's attitudes toward poverty. About half of the sample's respondents said that the poor are not doing enough to pull themselves out of poverty, while the other half said that "circumstances beyond their control cause them to be poor." Clearly, at that time, a substantial proportion of Americans believed that if you're poor, it's "your own fault." The economic stagnation that began in 2008 may have altered these attitudes somewhat. In 2010, a greater number of the population was recorded as living in poverty—just under 47 million—than in any previous year since the figure was calculated, at a stretch of fifty-two years. It's not clear that this increase has generated more empathy for the poor or a stronger feeling that poverty justly attracts blame and disrepute. But the social reality is that the odds are stacked against the poor, and creating a strictly equalitarian society requires more resources than any known society has been able to summon. Regardless of whether or not inequality stimulates achievement, the "chances are if you are poor you will stay poor. Through little fault of your own" (Mollman, 2011).

UNEMPLOYMENT

Currently, the United States work force is experiencing a roughly 7–8 percent unemployment rate. Unemployment is based in part on "fuzzy math" because it is the *official* rate; it includes only workers looking for work who have filed a claim for unemployment benefits. It does not include discouraged workers who have stopped looking for employment, workers who are still jobless when the benefits run out, or the part-time and under-employed. It also does not take into account employees in the "informal" sector, the

"shadow," black market, or *underground* economy—those working off the books, under the table, or in illegal enterprises. In such jobs, there are no unemployment benefits, no Social Security, no taxes—and no official records. In many less developed countries particularly in Latin America and Africa, according to some estimates (Portes and Haller, 2005; Schneider, 2012), the informal economy is larger than the recorded or official economy; it supports workers from street vendors to drug kingpins. In fully industrialized countries such as the United States, the informal economy makes up less than 10 percent of the total. Of course the officially unemployed may *also* work in the informal economy and receive an off-the-books income, so they are two partly overlapping categories. Still, for most workers, there is no shadow job, no alternate stream of earnings, and no extra money; for the traditional worker and ex-employee, unemployment is a humbling, demeaning, humiliating, and painful experience. It offers little but disrepute.

The classic study of the harmful impact of unemployment on self-esteem was conducted during the Depression by Bohan Zawadski and Paul Lazarsfeld (1935), who analyzed 57 autobiographies of laid-off Polish workers—reflecting a total of 774 that were submitted in a contest by a worker's institute—and found that others belittled them, causing them to suffer, lose their sense of dignity, and feel ashamed of themselves. These men were gripped by "ever-increasing perplexity," "hopelessness," and "fear of the future." "I look for a job," said one of the respondents. "I beg, I humble myself, and lose my ego. I become a beast, a humiliated beast, excluded from the ranks of society" (p. 238). "When I go out, I cast down my eyes because I feel myself wholly inferior. . . . I instinctively avoid meeting anyone. . . . Former acquaintances and friends of better times are no longer so cordial. They greet me indifferently. . . . Their eyes seem to say, 'You are not worth it, you no longer work'" (p. 239). "Hopelessness, bitterness, hatred, outbreaks of rage, gloominess . . . , flight into drunkenness . . . thoughts of suicide"—all appeared at least as a "momentary mood" of every one of these biographies.

The negative impact on the well-being of unemployed workers hasn't changed a great deal in recent times, though the unemployed today are less likely to express themselves in quite as flamboyant a fashion as they did decades ago. The current consequences of unemployment among American workers are dire, say two economists (Baker and Hassett, 2012)—a "human disaster." Workers over fifty who are laid off are more likely than their employed peers to commit suicide, contract a serious, potentially fatal illness; their life span is a year and a half shorter, and these disadvantages negatively impact on their wives' current and their children's future employability and earnings. In 2012, Connie Wanberg, a psychologist at a school of management, summarized the "individual-focused research" on unemployment from the unemployed person's perspective, stressing the first decade of the twenty-first century, a period during which financial crisis produced "the worst unemployment situation the world has encountered since the Great Depression." In 2010, over 200 million people worldwide were out of work, a 30 million increase since 2000 (2012, p. 379). A meta-analysis of dozens of studies on the impact of unemployment indicated that, independent of the selection process (that is, the fact that the unhealthiest individuals are more likely to be laid off), the unemployed experience higher rates of depression, psychological distress, feelings of helplessness, an erosion of the feeling that one can exert control over one's life outcomes, an increase in rates of suicide and "parasuicide" (i.e., self-inflicted injury), and poor physical health. Over a span of twenty years, the mortality rates are approximately 15 percent higher for job-displaced individuals. And job displacement was associated with a 15 to 20 percent decline in long-term earnings. Of course, not all studies had the same findings or reached the same conclusions, but the direction of the data pointed in the direction of these harmful outcomes (Wanberg, 2012). The unemployed stand among society's stigmatized sectors, outside respectable social circles; they are deviant in virtually every sense of the word, and the more long-term the unemployment, the more that this holds true.

WELFARE

Participation in welfare programs has sometimes been taken as evidence that recipients are lazy and hold deviant work orientations (Jarrett,

1996, p. 368). Over time, the Aid to Families with Dependent Children (AFDC) program has been broadened to include never-married women and their children, further evidence, to critics, that AFDC increasingly serves the "undeserving poor" (Murray, 1984; Katz, 1989)—in short, that they *should* be stigmatized and *deserve* to be treated as deviants. Many caseworkers treat recipients *as* deviants, asking them about their sex lives, berate them as reluctant workers and, overall, treat them disrespectfully (Jarrett, 1996). AFDC recipients frequently respond by adopting a passive, non-confrontational demeanor. To the recipient, stigma has often been the price the welfare client is forced to pay to receive services and benefits. The applicant "must adopt a suppliant role, like a medieval leper exhibiting his sores" (Rose, 1975, p. 152). The humiliation is simply part of the bargain; it is part of the "ritual of degradation."

According to Rogers-Dillon (1995), the "language of welfare stigmatizing relationships, as they are framed and defined" in concrete situations, is what demeans the recipient—although it comes in degrees of discreditation. Rogers-Dillon follows Goffman's distinction between a "virtual" and an "actual" social identity (Goffman, 1963, pp. 2–3) by arguing that the virtual identity of all Americans includes the possession of citizenship—but other citizens may challenge that identity. Self-definitions of recipients incorporate necessity; the stigma of receiving welfare becomes "almost meaningless in the face of pressing needs for food, shelter, diapers and other goods." Rogers-Dillon's respondents told her that going on welfare "was not a difficult decision to make," and "with no job or child support, they had no other options" (p. 445). "It's survival," said one of her interviewees. "You do what you have to do. It is demeaning. I hate it." In other words, though it was experienced by this woman as "demeaning," her very lack of options made it a necessity. The respondents were acutely aware of the stereotypes of welfare recipients, but economic "hard times" recast their experience as doing what they had to do to survive. "They saw the public's image of most welfare recipients as one of lazy, baby-making women living off other people's labor," but they felt it did not reflect their circumstances, feeling alienated from these stereotypes. Receiving food stamps can be something of a humiliation, given that in order to redeem them, recipients have to publicly display them, and to teach their children "how to manage food stamps and the information that food stamps convey." Yet even though food stamps "convey a degraded status," they "also provide essential goods." Though recipients "disliked the social meaning of food stamps," they found them necessary; all found this balancing act between assistance and necessity a "central task" (p. 450), sometimes choosing to avoid the dilemma by using up their reserve of cash. Hence, though the stigma of welfare "is inherent to the current American welfare system," just *how* degrading it is, is partly contingent on the recipient's necessity and partly on her management and presentation of self (Rogers-Dillon, 1995, p. 454). In short, stigma is not necessarily or *inevitably* internalized or accepted, though it is characteristically *conveyed*.

However recipients manage their feelings about their participation in welfare programs, they report negative treatment by their neighbors and peers as a consequence of using food stamp coupons, which can lower self-esteem and personal autonomy and efficacy. Hence, from the perspective of welfare clients, it is difficult to avoid participation as "cost" of the program, one that some potential recipients are not willing to bear. Stigma may be divided into two types—self-identity stigma, or "internal" stigma, and the stigma that emanates from being *observed* participating in a public assistance program, that is, external, or "treatment" stigma which stems from anticipation of negative treatment (Stuber and Schlesinger, 2006). In addition, stigma is exacerbated by poor health, minority status and facilitated by "the ways in which means-tested programs are implemented, including negative interaction with case workers, long waiting lines, and . . . applications for alternative enrollment" (p. 933). Manchester, Flaherty, and Mumford (2010) demonstrated that the cost of stigma, a powerful disincentive to client participation by the poor in welfare assistance, can be reduced when benefits come in the form of electronic benefits transfer (EBT) rather than in physical, identifiable vouchers. Hence, to reduce "treatment" stigma, and increase the efficiency of dispersing assistance, states have begun adopting electronic payment, which has resulted in 30 percent greater participation by eligible cli-

ents. Studies such as this one indicate the strong public health applications of the stigma concept.

THE INDIGNITY OF BEGGING

In the fifteenth century, European authorities arrested idle, seemingly able-bodied vagrants, "wandering rogues," and "sturdy beggars," and flogged, branded, expelled, and otherwise disgraced them in an effort to discourage idleness and encourage a life of wholesome labor (Jütte, 1994). Laws prohibiting panhandling or "aggressive behavior" such as "touching, accosting, continuing to panhandle after being given a negative response, blocking or interfering with a person's free passage" (Lankenau, 1999, p. 302), remain in effect and serve to exclude beggars from entering or loitering in public places. Today, this law is implemented when pedestrians and customers complain to store owners or the police, demanding that nearby beggars move on; sometimes, storeowners post signs announcing that panhandling is prohibited. Public reactions to begging are likely to be negative, reminding panhandlers of their status as pariahs. "Well, sometimes people just walk past you like you're nobody, like you're a piece of garbage," says Linda, a 25-year-old homeless, pregnant woman. Harlan, a 48-year-old homeless man, describes an incident in which a man knocked the change out of his cup. Now he puts it in his pocket. "Damn, man, your cup stay empty. Every time I see your cup, it's empty," people tell him. "They don't know why it's empty. That's why," he explains (Lankenau, 1999, p. 297).

Journalist Josh Shaffer decided to find out what applying for a permit to ask people for money feels like, so he went to North Carolina's Wake County's government office and applied for one, registering as county's twelfth registered panhandler. "It's humiliating. It's degrading. It's invasive." Filling out the paperwork, he tells us, he got the feeling "that it's meant to be." The form asked him to fill in his height, weight, hair color and eye color. "There's no mistaking what you're doing when you write down this information. You've completed a police profile." At the counter, in a room full of people, he was watched as someone placed "an official stamp" on his request to seek alms. And there was no mistaking how he felt: humiliated—very much like an outsider, a deviant. In the end, he decided not to go out and beg (Shaffer, 2011). Make no mistake about it: The experience of begging itself is also stigmatizing. Defying that stigma, Alison O'Riordan, an Irish reporter, got a polystyrene cup, placed a sign in front of him that read "Homeless, any donations appreciated," and sat down on a Dublin sidewalk, looking for a story. "I felt physically sick. Imagine if, in reality, life had turned this sour; abandoned by family and friends, without a job and a pillow to place my head at night, and so I let myself be consumed into that world for a few hours." He was invisible to the "high-powered men in pin-stripe suits," their jackets thrown over their shoulders in the blistering heat, a mobile phone at their ear. "People refused to meet my eye; they cast their gaze anywhere but where I sat. The odd person took a glimpse over their shoulder after they passed by when they thought I wasn't looking." He got the feeling that people "felt vulnerable" around him. "There I was," he says, "watching mothers with shopping bags, who whisked their little ones away like I carried some form of the Black Death as their toddlers pointed and stared" (O'Riordan, 2010).

Begging combines the indignity of admitting to being impoverished with humiliating oneself by abjectly asking someone else for small sums of money—and doing nothing in return, simply "getting something for nothing." Not only is begging a *manifestation* of one's exclusion from society—the activity, in and of itself, *affirms* that exclusion. Begging is actually hard work; one sacrifices one's self-respect by engaging in the activity, and the money one requests is frequently not forthcoming. One has to invest a substantial amount of time to receive handfuls of change. It is instructive to compare "getting something for nothing," that is, begging, with three activities that are similar to begging but which differ in the crucial respect of offering something of value to the community—"busking" or performing in public for handouts, (Harrison-Pepper, 1990), selling low-value items on the sidewalk that one has gleaned from the trash (Duneier, 1999), and collecting cans and bottles for cash (Gowan, 2010, pp. 147–159). Busking and selling recovered trash, such as books, bottles and cans, are widely regarded on the street

as "making an honest living." Begging is not the absolute bottom of the ladder—thievery is—but it is a substantial step down from engaging in sidewalk entertainment and peddling merchandise that one has rescued from rubbish. Begging is not considered "work," it adds no value to anyone except the receiver, and, unlike street enterprises that render a service or a product for cash, it does not resonate with any conventional activity. It comes as no surprise that begging is held in substantial disrepute. It is regarded as a form of deviance, but not nearly so depraved or wrongful as stealing. Once again, poverty appears in a wide display of manifestations, varying in degree of stigma.

HOMELESSNESS

Who are the homeless? And how would the sociologist calculate the rate of homelessness in the population. Homelessness is not like unemployment; homelessness is not a specific social and economic category. Studies attempting to measure homelessness are stymied by the fact that the total number is influenced by duration. People are undomiciled for periods of time; some are chronically homeless, while others don't have a roof over their heads for a night or two. If researchers draw a sample based on people who are out on the street on a single night, who have no place to go to during those eight or ten hours, they find a very broad cross-section of the population is likely to be homeless, and "no meaningful central tendencies in the distribution" (Shalay and Rossi, 1992, p. 142). In contrast, if they look at the long-term or persistently homeless, they find that the homeless are far more likely to be male, have considerably less education, more mental health and drug issues and problems, to have been incarcerated than the population at large. As a persistent or chronic problem, homelessness affects a relatively small percentage of the population who are "seriously disabled and deviant individuals from limited demographic subgroups" (Phelen and Link, 1999, p. 1336). When a research sample of "formerly" homeless individuals is selected, it will gather together people who look far more like the "single-night" or "occasional" sample—highly variable and not at all like the public stereotype. Gathering such a broad sample could make a political point—that all of us are only a few mishaps away from having to live on the street—but it would not be true to the reality of homelessness, and that is that the *persistently* homeless constitute a particular type of social denizen, one who is relatively rare, atypical, in serious behavioral difficulty, and in need of multiple social services. Hence, which sample is drawn conveys ideological, theoretical, and practical implications.

In an experimental study that entailed asking respondents about the degree to which they would put social distance between themselves and a hypothetical homeless man, the researchers found that identifying the person as homeless "engenders a degree of stigma over and above that attached to poverty" (Phelen et al., 1997, p. 332). Public perceptions of homelessness were at least as negative as those of the formerly hospitalized, even though mental hospitalization increased the public's perception of the person's dangerousness, while the homeless label did not. Moreover, mental hospitalization labeling is two-sided, engendering both positive and negative reactions, it did increase the likelihood of a compassionate response (greater support for government assistance), but this was not true of the homelessness label, which brought forth a virtually entirely negative or rejecting reaction. The authors argue that social rejection, or a disqualification "from full social acceptance" (Goffman, 1963, p. i), "lies at the heart of stigmatization" (Phelen et al., 1997, p. 328). Given that previous research has found that mental illness is stigmatized more severely than the ex-convict status, homosexuality, the diagnosis of mental retardation, as well as a number of physical disabilities and disorders, it follows, the authors argue, homelessness is not only more stigmatized than poverty, in all likelihood it is also more stigmatized than these other conditions (pp. 234–235).

Short of keeping someone out of one's country—which is the ultimate stigma—the most severe attempt to create social distance between the deviant and the person rejecting the deviant, the strongest denial of "full social acceptance," is the NIMBY reaction—Not In My Back Yard. In other words, NIMBY is the attempt by one or more persons to keep members of a deviant category *out* of that community. Community opposition to such social services began mobilizing in the 1980s—a populist ideology that says the government can't force deviants down our throat, this is *our*

neighborhood—and it creates a problem for public health and social services outreach programs. Most programs serving clients who are homeless, or who are infected with HIV/AIDS, often face NIMBY sentiment because a particular neighborhood does not want those deviant clients wandering around *their* streets. Lois Takahashi points out (1997) that such sentiment illuminates three distinct facets of stigma: nonproductivity, dangerousness, and personal culpability. Members of the community feel that homeless people are objectionable because they don't earn a living, they don't pay taxes, they mooch off the locals, they are failures and deviants, and responsible for their condition. But these community residents and activists also fear (not entirely unreasonably) that the homeless and the HIV/AIDS-infected will harm them, that they are a threat, they are dangerous, and hence, should not inhabit their neighborhood. There is, in other words, an *ecological* or *socio-spatial* aspect to stigma. Resistance to housing the stigmatized, or locating a service facility, in a particular neighborhood is not a mere matter of prejudice, discrimination, or an irrational fear of the deviant, says Takahashi; it is a complex and sometimes reasonable and understandable sentiment that must be understood before it is overcome or averted.

WHAT ABOUT DISEASE?

In his book, *The Status Syndrome* (2004), Michael Marmot, an epidemiologist at the medical school of University College, London, argues that a long, healthy life and good health are strongly related to education, income, and socioeconomic status (SES). All of this is true, he grants, but there is much more to longevity than social class; rather, there is much more to social class than the usual appurtenances of social class. Socioeconomic status pulls into its orbit a syndrome—the *status syndrome*—of positive qualities that goes along with social class that *encourages* long, healthy lives. Independence. Emotional and psychological satisfaction. Intellectual stimulation. Companionship. Good relations with others. Spiritual development. Being appreciated and respected by others. Experiencing a relatively stress-free life. None of these benefits is directly gauged by income, status, or education, but they float in with the tide of social class. The unequal distribution of these psychological and social benefits determines corresponding inequalities in the richness of our inner lives, hence, our well-being and the span of our earthly existence. Marmot conducts a mental experiment with the reader. Imagine four different parades of people filing past us, one by one. The first is ranked by education, the least well-educated first; as they walk by, we notice that they become increasingly healthy as their education increases—and that, if we have them with us long enough, their life's duration grows longer as well. Our second parade is sorted by income, and we notice exactly the same process taking place. The third parade repeats the same process, only this time sorted by the prestige of the occupation of the marchers' parents. And last, the prestige of their own occupations. The fact is, these are not four separate parades, since many of the same people who began the first parade will be in the same position in the second, third, and fourth one. This same process will be repeated at any age we select, and in any country on the planet. Researchers have conducted the study that Marmot summarized in the United States, but they also replicated it for the populations of ten comparatively well-off nations—Canada, Finland, Japan, France, Italy, Sweden, Germany, Belgium, Australia, and New Zealand. Wherever researchers look, they find precisely this same gradient. It is true that health and longevity have improved in all societies in the past century or two, and in all social classes. In fact, today, lower-SES categories live longer, healthier lives than higher-SES categories did in past centuries and decades. But today, in the twenty-first century, higher-SES categories also live longer, healthier lives than lower-SES categories; and persons living in poverty live the shortest and unhealthiest lives of all. And remarkably, even though different diseases have different etiologies or causes, *for virtually all diseases*, the same social gradient of inequality prevails. Each of the diseases that humans die of is caused by specific circumstances, but virtually all are related to the same social class and educational scale in the same way—with the poverty-stricken the most at risk. The links between social class and the personal and emotional benefits of life, and the corresponding links between these benefits and health and life span are a cruel fact of life, but they are implacable and consistent.

Once again, what matters in life expectancy is not only absolute poverty but also the *degree of income inequality*—the more inequality that exists in a society, other things being equal, the shorter the average life span. For the poor, in addition to being poor is the fact that inequality is bad for one's health. According to Marmot, we have to think of income in two ways—one, how much one has, and two, what one has relative to what others have. To the extent that all of the desirable societal accompaniments of organized social life—transportation, access to medical care, education, decent housing, recreational facilities, a healthful food supply, as well as freedom from street crime—are correlated with individual income, individual income serves as a measure or determinant of freedom and the ability to become a fully functioning member of the society, and hence, likewise, to that extent, one's capacity to live a long, healthy life is maximized. On the other hand, if these are provided by the community or the society, then individual income is of less consequence. Angus Deaton, an economist, found that states in the United States with the highest levels of inequality were also states with the highest proportion of African Americans in the population. But inequality itself may not be the causal factor here; the population's proportion of black people "is unlikely to be a cause of mortality" because the percent black is also correlated with the death rate among whites (p. 80). Marmot argues that both income inequality and proportion of African Americans in the population are indicative of the degree to which people have the opportunity to fully participate in society; both African Americans and the very poor do not, he says, fully participate in society's mainstream. Likewise, to the extent that the less affluent members of the society are restricted in their participation in the enriching and necessary institutions of social life, that society will not provide conditions that lead to the long, healthy lives of the numbers of such social strata.

Not only are the poor more likely to get sick and injured, they are less likely to be uncovered by medical insurance, which causes further impairment and a higher chance of premature death. The uninsured are more likely to suffer from undiscovered and untreated conditions, such as hypertension, diabetes, and elevated cholesterol (Wilper et al., 2009)—not to mention obesity, heavy drinking, smoking, and inactivity—and hence, become afflicted by more serious illness and debilitating medical disorders. The percentage of persons who are medically uninsured increases as real household yearly income decreases. Only 7.9 percent of persons living in a household earning $75,000 or more are medically uninsured; this figure doubles for those in households earning $50,000 to $74,999 (15.0%); increases again, to 21.4 percent, for those in households earning $25,000 to $49,999; and increases again for those who live in the poorest households, those earning less than $25,000 (25.9%). And the number of uninsured is increasing over time—from 13 percent in 1987 to 15.4 percent in 2012, and from 30 million people to 48.0 million (DeNavas-Walt, Proctor, and Smith, 2013, pp. 25–28). Though between 2010 and 2012, the percentage of the poorest Americans who are uninsured dipped slightly, taking the longer run, between 2002 and 2012, this figure actually increased by 2.5 percent.

Clearly illness—particularly mental disorders—are stigmatizing conditions that are inextricably intertwined with poverty. In a society where both respect and health partly depend on economic achievement, it must be pointed out that illness is strongly correlated with poverty and hence, disrespect (Twaddle, 1973). Illness, like poverty, results in Goffman's disqualification "from full social acceptance" (1963, p. i), though illness, like poverty, is mixed with compassion, and, as Goffman says, stigma (like deviance) is a matter of degree—physical illness perhaps being less socially discrediting. To the extent that physical illness is regarded as a *temporary* role out of which the usually normal person will emerge, it is correspondingly only temporarily deviant, but only to the extent that the normally well person refuses to do what he or she needs to do to get well, the condition is correspondingly socially regarded as deviant (Parsons, 1951a). *To the extent that* chronic physical illness and mental disorder disqualify the sick person from full social acceptance, they constitute stigmata—and hence, examples of deviance.

Virtually all generalizations come with qualification, and here's my qualification about poverty and ill health, and it's an important one: *Among the 17 most affluent, fully industrialized nations of the world, Americans live the shortest, most unhealthy lives, and are most likely to be killed or injured by accident and firearms homicide.* In 2013, the

National Research Council and the Institute of Medicine released a report, entitled *U.S. Health in International Perspective: Shorter Lives, Poorer Health*, indicating that the cumulative health and safety detriments added up to the conclusion that the United States occupied the worst ranking among the world's well-off nations with respect to health and safety. Americans had the second highest rate of death from heart disease, second highest for lung cancer, a rate of firearm homicide that is twenty times higher than other countries, and the highest with respect to diabetes. Three factors played a major role here, according to the panel that issued the report: First, because of its lopsided, inequitable income distribution, the United States has a substantially larger number and proportion of the population living in poverty; second, the United States harbors a "highly fragmented health care system," with poor primary care facilities and resources and a large uninsured sector of the population; and third, Americans tend to be more individualistic, more risk-taking, and are less likely to protect their safety—for instance, less likely to wear automobile seat belts, more likely to ride motorcycles without helmets, more likely to engage in risky, unprotected sex, more likely to get sick and die from illicit drug abuse. Hence, although all of my generalizations about the poor versus the less poor with respect to deviance and stigma still apply, we should keep in mind that with regard to matters of health and illness, *the United States is less well-off than the other affluent countries of the world.*

Everyone recognizes that leprosy has historically attracted contempt, scorn, disgust and horror (Cross, 2006). Although the stigma of HIV/AIDS has declined in recent years, Nyblade (2006) argues that shame and discrimination still accompany the condition. Has the stigma of tuberculosis disappeared? Not in many third world countries, although many health workers believe they can intervene in local settings to overcome it (Macq, Solis, and Martinez, 2006). Dalal (2006) details how intervention programs in India can remove discrimination against the physically challenged. In fact, interestingly, the entire health-related stigma issue is based on the "experience of activists, people 'in-the-field' with experiential knowledge of intervention designed to mitigate suffering as a result of labeling and discrimination." These activists aim to remove stigma from the lives of the unwell in order to "normalize" their lives (Scambler, Heijnders, and Brakel, 2006, p. 270). Stigma from which hospital patients suffer can be as debilitating as their diseases, and physicians have to battle on two fronts in order to cure them. In response, a group of physicians and scholars formed the "International Consortium for Research and Action Against Health-Related Stigma," and the editors of the journal devoted an entire issue of *Psychology, Health & Medicine* (August 2006, vol. 11, no. 3) to the topic. As I've said numerous times throughout this book, the social stigma of conditions that are "not the person's fault" is tragically unfair—but it is an aspect of the human condition in that life itself is unfair. Every one of us should struggle against injustice, but in order to do so, we must first recognize it. The stigma of both poverty and ill health is both unfair and manifestly true, and it is something that must be recognized so that it can be combatted.

RACE AND POVERTY

In the United States, race and poverty are densely and strongly intertwined; in comparison with persons of European and Asian background, those of African ancestry are statistically more likely to be poor. The same is true of person with a Latino or Hispanic heritage, though the tendency is not as pronounced, and many Latinos in the United States are recent arrivals, whose descendants are likely to rise in the class structure. The figures on race and poverty are stark and dramatic. According to the 2010 U.S. Census, conducted in 2010, African Americans (27.4%) and Hispanics (26.6%) are between two and three times as likely to live in poverty as whites (9.9%). Blacks are almost twice as likely to be unemployed (13.4% versus 7.0%). And consider Tables 4.1 and 4.2: Blacks earn 40 percent less than whites, and less than *half* of what

Asian Americans earn. And the total net financial worth of what African Americans own is roughly *one-twentieth* as much as that of whites. Moreover, during the second half of the first decade of the twenty-first century, the financial worth of blacks declined by half, 53 percent, while that of whites declined only 16 percent. The statistical difference in income and wealth between blacks and whites is substantial, and it is consequential—it has a strong negative impact on the material and emotional well-being of the lives of African Americans.

Consider this: Between 1995 and 2009, the ratio of the white-black median net worth rose from seven to one to nineteen to one; in other words, the *gap* between what whites have economically and what blacks have is growing over time. Many factors bring about income and net worth differences between the races, including one quite startling statistic: Blacks are much more likely to live in and grow up in a one-parent household (net worth: $2,850) than in a two-parent household (net worth: $81,250).

Our understanding of deviance is enriched by a consideration of the intersection of poverty and race. In the mid-nineteenth century, when immigrants of color arrived here from east and, later, south Asia, most entered the American economic structure as poorly-paid common laborers, and they encountered hostility, prejudice, and racial discrimination from the white majority. As they and their descendants rose in the economic ladder, Americans came to feel and express less racism toward them. But, as Herbert Gans explains (2005), for the most part, African Americans who have experienced upward mobility have not encountered reduced prejudice; why this is so, says Gans, "remains a mystery." Why does racial prejudice toward blacks remain so much stronger than that toward other nonwhites, even as the black middle class has expanded? Gans offers a variety of explanations, one of which is that the lowest economic

TABLE 4.1 MEDIAN INCOME OF FAMILIES BY RACE 2009

WHITE	BLACK	LATINO/ HISPANIC	ASIAN	TOTAL POPULATION
$62,545	$38,409	$39,730	$75,027	$60,088

Source: Pearson Education, Upper Saddle River, NJ.

TABLE 4.2   NET WORTH OF HOUSEHOLD, 2009, AND CHANGE IN NET WORTH, 2005–2009, BY RACE

WHITE	BLACK	LATINO/HISPANIC	ASIAN
$113,149	$5,677	$6,325	$69,590
−16%	−53%	−66%	−43%

Source: Pearson Education, Upper Saddle River, NJ.

quartile of the black population contributes a disproportionate share in the street crime which causes the substantial problems, not to mention fear and ill feelings, among the population at large. As a result, he says, "poor African Americans are more often considered undeserving" than members of other ethnic and racial categories and hence, are stigmatized; the stain of the troublesome sector of blacks has somehow not been removed by the mobility of those who have been successful (p. 20). Some scholars believe that the legacy of slavery continues to keep demonized stereotypes in play; African Americans "are still perceived as ex-slaves" (p. 20).

In addition, many whites believe that racial discrimination, even toward blacks, has virtually disappeared and the fact that a substantial proportion of blacks are stuck at the bottom of the class structure, "jobless and out of the work force," is blatant evidence to many in the white majority that they are lazy and aren't trying hard enough to escape poverty. Many whites have little empathy or even less understanding of the thousand and one ways that institutional racism blocks the upward path of striving African Americans and how shaky the footing is of those who lose their job in a sluggish economy and fall from middle-class grace. Gans also speculates that a considerable number of African American males feel that they must continually prove that they are worthy of "equal access to the American Dream" (p. 21). The resentment that some blacks feel as they watch white immigrants "pass them in the class hierarchy . . . gives whites additional evidence of their unworthiness, thereby justifying another cycle of efforts to keep them from moving up in class and status" (p. 21). Whether these or some other explanations account for the exceptionalism of racism against African American remains to be seen, but it's clear that a substantial percentage of whites are not ready to abandon their negative attitudes toward blacks, and that attitude bears strong parallels with those

that conventional members of society hold toward persons who have violated the norms of mainstream society. African Americans are, in the eyes of many white Americans, deviants. *In comparison with past decades*, whites are substantially less prejudiced toward African Americans than they were; *in comparison with their feelings toward other racial and ethnic minorities*, whites continue to harbor relatively high levels of ill-will toward blacks, even as they rise in the economic hierarchy.

SUMMARY

Achievement-oriented societies tend to stigmatize the poor; as it is measured—that is, by success— the value that virtually all Americans hold dear is one which the poor have failed to attain. Hence, even in societies with democratic, equalitarian ideals, shame and humiliation are likely to accompany poverty. For the most part, the rich, taken as a whole, feel superior to the poor who, in turn, tend to feel inferior to the rich. Hence, by itself, putting aside the relationship between income and engaging in deviant behaviors, *being poor is, by itself, a deviant condition.* Yet, with only a few exceptions, hardly any sociologists have discussed poverty as a *form* of deviance. Even so, a few sociologists and social commentators have made statements about the stigma of poverty, including Malthus, Marx and Engels, Weber, and, more recently, Matza, Lerner, Sen, Reyles, and Wacquant. For the most part, they have emphasized that the well-heeled construct a rationale for their good fortune and explanations for the ill-fortune of the poor. Throughout the world, although to a varying degree, the poor feel self-conscious about presenting themselves before persons better off than themselves, sensing themselves to be less worthy human beings. Being at the bottom of the heap results in marginality and powerlessness, exclusion, and indignity. Wacquant adds that the powerful have generated the means of further marginalizing the poor by disproportionately incarcerating them. Researchers have measured income levels and degrees of poverty in complex ways. Though these figures are precise, each yields slightly different numbers and percentages of the population as poor. The fact is, however, that roughly one American out of seven is officially living in poverty; unofficially, many more are poor.

The shrinking and, in some places, the collapse of the industrial economy has contributed to a hollowing-out of a substantial number of once-prosperous American cities, mainly in the Midwest, which depended on manufacturing. In addition, deindustrialization has reduced the "rippling out" effect of jobs and income, further impoverishing rural areas of the country that were poor to begin with. Both at the individual and the state level, education and income are linked; the higher the education, the higher the income, and vice versa. It's not clear which is the chicken and which the egg, but states with the lowest levels of education tend to be the poorest as well, and states with the highest per capita levels of education are also those with the highest income levels. Over time, in the United States, inequality in income distribution is growing. The old adage, "The rich are getting richer and the poor are getting poorer," is very close to the truth. In relative terms, the rich are earning an *enormously* larger percentage of the country's total Gross Domestic Production (GDP), while the income of the poor is earning a shrinking share of it, even though the total economic pie is immense, though, in recent years, stagnating. Among the twenty wealthiest countries of the world, that is, those with the highest per capita GDP, the United States has the greatest income inequality. In contrast, among all the countries of the world, in the small, affluent countries of northern Europe, income is distributed in the most equalitarian fashion; in contrast, in the less affluent countries of Africa, Asia, and Latin America, which encompass small, wealthy elites, the economies distribute income even less equitably.

In the United States, just under half of the population believe that the poor are responsible for their own poverty; in effect, they blame those at the bottom of the socioeconomic hierarchy for their economic condition. In contrast, just under half believe that factors beyond the control of the poor caused their economic circumstances. For much of the population, unemployment is considered shameful, and welfare, even more so; and for most of us, begging is the bottom of the economic barrel—that is, it is highly stigmatizing. The possession of good health, likewise is a valued commodity, and in affluent capitalist societies—especially the United States—the poor have less of it than the affluent. As a result of leading shorter, unhealthier lives, the poor are stigmatized and disvalued by the well-off, and by themselves as well. In the sense, the sick, especially the unhealthy poor, are stigmatized, held in disrepute. In the United States, and in some other affluent countries such as France and the United Kingdom, poverty is strongly correlated with race and ethnicity; the poor are more likely to belong to racial and ethnic minorities—in the United States, blacks and Latinos; in France, blacks and Muslims—than is true of the affluent. Racism is a stain on all democratic societies that is difficult for many American whites to wash away, even when they encounter affluent persons of African descent.

Account: Being Poor in Appalachia

The following two accounts were collected or written by students affiliated with Union College in Barbourville, KY; the authors choose to remain anonymous. I would like to thank Linda Silber for contacting these students and the students themselves for agreeing to allow me to use their accounts.

My Life of Poverty

Social stratification ranks people on a scale of social worth. This ranking influences life chances. How rich or poor people are is one such ranking. It can determine many aspects of a person's life, including friendships, how

(Continued)

Accounts: Being Poor in Appalachia   Continued

we are treated by others, our health, happiness, power, status—lots of things. When I grew up, my family was not completely destitute, but we did live on the poor side of town. I never felt as if I wasn't good enough or that I was missing out on anything. But in high school, the students started sorting themselves out into cliques. Money played a major part in how they made their friendships. If you came from a rich family, chances are, your best friend isn't going to be from the wrong side of the tracks, without a dime to his name; you're going to hang with someone who has money to do what you want to do when you want to do it.

I don't think we consciously chose not to be friends with someone outside of our own social class, we just found ourselves more comfortable around our own kind. In high school, the place where I fit in was with the kids who were living at or below the poverty level, where someone was automatically accepted—no questions asked. It seemed to me that you were either on one side of the poverty line or the other—you were either poor, or close to it, or you were comfortable, middle-class, whatever. I was supposed to feel grateful for just being in the same school and the same community as people who were well-heeled. "Don't bite the hand that feeds you" is a saying a lot of people live by. I guess I kind of expected equal treatment no matter what your background was. In my sophomore year, I got into a fight with a girl who called me a "fat-assed bitch." After I hit her, I was taken to an office where they sat us both down. After I explained what had happened, I was suspended for five days while the other girl was allowed to return to class. Once I went back to school I found out that her dad was a lawyer whose firm donated a lot of money to the school as well as various local causes. It wasn't a question of me being wrong and the other girl being right, it was that she came from money and I didn't. Throughout high school, I saw kids getting away with things that the poorer kids got a maximum punishment for, and it always came down to who their parents were in the community. Money seems to be the greatest form of power.

Everybody learns what their life chances are and where they are going to end up. You can see it in the way a shopkeeper stares intently at a poor kid because he thinks he's going to shoplift something, and he fails to notice that a rich girl drops a bracelet into her bag. You see it when a guidance counselor offers the poverty-stricken, straight-A student nothing but community college brochures, while the wealthy "C" kid gets applications to the more prestigious schools. You see it when local businessmen hire based on last names and not job qualifications. Everybody has expectations of who they meet, and it's usually based on how much money their parents have, not on who the person is.

Just because I came from a poor, lower-class family doesn't mean I had a horrible life. I love small-town life and I wouldn't give it up for anything. Class and status and money biases take place everywhere, not just in small towns. But in small, close-knit communities, these problems are more severe and more noticeable than in larger communities. When everyone knows everyone else and what family they came from, it's hard to make decisions about people based on anything else.

In my opinion, more emphasis is placed on money than should be. If we could look past the money and see who people really are, a lot of the problems of social class could be avoided. We should think about how to strengthen and grow our small towns rather than keeping them tight and closed off. Ruffling a few feathers might not be a bad idea. Money can't buy happiness but it does open up a lot of opportunities. Maybe everybody deserves the same breaks.

Poverty and the Drug Life

Growing up in Appalachia, I was exposed to the everyday abuse of alcohol, marijuana, and prescription drugs. I was the only girl in my family, and my childhood friends were mostly boys, so I had many early experiences that girls don't get exposed to until later in life. I started early, and my drug habits grew. Before long, I began selling, and eventually I was a major player in the drug game. Studies show that rural poverty, where job opportunities are rare, breeds illicit drug use and trafficking, and the rural areas of Kentucky are among the poorest in the country. Sometimes you just have to create your own economic opportunities.

When I was 13, I was introduced to alcohol. I'll never forget the experience. I was riding around with Tate, my best guy-friend, who was also 13. It was summer and it was hot. Tate drove his Dad's Trans-Am to our local bootlegger's house where we bought a couple of wine coolers. This bootlegger had hung the coolers from a tree branch in a cold mountain stream. Right off, first drink, I loved alcohol, and I drank like it was going out of style.

In my freshman year of high school, I was introduced to marijuana. I liked it, too. I smoked pot all through high school until I became pregnant. My child's father was a well-known drug dealer in the community, as were his brothers and many of his relatives. We grew marijuana and sold it. He often smoked pot but it was no big deal. I stopped smoking and drinking when I got pregnant, but I continued to sell marijuana. Since we had connections there, we moved to Georgia and built up a huge clientele. We made more money than I have ever seen before. After a year of selling pot, we returned home and bought a trailer and a new car with the money we made. After we returned, we tried to make a normal living to support ourselves, but we found that impossible, so we did what we do best—we grew and sold marijuana.

My son's father and I grew, cleaned, stripped, and sold marijuana to survive. I cleaned pot until my fingers were so sticky from the resin on the leaves that I couldn't pull them apart. Growing pot had become a way of life for many people in my community; doing it was a survival skill that had been passed down through the generations. Many local families depended on the leafy green plant to put food on the table and pay their bills. Poverty in Appalachia is real; some counties in southeastern Kentucky are nearly wholly dependent on the marijuana industry. But in recent years, prescription drugs have become a major recreational drug category, and selling them has become a major industry as well.

Substance abuse has been considered mainly a male problem and so, researchers have neglected the study of women's drug use. But a substantial number of women in my family have abused drugs, including my mother, who fell into prescription pill abuse. My mom became addicted to Xanax. She obtained legal prescriptions from her doctor, but when he retired, his replacement refused to write them for her, so she began buying them illegally from some people she knew. She eventually became addicted and, while I was in high school, she checked herself into rehab, kicked the habit, and, as far as I know, has remained clean. But many other people here in Appalachia have not received treatment for their addiction. Entering treatment is usually regarded as humiliating—evidence of the inability to take care of yourself. Fortunately, my mom recognized that she had a problem and she dealt with it.

In my opinion, people who enter a rehab program should not be humiliated; shame shouldn't be part of the treatment. All-too-often, stigma accompanies drug abuse and trafficking. If you are selling or using, society looks down on you. I never used prescription drugs, but I did sell them. My county ranks near the top with respect to number of prescriptions dispensed for painkillers. Sadly, one of the consequences of the abuse of pain-killers is drug overdoses; in our county, more people die from the abuse of pain-killers than from the use of illicit substances such as heroin or cocaine. Like marijuana, selling prescription drugs around here has become a way of life.

I'm convinced that poverty and drugs go hand-in-hand. If we understand why people abuse and sell drugs, we have the key to solving the drug problem. We also rank high in medical and psychiatric disability, such as depression; Kentucky is one of the most medicated states in the country, which makes prescription drug abuse highly likely. As for myself, while raising a family, there was always "too much month at the end of the money." In other words, there's never enough

(Continued)

Account: Being Poor in Appalachia   Continued

money for our basic needs—that's how my drug dealing evolved. To become self-sufficient, I had to learn the trade of drug trafficking, and I learned it well. I learned how to buy and sell drugs and earn money to pay the bills and provide for my son. I was never greedy and only sold to people I know really well. I didn't announce to the community that I was trafficking in drugs because it was shameful and embarrassing. My son's father died of an overdose of Oxycodone. His death was traumatic for me, and I explained to my son that he should never use drugs. You can't become addicted if you never use.

I obtained a college education so that I won't have to be in a position of selling drugs again. I don't want my children to learn that I have sold illegal drugs. I always try to be an example to my children and instill in them that it's not where you come from but who you turn out to be that counts. I tell them that if you work hard and try to be a good person, you will succeed in life. Unfortunately, lack of economic opportunity leads a great many people in poor communities to turn to drug selling to earn a living. The promise of quick money with little work makes trafficking appealing, especially when your family depends on you for support. In addition, in some communities, dealing is generationally entrenched. In order to dissuade children from selling drugs, an early education is necessary, and may mean the difference between living a happy, satisfied life and a lifetime in prison.

QUESTIONS

Are the poor stigmatized? Do the poor still feel shame in "going about" in shabby, dirty clothes, as Adam Smith said more than a quarter millennium ago? Is poverty a just cause for stigmatizing the poor? If it is unfair, why do people do it? How should sociologists treat, look at, or regard this process of poverty stigmatization? Should they ignore it—pretend it doesn't exist? Accept its reality but argue against it? Or do we accept the stigmatizing logic of the argument that people who live on government subsidies, many of whom are poor, are lazy, unmotivated, unwilling to work, and entitled to hand-outs—that the poor are legitimately a species of deviants? Do the poor have the right to engage in illegal activities to survive economically? Can we see a parallel between being poor and the stealing of a loaf of bread—as was depicted in *Les Misérables*—and being poor and selling marijuana? How do we explain poverty? Could any one of us, as a result of accidental, fortuitous circumstances, have become poor? Do you believe, with regard to poverty, "There but the grace of God, go I"? Why does poverty vary so much from one society to another? And why is it *distributed* so differently from one society to another? What generates wealth? Do the rich have a responsibility to help the poor? How do we equalize incomes? Can we? *Should* we equalize incomes? Is poverty a legitimate topic for the sociology of deviance?

Crime and Criminalization

Learning Objectives:

After reading this chapter, you will be able to:

- recognize the conceptual distinction between crime and deviance;
- compare and contrast common law with statutory law;
- understand the difference between constructionism and positivism;
- discuss the Uniform Crime Reports;
- define "violent crime";
- define "property crime";
- understand the social construction of murder;
- discuss how a criminologist looks at murder;
- understand the role of the National Crime Victimization Survey in the study of crime and deviance;
- define "forcible rape";
- examine property crime as deviance.

On December 14, 2012, a tall, thin man barely out of his teens, wearing combat gear and armed with a small arsenal of assault weapons, walked into Sandy Hook Elementary School near Newtown, Connecticut and, one after the other, entered two classrooms and began firing at children and adults alike. After he stopped, he shot himself in the head. He killed everyone he hit except one and left behind twenty dead children and six adults. The authorities identified the shooter as Adam Lanza of Newtown. Later, the police searched his home and found his mother's body; she had also been shot to death. His former classmates described Lanza as "intelligent and shy." No immediate motive seemed apparent for the attack (Barron, 2012). Coincidentally, that same morning, in a small village in China, a man with a knife attacked twenty-two children and one adult in an elementary school; nine victims were admitted to a nearby hospital, and not one was killed.

In Manhattan, a forty-five-year-old suburban mother pleads guilty to running a brothel. In Trenton, New Jersey, the mayor is charged with accepting bribes in exchange for selling city property at below market value. At the University of Colorado, authorities allow students to carry guns on the campus. A woman in the Bronx is charged with manslaughter for starting a fire that killed her boyfriend and injured several other people. The government of Turkey demands the return of a substantial number of art works now housed by several of the world's largest museums, including New York's Metropolitan Museum of Art, claiming they were stolen—illegally excavated without permit and sold without legitimate provenance. In China, a former communist leader is charged with numerous serious crimes, including taking bribes, abusing power, and having sex with women other than his wife. In Iran, a journalist is convicted of the crime of telling lies of "propaganda." At a college in Nigeria, attackers kill more than twenty-five students; authorities believe it to be the work of a factional conflict stemming from a campus election.

Just down the road from Cadereyta Jiménez, a Mexican town, residents discovered forty-nine headless bodies, "their hands and feet severed." Then they were towed away and buried. "Of course it is all scary," said Francisco Umberta, a resident, "but what are you going to do?" That night found him near a crowded Chili's restaurant waiting to buy tickets to *The Avengers*. He had heard about the slaughter, but commented that the regional soccer tournament attracted more public attention. "It's not like we're all paralyzed. . . . We still need to live while they do what they do." Over 16,000 organized crime-related murders took place in Mexico in 2011, and roughly 50,000 since 2006. "We know nothing is changing—it just goes on," said Imelda Santos, who was eating a hamburger with friends. "We try not to worry too much because we are not involved" (Archibold and Cave, 2012, pp. A1, A3). Why hasn't the human carnage spilled into the United States? El Paso, across the Rio Grande from Ciudad Juárez, is one of the safest cities in America, with a 2011 homicide rate of 2.40—only half that of the United States as a whole.

In this chapter, I'll indicate how crime both overlaps with and differs from deviance, and how explanatory theories and the constructionist approach diverge in the manner in which their practitioners look at them. Crime and deviance interpenetrate, yet the researchers who study each look at their subjects with a somewhat different mission in mind, and they usually study their subjects in different ways as well. Criminal homicide, or murder, and "nonnegligent manslaughter," are among the rarest yet most well-known and most publicized of crimes. The killing of a human being attracts a great deal of media and textbook attention; in contrast, to cite a common crime, the theft of a book or a CD—unless it is committed by a celebrity—does not. Though criminologists examine the full spectrum of crimes, their interest tends to be most attracted to the most paradigmatic of them—the "Index Crimes," meaning those crimes criminologists and the police believe reflect crime in general—which include homicide, rape, robbery, aggravated assault, motor vehicle theft, burglary, and larceny-theft.

CRIME AND DEVIANCE: A CONCEPTUAL DISTINCTION

Draw a four-fold table indicating crime and not-crime, and cross-tabulate it with deviance and not-deviance. In one of the four cells, you can write down instances or cases that are *both* crimes and deviance (for instance, murder and robbery); in another, instances that are *neither* crimes nor deviance (taking a shower once a day, reading a newspaper); in a third, those that are deviance but not crimes (over-eating, wearing out-of-fashion clothes). These three cells make intuitive sense; we can imagine examples of each. But in the fourth, you've created the possibility of acts that are *criminal but not deviant*. Is the fourth cell even possible? Or is it a "null" cell—theoretically conceivable but empty of real-world examples. Let's see. Crime is *official* deviance; it is wrong-doing that attracts *formal* sanctions—that is, possible arrest and imprisonment. Crime is deviance on steroids. It's no longer just a matter of ordinary people reacting interpersonally to offenses among them. In crime, the offender causes the criminal justice system—the police, the courts, and the jails and prisons—to get involved in the punishment of the supposed miscreant. The most serious crimes, particularly rape, murder, and armed robbery, represent instances of "high consensus deviance." They are the crimes, and the forms of deviance, that attract the most attention, the greatest condemnation, and the severest penalties.

Going back to our four-fold table, some deviant acts are criminal though most are not; in the United States, virtually no belief or physical condition is criminal. Obesity, being a creep, a loser, a geek, a dweeb, an eccentric, an atheist, and an alcoholic, are all deviant—but they are not crimes. In other words, clearly, crime is not a definitional precondition for deviance.

What about the other way around? Are all crimes deviant? Most of the mainstream public regards having been convicted of and, even more so, imprisoned for a crime, as stigmatizing. True, in some social circles, being an ex-con brings a certain measure of hip, edgy, romantic cachet. But the more conventional the audience, the more discrediting it regards imprisonment. And also true, many Americans harbor a reformist ethic, believing that in the heart of every ex-con is a former offender who is now a better person. Still, in that sense, yes—though, again, crime is not a *defining* criterion of deviance—criminality is one specific *type* of deviance, one that many offenders would like to put in their past. By itself, *being* a criminal is deviant because it can stigmatize a person in the eyes of many audiences.

But *independent* of its stigmatizing character, is violating the criminal code a form of deviance?

Are laws a type of norm the violation of which constitutes deviance? Here, we have to distinguish "formally illegal behavior" from criminal behavior. Many white collar crimes are against the law, but statutes criminalizing white collar and even corporate wrongdoing are difficult to enforce, are virtually never policed, and rarely attract the kinds of stigma that the Index Crimes do. On the other hand, *criminal* behavior is that which is likely to get the perpetrator arrested and prosecuted; by this definition, *all* criminal behavior is deviant behavior, since it attracts negative reactions—that is, formal sanctioning.

A broad definition of deviance sees *any and all* punishing or condemnatory reactions—regardless of whether they come from a friend, acquaintance, relative, or the criminal justice system—as the defining criteria of deviance. According to this definition, a crime is a violation of one specific *kind* of norm—a law—which generates formal, state-supported sanctions, including prosecution, conviction, and imprisonment. Clearly then, according to this definition, *all* crime is deviant. (Again, some laws are not enforced; hence, they are not actionable crimes in the sense that their violation does not generate formal sanctions.) But to repeat, the reverse does not hold: Crime does not *define* deviance. Instead, this definition sees laws as a *type* of norm, and criminal punishment a type of condemnation or punishment. Hence, crime is a *form* or *subtype* of deviance. Of course, there's also the possibility that a supposed offender *didn't do it*—is innocent of committing the crime. In that case, is being unjustly labeled or *defined* as a criminal offender so stigmatizing that the supposed offender has become a deviant? This is hypothetical since we are assuming a conviction without any guilt; no one knows it but us. And so, of course, such a person would be defined as *a* deviant.

The *analytic* or *theoretical* concepts that run through every course on deviance—and which will run through this book—also apply to any number of illegal actions. Such concepts include the social construction of reality, deviance neutralization, vocabularies of motive, stigma, stigma management, condemnation, identity, subculture, moral entrepreneurs, power, social conflict, and contingency. In addition, many theories of deviance are *also* theories of crime. The most important thing about both deviance and crime is not the specific details of each activity—important though they are—but the insight that studying them give us concerning how society works. What the study of both deviance and crime are "about" is primarily the exercise of social control, the dynamics of normative violations, and the possibility of punishment. The details about each form of behavior should serve the concepts, not the other way around. In other words, though there are important differences between stealing and abusing drugs, or being a transvestite and a robber, they all share a "common thread": Each is to some degree interpersonally stigmatizing from mainstream society's point of view.

A kind of rough "division of labor" exists between the fields of the sociology of crime and the sociology of deviance. By that I mean that different sets of scholars focus on somewhat different subject matters. Specialists in crime, often referred to as criminologists, tend to focus on behavior (almost never beliefs, and *never* physical conditions) that generate *formal* sanctioning, as well as the origin, dynamics, and consequences of that sanctioning itself. In contrast, deviance specialists tend to focus on behavior, beliefs, and conditions that generate *informal* sanctioning, as well as the origin, dynamics, and consequences of the informal sanctioning itself.

Consider the types of behavior discussed in a typical criminology text: violent crime, property crime, white collar crime, organized crime, and public order (formerly called "moral") crime, the last focusing mainly on drug use and sale, and sex offenses, such as prostitution (Siegel, 2011). In contrast, consider the kinds of behaviors (and conditions) discussed by the fourteenth edition of the classic, *Sociology of Deviant Behavior* (Clinard and Meier, 2011), whose first edition appeared in 1957: interpersonal violence, non-violent crime, white collar and corporate crime, drug use and addiction, drunkenness and alcoholism, suicide, heterosexual deviance, homosexuality, homophobia, physical disability, mental disorders, and "recent" forms of deviance, such as rudeness, bullying, cyber deviance, and teachers abusing their students. Again, we see both overlap and divergence between the topics investigated by criminologists versus those looked at by sociologists of deviance. Many actions that

attract interpersonal sanctioning are not against the law; they are not arrestable offenses. But virtually all offenses that can attract arrest and criminal prosecution are to a significant degree stigmatizing—or "deviantizing."

COMMON LAW AND STATUTORY LAW

Western society distinguishes two different types of criminal laws—common law (sometimes called "primal" law) and statutory law. (Here, we won't look at *civil* law—defined as all law other than criminal law—which includes *contract* and *property* law, and *torts*, or actions intended to obtain compensation by a wronged party.) Common law stems from ancient custom, tradition, and precedent. Most legal experts regard common law as a set of rules that defines acts as crimes that violate norms that have existed for thousands of years. Common law existed even before societies enacted norms into written statutes. These laws are based on the *unwritten* law (or, later, court decisions *based* on these norms, which were decided by a courtroom judge rather than adjudicated by a legislature). Laws against murder, robbery, and rape are examples of common or "primal" law. Their violations are referred to as "high-consensus" crimes because practically everyone in any society, practically everywhere on the globe, agrees that laws against them should exist and are valid and legitimate. The implication of common law is that it does not come into being as a result of the pressure of special interest groups but has the force of tradition behind it. In the United States, nearly all common law has been enacted into statutes by a legislature—a formal body of elected or appointed officials. Nonetheless, violations of these laws had been punished, with the force of sanction of the society as a whole, long before they were inscribed on paper, parchment, wood, or stone.

The history of common law, then, was a three-step process. First, such laws *began* as tradition (the violations of which were "primal" crimes); then (at least in England) were codified juridically, in the courtroom, by legal precedent; and finally (at least in the United States) they were enacted into statutory form.

In contrast, laws whose existence *began* as statutes (known collectively as "statutory law") have a history that is completely different from laws that began in the common-law tradition. Most statutory laws refer to crimes for which there are *no* roots in historical or cultural tradition. Most also tend to have less than complete public consensus concerning their legal status. Statutory laws arose because technological change made certain controls necessary (those regulating computer crimes, for instance); because conflict between social categories in the population resulted in the triumph of a more restrictive or moralistic group's views over those of more permissive groups (for instance, the liquor laws); or because social change or innovations or discoveries generate new situations, activities, or substances (such as laws criminalizing the possession and sale of psychoactive substances).

Consider gambling. Our current gambling statutes, such as they are, are statutory laws. Only a small percentage of the population currently feels that gambling should be a crime; in effect, the struggle over their criminalization has been lost. The government permits many forms of gambling, which substantially undermines the possibility of extending the reach and force of any proposed gambling statutes. And in Western society, gambling laws do not have the reach or heft of thousands of years of tradition behind them. Unlike murder, forcible rape, and robbery, gambling was not always considered a crime; for the past couple of thousand years, gambling was considered an entertainment or a pleasurable vice which some members of the society engaged in while others didn't, or feebly objected to.

Corporate and white collar crimes, likewise, do not carry the force and authority of historical tradition. For the most part, they came into existence by being defined *as crimes* only in the twentieth century, and only as a consequence of statutes, that is, the decisions of a legislature. In fact, many of the very activities proscribed by the laws against white collar crime *did not even exist* a few decades ago. Many statutes addressing corporate malfeasance are extremely technical, and a violation of them can be understood only as a result of knowledge not available to the general public.

The drug laws likewise are statutory in nature. In the United States, except for some local ordinances, most of the drug laws did not exist before the twentieth century. And, although nine out of ten Americans believe that possession and sale of the "hard" drugs (such as heroin and cocaine) should remain a crime, nearly three-quarters of the public believe that marijuana possessors and users should not be imprisoned. And a substantial majority of voters (about 80%) believe that the *medical* distribution, possession, and use of marijuana—which nonetheless violates federal law—should be legal. In short, there is a certain measure of disagreement over the criminal status of many statutory crimes.

Unlike the primal or common law that has a history of thousands of years, most illegal behavior defined by a set of statutes ("statutory law") is often subject to change over time, and may vary from one jurisdiction to another. Prior to 1973, abortion was illegal in the United States; today it is legal. The pro-life movement challenges the legitimacy of abortion legalization, aiming to return to some form of criminalization. Before the 1930s, the possession and sale of marijuana was legal; after that decade, they became illegal in every jurisdiction in the country. Then, beginning in the 1970s, more than a dozen states decriminalized small-quantity marijuana possession (no arrest, no imprisonment, no criminal record), and eighteen have made medical marijuana legal. In the early 1960s, homosexual acts between consenting adults were against the law; today, states have abolished their laws against such behavior, and the Supreme Court ruled such statutes unconstitutional. (Sexual solicitation in a public place, however, remains illegal in many jurisdictions.) The legislative status of the sale of alcohol has come full circle over the years, from legal to illegal to legal in most jurisdictions. Not possessing the force of tradition behind them, most statutory laws sway with the shifting winds of public opinion or malleable legislative mandate.

However, even for the primal or common-law crimes, a measure of relativity exists, not so much with respect to whether the actions are against the law or whether they are considered wrong, but with respect to judging the behavior criminal according to *when*, *by whom*, and *under what circumstances* such acts were committed. By that I mean that ancient societies often permitted *certain* parties to inflict harmful actions against others, but punished those same actions if they were inflicted against inappropriate parties. For instance, if a man committed forcible or violent intercourse upon a woman, the judgment of the members of a given society as to whether or not it was rape depended on a variety of factors, including the power, social standing, and tribal affiliation of the family of both the man and the woman. Likewise, the killing of a member of a society other than one's own was often considered acceptable—indeed, it may even have been encouraged—but if it involved a member of one's own society, clan, or tribe, the offender would be punished. Moreover, during periods of turmoil and widespread bloodshed—in Vietnam in the 1960s and early 1970s, Cambodia in the 1970s, Rwanda, Kosovo, Somalia, and Ethiopia in the 1990s, and Liberia in the early part of the twenty-first century—killings on a mass scale have been condoned by the regimes in power or by some sectors of the local populace.

While primal crimes have existed for thousands of years, the judgment as to the legality of specific instances of them has varied according to local custom and tradition. Even today, the taking of human life is condoned under certain conditions—for instance, legal execution, warfare, and in some jurisdictions, euthanasia. On one side of a border between Israel and the West Bank and Gaza, a killing may be regarded as an act of heroism, and on the other, murder. In Afghanistan, is a suicide bomber a murderer? To the relatives of the people he or she killed, and to the authorities in the jurisdiction where the act took place, the answer to this question is obvious: *absolutely*! To many of the bomber's friends, compatriots, political allies, co-religionists, and like-minded conspirators, the answer is equally clear-cut: The act was justified and the actor is a martyr—not a murderer. Murder may be a primal crime, condemned everywhere and at all times, but *what murder is*, is socially constructed. The term, "murder," refers not simply to a killing of one human being by another—but to an unjustified, unauthorized, unlawful, *deviant* killing.

WHAT IS OUR MISSION? CONSTRUCTIONISM VERSUS POSITIVISM

The fact that even common law crimes are interpreted differently according to who the perpetrator and who the actor are tells us that we can view crime *as* a social construct. It is constructed by definitions—called laws—and interpretations *of* those laws that regard certain actions as unlawful, worthy of punishment, while other, objectively similar actions are seen as acceptable and noncriminal. And, as we saw, even the same action may be regarded as a crime or not a crime according to the circumstances of the act; the constructionist is interested in these circumstances. What makes an act a crime *here,* but a law-abiding action *there*? For certain criminal statutes, consensus does not exist, and the laws change from one decade to another. Looked at as a social construct, legislation is not simply a product of abstract right or wrong but the outcome of conflict, with a different segment of the society attempting to gain the upper hand and pass a law favorable to its views and interests. If circumstances were to change, matters could reverse, and the law would be rewritten to reflect that fact. How the laws change, how they are interpreted, how they vary from one jurisdiction and society to another, how the circumstances of the act and the characteristics of the actor influence arrest, conviction, and incarceration: Answering these questions is the social constructionist's mission.

There is a big "*but*," however. We've all heard the phrase, "Everything is relative." With regard to crime, this platitude is not completely true. *In addition* to the relativity we see in what's a crime from one time period to another and from one society to another, there is also a *common core* to crime. As we already know, some crimes have existed—*as punishable offenses*—nearly everywhere, and for many thousands of years. Hence, crime remains a mixed bag. Many crimes look very similar the world over, in all societies that exist now or that have ever existed. (But again, just which specific *actions* committed by which specific *actors* against which specific *victims* is highly variable.) Murder is illegal and is prosecuted the world over, just as it has been from the dawn of humanity. But the word, "murder," is a loaded term; it refers specifically to what is considered a *deviant, unlawful,* and *illegitimate* killing. Taking property not one's own by force is regarded as an offense everywhere. (During warfare and violent ethnic conflict, stealing may be regarded as acceptable; during such times, many observers or audiences do not regard theft by their peers against outsiders as criminal.) But *who* steals, and *from whom* he or she steals, may transform the act from a punishable offense to a justifiable act. A man having sex, by force, with a woman is likewise criminal behavior in all jurisdictions known to criminologists—though it is not equally vigorously prosecuted everywhere—and whether or not sufficient force or sexual provocation took place is often disputed by an array of audiences; moreover, in many places of the world, who the perpetrator and who the victim is, will mitigate the nature and seriousness of the offense. *As a general rule*, there is a set of statutes that exists everywhere, and if violated, arrest, prosecution, and imprisonment are likely to follow, given certain preconditions. In contrast, consider the fact that such acts as blasphemy, heresy, professing atheism, and practicing a variety of minority religions were crimes centuries ago, but in the Western world, they are not. In Muslim countries, however, blasphemy is a crime. In Pakistan, in August of 2012, a Christian girl was jailed and booked on the charge of the country's blasphemy laws; her crime—burning the pages of a textbook designed for the instruction of the Quran to children. A crowd formed outside the police station where she was being held, demanding that the girl face the charges; some of her Christian neighbors fled the area, "fearing for their lives" (Walsh and Masood, 2012). Also in 2012, in Afghanistan, members of the Taliban attempted to murder a fourteen-year-old girl by shooting her in the face. Her offense? She attended school and urged other girls to do so, a violation of Taliban's notion of strict, pious Muslim behavior for females. The girl survived and good Samaritans rescued her and flew her to a hospital in the United Kingdom, where she is now convalescing. The majority of Muslims everywhere condemned Taliban's action and prayed for the girl's full recovery. Nonetheless, in certain regions of Afghanistan, Taliban's medieval notions of right and wrong—especially those having to do with *what constitutes murder*—have to be reckoned with.

One of the positivist's missions is the study of the causes of widely criminally prosecuted acts. Behavior that is regarded as criminal nearly everywhere is the principal subject matter of the field of criminology. "Common core" crimes also constitute the "common core" of the subject matter of criminology; nearly all criminology textbooks contain one or more chapters on what the Federal Bureau of Investigation (FBI) calls the Index Crimes: as we saw, murder, robbery, rape, aggravated assault, burglary, motor vehicle theft, and larceny-theft. (In 1979, by congressional mandate, the Uniform Crime Reports included arson as an Index Crime; few criminologists pay much attention to arson.) The majority of criminologists study the causes, consequences, and control of common law or street crimes, acts that are defined as criminal throughout history and in most or nearly all places of human habitation. The FBI collects and publishes information on crimes known to the police, and on arrests. The data on "crimes known to the police" are collected only for Index Crimes. The study of these classic "street" crimes is the "meat and potatoes" of the positivist's mission, and it makes up the bulk of the field's textbooks. There is a measure of consistency the world over in what is regarded as street or Index-type Crimes. So there is a common core to what's considered criminal behavior; what's regarded as a legally punishable offense is not random, not entirely dependent on the characteristics of the offender, and not completely relative from one time and place to another.

Criminologists *also* study non-Index Crimes. Just because statutes came into existence only in the past century or the past few decades does not mean that their violation is not harmful to society, or that their understanding is not important for the criminologist's mission. As we saw, drug laws are statutory laws, and understanding the whys and wherefores of substance abuse and trafficking is just as crucial as understanding why the drug *laws* came into existence and how they are enforced. The abuse of certain drugs may cause as much objective harm to a society as the common law crimes do—although whether the laws contribute to more harm or prevent a certain measure of harm is still hotly debated. Laws governing white collar and corporate crime are of an even greater impact on society than the commission of most street crime. One of the more interesting facts about the relationship of deviance and crime is that while corporate crime steals more money from, and inflicts more bodily harm on the public than is true of common property crimes, committing such offenses is not as interpersonally stigmatizing as engaging in street crime. In a like fashion, organized crime, political crime (such as treason), sexual offenses against children, violations of the laws against weapons possession, driving under the influence of alcohol, the sale of alcohol to minors, and fraud—none of which are Index Crimes—have important consequences for society, and are therefore studied by criminologists. Still, the Index Crimes are most characteristic, typical, and paradigmatic of crime in general, and when criminologists generalize about crime, they are the ones researchers generalize about.

THE UNIFORM CRIME REPORTS

The FBI divides the Index Crimes into violent crime—or rape, murder (or criminal homicide), robbery, and aggravated assault—and property crime (burglary, motor vehicle theft, and larceny-theft). The Index Crimes are *predatory* crimes: They entail one or more parties *victimizing* one or more other parties. The so-called "public order" or "moral" crimes include drug and alcohol offenses and sex crimes, a discussion of which is often found in deviance textbooks; they are not considered predatory crimes—they are consensual, "victimless," or non-victim crimes, "crimes without victims." (Of course, a person may victimize himself or herself, or victimize others *during the course of*, or as a result of engaging in, consensual crime.) Each type of crime, in its own way, highlights the relationship between deviance and crime.

The FBI's annual *Crime in the United States* (the Uniform Crime Reports, or UCR) is based on the population's reporting of crimes *to the police*. (Or the police coming upon such crimes themselves, through their own observation or investigation.) Critics have extensively and strongly criticized the UCR's data on the incidence and rate of crimes; officials representing cities that these data indicate are "unsafe" are especially critical (Rosenfeld and Lauritsen, 2008). The reporting by the police in some cities is no doubt more complete than for others. The main lesson to take away from this hailstorm of controversy and criticism is that some Index Crimes are substantially under-reported, as indicated by other ways of estimating rates of crime, for instance, victimization surveys (Truman and Planty, 2012); when researchers compare other data sources with the figures in the UCR, they find that criminal behavior is considerably more frequent than is indicated by police reports, and the discrepancies are systematic, not random. However, criminologists believe that the statistics reporting murder and motor vehicle theft are fairly complete—that is to say, they think that at least 75 to 80 percent of the time these two crimes take place, they are reported. But judging from victimization surveys, assault and rape are at least two or three times more common than the police data indicate. The FBI has collected the data reported in the UCR's *Crime in the United States* since 1930. Every year, roughly 12,500 law enforcement agencies, making up over 90 percent of the population, send to Washington such vital information as crimes reported (or "known") to law enforcement, the characteristics of victims, the geographic locale of the offense, number of offenses "cleared," usually by arrest, the demographic characteristics of arrestees, and information about law enforcement personnel.

In each jurisdiction, when Part I offenses (the Index Crimes) are reported to the police, they are "founded" (established as valid), recorded, and tabulated by each jurisdiction, then, yearly, the totals are sent to the FBI, which adds up their incidence nationwide. The FBI adds the number of murders, rapes, robberies, and aggravated assaults together to produce a *violent crime rate*. In 1992, this figure was 757.7 per 100,000 in the population (see Table 5.1), and in 2011, this rate was 386.3, a remarkable and unprecedented decline of almost 50 percent. Between 2010 and 2011, the violent crime rate dropped 3.8 percent. The FBI adds burglary, larceny-theft, and motor vehicle theft together to obtain a *property crime index*. In 1992, the property crime rate or index in the United States stood at 5,140.2, and in 2011, 2,908.7—a substantial drop of nearly 43 percent; the 2010–2011 property crime rate declined by 1.3 percent. For all of the Index Crimes, we see a substantial decline since the 1990s (Zimring, 2007); the same decline is demonstrated in victimization studies (Bastian, 1993; Truman and Planty, 2012), so this is not a figment of differential under-reporting.

This decline has not occurred in all jurisdictions or neighborhoods of the United States, but it did take place in the country *as a whole*. In 2011, roughly 9 million property crimes were reported to the police, and 1.2 million violent crimes—and property crime is *hugely* more under-reported in comparison to violent crime. Non-Index or Part II offenses include drug abuse violations, weapons possession, drunk and disorderly conduct, embezzlement, prostitution, and receiving stolen property; they are recorded in the UCR only when they result in arrest. The data in the UCR are referred to as "official" crime statistics. It's probably best to be skeptical of the UCR's tally of the incidence and rate of all the Index Crimes—except for criminal homicide and motor vehicle theft, which are as valid as we're likely to find. Still, we'll take a look at the UCR's data to give us a clue to the big picture of crime.

VIOLENT CRIME

The FBI defines murder and "non-negligent manslaughter" as the "willful . . . killing of one human being by another." Murder is willfully causing the death of another person. "Non-negligent homicide" refers to a killing in which one person becomes provoked and kills another "in the heat of passion." It encompasses all circumstances under which no prior intent to kill existed. Deaths caused by negligence, suicide, or accident, justifiable homicide (an officer of the law willfully killing a felon in pursuit of his or her legal duty), and attempted murder are not included. In addition, the killing of a felon, "during the commission of a felony, by a private citizen" (if so determined by law enforcement investigation) is not considered murder. But a non-intentional "felony murder," a death that occurs during the course of a felony, *is* murder. For instance, if a resident has a heart attack and dies when a perpetrator commits burglary, that's a felony-murder, and therefore, murder; the intent to kill someone is irrelevant. From now on, following the FBI, we'll refer to all criminal homicides, both "murder" and "non-negligent manslaughter," as *murder*. Murder is *by far* the least common Index Crime, and one of the rarer crimes on the books; in the most recent year, it makes up less than 1 percent of all violent crimes. In 2011, the FBI tabulated slightly fewer than 15,000 murders in the United States, a rate of 4.7 per 100,000 in the population, a decline from 9.3 in 1992—or just under 50 percent, a truly remarkable drop.

The FBI defines forcible rape as "the carnal knowledge of a female forcible and against her will. Assaults and attempts to commit rape by force or threat of force are also included; however statutory rape (without force) and other sex offenses are excluded." Sexual attacks on males "are counted as aggravated assaults or sex offenses, depending on the circumstances." Forcible rape is the most under-reported of the violent crimes. The rate of *reported* rapes declined sharply between the early 1990s (42.8 per 100,000 in 1992) and 2011 (26.8), a drop of 37 percent.

The FBI defines robbery as "the taking or attempting to take anything of value from the care, custody, or control of a person or persons by force or threat of force or violence and/or putting the victim in fear." By definition, robbery is an interpersonal, face-to-face, or *confrontational* crime. It always entails force, violence, or the threat of violence. Simple theft and burglary are not robbery. Robbery entails both violence—or the threat of violence—and the theft of property, but its violent character is much more interesting to criminologists than its larcenous quality, and it is also more significant to the general public; hence, the FBI classifies it as a crime of violence. Robbery is a very serious crime and, compared to simple theft, is relatively rare. Roughly a quarter of all robberies are not reported to the police. The decline of the robbery rate in the United States has been more spectacular than for any other violent Index Crime; in 1992, it stood at 263.7 per 100,000, while by 2011, it had dropped to 113.7, a decline of 57 percent. The FBI estimates that roughly $450 million was stolen in the latter year through acts of robbery, an average of $1,244 per offense. To put monetary value into perspective, consider the fact that Bernard Madoff, a recently-imprisoned stock market swindler, stole an estimated $50 to $65 billion dollars—more than a hundred times the value of what *all* the robbers supposedly took during 2011, added together. Obviously, the emotional impact of robbery far outweighs its relatively small monetary weight.

The Federal Bureau of Investigation defines aggravated assault as "an unlawful attack by one person upon another for the purpose of inflicting severe or aggravated bodily injury." The crime, to quote the FBI, is "usually" (but not always) "accompanied by the use of a weapon or by other means likely to produce death or great bodily harm." The line between "aggravated" (or serious) and "simple" (less serious) assault is not always easy to draw; it is a matter of degree. A punch in the nose is not usually classified as aggravated assault, though it is usually *simple* assault. Being shot or stabbed in the stomach and having to receive medical attention to survive, getting hit over the head with a baseball bat or being battered by an assailant's fists, resulting in a fractured skull, a concussion, broken ribs, and a trip to the hospital, *are* aggravated assault. Many serious assaults that take place in a domestic situation—most commonly, a husband battering his wife—are not reported to law enforcement. Like the other violent crimes, serious assault declined substantially between 1992 and 2011.

PROPERTY CRIME

As all data everywhere around the world indicate, property crime is *much* more common than violent crime; over 85 percent of Index Crimes that are reported to the police in the United States are property crimes. Burglary, a property crime, is "the unlawful entry of a structure to commit a felony or theft. The use of force to gain entry is not required to classify an offense as a burglary," although degrees of seriousness are determined by whether the entry is forcible or not. And nothing need be stolen for an act to qualify as a burglary. Only about a quarter of all burglaries are reported. In 1992, the country racked up a total of just under 3 million reported burglaries; by 2011, the total had dropped to 2.2 million, a decline of roughly 40 percent.

Larceny-theft is a grab-bag category; it includes acts of stealing that are not robbery, not burglary, not the theft of a motor vehicle, and not "embezzlement, confidence games, forgery, and [writing and attempting to pass] worthless checks." The FBI defines larceny-theft as "the unlawful taking, carrying, leading, or riding away of property from the possession or constructive possession of another; attempts to do these acts are included in this definition. This crime category includes pocket-picking, purse-snatching, thefts from motor vehicles, thefts of motor vehicle parts and accessories, bicycle thefts, and so forth." More larceny-thefts are reported to the police than all other Index Crimes put together; even so, proportionally speaking, larceny-theft is the most under-reported of all serious crimes, although in absolute numbers, more are reported than for any other crime. Roughly two-thirds of all property crimes reported to the police are larceny-thefts; 6.16 million larceny-thefts were reported in the United States in 2011, down from just under 8 million in 1992. Obviously, the greater the amount stolen, the greater the likelihood that the victim will report the theft to the police. According to the FBI, in 2011, larceny-theft offenses cost victims a shade over $6 billion, for an average of $988 per offense. The rate of larceny-theft in the United States declined during the 1992–2011 period by just under 40 percent.

And lastly, there is motor vehicle theft, "the theft or attempted theft of a motor vehicle. This offense includes the stealing of automobiles, trucks, busses, motorcycles, snowmobiles, etc." (About three-quarters of all vehicles reported stolen in 2011 were automobiles.) Today, the rate is fairly low, 229.6 per 100,000 in the population, considerably lower than it was in 1992 (631.6)—a stupendous 64 percent decline, more precipitous than for any other Index Crime. To judge by victimization surveys, among Index Crimes, motor vehicle theft is most likely to be fully reported (81%), except, perhaps, murder.

THE SOCIAL CONSTRUCTION OF MURDER

Paramount among the primal crimes is murder. Of all prohibitions, we might expect that the prohibition against murder is the one that is completely universal. As far as archaeologists, historians, and anthropologists are able to tell, every society that has ever existed has had a taboo against murder. If a primal crime can be said to exist, surely this is

TABLE 5.1   THE FBI'S INDEX CRIMES (UCR), 1992–2011

| | 1992 | | 2011 | | 1992–2011 |
	NUMBER	RATE	NUMBER	RATE	DECLINE
Violent Crime	1,932,274	757.7	1,203,564	386.3	−49%
Murder	23,760	9.3	14,612	4.7	−49%
Forcible Rape	109,062	42.8	83,425	26.8	−37%
Robbery	672,478	263.7	354,396	113.7	−57%
Aggravated Assault	1,126,974	440.5	751,131	241.1	−45%
Property Crime	12,505,917	5,140.2	9,063,173	2,908.7	−43%
Burglary	2,979,884	1,168.4	2,188,005	702.2	−40%
Larceny-theft	7,915,199	3,229.1	6,159,795	1,976.9	−39%
Motor vehicle theft	1,610,834	631.6	715,373	229.6	−64%

Source: FBI, Uniform Crime Reports, *Crime in the United States 2011* (2012); rate is number per 100,000 in the population.

it. In other words, it might seem that, for murder, the constructionist's mission is irrelevant, that only the essentialist and the positivist would have something to say about the subject. But the matter is not quite this simple. To understand what I mean, we have to make a distinction between "murder" and "killing."

It is true that *murder* is universally condemned. But as we saw, the word "murder" is a loaded, evaluative term. It is a predefined category and *implies* a negative judgment. *By definition*, murder is a deviant, criminal killing. To say that murder is universally a crime is like saying a dog is a mammal. Since that is how murder is defined, murder is *always and by definition* deviant, as well as a crime. Saying that murder is universally a crime is a *definitional* rather than a descriptive or empirical statement. But is the taking of human life—that is to say, *killing*—always and everywhere a crime? And the answer is, "Of course not."

Presumably, the Sixth Commandment says "Thou shalt not kill." Or so it reads, in English, in the King James Version of the *Holy Bible*. This is a serious mistranslation. The correct translation of the original text of the Sixth Commandment of the Hebrew Bible actually reads, "Thou shalt not commit murder," which specifically refers to an unauthorized, illegitimate, and *criminal* form of killing. The verb "to

kill" is objective and descriptive. It simply refers to the taking of human life, regardless of motive or circumstances. In contrast, the term "to murder" is subjective, a judgment that a particular killing belongs to a category of deviant acts. King David, who was unquestionably aware of the Sixth Commandment, killed in battle; he was a warrior, he took human life—he *killed*. And he did so, according to Jewish tradition (and, as later interpreted by Christian theologians) not *in violation* of God's law but *in pursuit* of it. To the ancient Hebrews, David's slaying of Goliath, the Philistine, was a righteous killing, most certainly *not* one prohibited by the Sixth Commandment. David *killed*, but he did not *murder*, Goliath. To shift to the Greek Bible or New Testament, in Romans 13:4, St.Paul declared that the God's representatives had the right to take an evildoer's life, and Matthew 5:21 contains the famous line, "An eye for an eye, and tooth for a tooth," which authorities interpret as sanctioning capital punishment.

All societies accept, tolerate, authorize, legitimate, and even encourage certain sorts of killing. In other words, a very hard, concrete, and seemingly indisputable fact—the taking of human life, the death of a human being—is judged very differently, subjectively evaluated, and placed into vastly different categories according to how it is seen by observers and audiences surrounding the killer and the victim. The legal status of a killing is determined by the law, the criminal justice system, and the courts. But in addition, we all have our own opinions on the matter. And whatever that opinion is, it is the result of a certain *judgment* that is made about the termination of human life. Making a judgment one way or another will transform a given act, in the blink of an eye, from criminal to noncriminal behavior according to who judges it. The point should be clear: *The taking of human life is tolerated, even encouraged, under certain circumstances.* Some killings are not seen by certain observers or audiences as murder, as criminal, or as deviant. Human life has never been an absolute value in this or in any other society in human history. What is evaluated as murder, as criminal homicide, or as a deviant form of killing, is the result of a socially and culturally based judgment. In other words, what is or is not murder is *socially constructed*. During certain periods in certain societies, governments have *authorized* the killing of dissidents and other undesirables. The three most prolifically murderous regimes in the history of the world wielded power during the twentieth century—Nazi Germany, during the Holocaust of the 1940s, the Soviet Union (roughly, the 1940s to the 1960s), in its gulags, and the People's Republic of China, in the Great Leap Forward (1958–1962), each of which deliberately slaughtered or looked the other way in the face of the deaths of tens of millions of political and ethnic "undesirables" or "expendables." At the time, and within each nation, the specifics of these acts were kept from the public, and few in power regarded such killings as "murder." Contemporary audiences disagree.

When someone jumps in front of a car and is run over and killed, the law usually considers the killing an accident. However, during times of intergroup tension, if the driver belongs to one group and the deceased, another, unruly mobs have deemed such seemingly accidental killings as murder, and have attacked, even killed, the driver. Justifiable homicide is a killing that results from the dictates of a legal demand, such as a police officer shooting a felon "in the line of duty" or a citizen who takes action against a felon, presumably to protect his or her life or that of another. Are "assisted suicides" criminal or noncriminal—acts of murder or mercy? In

Switzerland and the Netherlands, such actions are legal; in the United States (except for Oregon), they are not. An absolute pacifist would see *all* intentional killings, including those that take place in warfare, as murder. Pro-life advocates claim that abortion—the removal of a zygote, an embryo, or a fetus from a woman's body—is, in principle at least, murder. Again, the same objective fact—the willful termination of human life—results in differing subjective judgments.

These examples illustrate the fact that we should keep in mind *how* homicides are categorized and *why*. A basic question we have to ask here is: *What sorts of killings are judged as criminal—and deviant?* Which ones are tolerated, accepted, condoned—*not* considered criminal or deviant? What follows are fifteen empirically verified and widely agreed-upon generalizations about murder, that is, the willful killing of one human being by another, or a death which displays a reckless and depraved indifference for human life.

THE CRIMINOLOGIST LOOKS AT MURDER

Criminologists and sociologists do not collect statistical data on who commits murder, where, and under what circumstances, simply to construct empty generalizations. Policy-makers and planners generalize about data because they want to know how to prevent such intentionally lethal acts. Social scientists are also interested in the generalizations—but much more than that. Data and generalizations are in the service of a larger purpose: To understand *why* certain kinds of behavior take place. To *explain* or *account for* murderous acts in a cause-and-effect sequence. The data represent the first step; the generalization, the second step; and the final step, the prize, is the explanation or theory *accounting for* the regularity. By itself, the fact that members of population category A commit murder more than those in population category B is not of immediate theoretical value; understanding *what it is* about the lives of the people in population category A that causes them to kill more often than those in category B provides the criminologist with a key to unlocking the mystery of lethal actions. Is it stress? Indignation? Hostility? Does being stigmatized result in greater feelings of resentment? Does the key factor reside in the culture? Do the media play a role? How? Why? In other words, *what are the intervening variables* between these social characteristics and the behavior itself? What makes these people commit murder at higher rates, and others commit it at lower rates?

Theoretical criminologists can be divided into opposing two camps: the predispositionists, who believe that certain conditions early in life lead to a consistent, lifelong *tendency* to commit crimes such as murder (Gottfredson and Hirschi, 1990), and situationalists, who believe that the same people located in different situations or contexts will have differing likelihoods of committing crimes like murder according to present circumstances (Clarke and Felson, 1993). Both are right, of course: Other things being equal, certain predisposing tendencies *do* influence behavior over the lifetime of a given individual; likewise, other things being equal, certain situational factors *do* influence day-to-day or year-to-year behavior in many or most people. Neither approach negates the other. Most sociologists—with some exceptions—lean more toward situationalism, while most psychologists lean more toward dispositionalism. In Chapter 2, "Explaining Deviant Behavior," we saw that Michael Gottfredson and Travis Hirschi pointed toward this distinction between dispositionalism and situationalism in their discussion of the difference between *crime* and *criminality*. "Crime," they say, is the actual occurrence of sanctionable, illegal behavior; "criminality" is the *tendency* or *proclivity* to commit crime (1990, pp. 85ff). Certain locales or situations *encourage* the commission of crime, even by persons with a low-to-moderate tendency to commit crime; likewise, when faced with certain sanctions in a context with considerable surveillance, even persons with a strong tendency to commit crime ("criminality") do *not* engage in criminal behavior. Clearly, "dispositionalists" and "situationalists" look at different aspects of deviance, crime, and delinquency (Sampson and Laub, 2003).

Sociologically, we can summarize what is known about violent, intentional acts committed by one person that cause the death of another in the form of fifteen generalizations. Keep in mind

the fact that, when gathering homicide statistics, criminologists *start with* statistics on murder—not statistics on murderers. Initially, the police make suppositions about the criminal status of a given killing, and later, representatives of the district attorney's office (and still later, the courts) determine which killings are instances of criminal homicide. Hence, there is a "nexus" or sociological *construction* of a given killing *as* murder. Second, although most murders are committed by one killer, this is not always the case: Some (a few) murderers kill more than one victim, and some (a few) victims are killed by more than one killer. This complicates the ability of criminologists to reason from a given *killing* to a given *killer*. In addition, some factors associated with murder, such as gender, don't change over a person's lifetime, while others (like age) do change. The killer may be a given age at the time of the killing, another age at the time of arrest, and a third age at the time of conviction. Moreover, the same person can commit murders at different times during his or her life. Again, this complicates the ability of the criminologist to trace the characteristics of killers to known killings. Nonetheless, criminologists feel confident about their ability to generalize from the evidence about *who kills*, *where*, and *under what circumstances*. Hence, we can make the following generalizations about criminal homicide.

One: *The public and media images of murder are extremely distorted.* The image of criminal homicide that is conveyed in the news, television crime dramas, and in murder mysteries, as well as the image most people have of the typical or modal murder, bear only a loose relationship to the real thing. The public and media image exaggerate the role of mass and serial murders, murders committed during the course of a felony, such as a robbery or a rape, intentional or premeditated murder, murder for hire, murder for material gain, and murders committed either by deranged, psychotic killers or truly evil human beings. These tend to be relatively rare, producing a relatively low proportion of the total number of criminal homicides; they do not describe the typical, modal, or most common murder. Most murders take place in an unplanned fashion during the course of an altercation between two uneducated males with low impulse control who typically know one another. As callous as it sounds, the December, 2012 massacre in Connecticut of twenty schoolchildren and seven adults, including the killer's mother, by a lone, twenty-year-old gunman is not only atypical, it also does not appreciably alter the overall picture of criminal homicide. Likewise, the killing of twelve victims in a Colorado movie theater in July 2012, again, by a lone gunman, does not cause the criminologist to revise the picture of what is the modal or most common murder, because such killings do not add substantially to the total number of killings. Of the eighty-four gun-related murders that have taken place in the United States every day during the 2000s, only a minority departed from the picture I sketch out here. Again, the mass murders, serial killers, celebrity murders, whodunit murders, premeditated murders, felony murders—what have you—are more newsworthy; they attract a great deal of media attention, but they are *not* typical of the general pattern.

Two: *Most murders occur in the heat of the moment.* Unlike mystery murders, relatively few killings are planned or premeditated. Explosive altercations or escalating interpersonal disputes represent the circumstances of the vast majority of all criminal killings: an argument between husband and wife or boyfriend and girlfriend; a fight between friends or acquaintances in a bar; a dispute between and among neighbors. Over the past generation, drug-related murders by juvenile gangs have assumed a more central role in the criminal homicide picture, and in some locales, this is the most common form of murder; some are premeditated and some aren't.

Three: *Most murders are typically justified by killers as a form of vindication, a way out of an intolerable situation.* Assailants usually feel that in the killing they are obliterating, or defending themselves against, hostile circumstances. They have defined the source of their oppression or humiliation as an evil that *demands* retaliation. ("He deserved it," "He was in my face," "She slept with every guy in town," "He was my best friend—how could he *do* that to me?" "What the hell makes you think you can say that to *me?"* "You think you can get away with *that?"* "Wadda think—you can dis *me?"*) Only through a violent expression of rage are these killers capable of wiping away the disgrace of stigma, shame, and

humiliation. In the words of Jack Katz (1988, pp. 12–51), murder is very often "righteous slaughter." For gang-related murders, killing a rival is "taking care of business," and often retaliation for an invasion of turf.

Four: *The more intimate the relationship, the greater the likelihood that one person will violently kill another.* On a person-for-person basis, intimates—friends, acquaintances, neighbors, relatives, spouses, and lovers—are much more likely to kill one another than strangers are. Statistically speaking, that is, per 100,000 in the population, in the Western world, murder very rarely happens; as we saw, murder is less than 1 percent of all violent crimes. But *of* the willful killings that *do* take place, intimates figure in them extremely prominently. There are only a few dozen or a few hundred intimates in our lives, and many millions of strangers. However, only a quarter of all criminal homicides take place between and among strangers. Two plausible explanations: One, we are in the company of, or *with*, intimates, on an hour-by-hour basis, much more than we are with strangers, and two, though intimates are much more capable of stimulating positive emotions in us, they are also more likely to stimulate our negative emotions, including rage.

Five—and this is an extension of our fourth generalization: *Murderers and victims tend to look remarkably alike.* One stereotype of murder is that the killer selects a totally innocent victim and inflicts undeserved violence upon him or her. Of course, no one *deserves* to be a murder victim, but the fact is, given the circumstances and interpersonal dynamics of murder as well as the social circles in which people who kill travel, in the majority of cases, the person who kills and the person who is killed are often difficult to distinguish—with respect to age, race, social class, residence, prior criminal record and background, the use of drugs and alcohol, the locales they frequent, and lifestyle. There are exceptions, of course, but the majority of homicide victims resemble their killers in most important ways.

Six: Everywhere, *men are much more likely to commit homicide than women; and men are much more likely to be homicide victims than women.* In the United States, roughly nine out of ten killers are men; in 2011, the figure was almost exactly 90 percent. And about 70 to 75 percent of murder victims are men. When men kill, they tend to kill a man (in the United States, over seven out of ten of the criminal homicides that men commit are committed against another man); likewise, when women kill, they tend to kill a man (again, over 70 percent of the time that women kill, they kill a man). And when men *are* killed, they tend to *have been killed* by a man (this is true 90 percent of the time); when women are killed, they tend to have been killed by a man (again, this is true 90 percent of the time).

In other words, men loom much larger in the criminal homicide picture, both as killers and as victims. Whenever the exceptional woman kills, she usually kills a man; whenever the exceptional woman is killed, a man usually kills her. Men tend to be more directly governed by matters of dominance, hierarchy, competition, rivalry, rank, altercation, confrontation, aggression, and physical risk than women, and they are more likely to imagine that an explosion of violence will obliterate the frustrating, rage-inducing difficulty in which they feel they are trapped. And it tends to be other men with whom they are ensnared in these rivalries and confrontations. In contrast, when women kill men, they are most often defending themselves, whether directly or indirectly, in a physically abusive relationship, and feel the need to strike out at their abusers. In any case, the lethal rage of men is most often activated by another man, and the lethal rage of women, in a like fashion, is most often activated by men. And it is men who most often resort to violence—both the act of killing itself as well as the "duet" that leads up to the killing.

Seven: *Age is strongly related to lethal violence.* Putting together data from the Centers for Disease Control and Prevention (CDC)—which tabulates figures for homicide victims—the Department of Justice, and Statistics Canada, for males, the rate of criminal homicide peaks in the eighteen- to twenty-four-year- old or young adult bracket. Members of this category are three times as likely to commit murder as fourteen- to seventeen-year-olds, and five times as likely that those in the over twenty-five category. The median age of the killer at the time of his crime is twenty. Female killers are both slightly older than males at the time of the commission of their crime, and their ages are more dispersed, less concentrated in a narrow age range.

Eight: *Murder is strongly related to social class.* Socioeconomic status (or SES)—that is, occupational prestige, income, and education— is *very* strongly correlated with criminal violence generally and homicide specifically. Murders are *typically* committed by males toward the bottom of the SES ladder, that is, men who are relatively uneducated and are unemployed or who work at poorly paid, low-prestige jobs. (Let's keep in mind, however, that murder is an extremely rare event and thus, very few members of the lower or working class ever commit murder—but an even lower proportion of the members of the middle classes do so.) Just about every study that has ever been conducted on this relationship finds the same correlation. It is one of the most robust findings in the field of criminology. Researchers cite a number of factors to explain the relationship: being at the bottom of the heap; experiencing sharp social and economic inequality and its attendant deprivations; inadequate parental socialization, the relative absence of fathers or, more generally, living in non-intact families; having poor impulse control; living in neighborhoods and communities with high levels of disorganization and disintegration; being socialized into a "subculture" of violence; living in urban areas; and living in an environment that combines continual challenges to one's manhood with physical prowess, strength, daring, and a resort to violence as tests of manhood.

Nine: *African Americans are both more likely to kill and to be the victims of criminal homicide than whites are.* In the United States, each year (where the race of both victim and killer are known, where both are either white or black, and the killing is a single-victim, single-killer homicide), about half of all killers are white (this includes Latinos), half are black, and just under half of all murder *victims* are black, slightly more are white. This means that, relative to their numbers in the population, African Americans are roughly six times overrepresented as both killers and victims. In 2011, almost exactly the same number of blacks (4,149) were arrested for murder in the United States as whites (4,000); this can't be simple discrimination because for all the *other* crimes (except robbery), substantially more whites than blacks are arrested generally. Putting together census figures with UCR data, for 2010, of the fifty-two largest American cities, only one (Miami) of the dozen with a criminal homicide rate of 15 per 100,000 and higher, had a population less than 25 percent black; these are, in descending order according to criminal homicide rate: New Orleans (60% black, 55.16 murders per 100,000), Detroit (84%, 48.68); Baltimore (65%, 31.61); Kansas City, MO (30%, 24.61); Oakland, CA (28%, 24.00); Philadelphia (43%, 21.08); Atlanta (54%, 20.11); Cleveland (61%, 19.04); Memphis (63%, 18.25); Washington, D.C. (53%, 17.94); and Chicago (33%, 15.99). In Chicago, during the past twelve years (2001–2012), the population of the residential blocks on which *two or more* murders took place was 55 percent black; the population of the blocks in which *one or no* murders took place was only 14 percent black (Davey, 2013). Of America's 52 largest cities, only one (Raleigh, NC) of the dozen with the *lowest* murder rates, that is, below 6/100,000, has a population that is a quarter or more black. Honolulu, Hawaii, El Paso, Texas, and Mesa, Arizona, are the three least homicidal cities in America, with a murder rate of roughly 1.47, 2.40, and 2.68 respectively; their populations are only 3, 4, and 3 percent black.

Most criminologists argue that the reasons for this regularity are economic and demographic, that is, poverty, urban residence, and residence in more socially disorganized neighborhoods—not race per se. In addition, when discrimination and economic stagnation make economic achievement and mobility up the ladder of success extremely difficult, some residents of poorer neighborhoods will find street-level drug dealing attractive as a means of economic survival, and drug dealing is a dangerous way of making a living. Again, the reason for this very strong, striking, and noticeably in-your-face regularity has to do with income, class, and political marginality—not race. If class inheritance, economic achievement, and social mobility up the economic ladder were the same for African Americans as whites, such racial differences in violent crime would not exist. Hence, criminal homicide is *primarily* caused by poverty, social and economic marginality, drug dealing, and other factors associated with social class, income, and powerlessness—and only *secondarily* with race.

Ten: Relatedly and intriguingly, some experts suggest that *immigrants are less likely to commit murder than native-born Americans*. According to Jack Levin, a sociologist and criminologist, in a radio interview with a journalist (Balko, 2009), "If you want to find a safe city, first determine the size of its immigrant population. If the immigrant community represents a large proportion of the population, you're likely in one of the country's safer cities." Levin cites El Paso and San Diego as "teeming with immigrants" and, as it turns out, they are also "some of the safest places in the country." Immigrants, says Levin, work hard, are success-oriented, stay out of trouble, and "adjust well" to their adopted country's competitive ethic; it's even possible that immigration selects for a low potential for criminal behavior. Kathleen Dingeman and Rubén Rumbaut's research shows that the incarceration rate of native-born Mexican Americans is eight times that of Mexican-born immigrants (2010). While not all large cities with a high proportion of immigrants have low homicide rates—Miami ranks high on both scales— Levin's hypothesis is intriguing and worth future investigation.

Eleven: And this is also an extension of our fourth and fifth generalizations: *Murders tend to be overwhelmingly intra-racial*. This means that blacks tend to kill blacks, whites tend to kill whites. There are many exceptions to this rule, of course, but in the United States, roughly 90 percent of all willful killings by both blacks and whites conform to this rule. Interracial killings—those that take place between persons of different races—are slightly more common in large cities than in smaller communities, and they are likewise slowly inching up over time: Between the 1980s to the 2000s, white-on-black criminal homicides increased from 3 to 4 percent of all murders, and black-on-white homicides, from 6 to 8 percent (Hargrove, 2012). But in all communities and even today, intra-racial killings remain in the vast majority. The reason makes a great deal of sense: People who know one another stand a higher likelihood of killing one another than people who are more socially, emotionally, and physically distant. And people tend to be more intimate with persons of the same race, and more distant from persons of different races. People of the same race interact more with one another, they spend more time with one another, they are emotionally more significant to one another, they tend to marry one another—and they tend to kill one another.

Twelve: *In the United States, geography and demography are strongly related to criminal homicide*. As any criminologist will agree, the statistics in the FBI's Uniform Crime Reports' (UCR's), *Crime in the United States* for homicide are not complete. They are, however, the most complete crime statistics we have, and the UCR provides a solid basis for generalizing about how murder is distributed. As we've seen, murder varies enormously by city; the most lethal urban communities have murder rates forty times that of the least lethal ones. In addition, community *size* is correlated with criminal homicide. Cities or metropolitan areas have substantially higher rates of murder than non-metropolitan, specifically rural, counties, and Southern states tend to have higher rates of criminal violence than states outside the South—although the difference in the murder rates between the South and the rest of the country has been diminishing over time. The FBI tabulates the criminal homicide rate for all of the largest cities, that is, those with more than 250,000 residents, combined, at 10.1 per 100,000. For medium-sized cities, that is, those with a population between 100,000 and 249,999, the rate is 6.0; for the medium-to-small cities, those with a population between 50,000 and 99,999, it is 3.5; and for those with a population between 25,000 and 49,999, it is 3.1. The lowest rate is attained by the smallest communities—small cities of 10,000 to 24,999 souls (2.8), and those under 10,000 in number (2.9). Clearly, the *size of city* and its *murder rate* are closely related.

States likewise vary substantially with regard to lethal violence. Louisiana is the state with the nation's highest murder rate (11.2), and Mississippi has the second-highest (8.0). The state with the *lowest* murder rate is Hawaii (1.2), although the sub-regions of New England (2.6) and the upper Midwest (3.4) are the lowest in the country, with New Hampshire (1.3), Vermont (1.3), Rhode Island (1.3), Iowa (1.5), and Minnesota (1.4), along with certain states in the West, such as Idaho (1.3) and Utah (1.9) at or near the bottom. Puerto Rico, a Caribbean territory rather than a state, has by far the highest murder rate of any U.S. jurisdiction tabulated by the FBI (30.6); the rate of the District of Columbia, composed entirely of a city, is 17.5. Again, the *state* is a descriptive, not analytic category; murder rates vary by state because of sociological rather than geopolitical reasons—masculinist culture, economic status, urbanness, age and sex distribution, social conflicts, and hostility between and among categories in the population, and so on.

Thirteen: *In the Western world, violence, especially lethal violence, has dropped enormously since the Middle Ages* (Johnson and Monkkonen, 1996; Pinker, 2009). Europe, prior to industrialization, was an extremely dangerous place in which to live; violent death at the hand of another was a common event. One estimate has it that medieval Europe's homicide rate was ten to twenty times higher than it is today (Gurr, 1989). Five centuries ago, nearly everyone went about armed with a knife, a staff, a sword, or a club. Violence as a solution to disputes was routine; "murderous brawls and violent deaths . . . were everyday occurrences" (Givens, 1977, pp. 28, 34). Historians argue that the reasons for the decline in the homicide rate over the past half millennium or so include the growing power of a central authority, that is, the monarchy; the expanded role of courts of law to settle disputes; and what's called the "civilizing process" (Elias, 1994), that is, as a result of socialization through learning manners and civility toward others, propriety, and restraining the expression of one's emotion by controlling one's physical actions (Beeghley, 2003).

Fourteen: Even more specifically, *in the past two decades, criminal homicide has sharply declined*. As we saw in Table 5.1, the murder rate in the United States has dropped since 1992 by nearly half. In 2012, New York City posted the lowest number of murders (418) since records have been kept. A similar but somewhat less pronounced decline is also true of crime in general. This isn't true in all cities or neighborhoods, but it is true for the country as a whole. For instance, for 2012, Chicago, with one-third the population of New York City, posted almost 100 more murders (506); that total represented a 16 percent increase from the previous year. Still, for the United States as a whole, during the past two, three, or four decades, many, and in all likelihood most—though far from all—indicators of public health and safety, such as fatalities from accidents, including motor vehicle accidents (from nearly 25 per 100,000 in the population in 1978 to 12 per 100,000 in 2010), death by drowning (from about three to one) and death by fire (from roughly two to one), have also declined. From a number of disparate sources, with respect to both criminal victimization and accident, the United States has become a substantially safer place in which to live; not only accidental fatalities, but also intoxication while driving, and the incidence of most sexually transmitted diseases. (In this respect, let's keep in mind the qualification I issued in Chapter 4, "Poverty and Disrepute": In matters of health and public safety, the United States is at the *bottom* among the seventeen most affluent countries of the world. Americans are more likely to get sick and injured, and die prematurely, than is true of the populations of Canada, Japan, Australia, Germany, and so on. But these indicators have improved over time, even in the United States.) It is possible that the strengthening of a more progressive, civic-minded consciousness, along with the mentality Norbert Elias describes in *The Civilizing Process* (1994), could help explain these changes. As New York Mayor Michael Bloomberg said, about the City's decline in the murder rate: "The essence of civilization is that you can walk down the street without having to look over your shoulder" (Ruderman, 2012, p. A1). It's also possible that we can explain a major swath of the decline in these deaths by the application of numerous public safety measures, such as manufacturing safer cars, constructing safer roads and buildings, installing better lighting, deploying the police in the most strategic locations, using more sophisticated surveillance techniques, instituting alcohol and drug instructional modules into the school curriculum, and so on.

Fifteen: *The poor, economically less developed countries of the world have relatively high rates of criminal homicide, while, for the most part, the more affluent countries, with significantly lower levels of economic inequality, have much lower rates of murder.* In 2011, the United Nations Office on Drugs and Crime gathered the available worldwide data on criminal homicide, and published it in the form of a monograph, *Global Study on Homicide* (2011). Tallies of criminal homicide in industrializing counties are vastly more incomplete than they are for the United States, but they do give us clues to the size and direction of illegal killings internationally. In addition to lower levels of economic development and income inequality, factors that play a role in levels of lethal violence include the availability of firearms, fewer opportunities for employment, higher levels of political instability, social conflict, the role of organized crime, the presence of the drug trade, and the presence of an economic crisis. The worldwide rate of homicide was 6.9 per 100,000 in the population in 2010. As a continent, Africa has the highest overall rates of criminal homicide, with the Ivory Coast (56.9), Zambia (38.0), Uganda (36.3), South Africa (33.8), and Lethoso (33.6) leading the list. The murder rates for Central and South America and the Caribbean were likewise very high, especially Honduras (82.1), El Salvador (66.0), Jamaica (52.1), Venezuela (49.0), Guatemala (41.4), Belize (41.7), the U.S. Virgin Islands (39.2), St. Kitts and Nevis (38.2), Trinidad and Tobago (35.2), and Colombia (33.4) leading the list in these regions. The Muslim-Arab countries of North Africa have extremely low homicide rates—Tunisia (1.1), Egypt (1.2), Morocco (1.4), and Algeria (1.5)—as do China (0.5) and Japan (0.5), and nearly all of Western Europe: Iceland (0.3), Austria (0.5), Norway (0.6), Switzerland (0.7), Germany (0.8), Denmark (0.9), Spain (0.9), Sweden (1.0), and Italy (1.0). The United States, with a sizable drug trade, the ready availability of firearms, a substantial degree of economic inequality, and more than its share of social conflict, has a homicide rate considerably below the high-end countries, but several times higher than those of the least violent countries in the world—as we saw, 4.7 per 100,000 in the population for 2010. (In 2009, when the UN compiled its figures for the United States, the rate was 5.0.)

Drinking alcohol and using illicit substances are *strongly* related to homicide; I'll discuss the role of alcohol and drugs in the next chapter. In all of the above generalizations, positivists take the constructed nature of murder for granted—they put it on the back burner, so to speak—and examine the causal relationship between key factors and variables and criminal homicide as a consistent, coherent, materially real form of behavior, rather than a socially defined and judged phenomenon. As we've just seen, murder possesses enough internal consistency to reveal social patterning; it is not a "mere" social construction. Certain categories of people in the population, certain types of societies, and certain eras in American history, exhibit higher rates of homicide—as its features are spelled out by criminologists—than others. As a result, the evidence indicates, specific conditions are consistently and causally related to the likelihood of committing violence. (If cultural and historical instances stray too far from the contemporary American context, the notion of what a murder is, indeed—what a *crime* is—becomes ephemeral.) It is the job of the positivist social scientist to locate those conditions, establish relevant generalizations, and explain *why* homicide occurs—and, possibly, suggest ways to reduce a country's level of lethal violence.

THE NATIONAL CRIME VICTIMIZATION SURVEY (NCVS)

In 1965, in response to recent riots and the rising American crime rate, President Lyndon Johnson signed an executive order creating the Commission on Law Enforcement and Administration of Justice. The president charged the Commission with investigating the causes of crime and the adequacy of the then-current system of law enforcement, criminal justice, and corrections. In 1967, the Commission issued its report, entitled *The Challenge of Crime in a Free Society*, which recommended, among other things, that the government sponsor a national survey to determine the nature and extent of crime. Officials and experts recognized that the under-reporting of the Uniform Crime Reports made it unreliable for all its Index Crimes (except for homicide and motor vehicle theft). The way around the problem, they believed, was to use a completely different research method—self-report surveys on crime victimization.

In 1972, the Department of Justice sponsored, and the U.S. Census conducted, a survey called the National Crime Survey (NCS), based on a large, systematically selected sample of the population. As a result of criticisms of its methodology—particularly with respect to rape, which its questionnaire never asked about directly—the program's methodology was overhauled. The Census Bureau launched the new survey, NCVS—the

National Crime Victimization Survey—in 1993. Its surveys began with a sample of 45,000 households—huge by any standards; it is the second-largest household survey conducted by the federal government, the first being the decennial Census itself. After the first twenty years of such surveys, NCVS issued a summary report highlighting the findings from more than 800,000 victimizations reported by the respondents in its surveys (Zawitz et al., 1993). NCVS continues to draw samples, ask questions, and issue reports on criminal victimization. NCVS's surveys lend considerably complexity, shading, and accuracy to crime data. (As we'll see, it has also attracted considerable criticism.) Summarizing the findings of the dozens of NCVS surveys (Bastian, 1992; Zawitz et al., 1993; Rand, Lynch, and Cantor, 1997; Truman and Planty, 2012), we come to the following conclusions.

First, *roughly two-thirds of crimes are not reported to the police*. NCVS's crime rates are two-and-a-half times higher than those of the Uniform Crime Reports. Only four out of ten of all violent crimes, and only a third of all property crimes, are reported by the victim to the police. This under-reporting means that the UCR is worthless with respect to the incidence, extent, and rate of the Index Crimes. Motor vehicle theft is the crime that is most likely to be reported—in fact, about eight out of ten are reported to the police and hence, appear in UCR. (Obviously, murder is not included in these surveys because the victim is deceased and can't be interviewed!)

Second, *criminal victimization has declined*, albeit unevenly, *in the past two or three decades*, especially since the early 1990s. It is not methodologically correct to compare the crime data collected in the 1970s and 1980s by means of the old (NCS) methods with the 2011 figures, which was collected by the new (NCVS) methods, but the program's researchers have "adjusted" the 1992 data for the new methods, and the 1992–2011 decline in both property and violent crimes is considerable, even greater than those indicated by the UCR's data.

Third, *most criminal victimization is property rather than violent crime*. The NCVS estimated that in the United States in 2011, 5.8 million violent crimes took place (25%); for property crimes, the figure was 17 million, or 75 percent.

Fourth, *crime victimization varies considerably by social characteristics*. Specifically, blacks are more likely to be victimized by violent crime than whites are; males are more likely to be victimized than females; people living in large cities are more likely to be victimized than those living in smaller cities, suburban, and rural areas; and persons under the age of twenty-five are more likely to be victimized than those who are older. And the poorer the household, the greater the likelihood its residents will be victimized: Roughly three times as many members of the poorest households are victimized by crime as is true of those living in the highest-income category.

Fifth, with respect to crimes in which the offender confronted the victim, and the victim identified the characteristics of the offender, *the vast majority of the offenders* (85%) *are male*; for example, nine out of ten (more than 90%) of robberies are committed by males.

Sixth, *eight out of ten offender-identified crimes* (80%) *are intra-racial*—the offender and the victim are of the same race. This is true of assault and rape; it is also true of criminal homicide, which, obviously, the NCVS cannot count.

Over the past two decades, these generalizations have remained stable and robustly documented. What *has* changed is that over the past two decades, crime victimization has plummeted, by 72 percent, from 80 per 1,000 in 1993 to 23 in 2011. Likewise, all the categories of property crime have declined as well (Truman and Planty, 2012, p. 1). In other words, though the relationships between crime and other social factors and variables have remained the same, the frequency and rate of criminal behavior have declined substantially during the past two or three decades. Table 5.2 brings together the figures for 1992 (Rand, Lynch, and Cantor, 1997; Taylor, 1997), 2002, and 2011 (Truman and Planty, 2012). As we can see, the rate of each crime has declined for each decade, and for some crimes, the decline from the 1990s to the most recent figures is substantial. The degree of change and the consistency of the drop indicate that the recorded declines are real and not an artifact of measurement or methodology. We'll have a great deal more to say about the validity of the NCVS's figures on rape, which are vastly more controversial than for all the other crimes.

FORCIBLE RAPE

"Rape is horrible. . . . It is horrible because you are violated, you are scared," because "someone takes control of your body and hurts you in the most intimate way" (Abdulali, 2013). Rape is an outrage, a violation, a desecration—deeply shaming and humiliating to the victim. Men can be raped as well as women, and often are, usually in prison (Beck, 2010). But in mainstream society, rape is a crime largely committed *by* men *against* women. Conquerors have often employed rape as a weapon of domination in war and genocide (Rittner and Roth, 2012), and some feminists have argued that it serves that same function in maintaining patriarchy in everyday life for societies generally (Brownmiller, 1975); even more emphatically, others argue that it is a means of keeping women subservient, in an inferior position vis-à-vis men. Rape is a deeply personal form of victimization, in ways that robbery, for instance, is not. Whether or not the perpetrator is motivated primarily to humiliate his victim is irrelevant; the victim virtually always feels shamed—and usually outraged as well—and the

TABLE 5.2   CRIME VICTIMIZATION RATES, NCVS, 1992, 2002, AND 2011 (PER 1,000) FOR POPULATION AGE 12 AND OLDER

	RAPE/SEXUAL ASSAULT*	ROBBERY	AGGRAVATED ASSAULT	HOUSEHOLD BURGLARY	MOTOR VEHICLE THEFT
1992	2.9	6.1	11.1	58.6	18.5
2002	1.5	2.7	5.8	29.5	9.2
2011	0.9	2.2	4.1	29.4	5.1

*Includes rape, attempted rape, and sexual assault

Sources: For 1992, Rand, Lynch, and Cantor, 1997, and Taylor, 1997; for 2002 and 2011, Truman and Planty, 2012

reaction of the community ranges from empathy to pity to condescension and scorn. Rape is one of those crimes that attracts stigma to both perpetrator and victim. It is impossible to study and write about the subject of rape without entering the political arena. Of all crimes, it generates the most controversy. Some observers argue that rape is fairly rare, and that its frequency has been wildly exaggerated by polemicists (Gilbert, 1991, 1992; Roiphe, 1993; Sommers, 1995). Others write with a sense of urgency and anger, arguing that rape is widespread, even common—according to Susan Griffin, "the most frequently committed violent crime in America today" (1971, p. 27)—and has reached epidemic proportions. (Actually, aggravated assault was and remains ten times more common.) The crime, feminist observers assert, is encouraged by our society's aggressive, masculinist culture, and serves the function of keeping women subservient, docile, and subordinate. The estimates made by members of each of these conclaves—that is, skeptics and feminists—of rape's incidence, prevalence, and rate are so wildly different that they cannot be reconciled. In stating known facts about rape, an author is likely to stir up controversy by offending one or another of these congregations. And yet, when writing about this crime, the criminologists, epidemiologist, and sociologist of deviance cannot avoid the subject.

Virtually no one is *in favor* of or even indifferent to rape; almost everyone who writes about the subject regards rape as ugly and abhorrent. Moreover, nearly everyone regards it as a serious problem—although many chime in on the *degree* of its extent and seriousness. Some advocates of a certain stripe proudly describe themselves and their peers as "anti-rape"—although no one is "pro-rape"—but this tag embraces virtually everyone who writes on the subject; in fact, there is nothing particularly distinctive about being "anti-rape." Two dimensions enter the arena of controversy, however. The first is *how common* observers think rape is and hence, *how serious* they think the rape problem is. And the second is whether rape is paradigmatic or central to the oppression of women. These positions contrast with skeptics who insist that rape is simply a particular *type* of violent crime, essentially not appreciably different from, say, aggravated assault or robbery. Is rape the principal and foundational mechanism by which men dominate and tyrannize women? Or is it one of a number of many ways that both women and men—mainly, but not necessarily only, women—can be victimized by crime? Answering these questions locates the author's position in a political conflict that some authors foment and others are inadvertent, unwilling, and sometimes unwary—and even unaware—participants.

The FBI defines forcible rape as "carnal knowledge of a female forcibly and against her will." The law distinguishes statutory rape from forcible rape, even though a man past the age of eighteen who has consensual sex with a female below a legally stipulated age has committed a crime. Legally, an underage female is not capable of granting sexual access. Statutes regard any forced penetration of a woman's mouth, vagina, or anus by a man's penis as rape. Criminologists and other behavioral scientists regard forcible rape primarily as a violent rather than a sexual act. Rape is an *assault.* It employs force, violence, or the threat of violence. This is not to say that sex is not involved in any way—after all, there is a difference between beating a woman and sexually assaulting her. If there were no difference, acts of rape would be classified as assault and rape would not exist as a separate category. In rape, there is, to be technical about it, genital contact, or an attempt to affect genital contact, while there is no such element in simple assault by itself. But what defines an act as rape is that it is nonconsensual, a sexual act *forced on,* or *against,* a woman, against her will. Legally and by definition, forcible rape entails the use of force, violence, or the threat of violence. Thus, rape is *always* and *by definition* a violent act. Rape is *never* free of its violent character. Even if the victim, the offender, the general public, or law enforcement did not regard a specific rape as violent, legally, *if it is forced*, it is rape and hence, by definition, violent. What *defines* or *constitutes* it *as* a rape is that it is, *by definition and by its very nature*, against the victim's will. In that respect, it is similar to the act the law refers to as robbery. As we might expect, however, even this clear-cut and emphatic formulation hides a swarming host of social constructions. It is very likely that cultural and historical definitions of rape are even more variable than they are for murder. To put the matter more emphatically, it is possible that, at certain historical eras and in certain societies, the forcible sexual intercourse *of* certain women *by* certain men would not be defined as rape—under any circumstances.

Researchers have compared the findings of victimization surveys with official statistics (such as the UCR) and concluded that victims report to the police only 35 percent of rapes or sexual assaults, 40 percent of household property offenses, and 44 percent of assaults (Langton et al., 2012). Most criminologists believe that UCR's rape data are fatally flawed and cannot be used for incidence estimates; victimization surveys show a substantially greater tendency of women to report rape to an NCVS interviewer than to the police. Victimization surveys show a nearly 70 percent decline in rape in the past two decades, and an even more substantial decline since the early 1970s. Even in absolute numbers, we see a 30 percent decline between 2002 and 2011 (Truman and Planty, 2012, p. 2). But critics of victimization surveys have attacked NCVS's findings on rape, largely on the basis that, they argue, victims often—even usually—aren't even aware of the fact that they are raped. The basis of their argument is that the NCVS's definition of rape is too narrow; it should be broadened to include a range of aggressive acts not currently accepted by most victims or most researchers.

Rape: Sex versus Violence

Is rape a violent or a sexual act? Its violent character, as we saw, cannot be questioned. It is a violent crime; like robbery and assault, it entails violence, force, or the threat of violence. Consider the fact that, often, in addition to force and the threat of violence, women are often overtly injured *in the act of rape*; they can be punched, pummeled, beaten, scratched, strangled, and wounded with a weapon. But even if there is *no* overt or direct violence, and granting that the violence entails threat or force, does this mean that the rape is not a sexual act in any way whatsoever? Perhaps we have set up a false dichotomy here: a mutually exclusive formulation that insists that if an act is unquestionably violent, it cannot be sexual—for the perpetrator. As Diana Scully says, the arguments

that emphasize the violent and aggressive character of rape often "disclaim that sex plays any part in rape at all" (1990, p. 142). The fact that rape is—always, by definition, and by its very nature—violent, does not mean that it cannot be *other* things as well. The "rape isn't about sex—it's about violence" cliché is a bit too simplistic for sociological purposes. It sets up a false dichotomy, which assumes that rape is "about" *either* violence *or* sex—it cannot be "about" both. This formulation assumes that there is one and only one way of looking at rape, that there is an inner concrete or objective "essence" contained by rape—which is violence—that manifests itself to all reasonable and unbiased observers under any and all circumstances. *And* that this essence precludes other, very different, "essences," such as sex—whose essence is mutual consent. Since rape lacks the latter essence, it cannot, by definition, be "true" or "real" sex. But, as we've already seen, the same phenomenon can be regarded, defined, or experienced in different ways. What is rape to the woman and to the law *may* be sex to the man. This does not mean that it is any the less violent—and therefore not rape. What it does mean is that it may be experienced differently by the rapist. It may be both sex (to the man) *and* a violent assault (to the law, much of the public, and the female victim).

Diana Scully argues that rape can be sex *in addition to* being violence, and for the following reasons. First, for some men, violence and sex are fused. For them, violence against women has become sexualized. To these men, there is something erotic and sexually exciting about inflicting violence upon women; sex and violence do not exist in separate worlds. To the contrary, they are coterminous. Rape is sexual *because* it is violent. Of course, for their female victims, there is nothing erotic at all about rape. And second, for many men, rape is instrumental—to gain sexual access to otherwise unattainable women. For many men, rape represents a means of attaining sexual access to women who are otherwise unattainable to them. For these men, rape is not "about" violence because they do not imagine that what they do is particularly violent. "When a woman is unwilling or seems unavailable for sex, men can use rape to seize what is not offered" (Scully, 1990, p. 143).

Definitions of Rape: Exclusionism versus Inclusionism

While most observers regard rape in essentialistic terms, in fact, the social construction of rape is "relative" (Curra, 2000). This means that different audiences define it in variable ways. Two persons or audiences could watch a videotape or hear a description of exactly the same act—both of which qualify by the FBI's definition *as* rape—and one would regard it as an instance of rape and the other wouldn't. This does not mean that we cannot settle the issue of what rape is according to the law. In fact, the law is quite specific concerning its definition of rape. What it means is that social, cultural, group, and individual conceptions vary as to what acts constitute rape (Estrich, 1987; Bourque, 1989). What rape *is thought to be* or regarded as, is a matter of definition. What we have here is a striking contradiction between how the law defines rape ("the carnal knowledge of a female forcibly and against her will") and how many people judge concrete cases *that actually qualify as rape* according to the law. As a result, it is absolutely necessary to examine *how rape is seen, defined, and judged by audiences*. The central importance of these varying judgments becomes clear when we examine their role in subjective judgments of rape made by three crucial audiences: *the general public, the criminal justice system*, including the police and the courts, and *victims of rape*.

The general public can be divided according to a *spectrum or continuum* of judgments of what's rape. At one end, we have those that are *exclusive*, that is, the definition is very *narrow,* which judge *very few* acts of sexual aggression by men against women as rape. At the other end, we have judgments that are *inclusive*—that is, they are extremely generous, very broad—which include *many* acts as rape.

Perhaps the most extremely exclusive definition would be held by rapists, many of whom believe, in effect, that rape does not exist, that all or nearly all charges of rape are false. One convicted rapist expressed this view when he denied the existence of rape on the grounds that "if a woman don't want to be raped, you are not going to rape her" (Williams and Nielson, 1979, p. 131). A minuscule number of acts of intercourse against a woman's will would qualify as rape by the exclusivistic or narrow definition, which sees men as having nearly unlimited sexual access to women, regardless of their resistance, and women as having no rights at all—only the choice between death or being beaten unconscious on the one hand and being assaulted on the other. In one study of convicted, incarcerated rapists (Scully and Marolla, 1984), nearly a third said that they had sex with their victims but denied that it was rape. "As long as the victim survived without major physical injury," these men believed, "a rape had not taken place" (p. 535).

At the other end of the spectrum, equally as extreme, is the *inclusive* definition, held by the few remaining radical, militant, lesbian feminist separatists, who believe that *all* intercourse between men and women, however consensual it may appear on the surface, represents an assault, an act of aggression, an invasion, a violation—in a word, rape. According to this perspective, men exercise power over women—*every* man has power over *every* woman—and consequently, *no* sexual relationship between any man and any woman can be freely chosen by the woman. *All* heterosexual sex is coerced—that is, is not freely chosen by the woman—and hence, qualifies as rape. Heterosexual sex is, *by its very nature, tainted* by patriarchy, *saturated* with its sexist essence. In a patriarchal society, women are brainwashed to think they want male companionship and all that goes with it. In a truly equalitarian society, no woman would want to have sex with any man. Hence, *all* heterosexual sex is rape (Dworkin, 1981, 1987). Or so says the extreme inclusivistic definition of rape.

Very few Americans would agree with either end of the spectrum. Between these two extremes, we will find the *moderately exclusive* and the *moderately inclusive* definitions, which, together, encompass the views of the overwhelming majority of the American public.

The moderately exclusive definition tends to be held by sexual and sex and gender-role *traditionalists* and *conservatives*. Persons who hold to the moderately exclusive definition believe that a woman's place is in the home, and that she must have a man to protect her from the advances of other men. If she puts herself in a vulnerable position, this view holds, such as going to bars, acting flirtatiously or seductively, going alone to a man's apartment and allowing one in hers, wearing "provocative" clothing, dating a number of men, hitchhiking, or walking on the street alone at night, or even remaining single too long, perhaps she is responsible for provoking men's sexually aggressive behavior, maybe she provoked men into forcing intercourse on her. Maybe she wanted it all along—maybe it wasn't force at all. This definition does not see a great many acts of coercive intercourse as rape because it does not accept the view that women should have the sexual freedom that is granted to men. This view is summed up in the saying, "Nice girls don't get raped." In other words, if women don't engage in all these sexually provocative activities, they won't bring on men's sexual attention in the first place. The corollary of this saying is that if a woman is raped, maybe she wasn't so nice after all. It is possible that some version of this definition is held by a majority of the American public. It is possible, in other words, that most Americans hold a moderately exclusive definition of rape. Many, perhaps most, Americans—to a degree, and under a number of circumstances—will blame a woman for certain kinds of sexual attacks against her. They restrict their notion of what rape is to a relatively narrow or exclusivistic set of acts.

In contrast, the *moderately inclusive* definition tends to be held by sexual and sex and gender-role *liberals*. They believe that a woman has the right of sexual determination, the right to choose where and with whom she wants to go. Thus, she cannot be blamed for an attack against her. If a woman makes it clear she is not interested in a man's advances, and he persists, then he is forcing himself on her; she is being coerced, the act takes place against her will, and it is a case of rape. Moderate inclusionists feel women should not have to be "protected" by a man to live a life free of sexual assault. She has the same rights to go where and when she wants as a man has. And she has the right of control over her own body, whom she chooses to go to bed with, and whom she refuses to bed down with. Men have no right to force her to do anything sexual; if they do, it's rape. Men do not have the right to threaten to harm, or pin a woman's shoulders down, twist her arm, force her legs open, physically restrain her, jam an elbow into her windpipe—or do *anything* to physically overpower or coerce her—in order to have intercourse with her. If they do, it's rape. Likewise, if a woman is unconscious; sex with her is rape. And if a man threatens violence, the same principle holds. The moderately inclusive

definition is probably held by a minority, albeit a substantial minority, of the American public.

Redefining rape?

As we saw, for 2011, NCVS estimated the number of rapes during the prior year at less than a quarter of a million, for a rate of 0.9 per thousand women aged and older in the American population. In contrast, the various iterations of the National Women's Study (NWS), and the Centers for Disease Control and Prevention (CDC) yield an estimate of more than a million rapes in the United States for the 2000s (Kilpatrick et al., 2007; Black et al., 2011)—a difference on the order of four or five times. Likewise, an often-quoted study, the National Violence Against Women Survey (NVAWS), yields a total of *victims* perpetrated against women during the previous twelve months at 302,000, but an average number of rapes *per victim* at 2.9, and so, a total number of rapes 876,000 (Tadjen and Thoennes, 2006, p. 8)—clearly closer to the higher estimates than the lower.

Why do we find such a yawning gap between the highest and lowest figures measuring the incidence of such a fundamental social fact as rape? We do not see such variability in numbers—those that are taken seriously, at any rate—tabulated by different agencies or experts on criminal homicide. *Why is it true of rape?*

Recall that NCVS reports figures from a survey asking a sample of respondents if they have been victims of specific crimes within the previous year; it permits interviewees to define their own rape victimization. We can locate several reasons for this discrepancy.

First, the NCVS asks its question about rape directly. Its screen question reads as follows: "Has anyone attacked or threatened you in any of these ways. . . . Any rape, attempted rape or sexual threat?" In contrast, the CDC, as well as NVAWS and other surveys that generate much higher figures, ask respondents to answer specific questions that are much more detailed, about a number of specific victimizations that qualify as rape and attempted rape: "Has a man or boy ever made you have sex by using force or threatening to harm you or someone close to you? Just so there is no mistake, by sex we mean putting a penis in your vagina," and so on, asking questions about oral and anal sex, penetrating the respondent's "vagina or anus with their mouth or tongue," putting their fingers "or objects" into the respondent's vagina or anus," and so on. If the interviewees answer in the affirmative to any of them, they are recorded as have been victimized by rape. In other words, while NCVS assumes that respondents can self-define what constituted a rape, the 2010 CDC and other surveys that generate higher rape figures spelled out and defined what qualified *as* rape *for* the respondents. Hence, not only do questions about *specific* acts cue the respondent to answer affirmatively about rape victimization, but second, the CDC's questionnaire also includes many more acts that would not necessarily come to mind by victims *as* rape. The survey's rape tally includes cunnilingus performed by the man on an unwilling woman, and the penetration of one or more of her orifices by his fingers or an object as rape; again, such acts are not likely to be considered rape by most observers. Yet it was the researchers who decided that these specific acts should be tallied in the category of rape—not the respondents. In the NVAWS survey as well, the researchers count digital, lingual, and object-penetration of the woman's orifices, including her mouth, as rape (Tjaden and Thoennes, 2006, pp. 10, 11); as to whether victims agree is an empirical question. And, as we saw, NVAWS tabulates rape victimizations and number of rapes separately, yielding higher counts than NCVS's.

Third, consider the issue of facilitation. As we saw, the CDC's survey estimated that nearly 1.3 million women have been raped in the year prior; this includes "attempted forced penetration" (670,000 incidents) and "completed alcohol/drug facilitated penetration" (519,000 incidents). Hence, the third possible reason why the CDC's survey produces much larger figures on rape is that its definition of rape includes drug and alcohol facilitation. The survey includes unwilling sex when the respondent was "drunk, high, drugged, or passed out and unable to consent"—which encompasses a broad latitude of behaviors. Of course, if the woman *has* passed out, *any* sex with her by a man is unquestionably rape—according to the law, in virtually all courts, and to nearly all audiences; hence, this vehicle is noncontroversial—virtually all observers consider that rape. But if the woman is drunk or high—and the man is drunk or high—the sex act was not necessarily "facilitated" by

the psychoactive substances, and so, most audiences would not regard the ensuing sex ("penetration") as rape; they would regard drinking as freely chosen and mutual rather than a definition component of a violent act—rape. Hence, the differences between the NCVS's and CDC's definitions of rape may account for much, although far from all, of the discrepancy in their divergence in incidence and rate figures.

It is important to know that the inclusionist definition used by the Black et al. and the Kilpatrick et al. research teams and NVAWS does not *only* serve the goal of alerting the public and other researchers that rape is a larger and more distressing problem than many of us realize. These researchers also wish to stress that women (and men) who are victimized by actions that NCVS's survey may not define as rape suffer medical and psychiatric consequences as a result of their victimization. The CDC reports that women who had a "history" of rape *or* stalking *or* physical violence were more likely than those without such a history to suffer a range of health consequences, such as asthma (24 vs. 14%), frequent headaches (29 vs. 17%), chronic pain (30 vs. 17%), difficulty sleeping (38 vs. 21%), limitations on their physical activity (35 vs. 21%), and, generally, poor physical health (6 vs. 2%) and poor mental health (3 vs. 1%). In other words, regardless of whether all researchers agree that a definition of rape should be broader or more narrow, and include victimizations not all observers regard as rape, having experienced any one of a range of sexual victimizations takes a medical and psychiatric toll; this generalization also holds for men, who are nonetheless far less likely to be sexually victimized than women (Black et al., 2011, pp. 61–63). Likewise, the NVAWS survey asked questions about injury resulting from the rape as well as subsequent "mental health and lost productivity outcomes" (Tjaden and Thoennes, 2006, pp. 29–31).

PROPERTY CRIME AS DEVIANCE

Injunctions against property crime have ancient roots. Two of the Ten Commandments prohibit taking something of value not one's own: the

Eighth, which says "Thou shalt not steal," and the Tenth, which says "Thou shalt not covet thy neighbor's house . . . , his ox or donkey, or anything that belongs to thy neighbor." Indeed, we can trace back the taboo against theft thousands of years before the Bible was written, back before settled communities, agriculture, or the fashioning of metals, to hunting and gathering societies the world over, back to when the concept of movable property was institutionalized. In societies everywhere and throughout the span of human existence, whenever anything of value could be owned by individuals, some other individuals coveted, and stole, whatever it was, and societies promulgated rules that prohibited such theft.

Larceny, it has been said, is "in the American heart" (McCaghy et al., 2006, pp. 159–162). It is and has been in the hearts of the people of many societies the world over and throughout human history as well, since stealing is extremely widespread, practically universal. Polls as far back as the 1940s indicate that most people have stolen something of value at least once in our lives. But the popularity of property crime does not mean that we are all thieves. One study (Tracy, Wolfgang, and Figlio, 1990) found that, in the United States, roughly 5 percent of the population commits 70 percent of the serious property crime. Most of us steal very little and very infrequently, while very few of us steal a great deal, and steal frequently. Hence, there are significant differences between someone who says he or she has stolen "something" of value at least once and someone who steals routinely, as a living. Saying "we are all thieves," therefore, is misleading because, while hardly anyone is completely honest and never steals, relatively few of us make a *habit* of stealing.

Theft flourishes in societies in which some members do not care a great deal about the deprivations they cause to their fellow citizens, or where members of different societies come into contact with one another and the wants and needs of the members of the other society are deemed of no significance. Stealing is high in societies in which the collective conscience has broken down, in which the social community has become a fiction. Theft is common because some among us want certain things and how we acquire those things matters less than having them. We steal because we are successful at convincing our-

selves "it isn't really so bad," or "no one will miss it," or "it's covered by insurance," or "I need it more than they do," or "they're bigger crooks than I am." Basically, people are able to steal because persons from whom they steal have become impersonal, faceless, almost nonhuman to them. And stealing is particularly common in societies in which inequities in income and other resources are sharp, stark, and publicized, and, as anomie theory argues, where persons at the bottom of the hierarchy learn to *want* the things that the more affluent have.

The street thieves whose acts are tabulated in the pages of the UCR run the gamut from the rankest amateur who shoplifts to obtain items he or she sees others enjoying to the professional who earns a comfortable livelihood exclusively from larceny. For both, stealing seems to be a rational activity: It is a means to an end that many of us seek, although the means used are somewhat unconventional. Other benefits that may be derived from stealing ("kicks," fun, excitement, and so on) tend to be secondary to the monetary ones. A nation with high rates of theft, as Merton argues, is one that: (1) emphasizes material values; (2) manifests great material differences between rich and poor; (3) prominently displays the possessions of the affluent; (4) portrays the possessions of the affluent as attainable for everyone; (5) deemphasizes the means of attaining these possessions; and (6) makes it difficult, if not nearly impossible, for a substantial number of a society's members to obtain these possessions legally. It is these features that almost guarantee that a society or nation will have a high rate of theft. They make for a "rip-off" society, a "society organized for crime" (Messner and Rosenfeld, 1997, pp. 1–14).

Among the tugs and pulls inducing people to attempt thievery as a means of earning money, two are most prominent. The first would be the gap between poverty and having cash. In a nation with high unemployment rates in many neighborhoods, with a black unemployment rate twice that of whites, and an unemployment rate for teenagers three times that for adults, many people are induced to steal because they literally have no other means of earning money. In the neighborhood studied by anthropologist Philippe Bourgois, "El Barrio" or East Harlem in New York, 40 percent of all households earned no legally declared wages or salary at all. It is Bourgois's contention that its residents had no choice but to resort to a variety of activities in the "underground" economy, among them, stealing (1995, p. 8). Even if a family receives government benefits or one or more members work at a minimum wage job, there is no possibility of moving about in the world with physical dignity or comfort. Indeed, many minimum wage jobs put substantially less in one's pocket than many illegal activities. Clearly, poverty has to be counted as a major inducement to engage in property crime.

We experience a great deal of theft in this society because the economy does not guarantee enough people a decent livelihood and because our economy is incapable of distributing income in an equitable fashion. Many poor countries, likewise, experience high rates of theft as well, but this is far from an absolute rule. It is not poverty alone that guarantees high rates of property crime; theft tends to be rare in some nations of the world in which people are the most impoverished. This may be because the rule of the rich is far more tyrannical than is true here, or because the poor do not dream that they could, through simple acts of theft, acquire some of what the rich have.

The second factor that many thieves claim caused them to steal is that most jobs available to a poor, uneducated young person are not interesting or rewarding. Most are boring, tedious, alienating, and demeaning. So the choice for some of us is not between poverty and cash but between working at a legal job that pays little and that one despises, and doing something that is illegal but is less humiliating, or at least that doesn't consume eight or ten hours a day. Stealing for a living involves being one's own boss, choosing one's working hours, and doing jobs one decides to do. It is difficult to imagine more persuasive inducements. Of course, the downside is arrest and penal confinement, but some young people have a sense of bravado and invulnerability that insulates them from seriously considering the down side.

As we saw, according to both victimization surveys and the UCR, property crime has declined *very* sharply since the 1970s. In 1973, according to the NCVS, the total property crime rate in the United States was nearly 550 per thousand households. In other words, during that year, more than half of all American households were victimized by at least one property crime. In 1993, the figure was 319, a decline of nearly 40 percent. And by 2011, this was 138, less than a third of the 1973 figure and less than half of what it had been eighteen years before (Truman and Planty, 2012). This decline is remarkable, even startling, unexpected, and very possibly unprecedented. Numerous criminologists have devised explanations for why the crime rate declined in the United States during the 1990s and the 2000s (Blumstein and Wallman, 2000; Zimring, 2007), including an improvement in the economy, the aging of the American population, the imposition of longer prison terms, and declines in drug use. An economist (Levitt, 2004; Levitt and Dubner, 2005, pp. 117–144) even argues the drop came about as a result of the legalization of abortion and the disappearance of unwanted and therefore poorly supervised, troubled children who, chances are, would have been born and gone on to high rates of juvenile, criminal behavior. But no one predicted it in advance, and none of these explanations fully accounts for it. Whatever the cause, the American decline in the crime rate, including property crime, is perhaps the most remarkable development in criminal behavior during the past four decades.

A funny thing happened on the way into the second decade of the twenty-first century: American society experienced a slight uptick in violent crime, for both 2010–2011 and 2011–2012. The development was uneven—occurring for some categories but not others, and in some places but not others—but unmistakable. It was recorded by both the UCR and victimization surveys and thus, not an aberration of methodology. For instance, between 2011 and 2012, murder and manslaughter increased nationwide by 1.5 percent, and robbery by 0.6 percent. However, rates of violence increased in metropolitan areas (though not in New York), but down in rural areas; murder increased in large and medium-size cities but decreased in small cities. Robberies increased by 1.1 percent in metropolitan areas and decreased in nonmetropolitan areas by an identical 1.1 percent. Property crime was even more uneven: Nationally, burglary decreased 3.5 percent but motor vehicle theft increased 0.6 percent. If there is a trend in the making, its nature and form is not yet evident to criminologists.

SUMMARY

Deviance and crime overlap, although imperfectly. Many forms of deviance are not crimes—witness eccentricity and obesity. Some forms of crime are not deviant in the narrow sense, at least, they do not generate a great deal of informal condemnation, even though they may lead to arrest; many white collar offenses qualify here. The field of criminology focuses on criminal behavior. Rather than repeat what's in such courses, in this book I will devote my discussion mainly to acts, beliefs (and traits) that are interesting mainly because they generate *informal* negative reactions. However, it should be kept in mind that *conceptually* and *theoretically,* deviance and crime share much of the same territory; hence they cannot be neatly or clearly separated. This chapter is devoted to behavior that is both criminal and deviant—but its criminal character is more crucial here.

Both deviance and criminal behavior cover a diverse array of activities and phenomena, though deviance, as we might expect, is *vastly* more varied than crime, including, as it does, not only behavior but beliefs and conditions as well. Still, as with deviance, what is a crime—what is a *violation of the law*—is determined by judgments of a specific audience. A crime is not a "thing" in the material world but the result of a *decision* made by specific parties, from a victim or a private citizen to a police officer and a judge, that a punishable offense has been committed. After a report of untoward activity has been lodged to the police by a complainant, the audience that decides what a crime is, is made up of *agents of formal social control*—the police and the courts, including prosecutors, judges, and juries.

Some acts have been punished by agents of the society or tribe for thousands of years, even before a formal written legal code or a law-making body existed. It was custom, not legislatures, that determined their criminal status. These are the *common law* or "primal" crimes, which have existed pretty much everywhere and throughout human history. They include murder, rape, and robbery. It is difficult to refer to such offenses as being "relative" to time and place, since there is a *common core* of such offenses that exists everywhere and has always existed. Even so, even for

the common law crimes, judgments of *who* commits *what* offense against *what* party is variable, relative to time and place.

Legislature-created law is called "statutory" law; it rarely has the force of sentiment that is as strong as that behind common law, which is based on the force of tradition and custom.

As with deviance, crime can be studied both from the essentialist, or *positivist*, or "causal" perspective, and the constructionist perspective. The constructionist agrees with the positivist's argument that worldwide and over historical time there has been and continues to be a "common thread" or "common core" to a great deal of crime, the common law or so-called "primal" crimes. Still, in the past, and even today, in certain locales, who the perpetrator and who the victim are make a difference with respect to public judgments of whether or not a crime has taken place. Most criminologists are positivists, and most are interested in the objective causes (and consequences) of crime. Moreover, most criminologists focus on certain crimes as characteristic of crime in general; they are taken as a measure or index of criminality. For the most part, they correspond to the public's notion of "street" crime, which is entirely predatory in nature—they are committed against victims who are harmed by the criminal act. The FBI refers to them as "Index Crimes," and tabulates the incidence of seven of them, in the form of "crimes known to the police," in detail in a yearly volume entitled the FBI's Uniform Crime Reports, entitled Crime in the United States. These crimes are murder and nonnegligent manslaughter, rape, robbery, and aggravated assault (the violent crimes); and burglary, motor vehicle theft, and larceny-theft (the property crimes). Some criminologists study non-Index Crimes as well: illicit drug possession and sale, prostitution, unauthorized gambling, and public intoxication.

The taboo against stealing goes as far back in historical time as the ownership of private property; two of the Ten Commandments prohibit the faithful from thievery. It has been said that the United States, in comparison with other industrialized societies, is a particularly larcenous society. Merton's anomie theory predicts that any society, such as the United States, that prominently displays symbols of affluence, suggests that the poor can acquire the affluence enjoyed by the rich, and denies access to that affluence, is likely to have a great deal of crime. However, the property crime rate in the United States has declined sharply in the past two decades, while in Western Europe, it has increased. Moreover, most of the crime, including property crime, is committed by a relatively small percentage of the population, indicating that we are *not* "all criminals." Although, in a given society, certain property crimes are more likely to be committed by the poor, interestingly, the wealthiest countries have the highest rates of certain property crimes, such as auto theft and burglary. This is because there is a greater abundance of material goods to steal in the first place.

Some of the findings of criminologists and sociologists of deviance should remind us that conventional assumptions and biases do not offer a valid guide to the way things are in the world of crime. To put the matter another way, popular misconceptions are a type of social construction that may *become* valid by being believed and acted upon. Fear is an essential ingredient in the study of criminal behavior. The contrast between the findings of positivist criminology and the constructionist's perspective provides an interesting paradox: The classic crimes of violence, which we fear the most, tend to be relatively rare, while other, more common sources of harm tend to be feared far less. The sociologist of deviance is interested in paradoxes such as these.

The FBI lists murder and "nonnegligent homicide," rape, and robbery as its three violent Index Crimes. These form the "common core" of crimes that all humanity punishes—although this is tempered or relativized by contingent factors such as who commits the act, against whom, and under what circumstances.

Murder has been a primal crime since the dawn of humanity. Even though there has been a common core to the acts that are judged murder nearly everywhere and at all times, exactly what specific acts are deemed murder has varied from one time and place to another. In many societies and during much of human history, if a member of a society killed an "acceptable" victim (a member of an "out-group") the act was not deemed murder. If that same member of the society willfully and without reason or sufficient provocation killed an *unacceptable* victim (a member of the

"in-group"), this was deemed murder, a deviant, unauthorized, and criminal offense. In this sense, cultural relativity exists even for the most reprehensible and heinous of acts. Murder is patterned according to sociological lines; it varies substantially over time and by country, region, urbanness, age, gender, as well as social and situational context.

Even though condemned pretty much everywhere, rape exhibits even more relativity than murder. In the contemporary United States, audiences vary with respect to how "inclusive" (or broad) versus "exclusive" (or narrow) their definitions of rape are; the variation is sociologically patterned. As with virtually all forms of predatory crime, the incidence of rape in the United States has declined during the past two to four decades. Research on rape victimization in the United States has used one of two data sources that have produced two substantially different estimates of its incidence. The first, employed by the National Crime Victimization Survey (NCVS), has produced a lower figure of roughly one per 1,000 women in the population; the second, used originally by the National Women's Study (NWS) and later adopted by a number of offspring surveys, principally the NVAWS, found a figure that is four to five times higher. How to reconcile them? It is possible that both conceptual or definitional and methodological differences generated the vastly different tallies—the latter surveys used a definition of rape that is much broader, and used different ways of studying the crime. Either way, rape is a form of victimization that has enduring negative consequences on the woman's physical and mental health.

The deviant nature of property crime dates at least as far back as Biblical times, yet contemporary larceny in the United States displays its distinctively American character. We tend to justify thievery (while condemning it at the same time—no one wants to be stolen from!), but most of us steal very infrequently, while the majority of what's stolen is lifted by a small minority of more serious thieves. The Mertonian anomie theory seems to explain why the United States has such a high rate of theft, though other explanations are necessary to understand rates of thievery among sectors of the population with higher than average rates of larceny. Victimization surveys indicate that the Uniform Crime Reports hugely underestimate the incidence and total value of property crime. At the same time, over the past two or three decades, the United States has experienced a sharp and unprecedented decline in its rate of Index Crimes. As yet, no criminologist or sociologist has offered a satisfying or comprehensive explanation for this remarkable trajectory. To make matters even more complicated, between 2010 and 2012 in the United States, the rates of some crimes in many area increased, while those of other crimes, and in some areas, did not.

Account: My Life in and out of Prison

The following account was contributed by Clarence, an inmate of a correctional facility in New York State. His life illustrates some of the principles outlined in this chapter.

I was born in 1972 and grew up in Bedford-Stuyvesant, Brooklyn. As long as I can remember, I strove to be above average and make my mark as a positive individual. My dad left the family and took up another life in North Carolina. I was the youngest of five children, and was raised by my mom. I was an intelligent, happy, and athletic child. My brothers had teams and crews, and, since I loved sports and music, I followed behind my brothers. Everybody had a nickname; mine was "Wiz."

My brothers and I would meet every day after school and we'd indulge in whatever came to mind or was happening at the time. My brother "Flash," was the captain, and our leader. I was down with the skating crew, The Mysterious Chillers, and the baseball crew, The Destroyers, as well as the breakdancing crew, Rock the Rhythm.

Soon after the introduction of hip-hop culture in the 1970s, another brother, "Fame" (aka Salaam), along with some others, introduced us to The Nation of Gods and Earths [also known as the "Five Percenters," which was founded by Clarence 13X, a student of Malcolm X]. My attributed name became "Wizlaamic." The Nation helped me to become more independent, family-oriented, and motivated me to study everything in the world. (As an aside, I should say that I am no longer an active member of the National of Gods and Earth.)

Still, my brothers and my friends and I were rebellious, inspired by the spirit of the sixties and seventies. We believed that blacks were up against a wall, so we had to create our own opportunities.

I grew up near a drug-infested ho stroll [an area where prostitutes solicit customers]. We engaged in numerous illegal activities. We used to chase the cake factory truck and obtain free cakes by stealing them off the back of the truck. The older fellas would put a sleeper hold on drunk men and take their money. As for me, following along the path of non-righteousness, I often broke into lockers and stole their contents. I saw it as a way of getting ahead and getting over. I was blinded by the fun, the money, and the lifestyle. We had abandoned living a decent, righteous life. Growing up in Bed-Stuy, I had pretty much the same thing in mind that others had: personal gain. In the neighborhood, on the subway trains, and in other places—on the streets of the East Village and Brighton Beach in Brooklyn—I committed many acts that were sad and foolish.

In 1986, I began attending Sarah J. Hale High School, located in downtown Brooklyn, in Boerum Hill, only a block from the Wyckoff and Gowanus projects; it had recently been converted from an all-girls' school, specializing in cosmetology. I began venturing out of my neighborhood, and in one of my sojourns, in Wykoff Gardens, I met Beverly, who was to become my girlfriend. I began seeing her regularly.

In the Gowanus Projects, drug selling was rampant. The teenagers there were flush with money; they took cabs and rented cars and often had hundreds—even thousands—in their pockets. I began hanging out at Albee Square Mall on Fulton Street; it gave me a chance to learn new things and experience different styles. It became my second home. I'd hang out there, meet my friends, and we'd go play basketball and go to the nearby clubs. I wouldn't change anything about what I did. It was fun. I had a great time.

I went through the [criminal justice] system; I was in and out of jail, but I was never hit with a really serious charge as a juvenile—that didn't come until my adulthood. In 1991, I received my GED, and I even attended Borough of Manhattan Community College [BMCC], which is kind of a party school. I was young and smooth, I carried guns and sold drugs. When I was 20 years old, I participated in a heist with three of my friends. We stuck up a candy store somewhere in Queens. One of my friends was acquainted with the alarm system, the times and the settings, and how many people came in the early morning, so we went for it. It netted us $70,000; we split it four ways, each getting $17,500. With the money, I bought a white Jetta. That made me feel good.

At BMCC, I met a diversity of people from different ethnic and cultural backgrounds. I loved college, I learned a lot, and became more sophisticated—but still I was attracted to the bright lights and fast life.

In September 1991, I had a daughter, Freda, with Beverly; in July 1993, my son Jacob was born.

I got into a mindset of getting whatever I wanted by any means necessary. I wanted to be well-paid for my efforts, regardless of who or what stood in my way. This became my way of life, and I got charged with burglary in the first degree, which drew an eight-year sentence, with a consecutive of 18 months to three years for an attempted escape from Riker's Island. I was incarcerated in August 1997, at the age of 24, and released December 2005, at age 33.

In January 1998, my son Fulani was born.

Prison was a stressful experience, but participating in a variety of programs, like creating puzzles, playing basketball, and surrounding myself with good-hearted, business-minded guys, got me through. For me, the most interesting program was learning sign language. I also worked with the blind as a mobility guide. Ready to hit the neighborhood on a different note, I created a searchword puzzle book. I also created and registered a line of T-shirts, bags, and other items. To go along with the catchy name I designed a terrific logo, but I didn't attract any financial backing or encouragement. Since the eighties, a lot of the people in my neighborhood had good ideas—a barbershop, a laundromat, and so on—but hardly anyone managed to take steps beyond that, so basically I was on my own. Setting up a business turned out to be really complicated—getting a business license, setting up an account with a bank, paying a trademark patent attorney, trademarking a logo, doing name searches, printing up my book, putting up posters, flyers, business cards, running ads. I had to do all of my own footwork.

I had witnessed my two brothers' business plight, and I was determined to make my mark and have a positive influence in the community. They had to struggle to get their businesses off the ground. They had a record shop in Flatbush and an Internet café in Jersey City, but funds got low, sales got low, and they eventually had to close them down. I appreciated whatever money and support that came my way, but the truth is, in my neighborhood, we needed to be one another's crutches. No one can generate any energy or accomplishment from talking and drinking and watching the women work. You have to do everything yourself.

Whatever happened to our dreams and aspirations? Where's the "Let's go at it hard" attitude? Everybody I grew up with wanted to be wealthy and take care of our families, but when we were faced with opportunities, all of us got scared and acted like a bunch of illiterates.

In July 2006, my parole officer violated me for curfew, and I also sold some weed to an undercover officer in Times Square; I got sent to Attica. At the beginning of 2007, I was released—no more parole. I tried to find my way. Because of my criminal background, the TLC (Taxi and Limousine Commission) twice denied me a hack license. While I was in the building of the TLC offices, I noticed a publication called *The Taxi Insider*. I called the editor and got one of my puzzles published, but I didn't get a position, I guess because someone on the paper decided that anyone can do that, so they didn't ask me to send them another one. I figure it was because I didn't have the complexion for the connection. If I had been a Caucasian, I would have had a lot more chances in life. Sure, for some things, you have to meet the necessary criteria, the experience, a degree,

(Continued)

Account: My Life in and out of Prison   Continued

whatever. But in this case, it was racial discrimination, plain and simple.

Two years passed. In April 2009, my friend Jermaine, aka "Big Jerry," hooked me up with a limousine job. The company also had contracts with funeral homes throughout the five boroughs. Things began looking up for me. I drove a limo and worked catering at the Chelsea Piers. And I helped out the family more and more with financial assistance and other responsibilities. My two brothers invested in the printing of my puzzle book, which I named after my niece—the Amina Sharise Word Search Puzzle Book. I had two book signings, participated in several fairs and festivals, plus I got offers of collaboration and was invited to numerous gatherings.

In May 2009, my mother passed away from pancreatic cancer. Early in 2011, I found out that my son Jacob was not my biological child. And in May 2011, I was arrested for the sale of a controlled substance. The police informant attacked my desire to get ahead and now I'm back in the criminal justice system, feeling really empty. In prison you run into the same foul individuals you see on the streets of New York. There's a status hierarchy in prison. If you're not M.V.P. (money, visits, and packages) your status is that of a soft, lowlife punk. So you have to strategize how you move. And the answer to that is to surround yourself with positive, educated people. That's how you stay out of harm's way. Plus, I was never part of a gang. I mind my own business and try to educate myself.

Why did I do it? How did I get back into this fix? I guess I'm a mixture of good and bad—a product of the pulls and tugs of my beautiful mother, the educational system, and my environment and criminal experiences. Think about this. At the Brooklyn Bridge Marriott, which hosts puzzle tournaments, I met Caleb Madison, a young searchword puzzle master, whose work has been published in *The New York Times*. He even agreed to collaborate with me. Now look at where I am— behind bars, my dreams shattered.

Here's a message to the world and to my children: Being attracted to material things you can't afford can have an unhealthy influence on you. You have to live within your means. I never drank, I never smoked. Maybe stealing cash was like a quick fix for me. It's a very dangerous high. Having six Rolexes, jewelry, nice cars, walls full of electronic equipment, and lots of money, doesn't bring freedom, a life with loved ones, or happiness. As for me, that allure led me from being the community champ to the community chump.

QUESTIONS

Has Clarence failed the criminal justice system—or has it failed him? What role has his background of poverty played in his criminal career? Consider how ambitious he is and how much he has accomplished within the context of conventional values—his creation of puzzles and puzzle books, for example; his effort to get a job with a puzzle publication, his creation of a line of T-shirts, his effort to get a hack license. Do you think that if any of these had brought a regular, paying job, Clarence would have engaged in criminal behavior? What if he had had a middle-class background and had completed a college education—where would his abilities have taken him? What accounts for Clarence's ambivalence—on the one hand, pointing to racial injustice as the cause of his incarceration, on the other, blaming his own desire for glittery baubles as superficial symbols of his success? What does that say about the causal chain that led from Clarence's background to his long prison term? Do you have any thoughts with respect to the failure of his community college exposure to inspire him to seek a professional career? Think of Clarence's invocation of his lack of agency— his inability to admit that he is responsible for his fate. He says, "My parole officer violated me." Well, what did he do? He says, "I got charged with a burglary." "I was blinded by the fun, the money, and the lifestyle." How would Clarence explain this seeming contradiction, these dilemmas—the conundrums that life has placed in his path?

CHAPTER

White Collar Crime

Learning Objectives:

After reading this chapter, you will be able to:

- differentiate between individual and structural deviance;
- trace the history of the discovery and naming of white collar crime;
- understand white collar and corporate crime;
- discuss the correlative factors in corporate crime;
- answer the question "Was the 2008 financial crisis a form of deviance?"

Who's the biggest, baddest, most famous white collar criminal of all time? During the course of more than two decades, ending with his conviction in 2009, Bernard Madoff, an investment broker, committed the largest financial fraud ever conducted by a single individual. He swindled 4,800 clients out of roughly $50 to $65 *billion* dollars. His victims include charities and foundations, banks, schools and universities, corporations, a senator, a motion picture producer, a motion picture director, a famous motion picture actor, a Hall of Fame baseball pitcher, the owner of the Philadelphia Eagles, the owner of the New York *Daily News*, lawyers, accountants, and investors—the list is long, impressive, and for the most part, hugely monied. Many of his clients lost their entire investments to Madoff's flimflam.

Madoff ran what is called a "Ponzi scheme," named after a 1930s swindler who looted funds from later investors so that he could pay off earlier ones. And meanwhile, he and his wife enjoyed a lavish lifestyle beyond the imagination of most of us. In the courtroom, victims expressed their outrage at Madoff and his crimes, calling him a "monster," a "beast," "an evil lowlife." Judge Denny Chin, who presided over the case, noted that of the more than 100 letters he had received about the case, not one expressed support for the defendant or described a single good deed he had performed. "The absence of such support," said Judge Chin, "is telling." He sentenced Madoff to a 150-year term; the swindler's release date is listed as November 14, 2139. Barring a potentially fatal and/or debilitating illness and early release, Madoff will spend the rest of his life in a federal penitentiary in Butner, North Carolina. In addition, the court stripped Madoff and his wife of their financial assets, including a $7 million Manhattan apartment, an $11 million estate in Palm Beach, a $4 million property at the tip of Long Island, and a $2.2 million yacht. The federal asset forfeiture unit, whose job it is to "seize and freeze" criminal proceeds, seized a total of over $7 billion in assets from Madoff's plunder, of which $5 billion was distributed to the swindler's victims (Lattman, 2013).

For the purpose of examining white collar deviance, two features of the Bernard Madoff case are interesting: One, the perpetrator could not have committed his crimes without occupying the position of investor; and two, he did not commit his crimes by means of violence, the threat of violence, or physical stealth. Almost as interesting: Unlike the past, when white collar criminal received a "slap on the wrist" penalty for crimes that entailed frauds totaling huge sums of money, Madoff received a sentence characteristic of the most violent offenders, such as murderers. Perhaps this tendency will carry over into the future. But Bernard Madoff doesn't buy the legitimacy of the severity of his sentence. Speaking when he was in prison, a context in which self-righteousness and bravado tend to prevail, Madoff does not apologize—but he does self-exculpate. As he was standing in line to receive his medication, Madoff overheard another prisoner grousing about the $65 billion his victims lost in the trader's schemes. "Fuck my victims," Madoff spat out. "I carried them for twenty years, and now I'm doing 150 years" (Fishman, 2010, p. 32). "Everybody on the outside kept claiming I was a sociopath," Madoff declared to Steve Fishman, a journalist. "I am a good person" (2011, p. 24). Two years after Madoff confessed his crimes to his sons and wife, Mark, his older son, committed suicide by hanging himself with a dog leash; Mark's widow says she would "spit in his face" if she were to encounter her former father-in-law. Now, his younger son, Andrew, refuses to speak to him, and his wife, Ruth, remains angry; "It's hard not to be. I mean, you know, I destroyed the family," Madoff explains (Fishman, 2011, pp. 24, 25).

Clearly, Bernard Madoff's illicit activities, his arrest, and his incarceration—along with the enormous publicity surrounding these events—publicly shamed, stigmatized, and dishonored him and his family. He is, in the language of the topic under discussion, a *deviant*. But is he typical?

Bernard Madoff represents the tip of the iceberg—the most big-time and infamous of a long and wide tradition of bilking the public with pen and paper rather than a gun or a fist. The Bernie Madoffs of the world—the corporate swindlers who filched millions or billions—are wildly exceptional, very far from the rule. It's possible that white collar and corporate wrongdoing is as common as street crime, but its perpetrators commit their acts behind closed doors, in offices, behind desks, by means of actions that, even if we watched, we wouldn't immediately *detect* as criminal. But most white collar crime is not exciting, and, unlike what Madoff did, it tends to be petty, usually involving, as it does, diddles and fiddles, book-juggling and figure-finagling, cutting corners, making technically illicit transactions, purposely incorrectly adding up columns of numbers, then pocketing fairly small sums of money. White collar criminals are usually drab little people with a narrow vision and commonplace goals rather than colorful, flamboyant, romantic economic swashbucklers.

As a kind of template of the less exciting white collar story, consider the memoir by Jerome Mayne, *Diary of a White Collar Criminal* (2010). Self-published, it recites the tale of a real estate broker working with low-income, usually first-time buyers, who requested, he tells us, "loans from hell" (p. 17). Somehow, unwittingly, Mayne says, he made several transactions that were illegal. In one, he failed to record that a buyer had switched jobs in the middle of a contract settlement. In another, a colleague sold a house to someone before she had taken possession—a "legal loophole," he said (p. 19). In a third, an associate slipped him $100 for doing a good job on a loan application. In another, he was given "a wad of cash" consisting of $500 and a bottle of Sapphire Gin (p. 25). Once, he was the loan officer for the borrower who bought a house he owned, enabling him to make a profit on the sale. Mayne's book is rife with descriptions of small offenses such as these, yet he gets arrested, convicted, and slapped with a two-year sentence to a federal penitentiary (whose location he is allowed to choose), still wondering what he did wrong.

Today, because of the huge sums of money involved, high-level corporate criminality attracts a great deal of attention. A number of well-informed observers have created websites devoted to the "Top Ten White Collar Criminals"; Bernard Madoff is on everyone's list. Andrew Fastow, a former Chief Financial Officer of Enron—at one time an energy, communications, and services corporation that claimed over $100 billion in revenues—also appears frequently on these lists. Convicted in 2006 of fraud, money laundering,

and conspiracy to conceal Enron's financial losses, Fastow was released late in 2011. In the 1990s, *Fortune* magazine named Enron "America's Most Innovative Companies" for six consecutive years; today it no longer exists. Jeffrey Skilling, Enron's former CEO, was convicted in 2006 of insider trading—he sold his $60 million investment in the company in advance of its collapse—and he won't be released from prison until 2028. Bernard Ebbers is the former CEO of WorldCom and is now serving a twenty-five-year term for false financial reporting and defrauding investors out of $11 billion. *Time* magazine listed Ebbers as the "most corrupt" CEO in history. John and Timothy Rigas, a father-and-son team, founders of Adelphi Communications, were convicted in 2005 and sentenced to fifteen-year terms for fraud and converting $2.3 billion in corporate assets into their own personal funds. Dennis Koslowski, CEO of Tyco International, and Mark Schwartz, the firm's CFO, were found guilty of grand larceny, conspiracy, securities fraud, and falsifying business records, looting the company of $600 million. Perhaps the silliest white collar criminal of them all was Martin Frankel, who invested with the stars—literally—that is, he used astrology to play the stock market, persuading a substantial number of customers to capitalize his folly. He stole $200 million from insurance companies, hid his pilfered loot in flimflam accounts, and was apprehended and sentenced in 2004 to a sixteen-year prison term. The list of *caught* corporate criminals is long, but it's possible that more offenders escape prosecution than end up behind bars.

But as Mayne's case illustrates, most white collar crimes do not involve the huge sums—millions and even billions of dollars—that stick to the fingers of big-time corporate swindlers. But even the most lucrative conventional crimes—robbery, burglary, larceny, and auto theft—cannot possibly yield much more than a few thousand per heist. The glamorous cinematic jewel heist that nets thieves millions is so rare as to be added up on one's fingers every decade. There simply isn't enough value in what can be physically hauled away to resell for billions. In real life, the theft of readily negotiable stocks and bonds worth mammoth sums occurs only sporadically, if ever—even more uncommon, in fact, than the big-time jewel knockoff. On the silver screen George Clooney as Danny Ocean and his larcenous pals successfully rip off the Bellagio in Las Vegas, in addition to several *other* casinos, to the tune of $150 million in cash and get away scot-free; in real life, in 2010, Anthony Carleo stole $1.5 million worth of gambling chips from the Bellagio only to discover that the chips were embedded with tags that automatically deactivated their value, rendering them unredeemable and worthless plastic discs. A month after the heist, the thief was apprehended and he's now sitting in a Nevada state penitentiary, serving out a six-to-sixteen year period of incarceration. While both conventional theft and white collar crimes are mostly petty affairs, the sums that a small handful of top-of-the-heap corporate crimes entail are vastly larger than what all of the burglars, robbers, and larcenists steal, added together, in a single year. If we were to depict white collar crime in the shape of a pyramid, with number of occurrences as the *x* axis and sums of money as the *y* axis, it would have an immensely large base and a thin, needle-like pinnacle.

The white collar criminal has become well known to the American public. David Friedrichs opens his textbook, *Trusted Criminals* (2010, Chapter 1) with the punch lines from various cartoons making light and good-natured fun of corporate offenders. A man in a suit and tie enters his attractive house, and announces to his wife, "Sorry I'm late, honey. I was doing two to five at Danbury." Others may be found on the Internet. Two convicts are sitting on their beds in their prison cells. One has taped a dollar bill on the wall above his bed. "It's the first dollar I ever embezzled," he explains to the other. Two men are sitting at a desk. One is studying a document the other has handed to him. "This is an interesting proposal, he says. "The upside is huge profits but the downside appears to be court-ordered community service." Four men in suits sit around a conference table. A fifth, who is standing, announces to the others, "In a further effort to control costs and satisfy shareholders, we've decided to steal stuff." These cartoons convey the following message: The public is aware of the white collar criminal and understands the central point of corporate criminality: It is profitable but only rarely risky, and it's the unlucky offender who gets caught.

INDIVIDUAL VERSUS STRUCTURAL DEVIANCE

Some acts that are widely disapproved of and condemned are engaged in by individuals who act more or less on their own, although within a setting of their peers and a national, social, and cultural environment. We can trace the *agency* of most of the deviant acts we've looked at so far in the book to a single individual—again, within a larger ambience or environment. Murder, rape, robbery, drug use, alcoholism, and so on, are behaviors in which a specific, identifiable person (or group of individual persons) engages. Such acts are forms of deviance in which virtually *any* member of the society could engage or could be designated as "having." It is the *individual* who is the focus of the origin of judgments of deviance; *all* individuals in the society are designated with respect to the deviance or conventionality of their beliefs or mental or physical condition. Individual deviance corresponds to two of Goffman's famous trilogy—that is, first, behavior or conditions that indicate "blemishes of individual character," and second, physical traits that are considered "abominations of the body." And Goffman's "stigma of tribe, religion, and nation" likewise locates *each and every person* along an axis of degrees of supposed acceptability versus unacceptability (1963, pp. 4–5). They are relevant for *everyone* (or almost everyone) in *every* society on Earth. To repeat, such individuals act within a structural setting. Although structural conditions certainly *influence* individual actions, the fact remains that *most* people do not engage in the behavior discussed in the chapters of this book.

Other acts, disapproved of and condemned by other, relevant social collectivities, cannot be reduced to the added-up, discrete acts of individual actors. They are more or less purely the product of local or society-wide structures—nation-states, corporations, organizations, units within organizations—entities whose agency we can trace above and beyond the individual. These behaviors are more than a product of different people doing more or less the same thing at different times in different places. High-level corporation executives discuss and agree to dump illegal levels of mercury—a waste byproduct of their industrial process—into a nearby river. Across the state, the executives of another company agree to release high levels of a toxic, cancer-causing gas into the atmosphere rather than pay for "scrubbing" the waste to acceptable levels. Even if the Environmental Protection Agency (EPA) were to discover their contamination, the fines they'd receive, they agree, are so small that the violation will have been worth it. The likelihood of the pollution killing people is statistical and long-term, so why worry about it? they reason. "All of these things are just a roulette wheel anyway," one says; the rest chuckle. The head of state of an East African nation agrees to adopt a policy of "africanization" by expelling white settlers and farmers and Asian traders and merchants. He orders his cabinet, staff, security forces, and army to carry out his policy; anyone not complying with his order will have his property confiscated and be tortured and shot, along with his family, servants, and pets. Within six months, half the foreigners have left his country, and within a year, most of the rest follow. The country collapses into economic chaos. An American president meets with his cabinet and discusses the problems created to American interests by a particular Middle Eastern dictator. The consensus is that American forces should invade the country, capture the dictator, put him on trial, and execute him. The president calls the heads of several dozen allied nations, and creates a "coalition" of forces that coordinate in this endeavor. The resulting war kills roughly 5,000 coalition, mostly American, troops, and well over 100,000—possibly hundreds of thousands—locals, including the targeted dictator, but the war has created instability in the region, and violence between and among factions continues for some time after the execution.

Some of our other discussions address characteristics, such as poverty, race, and physical traits that do not require behavior at all. Mental disorder is a condition that *manifests* itself in the form of odd, eccentric, or often damaging or dangerous behaviors. Unconventional beliefs also represent a form of deviance, although they *may* not express themselves in overt actions. Like the deviant behaviors we've discussed, poverty, race, physical characteristics, mental disorder, and unusual beliefs are *structural in foundation*

but individual in manifestation. Poverty is generated by a nationwide and a global economy, but it is the individual who is judged by audiences to be poor; race is *constructed* by culture and society—but it is the individual who steps forward as the *representative* of a particular racial and ethnic category.

White collar crime is a hodgepodge category that consists of two types of offenses. One includes those acts that are illegal and can be engaged in only by persons who occupy the relevant positions, but whose dynamics are similar to the other deviancies we've discussed so far; within a particular environment and with or without the collaboration of peers, the occupants of these positions act more or less on their own. A second type of white collar crime is referred to as *corporate crime*; it is different from most forms of deviance. It entails individuals who act as embodiments of a particular organization and within a given organizational setting. The act could not have been performed without that actor's location *within* that setting, and the collective setting of the act dilutes or tamps down the stigma, condemnation, or deviance that adheres to the perpetrator. Of such illegal acts, we have two varieties. The first is lower-level *individual* white collar crime, and the second is *structural* or *corporate* white collar crime. In the first category, we find embezzlement by bank tellers, and other professional crimes, such as doctors making fraudulent statements in insurance forms, pharmacists stealing drugs from their shelves, and individual investors and entrepreneurs padding their expense accounts to receive greater refunds from the IRS. This is a form of deviance that results in condemnation and judgments against individual perpetrators, if apprehended, but nonetheless it is *not* a form of deviance that just anyone can enact. It is the individual's position within an organizational structure or occupation that *enables* the perpetration of the act. In other words, for these crimes, only some members of society—those who are embedded within a given organizational context—can be located along a continuum of deviance or conventionality. Most of society falls *outside* of the scope of this evaluation because they do not occupy the position that must be occupied to commit the behavior that attracts the condemnation.

The second type of "organizational" deviance is made up of those actions that are also located within a structural setting, but which are not enacted by one or a small number of specific individuals; its *setting* is organization, its *agency* or motivation is organizational, and its *enactment* is organizational. Corporate crimes are even more contextually located than our examples in that they represent coordinated actions that are enacted by *webs* or *networks* of interacting, orchestrated individuals engaged in behavior *in concert* with one another to produce the deviant action. In a sense, individual initiative is of no consequence. Any one actor in this network has no choice in the matter—or, rather, the choice is to comply with the act or quit one's job and leave the organization altogether. In all likelihood, the act was planned and mandated at or near the top of the power hierarchy by the major decision-makers—the CEOs, the presidents, the top-level executives, the directors. Top administrators may tell their underlings, "Do what you have to do to get the job done," and leave the nuts-and-bolts decisions to their assistants or henchmen. In this category we find most corporate crimes. Such schemes—dumping chemicals into streams, lakes, and oceans, making blatantly false claims in advertisements, dividing up a market among two or more corporations, selling meat with a higher bacteria count than is legal—are the collective products of a number of minds discussing what can be accomplished and what can't, what should be done and what shouldn't. They often, though not always, originate at the top, but if we take any other single actor out of the picture, the outcome would be the same because the replacement would do the same thing: collaborate in the commission of a corporate crime. Most people in the population cannot engage in such wrongdoing because they are not in a position do so, and they are not implicated in a cat's cradle of reciprocal relations that generates and sustains the illicit enterprise. The degree to which deviant corporate actions characteristically are not traceable to an individual's behavior can be seen in the fact that in *White Collar Crime* (1949), Sutherland treated *the corporation* as the criminal actor rather than the gaggle of executives and their subordinates who engaged in the illegal, unethical behavior that resulted in official action; it was the corporation that he labeled "recidivists," not the executives.

With respect to crime and deviance being enacted by actors whose behavior is coordinated by an organizational structure, the same can be said for organized crime and terrorist conspiracies. But criminologists do not regard the illegal behavior enacted by such organizations as "white collar crime" but a different species of crime altogether. Why? Because, for the most part, the actions that result from such conspiracies—murder, assassination, aggravated assault, arson, robbery, and so on—are ordinary street crimes that are tabulated by the FBI as Index Crimes. Just as some observers have (incorrectly) referred to corporate crime as "organized crime," it would be likewise incorrect to refer to organized crime and terrorist conspiracies as "white collar crime."

In this sense, organizational deviance stands outside Goffman's trilogy. They can *only* be enacted by a network of persons each of whom has a particular position in a particular organization. Only corporate executives and their subordinates can engage in a corporate crime, and only by consulting and interacting with a web of peers; they can do so if there's a give-and-take up and down and across the chain of command. Anyone can steal, virtually any man can rape, any person can commit robbery—but only actors located within a corporate or government setting can commit corporate or government crimes. In other words, with respect to *being judged as engaging in deviance*, the corporate and government crime categories are completely irrelevant for most of the members of society. This is not true of any of the other behaviors, beliefs, or conditions we've looked at in the other chapters in this book. Most of us do not stand at the judicial dock, waiting to be evaluated for corporate or government crimes; most of us *can* stand at the dock, potentially liable to be evaluated for sexual, racial, economic, criminal, drug, cognitive, physical, or mental irregularities, transgressions, or unacceptabilities—did we do it or not, do we believe it or not, do we possess the relevant traits or not?

Did somebody see us babbling to ourselves? Did the guy down the street walk by our window and see us sniffing a white powder off a mirror with a straw? Did we punch the annoying kid next door? Did we just move into a neighborhood where the skin of all our neighbors is a different color from ours? Did we lose our job?

Is our house being repossessed? Are we being kicked out on the street to fend for ourselves? All of these are likely to result in audiences judging us as *individual persons* engaging in *individual actions*, expressing individual beliefs, or possessing certain physical traits. But most of us never have to account for our corporate or government action—because we aren't embedded in a corporate or government network to begin with. Hence, corporate and government crimes are qualitatively different from everything else in this book. *As actors*, many forms of organizational deviance do not touch our lives, though many corporate and government crimes do place us at risk *as victims*—charging us more at the gas pump; being exposed to polluted soil, air, and water; eating tainted food; being exposed to the actions of unfriendly nations whose members consider the behavior of the American people, or the American government, wrongful; spying on us; taking away our rights; and illegally arresting us.

One of the more interesting features of behavior that takes place within an organization is that judgments of deviance vary considerably according to where one stands. The members of organizations, taken as a whole, seek to perpetuate the organization in which they are located—in a phrase, to ensure that it will survive and succeed. Certain actions that are regarded as deviant *outside* the organization are actually endorsed, encouraged, and rewarded *by* and *within* the organization. They are endorsed because they are thought to further the organization's interests. Other actions are discouraged, punished, and regarded as deviant by the organization. They are believed to be (and, objectively speaking, they actually are) harmful to the organization. In the former category we find much (although not all) corporate crime, where the perpetrator *is* the organization. To be more precise, the perpetrator is made up of the top echelon of the corporation. Corporate crime is by definition illegal behavior that is enacted *on behalf of* the corporation. In contrast, most (although not all) embezzlement, entails an employee stealing *from* a corporation.

The concept of organizational deviance helps us in our quest to understand and explain deviance in another way as well. Not only are some individuals embedded in organizations while most of the rest of us are not, causality also comes into the picture when we compare one organization with another. Some organizations experience high rates of deviance within their ranks while others have very low rates. Why? The main reason is the *institutional climate* that influences the enactment of deviance in a given organizational setting. Corporations whose top executives strongly and openly oppose, monitor, and sanction the illegal behavior of their underlings are likely to have less of it than those corporations whose executives seem indifferent to, or encourage, such behavior. Institutional climate is largely the product of social control emanating from the top of the organizational hierarchy. Institutional climate also applies to changes in time; after a corporation is seriously sanctioned for a business crime, accompanied by media reports and negative public opinion, there is likely to be a lull in illegal activities.

THE DISCOVERY AND NAMING OF WHITE COLLAR CRIME

The white collar crime concept had its origin in the work of the "muckrakers," a loose coterie of journalists, investigative reporters, historians, lawyers, and a few novelists, who, early in the twentieth century, delved into and wrote about a variety of illegal, unethical, harmful, and otherwise abominable and scandalous practices by corporations, bureaucracies, and other major organizations and institutions; these practices included corruption in municipalities, unhealthful, inhumane conditions in food-processing plants, dangerous conditions in coal mines, illegal and deceptive advertising, the abuse of mental patients by staff, the exploitation of factory workers, running "sweat shops," the exercise of monopolies and trusts, the use of child labor, bribery and corruption, the illegal use of prison labor, and so on. The four most famous examples of muckraking writing include two novels, *The Octopus* (1901) by Frank Norris and *The Jungle* (1906) by Upton Sinclair, and two works by journalists, *The Shame of the Cities* (1902) by Lincoln Steffens and *The History of the Standard Oil Company* (1904) by Ida Tarbell. Interestingly, many of these practices were not yet illegal, since laws had not yet been passed banning them; hence, were not white collar *crimes*. They were unethical, exploitative, and dangerous—but most were not yet technically criminal.

Almost certainly the passage of the Pure Food and Drug Act of 1906 represents the muckraker's greatest legislative triumph; it eventually forced the federal inspection of meat products, forbade the manufacture and sale of harmful or ineffective medical nostrums, imposed the labeling of habit-forming drugs, and paved the way for the creation of the Food and Drug Administration. In addition, a federal child labor law was passed in 1916, but declared unconstitutional, twice. Still, the legislative response to the exposés of these corporate malpractices was slow. But perhaps the most important overall impact the muckrakers achieved was in arousing the conscience of the public about harmful, dangerous, exploitative, unethical corporate practices; eventually, legislative reform caught up with what needed to be done, though business nearly always strenuously lobbied against such reforms. In effect, the muckrakers exposed, stigmatized, and deviantized a major swath of corporate and industrial practices that hadn't yet been criminalized.

Edward A. Ross (1866–1951) was one of the first social scientists to recognize the concept, and the import, of white collar crime. In *Sin and Society* (1907), Ross wrote that the railroad magnate "picks pockets with rebates" and the manufacturer murders "with adulterants instead of bludgeons," burglarizes with "rake-offs" rather than a crowbar, cheats with a "company prospectus" rather than a deck of cards, "scuttles his town instead of his ship" and, in the end, "does not feel on his brow the brand of a malefactor" (p. 7). Ross dubbed the white collar offender the "criminaloid." Before we pat the memory of the man on its back for his insightful discovery, we should keep in mind that he was also a racist who believed that whites were superior to all other races, opposed the mass, late-nineteenth and early twentieth-century immigration that populated the United States, and argued that the mingling of the races resulted in the degeneration and "suicide" of whites. Elected President of the American Sociological Society (now the ASA) for 1914–1915, E.A. Ross handed down a decidedly mixed legacy.

Sociologists and criminologists, almost universally, name Edwin Sutherland (1883–1950) as the most important historical figure in the development of the concept of white collar crime. In a talk before the American Sociological Society meeting in December 1939, Sutherland introduced the term, the "white collar criminal." He published that talk as an article in the *American Sociological Review* two months later, entitled "White-Collar Criminality." And his book on the subject, which appeared in 1949, morphed the title of his subject into its third and final version: *White Collar Crime*. In the original manuscript of the book, Sutherland provided names of the specific corporations he exposed, and the publisher thought it could be sued for defamation, so these names were expurgated from the first edition. An "uncut" version of the book which designated the firms involved, appeared more than three decades after its author's death (1983). "White collar crime," Sutherland wrote, "may be defined approximately as a crime committed by a person of respectability and high social status in the course of his occupation" (1949, 1961, p. 9, 1983, p. 7).

Unfortunately, Sutherland was vague and inconsistent about exactly what professions he wished to encompass in his conceptualization. In the footnote that accompanies his definition, he restricts his definition to "business managers and executives," and seems to *exclude* employees such as clerical and office workers, lower-level administrators, accountants, bureaucrats, minor officials and functionaries, and receptionists—not to mention government officials. But he is ambivalent, because lower-level white collar functionaries keep appearing in his text: Garage mechanics who overcharge (p. 11). Physicians who fee-split, conduct unnecessary operations, and sell illicit drugs (p. 12). A graduate student who takes a part-time job as a shoe salesman (pp. 236–238). It may be more productive to ignore Sutherland's conceptual delineation and *stress* corporate crime, but include any and all illegal activity that is committed by persons with high or middling occupational prestige within the context of their professions. Hence, while not corporate crimes, I regard professional, government, and computer-related cybercrime as *white collar crimes*.

Sutherland states that his principal motivation for developing the white collar concept was scientific and *theoretical*—that is, to argue for differential association or socialization as the explanation for white collar crime and to strengthen that theory's purchase as a general approach to crime and deviance. But Sutherland was a political progressive and interested in persuading criminologists that their belief that members of the lower and working classes were more likely to commit crime was false. Theories that relied on poverty, immigration, social ecology, divorce, the single-parent household, inadequate parenting, social pathology, and so on, failed to account for white collar crime since none of them cause it. Sutherland also mocked psychiatric theories as explanations of corporate crime; as Geis comments (1962, p. 160), Sutherland ironically stated that U.S. Steel does not have an unresolved oedipal problem nor does DuPont desire to return to the womb. The classic explanations for crime and delinquency that were based on social and psychological pathology were inadequate, he insisted because, again, they don't and cannot explain a major type of illegal behavior—white collar crime. Another theory is needed, he insisted, and that explanation is his own theory of differential association.

Sutherland's white collar crime concept, and his theory that claims to explain it, have met with both praise and criticism. This is because the concept and the theory offer pieces of a puzzle that do not quite fit together. To be more specific, introducing the *concept* represented a major innovation, whereas Sutherland's *theory*—that is, the explanation he offered in an attempt to explain it—is inadequate and misleading.

Donald Newman exclaimed that Sutherland's conceptualization of white collar crime may possibly be "the most significant recent development in criminology" (1958, p. 735). Karl Mannheim stated that if there were a Nobel Prize in criminology, "Sutherland would have been awarded it for his work on white collar crime" (1965, p. 470). Yet his detractors, while conceding that Sutherland's conceptualization of white collar offenses *as* crime opened up an immense fertile field of exploration for criminology, argued that he bungled in his efforts to account for its enactment *by* actors whose behavior need to be

understood. This is because Sutherland was fuzzy in his answer to the question: *Who is the corporate actor?* I've stated that corporate crimes are distinctly different from practically all other criminal acts in that they are, *by their very nature*, enacted by a collectivity rather than individual persons. Decisions are arrived at in consultation with higher-ups and approved—or initiated—at the top. It is the *corporation* that acts, as a whole, not scattered, isolated actors, one at a time. Often, after conviction, it is the corporation that is fined, not specific persons working for that corporation. On the other hand, individual corporate actors may be fined and, occasionally sentenced to a term of incarceration. (Clearly, a corporate entity cannot serve a prison sentence!) When the Pennwalt Corporation was convicted and fined more than $1 million for illegally dumping a toxic substance into Puget Sound, a federal district judge insisted on seeing the company's top executive in court before he would accept a guilty plea; "Who is the corporation?" the judge asked; "I think the public is entitled to know who's responsible" (Egan, 1989). Suffice it to say that, though individual persons act, they always do so within certain social structures. In the case of corporate crime, these social structures are formal organizations or bureaucracies. As to whether persons or organizations are responsible for a given corporate crime depends on the specific crime in question, and a single explanation cannot suffice (Gibbs, 1966, p. 323), just as a single explanation cannot account for all diseases (Geis, 1962, pp. 161–162). The realization that Sutherland's theory or explanation of white collar crime falls embarrassingly short the moment we realize that not only can it not account for all crime—it can't even distinguish between criminal and conventional behavior; both are learned as a result of individuals associating differentially with certain social circles of intimates.

The question of who the corporate actor is plays a central role when we attempt to determine the *incidence* or *rate* of corporate crime. If the corporation is considered as the actor (and if the entire period of its existence is considered as well), then clearly, *most* (and in Sutherland's pioneering study, *all*) corporations are guilty of committing corporate crimes at least once, since at least some executives made decisions that turned out to be illegal. Hence, their *rate* of corporate crime would be enormous. However, if all the executives are included in the total number of actors (and if a year-by-year tally is made), it is possible that rates of corporate crime would be quite low. Most observers who argue that corporate crime is rampant have not devoted much thought to determine its rate relative to the number of persons who are in a position to commit it. Sutherland's study was based on *corporations* as the unit of analysis, but his explanation for white collar crimes took place within them—differential association theory—was fundamentally *individualistic*, an obvious *contradiction* (Gottfredson and Hirschi, 1990, pp. 188, 191). In the words of Gilbert Geis, "Sutherland was led by his theoretical preconceptions into a concept of white-collar crime . . . of dubious utility" (1962, p. 160).

A another difficulty with Sutherland's original formulation of white collar crime is that he failed to distinguish acts that could draw a criminal sentence or a punitive fine from *civil* infractions—that is, acts that did not violate the criminal code. In fact, only 16 percent of Sutherland's cases were adjudicated in criminal court, which seeks a penalty or the punishment of the offender; the remainder was settled in civil court, which seeks restitution, or a return of the status quo, and where no arrest or incarceration is possible. Moreover, civil suits are initiated by private parties who feel that their rights are infringed by the offending party; unlike the criminal law, which presumably reflects government policy and the will of the people, civil law represents the will of an aggrieved party. In twenty-five civil cases, food-processing plants violated the Pure Food and Drug Act, and federal agents merely confiscated the goods (p. 19). General Cable Company was accused of interfering with the workers' right to organize and form a union; in response to the civil suit, the company "stipulated that it would desist" from its improper behavior (p. 31). In fact, in most of the cases Sutherland studied, the outcome was a mere "cease and desist" order. The same confusion wracks many contemporary analyses of the subject, and it weakens and muddies the analytic purchase of the concept. Many large firms consider lawsuits the price of doing business, but their top executives would think twice about committing an action that could land one of them behind bars in a federal penitentiary.

WHITE COLLAR AND CORPORATE CRIME

Corporate crime is a subset of white collar crime. That is, all corporate crime is white collar crime, but not all white collar crime is corporate crime. What is white collar crime? As we saw, as originally defined by Edwin Sutherland in a speech to the American Sociological Association in 1939 (and later formulated in print), white collar crime is an illegal action that is committed by the occupant of high occupational status in the course of his or her professional activity (1940, 1949).

Exactly how "high" the occupational status in question must be to qualify need not concern us; clearly, we are not referring to manual laborers, but it should include bank clerks, though Sutherland did not include them. Even embezzlement, a relatively lowly white collar crime, is committed by persons who work in occupations that rank close to the top half of the hierarchy of occupational prestige. But this definition *excludes* "common" or conventional crimes: an executive who murders his wife (or her husband), a professor who beats up a student, a bank teller who takes a gun and robs a bank. The concept also excludes theft and pilferage from the job; this is larceny-theft, an Index Crime category in the Uniform Crime Reports. In any case such acts are not committed *in the course* of the offender's job. And Sutherland's definition also excludes acts that someone may see as unethical and/or harmful *but are not against the law*, such as manufacturing and selling cigarettes, selling legal but dangerous products, taking "three-martini lunches," and paying workers low but legal wages. If an act is not a violation of a legal code and does not call for a punitive sanction, that is, a jail or prison sentence—or at least a punitive fine—then it is not a white collar *crime*. This introduces the dilemma that we face when looking back at unethical practices that prevailed in the late nineteenth and early twentieth centuries, when the muckrakers were conducting their investigations and writing their books, before the introduction of white collar legislation. Many acts such as the use of child labor, the dumping of toxic waste into the air and public waters, selling "embalmed beef," and so on, *were not crimes* yet were regarded as wrong by much of the public; a century or more ago, their exposure in muckraking newspaper articles created a scandal among their readers. Perhaps they could then have been regarded as "deviant corporate practices," but not white collar crimes.

The stereotype of white collar criminals is that they are all rich and powerful. In fact, this is far from true. As Weisburd et al. (1991), discovered by examining a cross section of offenders convicted in federal court of a variety of white collar crimes—including securities fraud, antitrust violations, bank embezzlement, and postal, tax, and credit fraud—most did not occupy high-status positions. True, given the fact that they are *white collar* offenders, by definition, they were not manual laborers. But a remarkably high proportion occupied the very lowest rungs of the white collar status hierarchy. Many were unemployed at the time of their arrest or held fairly humble jobs, did not have a college education, and did not own their own house. At the time of the arrest that led to their conviction, offenders were twice as likely to have had a criminal record than was true of the national average. These authors (p. 190) conclude that most white collar offenders are ordinary people who got into financial difficulty and who saw their way out of it through illegal and fraudulent measures. They were "struck by the banal, mundane quality of the vast majority of criminals" in their sample (pp. 45–46). The majority of their crimes, these authors say, "have an undramatic, local or regional quality," a "common, familiar ring." Say the authors, business fraud is "as familiar in their business context as are street crimes in poor communities" (p. 46).

What most people mean by "white collar crime" is *corporate crime*. As we saw, while all corporate crime is white collar crime, corporate crime is a specific *form* or *subtype* of white collar crime. To be precise about it, corporate crime entails executives and executive officers engaging in illegal actions that are intended to further the interests of that corporation; they are actions taken *on behalf of* the corporation. (In so doing, they may *also* benefit the careers of the individual corporate actors, but that is a different matter.)

This type of crime clearly contrasts with individual embezzlement, which is undertaken *against* the corporation *on behalf of* a given employee or several employees. In embezzlement, the victim is the corporation. In corporate crime, the victim, or potential victim, is the *general public* (in the case of illegal pollution), the *consumer* (in the case of price-fixing or the sale of illegally unsafe products), the *employee* (such as illegally unsafe working conditions), the *government* (for instance, illegal tax avoidance), or a *competitor* (two firms forming a price-fixing conspiracy against a third). And the criminal act was performed not only *in the context of* the corporation but also *on behalf of* the corporation. While, as we saw, the majority of white collar criminals are low-level, unsuccessful bottom-feeders who are trying to scrape by with petty, illegal scams to cheat and defraud their victims, the same is not true of corporate criminals.

Corporate crime is not a classic, clear-cut case of deviance. *In some respects*, it is a form of deviant behavior; in some respects, it is *not*. In the sense that audiences designate corporate actions that harm people physically and take money out of their pockets as serious crimes (Friedrichs, 2010), they are a form of deviance. To the extent that illegal corporate actions are likely to result in prosecution and a jail or prison sentence, they are deviant. To the extent that a conviction and a jail or prison sentence for a corporate crime is stigmatizing, *personally discrediting*, that it *taints* the character of the offender (for instance, if friends and loved ones regard mention of it in an obituary as inappropriate, a "smear"), then clearly, it is a form of deviance. To the extent that there are social circles in this society made up of persons who define executive misdeeds as serious wrongdoing, and attempt to legitimate that view in society as a whole, then they are indeed a form of deviance *in those circles*.

On the other hand, to the extent that harmful corporate crime, however serious, does *not* result in jury conviction for offenders or stiff prison sentences (Friedrichs, 2010), then it is *not* deviant. To the extent that social circles define the actions that corporate offenders engage in as acceptable and characterize their prosecution a "witchhunt," then, clearly, in those circles, such actions are *not* deviant. Just because corporate actions are unethical, harm people, and are formally against the law, does not automatically make them deviant *to relevant audiences*. Just because we, or persons very much like us, don't like what executives do can't magically make their behavior deviant. *Are corporate misdeeds condemned by the public?* Are they commonly *prosecuted* by the criminal justice system? Can corporate wrongdoers get into *trouble* as a result of their actions? Are such corporate actors socially *stigmatized* by their actions? If the answer is yes, then absolutely—corporate crime is deviant. If the answer is no, then corporate crime is *not* a deviant act. What we see, instead, is something of an in-between case. Clearly, corporate crime has one foot in conventionality and one in deviance. This is one of the reasons why it is so interesting.

Even today, though technically illegal, sentences for many white collar crimes entail criminal (along with civil) fines rather than jail or prison terms, and corporate executives responsible for wrongdoing rarely suffer from stigma or interpersonal condemnation. (They are often denounced in the press for their illegal behavior, however.) Consider the following event. On May 20, 2010, a tremendous explosion blew apart the Deepwater Horizon, a British Petroleum oil rig in the Gulf of Mexico, fifty miles off the Louisiana coast, killing 11 workers and injuring 27; the rig slowly sank into the sea, gushing, over the next few weeks, tens of millions of gallons of crude oil into the Gulf, contaminating the water and the shoreline from Texas to Florida and killing thousands of birds and other major wildlife and uncountable numbers of fish. The burning rig sent out a trail of smoke 30 miles long, and the spill sent out a floating scum of oil on the surface of the water 130 miles long and 70 miles wide. It was the worst environmental disaster in the history of the petroleum industry. As a result of a court settlement, BP "provisioned" $38 billion to clean up the spill, paid out $8 billion in civil damages, faces a $17 billion fine from the federal government, $4 billion specifically in criminal fines, and half a billion dollars in fines to stockholders who, the court argued, BP had "misled" as to the size and nature of the spill. Within two months, the pipeline had been capped, but a measure of environmental damage will remain forever. The BP oil spill was an environmental disaster,

and an illegal act, but not one BP executive was imprisoned for the crime. The disaster did fill the pages of newspapers and magazines and the airwaves with criticism for BP, but the corporation has spent the past three years engaging in a massive public relations campaign and a variety of good works to refresh its public image. Indeed, from the perspective of hundreds of years, environmental degradation remains a *negative* case of deviantization: extreme harm is often *unrelated* to outrage and condemnation—and only *rarely* to arrest and imprisonment.

Corporate crime is wrongdoing in high places. We do not expect the executive or lawyer to engage in crime, or to be prosecuted, convicted, and be sent to prison. Most of us have a conception of crime that *precludes* the respectability of the offender. The stereotype is that "crime" is what street people—or at least, poor people—do. There is, as many observers have pointed out, a certain *incongruity* in seeing an affluent, sixty-year-old banker in handcuffs and a prison uniform, being marched off to a prison cell, to serve time with murderers, rapists, and burglars. Many of us can understand the motives of poor, powerless criminals, who steal out of desperation or commit violence as a result of anger and frustration. The crimes of the rich and the powerful are puzzling to us, however; if someone can earn a sizable income legally, why try to earn even more in an illegal fashion? Why risk one's current material comfort and freedom simply to gain an edge over one's competitors? Is it greed? To many casual observers, corporate crime doesn't make a great deal of sense.

The fact is, corporate crime is similar to all *instrumental* actions, that is, those that are designed to achieve a certain goal; under certain circumstances, achievement of the goal assumes far greater importance than the means by which the goal was attained. One major *subtype* of—but by no means all—deviant behavior takes place when the actor resorts to *illegitimate* means to achieve a *legitimate* goal. If the likelihood of detection is extremely low, resorting to *legal* or *legitimate* means to attain that goal is actually quite *irrational*, since, typically, they are less efficient and less effective. Following legal procedures usually ties the corporate actor down to rules, regulations, and restrictions that may actually prevent or frustrate the achievement of desired goals. In the corporate world, we are forced to ask: "Given the great rewards and low risks of detection, why do so many business people adopt the 'economically irrational' course of obeying the law" (Braithwaite, 1985, p. 6)?

The same logic is not unique to the business world—nor even to capitalist society. Students often cheat on exams because it gets them what they want—a higher grade; shoppers may shoplift clothes, again, because it permits them to have what they cannot otherwise afford; many of us lie because, once again, in so doing, we attain what we desire—respect, admiration, or getting out of a sticky situation. Of course, there's the risk of apprehension, but the lower that risk is, the greater the likelihood of normative deviation. When legitimate or conventional avenues make the attainment of a goal difficult or impossible, many of us, whether as individual or as corporate actors, will resort to illegitimate or deviant avenues. The conditions that create the impulse to deviate are widespread, not confined to business dealings. "Some organizations seek profits, others seek survival, still others seek to fulfill government-imposed quotas, others seek to service a body of professionals who run them, some seek to win wars, and some seek to serve a clientele. Whatever the goals might be, it is the emphasis on them that creates trouble" (Gross, 1978, p. 72). The problem here is not the worm in the apple—it is the apple itself.

CORPORATE CRIME: CORRELATIVE FEATURES

There are also *correlative* features of corporate crime, aspects of what it is like that are a *product* of its defining criteria. What are they? Imagine describing corporate crime to someone who knows nothing about the phenomenon; what would our description look like? Let's look at eight of the most essential features of corporate crime.

First, as to the nature of the behavior itself: Corporate crime tends to be made up of *complex*, *sophisticated*, and relatively *technical* actions. Imagine witnessing or watching a videotape of a robbery or a murder; most of the time, we'd be able to unambiguously identify the act *as* a crime. In contrast, corporate crime would not be so readily identified. How do we know a corporate crime when we see one? When we watch a videotape of an armed robbery, we know an armed robbery is in process. In contrast, a videotape of a corporate crime would result in a more ambiguous judgment from an audience. It might even take an expert—an accountant, for example, an industrial chemist, a physician, or a government official—to determine its illegal status. The way that a corporate crime is committed is complex and interactional. At a board meeting of executives, a proposal is made and discussed. Memos are exchanged; decisions are made, policies are put into practice. Much of the time, it is not clear whether a crime in fact took place. Even experts may have trouble deciding. Even *victims* may not know that they have been victimized. Of course, the criminal status of some actions is more clear-cut than others, but for most, it is far less clear-cut than for most street crimes. This is because these actions tend to be complex, sophisticated, and technical. In contrast, the meaning of street crime is more direct and unambiguous.

Second, corporate crime tends to be *intermingled with legitimate behavior*. Illegal advertising claims are made in the context of a legal, legitimate advertising industry; some exaggeration is considered acceptable and is legal. But how much is too much? Monopolistic restraints of trade are carried out in a capitalistic business environment in which all corporations attempt to capture a larger share of the market; most of such attempts are legal and are considered good business practice, while some are illegal and "go too far." Even embezzlement is enacted within the context of ordinary, routine workaday activities, such as entering numbers into an accountant's ledger. While *some* traditional street crimes are also "intermingled with legitimate behavior" (date rape, for example, is a product of extremely aggressive courtship practices), most is not. It is difficult to imagine, let's say, what legitimate behavior a robbery or a burglary is "intermingled" with. With street crime, the crime act is illegal *in its totality*.

A third characteristic of corporate crime is that *victimization tends to be diffuse*. Harm is not always conceptualized or identifiable as such because it is usually spread out over a substantial number of victims. Again, this represents a sharp contrast with street crime. A rape harms a specific woman; a robbery, a specific store; a murder, obviously, the deceased victim as well as his or her survivors. But with corporate crimes, harm is usually spread out, usually thinly to many victims. Monopolistic practices may result in us being charged, let's say, $1,000 more for the purchase of a new car, a quarter more for a half-gallon of milk, $2 more for a pair of jeans. Even where there is physical harm, victimization can usually be measured in terms of *statistical odds* and *chances* rather than in a direct, one-to-one fashion. Pollution hardly ever kills or harms everyone exposed to it. Instead, it increases our *likelihood* of getting sick and dying prematurely. For instance, if a factory pollutes the air in a given area at a given level for a given period of time, the 10,000 people living nearby have a 1 in 100 lifetime chance of contracting a certain form of cancer as opposed to a 1 in 200 chance. The harm that embezzlement inflicts is usually more direct, but even here, the loss is pretty much always insured and hence is spread out over many policyholders.

A fourth characteristic of corporate crime is that the monetary sums that are involved tend to be quite large. The total amount of money that is stolen by a single extremely successful corporate criminal in a single year is usually considerably greater than, for example, the take of *all* of the robberies in the country in that same year. As we saw in the chapter on property crime, the FBI estimates that roughly $456 million dollars were stolen in all robberies in the United States during 2010, or about $1,239 per incident; this total is roughly the same sum of the *fines* the government levied against convicted stock swindler Michael Milken. The savings and loan scandal resulted in the "disappearance" of well in excess of $300 *billion*, perhaps 70 to 80 percent of which were a product of illegal acts. Since the money was insured, it will be the government—and ultimately the American taxpayer—who will foot the bill. The per capita cost? Roughly $1,500 for every man, woman, and child in the United States. As I said earlier, sums such as these simply *cannot* be stolen by ordinary thieves. Illegal price-fixing may add as much as $250 *billion* a year to the cost of the products we

purchase. It is *only* for "respectable" crime that thefts entailing sums in the hundreds of millions and the billions of dollars are possible.

There are two reasons why corporate crime is so much more lucrative than ordinary burglaries, robberies, and larcenies. The first is that street criminals have to steal money in the form of a *physical object*, and hundreds of millions of dollars are rarely found in the same place at the same time; even when it is, it is usually inaccessible except to trusted employees. In contrast, corporate criminals steal by *manipulating symbols*, which means that they can steal money they don't even have to pick up and carry away; indeed, that doesn't even have to *exist* in the form of a physical object. A second reason why so much more can be stolen by the executive thief than the street criminal: Street crime tends to be a "one shot deal," a single theft involving a specific sum of money. In contrast, white collar crime is usually made up of a *number* of *interrelated* actions that extend over a period of time—months, years, even decades.

A fifth characteristic of corporate crime is that it is *rarely* prosecuted; when prosecuted, and if a conviction is obtained, penalties tend to be *extremely* light. With respect to prosecution, evidence indicating that a crime has taken place is not as clear-cut as with street crime. Police officers do not patrol business suites looking out for corporate crimes being committed. Indeed, following up on the point on the complexity of corporate crime, how would the police even *know* when one is being committed? (In addition, business suites are private property and hence, the police cannot enter them until crimes are reported.) Relative to their incidence, arrests are very rarely made; the ratio of violations (were this known) to arrests almost certainly approaches and may even surpass that for crimes which entail no complainant, such as drug possession and sale. In addition, even if evidence does indicate criminal behavior, arrest is rare and business executives are rarely convicted for their crimes; conviction, when it does occur, is *extremely* unlikely to lead to a lengthy prison sentence. This is especially striking in view of the amount of money that is stolen. Jail or prison time tends to be almost nonexistent. As we saw, the recent cases of Bernard Madoff and the other swindlers we looked at earlier represent a few major exceptions to this rule; barring illness, Madoff will sit in a prison for the rest of his life, and the others will serve close to a decade, or more.

Sixth, for the most part, corporate crime does not fit our stereotype of "real" crime; it is rarely condemned to the same degree that street crime is, and there is very little public stigma attached to white collar crime. When harmful corporate actions are listed on rosters of actions the public is asked to evaluate the seriousness of, for corporate crimes, condemnation tends to be commensurate with harm. The public regards corporate crime in which injury occurs as *serious* crime. However, when members of the public are asked to act in the capacity of jurors and pass judgment on and sentence corporate suspects, they tend to be extremely lenient toward them. In other words, as Friedrichs says, although the public is perfectly willing to see corporate crime as having serious consequences, this does not always translate into being willing to impose harsh sentences on offenders or support legislation calling for such sentences (2010). To put the matter another way, as we've seen, in some ways, there is some question about whether corporate crime even *qualifies* as a form of deviance. As studies of the fear of crime indicate (Levi, 2009), white collar and corporate crimes rank very low on the public's roster of fearful crimes. Perhaps only identity theft comes close to the image of the predatory street activities that most people find fearful about crime.

Seventh, the media tend not to cover corporate crime in as complete or detailed a fashion as is the case with street crime. True, there have been a few notable exceptions in recent years: It's hard to ignore the theft of billions of dollars, and a sudden, dramatic eruption of millions of gallons of crude oil into the environment is certainly newsworthy—but corporations have huge resources to hire public relations firms to massage their image back to normal. The fact is, as we've seen, corporate crimes tend to be complex and technical; they are difficult to explain and understand, they are intrinsically unexciting, and there is virtually no way to present them on television in an even remotely dramatic fashion. They do not make "good copy," as members of the media say, they do not provide dramatic "sound bites." They do not make for juicy, sensationalistic stories that get page one coverage and a prominent place on the six o'clock news. When they do get space in newspapers, they tend to be buried in back pages, usually in the financial rather than the hard news section. In order for a story of a corporate crime to appear on television news, one of three conditions has to prevail: (1) as I said, the sums stolen have to be huge; (2) a scandal must be connected with the theft; or (3) the accused must be prominent. For the most part, the public finds news stories of corporate misdeeds boring. It is rare that we have the financial training even to understand the nature of corporate offenses; for most of us, there is little intrinsic *drama* in these stories. The shotgun robbery of a downtown bank, complete with hostages and a standoff with the police—now, that's a story! The gangland execution of a mob figure while he's eating a plate of linguine—that grabs our attention! A daring jewel heist from a famous store, again, captures our fancy and interest. We need not invoke conspiracies among the rich and powerful to account for this; the fact is, for most of us, corporate crimes just don't make it as news. Most of us would turn the channel or the page if confronted with such a story. With rare exceptions, we are just not as interested in such stories as we are in reports of meat-and-potatoes, nuts-and-bolts street crime, which most of us find exciting and entertaining. Of course, fanciful fictional depictions of supposed corporate misdeeds, complete with the murder of rivals or crusading journalists, always sells, but I'm talking about real-life corporate crime.

And eighth, as a result of its lack of correspondence to a crime stereotype and its lack of stigma, corporate criminals, even after being convicted, rarely think of themselves as "real" criminals. They use a "vocabulary of motives" that permits them to see themselves in a respectable, law-abiding light; they tend to "deny the guilty mind" and insist that, though their actions may have been technically illegal, they did not *intend* to commit a crime. While corporate criminals use a somewhat different "vocabulary," depending on the crime in question, to explain the crime, they are "nearly unanimous in denying [the] basic criminality" of their illegal actions (Benson, 1985, p. 591). While some persons convicted of street crimes and their defenders will insist that they "didn't do it," corporate criminals and their defenders take a different tack: They insist that, even though they engaged in the action of which they were accused, what they did *wasn't a crime.*

Another feature of corporate crime: For the majority of corporate crimes, the *intention* to do harm to a victim is usually absent. Instead, corporate executives expose parties to a certain measure of *risk*. Whether this risk is acceptable or unacceptable, legal or illegal, is a matter of interpretation. Some corporate actors *knowingly* expose other parties to risks that those parties, and the law, would regard as unacceptable, while other corporate actors do so in the *absence* of such awareness. But nearly all take risk into account and weigh their actions accordingly (Short, 1990). All executives would prefer that the actions they take *on behalf of* their corporation cause no one any harm. But in the real world, this is not possible. On the one hand, no work site, no product, no industrial waste, can be made completely safe; some level of risk is an inevitable feature of modern existence (Friedrichs, 2010); if corporate risk were to be eliminated altogether, all business activity would cease to exist (Perrow, 1984, p. 311). For instance, no automobile can ever be manufactured in which the likelihood of injury or death is zero. On the other hand, some work sites, products, or waste products are so *blatantly* unsafe, the risk so *immense*, that harm is nearly certain; some corporate actors can be said to *deliberately* expose potential victims to unnecessary and substantial risk.

How does the observer make a judgment that the risk was unacceptable and the action that brought it on is a crime? How do we assess risk? According to what criteria? And *who* assesses it?

Do persons who are themselves exposed to the risk of harm assess its magnitude and the acceptability of that exposure? (In effect, they often do, in civil cases, but only *after* the damage has been done, not at the decision-making stage.) One problem is that people assess risk in an extremely inaccurate fashion, exaggerating the likelihood of certain types of harm and minimizing others (Friedrichs, 2010; Erikson, 1990; Slovic, Fischoff, and Lichtenstein, 1980; Slovic, Layman, and Flynn, 1991). On the other hand, in determining the culpability of corporate actions, do we rely on corporate actors to assess what constitutes "acceptable risk"? Clearly, we do not, for it is members of the general public who sit on juries in civil trials, not hand-picked panels of corporation executives, who are likely to decide on the basis of what's good for the corporation, not what's good for the customer, the public, or the worker.

There is a second risk the corporate actor calculates in addition to risk of harm to customers, the public, and employees. This is the likelihood of *accountability*—in the case of the criminal law, the risk of arrest and prosecution, in the case of civil and administrative law, the risk of lawsuits and punitive fines. As we saw, corporate offenses rarely result in criminal prosecution, and administrative agencies rarely slap corporations with huge fines. But torts do result in a *great many* civil trials and, occasionally, extremely large settlements. In fact, today, product liability is the largest field of civil law (Priest, 1990). Here we see the inhibitory impact of civil law: It forces executive actors to consider, in their cost-benefit analysis, the cost of harmful consequences of their operations or products in the form of substantial settlements.

Let's be clear about this: We live in a capitalist society. Corporations are not philanthropic organizations; they are designed and run to earn a profit. So far, all government experiments based on a socialist economy, or any markedly noncapitalist alternative, have either collapsed or been seriously compromised. To a corporation, what counts is the "bottom line." This means that their executives make decisions based almost exclusively on *cost benefit analysis*: They weigh potential costs against earnings to determine possible or likely profit. To earn a profit, they make decisions to engage, or not to engage, in certain business ventures that may or may not pay off. Business ventures may be costly in various ways. Some may entail huge expenditures and offer little potential reward. Still others are likely to result in extremely unfavorable and irreparable public relations, and hence, be costly in indirect ways. Others are highly certain to result in criminal prosecution, while still others are so likely to cause damage to customers that extremely expensive lawsuits, along with the possibility of bankruptcy, loom on the horizon. Corporations do not avoid certain actions for the public good or as a service to humanity; they do so because they would be unprofitable.

Why do they do it? Why commit corporate crime in the first place? Aren't apprehension and incarceration inevitable? At the very least, doesn't the prospect of enormous corporate fines deter breaking the law? The answer is, to some extent, but not really. As we know in cases that have been prosecuted (the Great Electrical Conspiracy, for instance), executives do take steps to *conceal* their commission of offenses, but they continue to engage in such actions because *crime is profitable*. Of all explanations, the opportunity to make a great deal of money by bending or breaking the law (Benson and Simpson, 2009) remains the most convincing. The economic motivation is fairly straightforward: If the reward is substantially greater than the risk of getting caught and punished, and the penalty is trivial, then corporate executives will find it profitable to break the law. For instance, one investigation (Connor and Helmers, 2007) found that between 1990 and 2005, 283 corporation formed dozens of cartels that got together to overcharge to the tune of $300 billion, but they were fined only $2 billion—and none of their executives was imprisoned. For the corporations as a whole, median penalty-to-sales ratio averaged between 1.4 percent and 4.9 percent, depending on the product and the prosecution—and these were only the cases that came to light and resulted in apprehension and fines. Under these circumstances, it makes no sense to strictly obey the law because the bottom line—the profit margin—is improved by committing corporate crime. It makes the company's stock owners happy and it fattens one's own wallet by increasing one's salary. *Even getting caught* rarely results in imprisonment. The fact is, society at large and the criminal justice system see a major difference between street crime (say, the Index Crimes) and corporate crime: The latter takes place during the course of a legitimate economic activity, while all the thieves, rapists, and killers do is take and destroy, contributing nothing to the society.

Another important reason is fundamental to the dynamics of corporate crime: the vertical and horizontal group processes. The corporate setting entails a "dominance, despotism, ruthlessness, and egotism" of executives which allows superiors to intimidate subordinates, and subordinates to invoke the necessity of obedience to authority, which facilitate violations of established, conventional rules, codes, and laws. Even among peers, the interactional setting promotes "group think" which puts pressure on reaching a consensus in decision-making, thereby making it possible to "ignore critical external information," suppress dissent, and "intimidate doubters" who might otherwise reject an illegal solution, forcing them to "remain silent in the face of group pressure." The company is a kind of "total institution" that insulates actors from injunctions from the outside, making it possible to reach a seeming consensus to violate the law. Moreover, the corporate environment provides motives for deviance, which offer a verbal and mental template which answers all objections to illegal behavior when it comes to considerations having to do with "competition, rivalry, power, status, market share, profits, quarterly returns, speed to market, innovation," and so on. These vocabularies of motive "justify and rationalize" violations of the law by invoking a denial of harm, a denial of responsibility, and condemning the condemners (Punch, 2008, pp. 118–119). The outcome of these collective processes is the acceptance of "the organization did it," line of reasoning: I'm not responsible, the corporation is, and whatever the corporation does must be legal.

Four Examples of Corporate Deviance

According to the Securities Fraud InfoCenter, securities fraud occurs when one party deliberately misinforms another party during the trading of stocks, bonds, and other securities. Corporations are required to submit particular information to the Securities and Exchange Commission [SEC]; if this information is incorrect or incomplete, the company may be liable.

For years, WorldCom, once the nation's number two Internet services provider, hugely overstated its profits and assets to the SEC. By late 2002, the corporation admitted that it had juggled its books by concealing $9 billion in expenses by claiming them as assets, falsely inflating their company's net worth. The corporation is now in Chapter 11 bankruptcy and half a dozen of the corporation's top executives, including its former chief executive officer and its former chief financial officer, have been indicted for conspiracy to commit fraud; they face possible substantial prison sentences. In addition, WorldCom is in the process of settling its civil lawsuit with the SEC.

In 2002, the SEC filed civil fraud charges against Dennis Kozlowski, then chief executive officer of Tyco—a conglomerate selling a variety of products including health care products, electronic equipment, valves, and fire alarms—and two other Tyco executives. (All three have since been fired from the company.) The trio, said the SEC's Director of Enforcement "treated Tyco as their private bank, taking out hundreds of millions of dollars of loans and compensation without ever telling investors." The complaint seeks monetary penalties, a recovery of the ill-gotten gains, and barring the three from ever serving as officers or directors of a publicly traded company. In tandem with the SEC's suit, Kozlowski and one of the other executives faced criminal charges for stealing $170 million in company loans and obtaining more than $430 million through fraudulent sales of securities, as well as avoiding the payment of sales taxes totaling more than $1 million. As of 2002, Kozlowski owned a $30 million mansion in Florida and a $5 million house in Massachusetts; he gave a $17 million apartment to his ex-wife. He also used company funds to pay for a $1 million party for his second wife (which featured an ice sculpture of Michelangelo's David that spouted vodka from its penis), expensive trinkets for himself, including a $15,000 umbrella stand, a $2,000 wastebasket, and two sets of sheets for $5,900. Revelations caused Tyco's stock to plummet from $15.86 to six cents a share, snatching millions away from the portfolios of shareholders (www.sec.gov/news/press/2002-135.htm; http://money.cnn.com/2002/09/19/news/companies/kozlowski_jail/).

In 1997, Gary Winnick took on AT&T's request to lay an undersea cable linking Europe with the United States; the job raised billions of dollars in revenue, and Global Crossing was born. Eventually, the company laid 100,000 miles of fiber-optic cable connecting four continents and 27 countries. At one time, Winnick was the richest man in Los Angeles, with $6 billion in wealth. In 1998, he bought the most expensive single-family house ever purchased in the United States, at a cost of $60 million; renovations cost another $30 million. At its height, Global Crossing traded on Wall Street for $64 a share. In 2001, saddled with a debt of $12.4 billion and the company's stock down to 30 cents a share, Global Crossing filed for bankruptcy. During the quarter ending in September 2003, Global Crossing lost $3.3 billion as against a total revenue of only $286 million; demand for high bandwidth cable, it seems, was plummeting. The company simply never generated enough revenue to sustain its massive debt. Several months before the company filed for bankruptcy, Winnick cashed in $120 million in stock. In 2002, amid allegations of insider trading, he resigned from the company he had started up. Several lawsuits have been filed against the company (www.wired.com/news/business/0,1367,50114,00.html).

Between 1998 and 2001, executives at Enron, a company that shipped natural gas through pipelines, made false and misleading statements about the financial performance of the corporation. A growing debt problem was concealed by illegal, undisclosed transactions and partnerships; income was inflated and debts were incomplete and underestimated. The corporation's cooked books sent Enron stock to a high of $90.75 a share. But in 2001, news began leaking out that the corporation was worth considerably less than its stated value. Eventually the SEC stepped in and investigated Enron and Arthur Andersen, the accounting firm that audited the cooked books. A total of twenty-nine Enron executives have been charged with securities, wire, and mail fraud and accused of money laundering and conspiracy; Arthur Andersen was convicted of obstructing justice, paid a fine of a half million dollars, and was placed on probation for five years. The case is so complicated that it will take years for these many cases to be decided.

WAS THE 2008 FINANCIAL CRISIS A FORM OF DEVIANCE?

Late in 2008, the financial world—at first, in the United States and eventually, in every corner of the globe—suffered a catastrophic "meltdown." Banks, bonds, the stock market, property, businesses of every conceivable description, declined 30 to 80 percent in value. Investors lost fortunes practically overnight. Huge corporations that had stood for a century or more as beacons of stability and profitability filed for bankruptcy; unemployment inched close to 10 percent of the labor force; everyone began spending less money and so companies that relied on retail sales struggled to stay afloat; entire residential neighborhoods became festooned with "For Sale" signs. Between September and November, the stock market lost nearly half of its value. In October, the Federal Reserve lent the money market half a trillion dollars to stay in business; in November, it agreed to buy $800 billion in mortgage-backed investments. No one was immune; everyone was affected. Home mortgages, pension funds, insurance companies, mutual funds—financial instruments that affect all our lives—found themselves burdened with debt, undercapitalized, and on the verge of collapse.

The government took over Fannie Mae and Freddie Mac, the two largest and most venerable home mortgage corporations. Who owns General Motors and Chrysler? You do—the taxpayer owns most of these long-established auto giants, because they were unable to stay in business without huge government bailouts. The government converted Goldman Sachs and Morgan Stanley, previously unregulated investment banks each one of which owned more than a trillion dollars in assets, to ordinary banks, now subject to strict regulations. Lehman Brothers and Bear Stearns—together once worth a billion dollars in assets—now bankrupt. Merrill Lynch—taken over by Bank of America. And meanwhile, because of the "ripple effect," millions of ordinary workers find themselves on the unemployment line, unable to find a job.

Most financial experts point to two sources of the global financial crisis: Overvaluation of property and under-regulation of the finance industry. In the early 2000s, because of the low rate of interest from the Federal Reserve (1%), investors began borrowing huge sums of money to "leverage" financial deals. They began "packaging" bundles of mortgages, some safe, some risky, into investment instruments they bought and sold. The safe or *prime* "slices" of these mortgage investment instruments proved to be very profitable, so investors sought more mortgage investments and soon, they began dipping into the risky slices of these packages. The risky or *subprime* "slice" of the investment packages were made up of mortgages where the buyer needed no down payment, paid high mortgage rates, and was asked for no proof of income. Inevitably, a high proportion of such homeowners defaulted on their mortgages, and the lender got their houses; eventually the market was flooded with houses for sale, and all the houses in their neighborhoods lost value. As a result, the homeowners who were able to make their mortgage payments found themselves paying mortgages on houses worth a quarter of what they originally paid for them; increasingly, mortgage holders walked away from their payments, further swamping neighborhoods with unsold houses and further reducing the value of the occupied houses. Insurance companies that had insured the payment of mortgages lost billions on their investments, and, as I said, the "ripple effect" spread from there to non-financial companies and hence, to the jobs of ordinary worker. The world found itself in an economic crisis not experienced since the Great Depression of the 1930s, when one out of three workers were unemployed (www.mikesdailylockup.com/2009/02/the-financial-meltdown-explained.html). Most experts trace the global financial meltdown to the *subprime mortgage collateralized debt obligation*.

Sounds technical, doesn't it? It is, and there's no single villain in this drama. Many thousands of investors, homeowners, bankers, stock and bond traders, government employees, money managers, executives, ordinary workers—they're all tangled up in this fiasco, the toxic effects of which may last a decade or more. This crisis has snatched trillions from the pockets of people worldwide, turned houses worth half a million dollars into eyesores and liabilities, princes into paupers, and retirement funds into scraps of paper, and yet, though experts have some understanding of what caused it, it's not clear that such actions are criminal or deviant. The financial crisis that began in the fall of 2008 is a prime example of an interlocking set of actions that take place within an organization setting whose agency is likewise organizational. It's almost as if individual initiative played no role at all in the cascading meltdown.

SUMMARY

What makes white collar and especially corporate crime interesting sociologically is that, for all other types of deviance, *every single person in society can be evaluated as acceptable or unacceptable along a given axis*. All of us are fat, less fat, or not at all fat; honest or dishonest, or everything in between; atheists, agnostics, or believers; alcoholics, moderate drinkers, or abstainers; and so on. *Only* for organizational deviance is the relevant dimension *irrelevant* for most of us. Most of us cannot be placed along the relevant dimension because we are not members of the organization in question. Most of us do not have an executive position and hence, cannot be evaluated with respect to whether we have committed corporate crime or not.

However, even though most of us cannot *be* evaluated as having committed, or not committed a given form of white collar crime, all of us evaluate *others* for having done so. Since organizations are not always successful in shielding wrongdoing in their ranks from the prying eyes of others, the general public often becomes a crucial audience that evaluates organizational behavior. Often, the general public's evaluation of wrongdoing within a given organization is radically at odds with evaluations made by members of the organization. Some acts are judged more harshly by the general public than by organizational members; sometimes it is the reverse. Law enforcement, the courts, and the media are other relevant audiences who render judgments about organizational behavior.

White collar and corporate crime constitute an important form of organizational deviance. Most of the time, when the term "white collar crime" is used, it refers to corporate crime. Not all white collar criminals are rich and powerful. In fact, in the world of white collar crime, there are a lot more "small fry" than "big fish." Perhaps the best way of dividing up white collar crimes is those that are on behalf of an individual *against* the corporation (embezzlement) and those that are on behalf of the corporation against the general public, consumers, or employees (corporate crime). Other types include governmental crime (receiving bribes, violating international treaties) and professional crime (performing unnecessary surgery, overcharging a client).

As deviance, the public's reaction to corporate crime is ambiguous. On the other hand, public opinion polls reveal that most people regard corporate crimes that harm people as serious offenses. On the other hand, when corporate criminals are judged by a jury, they tend to receive penalties that do not match the seriousness of the offense. Whether corporate crime is a legitimate form of deviance isn't a cut-and-dried matter. Corporate crime tends to be made up of acts that are complex and not easily determined by nonexperts; are intermingled with legitimate business; cause diffuse victimization; entail sums of money that are substantially greater than those of street crimes; are prosecuted only rarely; don't fit the public's stereotype of what a "crime" is; are underplayed by the media (unless the sums are vast); are relatively unstigmatizing for the perpetrators; and are lacking in the intention to harm victims.

Corporate crime possesses several features that are uncharacteristic of or in comparison with ordinary or Index Crime: it tends to be made up of complex, and relatively sophisticated actions; it is intermingled with legitimate behavior; its victimization tends to be more diffuse; it entails sums of money that tend to be larger; it is less likely to be detected and prosecuted (and, characteristically, offenders receive relatively lighter sentences); it does not fit the stereotype of what crime is supposed to look like; it tends not to be covered in the news media, unless huge sums are involved; its corporate criminals, even after conviction, rarely consider themselves equivalent to common criminals; and its perpetrators very rarely set out to intentionally harm their victims (rather, they calculate public harm within the framework of "risk assessment").

In many respects, white collar crime, and especially its most well-known embodiment, corporate crime, are not instances of deviance. If deviance is behavior, beliefs, or traits that elicit negative, punishing, or condemnatory reactions from significant audiences, then admittedly the universe of white collar and corporate crime does not seem to draw as much outrage as the forms of deviance we've discussed throughout this volume. Even when a corporate offender is convicted, juries are loath to slap him with a serious prison sentence. Most of the public sees a fundamental incongruity in a respectable executive being marched off in handcuffs to a correctional facility that typically holds murders, rapists, and armed robbers. In most instances, the commission of white collar crime is not as serious, discrediting, or stigmatizing as most stereotypical forms of deviance are. Most of us pay lip service to condemning the harm that corporate crime inflicts, but its lack of intentionality and the diffusion of its impact are serious impediments to public censure. Of course, being an ex-convict can itself be stigmatizing, but on a crime-by-crime basis, the corporate offender is very unlikely—though increasingly so—to serve a prison sentence.

Account: Conspiracy to Defraud the IRS

Below, we find a transcript of an interview I conducted with Robert, a lawyer whose license was suspended for a white-collar crime. The offense he was originally charged with was "structuring," and the charge on which he was eventually convicted was "conspiracy to defraud the Internal Revenue Service." What these charges entail becomes clear in his explanations. (This interview has been lightly edited for readability.)

ERICH: Rather than have me ask specific questions, why don't you just tell me what happened.

ROBERT: OK, the ultimate charge was "conspiracy to defraud the Internal Revenue Service." My secretary had been working in this office even before I started—I was the sole practitioner. One secretary, one attorney. I trusted her completely, gave her the right to sign checks and everything else. She was, I thought, top-notch and beyond question, trustworthy. And I can't really blame *her*. I mean, obviously, I bear all of the blame for this. From time to time, I would have some clients who needed to borrow money, usually for a real estate transaction. And I had some other clients who, from time to time, would lend money. And I would prepare a mortgage and a note and that would enable these people to buy a house or a lot or whatever. Well, I had a situation where a client would borrow money. He was buying property in another state and ultimately he was going to sell his house here. But he hadn't sold it yet, and he needed to complete the transaction there. My secretary came to me—of course, she knew all of this—and she said that her cousin and her cousin's husband would lend the money. Later, she arrived in the office with [the cash]. And this is where my stupidity took over. I was under the impression that if a person deposits more than $10,000 in cash in a bank account, he had to notify the Internal Revenue Service.

ERICH: That was my impression, too.

ROBERT: A lot of people have that impression. That's as far as I knew. Number one, that's wrong, and number two, there's a lot more to it. I now know the actual facts are, if you deposit more than $10,000 in a bank account, the bank has a form, and the *bank* fills out this form. It's called a "currency transaction report." I thought

(Continued)

Account: Conspiracy to Defraud the IRS   Continued

I could avoid all of this aggravation by depositing the transactions in sums of $9,500. . . . And that's exactly what I did. And that was fine. It was deposited over many days. I went to the bank every single day . . . and the money was fully deposited, nobody did anything. And a week to ten days later, the check was written so that my client could buy the property. He signed the mortgage on his house here, and everything was fine. A couple of months later, again, my secretary said that her brother-in-law wanted to borrow some money. And again the same thing, that'll be fine, we'll put a mortgage on the property. . . . And again, she shows up with [the money] in cash. And it's in a small suitcase. Obviously, alarms should have gone off and didn't. Again, same thing. Deposited in the exact same way. The deal closed, no problems. Further period of time passed. I would say two to three months. And it now developed that the cousin and her husband wanted to buy a piece of property for themselves, in Arizona. And wanted me to represent them. I had *never talked* to these people. At the time I don't know that I had ever *met* them. But I explained to my secretary that I am not admitted to practice law in Arizona. I would be very happy to give them whatever expertise I had in real estate. I think I knew the procedure there, but I can't be an Arizona attorney. She relayed that message to them, they supposedly came back and said, we want you to give us whatever advice you can, we feel much more comfortable with you than picking a stranger in Arizona. The cousin's husband was an interstate trucker. Supposedly transporting produce from California to the East Coast. He lived in New York City, he had a number of trucks going back and forth. He had a Spanish surname and he was from Colombia.

ERICH: Fascinating.

ROBERT: I said, OK, we will do this. Give me the name of the title company and some various information and I will start to handle it. A few days later, his brother, I believe, arrived at the office with a *large* suitcase. And the purchase of this property was $191,000. And supposedly there was $191,000 in this suitcase. I said, wow, OK, now again, all communication was made through the secretary and the cousin. At this point, I had not had any direct communication with—their names were Maria and Freddie. Never had any contact with them. And I made it perfectly clear that, number one, I was not going to count this money, and that I am not responsible for it. If somebody breaks into my office at night and steals the whole thing, I do not want to be responsible for it. OK? I started to deposit the money.

ERICH: In bundles of $9,500.

ROBERT: Yes. I was informed that Freddie was going to put it in a safe in the office. So that's fine. And he almost immediately did so. The money was then put into the safe. Deposited *daily*, you know, with all the transactions, in the bank. This one also went fine. You can do the math as to how many transactions it takes. It took a long time. Went fine. When the full amount had been deposited, I got in touch with the title company in Arizona. Arrangements were made to wire the money to the title company who was acting as the escrow agent. The transaction went fine. And the title closed and there were not problems. A further period of months passed. And there were a couple of small transactions. When I say small, maybe $20–$25,000, [for] which again, the same procedure was used. And again, no problems with the bank, no problems with the Internal Revenue Service.

ERICH: You were dealing with only one bank.

ROBERT: Only one bank. Yeah. And went usually five days a week. I guess it was about a year after the first transaction, I was informed by my secretary that they now intended to buy a house in California. And the purchase of this house was $235,000.

ERICH: Who's "they"? Her cousin?

ROBERT: Freddie and Maria. Yeah. The same people who bought the house in Arizona. And frankly I was not paying too much attention to this thing. I had never kept a running balance of all of these transactions. I said, fine, we'll do exactly the same thing.

ERICH: Were you getting fees on these transactions?

ROBERT: I charged them a $350 fee for preparing the note and mortgage on the Arizona house, which was standard, if anything, it's a very reasonable fee. I charged a $2,500 fee for handling the real estate aspect of the Arizona property, but I never collected it. With the California property, I again started these deposits. Started to deposit the money. I had $205,000 deposited in the bank account for this transaction. Out of a total of $235,000. Again, I never counted it, but this was supposedly what he had given me. Then at this point my wife and I went on vacation. And while I was on vacation, the telephone rings. It's my secretary, calling to say the Internal Revenue Service had been to the office and left her with a piece of paper saying that they were seizing the account. And I was literally laughing. The secretary—she talked to my wife, not me—but she was literally crying about how upset she was over this. And when I heard about it, to show how naïve I was, I was laughing. I'm saying, look, this is not a problem for me. You'd better tell Freddie that *he* may have a problem. But as soon as I get home, I will notify the Internal Revenue Service that none of this is my money. And that if they have any questions about it, they should contact Freddie. I got home and saw the piece of paper that they left concerning this and realized that this was no longer a trivial matter, that this was serious. And at that point, I obtained an attorney. At first, the seizure was strictly a *civil* matter. My attorney contacted the U.S. attorney who was in charge of this case. And explained to her that we were more than willing to cooperate in any respect, but in order to resolve the civil aspects of the case, we also [had] to resolve the *criminal* action that they may be contemplating. She said, I'm only handling the civil aspects, I can't tell you what's going on in the criminal action. Months passed, nothing was done. They moved the case to a more nearby federal court. The case was assigned to a federal prosecutor who had a terrible reputation. He's very hard-nosed, but we have to deal with him. He made arrangements to meet with me, my lawyer, a U.S. attorney, the IRS investigator, and the chief U.S. attorney in that court, and we all sat down. And I told my story. The, quote, hard-nosed

U.S. attorney apparently didn't believe it. Months and months passed. We went in one day, and my attorney was informed that the U.S. attorney has refused to make any deals. That he will allow me to plead guilty to "structuring." And that under the federal sentencing guidelines, I will be sentenced to thirteen months in prison.

ERICH: What exactly is "structuring"?

ROBERT: OK, I subsequently learned that in addition to the *bank* filling out this form and not the customer, that it is also illegal for anyone to *structure* the deposits so that the amounts appear to be less than $10,000 when the overall amount deposited is more than $10,000.

ERICH: I didn't know that.

ROBERT: I'm glad you said that because not only I didn't know that, but I've talked to a number of attorneys and they didn't know either. The one thing that was very upsetting to me was that the *bank* didn't know this. I had been dealing with this bank for many, many years. I had a very close relationship with the branch vice-president, the tellers, they have referred me clients over the years. And the middle for the California transaction, the head teller came to me and said, look, this is silly, why don't you go ahead and deposit the whole thing at one time? And I said, well, I don't want to get involve[d] with the Internal Revenue Service. I've got enough problems without dealing with them. And she gave me the *form*. That's when I learned that it's a form that the bank is supposed to fill out. I read through the instructions on it, and it *clearly* says this form is filled out when a cash deposit is more than $10,000. And made no mention of the fact that there is this crime of "structuring." So I said, look, you know, this form says that we don't have to fill this out. And she didn't say anything else. It was *almost a joke*, when I walked into the bank. One of the tellers would see me coming, and would literally duck behind the counter, saying, "Oh, my God, here he comes again, I don't want to be responsible for counting this money."

ERICH: How did the IRS get wind of this?

ROBERT: Well, we're getting to that. [Laughs.] Shortly after the head teller gave me the form, within, say, a week, I was making another deposit,

(*Continued*)

Account: Conspiracy to Defraud the IRS   Continued

and she said the branch vice-president would like to see me. So I went in to talk to her. And, you know, we were on a first-name basis. And she explained that the bank had recently gotten itself into some very serious trouble with the Internal Revenue Service over this type of thing. I said, OK, what would you like me to do? And she said, we're going to fill out these forms. I said, OK, *you* know that of course it's not my money. And I told this to the various tellers. So I said, you have all the information in your records to fill out this form, do what you have to do, you know it's not my money. Within days of that conversation, the account was seized. And supposedly, the bank had some person in their main office whose job it was to look for cash deposits. And if it looks suspicious, they notify the Internal Revenue Service. And that's how I got trapped.

Fortunately, the U.S. attorney who said that he wasn't going to make any deals with me, he was taken off the case. And it was assigned to another U.S. attorney, a woman who had just come in from California, who turned out to be very nice, very understanding. I met with her and we went over again all of these facts, and she believed me. Subsequently, she offered a plea of "conspiracy to defraud the Internal Revenue Service" which my attorney thought would go better with the bar association than structuring. Because in the back of our minds, we were worried about what the bar association was ultimately going to do. And she offered a letter that shows the defendant has cooperated in their investigation and has rendered valuable assistance to them. Which frees the judge from sentencing guidelines, so that he can now sentence somebody to a much lesser sentence. That is the thing my attorney was desperately trying to get all along, otherwise the guidelines say that they judge had no choice, he would have to sentence me to a prison term of thirteen months.

ERICH: That was the thirteen months you talked about earlier.

ROBERT: Yeah. Again, it dragged out and dragged out. We signed a plea agreement.

Meanwhile, they arrested Freddie, Maria, Freddie's brother, and my secretary. And there was a travel agent, who I didn't know at all at the time who had been doing some things with [the] cash. They arrested a number of people. Now, the first transaction . . . , we were on vacation when I got the call. . . . I entered the plea, it must have been two years later that I entered my plea. And then sentencing was put off and put off. I was ultimately sentenced six months later. I had to do 300 hours of community service, pay a $40,000 fine, and I was subject to three month's house detention. A three-year probation was put off until I completed the other things. Within two months, the bar had suspended me. They had issued their interim suspension. I was confined to the house for three months, which was no punishment for me, but it punishes the family. I was able to leave the house, I believe they gave me from seven o'clock in the morning until seven o'clock at night. Clearly if I wanted to flee the jurisdiction, I could have been halfway around the world by the time they would have known about it. It did nothing but inconvenience the family, it did nothing to me, the criminal. As soon as possible, I completed my 300 hours of the community service. And we went back to court. The three-year probation was immediately lifted. By that time, probably eleven months had passed since the sentencing. Everybody agreed that we'll change it to a one-year probation, which will be up in a matter of weeks. And that ended all of my exposure to the criminal justice system. I had completed everything that was required of me by then. I was at that point in the interim suspended from the practice of law. I was interimly suspended in March. The hearing wasn't actually conducted until a year later, and the return date of the motion was a year after that. The court did not render their decision until February of the following year. And their decision was to suspend me from the practice of law for two years. For whatever reason, the decision was, he is suspended effective immediately. In other words, I thought I had *already* served the suspended period—and I *had* been suspended since just after the sentencing—and my license was [then]suspended for an additional two years. My attorney thought they had made a mistake. He argued that surely you can't want to suspend this individual for a total of, really, four years. The decision came back, oh, maybe a month ago, no, motion denied, so [two years from *now*], I could apply for reinstatement. And that is my tale of woe.

ERICH: That's an interesting story. So, what are you doing at this time.

ROBERT: I've done some income tax work. I've done some work for a builder who's selling big pieces of property. And I represent him at closings, but I can't prepare deeds or anything like that. And basically, we are living off investments. You know, we were very fortunate. We have the wherewithal to support the family. Without that, I don't know what I could have done. The suspension effectively ended any of the legal work that I was doing. The practice of law is such that, the work you do, usually you don't get paid for some period of time. So there was some overlap of income coming in which carried us for quite a while. And as I said, then we we've been living on investments.

ERICH: Do you know what happened to Freddie and Maria?

ROBERT: They were both ultimately sentenced to prison time. Apparently absolutely nothing happened to my secretary. She was pregnant at the time of her arrest. And I believe that because of her circumstances, they decided, well, we'll leave her alone. For whatever it's worth, she insisted all along that this was all legitimate. That they make this money on the trucking, that everything was above board. It's easy to blame someone else, but I was the one who did what I did.

ERICH: Do you know if any of that was drug money?

ROBERT: I know it now, yeah. Yeah. Certainly once the arrests were made, I was 100 percent convinced now that that was drug money. I have a copy of their [Freddie's and Maria's] sentencing minutes. Their attorney tried to blame me

completely. He made this little speech to the judge, but obviously it didn't work. Yeah, they're in prison.

ERICH: Do you know what kind of time they got?

ROBERT: I think Freddie got eight years. I think his brother got three years. And his wife got a shorter term, but it was not something that I would want to spend.

ERICH: Right. Well, this is really interesting. Thank you.

QUESTIONS

Do you regard Robert's crime as heinous? Should he have lost his license to practice law for four years? Do you feel he should have been aware that Freddie and Maria were drug dealers? Why do you think he was so naïve about his complicity in their crimes? Was he simply trying to cover up his part in a major criminal conspiracy? Or was he an unwitting dupe in a scheme about which he was kept in the dark? Would you have done the same thing? What does this case say about our responsibility as citizens in reporting or discussing wrongdoing with others? Where do we draw the line between complicity and tolerance? Is every adult citizen aware of the criminal status of "structuring"? Does Robert's conviction of a federal crime make him a *deviant*? Should he have been included in a book on deviant behavior? Or is the impulse of the sociologist of deviance not to discuss major corporate or white collar crimes, as Alexander Liazos says, a bias that indicates that the field is simply interested in "nuts, sluts, and deviated preverts"? How should we approach or think about white collar crime? If crimes are major in their impact on the society, does that mean they are of major theoretical significance? Should the IRS be regarded as an important "audience" that determines what's deviant? Or should we ignore what the federal government says about who's guilty of wrongdoing? Would you predict that Robert's conviction would have a long-term impact on his career? What do you speculate he's doing now?

Drug Use as Deviance
An Introduction

Learning Objectives:

After reading this chapter, you will be able to:

- assess data sources, answering the question "How do we know it's true?";
- understand how alcohol consumption fits into the discussion of deviance;
- discuss the questions "Who drinks? Who doesn't" in the context of a conversation about deviance;
- recognize the acute effects of alcohol;
- understand the relationship of alcohol abuse to risky, deviant behaviors;
- understand the correlation between alcohol consumption and sexual victimization;
- discuss the relation between alcohol and drug use;
- examine drug use as deviant behavior;
- classify drugs and drug effects;
- detail the history of marijuana use in the United States from 1960 to 2011;
- relate marijuana use to deviance and crime.

What defines psychoactive substances is that they transform how the human brain works—how we think, feel, and act. They produce an "out of the ordinary" state of mind that some observers consider inappropriate. At a sufficient dosage, we call this state "intoxication," and the achievement of the state, "getting high." If we are sufficiently high or intoxicated, we are likely to engage in behavior that, norms dictate, we shouldn't engage in, that may be deviant or even criminal. We do what we're not supposed to do, according to authorities, and we don't do what we're supposed to do—such as perform adequately at our jobs, attend to our families, go to school, study and learn, be a functioning member of mainstream society. Under certain conditions—such as driving, working, and even appearing in public—our very intoxicated state may be considered deviant or criminal. As a result, legislatures have deemed our possession of a number of these substances to be against the law and dominant medical opinion considers any and all use of them to be a form of drug "abuse." Hence, we look at their use in a course or book on deviant behavior.

We must keep in mind two absolutely crucial facts about the consumption of psychoactive substances, which are by definition drugs, including alcohol, that influence the workings of the brain, that influence how the mind works, that influence mood, emotion, thinking, feeling, and acting. The first is that legal drugs (alcohol and tobacco) are vastly more likely to be used than illegal drugs. The consumption of psychoactive substances is *mainly* the consumption of alcohol. And the second important fact about psychoactive drug use is that marijuana is *vastly* more likely to be used than any of the other illicit drugs (cocaine, the amphetamines, including methamphetamine, Ecstasy, narcotics, the hallucinogens, including LSD, and PCP). No systematic study of a major area of the United States has shown any contrary finding to be true. Almost three-quarters of all the episodes of the consumption of illicit drugs are with marijuana. Illegal drug use is *mainly* marijuana use. The same applies to drug consumption worldwide: In its *World Drug Report 2012*, the United Nations Office on Drugs and Crime estimated that in 2010, the annual prevalence of marijuana was five percent—*ten times higher* than that of any other illicit drug.

HOW DO WE KNOW IT'S TRUE? DRUG DATA SOURCES

Aside from conducting surveys themselves and studying the work of other social and behavioral scientists, drug researchers rely on several large, systematic, ongoing, government-sponsored data sources to generalize about substance use and abuse. They include ADAM (the Advanced Drug Abuse Monitoring program), DAWN (the Drug Abuse Warning Network), MTF (Monitoring the Future), and NSDUH (the National Survey on Drug Use and Health). All include data on alcohol consumption, which can also be located in the sale of legal alcohol products, Driving Under the Influence (DUI) and other drug arrest statistics, and the intermittent data published by the National Institute of Alcohol Abuse and Alcoholism (NIAAA). In addition, from time to time, the United Nations (UN) publishes surveys of both drug and alcohol consumption.

The reason why these four data sources are so important for our investigation of deviance is that they emphasize society's problematic and troubled stance toward certain forms of drug consumption. Substance abuse becomes deviance insofar as it is defined as such, and when substances are consumed to the point where society must mobilize its representative agents to protect its constituent members against harming themselves and others—and collects data designed to inform authorities so that they may take such precautions—said consumption is *by definition* a deviant act. ADAM collects data on actors who have triply engaged in deviance—first, by getting high during the course of recreationally consuming a psychoactive drug, secondly by committing a crime, and third, by getting arrested for said commission of a crime. DAWN collects data on people who have inappropriately misused or abused drugs, whether licit or illicit, to the point where they need medical assistance—or where they go so far as to kill themselves. NSDUH investigates the full spectrum of drug use— the consumption of some of these drugs (meth, crack, PCP, heroin) is, by its very nature, deviant, while with others, the upper reaches of use are likewise seriously deviant; the same applies to MTF's survey.

ADAM

If you want to know about the relationship between drugs and crime, what better place to begin than the drug use of people who have been arrested for criminal behavior? In 1987, the National Institute of Justice established the Drug Use Forecasting (DUF) program. In 1997, the name of the program was changed to the Arrestee Drug Abuse Monitoring program (or ADAM); its current incarnation, referred to as ADAM II, is based on a sample of arrestees for violent, property, and drug crimes; it is drawn in ten counties in which several of the nation's large cities are located. The 2011 sample, all male, was made up of about 6,300 interviews and data from 5,900 urine samples from arrestees in five major American cities—Charlotte, NC; Denver, Colorado; Minneapolis, Minnesota; Portland, Oregon; and Washington, DC What is so useful about ADAM is that it accesses populations that would be inaccessible by means of more conventional research methods, such as the surveys conducted by the National Household Survey on Drug Abuse or Monitoring the Future. This is the case because many of ADAM's samples do not live in conventional households, nor can they be located in a conventional institution, such as a school or place of employment. Over half of 2011's sample were unemployed, over half were uninsured, and one in ten was homeless. Unfortunately, ADAM does not test for the presence of alcohol. For someone interested in the relationship between drug use and crime, however, ADAM is probably the best place to start (Wish, 1995; Yacoubian, 2000).

Over 60 percent of the arrestees in the sample tested positive for at least one drug, and the congruence between self-reports and the results of a drug test was extremely high for the sample as a whole—84 percent for marijuana, 88 percent for cocaine, 93 percent for opiate drugs, and 97 percent for methamphetamine. Marijuana is by far the drug that arrestees are most likely to be tested for; roughly half of all persons apprehended in 2011 for a crime in the United States had a measurable quantity of marijuana in their body; the drop-off from marijuana to the second most popular drug, cocaine, was sharp—only one in five both tested positive for and self-reported cocaine within the prior month. ADAM's data show an extraordinarily high rate of illegal drug use among arrestees, as we'll see when we compare these figures with surveys of drug use among the general population, including school populations. These figures indicate that deviancies tend to cluster—that is, persons who get arrested, pretty much all of them having committed a crime, tend to have engaged in other deviancies, illicit drug use included. In addition, a higher-than-average proportion of them are also outside the mainstream in other ways, such as being unemployed, uninsured, and homeless. The connection between and among these unconventional behaviors is statistical rather than absolute; nonetheless, one type of unconventionality is *related* to others (see Table 7.1).

DAWN

DAWN replies on two data collection efforts: emergency department (ED) episodes and medical examiner (ME) reports. DAWN tabulates the number of acute medical complications that are caused by or associated with the use of certain drugs. Comparing DAWN's figures with the percentage of the population who use these drugs gives

TABLE 7.1   ADAM, ADULT MALE ARRESTEES, MEDIAN CITY FIGURES, 2011

URINE TEST		SELF-REPORT (PAST 30 DAYS)	
Marijuana	50	Marijuana	48
Cocaine	19	Crack Cocaine	10
Opiates	10	Powder Cocaine	7
Meth	3	Heroin	4
		Meth	4

Source: ADAM II, 2011 Annual Report, 2012.

us a rough (but far from exact) idea of how dangerous their use is, at least within the time frame of a particular episode of use. Though DAWN attempts to cover all 50 states in its examination of ED visits, unfortunately, its ME reports are far from complete; in fact, in 2010, only 373 jurisdictions in 157 metro areas and all the counties in13 states submitted detailed data—a very spotty coverage of the United States. (DAWN virtually ignores rural areas.) ME data covers catchment areas that encompass about a third of the American population, though a skewed third at that. As its 2011 report states, ME and coroner participants in DAWN do not constitute a scientific sample "at either the metropolitan or the national level." Meanwhile, the diligent researcher must make use of such data as are available, and interpret them accordingly. As a general rule, incomplete and unrepresentative data cannot be used for drawing inferences about the absolute size of numbers, but can often be used, with caution, to determine relationships between variables. The procedures for recording DAWN data are becoming more standardized over time. Still, we should take DAWN's data with the proverbial grain of salt.

An *ED episode* is any nonlethal, untoward, drug-related event that results in an ED visit to a facility with 24-hour services. Such episodes include a suicide attempt, a panic reaction, a psychotic episode, a hallucination, unconsciousness, poisoning, accidental ingestion, extreme allergic reaction, and dependence for which the patient demands treatment. (A patient who comes or is brought to the emergency room for drug "detoxification" is the only non-acute episode that is tallied in ED figures.) In a given episode, recorded by a designated member of the ED staff, up to four different drugs may be mentioned as the cause of the untoward effect. ED visits involved an average of 1.6 drugs. In a given year, the same patient could visit one or more ED on two or more occasions; hence, the yearly tabulation of episodes does not indicate the number of people who experienced untoward, drug-induced ED visits during that year. And since several drugs could be mentioned as having been used in a given episode, the number of times a drug is mentioned is greater than the number of drug visits or episodes (in the case of ME reports, an "episode" is the drug-related death of the user) that took place. It should also be emphasized that drugs may be adulterated or bogus and so tabulations of ED episodes may be misleading in that they may not tell us about the inherent dangers of a particular drug, another reason why DAWN figures should be read with a measure of skepticism.

DAWN's ED figures indicate that, out of all the non-fatal drug-related visits to America's ED in metropolitan communities around the country in 2011, nearly half (46.8%) are associated with the abuse or misuse of or an overdose of a legal pharmaceutical drug (see Table 7.2); a substantial

TABLE 7.2   DAWN: DRUG-RELATED ED (EMERGENCY DEPARTMENT) VISITS, 2011

	NUMBER	PERCENTAGE
Total	4,916,000	100
Pharmaceuticals	1,345,000	46.8
Benzodiazepines	408,000	8.3
Anti-depressants	105,000	2.1
Hydrocodone	116,000	2.3
Oxycodone	183,000	3.7
Cocaine	488,000	9.9
Heroin	225,000	5.4
Marijuana	1,346,000	27.4
Alcohol-in-combination	564,000	11.5
Underage drinking	189,000	3.8

Source: "The DAWN Report," ED visits, July 2, 2012

TABLE 7.3   DAWN: ME (MEDICAL EXAMINER) REPORTS, PERCENT OF TOTAL EPISODES, 2011

Opiates	71%
Methadone	14%
Heroin	13%
Alcohol	25%
Benzodiazepines	25%
Cocaine	23%
Anti-Depressants	14%
Stimulants	8%

Source: *DAWN*, Area Profiles of Drug-Related Mortality, 2012

proportion are nonlethal suicide attempts. Of the illicit drugs, over a quarter (27.4%) result from cannabis use, whether its source is a panic attack, a psychosis-like outbreak, or the request for treatment for a dependency.

ME reports are tabulations of deaths caused directly or indirectly by one or more drugs, as reported by a city or a county coroner or ME (see Table 7.3). In the case of a non-routine death— a death that requires investigation, an autopsy is performed on the decedent. If drugs are deemed to be a factor in (are "involved in" or "related to") the death, it is counted as a ME episode. Roughly two-thirds of all the ME episodes were deemed directly drug-induced (were deemed drug "overdoses") in 2011; in about one-third of cases, the drug or drugs played a contributory role. The rules ME follow for including a case in their DAWN reports are not completely standardized. Hence, a case that is included in one jurisdiction may be excluded in another. DAWN's ME data on drug-related death and suicides are tabulated separately; drug-related death is about six times more frequent than deaths that the ME deems are suicides. About two-thirds of all drug-related deaths entail the use of two or more drugs.

DAWN does not say that say that the drugs named *caused* the drug overdoses it tabulated— only that these drugs are *associated* with the user's demise; they tend to be found in the bodies of persons who died and, very likely, the death was caused or influenced by the abuse of the indicated chemical substance or substances. Most people die with several drugs in their bodies, and some of them may be causally related to the death

while others are unrelated. County coroners and MEs make such judgments, and they are fallible. Alcohol is mentioned only if taken *in combination* with pharmaceutical or illicit drugs *or* if the deceased is underage. Clearly, opiates, taken as a whole, are most often associated with a drug-related demise. In a majority of cases of a drug-associated death (71%), the ME found one or more of the narcotics in the deceased's body; two in particular (methadone and heroin) were singled out for detailed examination, although the prescription narcotics, oxycodone and hydrocodone, have become more often used. Two legal drugs (benzodiazepines, a Valium-type sedative, and anti-depressants) also tend to be associated with a premature drug-related demise (25% and 14%). MEs rarely or never mention marijuana as a drug that is associated with or may facilitate an acute drug-related death.

NSDUH

In 1971, the federal government sponsored the first national survey of drug use in the United States among a randomized sample of Americans; conducted by the National Commission on Marihuana and Drug Abuse, this survey gave us our first accurate look at patterns of drug consumption in the United States. The National Institute on Drug Abuse (NIDA) conducted nine similar surveys between 1975 and 1991. Beginning in 1992, the Substance Abuse and Mental Health Services Administration (SAMHSA), a division of the United States Department of Health and Human Services, conducts yearly surveys of drug use in the American population. In 2002, the survey's name was changed from the National Household Survey on Drug Abuse to the *NSDUH*. The 2011 NSDUH survey was based on a sample of 67,500 respondents. The resultant report, released in 2012, provides, in the words of SAMHSA, national estimates of rates of use, number of users, and other measures related to the use of illicit drugs, alcohol, cigarettes, and other forms of tobacco by the population, ages 12 years and older. (As of this writing, NSDUH's 2010 survey has more detailed and complete presentation of its data than its 2011 survey.) And as with the MTF study, the NSDUH survey asks about lifetime prevalence, yearly prevalence, thirty-day prevalence, and daily prevalence for each drug. SAMHSA's national survey divides its sample into youths ages 12–17, young adults ages 18–25, and adults ages 26 and older.

Large as its sample is, even the NSDUH is less than useful for subsamples in the population that are statistically very rare. For instance, estimating heroin or crack use from NSDUH's data is misleading. Not only do they turn up fairly infrequently in its sample (since they make up a tiny number even in a sample of 67,500), they are also difficult to locate. Most addicts do not live at a fixed address and so a sample based on a household survey will not be able to locate them. Many are homeless, many avoid responding to surveys, and relatives often refuse to acknowledge their existence. Hence, as with surveys on serious crime, self-report drug surveys are

increasingly inadequate the more serious—and therefore, the less common—a particular form of drug use, which is why the ADAM data are so valuable. In spite of its limitations, the NSDUH is probably the best survey on the consumption of psychoactive substances that has ever been conducted among the American population as a whole. And future surveys will be improved yearly.

As we can see from the National Survey, (see Table 7.4) legal drugs are more widely used than illegal drugs, marijuana is the most popular illicit drug in the United States, and the "hardest" of the illicit drugs, such as heroin, crack, methamphetamine, and PCP, are the ones that are least likely to be used. NSDUH offers a correction to the sensationalized media reports that the use of certain extremely dangerous and exotic drugs "is sweeping the country like wildfire," that one or another dangerous substance has "become the drug of choice among America's youth," or "will destroy an entire generation." These sensational headlines are quickly refuted by a perusal of NSDUH's serious, sober, and systematic survey of the real-life drug incidence and patterns on the consumption of psychoactive substances, legal and illegal.

MTF

Each year since 1975, the Institute on Survey Research at the University of Michigan surveys a nationally representative sample of 15,000

TABLE 7.4   NSDUH, DRUG USE PAST MONTH, PERSONS AGE 12 AND OLDER, 2011

Alcohol	51.8%
Binge drinking	22.6%
Cigarettes	22.2%
At least one illicit drug	22.5%
Marijuana	18.1%
Psychotherapeutics	6.1%
Cocaine	1.4%
Hallucinogens	1.0%
Inhalants	0.6%
Heroin	0.3%

Source: *NSDUH*, Summary of National Findings, September 2012

TABLE 7.5   MTF (MONITORING THE FUTURE), 12TH GRADE, 2011

Alcohol	40.0%
Been Drunk	25.0%
Cigarettes	18.7%
Any Illicit drug	25.2%
Marijuana	22.8%
Amphetamine	3.7%
Ecstasy	2.3%
Hallucinogens	1.6%
Cocaine	1.1%
Inhalants	1.0%
LSD	0.8%
PCP	0.8%
Methamphetamine	0.6%
Crack	0.5%
Heroin	0.4%

Source: Johnston et al., *Monitoring the Future: National Results on Adolescent Drug Use, Overview of Key Findings*, February 2012

or so high school seniors about their use of and attitudes toward legal and illegal drugs. Beginning in 1977, adults, both college-educated and non-college educated, who completed high school one or more years earlier were also questioned. The adult sample was divided into college students and non-college respondents, whose answers are tabulated separately. In 1980, a specifically college sample was drawn and surveyed about drug use. In 1991, samples of eighth and tenth graders were included. In 2011, its survey of drug use among eighth, tenth, and twelfth graders drew a sample of 46,000 students in 400 secondary schools around the country. This ongoing survey is referred to as *MTF* survey. The MTF's surveys are conducted in the classroom, and its questionnaires are self-administered by each respondent. For each drug, four levels of use are asked about: lifetime prevalence—whether the respondent ever used the drug in question; annual prevalence, or use during the prior year; thirty-day prevalence, or use during the prior month; and daily use, or use on twenty or more days during the previous thirty days. Respondents are also asked about perceived risk, their disapproval of drug use, and perceived availability of specific drugs.

MTF's survey (see Table 7.5) reminds us that drug use patterns among youths (MTF also surveys 8th and 10th graders, college students, and college-age persons not in college) parallels those in the general population; again, among youth, alcohol is more popular than illicit drugs, the use of tobacco is declining, marijuana is the most popular illicit drug, and the quartet of the most dangerous drugs—methamphetamine, PCP, heroin, and crack—are the least popular of the illicit substances. As with the National Survey, MTF draws a huge sample, and so it is possible to tabulate relationships between and among variables—for instance, that drinkers, especially those who have drunk often and been drunk, are more likely to use an illicit drug than non-drinkers, that students who do poorly in school are more likely to use illicit drugs than students who excel.

ALCOHOL CONSUMPTION: AN INTRODUCTION

Fermentation is one of the most ancient of human discoveries, dating back to the Stone Age. Alcohol emerges spontaneously from the fermented sugar in overripe fruit; the starch in grains and other food substances also readily converts to sugar and from sugar to alcohol. Because this process is so simple and basic, the discovery of alcohol by humans was inevitable and early. Alcohol consumption, in all probability, began when a prehistoric human consumed fermented fruit and experienced its effects, enjoyed them, and communicated his or her discovery to others. Alcohol can induce pleasure, euphoria, intoxication, a sense of well-being, a state of relaxation, a relief from tension, a feeling of goodwill toward others, the alleviation of pain, drowsiness, and sleep. Unpleasant effects occur at higher doses, but nearly everywhere, such levels of use tend to be the exception rather than the rule. As a result, it is an almost universally accepted beverage. Consequently, as paleontologists and anthropologists tell us, alcohol's use tends to be both ancient and nearly universal: Humans have been ingesting alcohol for more than 10,000 years, and it is the most widely imbibed psychoactive substance in the world—ubiquitous, almost omnipresent the world over.

In spite of its universality around the globe, societies differ vastly in their average level of alcohol consumption. Every society that has some acquaintance with alcohol has devised and institutionalized rules for the proper and improper consumption of alcohol. These rules vary from one society to another and from one social category to another. Although alcohol does have objective biochemical effects, both short-term and over the long run, these effects can be influenced, mitigated, or altered by the observance of cultural rules for consumption. For instance, if alcohol is consumed on an empty stomach, its effects will be more drastic and debilitating than if taken in conjunction with the consumption of food. If male drinkers are surrounded by intimates, especially women and children—who usually control or mitigate their behavior—their tendency to take harmful risks will be diminished. In most societies, the vast majority of episodes of alcohol consumption pose little or no problem to society. The drug is consumed in moderation and associated with very little untoward behavior. But in other societies, drinking, whether on multiple occasions or taken as a whole, has been catastrophic. The impact of alcohol consumption is not determined solely by the biochemical effects of the drug but by the relationship of those effects to the characteristics of the people drinking it, constrained by the culture and the society in which it is used.

The critic in us is likely wonder what's so deviant about drinking. The polls say that eight out of ten in the American population age 12 and older drink once in a while and more than half of us drink regularly. Even many kids drink. Most high school seniors drink, all of them are seriously underage, and drinking in college is expected. Do legislatures think that it is possible to criminalize drinking *in college*? Isn't the ban on drinking under twenty-one a case of over-legislation, too much control, a case of "big brother is watching you"? What's so *deviant* about drinking alcohol? Shouldn't we acknowledge that drinking represents the widespread consumption of a more or less benign substance, which is the basis of a huge industry, the alcoholic-drinks market, one that generates revenues, in the United States, in excess of $150 billion dollars annually? Isn't drinking alcohol a perfectly conventional activity as well? Isn't the consumption of a glass of wine or two at dinner well within the normative framework of nearly all the social circles in America? Shouldn't sports fans be allowed to enjoy a brew or two while watching a ball game? Isn't the *refusal* to drink considered a bit odd, eccentric, unconventional—in a word, *deviant*? These are all rhetorical questions, of course, and so sociologists of deviance quiet down the inner critic by pointing out that five reasons drive their interest.

First, the *excessive* consumption of alcohol makes it difficult for most people to effectively perform their expected institutional roles—marital, familial, economic, and educational. Swill down five or six drinks during lunch, stagger around your office, slur your words, appear dazed and confused while wandering the halls, fall asleep at your desk—and you're likely to be told to stop drinking or lose your job. Drink too much before class or when you should be doing your homework and you'll find you can't learn as much and you may flunk school. All societies depend on an adequate performance in their fundamental institutions; an overly generous consumption of alcohol imperils that performance. No doubt about it: Failing to perform expected roles as a result of intoxication is a form of deviance. And it's true that *most* people don't drink so much that they fail at the tasks they are expected to perform.

But many of us do—millions of us. And *when* we do, we're engaging in a form of deviant behavior. And it happens enough times for authorities, legislatures, people in positions of responsibility—parents, teachers, friends, employers, traffic cops, you name it—who are distressed or disappointed to act to curb it. We can't perform at jobs and assignments, or we do them badly. We don't get paid. We fail an exam. We get into an accident. Somebody gets killed. Is it necessary to continue?

Second, the effects of alcohol *facilitate* or *are associated with* the enactment of many forms of deviance, including crime, violence, sexual transgressions, and needless, avoidable accidents. Epidemiologists find that the greater the amount of alcohol someone consumes, the greater the likelihood that he or she will engage in most deviant and criminal activities. Sadly, even being a *victim* of rape, robbery, murder, not to mention a range of other predatory crimes, are associated with drinking. Here, the deviant is not the victim but perpetrator, but the victim is *forcibly* yet *causally implicated* in the act by being victimized. Some critics have referred to this line of reasoning as "blaming the victim" (Ryan, 1976), but factually, the researcher can separate the concept of *blame* from that of *cause* (Felson, 1991). Again, most of us don't drink so much that our lives are imperiled, or that we imperil the lives of others. But *how much* drinking, which causes *how much* untoward behavior, do we think is acceptable? And how much drinking do we grant the innocent party before we acknowledge that he or she may be victimized by said consumption? At some point, most of us draw a line. We *know* that certain forms of drinking result in deviant, predatory behavior, as well as a person's becoming the victim of deviant behavior, and hence, when those instances take place, we know that a connection between alcohol consumption and deviance has been forged.

The third reason the student of deviance is interested in alcohol consumption is that at certain times and under certain circumstances and in certain social circles, the mere consumption of alcohol—*regardless* of its consequences—has been or is regarded as both legally and informally non-normative. For instance, the distribution of alcohol was banned in the United States during Prohibition (1920–1933); it continues to be banned in a number of "dry" counties in the United States, and it is banned in certain jurisdictions around the world, mainly in Muslim nations. It is also regarded as unacceptable and untoward behavior among most evangelical, conservative, and fundamentalist Christians. Whether we like it or not, and whether drinking is associated with other untoward behaviors, understanding the *social construction of deviance* is one of our jobs here, and banning any and all alcohol consumption has taken place enough times in history for the interest of the sociologist of deviance to be aroused.

Fourth, while very few sociologists *define* deviance by harm (one exception: Costello, 2006), harm and deviance are not randomly related to one another; many of the most harmful activities are condemned. So our fourth concern is the "flip side" of our first one. The fact that alcohol causes, generates, or is implicated in, as much harm as it has, mostly without being banned or strongly condemned pretty much everywhere, is interesting, and one worth exploring. Given the harm it causes, and given its harm relative to that of more severely condemned activities, why do we tolerate or mainstream or *conventionalize* alcohol consumption as much as we do? The enterprising sociologist of deviance wants to know *why* alcohol has received such fitful and mild, "slap-on-the-wrist" condemnation, while many less harmful activities are illicit, illegal, and strongly condemned. Certainly proponents of marijuana legalization have made this observation in advocating their cause. There may be a cultural or historical explanation, and perhaps the facts support a more rationalistic explanation. To the student of deviance, this issue should be discussed.

And fifth, there's the concern that practically all adult members of society harbor when it comes to drinking: alcohol consumption among minors. The majority of adults consider drinking *at all* among young people as non-normative because they don't believe that young people can "handle their liquor." Among adolescents, intoxication is more likely to lead to problematic behavior, they believe, than among the mature. Even if *most* episodes of teen drinking result in unproblematic consequences, factually speaking, enough teens get into sufficiently serious trouble for adults to regard youthful alcohol consumption as unacceptable, non-normative—and deviant.

WHO DRINKS? WHO DOESN'T?

Who drinks and who doesn't? Are certain groups or social categories significantly and consistently more likely to drink than others? Do the social origins of drinkers influence the tendency to label their behavior as deviant?

There are at least two crucial measures of alcohol consumption: first, drinking versus abstention, and second, among drinkers, drinking at all versus drinking to excess. Drinking varies dramatically from one category in the population to another; likewise, drinking heavily, compulsively, and abusively—that is, to excess—varies along sociological lines. We might expect that categories in the population that have a high proportion of drinkers (and, contrarily, a low proportion of abstainers) would also rank high in the likelihood that their members are alcoholics, that is, those who drink to excess. The opposite side of the coin should be expected as well: The lower the proportion of drinkers in a given social category, the lower the likelihood that the members of that category will be abusive drinkers. This is not always the case, however; some groups in the population have extraordinarily high proportions of drinkers but low proportions of alcoholics, while some other groups are more likely to abstain, but its drinkers are more likely to drink compulsively and abusively. For instance, persons of Jewish and Italian ancestry are highly likely to drink, but their rates of alcoholism are comparatively low. In contrast, men over the age of sixty have higher than average rates of alcohol abstention and also higher than average rates of alcoholism.

Social class or socioeconomic status (SES), which is usually measured by income, occupation, and/or education, correlates strongly and consistently with the consumption of alcohol. As a general rule, in the Western world, the United States included, the higher the social class or SES, the greater the likelihood of drinking; members of the lower and working class are much more likely to be abstainers. This generalization is confirmed by the 2010 *NSDUH*, which found a remarkably strong correlation between education and drinking during the previous year. Among respondents

eighteen and older, only 37 percent with less than a completed high school education drank at all during the prior year, but 69 percent of college graduates had done so. But when the NSDUH researcher used measures indicating *binge* (having five drinks on the same occasion at least once in the prior 30 days) and *heavy* drinking (having five drinks on the same occasion five or more times in the prior 30 days), this pattern was reversed. Among respondents twenty-six or older, 23 percent of high school dropouts had engaged in binge drinking during the past month versus 20 percent for college grads; and for heavy drinkers, these figures were 7 versus 5 percent (SAMHSA, 2011). High school dropout drinkers were two-and-a-half times more likely to be "heavy" drinkers (about 18%) than was true of college graduate drinkers (7%). In short, the lower the SES, the greater the likelihood of *abstaining* from alcohol use but, among drinkers, the higher the likelihood of binge and heavy drinking.

Gender, too, correlates strongly with drinking. Of all variables (except age), perhaps gender correlates most strongly with alcohol consumption. Men are consistently more likely to drink than are women, and they drink more when they do drink. Both the 2010 and 2011 NSDUH found a sizeable male–female difference in drinking: 57 percent of the males but only 47 percent of the females in the study had drunk alcohol during the past month. And men were twice as likely as women to be binge drinkers and three times as likely to be heavy drinkers. The interesting thing about gender, though, is that the use of alcohol in the prior month among male and female youths age 12 to 17 was identical: 14 percent for both sexes for 2011, and 13 percent for both for 2011. Is the female's tendency to drink catching up with the male's? Possibly. The MTFs 2002 survey found that, among 8th graders, girls overtook boys in their thirty-day prevalence of alcohol consumption; they have had higher rates since then (Johnston et al., 2012, p. 44).

Age is also strongly correlated with drinking. Drinking tends to be extremely low in early adolescence, shoots up in the middle-to-late teenage years, reaches a peak in the twenties, and declines slowly after that. This pattern differs from that drug use, which peaks more sharply at the younger ages and drops off more sharply with age. Of course, drinking during the past month is not as "deviant" as illicit drug use; in moderation, it is conventional, very much in the mainstream. In the 2010 NSDUH, binge alcohol use was only one percent in the twelve-to-thirteen-year-old bracket, rose to 6.7 percent among fourteen- and fifteen-year-olds, to 15.3 among sixteen- and seventeen-year-olds, 33.3 among persons eighteen-to twenty, and peaked among those age twenty-one to twenty-five, at 45.5 percent. Current use (during the past 30 days) was 51.6 percent among twenty-six- to twenty-nine-year-olds and declined to 38.2 percent among persons 65 and older.

But consider this: Heavier drinkers are more likely to be drawn from the social sectors of the population who contribute the highest proportion of participants in deviant behavior: less-well educated, lower-SES, young males. While drinking once or more in the past month is hardly a form of deviance, drinking five or more alcoholic beverages on repeated occasions, month after month, is certainly non-normative. Moreover, as we saw, such an activity opens the door to other deviant activities. Not only are the people who engage in such drinking patterns also likely to get into other kinds of trouble, but intoxication may contribute to that tendency. Binge and heavy drinking is deviant in and of themselves, *and* the social characteristics of binge and heavy drinkers may facilitate *further* and *related* deviant behavior.

ACUTE EFFECTS OF ALCOHOL

Chemically, alcohol is known as "ethyl alcohol" or *ethanol*; it is one of dozens of other substances chemists call "alcohol." (Methyl alcohol, a poison, is another.) Scientists measure the potency of alcoholic beverages by the percentage of alcohol (often referred to as "absolute" or *pure* alcohol) they contain. Pure ethyl alcohol is 100 percent "absolute" alcohol. Beer contains 4 or 5 percent alcohol; wine is 10 to 13 percent alcohol. "Fortified" wine, (wine to which alcohol or brandy is added), is legally set at 20 percent. Sherry is a fortified wine to which brandy has been added. The process of distillation (boiling, condensing, and recovering the more volatile,

alcohol-potent vapor from the original fluid and adding an appropriate quantity of water) produces drinks such as Scotch, vodka, gin, and tequila, which are 40 to 50 percent alcohol, or 80 to 100 "proof." In order to consume one ounce of alcohol, the drinker would drink two 12-ounce cans of beer, *or* one 8-ounce glass of wine, *or* a mixed drink containing about 2 or 2½ ounces of Scotch or gin.

The *rule of equivalency* states that, other factors being equal, the effects of alcohol are determined by the volume that is consumed rather than the type of drink itself. Hence, if consumed in the same period of time by the same person under the same conditions, two 12-ounce cans of beer, or one 8-ounce glass of wine, or a mixed drink containing 2 to 2 ½ ounces of Scotch or gin—they'd have the *same* effects. With respect to the drink that is consumed, nothing else makes a difference except the quantity of alcohol, consumed within the same period of time. (Of course, it generally takes longer to guzzle two cans of beer than to sip one mixed drink.) In other words, alcohol is alcohol is alcohol; nothing else matters in its impact, except of course the usual mitigating physiological factors. Drinking lore has it that different *kinds* of drinks—wine versus Scotch; gin versus beer; tequila versus vodka—have different capacities to make drinkers drunk. This is false; aside from mitigating factors (which I discuss later), how much "pure" or "absolute" alcohol one has consumed is the *only* factor that matters in determining level of intoxication. But this is a crucial point: Level of alcohol intoxication does *not* automatically translate into behavior under its influence. Two people with the same *measurable* level of intoxication may exhibit very different behaviors; people in the same society but drinking in two different locales or situations may reach a given level of intoxication but behave substantially differently; people in different societies may react differently to the same level of intoxication. Here's where our story gets really interesting: Alcohol is both a drug, with objective, measureable effects, and a social phenomenon the impact of which is shaped by culture, society, and social context.

But the objective level of alcohol in the body is crucial as well; beyond a certain level of intoxication, it is practically the only thing that matters. "Alcohol is the only addictive drug that alters behavior dangerously, yet at the same time is freely and legally available without a prescription" (Goldstein, 2001, p. 137). When it enters the body, a given quantity of alcohol translates into what pharmacologists call *blood–alcohol concentration* (BAC).This corresponds to the percent of the volume of one's blood that is made up of alcohol. Goldstein describes a given BAC as "bathing the brain" in a given alcohol concentration (p. 137). A close relationship exists between BAC and behavior. The effects of alcohol are drug-related: As a general rule, the greater the amount one consumes, the more intoxicated one becomes, and the more extreme is any given effect.

The effects of alcohol are contingent on, or influenced or mitigated by, a number of crucial physiological factors in addition to the total volume of alcohol in the drinker's body. Women are more sensitive to the effects of alcohol than men; the smaller the person (and therefore the less blood someone has to dilute the effects of alcohol), the more substantial the effect; the less body fat someone has, likewise, the more substantial the effect. And the less food (and water) one has in one's stomach, the more substantial the effect that the same quantity of alcohol has. And, as with practically all drugs, alcohol builds up pharmacological tolerance: It takes more alcohol to achieve a given effect in a regular, experienced, or frequent drinker than in an abstainer or infrequent drinker.

Alcohol is a depressant, much like the sedatives, such as barbiturates. Ethyl alcohol depresses, slows down, retards, or *obtunds* many functions and activities of organs of the body, such as heartbeat rate and neurological response time. Organs become more sluggish, slower to respond to stimuli. This is especially true of the central nervous system. If the dose is too high, the body's organs will shut down, and death will ensue. Alcohol also disorganizes and decreases the ability of the brain to process and use information and hence, impairs most perceptual cognitive and motor skills needed for coordination and decision-making. One ounce of alcohol, or roughly two mixed drinks, consumed in less than an hour will result in a BAC of roughly .05 percent in a man roughly 150 pounds. This BAC produces in most people a mild euphoria, a diminution of anx-

iety, fear, and tension, a corresponding increase in self-confidence, and, usually, what is called a "release" of inhibitions. Decreased fear also typically results in a greater willingness to take risks; this effect has been observed in laboratory animals. Alcohol is, for most people, a mild sedative, anxiety agent, and tranquilizer. This is not universally the case, however; in many people, alcohol ingestion results in paranoia, fear, distrust, and heightened anxiety, even hostility. These effects typically occur, when they do, at moderate to higher doses.

Alcohol's effects on motor performance are familiar to us all: clumsiness, an unsteady gait, the inability to stand up or walk straight, and slurred speech. One's accuracy and consistency at performing mechanical activities dramatically decline as one's BAC increases. And the more complex, abstract, and unfamiliar the task, the steeper the decline. The most noteworthy instance of such a decline is one's decreasing ability to drive an automobile. It is clear that drinking, even moderately, impairs the ability to drive, and contributes to highway fatalities. How intoxicated does one have to be to lose the ability to perform highway tasks? What does one's BAC have to be to produce a significant decline in motor coordination? And how many drinks does that represent? All drinkers experience a loss of motor skills at a certain point, and it occurs at a fairly low BAC. At about the .025 blood-alcohol level, that is, after finishing an average drink, some very inexperienced and particularly susceptible individuals will display a significant decline in the ability to perform a wide range of tasks. At the .10 level, even experienced drinker will exhibit measurable impairment in coordination; this is the consumption of roughly four drinks, each containing a half-ounce of alcohol, that is, an ounce of Scotch, rum or tequila. And many drivers seem to be willing to get behind the wheel while intoxicated: According to the FBI's Uniform Crime Reports, in 2011, the police made 1.2 million arrests for driving under the influence, and 534,000 for "drunkenness," and half a million for the violation of the liquor laws. And, specifically to the point of this book, the overly-generous consumption of alcohol is likely to co-occur with, and may cause, *risky, deviant behavior.*

THE CO-OCCURRENCE OF ALCOHOL ABUSE AND RISKY, DEVIANT BEHAVIORS

To understand the relationship between the heavy use or abuse of alcohol and other forms of deviance, it is essential to define our terms. Here, we have two terms that refer to concepts that point to things in the real world. The first is alcohol "abuse" and the second, "risky, deviant behavior." It's important to define terms in such a way that they are independent of one another. By that I mean if we want to establish an empirical or factual relationship between two things in the world—in such a way that we can argue that one has an impact on the other—we have to make sure we don't *define* one by the other. If we were to define alcohol "abuse" as problem alcohol consumption, that is, drinking to the point where one gets into trouble (DUI/DWI, arrest, divorce, alienation of friendship, accident, *etc.*), that would mix up cause with consequence. It is only by defining our terms along separate dimensions that we can determine what their co-occurrence or empirical relationship is (Mills, 1963, pp. 42–43).

Thousands of researchers have investigated the relationship between alcohol consumption and untoward, risky, criminal, violent, and/or deviant behavior. Of course, different researchers or research teams have measured different aspects of these phenomena and have used somewhat different definitions of their key concepts. How does the researcher define alcohol "abuse"? And what is untoward, risky, criminal, violent, and deviant behavior? Most researchers regard *binge* and/or *heavy* drinking as a form of alcohol "abuse." One common operationalization of "binge" drinking is the consumption of five or more alcoholic drinks three times during the prior month (some researchers set this figure at two; others, four; some track such drinking over a month, others, two weeks; etc.), and "heavy" drinking (one way of defining this is consuming more than three drinks per day during the past month; another is five or more episodes of five or more drinks on a single occasion). And by risky, deviant behavior, researchers tend to be interested mainly in behaviors that society

regards, likewise, as non-normative, or those that physicians and epidemiologists regard as actually or potentially harmful. Risky, deviant behavior includes: driving under the influence; engaging in criminal and violent behavior; putting oneself into a situation in which becoming a *victim* of criminal and violent behavior is likely; engaging in risky sexual behavior (multiple partners, unprotected sex, sex with strangers); using and abusing illicit drugs; and suicide attempts, successful suicides included.

Empirically, drinkers, taken as a category, are more likely to engage in risky, deviant behavior than non-drinkers, and the more they drink, the greater this tendency is; and people who are intoxicated are more likely to engage in risky, deviant behavior than persons who are not intoxicated, and the more intoxicated they are, the greater this tendency is. One study even found that the *sale* of alcohol in an area was strongly correlated with the likelihood that local residents will be hospitalized for assault. If you live near a place that sells a lot of alcohol, you're more likely to be seriously injured by a heavy drinker than if you live near a place that sells very little alcohol (Ray et al., 2008). In this case, the victim isn't the deviant, the victimizer is.

Here's a sociologically important qualification: The relationship between alcohol abuse and risky, deviant behavior is strongly *contingent* on drinking locales or contexts, that is, the social and physical circumstances or situations within which drinking takes place. Here are a few examples of social and physical drinking locales: a bar, a restaurant, a beach, a park, in the drinker's own home, in the home of friends, in a moving car, at a party, among intimates, among relatives, among strangers. For instance, aggressive and other problematic behaviors, such as arguments, fighting, and drunk driving, are more likely to occur in or follow drinking in a bar than at home (Nyaronga, Greenfield, and McDaniel, 2009). And *where* people drink and *what they are doing* when they drink determines how, and how seriously, they get injured. Compared with other locales, a relatively low proportion of people drink on the job; hence, again, relatively speaking, few show up at an emergency room (ER) as a result of an alcohol-impaired injury incurred on the job. On the other hand, again, a very high proportion of people in bars (and restaurants) do drink and hence, by that factor alone, a great many people show up in ERs, and have been injured in those locales as a result of alcohol impairment. In fact, in a summary of data from dozens of studies gathered in sixteen countries, a team of researchers (Macdonald et al., 2006) found that injuries in bars were significantly more likely to involve alcohol impairment than any other setting. Of all injuries that took place in a bar in which the injured party was taken to an ER, nearly 35 percent entailed alcohol impairment; this was true of only 2 percent where the injured person was in a school or workplace, 5 percent in a park or beach, just under 10 percent in a house, and just under 15 percent in a vehicle on the street or highway (Macdonald et al., 2006).

Broadening our conception of context or locale, and addressing violence specifically, we could include the society or country in which drinking takes place. In some countries, such as France, Italy, Portugal, and Spain, a high proportion of regular drinkers consume alcohol, usually in the form of wine, in a convivial setting with family and other intimates present, often during mealtimes, such as dinner. Such societies tend to have low rates of violence, especially criminal homicide, following drinking, and the relationship between alcohol consumption and violence is weak. In other countries, such as Russia and the other countries of Eastern Europe and the former Soviet Union, a high proportion of drinkers are single men who consume alcohol, mainly in the form of distilled spirits and mainly for the purpose of getting drunk, in the presence of other single men, often in a public place, such as a bar, with few females or family members to restrain their aggressive, argumentative, confrontational behavior. These societies manifest higher rates of violence and a closer relationship between heavy drinking and violent behavior. Hence, it is not *only* heavy alcohol consumption that counts in this relationship, but the social, cultural, and local contexts of drinking behavior, as well as the specific alcoholic substance (wine versus distilled spirits) that is consumed.

Here, the key question is *why*. What *causes* higher (and non-normative) levels of alcohol to covary with risky, deviant behavior? Hypotheses differ somewhat among one another and hence, the mechanism by which this relationship occurs differs according to the hypothesis. Researchers have offered at least three paradigmatic

explanations—the *pharmacological*, the *situational*, and the *dispositional*. Some hypotheses argue that *being under the influence* is the key mechanism causing this relationship. Others argue that the *context* within which drinking occurs is the culprit. Still other hypotheses argue that it is the *kind of person* who drinks, and drinks heavily, that is the key explanatory factor here; hence, it doesn't matter whether the drinker is under the influence at the moment the act is committed, or the situation that he or she is in, what counts is the *kind of person* who drinks, especially in substantial amounts. All in all, the relationship is most likely to be caused by a combination of these three factors.

In any case, pushing the cause-and-effect mechanism back even further, what is it about alcohol specifically that brings about an increase in risky, deviant behavior? Whether pharmacological, dispositional, or situational, Factor A (drinking) is related to or correlated with Factor B (risky, deviant behavior). Three possible mechanisms of our relationship come to mind (Young, Sweeting, and West, 2008, pp. 204–205).

First, we have the *disinhibition* hypothesis: Alcohol's effects *cause* risky, deviant behavior. Because alcohol offers a "release" from the inhibition that result from normative constraints on dangerous acts, under the influence, the drinker is more likely to engage in those acts. Sober, we rarely engage in these behaviors; intoxicated, we often do because of this "release of inhibitions" effect. A variation on the disinhibition hypothesis is the "alcohol-myopia" model: Alcohol disorganizes the brain's capacity to pay attention and process information and hence, "do the right thing" (George and Norris, 1991).

Second, there's the *susceptibility* hypothesis: Alcohol abuse and engaging in risky, deviant behavior are related because they are *effects of a common cause*. The abusive drinker is more likely to engage in risky, deviant behavior because the person who drinks heavily is *also* the sort of antisocial person who engages in behavior that either harms others or himself or herself. These are people who are unable to regulate or control their own behavior: They tend to be impulsive, sensation-seeking, aggressive, and highly risk-tolerant. Getting drunk and engaging in risky behavior are *both* caused by the antisocial proclivity of the drinker.

Third, there's the *reciprocal* hypothesis: Alcohol abuse and risky-antisocial behavior feed back into and fuel one another. True, a certain type of individual seeks out certain types of risky behaviors; but getting intoxication also disrupts one's judgment and further behavior, and contributes to both further heavy and binge drinking and impulsive, risky, deviant behavior (Young, Sweeting, and West, 2008).

ALCOHOL CONSUMPTION AND SEXUAL VICTIMIZATION

In the area of alcohol-related violence-victimization, more research has been conducted on *sexual* victimization than any other type. A woman who is intoxicated is substantially and significantly more likely to be sexually victimized than a woman who is sober. Students of deviance are curious to know why. Is it spurious, that is, an *artifact* of the situation? Are women more likely to drink on *dates* and hence, more likely to be in situations in which they are confronted by men who may force them to have sex? Are dates who offer women drinks more likely to be sexually aggressive than men who do not? Are men who offer women a drink on a date more likely to *perceive* women who accept drinks as sexual victims than they would women who refuse drinks? Do the physiological effects of alcohol render the intoxicated woman more sexually helpless than a woman would be if sober? Many causal explanations present themselves to account for this relationship. Which one is—or which ones are—valid?

Maria Testa (2004) surveyed four bodies of research on the role of substance use, alcohol included, when men commit violence against women: non-sexual physical violence perpetration; sexual violence perpetration; non-sexual violence victimization; and sexual violence victimization. We already know that men under the influence are more likely to commit violence, including sexual violence, against women than men who are sober. The weakest relationship of the four, Testa concludes, is that between alcohol (and drug) consumption and non-sexual violence

victimization. However, the evidence supporting the relationship between substance use and a woman's experience of sexual victimization is substantially stronger. This is especially the case at the "proximal" or *event* level—that is, in the immediate context or situation of the victimization itself. Sexually aggressive dates are more likely to include alcohol (and drugs) in their dating agenda and attempt to inflict sexual violence on their dates than is true of non-aggressive dates (Testa, 2004, p. 1497). Nonetheless, Testa concludes that women who have consumed alcohol "show impairment in their ability to recognize and respond to sexually aggressive risk" than women who are sober (2004, p. 1497). While Testa qualifies her literature summary by stating that the substance use–violence relationship is not universal for all people, all circumstances, or all measures of use, the pattern is strong enough to merit the generalization: Alcohol (and drug) intoxication increases the likelihood that women will be sexually victimized by men.

Muhlenhard and Linton (1987) report that, when college women describe their alcohol consumption on a date as "heavy," she is four times as likely to experience sexual aggression from the male than if it is "light" or none at all. About 15 percent of the women say they engaged in "unwanted sexual intercourse" (p. 186). Clearly, along with other factors, alcohol is strongly related to, and seems to facilitate, sexual aggression and tacit victimization in a college dating situation. In another study (Parks and Fals-Stewart, 2004), during a six-week period, college women were nine times more likely to experience sexual aggression on days when they are drinking heavily and three times more likely when it was lighter than when they are not drinking at all. Of course, these could be days specifically when they are out on a date and hence, vulnerable to men's aggressive sexual advances. As the authors say, the "temporal association" between college women's alcohol consumption hugely increases their risk for sexual victimization (p. 625). Finally, in another study (Ullman, Karabatsos, and Koss, 1999), drinking by victims (and offenders as well) was associated with riskier, unplanned situations in which the victim did not know their offenders well prior to the assault. In addition, victim (and attacker) drinking was associated with more severe levels of sexual victimization (coercion, force, hitting, slapping, choking, etc.), though if she was drunk, her resistance was more easily overcome than if she was sober. In short, the study suggests that "alcohol use plays both direct and indirect roles in the outcomes of sexual abuse," including completed rape (p. 603).

Again, researchers do not "blame" the victim when they document that intoxication makes sexual victimization, again, including forcible rape, more likely. Victimizers, exploiters, and brutalizers are more likely to seek out vulnerable targets, and their perception that an intoxicated woman is more vulnerable to sexual victimization results in her *actual* sexual victimization. Here, women are unwillingly coerced into victimization partly as a result of their excessive use of alcohol.

The tendency of women to be victimized while intoxicated frequently leads to another victimization, some critics say. In a study using mock rape trials (Finch and Munro, 2007), juries regard complainants as *more* responsible than their sober attackers—a *true* case of "blaming the victim"—while their attackers are held to be *less* responsible than the sober defendants. In effect, if a woman who is drunk when she is raped is regarded as guiltier than a sober victim, a drunk rapist is seen as less guilty than a sober rapist.

The social construction of the intoxicated woman's vulnerability is two-fold: First, there is the men's construction of intoxicated women's vulnerability as well as their belief that taking advantage of such women is permissible and non-culpable. And second, there is society's after-the-fact interpretation or construction of the meaning of such assaults. Objectively, intoxication lowers the woman's "awareness of risky situations and impairs the ability to resist assault" (p. 592). As a result of the woman's involvement of intoxication in sexual consent scenarios often influences the way in which observers assign responsibility to the parties involved" (p. 592). When the female is intoxicated, audiences regard her drunkenness as her responsibility. But when the male perpetrator is intoxicated, his drunkenness is a partial exoneration for his crimes" (Stormo, Lang, and Strizke, 1997; Finch and Munro, 2007, p. 593).

Audiences regard alcohol intoxication "as a culturally sanctioned masculine activity" (Finch and Monro, 2007, p. 593), whereas when the female drinks too much, audiences regard her as deviating from gender-role norms. Hence, in a rape case, observers "tend to hold a voluntarily intoxicated complainant more responsible than her sober counterpart" (p. 594). She "has exhibited a reckless disregard for her own safety by sending out a message of sexual interest through her intoxication and by placing herself in a position in which she is vulnerable to the inevitable sexual aggression of an intoxicated male companion" (pp. 594–595). These stereotypes tend to govern the way that juries or potential juries think about the culpability of a rape defendant. A member of a mock jury assigned less responsibility toward the intoxicated defendant if he had sex with the woman when she was drunk than they did to her attacker because she accepted the drinks. Even if the defendant spiked her drinks with alcohol, they were unwilling to charge him with rape. It was only when his motive was to render the woman helpless and force her to have sex that they were willing to convict him of rape. In addition, this study showed, if the drug was Rophynol rather than alcohol, in contrast, the mock jury attributed less responsibility to the female victim and were more willing to convict the perpetrator with rape. In other words, alcohol is "heavily normalized" and hence, not regarded as a "demon" substance instrumental in the heinous crime of rape. It was apparent, say the authors, that jurors "were often prepared to attribute responsibility for the rape to the defendant but are reluctant to translate this into an attribution of blame [to the defendant] in the form of a guilty verdict, possibly because they were simultaneously attributing some responsibility for the subsequent sexual events to the intoxicated complainant" (p. 603).

ALCOHOL AND DRUG USE

The consumption of alcohol and the use of illicit psychoactive drugs are related in revealing and important ways. But since fewer people use illicit drugs than use alcohol, the relationship is far from perfect. Let's express their relationship in the following two generalizations. First: *People who drink alcohol are more likely to use illegal drugs than people who don't drink.* And second: *Most people who drink don't use illegal drugs.*

TABLE 7.6   ILLICIT DRUG USE BY ALCOHOL USE IN PAST MONTH

	No Use	Use But Not Binge Use	Binge Use But Not Heavy Use	Heavy Use
Marijuana	1.9	4.0	12.4	25.1
Cocaine	0.2	0.4	1.5	5.5
Hallucinogens	0.1	0.2	0.9	2.2
*Non-Medical Prescription Use	1.6	1.9	4.6	10.5
**Illicit Drug Other than Marijuana	2.0	2.4	6.5	15.4
ANY/ALL DRUG USE	3.4	5.5	16.1	31.3

*Non-medical prescription use indicates the use of at least one prescription drug without a physician's prescription and includes pain relievers, tranquilizers, stimulants, and sedatives.

**Illicit drug other than marijuana refers to the use in the past month of at least one illegal drug in addition to or aside from marijuana.

Source: SAMHSA, 2007, "Detailed Tables" (not in SAMHSA, 2008). I thank James Colliver for supplying me with these tables and helping me interpret their significance.

The data on the relationship between alcohol consumption and drug use are instructive. Drinking alcoholic beverages is significantly related to the use of *all* psychoactive recreational drugs. Drinkers consume alcohol *mainly* for its effects; illicit drug users take illicit substances *mainly* for their effects. Drinkers are more likely to know the users of illicit drugs than non-drinkers are, and hence, become socialized to accept the desirability of drug use as well as have access to illicit drugs. Statistically speaking, people who drink are more unconventional and more willing to take risks than people who do not drink; as a result, they tend to be more open to the experience of getting high on illegal drugs. In a nutshell, these are the most informative explanations for why we observe such a strong and irrefutable relationship between alcohol consumption and illicit drug use. To repeat: Not all drinkers take illegal drugs; most don't. But they are a lot *more likely* to use drugs than non-drinkers. In fact, as the ongoing NSDUH reports indicate, drinkers are roughly *ten times* more likely to use illicit drugs than non-drinkers. But let's also keep in mind the following truism in the world of the consumption of illicit substances: *Most illegal drug use is with marijuana.* About three-quarters of all episodes of illicit drugs are with marijuana alone. When anyone refers to illicit drug use they are talking *mainly* about marijuana use. Tables 7.6 and 7.7 document the relationship between alcohol consumption and illicit drug use.

TABLE 7.7   USE OF ILLICIT DRUGS BY USE OF ALCOHOL AND CIGARETTES IN PAST MONTH

	No Cigarettes, No Alcohol	Alcohol, No Cigarettes	Cigarettes, No Alcohol	Cigarettes and Alcohol
Marijuana	0.9	4.6	7.0	20.3
Cocaine	0.0	0.3	1.1	3.8
Hallucinogens	0.1	0.2	0.4	1.7
*Non-Medical Prescription Use	1.2	2.1	3.4	7.9
**Illicit Drug Other than Marijuana	1.4	2.6	4.6	11.5
ANY/ALL DRUG USE	2.2	6.4	9.7	25.3

Source: SAMHSA, 2007, "Detailed Tables" (not in SAMHSA, 2008). I thank James Colliver for supplying me with these tables and helping me interpret their significance.

Tables 7.6 and 7.7 convey a simple message with a complex explanation: The consumption of alcohol and the use of illegal drugs are strongly related; not only are users of alcohol more likely to also use illegal drugs, but the more alcohol the drinker consumes, the greater the likelihood that he or she will *regularly* use psychoactive drugs. Of all the respondents in NSDUH's survey who did *not* drink alcohol in the past month, only 1.9 percent used marijuana in the prior month—but 25.1 percent of the persons defined as "heavy" drinkers had done so. Only 0.2 percent of the non-drinkers had used cocaine in the previous 30 days, but 5.5 percent of the heavy drinkers had done so. There is a step-wise and linear relationship between alcohol and illicit drug use; the heavy drinker is between 6.5 and 27.5 times as likely to have used drugs (depending on the drug) than the non-drinker, and increasing alcohol use also increases the likelihood of using one or more illicit drugs. The relationship is even stronger when we introduce smoking cigarettes into the picture, which is remarkable because Table 7.7 compares alcohol use during the past month with non-use, whereas Table 7.6 compares degrees of alcohol use, and has no category for simple use during the

past month. Smoking cigarettes seems to correlate *even more strongly* with illicit drug use than drinking (compare the figures in the "alcohol, no cigarettes" column with the "cigarettes, no alcohol" column). This may be because monthly-or-more cigarette smokers are less numerous and more committed substance users than the mainstream of monthly-or-more drinkers—and, very possibly, a bit more unconventional. But of course, using *both* tobacco and alcohol is even more compatible with psychoactive drug use than is using one but not the other. This is especially the case with smoking marijuana: Consumers of alcohol and cigarettes are *twenty-two and-a-half times* more likely to have used marijuana in the prior month than non-smokers *and* non-drinkers.

As we can see in Table 7.8, as with the population at large, adolescents in the 8th, 10th, and 12th grades who drink alcohol are much more likely to use illicit drugs than those who do not drink; this pattern is true of drugs in general as well as with marijuana specifically, and it is true of each grade level separately. Moreover, the more that secondary school students drink (1 to 19 versus 20 or more occasions), the greater is the likelihood that they also used drugs during the prior thirty days.

TABLE 7.8   ALCOHOL AND ILLICIT DRUG USE, 8TH, 10TH, AND 12TH GRADERS

30-DAY ALCOHOL USE	*PERCENTAGE OF N*	*ANY ILLICIT DRUG*	*ANY ILLICIT DRUG OTHER THAN MARIJUANA*	*MARIJUANA*
8th Grade (N = 15,260)				
0 Occasions	84.3	2.7	1.3	1.7
1–19 Occasions	15.2	31.0	14.9	25.0
20+ Occasions	0.6	73.9	53.3	62.1
10th Grade (N = 15,423)				
0 Occasions	66.8	6.1	2.3	4.5
1–19 Occasions	31.8	37.8	16.0	32.5
20+ Occasions	1.4	62.2	27.6	57.7
12th Grade (N = 14,116)				
0 Occasions	55.7	6.2	2.6	4.6
1–19 Occasions	41.2	39.4	16.1	34.7
20+ Occasions	3.1	71.5	41.3	63.1

Source: Tabulations of the 2007 Monitoring the Future data, not in published report; I would like to thank Patti Meyer for supplying me with these figures.

N = sample size

For instance, of the majority of the 8th graders who drank no alcohol in the past thirty days (84% of the total), only 2.7 percent had consumed any illicit drugs during that period—but 73.9 percent of the tiny minority who had drunk alcohol 20 or more times (0.6%) had used at least one illicit drug one or more times—a difference of 27 times! For 10th graders, this figure was 10 times, and for 12th graders, 11.5 times. Clearly, an extremely strong relationship exists between alcohol consumption and illicit drug use. Of course, for teenagers, the purchase and possession of both alcohol and illicit drugs are illegal.

The question is why? Do we have a *direct* cause-and-effect relationship on our hands, that is, is the relationship the result of feeling the *effects* of drinking alcohol that impels the drinker to want to seek the effects of a *cognate* psychoactive substance? Is it that "heavy" drinkers are the kinds of unconventional people who are likely to do other unconventional things, like getting high on marijuana or taking a "toot" of cocaine? Or, alternatively, are the social networks that "heavy" drinkers, and regular drinkers, *and* cigarette smokers hang out with and among *also* the kinds of social networks whose members encourage and practice the use of one or more illicit drugs? My guess is that it's all three; many deviant behaviors "cluster" together in the same social circles, and attitudes toward unconventional behaviors in one sphere of life tend to "spill out" into other areas of life. The *generalizability* of deviance is one more of the more firmly established patterns in crime and deviance, and may be taken as something of a truism (Gottfredson and Hirschi, 1990; Hirschi and Gottfredson, 1994).

DRUG USE AS DEVIANT BEHAVIOR

We can look at drug use as deviant behavior from both the positivist and the constructionist perspectives. With both, when looking at drugs, we must ask the same two questions I raised earlier: *What is our mission?* And: *What is to be explained?*

From a positivistic perspective, the issue that needs explaining is *why some people use illegal substances*. This perspective places the deviant nature of drug use in the background, of only secondary interest. To positivists, the issue of why the use of certain drugs is regarded as deviant does not need to be answered; it is irrelevant to their mission. In contrast, they believe, "Why do they do it?" *is* the question that needs to be answered.

Of course, each positivistic theory attempts to answer the "Why do they do it?" question in its own way. Some focus on individualistic explanations—such as biological or personality factors. Others examine differences between and among people living in certain types of social and economic structures, such as different types of neighborhoods, different societies and social structures, cities versus small towns, and so on. And some positivist theories ask "Why *don't* they do it?"—which is simply the flip side of exactly the same question. But *all* positivistic explanations seek to reveal the causes of drug use; all take drug use as the *dependent* variable, as the variable that needs to be explained. And the factor they isolate as the cause, usually their theory's name, is the *independent* or explanatory variable. All positivistic theories have the same structure or form: Factor A (the explanatory or independent variable) causes Outcome B (drug use, the dependent variable).

In addition, positivists examine the *consequences* of actions such as drug use. This is important to someone with a scientific or empirical approach to the consumption of psychoactive substances because it helps explain *why* those drugs are used. The appeal of psychoactive drugs is largely a result of their effects. For instance, certain drugs are highly reinforcing; they activate and "hijack" pleasure centers in the brain. They are so rewarding, some scientists argue, that the user takes them again and again, becoming dependent, abandoning what was previously valued, such as family, school, a job, a home (DuPont, 1997). There is also an unstated or background assumption in the positivist's approach to drug use that the objective consequences of the use of certain substances are so harmful that society wisely attempts to control or limit their use through law enforcement. In other words, the condemnation of illicit use is a rational response to the very real and present danger such use poses and hence, so commonsensical as not to require detailed, systematic study. A different sort of explanation is not so much that the use of psychoactive substances "hijack" the brain and cause untoward behavior as that it *covaries* with other variables, but does not necessarily cause them. Hence, drug use and grades in school could be related to one another, but a third or prior factor, such as the susceptibility to engage in deviant behavior, could cause them, as we saw with Gottfredson and Hirschi's social control theory or "general theory of crime" (1990).

In contrast, for the constructionist, the very issue that for the positivist is theoretically unproblematic and taken for granted, becomes central. This issue is: *Why is the use of certain substances regarded as deviant?* For the constructionist, it is the "Why do they do it?" question that is assumed or in the background. The constructionist raises questions such as: Why are certain substances regarded as "drugs" while others aren't? Why are the possession and sale of some "drugs" legal while those of others illegal? What are the processes through which influential segments of society mount an antidrug campaign to convince the public that substance abuse is wrong and more dangerous than other threats that are ignored? Why does so much of the public believe that the drug war should be fought with such ferocity? How did the drug "war" get started in the first place? Why are the use and distribution of heroin and cocaine widely seen as evil while the use of alcohol and tobacco is regarded as acceptable, respectable, recreational—or, at worst, a bad habit, or an illness? Is it solely a product of the former drugs' objective dangers and the latter drugs' safety? These are not ideological or rhetorical questions, but ones that demand serious investigation (Duster, 1970; Reinarman and Levine, 1997).

The constructionist does not assume that social constructions of drug use are "irrational," illogical, or unreasonable, that all crusades to stamp out the consumption of illicit psychoactive substances are "moral panics." For the most part, societies do not condemn or criminalize the possession and sale of drugs out of prejudice, ignorance, or perversity, simply because their culture

or history or religion or sense of morality told them to do it. It would be wrong to trace society's condemnation of drug use and the drug laws exclusively to politics, ideology, economics, or religious edicts. All of these factors and processes may play a role. The simple fact is that most forms of drug use *are* harmful—to some people, under certain circumstances, and in varying degrees, according to the drug in question, the dose, and the frequency of use. But so are many activities that are not widely condemned or banned—scuba diving, hang gliding, NASCAR racing, hunting, possessing handguns, rock climbing, boxing, and playing football. Each of these activities has its supporters who are willing to offer a justification explaining how and why drug use is different. But all of these activities, drug use included, share several characteristics in common: All result in some harm, even the loss of human life, all are pursued because some people find them enjoyable, and all become an obsession for a substantial percentage of participants. Activities involving excitement and danger tend to trigger chemicals in the body ("endorphins") that are analogous to the dependency-producing substances we refer to as drugs. Hence, the question becomes: Why condemn and outlaw one type of dangerous behavior but accept and permit another? Again, this is not a rhetorical or argumentative question but one that should be seriously considered.

Moreover, many activities, whether harmful or benign, are legal in some jurisdictions and at certain times but illegal in others. Gay marriage is legal in several states of the United States, in Canada, and several countries of Europe, but not permitted by law in the vast majority of the United States. Marijuana can be obtained in the Netherlands but not in most American jurisdictions. The age of sexual consent is, variously and depending on the jurisdiction, fifteen, sixteen, seventeen, eighteen, and even, in some places, twenty-one. In Iran, China, Saudi Arabia, Pakistan, and Syria, the government blocks access to politically and sexually sensitive websites; in most other countries, such access is free, open, and unlimited. Before 1920, the sale of alcohol for recreational purposes was legal in most of the United States. Between 1920 and 1933, it was illegal everywhere, and after 1933, again, it became legal in most places. In other words, arresting and prosecuting for, and condemning, certain behavior is not a simple product of that behavior's objective negative consequences. It's an obvious point but one worth making: The difference in the law of these many jurisdictions is not solely based on the threat or the harm or danger posed by the activity—that is pretty much the same everywhere—but on political, ideological, economic, and cultural factors. In short, these laws are *social constructions*. What the constructionist is interested in is how these factors influence the law and the condemnation of certain activities. The harm of an activity is not the only factor influencing its illegality and its condemnation—it is one among many. Even the laws against and prosecution of murder, rape, and robbery, unarguably harmful acts with genuine victims, are constructed in certain ways for certain reasons.

A CLASSIFICATION OF DRUGS AND DRUG EFFECTS

Stimulants speed up signals passing through the central nervous system (CNS), that is, the brain and spinal column. They enable the user to feel more alert and awake. Strong stimulants include cocaine, amphetamine, methamphetamine, Adderall, and Ritalin. Caffeine is a stimulant so weak that most of us do not think of it as a drug at all.

Narcotics, or "narcotic analgesics," diminish the brain's perception of pain. This category includes the opiates—opium and its derivatives: morphine, heroin, codeine. This category also includes the various synthetic and semisynthetic narcotics, called opioids (or "opium-like" drugs), such as Percodan, Dilaudid, methadone, and meperidine (or Demerol), and oxycodone (including OxyContin). In addition to their painkilling property, all narcotics are also physically addictive, that is, they generate a physical dependency after regular, long-term use. In addition to dependence, their effects include mental clouding and euphoria. It is their euphoria-generating property that causes many people to use narcotics recreationally, that is, for the purpose of getting high.

Unlike the narcotics, which have a depressive effect principally on one bodily function—the perception of pain—*sedatives* or *general depressants*, while not effective painkillers, have a depressive effect on a wide range of body organs and functions. They tend to induce relaxation, inhibit anxiety and, at higher doses, eventually result in sleep. The most well-known of the general depressants is alcohol, which scientists refer to as ethyl alcohol or ethanol. Other examples include sedative-hypnotics such as barbiturates, methaqualone (once sold under brand names such as Quāālude and Sopor) and GHB; and tranquilizers, including Valium, Xanax, Librium, lorazepam, and Rohypnol ("roofies"). In sufficiently high doses, general depressants induce mental clouding, drowsiness, and physical dependence; an overdose can produce unconsciousness, coma, and even death. Some users seek the woozy, cloudy, drowsy feeling that depressants or "downers" generate. Since such a psychic state is potentially dangerous, such drugs are controlled. Still, let's recognize that alcohol has many of the same effects as the other sedatives, and it is available to anyone over the age of twenty-one.

Hallucinogens (once referred to as psychedelics) have effects on the central nervous system that cannot be reduced to a simple stimulation-depression continuum. These are the drugs that induce profound sensory alterations. They occupy their own unique and distinct category and include LSD, peyote and mescaline, and psilocybin or "magic mushrooms" ("shrooms"). The principal effect of the hallucinogens is not, as might be expected from their name, the inducement of hallucinations, but extreme psychoactivity, a loosening of the imagination and an intensification of emotional states.

Most recent classifications include a drug called PCP or Sernyl, once referred to as "angel dust," as a hallucinogen. Originally used as an animal tranquilizer, this drug has almost none of the properties associated with hallucinogens, such as dramatic sensory transformations. More sophisticated classification schemes see it as a disassociative-anesthetic. Ketamine ("special K") is a milder version of PCP. These drugs produce drowsiness, discoordination, a distorted sense of the reality of one's physical surroundings, and a feeling of invulnerability.

MDMA or Ecstasy ("Molly") is sometimes referred to as a hallucinogen, but it does not produce sensory alterations; a more accurate term to describe it would be "empathogen," that is, capable of inducing empathy, or an emotional identification with others. In animals, research indicates, the drug causes brain damage.

Marijuana has, at different times, been classified as a depressant, a stimulant, and, as late as the 1970s, a hallucinogen. Most observers nowadays feel that it belongs in a category by itself.

As we saw, according to the 2011 NSDUH, conducted in the general population, sponsored by the SAMHSA, slightly over half (52%) of the sample said that they drank alcohol within the past month, and were therefore defined as "current" drinkers. Alcohol is by far society's most popular recreational drug. A bit more than a quarter of the sample (27%) said they used at least one tobacco product, mostly cigarettes, in the past month. We can use these two "benchmark" figures against which to measure illicit drug use.

The illegal drug trade is an enormous economic enterprise, variously estimated to represent a $65-billion-a-year business in the United States (Rhodes et al., 2001, p.3). Other estimates vary somewhat from this one. In 2005, the United Nations estimated the illicit *global* drug market at 285 billion Euros (at the current rate of exchange, about $400 billion). But in 2009, a team of RAND social scientists scaled this figure down by half (Reuter and Trautmann, 2009). Most observers argue that drug expenditures have declined since the 1990s. In any case, clearly a great deal of money is spent on illegal drugs in the United States (certainly tens of billions of dollars a year) and worldwide (possibly hundreds of billions). And these sums represent a corresponding *immense* demand for illicit drugs.

Roughly a third of the American population has used one or more illicit drugs at least once during their lifetime. The NSDUH found that, in 2011, 9 percent, or 22.5 million people, had used an illicit drug within the past 30 days and were defined as "current" users. As we might expect, of all age categories, young adults were most likely to have used illegal drugs: for 2011, for eighteen-to-twenty-five-year-olds, the figure was 19 percent.

The most frequently used illegal drug in America is, again as we saw, marijuana; in 2011,

7 percent of the population age 12 and older were "current" users, that is, had used marijuana during the past month—a figure seven times as high as for cocaine (1.0%) and eighteen times as great as for hallucinogens (0.4%). In fact, again, almost three-quarters of current illicit use was with marijuana specifically, and over half of current drug users took *only* marijuana (SAMHSA, 2012). Allow me to reiterate: *Most illegal drug use is marijuana use.* About 2.4 percent of Americans had used one or more of the psychoactive pharmaceuticals—stimulants, analgesics, tranquilizers, and sedatives—non-medically in the past month. Heroin, a well-known and highly publicized illegal drug, was used by only 0.2 percent, or 620,000 people during the past year. Just over half a million (439,000) were current users of methamphetamine (SAMHSA, 2012). However, the NSDUH is almost certainly least useful for estimating the drug consumption of heavy users of relatively rarely used drugs such as crack, heroin, and meth because of the problem of locating them. Hence, these figures for the hard drugs are almost certainly substantial underestimates.

A study of drug use among high school seniors, college students, and young adults not in high school or college (the "MTF" survey) found much the same picture with respect to illegal drug use, except that their level of use was slightly higher than is true for the population as a whole (Johnston et al., 2012). In 2011, a quarter of high school seniors (25%) had used one or more illicit drugs at least once in the past thirty days, a fifth of tenth-graders (19%), and less than a tenth of eighth-graders (8.5%). For students in all grades—as with the population as a whole—again, marijuana was by far the most popular illicit drug. All of these figures represent slight but significant increases since 2007.

As a source of illegal and deviant behavior, drug use is substantial. But three qualifications are in order at this point: 1) in spite of small increases among teenagers, the use of nearly all illegal drugs declined *substantially* after the late 1970s; 2) illegal drug use is not nearly as high as many sensational media stories claim; and 3) illicit drug use is considerably less widespread than the use of alcohol and tobacco.

Both legal and illegal drugs vary considerably in user loyalty or continued use. Users are much more likely to "stick with" or be "loyal to" certain drugs, while users are much more likely to take other drugs episodically or infrequently, or to abandon them after a brief period of experimentation.

As a general rule, *legal* drugs tend to be used much more often on a continued basis, while *illegal* drugs tend to be used more infrequently and are more likely to be given up after a period of time. Of all psychoactive substances, legal or illegal, *alcohol* attracts the greatest user loyalty: Roughly six persons in ten who say that they ever drank, even once, did so in the past month. For cigarettes, just under four in ten of all at least one-time smokers are still smoking. Among all illegal drugs, marijuana tends to be "stuck with" the longest—16 percent of all Americans who have tried it remain users. For cocaine and methamphetamine, the figure is 6 percent and 4 percent, respectively, and for heroin, it is 4 percent; only six-tenths of 1 percent of at least one-time users has taken PCP in the past month (SAMHSA, 2012). In other words, *the more legal the drug, the more loyal users are to it*, the more they stick with it, the more likely they are to *continue* using it over time, the less likely they are to give up its use. Turning the equation around, the more illegal or illicit the drug, the less likely it is that one-time users will stick with it or continue to use it. Marijuana, the "least illicit" of the illicit drugs is the one that one-time users are most likely to continue using.

MARIJUANA USE IN THE UNITED STATES, 1960–2011

We already know that widespread behavior, beliefs, and conditions are not necessarily conventional or normative, and that rare behavior, beliefs, and conditions are not necessarily deviant. In other words, infrequency of occurrence is not a *defining* characteristic of deviance. Still, knowing how rare or widespread something is a relevant piece of information in any investigation of deviance.

At the beginning of the 1960s, very few Americans used illegal drugs. Even the use of marijuana, by far the most widely consumed illicit substance, was at an extremely low level.

The precursors to the national surveys, which were launched in 1973, asked respondents about their use at earlier ages; putting the age of respondents together with their estimates of earlier drug use, researchers were able to retrospectively estimate use in the early sixties. In 1960, less than 1 percent of youths age twelve to seventeen, and less than 5 percent of young adults age eighteen to twenty-five, had even tried marijuana. By 1967, these figures had nearly quadrupled, to over 5 percent for youths and over 15 percent for young adults (Miller and Cisin, 1980, pp. 13–16). The percent trying and using marijuana increased throughout the decade from the late 1960s to the late 1970s, and reached its peak roughly in 1979, when nearly a third of youths age twelve to seventeen (31%) and two-thirds of young adults age eighteen to twenty-five (68%) had tried marijuana. The use of marijuana declined during the 1980s but then rose again after the early 1990s. In 2011, in the most recent NSDUH available at this writing, only 7.9 percent of twelve-to-seventeen-year-olds and 19.0 percent of eighteen-to-twenty-five-year-olds said that they had used marijuana in the past month. For the population as a whole, this figure was 7.0 percent (SAMHSA, 2012). This up-and-down pattern was also revealed by surveys conducted by the MTF study; an almost identical arc was traced by college students during this same era.

During the 1980s, after the all-time high figures for the late seventies and early eighties, it seemed as if the use of marijuana among young people was diminishing. Many commentators argued that marijuana specifically and illegal drug use generally would decline to the point at which they would cease to be a problem in the United States. But after the early 1990s, for both high school seniors and college students, the percent who used marijuana had increased to the point where well over a third had used it during the past year (Johnston et al. 2012). Among high school seniors and college students, during the 1990s, the use of marijuana had become more widespread, more common. (In 1991, the MTF study began surveying eighth- and tenth-graders, and researchers found the same increases among these younger age brackets.) While the prevalence of marijuana use today does not reach the late 1970s to early 1980s levels, it is significantly higher than it was in the early 1990s and *vastly* higher than it was in the late 1960s. Marijuana use would have to decline substantially to reach the vastly lower figures that prevailed in the 1960s. This is unlikely to occur early in the twenty-first century.

MARIJUANA USE AS DEVIANCE AND CRIME

In the United States, the use and criminal status of marijuana have had a remarkable and complicated history. In the 1920s, very few Americans had even heard of marijuana or even knew anyone who used it and, consequently, very few thought of it as deviant. Until well into the twentieth century, the few who did know of the drug thought of it as a kind of medicinal herb. In the eighteenth century, George Washington grew marijuana plants on his plantation, probably for that very purpose. By the 1930s, however, marijuana had become the subject of hundreds of sensationalist newspaper and magazine articles. The drug was dubbed the "killer weed," the "weed of madness," a "sex-crazing drug menace," the "burning weed of hell," a "gloomy monster of destruction," the "green monster." Journalists and propagandists gave almost unlimited reign to the lurid side of their imaginations on the marijuana question. Every conceivable evil was concocted concerning the effects of this drug, the principal ones being insanity, sexual promiscuity, and violence. A popular film distributed in the 1930s, *Reefer Madness*, illustrates this: "marijuana causes you to go crazy, become sexually promiscuous, and want to kill people" theme. But by the 1960s, this movie had begun to be shown to pro-marijuana audiences, who found it so ludicrous as to be hilarious—evidence that confirmed their view that the drug was in fact harmless.

By 1937, partly as a result of the hysterical publicity surrounding the use of marijuana, laws criminalizing its possession and sale had been passed in every state and at the federal level as well. Several observers argue that racism against Mexican Americans was one of the principal reasons for the white majority's belief in the drug's evil effects, as well as for the swiftness with which these laws were passed (Musto, 1987, pp. 219, 245, 1999). The majority of states that passed the earliest anti-marijuana laws were Western states with the largest concentration of Mexican American populations. At times, an activity can be condemned, even criminalized, less as a result of a sober assessment of its objective impact than because of the majority feeling about the group that is thought to practice it.

Marijuana remained completely illegal and deviant throughout the remainder of the 1930s, and during the 1940s and 1950s; consensus has it that during this stretch, use was extremely low. During the course of the 1960s, however, the popularity of this drug increased dramatically. Along with this increase in use came the widespread awareness that it was not simply the poor or members of minority groups but also the sons and daughters of affluent, influential, middle-class folk who used it. Marijuana acquired a mantle of, if not respectability or conventionality, at least not complete deviance either. Attitudes began to soften; in the 1970s, eleven states comprising one-third of the United States population decriminalized the possession of small quantities of marijuana. Then, beginning roughly with the election of Ronald Reagan as president in 1980, the tolerant sentiment toward marijuana that had been growing during the 1960s and 1970s began to dissipate and a more condemnatory mood set in. The tide had been reversed: Marijuana, its possession, use, and sale, had become deviant once again.

One measure or indicator of the deviant status of marijuana use is the growing percentage of high school students who said that marijuana use should be illegal, that the regular use of marijuana is harmful, and that they disapprove of regular marijuana use. The late 1970s represented an era when tolerance and acceptance of marijuana were at their peak. After the late 1970s, a growing percentage of Americans said that the drug's use should be illegal, that the use of the drug is harmful, and that they disapproved of its use. In 1979, the MTF survey showed that only a quarter (24 percent) believed that using marijuana should be a crime; only an eighth (14 percent) believed that people who smoked marijuana "occasionally" risked harming themselves; and under half (45 percent) said that they disapproved of the occasional use of marijuana.

What happened roughly after the late 1970s and throughout the 1980s was truly remarkable. Tolerance of marijuana use among high school seniors evaporated and a far more condemnatory attitude replaced it. By 1991, high school seniors' belief that marijuana use should be a crime doubled, to 49 percent; the belief that one risks harming oneself by smoking marijuana occasionally more than doubled, to 41 percent; and those saying that they disapproved of the occasional use of marijuana increased to 79 percent (Johnston et al., 2005, pp. 354–363). In short, over the 1980s, marijuana use came to be seen as *more* deviant. In the sense of supporting the arrest and imprisonment of users, believing that use is medically dangerous, and disapproving of use, American's high school seniors moved *away* from seeing marijuana use as conventional, acceptable, safe, and ordinary, *toward* seeing it as unconventional, unacceptable, dangerous, and out of the ordinary—in short, as deviant.

As with use itself, after the early 1990s, a significant (though far from complete) reversal in attitudes toward marijuana occurred. The 1990s and the early years of the new century witnessed a growing tolerance and acceptance of the drug. Between 1991 and 2011, the proportion of high school students saying that people who smoked marijuana more than occasionally risked harming themselves declined from 41 to 23 percent, and the proportion saying that they disapprove of someone using marijuana occasionally declined during that same period dropped from 79 to 61 percent. Acceptance and tolerance of marijuana at the beginning of the twenty-first century was not as great as it was during the late 1970s to the early 1980s, but clearly, today it is significantly—and strikingly—greater than it was just than a decade and a half ago. We can assume that this pattern is not confined to high school seniors because, after 1980, the same questions were posed to 8th and 10th graders and to college students and young adults not in college, and the researchers found the same results. In short, the deviant status of marijuana use reached an all-time low in the late 1970s, grew throughout the 1980s and then retreated again during the 1990s and into the second decade of the twenty-first century. One indication: The decriminalization movement is

back on track, energized by the issue of medical marijuana. As of October 2012, more than a dozen states permitted small-quantity marijuana possession, without arrest, and eighteen of them permitted medical marijuana. In the 2012 election, two states, Colorado and Washington, voted to legalize recreational marijuana—a violation of federal law—and Massachusetts voted to legalize medical marijuana. The decline in the deviant status of marijuana consumption among teenagers and young adults will probably continue beyond the first two decades of the new millennium.

Among adults, the polls indicate complicated attitudes toward marijuana legalization. During April 2009, *The Washington Post* and ABC News conducted a poll that indicated qualified attitudes both for and against legalization. When asked about the legalization "of small amounts of marijuana for personal use," those who opposed were a bare majority, 51 percent, while those in favor stood at 46. But when respondents were asked if people should be jailed for the possession of small amounts or pay a small fine "but without serving any jail time," only 19 percent favored jail time. In 2012, *The Christian Science Monitor* conducted a poll that revealed that a clear majority, 56 percent, favored the legalization of marijuana similar to that for alcohol and tobacco (Wood, 2012). And 80 percent of the respondents in a CNN/*Time* magazine favored legal marijuana for medical purposes. Today, the possession of marijuana—although not quite legal—isn't entirely deviant, either. Again, though illegality is not defining criterion of deviance, when a growing and substantial proportion of the population favors the decriminalization of a previously illegal act, that act is losing its deviant status.

These shifts show that the deviant and criminal status of some activities, as well as their incidence, are dynamic, shifting affairs. And just as activities can become more, or less, common, they can become more, as well as less, deviant and criminal over time. We witness historical fluctuations in the deviant and criminal status of marijuana use, possession, and sale. During the 1990s and the early 2000s, both the hostile attitudes that prevailed in the 1930s and beyond, and, on the other side, during the late 1970s and early 1980s, the blatant openness and tolerance that dominated, as well as the extremely widespread use, have all dissipated, and been replaced with more moderate feelings and behavior on both sides.

During the 1930s, the deviant status of marijuana use flowed mainly from the marginality, unconventionality, and stigmatized status of its users and the drug's supposed tendency to trigger immoral behavior and cause users to freak out and go crazy, perhaps to rape, possibly to commit suicide. During the 1940s and 1950s, a new sin was added to the weed's arsenal of malefic effects: The drug stimulated the urge to escalate to the use of harder, more insidious, more dangerous drugs—heroin being the ultimate kick, and a trip to oblivion. During the 1960s and beyond, scientists began searching for scientific evidence that would demonstrate that marijuana caused bodily and physiological harm—to the liver, the lungs, white blood cells, testosterone, and, most especially, the *brain*. The brain is the mother of all organs; it domiciles the mind, and the mind determines behavior. Currently, researchers continue to generate findings that indicate that marijuana use causes chronic mental and cognitive deficits, specifically among youths, that persist beyond the immediate occasions of intoxication (Gruber et al., 2012; Meier et al., 2012). These and numerous such studies seem to imply that, given marijuana's harmful effects, its use should remain illegal, deviant, and confined to the margins of the society. In other words, the studies seem to broadcast the message: "Legalizing Marijuana Raises Health Concerns" (Rabin, 2013).

Whether such conclusions are warranted remains to be seen. But, as with all drugs—alcohol and tobacco included—we may apply several impeccable and iron-class generalizations about marijuana use that cannot be ignored: *First, the earlier the onset of marijuana use, the more deviant use is, and the greater the likelihood of psychophysiological harm.* The teenage brain is still growing, and it may not welcome the introduction of an alien, potentially toxic, psychoactive substance into its operation. Second, *the greater the quantity of use* (whether daily, several times daily, or all of the user's waking hours), *the more deviant the use, and the greater the likelihood of physiological harm.* The human brain did not evolve to perform at maximum capacity saturated

with psychoactive chemicals. When recreational use becomes abuse, and abuse becomes addiction, and addiction becomes oblivion, it's almost certain that the user is visiting serious harm to his or her most vital organ. *And third, the greater the marijuana use, the greater the likelihood that the user will consume drugs in addition to, and more harmful than, weed itself.* At a certain point, the biophysical consequences of marijuana use may become entangled with those of meth, cocaine, LSD, PCP, Ecstasy, and heroin.

SUMMARY

All societies recognize that certain substances induce an altered state of consciousness, and some members of all societies consume consciousness-altering substances. Writing and research on drug use constitutes an enormous enterprise; it is one of the most widely-discussed, studied, and written about activity in which humans engage. Most members of society regard the consumption of too much of, or dependence on, a given substance a form of deviance. Indeed, even the very use of a number of substances constitutes deviant behavior; their possession and sale are likewise against the law. Alcohol induces a consciousness-altering state, and, although legal, becoming drunk, especially habitually, and especially in situations which demand mental acuity and physical coordination, is a violation of society's norms. Given the crucial role that drug use plays in society, it should come as no surprise that the American government invests millions of dollars in studying its use and abuse.

Humans are almost certainly hardwired to enjoy the low-to-moderate effects of alcohol; hence the use of this substance is both ancient and nearly universal. But at higher doses, drinking exacts a heavy and sometimes tragic toll: discoordination, mental confusion, risky behaviors, and, in the long run, mental and physical maladies. All societies regard excessive drinking as deviant and condemn the heavy drinker. Patterns of drinking are probably more influential in determining social problems and deviant behavior than the quantity consumed: who drinks it, why, how much during a single occasion, and socially, where.

Men tend to drink more than women and the young drink more than older adults. Socioeconomic status (SES) displays a complex relationship with drinking: The higher the SES, the greater the likelihood of drinking; lower SES members of the society are more likely to abstain from alcohol than those higher up in the class ladder. However, among persons who drink, lower SES individuals are more likely to engage in deviant drinking and to get into trouble as a result of their intoxication.

As with all forms of deviance we've considered in this book, alcohol consumption can be looked at both through the lens of essentialism and constructionism. Essentialism examines the "objective" properties of alcohol: its effects, the consequences of its use, and the causes of excessive consumption. Alcohol is a sedative with complex, even contradictory properties, and some individuals react to it idiosyncratically. But as a general rule, the greater the amount of alcohol consumed, that is, the greater the degree of intoxication, the greater the likelihood that the drinker will engage in risky, deviant behavior, including fatal automobile accidents, risky sex, violence, and the greater the likelihood that one will be a victim of violence, including sexual violence.

Some alcohol researchers argue that alcohol "releases inhibitions" from normative constraint and disorganizes and diminishing the mind's capacity to reason effectively, making certain deviant behaviors more likely. In addition, the people who engage in deviant drinking are also the kinds of people who are more likely to engage in risky behaviors in the first place, alcohol or no alcohol. And third, the occasions and locales of drinking are also the kinds of times and places when untoward events take place; alcohol may be little more than an accompaniment of risky, deviant settings.

Drinking alcohol (in moderation, a conventional act) is strongly correlated with the use of illicit drugs (not only an illegal but, in many social circles, a deviant act). Perhaps many of the intersections of these two activities that researchers observe explains many of the correlations they also see between the most common form of drug use, marijuana smoking, and a substantial number of deviant activities.

Drug use has both an objective (positivistic) and a subjective (constructionist) side. On the one hand, it is an identifiable form of behavior; it has certain concrete, measurable consequences; and it is caused by and has consequences that are a product of scientific, discoverable factors. On the other hand, drug use is also categorized in a certain way by the general public, by the law, and in the media, and users, likewise, are thought about and dealt with a certain level of public concern that is not always an accurate reflection of the degree of objective danger or damage represented by drug use.

Often, there is great concern at a time when the harmful effects of drug abuse are declining and, contrarily, concern is often relatively low when these drug effects are on the rise. In addition, the specific drug that attracts public concern has shifted over time—from marijuana in the 1930s, to LSD in the 1960s, to heroin in the early 1970s, and to crack cocaine in the later 1980s. Sociologists refer to a period in which concern over a given condition, such as drug abuse, is intense and disproportionate to its concrete danger as a "moral panic." Usually, in a moral panic, a specific agent is held responsible for the condition or threat—a folk devil. Of course, sometimes, the concern is commensurate with or reflects the potential harm of an activity, in which case, it does not manifest a moral panic.

Humans have ingested psychoactive or mind-altering substances for thousands of years. Drug use is very close to being a human universal in that nearly all cultures use psychoactive drugs substances. But drug use inevitably has a deviant side as well. Sometimes the wrong substance is ingested, or it is taken too often, or under the wrong circumstances, or with undesirable consequences. In such cases, we have instances of deviant behavior.

Marijuana use has gone through several drastic changes as an illegal and deviant activity. In earlier centuries, marijuana was used as a medicine. Early in the twentieth century, the recreational use of marijuana was not well known; users were rarely condemned as a separate category of deviants. During the 1930s, numerous articles in popular magazines and newspapers created something of a marijuana scare or panic; in that decade, possession and sale of the drug became a crime in all states of the United States and at the federal level as well. Harmful medical effects of marijuana have been asserted but never fully documented; the jury is still out on this question. In the United States, during the 1960s and 1970s, marijuana use became much more common, more accepted, and less deviant, and the small-quantity possession has been decriminalized in more than a dozen states. In addition, it is legal as medicine in seventeen states; this figure will inevitably grow. Since 1990, marijuana use has become somewhat more common and a bit less deviant among the young. Nonetheless, in some jurisdictions, with respect to arrests, the "war on drugs" has become a "war on marijuana."

Account: Using Marijuana

One interesting aspect of illicit drug use is that there is a gulf between what the law says on the one hand, and public opinion and law enforcement on the other. Illegal is illegal. Though penalties vary from drug to drug, the fact is that both in a number of states and by federal law, one can receive a lengthy sentence for the possession of a usable quantity of marijuana— a crime most of the American public thinks should not draw a jail or prison sentence at all. In Arkansas, possession of an ounce or more draws a sentence of four to ten years in prison; in Connecticut, a second conviction of simple possession of any amount draws a sentence of five years; and in Florida, possession of 20 grams (less than an ounce) calls for imprisonment for five years. Moreover, while the federal government seems adamant about retaining marijuana's criminal status, possession of small quantities of the drug is extremely low on law enforcement's radar screen. As we saw in this chapter, 80 percent of the population favors medical marijuana and 72 percent is opposed to incarcerating recreational pot smokers. Hence, we observe a disconnect between the law on the one hand and how the public feels and what the police and prosecutors are willing to do to enforce the law, on the other.

Brad is in his forties and is a recreational pot-smoking parent. His daughter, Tiffany, is a college student. In the eighth grade, she took a drug education course under the auspices of D.A.R.E., and was shocked, angered, and appalled when she discovered that her dad smoked marijuana.

"I had been force-fed the notion that people who use drugs are all criminals," she explains, "and addicts. It angered me that he would want
to do that to his body. To me, smoking pot was the equivalent of shooting heroin. A drug was a drug, and I was ashamed to have such an out-of-control father who was stuck in his little seventies world. Somehow, the fact that he took me skating every day, went to work, helped my mom, made dinner, and cleaned the house, did not matter. . . . Granted, he never smoked in front us [Tiffany and her brother]. It was just always there in the background somewhere in a smoked-filled bathroom. . . . In my family, as well as our family's friends, my dad is not considered deviant. Some of his musician friends do much harder drugs than he does.... In our neighborhood, though, as well as in America as a whole, his marijuana use would definitely be seen as deviant. I think this is because of the belief that fathers and mothers should set a good example for their children and that parents who use drugs are not good parents. A lot of conservative people would argue that Brad's drug use is irresponsible and immature." Tiffany adds: "Brad is an example of a person who shatters the stereotype of a parent who uses marijuana. He is hard-working, family-oriented, and responsible. That is not my own personal opinion, it is a fact. he proof is the roof still over my house, the wedding ring on my mom's finger, and the diploma I will receive in a year." In this interview, Tiffany is asking her dad questions.*

TIFFANY: How regularly do you smoke?

BRAD: Daily. I stop drinking alcohol when I'm stoned. I get my stuff from one of my fraternity brothers from college. He gets me a whole bunch so I don't have to go through some dealer I don't know. I don't think I'd do it half as much if it was hard to get. But it's cheap and easy for me. I don't smoke a lot at a time. I just pack a bowl

(Continued)

Account: Using Marijuana   Continued

with about half a gram, about the size of a dime [there are 28 grams in an ounce], watch TV, and don't remember what I saw, I kind of zoom out. Anyway, pot's so strong nowadays, I get much higher with less than I used to. I don't have to smoke as much pot to get the same effect that I got years ago. Strong stuff.

TIFFANY: What kind of jobs have you had?

BRAD: I've worked in the telecommunications field for a long time for a lot of different companies. I also helped my wife when we ran a daycare business out of our house. It was a great little thing we had. Just a handful of infants and toddlers—we were great at it.

TIFFANY: Were you ever high at work?

BRAD: Usually I don't smoke until I get home. I have to get up too damn early for that.

TIFFANY: How is smoking [marijuana] seen in those circles [that is, among the people Brad works with]?

BRAD: I only talk about it with people I know smoke too. Like, you could tell who did it and who didn't. The people who didn't, yeah, they probably have a big stick up their ass about it, but I really don't care. I don't advertise that I smoke or anything.

TIFFANY: So if everybody knew you smoke, how do you think they'd react? Do you think they would consider you somehow deviant?

BRAD: By a small percentage, I'd be seen as a deviant.

TIFFANY: Do you think you'd be fired?

BRAD: I don't know. I guess it depends on the boss. I don't really think about getting fired or not. That's not why I keep it hidden. It's more the fact that I don't want people judging me on their limited knowledge. . . . They lump pot in with heroin. I think pot's not even in the same galaxy as the hard drugs. It's like alcohol or cigarettes. But a lot of people think that way because they haven't had the same experiences as I have. Ignorance is bliss and there's a lot of blissful people in the world.

TIFFANY: How do you think you have been as a parent?

BRAD: Above average. I've come home every night, done laundry, washed dishes, haven't fooled around, haven't beaten my kids, sexually abused them, I've encouraged them to excel in whatever they were interested in. I've been open, honest, and supportive. We've lived within our means, sometimes above our means. We always ate well, and my kids' friends were always welcome and fed. I have the greatest relationship with my kids. They're awesome. Much better than I could have hoped. They know self-reliance, they know they can trust me with a secret, and I've continued to earn that trust by not revealing any of those secrets. They know that they can come to me with anything, day or night as a dad, friend, nurse, sounding board for ideas, devil's advocate, accountant, or a resource for information. I think I'm just a nice guy.

TIFFANY: Has being high ever affected your parenting?

BRAD: No, I don't think so. I've always been there for my family. They're the most important thing in my life. Career's a distant fifth, and pot's a little after that.

TIFFANY: If your drug use were public and obvious, how do you think people in the community would see you?

BRAD: In our community, about 10 percent would think I'm extremely deviant and the rest would think I'm normal. I know there's a ton of people out there who do a whole lot worse shit than I do. I think I'm somewhere in the middle there.

TIFFANY: How about how you're seen in your social circle?

BRAD: In my private social circle there's marijuana use and some limited cocaine use. You know, wussy stuff. And [with the cocaine], it's just snorting. I'd say a lot of my friends go further than I do. We're a diverse mix of guys, and I'd say that in that mix, I'm one of the more conventional ones.

TIFFANY: If it's no big deal to you and you don't think that most people would care, why do you keep it a secret? Do you have any fear of stigmatization?

BRAD: Not fear of stigma really. I just don't need the hassle with cops or anything. I don't want rehab, parole, or community service. Cops are the biggest hassle [with using an illegal substance]. There's just no reason for me to flaunt anything in front of them or anybody else. I don't want to be the poster boy for middle-aged marijuana use.

TIFFANY: Would you consider yourself an addict?

BRAD: Hell, yes. Just like I'm addicted to cigarettes. I quit for nine years, but when I wanted to smoke again, I did. I don't need pot to live, but it doesn't hinder my life or change how I act, so there's no need for me to quit.

TIFFANY: If your life were put into a newspaper, how do you think a lot of people would react to your drug use?

BRAD: If my life were put into a newspaper I guess I'd be considered deviant. But I don't believe in organized religion, and that's deviant too. Let me put it this way. On Dr. Phil or Oprah, yeah, I'd be considered deviant. On The Man Show, I'd be a minor hero.

TIFFANY: Do you think you're a part of a small group of people who do this? Do you feel connected to adults like you who smoke pot—maybe feel like you belong to a subculture?

BRAD: No, I'm just a guy who likes to drink beer and get high in my basement. Life is short and some things are fun.

QUESTIONS

Brad is a regular pot smoker and unconventional though not entirely deviant parent. Is there or is there not something about the specific drug used that makes a certain lifestyle possible, and precludes other lifestyles? Is the regular use of certain drugs more demanding and forceful in intruding into the life of the user, making certain ways of life necessary, and others impossible? In other words, can you imagine Brad living the life he does and using methamphetamine or heroin? What other illicit drug could he have used and still maintained his role as a parent and reliable worker? Do you buy Brad's claim that he could quit any time he wanted? Do you feel he is irresponsible for smoking marijuana while parenting his children? Do you accept Tiffany's defense of her dad's use of pot? If you were to guess, would you agree with her that the fact that he has performed in a number of conventional roles while continuing to smoke pot indicates that the stereotype of a marijuana smoker is inaccurate?

Drug Abuse

Learning Objectives:

After reading this chapter, you will be able to:

- categorize hallucinogenic drugs;
- understand the effects of cocaine and crack;
- discuss heroin and narcotics;
- define "methamphetamine" and understand its effects.

Pharmacologists refer to all substances that influence the workings of the brain, that is to say, any and all mental and emotional processes—thinking, cognition, understanding, feeling, sensing, intuiting, empathizing—as *psychoactive*, and by definition, all psychoactive substances are drugs. Drugs have a range of effects and degrees of influence, but all can be abused. To be more specific about it, one does not abuse *the drug*, one abuses oneself—and others—with the use of the drug. As we already know, alcohol can be abused—by becoming physically and/or psychologically dependent, by harming oneself and the organs of one's body through excessive use, or by getting drunk and harming oneself or placing oneself in harm's way. It's more difficult to abuse marijuana, but anyone who uses frequently and puts oneself into a condition that makes it difficult to perform conventional roles—studying, working, relating to others, navigating the material world—is guilty of marijuana abuse.

Most of us make a distinction between "soft" and "hard" drugs. This is a partly misleading distinction, since all drugs, alcohol, and marijuana, pack a potential for harm, though on an episode-for-episode basis, some are "harder" or more potentially dangerous than others. *However*—and with drug use, there's always a "however"—virtually no one dies of an "overdose" of marijuana. And though alcohol is seriously discoordinating and its overuse causes a range of physical ailments, on an episode-by-episode basis, its use is far safer than that of the narcotics, phencyclidine (PCP), methamphetamine, and cocaine. And it is cocaine that stands at the top of the hierarchy in the emergency department data of drugs that causes or is associated with nonlethal medical crises requiring trips to the hospital. Clearly, cocaine is far from a safe drug; it is, in short, a dangerous or "hard" drug. And as we saw, by a wide margin, the opiates or narcotics stand at the top of the list of drugs that cause or are associated with dying as a result of overuse. Clearly, the narcotics are "hard" drugs. And heroin, one of the least frequently used drugs, kills perhaps one of seven of all people who die of a drug "overdose." Perhaps even more to our focus of interest, the casual use of alcohol and marijuana are not deviant at all, or only mildly so, and in certain conventional circles, whereas any and all use of the "hard" drugs—and especially their heavy or abusive use—is most decidedly and *seriously* deviant. Hence, our division of drugs into categories of *relative* harm, dangerousness, or "hardness."

HALLUCINOGENIC DRUGS

Hallucinogenic drugs are substances that produce severe dislocation of consciousness, those that act on the nervous system to produce significant perceptual changes. While all psychoactive drugs, by definition, influence the working of the mind, hallucinogens are specifically, powerfully, and exquisitely psychoactive in their effects. They are the preeminent example of a category of psychoactive drugs. In the 1960s, hallucinogens were commonly referred to as "psychedelics," a term that implied that the mind is "made manifest"— or is more perceptive than ordinarily—under the influence. In those days, substances such as mescaline (the major ingredient in the peyote cactus) and psilocybin (the major ingredient in the "magic mushroom") were much discussed but relatively little used. Today, the term "psychedelic" is used less frequently among drug experts than "hallucinogen." And virtually the only representative of this category that is currently used with any frequency is LSD. (I do not consider Ecstasy or PCP as hallucinogenic drugs; neither one has the vision-inducing properties of LSD, mescaline, and psilocybin.)

It is in the mental, psychic, and "subjective" realm that the effects of LSD and other hallucinogens have their most profound, dramatic, and interesting effects. Experiences take on an exaggerated emotional significance under the influence. Moreover, huge emotional mood swings tend to dominate an "acid" trip. On the other hand, in spite of their name, hallucinogens typically do not generate full-blown hallucinations— that is, cause users to see things in the concrete world they know "aren't really there." More often they will have experiences or visions they know are a product of the drug—that is, that are in their minds rather than a reality, which is located "out there" in the material world. (These visions are sometimes referred to as "virtual" hallucinations.) Many users will experience synesthesia, or the translation of one sense into another—that is, "hearing" color and "seeing" sounds. Many LSD users, under the influence, experience the world as in flux—fluid, dynamic, wobbling, flowing. The effects of LSD are experienced as vastly more incapacitating than those of marijuana (depending on the dose, of course); many users imagine that they can cope (drive a car, converse, interact with others, especially parents and the police) on marijuana, whereas very few will say that they can do so at the peak of the LSD trip. Very few users of hallucinogens experience a psychotic outbreak sufficiently serious as to require hospitalization. Such reports reached their peak in the 1960s (when use was actually quite low) and declined sharply after that.

Psychedelic drugs have been used for thousands of years: psilocybin, or the so-called magic mushrooms, by Indians in Mexico and Central America; the peyote cactus by the Indians of northern Mexico; the Amanita (or "fly agaric") mushroom among the indigenous Siberian population; the mandrake root among pre-Christian Europeans, to name only a few (Schultes and Hofmann, 1979). In 1938, a Swiss chemist named Albert Hofmann discovered the chemical that was later to be called LSD. Hofmann did not experiment with it until 1943, when he ingested a minuscule quantity of the substance himself. He experienced an extraordinary and intense "play of colors," a sense of timelessness, depersonalization, a loss of control, and fears of "going crazy." The early researchers on LSD thought the drug might be the key to unlock the secrets of mental illness, especially schizophrenia. Later they found that the differences outweighed the similarities, and this line of research was abandoned. In the 1950s, the English writer Aldous Huxley, author of the classic novel *Brave New World*, took mescaline (the psychoactive ingredient in the peyote cactus) and wrote about his experiences in a slim, poetic volume, *The Doors of Perception*. Huxley drew the parallel with insanity, but he added a new dimension not previously discussed. Psychedelic drugs, he claimed, could bring about a view of reality that washes away the encrustation of years of rigid socialization and programming. These drugs, Huxley argues, enable us to see reality without culture's blinders—reality "as it really is." Taking psychedelic drugs could bring about

a kind of transcendence, much like religious insight.

Huxley's book was read by Timothy Leary, holder of a PhD in psychology and lecturer at Harvard University. Leary took a dose of psilocybin and had a "visionary voyage." Soon after, he began a series of experiments that entailed administering the drug to convicts, theology students, and undergraduates; he claimed the drug "changed their lives for the better." Authorities at Harvard felt the experiments were casually administered, lacked sufficient safeguards, and were aimed mainly at proselytizing. Leary brushed off such concerns as so much "hysteria" that was hampering his research. In the spring of 1963, Leary was fired from his job, an event that touched off national headlines. In the decade prior to Leary's firing, a total of fewer than a dozen articles on LSD had ever been published in the national magazines indexed by *The Readers' Guide to Periodical Literature* (excluding *Science*, which is not really a popular magazine). These articles exploded after the Leary incident; publicity surrounding his firing focused an intense public glare on the use of LSD and the hallucinogens.

Prior to 1967, nearly all the articles discussed the drug's supposedly bizarre effects, especially those that seemed to indicate that it caused users to go insane. The effects of LSD were described as "nightmarish"; "terror and indescribable fear" were considered common, even typical experiences under the influence. *Life* magazine ran a cover story in its March 25, 1966, issue entitled "The Exploding Threat of the Mind Drug That Got Out of Control." *Time* ran a feature essay on LSD emphasizing the "freaking out" angle. "Under the influence of LSD," the story declared, "nonswimmers think they can swim, and others think they can fly. One young man tried to stop a car . . . and was killed. A magazine salesman became convinced he was the Messiah. A college dropout committed suicide by slashing his arm and bleeding to death in a field of lilies." Psychic terror, uncontrollable impulses, violence, an unconcern for one's own safety, psychotic episodes, delusions, and hallucinations filled the bulk of the early news stories on the use of LSD.

On March 17, 1967, the prestigious journal *Science* published an article, which indicated that

LSD damaged chromosomes (Cohen, Marinello, and Back, 1967). The media immediately surmised that the drug would cause birth defects; this wave of media hysteria was not quite as intense or as long-lasting as that touched off by the "insanity" angle, but it did convince much of the public—some users included—that the drug was uniquely and powerfully damaging and dangerous. An article that appeared in *The Saturday Evening Post* (Davison, 1967) was typical. It explained that "if you take LSD even once, your children may be born malformed or retarded" and that "new research finds it's causing genetic damage that poses a threat of havoc now and appalling abnormalities for generations yet unborn." Scientists learned soon after that the whole issue was a false alarm; in the doses taken on the street, LSD is an extremely weak mutagen or gene-altering agent, extremely unlikely to cause birth defects (Dishotsky et al., 1971).

In the 1960s, many critics and observers believed that LSD posed a major threat to American young people and possessed a uniquely deviant potential. In 1966, the New Jersey Narcotic Drug Study Commission declared LSD to be "the greatest threat facing the country today" (Brecher et al., 1972, p. 369). And yet this hysteria and fear evaporated in what was probably record time. Today, the use of the hallucinogen is no longer a public issue, at least not apart from the use of illegal drugs generally. LSD has been absorbed into the morass of drug taking in general—less seriously regarded than crack and heroin use, but more so than that of marijuana. LSD never really materialized into a threat to the society that many observers and critics (or, for that matter, it supporters) claimed it would. The drastic, dramatic, cosmic, philosophical, and religious claims originally made for the LSD experience now seem an artifact of an antiquated age. The psychedelic movement—whose members glorified the drug as a superhighway to an astounding new vision, perhaps a new way of life for the society as a whole, but who never made up a majority of even regular users in the 1960s— simply disappeared. The fear of the conventional majority that users would go crazy, drop out, or overturn the social order never came to pass. LSD became simply another drug taken on occasion by multiple drug users for the same hedonistic, recreational reasons they take other drugs—to get high.

One of the most remarkable aspects of the use of LSD and the other hallucinogens is how episodically and sporadically it takes place. In fact, of all drugs or drug types ingested currently in the United States (with the possible exception of PCP), it is possible that, among the universe of everyone who has taken the drug at least once, the lowest percentage is made up of current or recent users. Recall that alcohol generates very high continuance or loyalty rates: About six out of ten of at-least-one-time drinkers consumed one or more alcoholic beverages in the past month. But only one out of twenty persons who ever used LSD had taken it within the past month— one-twelfth the figure for alcohol and one-tenth that for cigarettes. LSD is simply not a drug that is taken very often or regularly—even among users. Psychopharmacologists rank the "dependence potential" of the hallucinogens as extremely low—in fact, close to dead last among all drugs and drug types.

There is a perception of the 1960s as a "psychedelic" era, a period of history when the use of LSD was not only widespread but characteristic of the period. Evidence points to the fact that the incidence of LSD use was extremely low (although climbing) in the 1960s; it reached something of a peak in the 1970s; it declined into the 1980s; and it has remained at a fairly stable level for the past twenty years or so. In 1967, according to a Gallup Poll, only 1 percent of American college students (in all likelihood, the category that was most likely to have taken the drug at that time) said that they had tried LSD, at least once; by 1969, this figure had grown to 4 percent, and by 1971, 18 percent. In other words, precisely at a time when use was mushrooming, media attention to LSD dropped off. But in the past thirty years, the drug's use has declined; in 1980, the *lifetime* prevalence figure among high school seniors for LSD was 9 percent; by 1985, this had declined slightly to 7.5 percent; in 1990, it was 8 percent. In 2011, the latest year for which we have data at this writing, it was only 4 percent; use during the prior thirty days stood at only 0.8 percent (Johnston et al., 2012). For college students and noncollege young adults, the trend lines are similar. Thus, although again, LSD and the psychedelics are used extremely episodically by those who use it, their use have not entirely disappeared, though their slope have been tilted downward.

The use of LSD in the United States should teach us some very important lessons about the perception of social problems and the imputation of deviance to an activity. *First*, the public hysteria generated over an activity, a belief, or a condition may be substantially disproportionate to its objective threat to the society; some activities or conditions attract considerably more than their fair share of public hysteria, while others attract far less. *Second*, media attention does not necessarily reflect how common or frequent an activity is; some commonly enacted behaviors receive little or no media attention, while some rare or infrequent activities receive an extensive coverage. As with LSD, media attention to an activity could very well increase at a time when it is declining in frequency, or decline when its frequency is increasing. *Third*, it is likely that people base their notions of the frequency or commonness of behaviors, beliefs, and conditions, and the threat they pose to the society more on how well known these are than on the objective, concrete facts of the matter. A study of LSD is more instructive for what it tells us about deviance in general than for what it tells us specifically about drug use. LSD use moved from an unknown phenomenon to moral panic to ho-hum in what may be record time.

COCAINE AND CRACK

Cocaine is a stimulant. Its most commonly described effect is exhilaration, elation, euphoria, a voluptuous, joyous feeling. Probably the second most frequently described effect by users is a sensation of mastery and confidence in what one is and does. And third, users most commonly report a burst of increased energy, the suppression of fatigue, a stimulation of the capacity to continue physical and mental activity more intensely and for a longer than normal period of time.

In the nineteenth century, before its effects were fully understood, cocaine was used by physicians for a variety of illnesses, ailments, and complaints—first, to offset fatigue and depression; later, to cure morphine addiction. Today, one of its very few medical uses is as a local anesthetic—that is, to kill pain when applied topically to delicate tissues and organs, such as the eye or gums. The earliest papers of Sigmund Freud were devoted to singing the praises of this drug; when he became a dependent on it, he realized his mistake (Byck, 1974; Andrews and Solomon, 1975; Ashley, 1975, pp. 21–28). At the end of the nineteenth and the beginning of the twentieth centuries, cocaine, like morphine and opium, was an ingredient in many patent medicines. Cocaine was even contained in many "soft" drinks, including Coca-Cola, until 1903, when it was removed because of pressure applied by "Southerners who feared blacks getting cocaine in any form" (Ashley, 1975, p. 46)

Many observers feel that a major reason for the criminalization of cocaine after the turn of the century was racism. Although there is no systematic evidence that African Americans were any more likely to use cocaine than whites, or that those who did were any more likely to become dangerous or violent under the influence, the fear among many whites that both were true may have been responsible for bringing the drug under state and federal control. Numerous articles published in the early 1900s made the claim that cocaine stimulated violence among blacks.

In 1903, *The New York Tribune* quoted one Colonel J.W. Watson of Georgia to the effect that "many of the horrible crimes committed in the southern states by the colored people can be traced to the cocaine habit." A Dr. Christopher Koch, in an article that appeared in the *Literary Digest* in 1914, asserted that "most of the attacks upon white women of the South are a direct result of a cocaine-crazed Negro brain." *The New York Times* published an article in 1914 entitled "Negro Cocaine Fiends Are a Southern Menace," which detailed the "race menace" and "hitherto inoffensive" blacks "running amuck in a cocaine frenzy" (Ashley, 1975, pp. 66–73; Grinspoon and Bakalar, 1976, pp. 38–40). "All the elements needed to ensure cocaine's outlaw status were present by the first years of the twentieth century: It had become widely used as a pleasure drug . . . ; it had become identified with [groups that were] despised or poorly regarded [by middle-class whites] . . . [that is], blacks, lower-class whites, and criminals; and it had not . . . become identified with the elite, thus losing what little chance it had of weathering the storm" (Ashley, 1975,

p. 74). By the time of the passage of the Harrison Act in 1914, which included cocaine as a "narcotic," forty-six states had already passed state laws attempting to control cocaine. This indicates that cocaine was seen at the time as a serious drug problem. And a reason for the criminalization of cocaine was, in all likelihood, racial hostility toward African Americans on the part of the white majority.

Most experts argue that the use of cocaine declined sharply during the 1920s and remained at an extremely low level until the 1960s (Ashley, 1975; Spillane, 2000). The increase in cocaine use during that decade and into the 1970s paralleled that of marijuana use, though on a much smaller scale. Although no systematic, nationally representative surveys were conducted on drug use in the United States until 1972, a 1979 study "reconstructed" estimates for the 1960s based on dates interviewees gave for when they began drug use (Miller and Cisin, 1980). This study estimated that only 1 percent of all Americans who were aged eighteen to twenty-five in 1960—the category most likely to use the drug—had used cocaine at least once in their lifetime; by 1967, this had doubled. In 1972, when a full-scale survey was conducted, lifetime prevalence figure for young adults stood at 8 percent, and by 1979, it had shot up to 27 percent. In 2011, for young adults, this figure stood at 13.3 percent—almost exactly *half* of what it had been three decades earlier (Substance Abuse and Mental Health Services Administration, 2011).

For the general population, current or past month use of cocaine decreased from 1 percent (2.4 million people) in 2006 to 0.7 percent (1.6 million) in 2009 to 0.5 percent (1.4 million) in 2011 (Substance Abuse and Mental Health Services Administration, 2012). For high school seniors, the thirty-day prevalence figures for cocaine were 2.5 percent in 2006, 1.9 percent in 2008, and 1.1 percent in 2011—a small but distinctly downward trend (Johnston et al., 2012). Among eighth graders, the decline was barely perceptible—from 1 percent in 2006 to 0.8 percent in 2009 and 2011. These numbers do indicate some diminution in both the general population's and school children's demand and use for cocaine, but the declines are not so strong as to make us feel confident that they will continue.

Practically all surveys show a decline in the use of cocaine in the general population over time since the late 1970s. This sounds encouraging, and it's possible that yearly, even monthly, use may not present a serious problem to the society. What most experts are concerned about are the problems posed by cocaine addicts—frequent, chronic, heavy, compulsive abusers who stand a high likelihood of causing medical damage to themselves as a result of overdoses and heavy use, and of victimizing others in the form of violence and property crime. The problem for researchers is that such users are difficult to locate. What indicators we do have however, indicate a trend line that is not nearly as encouraging as for casual use. While the casual, recreational use of cocaine in the general population has declined in the past decade or two, it is possible that the heavy, chronic abuse of the drug has actually increased. What we see is something of a polarization in cocaine use, with the least involved (and least criminal and least deviant) user most likely to give up the drug, and the most involved (and most criminal and deviant) abuser least likely to abstain. Abusers who are most likely to harm themselves and victimize others are also most likely to stick with cocaine over an extended period of time.

The Drug Abuse Warning Network or DAWN plots two drug-related events over time: non-fatal drug-related emergency department (ED) admissions or visits, and medical examiner (ME) and coroner's reports on lethal drug-related deaths or mortality. Government researchers originally tagged DAWN with its name because they believed that drug "overdoses" would predict future trends in drug use and abuse for the population as a whole—in other words, the extreme levels of use (ED admissions and fatal episodes) would predict the future of the more modal or most common levels of use. While there are many reasons why these figures would change over time (including changes in drug potency, trends with respect to taking different drugs simultaneously, taking drugs via different routes of administration, and an aging addict population), one reason is the change in the number of heavy abusers, resulting in changes in the medical problems they exhibit. An estimated 4.9 million emergency department hospital visits associated with drug-related causes took place in 2010, over half of which (47%) were for drug misuse or abuse—half (47%) for adverse drug reactions, a 12 percent for alcohol alone, 14 percent for alcohol in combination with illicit drugs, 4 percent for "underage drinking," a quarter (27%) for prescription drug misuse or abuse. And among all illicit drugs, cocaine ranked at the top of the list, figuring in 43 percent of all ED visits, with a rate of 157.8 ED visits per 100,000 in the population—more than twice that of heroin, which had a rate of 72.6. Marijuana, surprisingly, caused or generated nearly half a million trips to the emergency room, with a rate nearly equal to that of cocaine—149. But the legal drugs far outstripped these three illicit substances—182.5 for alcohol in combination with other drugs; 215.4 for underage drinking; 213.3 for pain relievers; and a whopping 434.9 for pharmaceuticals generally. Experts warn that DAWN's data are not trendable over time. What is crucial, however, is that cocaine causes or is related to more untoward emergency department episodes—non-fatal overdoses—than any other drug.

Medical examiners (ME) reports are tabulated only in metropolitan communities (SMSAs), and not all counties in a given SMSA contribute to DAWN's program. And even within a given area, not all the programs cover the entire population within their jurisdiction. Moreover, year-by-year, some jurisdictions enter then leave participation in DAWN's. Hence, ME figures are extremely incomplete—but they do give us a good idea of which substances cause or are related to drug-related mortalities (or death by "overdose"). The narcotic and opiate drugs are, by far, the most lethal drugs in causing or being related to drug-induced deaths. In 2010, in seven out of ten (71%) deaths the coroner or medical examiner determines that a death is drug-related, one or more of the narcotics or "opiates" is involved, including heroin, methadone, codeine, oxycodone, morphine, and "opiates," not otherwise specified. Alcohol, mentioned for adults only in conjunction with another drug, ranked second, with 25 percent; and the benzodiazepines, or the Valium-type sedatives and tranquilizers, was tied for second also with 25 percent mentioned in such deaths. Cocaine ranked fourth at 23 percent, and the antidepressants (such as Zoloft, Prozac, and Paxil),

ranked a distant fifth, with 14 percent. Stimulants (in large part, methamphetamine) were mentioned in 8 percent of drug-related deaths. No other drugs or drug types were close to these five. Hence, cocaine ranks *among* the five deadliest drug types with respect to fatal overdoses, but the opiates rank *at* the top.

In its powdered form, cocaine is usually sniffed or snorted—that is, inhaled sharply through the nostril. The user usually chops the drug on a smooth surface and arranges it in the form of a fine, thin line. The user snorts each line up either directly off the surface into a nostril, or through a tiny tube, such as a short, cut-off soda straw or a rolled-up bill. Some users prefer to scoop up the powder with a tiny spoon, place it in the vicinity of the nostril, and then snort it. Snorting cocaine is slower, less efficient, less reinforcing, and less intensely pleasurable than smoking it. Perhaps nine users out of ten will snort cocaine most of the time they use it. Until 1985 or 1986, users smoked pure cocaine in the form of "freebase." After 1986, smoking users moved to crack making it the most popular smoked cocaine substance. Crack is an impure crystalline precipitate that results from heating cocaine with baking soda; it contains only 30 percent or so cocaine.

The difference between powdered cocaine and crack is mainly in route of administration, or the way users take these substances. Taking powdered cocaine intranasally produces a high that takes roughly three minutes to take effect and lasts perhaps thirty minutes. There is no real "rush" or intense orgasm-like explosion of pleasure. Injected, the rush takes only twelve to fifteen seconds to appear, and it is described as a vastly more voluptuous feeling than the high that occurs when cocaine is snorted. Users do not as often smoke powdered cocaine since the combustion temperature is extremely high. When cocaine is smoked in the form of freebase or crack, the onset of the drug's impact is even faster than injection, a matter of six to eight seconds, and the intense, orgasm-like high or rush lasts for perhaps two minutes, followed by an afterglow that lasts ten to twenty minutes. The euphoria achieved in this experience is extreme—in the terms of the behaviorist psychologist, it is highly *reinforcing*—and, often, this impels users to want to take the drug over and over again. Since it is impossible to detect the difference between crack and powder cocaine after metabolization, DAWN does not distinguish between them.

To say that smoked crack cocaine is highly reinforcing—more so, in fact, than almost any other drug—is not to say that most experimenters become chronic abusers. As with nearly every newly introduced drug, sensationalistic exaggeration in the media accompanies its widespread use. *Feeling the urge* to take a drug over and over again does not always, necessarily, or even mostly, results in actually doing so. In the mid-1980s, newspaper headlines and television reports implied that all teenagers in the country had used, or were in imminent danger of using, crack—that every community nationwide had been "saturated" by the drug. The reality is not nearly so terrifying. The first year that the Monitoring the Future study asked about crack (1987), only 5 percent of high school seniors questioned said that they had *ever* used crack, even once in their lives; in 1998, the figure was 4 percent; and in 2011, it was 2 percent (Johnston et al., 2012). The figure for thirty-day prevalence stood at only 0.5 percent. (Again, unfortunately, high school dropouts, whose crack use is likely to be considerably higher, could not be included in this survey.) For 2010, the national survey, SAMHSA reported 3.6 percent lifetime crack use for the population at large and 0.6 percent for thirty-day or last-month use; it did not report crack use figures for young adults and youths separately.

Just as the incidence or frequency of crack use from the 1980s into the 2000s was exaggerated by the media, the drug's demonic addictive power was sensationalized as well. A June 16, 1986, story in *Newsweek* claimed that using crack immediately impelled the user into "an inferno of craving and despair." "Try it once and you're hooked!" "Once you start, you can't stop!" These and other slogans were repeated so often that they seemed to take on a life of their own. In fact, they are a serious distortion of reality. Crack may be among the most reinforcing drugs known, and it is possible that a compulsive pattern of abuse builds more rapidly than for any other well-known, widely used drug. Still, only a minuscule minority of users take the drug compulsively and destructively.

In one Miami study of over 300 heavily involved drug users aged twelve to seventeen, 96 percent of whom had taken crack at least once and 87 percent of whom used it regularly, only a minority, 30 percent, used it daily, and half used it weekly or more, but not daily. A majority of even the daily users limited their use to one or two "hits"—"hardly an indication of compulsive and uncontrollable use. Although there were compulsive users of crack in the Miami sample, they represented an extremely small minority" (Inciardi, 1987, p. 484). While there is unquestionably a certain risk of dependence in smoking crack, the hellish experiences that were described in the media in the 1980s did not typify what most users went through when they took the drug. Once again, drug users are often characterized as extreme deviants by the media, a characterization that assumes a reality in the way they are pictured by much of the public.

A good example of the way that crack use was demonized in the media is provided by the "crack babies" phenomenon of the late 1980s and early 1990s. In his *Folk Devils and Moral Panics*, Stanley Cohen (1972, pp. 77–85; 2002) refers to the process of sensitization in the early stages of a moral panic—that is, "the reinterpretation of neutral or ambiguous stimuli as potentially or actually deviant" (p. 77). Thus, a familiar, non-deviant source that causes a certain measure of harm does not generate much concern, while an unfamiliar, deviant source that causes the same level of harm will touch off a firestorm of concern, fear, and hostility. We already saw the sensitization process at work in the 1960s with LSD: Panic reactions were interpreted as an epidemic of psychotic episodes, and peculiar-looking chromosomes drawn from one mental patient who was administered LSD were interpreted as a future tidal wave of malformed, abnormal children.

The findings of the initial studies on children born to cocaine-dependent mothers were extremely pessimistic. Babies whose mothers were exposed to crack and powdered cocaine during pregnancy, compared with those whose mothers were not exposed to the drug, are more likely to be born prematurely, have a lower birth weight, have smaller heads, suffer seizures, have genital and urinary-tract abnormalities, suffer poor motor ability, have brain lesions, and exhibit behavioral aberrations such as impulsivity, moodiness, and lower responsiveness (Chasnoff et al., 1989).

Findings such as these were picked up by the mass media with great speed and transmitted to the general public; within a short period of time, it became an established fact that crack babies made up a major medical and psychiatric problem for the country. It is possible, some argued, that they could never be cured. Crack babies, they said, could become a catastrophe of monumental proportions. William Bennett, then federal drug "czar," claimed that 375,000 crack babies annually were being born in the United States in the late 1980s—one out of ten births!—a figure that was echoed by *Washington Post* columnist Jack Anderson and *New York Times* editor A.M. Rosenthal (Gieringer, 1990, p. 4). One reporter, in a major and widely quoted article published in *Time* magazine, claimed that the medical care of crack babies would cost society thirteen times as much as normal babies. There is fear, she said, that these children will become "an unmanageable multitude of disturbed and disruptive youth, fear that they will be a lost generation" (Toufexis, 1991, p. 56). Visitors to hospital pediatric wards describe crack babies in heart-wrenching terms— premature babies, tiny babies with thin arms and wrinkled skin, babies weighing roughly two pounds, babies looking sick, like old, dying men. It is a pathetic sight, enough to bring the observer to tears.

It was not until the early 1990s that enough medical evidence was assembled to indicate that the crack baby "syndrome" was, in all probability, mythical in nature (Neuspiel et al., 1991; Coles, 1992; Richardson and Day, 1994). The problem with the early research on the babies of mothers who had used cocaine and crack was that there were no controls. Most of these women also drank alcohol, some heavily—and medical science has documented at least one damaging outcome of heavy drinking by the expectant mother: fetal alcohol syndrome. Likewise, no controls were applied for smoking, which is associated with low birth weight in infants; nutritional condition; medical condition of the mother; medical attention (receiving checkups, following the advice of one's physician—indeed, even seeing a physician at all during one's pregnancy); and so on. In other words, factors that vary with cocaine use are known to determine poorer infant outcomes; mothers who smoke crack and use powdered cocaine are more likely to engage in other behaviors that correlate with poorer infant health. Is it the cocaine or these other factors that cause these poorer outcomes? Expectant mothers who use cocaine are more likely to get sexually transmitted diseases; such mothers are less likely to eat a nutritious, balanced diet, get regular checkups, and so on. Were these factors at work in their children's poorer health? Or was it the independent effect of the cocaine itself that produced these medical problems?

When the influence of these other factors was held constant, it became clear that the poorer health that was observed in very young babies was not caused by the effects of cocaine use itself. Instead, it seemed to be a function of the impact of the other drugs these pregnant mothers were using, including alcohol and cigarettes, and a lifestyle that included an inadequate diet and insufficient medical care. In short, it is likely that the crack babies issue was a "hysteria-driven" rather than a "fact-driven" syndrome. In the late 1980s and early 1990s, the public, the media, and even the medical profession were sensitized to believing in the harmful effects of cocaine on newborns with scanty, skimpy evidence; at the same time, influence of the more conventional factors was normalized and ignored. Such processes are characteristic of the moral panic; in the moral panic hostility to and condemnation of deviant behavior and deviant actors are intensified and reaffirmed.

HEROIN AND THE NARCOTICS

Of all well-known drugs or drug types, heroin ranks among the lowest in popularity. Assuming the polls are reasonably accurate, only 1.6 percent of the American population has even tried heroin, and a fraction of that figure (one-tenth of 1 percent) has used it, even once, in the past month (Substance Abuse and Mental Health Services Administration, 2011). For high school seniors for 2011 its use is extremely low as well: 1.4 percent has at least tried heroin, and less than one-half of 1 percent (0.4%, to be exact) has done so in the past month (Johnston et al., 2012). In its *World Drug Report 2012*, The United Nations Office on Drugs and Crime estimates that, worldwide, the annual prevalence of opiate drugs for the population age fifteen to sixty-four in 2010 is only 0.5 percent.

Remember, however, that school surveys do not interview dropouts; in addition, infrequent school attenders and truants are less likely to show up in a survey's sample. And it is almost certain that dropouts and truants are significantly more likely to use heroin. In addition, studies of the general population are based on households. Homeless people, the incarcerated, and people who crash on the couches of acquaintances do not live in stable households, and the chances are they are more likely to use heroin than members of stable households. Nonetheless, by any measure and in every broad-based study that has ever been conducted, heroin ranks extremely low on America's list of well-known illicit drugs.

The question that arises, then, is: Why study heroin use at all? If, compared with marijuana, cocaine, and the hallucinogens, it is used with such rarity, why study it? Why discuss heroin in a general overview of drug use and abuse as a form of deviance? One answer is that, until the advent of crack in the mid-1980s (and, more recently, the abuse of methamphetamine in the late 1980s to early 1990s), in the public mind, heroin use and addiction have been the most deviant form of drug use. They have usually been regarded as the ultimate or most serious forms of drug use known. In addition, although many users take heroin once, twice, a dozen times, and abstain from it from then on, and many use it occasionally, or, if regularly, confine their use to weekends or special occasions, nonetheless, a substantial proportion of heroin users become addicts. Most estimates of the number of narcotic addicts in the United States hover in the half million range, though it is possible that, according to more generous definitions, there may be as many as a million American heroin addicts or abusers, or two. (It must be stressed that defining just who is an addict or abuser is not as obvious or straightforward as might be supposed.)

One reason why heroin is such an important drug for the sociologist of deviance (aside from its strongly negative image in the public's mind) is that its use seems to generate social problems of enormous seriousness and magnitude. This is not merely a matter of the society subjectively constructing a problem in a certain way; objectively speaking, heroin causes a great deal of damage to users and nonusers alike. As we've seen, it is clear that alcohol and tobacco kill more Americans than the illegal drugs. But quite obviously, on a dose-for-dose, episode-by-episode basis, heroin kills vastly more users than alcohol and tobacco, and cocaine as well—and very possibly more than any other psychoactive drug currently in use in the United States. If heroin were to become as popular as these legal drugs—an obvious impossibility, given how disruptive the drug is in the user's life—its death toll would be vastly higher than it currently is. Even if the use of heroin would double, bodies would begin piling up; the use of the drug is extremely unsafe, even under controlled circumstances. Hence, in spite of the relatively small number of its users, heroin is worth paying attention to by the sociologist of deviance. Consider the fact that cocaine is used ten times as frequently as heroin, yet DAWN's ME data tabulated only 10 percent more drug-related deaths for cocaine (23% of the total) as for heroin (13%). That suggests that, along with other factors (such as who uses it), heroin's use is potentially more fatal than cocaine's—and by a substantial margin.

METHAMPHETAMINE

The stories were terrifying. The abuse of methamphetamine, a more potent sister of the amphetamines, was sweeping the country like wildfire. Within just a few years, the United States would be awash in "ice"—recrystalized methamphetamine sulfate. Methamphetamine, according to the media in the late 1980s, was the drug of choice for a "new generation." It would replace heroin, cocaine, and even marijuana as the nation's premier problematic drug. Law enforcement was put on notice; "crystal meth" or "crank" (other terms for illicit methamphetamine sulfate) was the drug to watch. Or so the media announced in the late 1980s (Lerner, 1989; Young, 1989).

Every decade or two, a particular drug or drug type is designated by the media as, in the words of criminologist Ronald Akers, the "scary drug of the year." A panic or scare is generated about its use, and headlines scream out the danger its use poses. A tidal wave of abuse has hit or is about to hit our shores, these stories have asserted, and we should be prepared. In the 1930s, that drug was marijuana; in the 1960s, it was LSD; in the late 1970s, it was PCP; in the 1985–1990 era, it was crack cocaine. Just as the crack scare had begun to die down, a smaller but no less terrifying scare cropped up. Beginning in the late 1980s, the use of methamphetamine emerged and moved throughout the 1990s and into the early 2000s, generating periodic scares throughout this period. In every case, the headlines were exaggerated. Experts do not doubt the dangers attendant upon compulsive drug abuse, but they do argue that the headlined drugs are not nearly as harmful, nor are they likely to be used as compulsively, or as widely, as most of these headlines claimed. Sober, systematic evidence eventually revealed that the vast majority of episodes of PCP use did not result in self-destructive or violent behavior, that neither LSD nor crack use by expectant mothers produced birth defects in their babies, and that very few crack users were caught up in the "inferno of addiction" described by the press.

What of methamphetamine? Is or was the country "awash" in "ice"? Has "crystal meth" become the drug of choice for our younger generation? Is it as dependency producing as the headlines proclaimed? What evidence do criminologists, epidemiologists, and sociologists have of the use of this powerfully reinforcing drug?

Compared with the amphetamines, methamphetamine use all-too-often escalates to high-dose, compulsive abuse. Methamphetamine is more potent than any of the amphetamines; it crosses the blood-brain barrier more rapidly, and is metabolized more efficiently. A dose of methamphetamine generates more dopamine, a chemical neurotransmitter that regulates pleasure, than amphetamine or even cocaine. But a drug's effect is also influenced by route of administration—that is, *how* it is taken. Amphetamine has traditionally been taken orally via capsule or sniffed in powder form, while methamphetamine, in addition to being snorted, is injected and smoked; less commonly, although occasionally, it is ingested in pill or other form. John Kramer, a pharmacologist who studied amphetamine addiction in the 1960s, said at the time

that the drug, administered IV, "is an ecstatic experience." The user's first thought is, "Where has this been all my life?"

At one time, methamphetamine was prescribed under the brand name Methedrine; it is no longer legally manufactured in the United States. (Another methamphetamine is currently marketed in pill form under the brand name Desoxyn; it is a Schedule II drug.) In the 1960s, Methedrine was injected intravenously in high doses; a sizable "speed scene" developed, which involved tens of thousands of youths taking huge doses day in and day out. Use peaked around 1967 and declined sharply thereafter. Many "speed freaks" (as compulsive, high-dose users of Methedrine were called) at the time eventually became heroin addicts, because they alternated the use of methamphetamine, a stimulant, with heroin, a depressant, so that they could come down from their Methedrine high. They began to use more heroin and less methamphetamine, and eventually the heroin took over. Considering the way that Methedrine was used by speed freaks, heroin turned out to be a safer, easier drug to take, and it had less of a deleterious impact on their lives.

Although the street speed scene did not last very long, it had a tremendous impact on its participants' lives. What was it like? The speed freak of the late 1960s took Methedrine to get high. More specifically, the drug was injected IV to achieve a "flash" or "rush," whose sensation was likened to an orgasm—a "full body orgasm"—or a jolt of electricity. Users took extremely large quantities of the drug. While 5 to 10 milligrams of Dexedrine or Dexamyl taken orally via tablet or capsule would represent a typical therapeutic or instrumental dose of an amphetamine, the speed freak would inject as much as half a gram or a full gram (500 or 1,000 milligrams!) of Methedrine in one IV dose. Such massive doses of speed would cause unconsciousness or even death in a non-habituated person but an orgasmic rush in the experienced user. Since amphetamine inhibits sleep, IV administration every four hours or so causes extended periods of wakefulness, often two to five days at a stretch (called a "run"). This would be followed by long periods of sleep ("crashing"), often lasting up to twenty-four hours. The speed epidemic burned itself out within a year or so.

But in the late 1980s, the heavy use of methamphetamine made a comeback; it began in Hawaii and spread to California. The current form of methamphetamine is considerably more potent than its older version, Methedrine. (Its current manufacturers use ephedrine or pseudoephedrine, a heart and central nervous system stimulant, as its precursor drug.) The effects of a substantial dose of methamphetamine last a long time, twelve hours, its half-life is at least as long, and it takes two days to be totally eliminated from the body. Its relatively slow breakdown rate means that if taken daily, accumulation can occur. This both boosts the effect of each subsequent dose and potentiates serious organic harm.

The chemical process to produce methamphetamine is extremely simple and its precursor chemicals are readily available. As a consequence, until the mid-1990s, most of the meth used in this country was manufactured either by biker gangs or very small "mom and pop" operations, mainly in the Southwestern United States, usually California. According to the Drug Enforcement Administration (DEA), however, beginning about fifteen years ago, Mexican gangs began muscling into the bikers' turf and managed to wrest a majority of the business away from them. Within the last five years, authorities began seizing methamphetamine originating from Canada. In addition, methamphetamine tablets that had its origin in Southeast Asia began to show up on the streets of America's cities (www.dea.gov/pubs/intel/01020/index.html).

Recent media accounts on methamphetamine abuse have warned the public and put law enforcement on alert: Methamphetamine is the drug to watch. Does systematic evidence bear out these journalistic claims?

The Arrestee Drug Abuse Monitoring Program (ADAM) drug tests and interviews arrestees who have agreed to volunteer information about their use; most percentage agree to be interviewed and of these, and 88 percent agree to be urine-tested for the presence of drugs. Hence, in ADAM's 2010 study, we have two different looks at the drug use of a non-traditional sample—an objective indicator (drug tests) and a survey, for the same set of respondents—that is, arrestees. ADAM looks at arrestees from the counties in and around the nation's largest cities.

In the past decade, cocaine has declined as the drug of choice among arrestees, and marijuana has remained more or less stable. Even so, nationwide, only *one-tenth* as many arrestees test positive for methamphetamine as for cocaine. Perhaps the most remarkable of ADAM's findings, however, is that the use of methamphetamine remains *extremely* regionalized—which is not true of cocaine. In 2010, ADAM drug-tested over 4,700 arrestees in ten cities across the country. In only two of these cities, Sacramento (33%) and Portland, (20%), both in the West, arrestees tested positive at a substantial level. In three others, Denver (4%), Indianapolis (3%), and Minneapolis (2%), the proportion of positive tests was low but not insignificant. And in the remainder, Chicago, plus mainly Eastern and Southern cities (New York, Washington, DC, Charlotte, and Atlanta), arrestees tested at the 1 percent or lower level. This pattern may change in the future, since some cities which, a decade ago, tested 0 percent for methamphetamine among arrestees, now find that a tiny percentage test positive. But for the last quarter century, regionalization has characterized meth use, and it's possible that this pattern has developed into a stable tendency. Hence, the predictions that meth abuse was "marching across America like wildfire," as numerous media stories claimed, were not only completely wrong, but irresponsible as well.

Almost as important as ADAM's revelation of the regionalization of meth distribution and use is the fact that its sample accessed a sector of the population that has remained nearly invisible to polls, surveys, and systematic research investigation. A substantial number of the arrestees who tested positive for the presence of a drug, ADAM's 2010 study found, *denied* using that very drug in its survey—and the percentage varied substantially by the drug in question. "Truth telling" for the marijuana users was high (83%), but it was lower (62%) for meth-positives, lower still (45%) for cocaine-positives, and only 37 percent for those who tested positive for heroin. Since a high percentage of the arrestees lived in rooming houses, on the street, in shelters, or were frequently housed in jails or prisons, conventional surveys rarely captured them in their surveys. And since transients exhibit such a high proportion of drug users, and such a low percentage tell the truth about their use, even when surveys manage to locate them, it is clear that the percentage of respondents in conventional surveys who say they have used drug is seriously *under-estimated*. Hence, ADAM's data "present a cautionary tale regarding underrepresentation of use of highly stigmatized drugs when only self-report data are the source" (ADAM, 2011, p. 12).

As we've seen, Monitoring the Future is a yearly survey of eighth, tenth, and twelfth graders, as well as college students and adults not in college. Questions about methamphetamine began in the late 1990s and declined since then; in 2011, for high school seniors, lifetime use was 2.1 percent, and thirty-day prevalence was 0.6 percent. The data from the 2011 National Household Survey on Drug Abuse indicate that methamphetamine use has declined recently, and nationwide, it is far below that of marijuana and even cocaine; only one-tenth of 1 percent of the study's respondents said that they had used it in the past 30 days, a decline of two-thirds since 2006 and a drop of nearly 400,000 users—and a drop of 150,000 within only the prior year, from 2010 to 2011. Methamphetamine is not among DAWN's ME "top five" drugs with respect to its 2010 tally of mortality (the generic category, "stimulants" appears as the sixth most common drugs in ME drug-related deaths), and in recent years, methamphetamine appears in emergency department (ED) visits less than a sixth as often as for cocaine.

These nationwide figures mask not only regional differences but rural-urban differences as well. In some rural communities, methamphetamine has become *the* drug of abuse. In some areas, in the past few years, narcotics law enforcement spends most of its person-hours on methamphetamine, and, in these same areas, admissions to treatment programs for meth abuse have shot up several fold and have overwhelmed regional and local facilities. Clearly, the national picture is not the same everywhere; it is clear that to get the big picture, it is necessary to piece together many smaller pictures.

At the same time, the nationwide picture does not warrant alarm—yet. Methamphetamine has been dubbed "redneck cocaine," and it is principally in the poorest, more rural areas of the country that meth has taken root. Even today, almost

everywhere, methamphetamine abuse is dwarfed by the use of cocaine and, as measured by harm if not by its volume of use, even heroin. That may change in the years to come, but the current picture does not justify a recent *USA Today* headline: "'Meth' Moves East" (www.usatoday.com/news /nation/2003-07-29-meth-cover_x.htm), whose story quotes a DEA agent who says, "It looks almost like a wildfire moving east." Between 2004 and 2006, *The Oregonian* devoted over 250 stories reporting on the horrific threat of the meth epidemic. Meth was certainly a problem in Portland, but the hysterical prediction of its eastward march was not warranted. Nationwide, meth is (and was) used *vastly* less than the media indicate, and the harm it has caused is likewise substantially lower. And by 2006, reporters and scholars began recognizing that much of the media had exaggerated the extent of methamphetamine use and the damage it caused. In an online story, Angela Valdez took *The Oregonian* to task, referring to its invocation of "Meth Madness," charging the newspaper with manufacturing an epidemic (www.week.com/editorian/3220/7368). In *Newsweek*, a highly respected news magazine, reporter David Jefferson declared that meth was "America's Most Dangerous Drug" (2005). Nonsense, argued Jack Shafer, charging *Newsweek* with "scaremongering" for its cover title, "The Meth Epidemic: Inside America's New Drug Crisis" (Shafer, 2007). Meth is not and never was America's "most dangerous drug," Shafer averred. Late in 2007, in an academic journal, sociologist Edward Armstrong asserted that the concern over meth constituted a *moral panic* (2007).

As we've seen, different drugs generate different rates of "loyalty" or continuance rates. Most one-time users of any and all illicit drugs do *not* go on to continued use; most give it up after a few trial experiments, and even most of those who use it for a longer period of time eventually stop using. We can measure a drug's continuance rate by comparing the number of persons who have used it at least once, or lifetime use, with the number who have used in the past month. As we noted, over six out of ten of one-time users of alcohol have drunk within the past month; for tobacco cigarettes, the figure is about a third. Among all illicit drugs, roughly one out of seven lifetime marijuana users or triers (16%)

consumed the drug in the past month. Some drugs, such as LSD (0.7%) and PCP (0.5%), are used extremely episodically. According to the national survey, among the 13 million people in the United States who had *ever* used meth, a third of a million, 353,000, said that they had taken it in the past month—a "loyalty" rate of 3 percent; just over a third (37%) of once-or-more users within the past year have also taken it within the past month. In other words, a minority—albeit a substantial minority—who graduate from the experimental use of methamphetamine, begins taking it more or less regularly. And if we had more precise data, we'd see that a minority *within* that minority—but again, a fairly substantial minority—begin taking the drug compulsively and abusively. It is this minority within a minority that law enforcement has to worry about. (Again, keep in mind that conventional polls undersample unconventional populations.) No, "tasting" crank does not even inevitably lead to a "maelstrom of addiction." But yes, if a user escalates from tasting to occasional use, the risk is almost as high as it is for the other hard drugs currently available on the menu, except marijuana, alcohol, and tobacco—6 percent for heroin and 4 percent for crack and cocaine. As small as the proportion who escalates is, they are significant and important to the researcher of deviant behavior.

SUMMARY

Hallucinogens or psychedelics include LSD as their best known representative. During the 1960s, an LSD scare or panic erupted. Users were said to suffer temporary insanity and irreparable chromosome damage. The first effect is now regarded with suspicion by experts, while the second has been entirely discounted. LSD use has not disappeared. If anything, it has stabilized over the past decade or two. LSD is taken sporadically, with episodic infrequency. It rarely becomes a drug of serious, heavy, or chronic abuse.

Although once an ingredient in some medicines and beverages, for recreational purposes, cocaine was never a drug of widespread popularity in the United States until the 1970s. Cocaine was criminalized, along with narcotics, in the aftermath of the Harrison Act. In the

1980s, a new form of cocaine, "crack," became popular. Crack is smoked and thus produces an intense and extremely rapid high. Never widespread in the country as a whole, crack quickly became popular among a minority of poor, inner-city youth. Its use declined during the course of the 1990s. Crack use, while far from safe, was demonized by the media; its harmful effects were hugely exaggerated. Babies born to cocaine-dependent mothers were said to be permanently disabled mentally and physically. In fact, it is now clear that their medical problems were due more to the lifestyle of their mothers than to the effects of cocaine per se. In other words, the fear that crack will severely harm the fetuses of the dependent mothers was a "fear-driven" rather than a "fact-driven" syndrome. Crack abuse became another in a long line of drug panics. During the 1990s cocaine use declined in the general population but increased slightly among the young.

Heroin is perhaps the least popular of all widely known drugs in America. As it is used, on an episode-by-episode basis with respect to lethal overdoses, it is also one of the most dangerous. Considering the small number of heroin users in the United States, a surprisingly high number of addicts die of heroin overdoses and other related ailments. Some observers argue that this has as much to do with the legal situation as to the effects of the drug itself. Since the early 1980s, heroin has become increasingly pure and abundant. It is now imported from a much wider range of sources than was true in the past.

Since 1989, methamphetamine, a powerful chemical analogue of amphetamine, has created a media stir. Pundits and journalists predicted that the drug would sweep the nation like wildfire. Methamphetamine has caused major disruption and devastation in Western and Midwestern cities such as Honolulu, Portland, San Jose, and Omaha, as well as in many rural areas of the West and Midwest, but its abuse is low in the cities of the Northeast. The ranking of methamphetamine among the drugs that cause "overdose" problems—both with respect to emergency department (ED) visits and Medical examiner (ME) reports —is extremely low. Meth rarely appears among the top five of either of these abuse indicators. Surveys, both of the population at large and among schoolchildren, indicate that relatively few people use meth, and that this figure is declining. Cocaine, for example, is vastly more frequently used and by a substantially higher percentage of the population, by a factor of five times. In 2010, ADAM (the Arrestee Drug Abuse Monitoring Program) drug-tested over 4,700 arrestees in ten cities across the country. Only in Sacramento (33%) and Portland (20%) were the positives for meth substantial; in the Rocky Mountain city of Denver (4%) and the Midwestern cities of Indianapolis (3%), and Minneapolis (2%), the proportion testing positive tests was low but not insignificant. In the city of Chicago, in the South (Atlanta and Charlotte), and in the Northeastern corridor (New York, Washington, DC), the proportion testing positive was 1 percent or less. The percentage self-reporting methamphetamine use in ADAM's survey revealed virtually identical figures. It is possible that meth use is higher among rural, more inaccessible regions that these data collection enterprises do not tap, but some skeptics are dubbing the concern over meth as a "moral panic."

Account: Substance Abuse in the Family

The author of this account is a college student.

Sociologists define deviance as behavior, belief, or traits that depart from a norm and elicit a negative reaction in a social collectivity or in the society at large. They consider drug addicts and alcoholics as deviants because people tend to look down on them, stigmatize them, and treat them as abnormal because of what they do or have done. I know this from experience. Even family members who don't use drugs treat family members who do as deviant. When he was growing up, my brother took the wrong path, and he became a drug addict. It was difficult for me to watch him struggle with his addiction. I was close to him before he became addicted, but when he got involved with drug abuse, we fell apart. Once he got involved, he refused to have anything to do with the family. He used hard drugs and got in trouble a lot. He got caught stealing because he needed money for his habit. He even stole from our mom and from me. When I left anything of value in my room, he stole it. Any little thing he could find around the house that he could take to a pawn shop, he'd steal it. He began manufacturing methamphetamine, and the authorities discovered his lab, arrested him, and he did a pretty long prison stretch. Since we live in a small town, everyone found out about the trouble my brother got into. You can't hide anything in this town. Pretty soon, the whole county knew about his troubles.

Our dad is a serious alcoholic. He can't keep a job because of his drinking problem. He's always coming home late; he comes in, falls down, breaks stuff, and curses at my mom and me. Every time you see my dad, he's drunk. Often, his drinking leads to arguments and fights. It just about kills my mom having to live with a drunk, so I have to reassure her that everything is going to be all right. She worries herself practically to death about whether I will end up in the same condition as my brother and my dad.

I have to deal with the problems my brother and dad create for me, along with the deviant label I've attracted from the society. Most folks think that because my brother and my dad have substance abuse problems, I do, too. I may not be perfect, but I'm not an alcoholic or a drug abuser—but I still get stigmatized. The parents of some of my peers won't let their kids hang out with me because they figure I'm like my brother and my dad and assume that if I'm with their kids, we're going to use drugs and get drunk. This is a good example of labeling theory: Deviance is a consequence of judgments that people make and labels they apply that influence a person's self-concept and behavior. I wanted to date a girl in high school but her parents wouldn't let me see her because they had tagged me with a label; they figured I'd get drunk, do drugs, and have a bad influence on their daughter. That same sort of labeling took place throughout high school. I couldn't hang out with anyone or date any girls because of my bad reputation.

Everyone knew me as Jim's little brother. They knew bad things about Jim because of what they had heard about him, and I couldn't do anything about it. As long as I lived in the county, I'd be stigmatized, disvalued, held in low esteem, excluded from full social acceptance. I've experienced many instances of being left out of activities and relationships because people think badly of me. Their parents don't like me and tell their kids not to associate with me. I try not to feel hurt by this rejection, but I am hurt by it.

My brother got out of jail about six months ago. He's doing much better now. He's off drugs, he's holding down a job, and he's taking care of his kids. He recently got baptized and he attends church every Sunday. Before he went to jail, he weighed 120 pounds; he now weighs about 200, and he looks a lot better. Yet people will still label him a "meth head" and a "druggie." He's a convicted felon, so there are a lot of jobs he can't hold. He'll be tagged as a deviant for the rest of his life because he made some mistakes when he was younger. As for me, I don't like having the bad name that's been attached to me and I don't like being kept from developing social relationships I'd like to have. I didn't do anything wrong and it's unfair to judge me for something I didn't do.

Questions

Does this account say something about the influence of the family on a person's drug and alcohol abuse? While the author's brother was a drug addict and abuser, he himself was not; how do we account for differences within a given family? Do the author's experiences verify some of labeling theory's central tenets? Yet, even though deviance labeling is influential, it did not *cause* the author to become a drug abuser. How should we qualify the labeling perspective to account for exceptions to the rule? Do you think that, in spite of being an ex-convict and being labeled a deviant, Jim has a chance to stay clean?

Sexual Deviance

Learning Objectives:

After reading this chapter, you will be able to:

- differentiate between essentialism and constructionism in the discussion of sexual deviance;
- discuss the history and purpose of sex surveys;

- answer the question, "What's deviant about sexual behavior?";
- examine attitudes regarding homosexuality;
- discuss adultery in the context of deviance;
- examine gender as a crucial ingredient to understanding sexual behavior.

A popular Catholic priest confesses to fathering a child, makes a public apology, and agrees to take a leave of absence from his pulpit (Goodstein, 2012a). President Barack Obama puts gay marriage—a controversial position supported by a bare majority of the electorate—on his campaign agenda (Landler and Zeleny, 2012); Former Vice President Dick Cheney, a staunch conservative, admits that his daughter's lesbianism has changed his position on the question of homosexuality (Cooper and Peters, 2012). The Vatican denounces a nun, Sister Margaret Farley, for publishing a theological tract entitled *Just Love: A Framework for Christian Sexual Ethics*, which supports same-sex marriage, masturbation, and remarriage after divorce (Goodstein and Donadio, 2012). In Minneapolis, twenty-nine Somali immigrants and Somali Americans are charged with sexual trafficking (Eckholm, 2012). A scandal erupts when reporters reveal that U.S. Secret Service agents are paid to protect the president who had hired prostitutes two days before at an international summit in Cartagena, Colombia. Eight agents are fired from their jobs; more are likely to follow (Leonnig and Nakamura, 2012). Tek Young Lin, a retiree, publicly admits that when he taught English at the Horace Mann School, a preparatory school in the Bronx, he had sexual relations with his fourteen- and fifteen-year-old students (Anderson, 2012).

At least one critic of the sociology of deviance (Liazos, 1972) has accused its researchers and authors of inappropriately dwelling on "nuts, sluts, and preverts" forms of behavior—in other words, focusing on "trivial" forms of deviance such as mental disorder, prostitution, and sexual depravity, thereby ignoring the momentous "big bang" types of deviancies such as corporate crime and political machinations. But the fact is that it *is* more interpersonally discrediting—and therefore more *deviant*—to engage in sexual improprieties and transgressions than in corporate crime and high-level political malfeasance. In spite of the supposedly "misguided" and "biased" emphasis that such critics charge the field with, sociologists of deviance continue to focus on the study of, and discuss, sexual deviance more than the "big bang" deviant behaviors. There is a good reason for this: Sexual transgressions represent a prime example of deviance. Sociologists discuss

them *as deviance* because such behavior tends to be more discrediting and stigmatizing than most other forms of normative violations. Indeed, it seems wrongheaded and ignorant *not* to emphasize sexual transgressions in a deviance course. It is the field's critics who hold the "bias"—not the sociologists of deviance. Such critics are asking the wrong questions. The *right* questions are: *Why do societies devise and enforce so many norms about sexual behavior?* And: *Why is the violation of sexual norms so interpersonally shameful?*

The ways we violate mainstream society's norms by engaging in variant sexual acts are almost infinite. And the *severity* of society's punishment for many sexual transgressions is substantial. How many husbands or wives divorce their spouses for committing corporate crime? Very few. How many people become the town gossip as a result of cheating on their income tax? A few—but not many. (Of course, the latter may risk a jail sentence, while the former will not—a separate issue altogether.) In contrast, *many* sexual acts are transgressive or unacceptable to most of the members of this—indeed, almost any—society. The fact is, societies pretty much everywhere have set forth and enforced an *immense* number of norms dictating acceptable and unacceptable sexual behavior. The do's and don'ts of sex are staggering in their number, variety, and complexity. And violating the "do's," and engaging in the "don'ts," usually carry with them interpersonal penalties. It is in the sphere of sexual transgressions that we find the greatest number of discrediting acts—in fact, where the most illuminating instances of *deviant behavior*—may be found.

We construct almost uncountable *social identities* on the basis of what we do, or have done, sexually. We construct *categories* for people as a result of the fact that they, or we, engage in, have engaged in, prefer, or want to engage, or try to engage, or can't engage, in certain types of sexual acts. Think of just a handful of these categories: homosexual, heterosexual, bisexual, adulterer, cuckold, faithful husband, faithful wife, impotent man, frigid woman, necrophiliac, pedophile, child molester, rapist, rape victim, cougar, gigolo, escort, call girl, "dirty old man," sexual harasser, "slut," "tramp," whore, prostitute, pimp, sex fiend, sex addict, pornographer, sadist, masochist, exhibitionist, peeper, lap dancer, stripper, nude dancer, exotic dancer, "tease," a "lousy lay," "limp dick," gay, queer, faggot, pansy, Mary Jane, dyke, "butch," "femme"—the list goes on and on. Obviously, sex plays a very *central* role in defining who we are in this (and virtually any) society. And its importance, so intricately and intimately tied in to social relations, is indicated by the number and strength of the norms attempting to govern it. Clearly, sexual deviance is a very *important* type of deviant behavior. With respect to interpersonal stigma, corporate crime is an extremely *minor* form of deviance since only a *small* number of people can engage in it, the interpersonal sanctions for transgressions are usually *minor*, and it is *rarely* relevant to actors' identities; the opposite is true of sexual deviance.

Consider the Bible's sexual prohibitions. It is true that, for most people, *The Holy Bible* is not the primary source of sexual norms. In fact, many people ignore most of the injunctions in the Bible as more or less irrelevant for their lives. Still, when we want to understand how sexual norms work, a good place to start is the Old and New Testaments; these texts give us a clue to what's considered wrong. A perusal of the Bible tells us a great deal about sexual norms. The number of injunctions and prohibitions against sexual acts considered wrong by the ancients, and the severity of the punishments for violating them, are impressive. Consider the fact that the Bible contains sixty-nine different passages that refer to "adulterer," "adulterers," "adulteress," "adulteresses," "adulteries," "adulterous," and "adultery," and forty-four refer to "fornication," "fornications," "fornicator," and "fornicators." In addition, the Holy Book prohibits sex with one's father's wife, daughter-in-law, mother-in-law, sister, father's daughter, mother's daughter, mother's sister, father's sister, uncle's wife, and brother's wife—not to mention animals, another man, and one's own wife during menstruation. (It is interesting that these prohibitions are spelled out mainly for men, less often for women; the compliance of women to the norms is more likely to have been taken for granted.) Several of these injunctions carry a penalty of death, in some cases, stoning. Clearly, the control of sexuality and the punishment of deviant sexuality were major tasks of the prophets. And the importance of sexual prohibitions remains the case to this day.

ESSENTIALISM VERSUS CONSTRUCTIONISM

Positivism—the application of the strict scientific method to the social world—is related to a perspective that, in philosophy, is referred to as "essentialism." There is perhaps no arena of human life in which a contrast between essentialism and constructionism is sharper than with sexual behavior. The *essentialist* position sees sexuality as "real," as something that exists, in more or less standard form, everywhere and for all time. Sex is a "thing," a pregiven entity, a concretely real phenomenon, much like an oxygen molecule, an apple or an orange, or gravitation. From the essentialists' perspective, sex is an imminent, indwelling inherent force, it is *there*; it exists prior to the human consciousness. "Everyone knows" what sex is; sex is sex is sex. Essentialists recognize that sex norms and sexual custom, and behavior, vary the world over and throughout recorded time. But the sexual conservative would say that certain variations are a perversion of our "true" or legitimate sexual expression, while the libertarian would say that sexual *repression* is a perversion of our "true" or legitimate sexual expression. Both agree, however, that the essence of sexuality is a "thing" that can be characterized in a more or less standard fashion. In other words, both are essentialists.

A completely different view of sex is offered by *constructionism*. This perspective asks questions about the *construction* and *imputation* of *meaning* (Gagnon and Simon, 1973, 2005; Plummer, 1975, 1982). Instead of assuming beforehand that a phenomenon bears an automatic sexual meaning, the constructionist asks: *How is sexuality itself constructed?* What *is* sexuality? How is the category put together? What is included in it, what's excluded? What are the *meanings* that are attached to it? How is sex thought about? Talked about? What rules do societies construct for appropriate and inappropriate sexual behavior? Constructionists argue that sexual meanings vary from person to person, setting to setting, social circle to social circle, and society to society.

Constructionists insist that behaviors or phenomena that are superficially, mechanically, and outwardly the same—that might seem *formally* the same to an external observer—can have radically different meanings to the participants. And the opposite is true as well: Social phenomena that, if examined from the outside, are objectively radically *different* can actually bear very *similar* meanings to observers or participants. What is sexual to one person may be totally *lacking* in sexual content or meaning to another.

For instance, is being strangled with a nylon cord sexually exciting? Very few of us would feel that way, but sexual asphyxia—strangling oneself to achieve sexual excitation (Sheleg and Ehrlich, 2006)—is common enough to be well known to every coroner and medical examiner in the country. Does wearing rubber and leather arouse our passion? What about engaging in dominance and submission games with your partner? Are children your sexual cup of tea? Do strippers become sexually aroused when they perform? Many members of their audiences certainly do; in contrast, these performers are usually going through the motions, utterly unmoved by their act. Receiving an enema or watching an entire family playing volleyball at a nudist colony may be sexual to one observer or participant and totally asexual to another. Is a vaginal examination by a gynecologist "sexual" in meaning? An act that sickens one person leaves another cold and indifferent, and causes a third to become aroused to orgasm.

Consider same-gender sexual behavior in ancient Greece. Such practices were accepted, even expected, if one male was older and the other was an adolescent and the older male continued to have sex with women as well, while sex between two grown or older males was frowned upon. Now consider same-gender sexual behavior in the contemporary United States where homosexual contact is more likely to be stigmatized, the partners tend to be age peers, and it is not typically accompanied by heterosexual activity. It is improper to regard the two as precisely "the same" sort of behavior? It's not even clear if we can refer to both as "homosexuality." Yes, both entail homoerotic sex, but in each

time and locale, each has distinctive features the other doesn't have. In Inuit society, a custom exists of husbands offering their wives sexually to male guests (or once did—it's almost certainly obsolete nowadays); in the contemporary United States, in some social circles, married couples "swap" or "swing" or engage in "co-marital" sex. Are these two practices similar to, or very different from, one another? They are likely to serve entirely different functions and be experienced by the relevant parties in radically different ways. Hence, to the constructionist, they are different acts; their similarities are likely to be more superficial than meaningful.

Constructionists argue that *sexuality is in the service of the social world.* Sexuality does not shape our social conduct so much as social meanings give shape to our sexuality (Plummer, 1982, p. 232). We are sexual because we are social. It is social life that *creates*, *motivates*, and *shapes* our sexuality. The social constructionist argues that sex is not a given, not a hard-and-fast reality or a bedrock biological constant—something that simply "is"—but something that is created or *fashioned* out of our biological "raw material," partly by our culture, partly by our partners and our interaction with them, and partly by the richness of our imagination. It is not sex that makes us who we are but it is *we who make sex what it is.*

The constructionist position goes considerably beyond the insight that understanding symbolic meaning is necessary to understand sexual behavior. It argues that not only is the very *category* of sexuality constructed, in addition, a specific *evaluative* meaning is read into it as well. By "evaluative" I mean, sexual categories are rendered "good" or "bad"—that is, conventional and norm-abiding, or deviant, in violation of the norms—through the construction process. For instance, not only are the categories "homosexual" and "heterosexual" constructed, but they are *infused with positive or negative meanings.* Different forms of sexual expression do not bring with them an automatic response; they do not drop down, pregiven, from the skies as an automatic reaction to their essence or basic reality. What *creates* the phenomenon of deviance is condemning reactions and these reactions are variable in societies the world over, from one historical period to another, and from one social circle or context to another in the same society. What's good in one place and time is regarded as bad in another. This variability reflects the construction process that makes up the very stuff of deviance.

Traditionally, the imputation of pathology has been an aspect of the way that deviance was constructed by psychologists and psychiatrists. This has been *especially* true of deviant sexuality. Until the 1960s and 1970s, the vast majority of research and writing on non-normative sex cast it beyond the pale of normality. Sexual deviants, these early researchers were saying, are distinctly *not like the rest of us*. When the words, "sexual deviant" was used to describe someone, the image that came to mind was someone who is impelled to act as a result of uncontrollable and distinctly abnormal, motives—someone whose behavior is freakish and fetishistic.

Today, when discussing deviant sexual behavior and proclivities, we are not referring to something, which is sick or pathological but what's *socially disapproved*. Such a discussion includes no taint of disorder whatsoever, no implication of harm, sickness, or illness. Sociologists of deviance do *not* mean "abnormal" or "sick" when they refer to sexual transgressions. To repeat the theme of this book: Sociologically, *deviance* is made up of actions (and beliefs, and conditions) that violate one or more norms in a given place and at a given time, and are likely to touch off negative reactions.

Let's put the matter another way: *Psychological* and *social* (or sociological) deviance are not the same thing. They delineate two separate and independent dimensions. They overlap, of course; the chances are that nearly all cases of *psychological* deviance would qualify as *sociological* deviance. But the reverse is not the case. Psychologically, sexual deviance implies a *disorder*, a *dysfunction*; socially and sociologically, sexual deviance refers to a violation of norms and a subsequently high likelihood of condemnation and stigma. What violates the norms in a given society may in fact be regarded by psychiatrists and clinical psychologists as quite normal (although it may not). What is accepted, practiced, and even encouraged in one society may be savagely condemned and harshly punished in another. What is a normative violation at one time may be the norm at another. Again, because the link between sexual deviance and psychological abnormality is so strong in many observers' minds, we have to be reminded of their conceptual independence.

SEX SURVEYS

How do we know about sexual behavior? Some observers argue that we can't know—that this sphere of human existence is too secretive and controversial to study (Lewontin, 1995). Still others insist that we shouldn't study sex, that it is a world apart, a dimension of life that should be protected from the probing, prying gaze of the social scientist. The former U.S. Senator Jesse Helm exemplifies this position—which we can call the "know-nothing" point of view. Fortunately for intellectuals, researchers, and the inquisitive public, a substantial number of social scientists have ignored such objections, forged ahead anyway, and tried to bring the world of sex into the clear light of day for all to see and understand. Such research does not identify anyone personally—everyone's entitled to their own privacy—but it does look at sexual behavior, like all human behavior, as part of general patterns that help us understand what social life is like; that's what social scientists *do*—it's their *career*.

In the 1940s and 1950s, Alfred Kinsey and his associate investigated sexual behavior among men (1948) and women (1953); their reports created a sensation, including thousands of newspaper and magazine articles, a firestorm of criticism, and Kinsey's face on the cover of *Time*. We learned a great deal from the Kinsey surveys, but at least one of the lessons they taught was that it is extremely important to draw a *nationally representative sample*, which Kinsey's research team failed to do. Its samples were huge—in the tens of thousands. The survey's questions were detailed, but it failed to address the matter of representativeness, which means that its sample was biased or *skewed*, which means the answer to its questions were misleading. For instance, Kinsey sought cooperation from voluntary associations, and the *kinds* of organizations he got cooperation from were more likely to draw samples (or "chunks") of people who were more middle class, less African American, more homosexual, and so on, than is true of the population at large. Hence, it's biased. Clearly, researchers needed methodologies that better reflected the realities of human sexuality.

Ken Plummer (1982) classifies sex research into four main "traditions": the *clinical* tradition, initiated by Sigmund Freud and the psychoanalysts, and continued by psychiatrists and clinical psychologists in other theoretical traditions; the *social bookkeeping* tradition of Alfred Kinsey and the other survey-takers; the experimental method of Masters and Johnsons and the other many psychologists and physiologists; and the *descriptive/ ethnographic/symbolic interactionist* tradition of anthropologists and participant observation sociologists, including Plummer himself. Each of the traditions is appropriate for a somewhat different set of issues. Although Freud's reputation has suffered a virtual eclipse in psychology and the social sciences (Crews, 1995; Webster, 1995), it lives on in the field of literary criticism, where statements are insulated from empirical falsification. Still, thousands of researchers using non-psychoanalytic clinical approaches continue to investigate sexual behavior, mainly disorders. With respect to the laboratory "tradition," one learns virtually nothing about how widespread sexual practices are by putting couples in rooms and strapping monitors to their bodies, asking them to engage in intercourse, then measuring their responses, as the Masters and Johnson team did (1966, 1970, 1979). On the other hand, laboratory method does have applicability with respect to physiological and anatomical sexual responses, and many behavioral psychologists and researchers in related fields have found that measuring patterns of sexual arousal in the laboratory are reliable and valid, and they continue to pursue this line of research (Roche and Barnes, 1998; Ariely and Loewenstein, 2006). Some laboratory researchers study arousal by means of pupillary dilation (Rieger and Savin-Williams, 2012), which is an indirect measure of sexual arousal.

The "social bookkeeping" method of studying, too, has its strengths and weaknesses. Following the interactionist theoretical perspective, many sociologists of deviance regard social bookkeeping deficient in a number of respects—for instance, what these behaviors *mean* to their participants.

Still, some social bookkeeping is necessary for knowing a wide range of facts, including matters crucial to sexual deviance or "transgressions." For instance, we know that the HIV/AIDS virus is far more likely to be transmitted to the extent that sex partners are anonymous and large in number. Without knowing who does what with whom, we would be in the dark about this important fact. We know, as we've already seen, that the heavy consumption of alcohol is correlated with risky, deviant sexual behavior—an extremely important fact when it comes to making generalizations about the consequences of drinking and risky sex. If we want to know the likelihood that unmarried teenagers will become pregnant and either have an abortion or bear out-of-wedlock children, again, some social bookkeeping becomes necessary. It is only by means of social bookkeeping that we can discover *correlations* or *relationships* with key factors or variables of importance to social scientists. Answers to most questions tend to be internally consistent; they usually fit together like a jigsaw puzzle. Hence, when we ask questions about a respondent's attitudes toward homosexuality, typically, the responses correspond to a conventional-unconventional outlook on life: conventional attitudes and behavior in one sphere of life often predict those in another. Likewise, social characteristics predict behavior and attitudes: For instance, men are more likely to drink heavily, use drugs, and engage in risky, deviant sexual behavior than women; the same is true of the young versus the old, urban dwellers versus residents of small towns and rural areas, Westerners and Northeasterners versus Midwesterners and Southerners, and so on. All of this is a preamble to saying that, in spite of their limitations, surveys and polls ("social bookkeeping") do have great value in the study of sexual behavior, including sexual deviance. We can often cross-check the validity of an answer to one question through asking another, including those that we have reliable data for. Surveys, including those about controversial, touchy, private matters, produce answers that are a great deal more valid and reliable than most people thing.

In 1987, an agency of the federal government sent out a request for researchers to submit proposals to conduct a survey of sexual practices as a means of understanding ways to combat the spread of the AIDS virus. A team of researchers, based principally at the University of Chicago, submitted a proposal that was accepted and funded. However, in 1991, ultraconservative Senator Jesse Helms (1921–2008) got wind of the project and successfully lobbied to have its funding cut off. The research team managed to obtain funding from private sources. Although its sample size was much smaller than the team had originally intended, the researchers managed to conduct the study without political interference. They interviewed nearly 3,500 adults aged eighteen to fifty-nine; the sample was nationally represented and reflected the composition of the population as a whole. The study was conducted by Edward Laumann, John Gagnon, Robert Michael, and Stuart Michaels, and was published in two volumes—a research monograph, *The Social Organization of Sexuality* (Laumann et al., 1994), and a briefer work for a wider audience, *Sex in America*, coauthored with science and medical writer Gina Kolata (Michael et al., 1994). Among other things, this survey demonstrates the political pitfalls such research entails; conservatives do not *want* sociologists to conduct sexual research on the general population, and chances are, will attempt to block surveys such as these, which is one reason why they are so rare.

The results of the study were surprising, in that the sexual behavior of the American people turned out to be a great deal more *conservative*, *traditional*, and *conventional* than almost anyone, the researchers included, had expected. Perhaps the most consistent finding, one that ran throughout all aspects of the study was that, whether or not marriage was the aim of a relationship, people usually have sex with partners who are similar to themselves—in age, race and ethnicity, and socioeconomic status, especially education. There are three reasons for this, the authors argue. First, even *meeting* someone takes place within social boundaries. The fact is, one rarely interacts with a random cross-section of the population. Social relations are constrained by religious membership, neighborhood or community residence, school or occupational setting, friendship networks, and so on. Statistically speaking, the people one runs into in one's social circles and settings are likely to be similar to oneself. Even bars are constrained by locality. And it is in these social circles and

settings that one usually meets romantic and dating—and sexual—partners. Second, "stakeholders," that is, third parties—parents, friends, peers, relatives, coworkers, acquaintances, associates—are likely to put pressure on one to date within certain social boundaries. And the more serious the relationship, the more intense that pressure is. And third, similarity makes compatibility more likely which, in turn, increases the chances of liking and intimacy. Sharing the same social background or characteristics is far more likely to lead to a sexual and romantic and, eventually, marital relationship than having different backgrounds or characteristics. "Like has sex with like" is a far more accurate and realistic aphorism than "opposites attract."

In addition to the conventionality of the avenues through which partners meet and from which they draw their "pool" of sexual candidates, there was the conventionality of the behavior itself. More than eight Americans in ten had sex with either no partners (12%) or only one partner (71%) during the past year; only 3 percent had sex with five or more partners. Since the age of 18, not quite six in ten (59%) said that they had had sex with four or fewer partners, and only 9 percent said that they had had sex with more than twenty partners. Three-quarters of the married men in the sample (75%) and 85 percent of the women said that they had had sex only with their spouses during the course of their marriages. Among married respondents, 94 percent said that they were faithful during the past year. The data on homosexual behavior were even more surprising, given the widespread belief, fostered by Kinsey's research, that one in three American men has had at least one homosexual experience and one in ten is *a* homosexual. Only 2.8 percent of the men in the sample and 1.4 percent of the women identified themselves as homosexual or bisexual. Only 2 percent of both the men and the women said that they had had sex with a same-gender partner during the past year; only 5.3 percent of the men and 3.5 percent of the women said that they had done so since the age of 18. And only 9 percent of the men and 4 percent of the women said that they had done so since the onset of puberty. These figures were a small fraction of those obtained by the famous "Kinsey Reports" of a half-century earlier which, as I said, were based on biased samples. In short, regardless of how we feel about the "bookkeeping" method of research on sex, clearly it has something to offer to any inquisitive and skeptical observer of the subject.

A third set of findings that the media, the general public, and the researchers themselves found surprising related to sexual *frequency*, which was considerably lower than many observers had anticipated. Only one-third of the sample (34%) had sex as often as twice a week, and of that total, only 8 percent said that they had sex as often as four or more times a week. One out of ten of men in their fifties (11%) and three out of ten of the women of that age (30%) did not have sex at all during the prior year. Perhaps even more surprising, the *married* members of the sample were significantly more likely than the single members to have had sex twice a week or more (41% versus 23%), though unmarried cohabiting partners were even more likely to have sex this often (56%). In addition, the marrieds were most likely to report being physically and emotionally pleased with their sex and its frequency. The image of the wild, free, and easy sex life of the "swinging singles" received a serious body blow from the findings of this study. Ironically enough, Jesse Helms, who tried to prevent the study from having taken place, would have been pleased by the results it turned up.

And a fourth set of findings the Chicago team discovered pertained to the sexual activities that were most appealing to the sample. Traditional penile-vaginal sex turned out to be the only activity that was almost universally appealing: 83 percent of the women and 78 percent of the men said that that particular activity was "very" appealing to them. Moreover, 80 percent of the sample said that *every* time they had sex during the past year, they had traditional penile-vaginal sex. Half the men and a third of the women said that watching their partner undress was very appealing; the same proportion said that receiving oral sex was very appealing. Of the remaining sex acts asked about, only giving oral sex (37% for the men, 19% for the women) was appealing for a substantial proportion of the sample. All the other activities attracted only a small fraction of these figures. For instance, only 5 percent of the men and 1 percent of the women said that having sex with a stranger was appealing. All in all, the

activities the respondents said that they found appealing were quite traditional and conventional. Unusual, far-out, or "deviant" activities attracted very, very few positive evaluations.

Similar or almost identical surveys have been conducted in other countries, for instance, in France (Spira et al., 1992, 1993) and the United Kingdom (Johnson et al., 1994; Wellings et al., 1994). In 2010, Durex, a company that makes condoms, conducted a "global" sex survey, as well as one in the United States, whose questions focused mainly on the factors that make for condom use by men. Numerous other surveys, sponsored by a variety of institutions and agencies, have been carried out in the twenty-first century. ABC News conducted a poll that offered "a peek beneath the sheets," which seemed to have come up with findings that, at first glance, seemed to challenge the views engage in fairly conventional sex. But a closer look at the results of this survey indicated pretty much the same picture that the Chicago report gave us a decade or more earlier. But it did ask whether respondents had "ever" engaged in certain unconventional sexual behaviors. Over half (57%) said that they had sex outdoors "or in a public place," almost three in ten have had sex on a first date, about as many have had an "unexpected sexual encounter with someone new," 15 percent of men—three in ten (30%) of single men age 30 and older—have paid for sex, 16 percent of the total sample said that they had "cheated" on a partner, and one in five indicated that they had visited a porn Website. But again, these are figures for respondents who have *ever* had such experiences, even once; they do not indicate anything about their more typical or ongoing experiences.

The ABC News Primetime survey turned up some of the same findings concerning sex that earlier ones did. For the sample as a whole, only 5 percent described themselves as homosexual or bisexual. And heterosexual monogamy, the report states, "rules the roost." The median lifetime number of sexual partners is three for women, eight for men; among those who have had sex in the past year, 86 percent said that they only had a single sex partner during that period. As with all other surveys conducted on sexuality, men's behavior and attitudes are more unconventional than women's. For instance, twice as many men say they think about sex every day (70%) as women do (34%), considerably more men than women say they enjoy sex "a great deal" (83% versus 59%), and over twice as many men say they have had the experience of having had sex on a first date (42%) than women did (17%). The data are internally coherent; respondents who report more sexual partners are more apt to describe themselves as sexually adventurous and report more sexual partners than those who do not use this description for themselves—for instance, the self-described sexually "adventurous" women had an average of nineteen partners as compared with four for the other women. Not surprisingly, religiosity strongly influences sexual attitudes and behavior. Those who attend church never or rarely are much more likely to say that homosexuality is "OK" (70%) than is true of respondents who attend weekly or more (31%). The same prevails for those who have ever visited a porn site (29% versus 10%) and those who say they have had first-date sex (37% versus 14%). And political ideology follows a similar pattern as religious observance, with conservatives, along with the religiously observant, tending to be more conventional in sexual practices and attitudes. In short, political and religious conservatives are less sexually adventurous and more likely to consider sexual adventurousness—specifically, homosexuality, paying for sex, visiting a sex Web site, having sex before marriage, sex outside of marriage, sex with a number of partners, first-date sex, and sex at work—as a form of deviance. In other words, sexual behavior tends to be predictably related to sexual attitudes, and both tend to be correlated with key sociological variables, especially religiosity, religious practice, political ideology, and generic unconventionality and tolerance for deviance.

WHAT'S DEVIANT ABOUT SEXUAL BEHAVIOR?

In contemporary society, what are the *ways* in which sex may be considered deviant? With sex norms, as with laws governing sexual acts, there are the *who, what, how, where,* and *when* questions. Who one's partner is, is clearly an important source of prohibition; "what" one's partner is, likewise, determines right and wrong in the

sexual arena; how the sex act takes place also can determine its inappropriateness; where and when sex is performed, too, can be a source of right and wrong. What *makes* a sexual act illegal—and deviant—is an *inappropriateness along one or another of the following dimensions:*(1) the degree of consent, one aspect of the *how* question; (2) the nature of the sexual object, the *who* and *what* question; (3) the nature of the sex act, another aspect of the "how" question; and (4) the *setting* in which the sex act occurs, the *where* question (Wheeler, 1960).

Rape, which is regarded by most observers as more an act of violence than a type of sexual behavior, and which is discussed in Chapter 5 as a type of crime, is deviant along dimension (1)—*consent* on the part of the woman is lacking; force, violence, or the threat of violence is used to obtain sexual intercourse.

All societies proscribe certain sex partners as unacceptable, and sex with them as deviant—dimension (2), or *nature of the sex partner*. The number of sex partners who are regarded as inappropriate for all members of societies around the world is enormous. In our society, close relatives may not have sex with one another (again, the "who" question); if they do, it is automatically an instance of deviance. The same is likely to apply to members of the same sex, nearly always to strangers, anyone except our spouse if we are married, and so on. Adults may not have sex with underage minors—indeed, violating this injunction is a crime, punishable by a jail or prison sentence. Catholic priests may not have sex with anyone; psychiatrists may not have sex with their patients; on most university campuses, professors should not have sex with students; and so on. Many of these restrictions pertain to the relationship we might have (or can't have) with certain persons—brothers and sisters, strangers, and so on. Dimension (3), the nature of the sexual partner, also includes nonhuman sex objects, such as animals or sex dolls. (This is a "what" rather than a "who" question.)

"Kinky" sex, encompassing dimension (4)—the nature of the sex act, or the "how" question—is made up of sexual behavior that is bizarre to many people, constituting what used to be referred to as "perversions." Some people receive a sexual charge out of receiving an enema; this is regarded as "kinky." Others like to be tied up when they have sex, or to tie their partner up; this too may be referred to as "kinky." Sado-masochistic practices (giving or receiving pain during the sex act) likewise fall under the "how" umbrella of dimension (5). Some acts that were once considered perverted are likely to be accepted and considered normal today—for instance, oral and anal sex—a fact that demonstrates that sexual norms change over time. "Kinky" sex is considered deviant specifically because what is done—the nature of the act—is considered weird, unwholesome, and worthy of condemnation. Sex with a partner of the same gender is condemned and therefore deviant in most social circles of Western society. Another widely controlled sex act in this society—by custom, if not by law—is masturbation. Adolescent boys and girls are admonished not to "touch" themselves, and adults are rarely willing to discuss their participation in it, even to their close friends.

And lastly, some people find sex in public and semipublic places exciting and practice it because they have a certain chance of being discovered by others. Pushed to its extreme form, this is referred to as exhibitionism, and it is regarded as deviance because of dimension (6), the "where" question—sex in an inappropriate setting. Sexual fantasies indicate that sex in an inappropriate setting excites the imagination of many people. Table 9.1 gives us some idea of public attitudes toward various sexual practices. As we can see, a substantial majority of Americans disapprove of extramarital sex, but, for the most part, premarital sex is not widely condemned.

There are other dimensions that are not covered by the law or are less strongly governed by law than by custom that, nonetheless, dictate the inappropriateness of certain sexual behaviors. There is, to begin with, the *how often* question: The desire for sex that is widely deemed *too often*

may court the charge of being a "sex addict" (Carnes, 1983) or being "sexually compulsive" (Levine and Troiden, 1988). On the other hand, desiring or having sex *not often enough* may result in being labeled "impotent" or "frigid." Generally, sex at *too young* an age, even if the partners are the same age, generates condemnation and punishment among conventional others, parents especially. Not uncommonly, persons who are deemed too *old* will experience some negative, often condescending, reactions from others—often their own children! Sex with *too many* partners (a pattern that is conventionally referred to as "promiscuity," a loaded and sexist term) will attract chastisement, although more often for women than men, and more often homosexual men than heterosexuals. Exposing one's sex organs to an unwilling, coerced audience (exhibitionism), too, qualifies as an unconventional sex act, and is illegal as well. Selling, acting in or posing for, making, or, in some quarters, purchasing and consuming material that is widely regarded as pornographic is widely regarded as deviant. Selling and buying sexual favors is a clear-cut instance of sexual deviance in most people's eyes; prostitution is one of the more widely known and condemned forms of sexual deviance.

When we ask people whether certain acts are wrong, whether they should be illegal, or whether a certain behavior should even exist in the first place, we are asking whether these people consider these acts deviant. As we just saw, the sex survey conducted by members of the sociology department at the University of Chicago and published in two volumes, *The Social Organization of Sexuality* (Laumann et al., 1994) and *Sex in America* (Michael et al., 1994), and included a number of attitudinal questions in its interview

TABLE 9.1   ATTITUDES TOWARD NON-TRADITIONAL SEX

Percent Agreeing	
Extramarital sex is always wrong.	77
I would not have sex with someone unless I was in love with them.	66
Same-gender sex is always wrong.	65
Premarital sex among teenagers is always wrong.	61
There should be laws against the sale of pornography to adults.	34
Premarital sex is always wrong.	20

Source: Pearson Education, Upper Saddle River, NJ

schedule. From this survey, we get a pretty good snapshot of the American public's attitudes toward certain sexual acts and hence, what residents of this country consider sexually deviant. Here are the results of several of its questions.

What do these figures from the "Sex in America" survey tell us? First of all, the vast majority of Americans do not believe that premarital sex is "always" wrong or deviant. Today, it is expected that couples will have sex before marriage. However, the answers to the next question qualify this position: Most Americans consider teenage premarital sex to be wrong (61%). In other words, the public makes an age-specific or "relativistic" judgment about the appropriateness of having sex outside of marriage. The majority of Americans do not consider teenagers mature or responsible enough to engage in a sexual relationship. Extramarital sex—sex with a partner other than one's husband or wife, when one is married—is very widely condemned; over three-quarters of the sample (77%) said that it was "always" wrong. (The fact that roughly three-quarters of the married members of this sample also said that they *never* engaged in extramarital sex increases our confidence that they consider adultery "always wrong," and therefore deviant.) Interestingly enough, although most of the respondents in this survey said that they disapproved of homosexuality, that disapproval is weaker than it is for adultery. Criminalizing the sale of pornography to adults attracted approval from only a third of the sample (34%), suggesting that indulging in or consuming porn is not seriously deviant in the United States. Two-thirds of the sample (66%) said that they wouldn't have sex with someone with whom they were not in love, by implication indicating that for most Americans loveless sex is unacceptable and possibly deviant.

In short, Americans tend to be qualified about their sexual attitudes. A few behaviors are condemned more or less across the board (extramarital sex and homosexuality), but even here, disapproval, though fairly widespread, is far from universal. And behaviors that were strongly disapproved of in the past (such as premarital sex and the use of pornography) are acceptable or at least tolerated under certain circumstances. Sex before marriage is acceptable if it takes place among adults but not among teenagers. Far from

revealing Americans to be simple-minded Puritans, ready, willing, and eager to condemn any and all sexual behavior that departs from the mainstream, the "Sex in America" survey reveals a complex, nuanced, and highly qualified set of attitudes and reactions that are contingent on who engages in the behavior, why, and under what circumstances. We'll have a thing or two more to say about these complexities momentarily; recent public opinion has softened considerably about some, but not all, of these opinions.

HOMOSEXUALITY: DEPARTING FROM DEVIANCE

Of the many ways that humankind is divided into categories, using the sex or gender of one's sexual partners and the objects of one's sexual desires as a basis for this division is one of the most fundamental and ramifying. Why is the sex of one's partner such a crucial part of our identity? Why do we divide humanity into "straight" and "gay"? Why is such a division so much more important for us than one that divides us into "egg-eaters" and "people who don't eat eggs"? Or people who wear boots and those who don't? And why does the sexual division include an evaluative component? Not all societies condemn sex with members of the same gender, and even within the United States, we see substantial variation in attitudes toward homosexuality. In the United States, a sizeable—although slowly and unevenly shrinking—percentage of the straight population believe homosexual acts to be an "abomination" and support the laws banning them. Is homosexuality "deviant" in the United States? It depends on who you ask. It is most decidedly "deviant" in more conservative and evangelical social circles, but to the majority, it is decreasingly deviant, and in certain collectivities, it is a perfectly acceptable sexual orientation. The hatred and dread of homosexuality and homosexuals is referred to as *homophobia*; it is a form of prejudice toward and discrimination against a sexual minority. Some men feel homophobic because it affirms their heterosexuality and masculinity, but this is not a necessary component of this feeling, since such hatred has an ancient and deeply rooted pedigree.

"Homosexuality" is a socially constructed category; it has no meaning in and of itself. To render it meaningful, we need to specify its components—what the term refers to. We can distinguish between overt, same-sex sexual behavior, the gender of one's sexual desire or most intense arousal, and one's self-identification. As Alfred Kinsey said in his monumental surveys, published in the 1940s and 1950s, these sexual elements may vary with one another. In addition, the term, "lesbian," is typically used to refer to female homosexuals, since "gay" and "homosexual" are most often used to refer to males. And today, the term "queer" is used, with pride, by male homosexuals. It is possible to engage in heterosexual sex, have homosexual desires, and identify as gay; to engage in homosexual sex, have heterosexual desires, and to self-identify as straight; and so on. In addition, *degrees* of overt sex, desires, and identity, each theoretically independent of one another, are possible. The possible combinations are multiple and varied. Today, however, in the United States, most men and women who are sexually aroused by persons of the same sex act on those desires and, eventually, adopt a gay or lesbian identity.

Until June 2003, eleven states of the United States had laws on the books criminalizing "sodomy," which applied equally to homosexual and heterosexual acts; four states had sodomy laws that applied only to homosexual acts; and thirty-five states had by then repealed their sodomy laws. At that date, the Supreme Court of the United States ruled that the Texas sodomy laws were unconstitutional, a decision that repealed these statutes everywhere. This decision, referred to as *Lawrence v. Texas*, overturns a 1986 ruling, *Bowers v. Hardwick*, which affirmed the right of states to criminalize homosexual sodomy. The 2003 Supreme Court decision, say legal scholars and movement spokespersons, represented a "landmark victory for gay rights" (Lane, 2003). Homosexual acts remain a crime in roughly seventy countries worldwide, including most African states, a substantial number of Caribbean and Pacific island nations, Belize, Burma, Guyana, Singapore, and the majority of Muslim Asia. In Iran, the penalty for homosexuality behavior is death. No European country criminalizes homosexuality.

For American society, attitudes, once solidly negative, are changing. In the United States, homosexuality is "departing from deviance" (Minton, 2002). A substantial proportion of Americans still regard homosexuals as deviants and feel that homosexual behavior is abnormal, unnatural, and unacceptable—but that proportion is dwindling. As we just saw and will see in more detail, the segment that is consistent in its strong condemnation of homosexuality is increasingly confined to political conservatives and fundamentalist Christians. This remains a substantial segment of the public, but before long, that sector may become practically the only one that feels and acts this way. Among more well-educated social circles, and in many urban communities, especially in the West and Northeast, it is homophobia that is, and the homophobes who are, regarded as deviant rather than homosexuality and homosexuals.

Public Opinion

Public opinion has become *much* more accepting of homosexuality than was true a generation ago. Today, as compared with twenty or thirty years ago, the public is significantly, and in some cases, strikingly, more likely to believe that homosexual relations should be legal (63% in 2011 versus 43% in 1977); that homosexual relations are "morally acceptable" (54% in 2012 versus 34% in 1982); that homosexuals should have the right to get married on an equal par with heterosexuals (53% in 2011 versus only 27% as recently as 1996). *In many respects*, a majority of Americans no longer regard homosexuality as a seriously deviant form of behavior, or homosexuals as deviants. These public opinion polls suggest that homosexuality is in a transition phase with regard to its deviant status; it is exiting or *transitioning* away from a deviant status through a half-way house between deviance and near-conventionality (see Tables 9.2, 9.3, and 9.4).

One indication that the condemnation of unconventional sexual practices is slowly declining is that younger sections of the population condemn homosexuality less than older sections do. For instance, consider the question, "Do you believe that marriages between same-sex couples should or should not be recognized by the law as valid, with the same rights as traditional

TABLE 9.2   ATTITUDES TOWARD SAME-SEX MARRIAGE

Do you think that marriages between same-sex couples should or should not be recognized by the law as valid, with the same rights as traditional marriages?

	Yes	*No*
1996	27	68
1999	35	62
2004	42	55
2007	46	53
2009	40	57
2010	44	53
2011	53	45

Source: Copyright © Gallup, Inc. All rights reserved. The content is used with permission; however, Gallup retains all right of republication.

TABLE 9.3   ATTITUDES TOWARD HOMOSEXUAL RELATIONS

Do you believe that homosexual relations are:

	Morally Acceptable	*Morally Wrong*
2001	40	53
2002	38	55
2003	44	52
2004	42	54
2005	44	52
2006	44	51
2007	49	47
2008	48	48
2009	49	47
2010	52	43
2011	56	39
2012	54	42

Source: Copyright © Gallup, Inc. All rights reserved. The content is used with permission; however, Gallup retains all right of republication.

marriages?" As we saw, a slight majority of the respondents who were polled agreed, 54 percent. But the 2011 Gallup poll that asked this question also found that the older the respondent, the lower the support for gay marriage: Fully 70 percent of the eighteen to thirty-four-year-olds said that gay marriage should be legal; 53 percent of the thirty-five-year-olds did so; but only 39 percent of those 55 and older agreed. The older segments of the population grew up in an era when homosexuality was condemned, an attitude many or most retain. But as the younger segments of the public grow older, they tend to retain their more tolerant and permissive attitudes, and continue to support a more permissive interpretation of morality. In other words, the view that homosexuality is deviant is in fact dying out; homosexuality, it seems, as I said, is "departing" from deviance. In the

TABLE 9.4   ATTITUDES TOWARD LEGAL STATUS OF HOMOSEXUAL RELATIONS

Do you think gay or lesbian relations between consenting adults should or should not be legal?

	LEGAL	NOT BE LEGAL
1986	32	57
1989	47	36
1998	50	43
2003	60	35
2005	51	45
2007	55	40
2008	56	40
2009	56	40
2010	58	36
2011	64	32
2012	63	31

Source: Copyright © Gallup, Inc. All Rights Reserved. The content is used with permission; however, Gallup retains all rights of republication.

National Opinion Research Center (NORC) poll I cited before, only a quarter of the eighteen- to twenty-nine-year-old respondents (26%) said that homosexuality is "always wrong," an attitude that nearly two-thirds of the respondents who were of age seventy and older agreed with (63%). Moreover, attitudes toward homosexuality are *strongly* related to education. Roughly seven out of ten respondents in the NORC study who did not graduate from high school said that homosexual relations are "always" wrong, but the more educated someone is, the smaller this figure became: Forty-three percent of the sample who were college grads said this, and only 33 percent of the respondents with a postgraduate education did so. Clearly, as American society becomes increasingly educated, its condemnation of homosexuality will almost certainly decrease.

Correlates of Homophobia

"Homophobia" is the hatred of homosexuals. The homophobe is a person who says that homosexuals should be regarded as deviant and treats them as such. Which segments of the population are more likely to be homophobic? Which ones are less so? As we just saw, *age* and *education* are two major factors: The older and the less educated the person, the greater the likelihood that he or she says that homosexuality is wrong and that homosexuals should not have the same rights as heterosexuals. Gregory Herek, poured through the polling data and found that men, Southerners and Midwesterners, rural dwellers, Republicans, frequent churchgoers, the religiously fundamentalist, and political conservatives are more prejudiced against gays; women, people living in the Northeast and on the West Coast, urban residents, Democrats and independents, people who attend religious services infrequently or not at all, and those with a more secular view of religious beliefs, and political liberals and moderates are less homophobic (http://psychology.ucdavis.edu/rainbow/html/prej_corr.html). The Gallup poll, taken in 2011, revealed that in nearly seven out of ten Democrats (69%) support gay marriage but only slightly over a quarter of Republicans (28%) do so.

Two psychologists used polling data from the General Social Survey, conducted by NORC and determined that the most important variable determining whether and to what extent the public condemns homosexuality is the degree to which the respondent held a *general traditional belief system* (Shackleford and Besser, 2007). Someone who is "open to novel experience" ranks low in traditionalism; being open to experience involves being curious, imaginative, and willing to entertain novel ideas and unconventional values. People who are closed to novel experience tend to be conventional in beliefs and attitudes, conservative in tastes, and more dogmatic, rigid in their thinking and beliefs (p. 108). The open-closed dimension is related to age, education, political conservatism, as opposed to liberalism and religious fundamentalism. Persons who are more "closed" tend to be older, more politically conservative, and religiously fundamental, and have lower level of education; those who are more "open" tend to be younger, politically liberal, secular or religiously moderate and ecumenical, and have a higher level of education (p. 108).

Psychotherapeutic Opinion

Until the early 1970s, the majority of psychiatrists and clinical psychologists argued that homosexuality represented a neurosis, illness, or disorder, much like depression or obsessive-compulsive personality, that was caused by an adaptation to an overbearing, too-intimate mother and an absent, weak, or punishing father. Advocates of this position included the most important figures in the field, most notably Edmund Bergler (1899–1962), author of *Homosexuality: Disease or Way of Life?* (1956), Irving Bieber (1909–1991), coauthor of *Homosexuality: A Psychoanalytic Study of Male Homosexuals* (1962), Lionel Ovesey (1915–1995), who wrote *Homosexuality and Pseudohomosexuality* (1969), and Charles Socarides (1922–2005), author of *The Overt Homosexual* (1968). These therapists claimed that they could "cure" or treat this neurosis. The case of Socarides was especially ironic, since Richard, Socarides' oldest son (b. 1954), a lawyer, is not only openly gay but he has held important positions in the Clinton administration, including special assistant to the president and senior advisor for public liaison on gay and lesbian civil rights issues (Bull, 1999).

In 1973, the membership of the American Psychiatric Association voted to remove homosexuality from the *Diagnostic and Statistical Manual of Mental Disorders*—a close vote and controversial position at the time, but it represented the tocsin of changes to come. By the 1980s and 1990s, the "pathology" theory of homosexuality, once dominant, had become discredited. It is accepted by very few practicing clinicians today; those who do are older and they are dying out. In 2005, in an obituary, Gilbert Herdt, a sex researcher, wrote that the pathology theory that Socarides advocated "went from being the reigning paradigm to being considered eccentric" (January 2, 2006, *The Washington Post*). The collapse of the "pathology" orientation toward homosexuality was swift, spectacular, and, for its adherents, humiliating.

Conservative, Evangelical, and Fundamentalist Christians

Who are the "holdouts," those segments of American society who continue to regard homosexuality as deviant? One such segment is, as we might expect, conservative Christianity, both among the clergy and the laity. Contemplating the election of Bishop Robinson, Richard Land, head of the Southern Baptist Convention's Ethics and Religious Liberty Commission, stated: "Homosexual behavior is deviant behavior according to the clear and consistent teaching of Scripture, from the Book of Genesis to the end of the New Testament." Bishop Robinson's election is, he said, "the antithesis of Scripture" (Broadway, 2003, p. B8). Adopting a vastly more extreme position, Jim Rudd, writing in the June 7, 2006, issue of *The Covenant News*, a publication of Liberty University, proclaimed, "Put homosexuals to the sword." "Homosexuality is a crime," he asserts in the December 9, 2008, issue. Christianity has moved from monolithic opposition to homosexuality to a reluctant acceptance, with pockets of resistance among evangelical and fundamentalist wings. It is likely to be decades before its more conservative wing accepts gay sex, and it is even possible that such a change will never take place. Their current position is occupied by a mixture of critics who proclaim that homosexuality can be "cured," to those who believe it is a demonic "curse" to the extreme of execution and isolation. Pat Robertson, presumably a more moderate spokesperson for conservative Christianity, stated on his program on March 27, 2012, of the Christian Broadcasting Network that gays were under the spell of a "demonic possession." After hearing a man's story about picking men up off the street and having sex with them, Robertson replied: "The world says, 'OK, so you are gay, you want to have affairs with men—that's cool. You have an absolute right to do that, why not?' That's not the right attitude. The [right] attitude is that this is sin. It's wrong. And [this man] realized it was wrong but couldn't control it. But that kind of conduct is wrong. . . . [He] is obsessed. I would think that it is somehow related to demonic possession."

"I figured out a way of getting of all the lesbians and queers, but it couldn't get past the Congress," says Pastor Charles Worsley of the Providence Road Baptist Church in Maiden, NC, in a sermon delivered on May 13, 2012. "Build a great large fence 50 or a hundred miles long. Put all the lesbians in there. Fly over and drop some food. Do the same thing with the queers and homosexuals. And have that fence electrified till they can't get out. And you know what? In a few years they'll die out. You know why? They can't reproduce. . . . God have mercy! It makes me pukin' sick to think about. . . . I don't even know whether you ought to say this in the pulpit or not. Can you imagine kissin' some man? [Long pause.] Our president gettin' up and sayin' it's all right for two women to marry and two men to marry. I'll tell you right now, I was disappointed bad. The Bible's agin' it, I'm agin' it. And if you've got any sense, *you're* agin' it."

Fundamentalist Christians and political conservatives point to the Bible to justify their opposition to homosexuality. As we saw, Leviticus clearly states that homosexual behavior is an "abomination." "It's God's judgment, not just mine!" these opponents of homosexuality will state. But this conveniently omits the fact that the Bible also permitted and condoned slavery, patriarchy, and polygamy. Moreover, the Bible calls for the death penalty for a number of taboos besides engaging in homosexual relations—adultery, engaging in sex with an animal, cursing and hitting one's father and mother, and working on the Sabbath. The Scriptures commanded the ancient Israelites to "annihilate"

the non-monotheistic peoples—the Hittites, the Ammonites, the Canaanites, and the Jebusites—who lived in their region. Today, hardly any fundamentalist Christian supports capital punishment for such practices. Homosexuals feel that strict Bible Christians cherry-pick certain injunctions while pretending that others don't exist. They wonder why fundamentalist Christians consider homosexuality an abomination while they tolerate or ignore so many other actions that the Bible sternly and savagely condemns.

Is Homosexuality Departing from Deviance? A Summary

In many respects, homosexuality is "departing from deviance" (Minton, 2002). Gay couples are, increasingly, permitted to adopt children (Brody, 2003); the media are depicting homosexuals in a more realistic, less negative light; three-quarters of gays and bisexuals feel more accepted by society today than a few years ago; an increasing percentage of Christians, both clergy and laity, believe that homosexuals should be accepted on an equal basis; sodomy laws outlawing homosexual acts have been struck down as unconstitutional; the majority of psychiatrists and psychologists no longer believe that, in and of itself, homosexuality is the manifestation of a mental disorder; gay marriage is legal in Canada, and marriage-like "civil unions" between two persons of the same sex are legal in several states of the United States; today, heterosexuals are vastly more accepting of homosexuality than was true even a decade ago; and in society's more traditional sectors and institutions, monolithic opposition to homosexuality has given way to conflict, dissension, and schisms. In short, the deviant status of homosexuality is eroding. "The war for acceptance" of gays, says a *New York* magazine writer, "is practically won" (Green, 2001, p. 27). Although, as we saw, in some sectors of the society, homosexuality is still seen as an "abomination," those sectors are shrinking, and this position is becoming, increasingly, a minority view, much like belief in creationism, masculine dominance, and uncompromising opposition to abortion. In other words, if we look at deviance in *horizontal* terms, we will still be able to find categories in the population—political conservatives and strict Bible Christians—who retain the view that homosexuality is immoral, a sin, and hence, deviant. At the same time, in the past two decades, public opinion toward homosexuality moved from a majority opposed to a majority believing it is morally acceptable, should be legal, and should be sanctioned by marriage. It is entirely likely that within a generation, for the society as a whole, homosexuality's deviant status will shrink to the point where it will no longer be a form of *societal* deviance. At which time, homosexuality will no longer be discussed by sociologists as a form of deviance, except as a historical artifact.

ADULTERY

According to traditional Jewish and Christian beliefs, Moses received the Ten Commandments directly from God. Among them, the seventh is: "Thou shalt not commit adultery." Like the other proscriptions, it forbids an action that is tempting to many and hence frequently engaged in, and deviant as well. In fact, *because* it is so tempting—and because of its potentially harmful consequences—it *had to be* prohibited. In the absence of the prohibition, adultery would be far more commonplace than it is. In the Old Testament, adultery—having sex with someone other than one's marital spouse—was a capital offense. The prohibition was principally aimed at the wife, and the reason is clear. Linguistically, the term described the contamination, pollution, or "adulteration" of the bloodline that could result when a married woman engaged in extramarital sex and hence, risked having a child that was not her husband's. In short, the original laws condemning and punishing adultery were concerned about *property* and *inheritance* (Nicholas, 2011).

Laws criminalizing extramarital sex remain on the books in twenty-four states. Today, the likelihood of an offender being arrested and serving a jail or prison term is zero, but it is a useful tool for divorce lawyers and in child custody cases. Few politicians are willing to risk their careers crusading for the decriminalization of adultery;

most Americans believe that the law spells out an idea by serving as a reminder to us that marriage is sacred and that adultery corrupts the very foundation of the society. To many of us, wiping the adultery laws off the books sends a message that cheating on one's spouse is acceptable (Bronner, 2012).

"It used to be, I'd get in the shower and my wife would come in there, too, impulsive and sexy and all," says Anthony. Not long ago, he snuck up on her in the shower. "What are you doing?" she asked. "Grow up. The kids will hear us." Anthony and his wife no longer have sex. He has had three extramarital liaisons; they only take place on business trips, far from home. "I've cheated because I just wanted to have sex and that was something my wife and I weren't doing. . . . And if what I did was away from home it doesn't count" (Konigsberg, 1998).

We already know a thing or two about the deviance of adultery.

One: Most Americans disapprove of it. In the "Sex in America" survey, as we saw, three-quarters of the sample (77%) agreed with the statement, "Extramarital sex is always wrong." This condemnation is even more widespread than that of teenage sex and same-gender sex. The same finding turned up in a comparable survey conducted in Great Britain (Johnson et al., 1994, pp. 238–240, 471). The General Social Survey conducted in 2010 found that 75 percent of respondents said that extramarital sex is always wrong; respondents with a graduate education were *less* accepting of adultery over time, whereas the reverse is true of homosexuality. Interestingly enough however, given how widespread the condemnation of marital infidelity is, the strength of this condemnation is rather muted and qualified. In a recent national poll, only a third of the population (35%) said that adultery should be a crime (Goldberg, 1997). Laws left over from Puritan times still remain on the books in two dozen states, and in several (Illinois, Minnesota, and New Hampshire), conservatives opposed repealing them (Turley, 2010). A majority of the American population opposed the impeachment of President Bill Clinton (in office 1993–2001), an event that was launched by his lies, under oath, about an extramarital liaison with a White House intern. Clinton was impeached—voted to be removed from office—by the House of Representatives in December 1998 but acquitted by the Senate in February 1999. In spite of his affair and his lies about it, Clinton left the White House, in 2001, with a 65 percent approval rating. In a *Newsweek* poll, only a third of the sample (35%) considered the adultery of a political candidate a sufficient reason to vote for someone else (Adler, 1996).

Two: In every Western society in which a nationally representative survey has been conducted—France, the United Kingdom, Finland, and the United States—the majority of married respondents said that they were faithful to their spouses for the entire length of their marriages. In the United States, only a quarter of the men (25%) and a bit more than one-seventh of the women (15%) in intact marriages said that they had ever had even one "extramarital affair" (Laumann et al., 1994, p. 216). If this survey is valid, it is clear that adultery is far less common than most of us imagine.

Three (and related to point two): As we just saw, men are significantly more likely to engage in extramarital sex than women. However, the gap may be closing: Among the *oldest* respondents (age 54 to 63) in the "Sex in America" survey, the male-to-female infidelity gap was three to one (37% versus 12%), whereas among the *youngest*, the gap was much smaller—12 percent versus 7 percent (Adler, 1996, p. 60).

And *four*: In most of the societies of the world, a double standard exists; women are more likely to be condemned for adulterous sex than men are. As we saw, it is extremely common for societies around the world to completely tolerate (43% of all societies studied did so) or at least condone (22%) extramarital sex for the man but condemn the same behavior for the woman (Broude and Greene, 1976, pp. 415–416). Some feminist observers have argued that the reverse is becoming true: "When men cheat, they're pigs. When women do it, they're striking a blow for sexual freedom" (Roiphe, 1997, p. 54).

The motives for extramarital sex are many and varied (Hunt, 1971; Wolfe, 1976; Atwater, 1982; Lawson, 1988). The simplest reason for men and women straying from the marital bed is a response to a failing marriage. This is indicated by the fact that couples in marriages, which end in divorce are vastly more likely to have adulterous sex than those in intact marriages. In this case, extramarital sex may be both cause and consequence of marital instability. At the same time, it is clear that a substantial number of stably married men and women (though not, as we saw, a majority) have intercourse with partners other than their spouses. Why? Why risk getting into trouble, being defined as a deviant, disrupting a marriage that is more or less satisfying?

Evolutionary psychologists think they have found the answer. The key, they say, can be located in the tendency of organisms, humans included, to act in such a way that they maximize the transmission of their genes to later generations. And one way of understanding this process, they claim, is the differences between males and females in responses to questions about what would be most upsetting about the infidelity of their spouse or partner. "What would distress you more," these researchers ask respondents, "discovering that he or she has formed a deep emotional attachment" to another person, or discovering that your spouse or partner "is enjoying daily passionate sex with the other person"? As it turns out, women are much more likely to be distressed by the emotional involvement of their partner, while men become more upset at their partner's sexual infidelity. Evolutionary psychologist David Buss has asked this question to samples of respondents in Germany, the Netherlands, and the United States; the differences are, says Buss, "quite solid."

The reason for the findings? This "jealousy gender gap" is encoded in our genes, says Buss and his colleagues (1994, pp. 125–131). Think back to the early ancestors of humans, these researchers argue. Since men could never be certain of the paternity of their children, they are most threatened by their partner having sex with another man; if their partner becomes pregnant by him, they will thereby end up being tricked into supporting offspring who are not biologically their own. Moreover, when the male's partner is pregnant with another man's child, he is thereby prevented from impregnating her himself. What heightens a man's chances of ensuring the survival of his genes is a faithful wife. It is the winners in this competition to keep their female partners faithful who are our ancestors, evolutionary psychologists claim.

The female has a different task, they argue. If a woman's partner strays, the sexual aspect of the encounter could be over in minutes, or even seconds, and that may very well be the end of it. No threat to the long-term relationship is implied by such a liaison. But if he were to become emotionally involved with another female, he might abandon his long-term mate and thus threaten her likelihood of survival and that of her children as well—and therefore, the survival of her genetic material. In short, women are "evolutionarily programmed to become more distressed at emotional infidelity than sexual infidelity" (Begley, 1996/1997, p. 58).

Not all observers agree that jealousy is genetically encoded. Enormous variation exists from one society to another with respect to how jealous its members are at the infidelity of their partners. The male–female gap predicted by the evolutionary biologists is found everywhere, it is true, but the size of the difference varies considerably. In the United States, three times as many men as women are upset at their partner's sexual faithlessness versus their emotional infidelity; in Germany, the gap is only 50 percent. Moreover, while the *relative* differences between men and woman support the theory, the absolute *size* of the percentages runs counter to it. Evolutionary biologists predict that more men would care about sexual than emotional fidelity, in fact, *most* men are *not* disturbed more by sexual than emotional infidelity, which is totally contrary to the theory (p. 58).

What triggers sexual jealousy, many observers argue, is how members of each sexual category picture the connection their partner has in his or her mind between sex and love. Men's conception of female sex has it that her sexual infidelity implies emotional infidelity as well. In other words, if she has sex with another man, he assumes, that pretty much means that she loves him, too. In addition, some women can be in love with another man but not have sex with him. Hence, the man loses twice when his partner is sexually unfaithful, a more threatening situation

than simple emotional infidelity, which may imply nothing beyond that. In contrast, women are aware of the fact that their male partner can have sex with another woman without loving her. But when a man forms a romantic or loving attachment to another woman, it is much more likely to be a serious threat to his relationship with the first woman.

Our awareness of what sex and sex roles *mean* to our partners determines the differences researchers observe. The jealousy gender gap, critics of evolutionary psychology argue, is the result of a cultural, intellectual, and to some degree "rational" process, not the nagging and largely unconscious demands of our genes. Regardless of which explanation is correct, marital infidelity is not likely to be accepted any time soon. It remains a major form of sexual deviance.

GENDER: THE CRUCIAL INGREDIENT

Understanding sexual behavior demands that the observer and analyst have a firm grasp on gender. "Heterosexuality," writes Diane Richardson, "is a category divided by gender" (1996, p. 2). The same applies to homosexuality; gay males and lesbians are not merely homosexuals but also—it seems almost obvious to say this—men and women. With regard to sexual behavior, a "gender disparity" looms between men and women. Male sexual behavior "is less subject to social strictures than female sexual activity" (Weitzer, 2000, p. 7). For instance, evaluations of sexual behavior vary according to the sex or gender of the actor. Thus, a sexually active teenage girl is condemned more strongly than a teenage boy; an adulterous wife is condemned more harshly than an adulterous husband. Hence, the very foundation of deviance—that is, stigma or condemnation—is dependent on who is being stigmatized or condemned which, in turn, is based on the sex or gender of the enactor. The problem of teenage sex, pregnancy, and subsequent out-of-wedlock births is widely regarded as a problem almost exclusively for the behavior of girls. The sexual behavior of boys is considered natural, understandable, inevitable, and beyond society's control. When the authorities attempt to "control" teenage sex, it is specifically the sexual behavior of teenage girls that is the target of such control. Even more specifically, "female sex workers are [regarded as] quintessential *deviant women*, whereas [their] customers are seen as essentially *normal men*" (Weitzer, 2000, p. 7). Condemnation for participating in sexual deviance is much stronger for women than for men. (Of course, most of the time, for women, the behavior is more central: it is a full-time paying job; whereas for men, it is little more than a part-time recreation.) The stigma of having to pay for sex is vastly less than the stigma of being paid. "The very terminology used [for women]—whore, hooker, harlot, slut—is heavily laden with opprobrium." By contrast, the terms used for male customers are "fairly tame labels." In short: "You may be a bit surprised to learn that a male friend has visited a prostitute, but shocked to learn that a female friend *is* a prostitute" (p. 7). The same applies to a one-time experience.

An experiment conducted by Russell Clark and Elaine Hatfield, two social psychologists, indicates that men are much more likely to take up sexual offers from female strangers than women are to do so with male strangers; in fact, the authors suggest, women *hardly ever* take men up on such offers, whereas men often, even *usually*, do (Clark and Hatfield, 1989; Clark, 1990). Sexual behavior generally and sexual deviance more specifically are expressions or manifestations of the roles of men and women. Sex as behavior cannot be understood independent of sex as a role. In short, sex is "gendered," and our understanding of sex, sexual deviance included, must incorporate gender as its foundation. It is naïve to assume that a given sexual encounter between a man and a woman means the same thing to the two participants, has the same consequences, or is interpreted by members of the society in the same fashion. While men and women act and interact together, in a way they inhabit social worlds that are in large measure separate and distinct. Gendering must always inform our view of sexual deviance. Sexual non-normativeness is usually more deviant when engaged in by women than

by men; women are expected to conform more closely to sex and gender roles than men, and their transgressions are typically noticed and condemned by men (Schur, 1984).

When the paper reporting a study concluding that men are more likely to accept invitations to engage in adventurous, risky sex than women—documenting what may be the most important and significant difference between men and women—was first circulated for consideration for publication to academic journals, it attracted a great deal of hostility among researchers. One reviewer's evaluation branded the "nature and situations" of the study as "comical" and "hilarious," its propositions "incredibly naïve," its conclusions likewise "naïve." It should, said one reviewer, "be rejected without possibility of being submitted to any scholarly journal." The study itself, "lacks redeeming social value," said another reviewer. It "is too weird, trivial and frivolous to be interesting. Who cares what the result is to such a silly question"? (Clark and Hatfield, 1989, pp. 229, 230). The paper, rejected by numerous journals, sat on the shelf for four years before it was sent to *Journal of Psychology and Human Sexuality*. "Times have changed," say the authors. "Today, most scientists recognize the importance of scientific knowledge about topics that were once considered taboo—love, emotions, sexual desire, sexual behavior" (p. 230). Clark and Hatfield experienced a transition that Kinsey never went through: Research on sexual behavior, once itself a deviant activity, had become important and scientifically respectable.

SUMMARY

The essentialist sees sex as a drive that exists to some degree independent of and prior to social context or definition. In contrast, the constructionist position argues two points. One, sex is *constructed* by the society and social contact through the *imputation of meaning*. And two, the sex drive itself is, in large part, a *product* of human contact. Constructionists argue that social dynamics are lurking behind all things sexual; sexuality is *in the service of* the social world. Sexuality does not shape our social conduct so much as social meanings *give shape to* our sexuality. We are sexual *because* we are social; it is social life that *creates, motivates, and shapes* our sexuality (Gagnon and Simon, 2005).

The construction process applies not only to infusing phenomena and behavior specifically with *sexual* meaning, but also to filling the content of "sexual" definitions with a certain type of evaluation—positive, negative, or neutral, "normal" or "abnormal," conventional or deviant. How deviance is socially constructed is central to any understanding of sexual behavior. It is likely that sexual deviance is more likely to be regarded as "sick," abnormal, and pathological than any other type of deviance. A central feature in the psychiatrist's and the psychologist's conception of sexual deviance is *dysfunction* or *disorder*—an undesirable condition in need of treating or curing. However, the notions of dysfunction and disorder are alien to the sociologist's, particularly the constructionist's, notion of sexual deviance. Sociologically, what defines sexual deviance, as with all other varieties of deviance, is that it is a violation of societal norms and *likely to result in the condemnation of the actor*. No implication of dysfunction or disorder whatsoever is implied. Hence, the sociological conception of sexual deviance overlaps extremely imperfectly with the psychological conceptions.

A variety of dimensions determine judgments of deviance with respect to behavior in the sexual arena. Several include degree of consent, who (or what) the sexual object or partner is, specifically what behavior is engaged in, where it takes place, who engages in the sex act, how often, when, with how many partners, and so on. These dimensions proscribe or render deviant a substantial number of sexual acts. How does the sociologist of deviance decide which ones should be studied? How strongly a given behavior is condemned (some acts are not deviant enough to be considered "deviant behavior"), how frequently it is enacted (some acts are too rare, too unusual), whether it makes up a category that is well known enough to be a form of deviance in the public's mind (some acts are not conceptualized as a deviant category,

and some are too obscure to be thought about or condemned), and whether it generates a social structure (some acts are enacted by scattered, isolated individuals), will all influence the sociologist of deviance's decision.

In Western society, homosexuality is decreasingly regarded as a form of sexual deviance. Over time, a decreasing proportion of the American population believes that homosexual relations should be against the law, the media are increasingly depicting gays in a non-demeaning, non-stereotypical fashion, a growing number of Christian denominations are accepting gays both as members and as clergy, the sodomy laws have been struck down as unconstitutional, Canada has legalized gay marriage and in a growing number of jurisdictions, "civil unions," which grant partners the same rights as married couples, have been legalized. Albeit with important exceptions, increasingly, homosexuality is "departing from deviance." Still, fundamentalist and evangelical Christians condemn homosexuality more than seculars, non-Orthodox Jews, and ecumenical Christians.

Sexual jealousy is a powerful emotion in our society. Extramarital sex is widely condemned yet far more rarely practiced than most of us believe. Men and women differ in their response to their partner's infidelity. Women are more likely to be distressed by their partner's emotional faithlessness, while men are more likely to become upset about their partner's sexual infidelity. Evolutionary psychologists believe that these responses are dictated by messages encoded in the genes; social psychologists argue that it is a result of reasonable inferences about the meaning of sex roles in our society.

Sexuality is "gendered." By that, sociologists mean that it is impossible to understand sexuality of any kind apart from men's and women's gender roles. Everything that we do sexually is informed or saturated by our maleness or femaleness. What are seemingly the same acts mean very different things if performed by men versus by women—both to the participants and to the society at large. We cannot understand sexual behavior without simultaneously considering who we are as males and females.

Account: Prostitution

The following is an account, narrated by an anonymous acquaintance, of the life of Sue, a white female living in a lower-middle-class neighborhood in a suburb of a large Eastern city. The interviewer writes: "I took notes during our interview. I was aware of most of what Sue told me, so much so that I could have recited much of it myself. I was present during many of her escapades, and as for the others, she had already told me about them. It is unfortunate that our relationship has deteriorated due to her life's difficult circumstances. Still, I'm glad she agreed to do the interview. I sincerely hope that she gets the help she needs to stop drinking and goes on to live a long and prosperous and happy life."

We were considered the crazy family in the neighborhood. My father was always in the bars drinking, and I had a reputation for being promiscuous. Two of my brothers were heavy drinkers as well. They would hang out all night in the local bars and get into fights and as a result, they'd be arrested. They also became regular users of marijuana and cocaine. My family's behavior was very visible in our community and so our neighbors would not speak to us. If we ran into them at local store, they would pretend we weren't there. We also had a reputation for being bad and tough, so no one messed with us.

When I was 17, I became friendly with a girl I'll call Donna. She introduced me to another friend, Silky, who smoked marijuana. Silky ran with a crowd of marijuana-smoking friends whose homes we'd go to and hang out with. We'd watch TV, veg out, talk, laugh, and smoke pot. One day, Donna asked me to meet her at work and talk to her boss; maybe I could get a job there, she said. A woman greeted me at the door and explained that Donna was with a customer and that she'd be out soon. Two women were sitting on the couch in the waiting room, watching TV. They were dressed provocatively and were wearing a lot of makeup. I suspected they were put off by my presence. I was young, attractive, blonde, and had blue eyes. Men were crazy about me, and I'd sleep with just about any man who asked. Most of the time I was drunk and often, I'd wake up the next morning in a stranger's bed. I'd go out drinking in a bar, bring home a man I just met, and have sex with him.

When Donna came out, she and the woman she worked for, who was the madam, explained to me that if I had sex with men, I could make $300 a day. I said, I don't know, it sounds kind of disgusting to me. I had just seen Donna walk out of a room with a man in his fifties, and he wasn't even that attractive. They explained that it was easy, you just close your eyes and pretend you're someplace else, and before you know it, they're done. Most of the tricks are so excited to be with a working woman that they came very fast—and they're only allowed to come once.

What finally convinced me to agree to work there was two things that Donna told me: One, that I could earn enough money to buy my own place, and two, that I already sleep with a lot of men for nothing—why not get paid for doing something I'm already doing? A week later, when I told Donna that I had decided to work with her, she told me that she didn't like working there any longer, she had located an escort service that was a lot better. She only has to talk to the woman who runs the service once a week, whereas the madam she worked for before was bossy, always telling her what to do, which she didn't like. This sounded fine with me; she seemed to know what she was doing, so I followed her lead without question.

Donna explained that a driver will pick us up and drive us to our calls. When customers call the agency, a woman calls the phone girl, explains what type of girls are working that night—what we look like, our measurements, and any other necessary information. If the customer wants to see one of us, the phone girl calls the driver, he gets the address of the customer. He then tells us which one of us the call is for. Sometimes he asks which one of us wants to do it, and maybe he'll tell us a little about the guy, if he's a regular, or what kind of sex he's into. This particular piece of information is very useful because one of us might not be interested in performing the kind of sex

(Continued)

Account: Prostitution   Continued

he wants. For instance, he may be into anal sex, which a lot of the girls don't want to perform, although some will, for extra money.

My first night was a slow night. We drove around drinking beer. The driver asked if we'd like to go to his place and do some coke. I had never done it before but I was game for anything. He said that if we get called, we can just leave from there. When we got to his place, I took off my high-heeled shoes, which were killing my feet. I wasn't dressed like a street prostitute—more like a Wall Street business woman than a call girl. The agency wouldn't allow us to dress too provocatively, so I wore a skirt and a blouse. Our customers were respectable-looking men and we had to look inconspicuous. So if a customer's neighbor saw us going to his home, he could say we were a friend of his—it wouldn't be obvious that he was seeing a prostitute.

Donna and I made ourselves comfortable at the driver's house. We lay down on his king-sized bed and turned on the TV. He brought in a mirror and some powder cocaine. He poured about a gram of coke on the mirror, took out a razor blade, and chopped the coke into long, thin lines. He rolled up a dollar bill and snorted a line really fast up his nose, then handed the bill to me. I began snorting a line, but the driver told me I was doing it wrong; I was snorting it too slowly. You have to do it fast to get a really good high. I did it again, and it was strong. Every time I snorted it, I jumped back a little. We spent an hour snorting up the coke, and I got really stoned. It felt great, I was talking a lot, I had a lot of energy, and I was ready to face anything. I said, Bring on the customers—I can handle all of them!

Before long, we got a call. They decided to give the job to me. It was a new customer, but they assured me that they had checked him out. I later found out that the only checking they did was to locate the customer's name in a phone book and call him to make sure he's not a cop. We had to drive 45 minutes to get to this guy's place, which they usually don't do. This guy didn't seem to mind paying extra, which meant that he probably had plenty

of cash. Normally, the driver would take Donna to another call, but since we drove so far to get there, that wasn't possible, so she had to wait in the car. I was a little nervous going in, but fortunately, my first customer was a handsome young man. We began having sex, and he was so gentle and clean that I felt really comfortable. He was really nice, he was the type of guy, outside of my work, I would date in a second. He wasn't weird at all—he just wanted straight sex. When we were finished, I began leaving, not realizing that I had forgotten the money. As I was going out the door, he stopped me. "Wait—you forgot this," he said, and handed me the money, plus a hundred dollar tip. I told him it was a pleasure and he didn't have to tip me. I actually tried to hand back the hundred, but he insisted so I took it.

When I got into the car Donna and the driver told me I was a few minutes over the hour, which isn't good in this business. Then both of them asked me how it went. I told them it was great—it was so great, I raved, that I didn't even want the money. They reminded me that I was in this business for the money; if I just wanted to get laid, I could do it on my own time. Not every call is going to be like this one, they reminded me; this business is about making money—nothing else. I had deluded myself that I could have a relationship with this guy. Boy, was I naïve! I later found out that this guy was married, and he requests a different girl from the agency each time—he likes a variety of women, and that's why he's doing it.

I continued in this profession for a number of years. I became more knowledgeable about the work, and I made a lot of money. I got an apartment with Donna. We rented a really nice two-bedroom duplex apartment. The rent was high, but we could definitely afford it. We continued to work for the escort service and drank a lot of alcohol and used marijuana and cocaine on a regular basis. We even tried a variety of different drugs—mescaline, hash, acid, angel dust (PCP), and Quaaludes. Our families and friends didn't know anything about our lifestyle, though many must have suspected something. After all, we slept all day and were out all night.

Sometimes the customer wants to be with the girl for more than an hour. Once, I stayed with a customer for five hours. The customer took his time and performed oral sex on me. He asked me if he was doing a good job, and so I'd have to fake orgasms to show him that he was. As I got more professional, I realized that if a customer has a lot of money and wants to keep me for hours, why give the agency half? I got my own phone just for professional purposes, and if the customer wanted to see me, he'd call me, we'd meet at a hotel, and the money would be all mine.

Once, Donna and I were with a customer for nine hours. He paid each of us $100 an hour. He was a coke fiend, and we were doing coke with him. He was the most deviant trick I've ever been with. He wanted to watch us perform oral sex on each other while he masturbated. We weren't bisexual, so we had to fake it. We did this until seven in the morning; he wanted us to keep on doing this, but we had had enough. We told him we'd do it another time, and left. It was an easy call because the guy was doing coke the whole time and couldn't get it up, and we made 900 bucks each. Most coke calls don't involve a lot of sex.

One night Donna and I were in our new apartment, sitting on the couch talking. We had just gotten home from work. At four in the morning, we heard a knock on the door. We had just moved in and were scared, we didn't know anybody, so we started screaming. Then we heard a voice saying, "It's the guy from downstairs. Do you want to come down and smoke a joint?" Donna didn't trust the guy, but I agreed to go and told him I'll be right down. This guy turned out to be my future husband.

We were married a year later, and technically we still are. We began having sex four or five times a day. He was a pothead and I was a drinker. I drank at least two six-packs a day. Actually, I drank anything I could get my hands on. I've always been so wild that no one attributed my strange behavior to the alcohol alone. It's difficult for me to admit this now, but calling up all these memories is really upsetting for me. It makes me realize I've made a lot of mistakes in my life.

Donna met a trick at work. He was married and a multimillion-dollar businessman. He fell in love with her, and she never had to work again. She stopped working for the agency and she'd meet him in hotels. He paid her $200 an hour for straight sex and he'd stay with her for hours. This guy was crazy about her. He bought her all kinds of expensive jewelry—diamonds, rubies, and plenty of gold. She had a boyfriend who didn't know about this relationship, but he was suspicious. He used to come over to her apartment and they would get into fights, and sometimes he'd hit her. At some point, it was about all I could take, so I told her either he leaves or I move out. Eventually, I moved downstairs to my future husband's apartment, and Donna's boyfriend moved in with her.

My boyfriend and I got married. We got along great until I started going out and hanging out in bars and coming home drunk all the time. Though he stayed home nights, I always thought he was cheating on me. He told me he never cheated on me, that I just invented that for getting into fights then using that as an excuse for going out to bars and getting drunk. In essence, he became my father. I had so much anger toward him. I never really trusted any man, and to this day I think all men are scum. My drinking became so bad, I had blackouts. I'd go out, get drunk, go to some guy's home, or different guys, sleep with them, and stumble home the next day. This went on for some time until my husband and I went into therapy, and I began going to AA meetings. For a while we began getting along better, and we had a daughter as a result of our new-found happiness. Our daughter was very colicky, and I suffered from postpartum depression. Often, my husband had to stay up all night taking care of our daughter. He almost lost his job because of this.

Our life was no bed of roses. We fought, I was raped by several men, I was chronically depressed, I was accused by child services of being a neglectful mother, my husband and I separated, we had a custody battle over our daughter, I entered a rehab center, and I continued with my abusive drinking; several times, I tried to commit suicide. My brother died of AIDS. My father died of a heart condition. My husband got custody of our daughter. Eventually, I want to get my daughter back—I got my

(Continued)

Account: Prostitution   Continued

tubes tied after becoming pregnant by a trick, and I had an abortion. I have supervised visitations with my daughter, with my mother there—she's even more unstable than I am. I'm trying really hard to get my life straightened out. I go to AA meetings, though I fall off the wagon from time to time. What can I say? My life is difficult and I have to drink to get through it.

QUESTIONS

Why did Sue become a prostitute? Does her explanation make sense to you? Was her transition from promiscuity to prostitution convincing? As we saw in Chapter 2, criminologists Michael Gottfredson and Travis Hirschi argue that the commission of deviance is generic and generalizable—that is, people who engage in one type of illegal, illicit, self-interested activity are more likely to engage in others. Sue engaged in promiscuous sex; she moved on to prostitution; she was an alcoholic; she used illicit drugs; she was chronically depressed; she attempted suicide; she was a neglectful mother and the court removed her daughter from her custody; she was the *victim* of violent crimes against her. Her life was an unremitting march of misery from her childhood to the present. Do you think Gottfredson and Hirschi's argument makes sense? Or is another process at work here? Is it possible that genetic or physiological processes cause Sue's deviance, or her clinical depression? Or did the labeling process, or abuse she may have suffered as a child make her into what she became? Does Sue's case arouse the sociologist in you—do you search for sociological causes and consequences, labeling and constructionist processes at work, the biases of the court system, dynamics of stigmatization, all the factors and variables we've looked at so far? Do you feel compassion or empathy for Sue? Or do you feel that "she made her own bed, now she has to lie in it"? How would most of the public regard Sue's life and activities?

Unconventional Beliefs

Learning Objectives:

After reading this chapter, you will be able to:

- discuss the social functions of belief systems;
- identify religious sects and cults;

- contrast creationism and intelligent design with evolution;
- answer the question, "what makes paranormal beliefs a form of cognitive deviance?"

The most commonly discussed instances of deviance discussed in textbooks are behavioral, but holding and expressing deviant *beliefs* can get the individual in trouble as readily as engaging in what is considered unacceptable or wrongful acts. Hence, what's referred to as "cognitive deviance" is as important as unconventional behavior that manifests itself in actual behavior (Perrin, 2007). Not all expressions of belief lead to specific actions; even the mere *expression* of those beliefs is likely to result in negative reactions from audiences. Is atheism deviant? Indeed it is! In the United States, year after year, polls indicate that 80 to 90 percent of the population believes in God. A substantial proportion of theists feel that someone who doesn't believe in God is not a moral person and "might not be fully trustworthy," hence, might vote for a self-admitted atheistic political candidate, for instance, for president. But there is good news and bad news for our nonbelieving presidential aspirant. Interestingly enough, according to a Gallup poll taken in July, 2012, 54 percent of the U.S. public said that they *would* vote for a self-proclaimed atheist presidential candidate; 43 percent said that they would not. In 1958, only 18 percent proclaimed that they would vote for an unbeliever—an enormous change in more than a half century. Times have changed, true, and the chances of success for an atheist politician are looking up. But consider the matter the other way around: If you're a political candidate and you give up on nearly half of your potential voters, you'll never get elected. And among all the categories the poll asked about, respondents were *least* supportive of the atheist; Muslims received 58 percent positive responses, and gays and lesbians, 68 percent. Democrats were more supportive of atheist politicians (58%) than the Republicans were (48%), and the young respondents aged eighteen to twenty-nine (70%) more than the older ones, aged sixty-five and over (40%). As much as atheism has stuck a toe in the water of the mainstream, many segments of American society—evangelical Christians and Orthodox Jews—still don't trust the unbeliever. And, more generally, beliefs and notions of right and wrong, and what ideas are right and wrong, vary by social category and historical time period. And political ideas make up a major constellation of our belief system. The fact is, in the United States, among the more conventional voters, a professed atheist has virtually no chance of winning a presidential election and, other things being equal, atheism has very little moral traction with believers.

Cognitive deviance often reveals cultural differences so vast that, when revealed and reactions play themselves out, people on one side of a divide denounce those on the other, and may even kill them; relations between and among nations, based partly on clashes in belief systems, are stretched to the breaking point; international trade is terminated and millions of dollars of revenue lost to one or the other side of the dispute; major institutions are undermined; and riots break out in the street, angry crowds smash windows, burn buildings, and hang figures in effigy. Such unbridgeable differences between contending parties speak eloquently of the relativity of deviance, of cultural and subcultural *definitions* of deviance, of clashing norms about what views can and cannot be expressed, and what the appropriate reaction is when norms are violated. Cognitive or "intellectual" deviance often generates enormous hostility and punitive official reaction, and the exercise of power, or the manifestation of powerless, on one side or the other. But remember, as I've emphasized throughout, what is regarded as deviant in one collectivity may be repugnant to the members of another.

A striking example of *mutual deviantization* or mutual vilification may be seen on the Internet under the category "deviant beliefs." Googling that phrase in 2012 reveals that, in enormous profusion, leaders and followers of one branch or wing of Islam post denunciations of the tenets of another, insisting that their rivals and enemies are intellectually, cognitively, and spiritually misguided, with each side purporting to affirm the "true" expression of Islam. These sites are given titles such as "Deviant Sects You Should Beware of," "A Refutation of the Deviant Beliefs of," "Spreading Deviant Beliefs of the Almighty," "The Deviant Beliefs That Drive the Followers of," "The Deviant Nature of Preacher Exposed," and so on. For the non-Muslim, this thicket of charges and countercharges is bewildering, impossible to untangle, but it is clear that the struggle to establish the hegemony of one interpretation and the falsity or illegitimacy of the others is virtually without end. Clearly, cognitive unconventionality or deviance is of earthshaking importance in a number of social circles.

Of course, in hierarchical power contexts, more hegemonic structures are able to effectively define certain beliefs as false—and hence, *deviant*—in ways that scattered, powerless, and marginal individuals cannot. In Iran, China, Pakistan, and Saudi Arabia, government censors block access to certain Web sites; in China alone, the government employs 40,000 censors. In 2008, sites offered a new software that allowed users to evade government censors; within a few months, "more than 400,000 Iranians were surfing the uncensored Web" (Markoff, 2009, p. 1).

In Rome, Richard Williamson, an excommunicated Catholic Bishop who had earlier made a speech denying the existence of Nazi gas chambers and to the extent, even the very fact, of the Holocaust, under pressure from the Vatican, apologized for having made such schismatic statements. His statements did not, however, address the issue of whether he still thought his statements were truthful (Donadio, 2009). Still, observers wondered whether such a tepid recantation was enough to stop the erosion of the Church's moral authority caused by his original statement.

Did NASA land astronauts on the moon, on six occasions? Or was the moon mission a hoax, a conspiracy perpetrated by nefarious politicians and their agents to bolster the sagging morale of an increasingly pessimistic public during dark times? Polls indicate that about 6 percent of the American population believes that the moon landings never happened, that they were staged on a secret movie set somewhere in the desert for political purposes. Bart Sibrel, a filmmaker and director of *A Funny Thing Happened on the Way to the Moon*, has made a career of moon-landing denial. He even pestered astronaut Buzz Aldrin by waving a Bible in his face and calling him "a coward, and a liar, and a thief." Mr. Aldrin became exasperated to the point where he punched Sibrel in the face; law enforcement refused to charge the astronaut with a crime. "I have suffered only persecution and financial loss," Sibrel told a reporter. "I've lost visitation with my son. I've been expelled from churches. All because I believe the Moon landings are fraudulent" (Schwartz, 2009).

Cognitive or intellectual deviance is the expression of beliefs that are contrary to the views of specific audiences, one being of course the mainstream. Such expressions of belief are deviant *in context*, so that criticisms that undermine the foundation of Mormon theology—which itself is deviant to many Americans—would be deviant *among Mormons*. The expression of some beliefs is hostile to established interests, the ruling elite, the regime in power; some are hostile to the views of the majority of the public; and some, to particular sectors or social circles within the society.

It might seem controversial to argue that beliefs and their expression make up a form of deviance. After all, isn't it true that, though you can get arrested for enacting certain *behavior*, you can't get arrested for holding, or even expressing, a certain *belief*? How can holding unconventional beliefs be a form of deviance? Doesn't everyone have a right to believe whatever they please? Isn't what you believe "nobody's business but your own"?

Well, ideally, but not in practice. First of all, you *can* be arrested for expressing a belief. Not in contemporary Western society, but in past centuries, yes, one could be arrested for expressing many beliefs. In Europe a few hundred years ago, the air was rank from the burning flesh of heretics and blasphemers, or supposed heretics and blasphemers. And over the centuries, even in the West, religious wars have led to the slaughter of millions of Catholics, Protestants, unbelievers, Muslims, and Jews. And people are still arrested elsewhere—Iran, China, Saudi Arabia, parts of Africa, and so on—for expressing certain views. Even more important for our purposes, *informal* reactions to definitions of right and wrong verify that expressing certain beliefs is deviant. Cognitive deviance may not be an appropriate subject for a *criminology* course, but it is for a *deviance* course.

The fact is, many audiences *do* react negatively to the expression of certain beliefs. Certain audiences do *not* feel that beliefs and their expression are "nobody's business but your own." In the West, even if people aren't arrested for expressing unconventional views today, they can be criticized, denounced, and lose their jobs; depending on the belief, some will have their sanity questioned. Almost as many—and in some eras of history, even more—people have been punished, stigmatized, and condemned for expressing their beliefs as for their behavior. One of Erving Goffman's types of stigma is "blemishes of individual character," one portion of which includes "treacherous and rigid beliefs" (1963, p. 4). And a belief that one person regards as "treacherous and rigid," another sees as just and righteous, and vice versa. So, *of course*, holding beliefs that wander off the beaten path is a form of deviance. William Newman identified three minority groups: behavioral, cognitive, and physical. "Behavioral" minorities varied from the norm in conduct; an example: homosexuals. "Cognitive" minorities vary from the norm with respect to their beliefs. An example: members of religious sects and cults. And "physical" minorities varied from the norm in appearance; for example: the handicapped (Newman, 1973, p. 35). Holding unconventional beliefs is an *important* form of deviance.

Cognition refers to knowing—that is, what one believes to be true. It encompasses "beliefs, disbeliefs, guesses, suspicions, judgments, and so forth" (Douglas and Waksler, 1982, p. 364). When sociologists refer to "knowing," we do not imply that these views are empirically correct (or that they are wrong). What we mean is that people *think* that they are true. Cognition refers to the belief that a given assertion or claim is valid. Cognitive deviance refers to holding beliefs that are unconventional and non-normative, which, in some social circles, causes their believers to be shunned, isolated, marginalized, rendered powerless, criticized, condemned, or punished. And it is the *expression* of beliefs that gets the believer in trouble. After all, the belief has to be *known* to disapproving audiences.

With respect to the central analytic features of deviance—what makes something *deviant*—in principle, deviant beliefs are identical to deviant acts. The same basic principles apply: Someone, or a category of persons, is regarded by the members of one or more audiences as violating a rule or norm, and the members of those audiences are likely to condemn or punish them. The content of the belief is less important than the fact that that belief is deemed normatively unacceptable. Thus, being an atheist violates a rule that says one must believe in God; belief in creationism violates the principles of scientific reasoning; belief in evolution violates a literal reading of the Bible; belief in alien spaceships violates a law that says that objects cannot travel faster than the speed of light; and so on. Because specific audiences hold certain beliefs to be non-normative, unconventional, unacceptable, scandalous, heretical, vulgar, unseemly, improper, and/or just plain wrong, they isolate, stigmatize, condemn, and/or punish the persons who hold them. Of course, precisely the beliefs that *one* audience finds unconventional *another* accepts as normatively correct. In these respects, holding unconventional beliefs is no different from engaging in unconventional behavior. Both result in stigma and condemnation. In other words, social rules apply "not only to how one behaves but also *how and what one thinks*" (Douglas and Waksler, 1982, p. 366). And to the extent that audiences treat others negatively—for instance, that they consider them immoral, unpatriotic, and, let's say, refuse to vote for them if they are a political candidate—"how one thinks" is a form of deviance.

It is not always a simple matter to separate beliefs from behavior. Often, unacceptable beliefs *translate into* or *become a basis for* unacceptable behavior. Someone who holds a certain belief announces to the world that he or she has the potential to act in a certain way. In other words, the *believer* can become an *actor*.

The belief that Jews are parasites who are organized into an international conspiracy to enslave the rest of the world (Greenberg, 2001; Webman, 2011) is far more than a "mere" belief: Some members of organized groups who hold such beliefs have committed overt violence against Jews. In the 1950s and 1960s, many politically mainstream Americans feared and stigmatized communists not merely because of their unconventional political ideology but also because they sincerely believed that communism was actively dedicated to the destruction of everything they valued: religion, spiritual values, the conventional family, democratic elections, the work ethic, a free market economy, a free press—in other words, that which defined the "American way of life." Hence, audiences may label or condemn people who hold unconventional beliefs because they fear that these believers pose a clear and present danger to the way of life—indeed, the very physical existence—of right-thinking people everywhere. Hence, many cognitive belief systems are not deviant *merely* because they violate mainstream notions of what's true. Their proponents are *also* regarded as deviants because of the behavior those beliefs could potentially call forth. The deviant nature of terrorists is not that they criticize the U.S. government; it is that they are likely to commit violence against innocent victims. Still, *independent of behavior*, the mere expression of unconventional beliefs is a form of deviance.

Cognitive deviance overlaps with mental disorder. Psychiatrists and clinical psychologists regard the expression of certain beliefs as a manifestation or an indicator of a pathological psychic condition. For instance, schizophrenics are said to suffer from *delusions* and *hallucinations*. One man describes a transmitter that has been implanted in his teeth that receives signals from a distant galaxy commanding him to deliver a message to everyone on Earth about a coming catastrophe. A woman believes that her thoughts have been sucked out of her mind by a "phrenological vacuum extractor" (Kring et al., 2010). A man believes that X-rays have entered his body through his neck, passed down to his waist, and settled in his genitals, preventing him from getting an erection. A woman claims that she is "just a puppet who is manipulated by cosmic strings. When the strings are pulled my body moves and I cannot prevent it." Clearly, then, people who are diagnosed as having a mental disorder often hold deviant beliefs.

Just as there are parallels between mental disorder and cognitive deviance, however, there are differences as well. Schizophrenia is nearly always accompanied by a number of other disturbances in addition to cognitive delusions and hallucinations. Some of these include flat or inappropriate emotions, bizarre motor activity, and the use of jumbled words ("word salad") and thoughts. Clinical depression, too, is marked by inappropriate beliefs, but in addition, it is a *mood* disorder characterized by feelings of sadness, dread, apprehension, worthlessness, guilt, and anhedonia, or an inability to take pleasure in life.

In contrast, *by itself*, cognitive deviance, or holding unconventional beliefs, is not necessarily linked with any psychiatric disorder. Mental disorder and cognitive deviance are *empirically* related but *definitionally* separate and distinct. In other words, while mental health professionals would classify many cognitive deviants as mentally disordered, and many of the persons they classify as mentally disordered would also be regarded as cognitive deviants, neither category demands or necessitates the other.

Beliefs are not deviant simply because of their content. No belief, however bizarre it might seem to us, is *inherently* or *objectively* deviant. A belief is deviant in two ways—one, normatively; and two, reactively. In other words, one, because it violates the normative tenets of the dominant belief system, or simply a different belief system, and two, because its adherents are likely to be condemned or punished by the members of the society at large or specific subgroups within that society—that is, a given "audience." A belief is deviant both because it is *considered* wrong and its believers are *treated* as socially unacceptable—*in* a given society or collectivity.

As we saw earlier, many ideas have been regarded as heretical—and therefore *deviant*—at one point in time, yet later *came to be* accepted as true or valid. In 1633, the Catholic Inquisition imposed the penalty of house arrest of Galileo because he argued that the Earth revolved around the Sun, an assertion that was contrary to Catholic dogma, which held that the Earth is the center of the universe. In 1854, Viennese physicians ridiculed Ignaz Semmelweis for asserting that physicians could transmit disease to patients after they dissected rotting cadavers; *in* the 1850s, the medical establishment regarded Semmelweis as a deviant. Today, any physician asserting that physicians should *not* wash their hands before thrusting them into patients' bodies would be regarded as the deviant, not to mention medically irresponsible and very possibly criminally liable. Beginning in 1915, and, in revisions throughout the 1920s, a German astrophysicist Alfred Wegener proposed the theory that, 300 million years ago, the Earth's crust formed one giant continent, Pangaea, that broke apart over time into the continents we know today. They are still drifting, and will continue to do so for as long as the Earth exists. For nearly a half century, Wegener's theory met with scathing derision and almost uniform hostility; it was not until the 1960s that virtually all geologists accepted continental drift and plate tectonics as a valid description of geological processes.

Because of his astronomical statements, *to* the hierarchy of the Catholic Church, *in* the 1600s, Galileo was a cognitive deviant; *because* of his medical claim, *to* physicians *in* the 1800s, Ignaz Semmelweis was a cognitive deviant; *because* of the publication of his books espousing the theory of continental drift, *to* geologists between 1915 and the 1950s, Alfred Wegener was a cognitive deviant (Ben-Yehuda, 1985). The fact that these theories have proven to be valid is *irrelevant* to the fact that *at* one time, *to* a certain audience, these theories *were* heretical and hence, their creator *was* condemned and punished—and hence, deviant.

To repeat a point I've made throughout this book: Deviance makes sense *only* with reference to the beliefs and reactions of certain audiences. Beliefs that are regarded as wrong, unacceptable, and deviant in one social circle may be considered right, good, proper, and true in another. In social circles of political radicals, conservatism is unacceptable, objectionable, deviant. Contrarily, among conservatives, radicals are on the hot seat. To the fundamentalist Christian, the atheist is the spawn of Satan, most decidedly a deviant. Turn the picture around: To the atheist, fundamentalist Christians are ignorant, narrow-minded fools. Here, we encounter the process of "mutual deviantization" (Aho, 1994, p. 62).

But let's be clear about this: Deviance is never *solely* a matter of the members of one social category's word against the word of another. Yes, we live in a society, which is an assemblage of different and mutually antagonistic belief systems. But society is as much a ladder as a mosaic. This means that some beliefs are more *dominant* than others; their adherents have more power and credibility and hence, can legitimate their beliefs and discredit those of their opponents. To the extent that a particular belief is taught as true in the educational system, it is dominant, legitimate, and credible; to the extent that, when a belief is expressed in schools, its proponents tend to be *disparaged*, that belief is deviant. To the extent that holding a certain belief is a criterion among a majority of the electorate to vote for a given political candidate, it is

a dominant belief. To the extent that a substantial segment of the electorate *refuses* to vote for a political candidate because he or she is known to hold a certain view, that view is deviant. To the extent that a given belief is taken for granted as true in the mainstream media, it is dominant; to the extent that holders of a given belief are scorned, rebuked, and ridiculed—that belief is deviant. In each of society's major institutions, we can locate beliefs that are mainstream, "inside the lines," conventional, dominant or hegemonic; *and* we can locate those beliefs that are nonmainstream, outside the lines, beyond the pale, unconventional—in a word, from the societal point of view, *deviant*.

THE SOCIAL FUNCTIONS OF BELIEF SYSTEMS

Are beliefs just beliefs? To put the matter even more emphatically, are beliefs *ever* just beliefs? How does the sociologist approach deviant beliefs? More generally, how do *we*, as students of the sociology of deviance, approach beliefs? As Berger and Luckmann say, the task of sociologists who study beliefs is not to look at beliefs for their own sake, to take them as "just" beliefs, and attempt to prove them right—or, on the other hand, debunk or prove them wrong. Instead, sociologists attempt to understand the social conditions that *generate* or *encourage* them (1966, p. 12). The basic insight of sociology is that beliefs serve social functions that *transcend* their uniqueness *and* their empirical validity or truth value. We argue that the way humans think is rooted in the material and social world. Beliefs usually grow out of real-world conditions and tend to have real-world consequences.

For thousands of years, theorists, philosophers, intellectuals, academics, social scientists, and other observers of social reality have commented on the relationship between the *ideational* world—the world of thoughts, beliefs, and ideas—and the *material* world, such as how people make a living, where they live, and what social categories they belong to and participate in. Theories have been proposed to account for the relationship between the material and the ideational worlds. The central thrust of these writings is that beliefs spring from social conditions, they serve social functions, and they have social consequences.

Most of us think that what we believe comes from our own special, unique individuality. We convince ourselves that our beliefs would be the same, even if we had been subject to very different social influences. Sociologist Joel Charon asks the question "Why do we believe what we believe?" To answer it, he invites the reader to ask the following questions: "If my life had been different, if I had been born at a different time or place, would I still believe in God? Would my beliefs about God be the same as they are now?" (1995, p. 99). Do you really think your beliefs would be the same if you had grown up in a different time and place? If you had grown up two centuries ago the child of a white slave owner, would you have believed that slavery is evil? If you had been a gentile child in Nazi Germany, would you have believed that Jews are good, decent people who deserve the same rights as everyone else? If you had been born a thousand years ago in the New Guinea Highlands, would you have had the same religious beliefs you have now? Or had you been born on a Polynesian island half a millennium ago, would you have thought that public nudity was immoral? Do you really believe that, in a different society in a different time period, you would have had exactly the same notions of right and wrong and true and false that you have now? "Can you think of *any* idea you believe that does not have primarily a *social* foundation? Is there anything we believe that has not arisen primarily through *interaction* with others?" (p. 99). The first and more or less universally accepted sociological principle of beliefs is that they arise through social interaction with others. In short, *human consciousness is determined by social existence* (Berger and Luckmann, 1966, pp. 5–6).

Karl Marx, a nineteenth-century German intellectual who, for more than a century and a half, had a profound impact on sociology, philosophy, history, and economics, argued that the way we think at a particular time and place is a *reflection* of the economic arrangements of the society in which we live. "Morality, religion, metaphysics, all the rest of ideology and their corresponding forms of consciousness," Marx and Engels wrote, "thus no longer retain the semblance of independence. . . . Life is not determined by consciousness, but consciousness by life" (1846/1947, pp. 14, 15). And by "life," they meant *economic* life. It is the nature of the economy that determines the nature of a society's art, politics, religion, science, system of justice—in short, the ideational world, the world of beliefs and ideas. Moreover, in any society, it is the dominant social class whose ideas tend to be most influential. "The class which has the means of material production at its disposal, has control at the same time over the means of mental production. . . . The individuals composing the ruling class . . . rule also as thinkers, as producers of ideas, and regulate the production and distribution of the ideas of their age: thus their ideas are the ruling ideas of the epoch" (p. 39).

The influence of Marx's theories has declined considerably during the past generation or so. Most social scientists and intellectuals see a much more complex and less deterministic relationship between the economy and beliefs. They argue that ideas can influence the economy as much as the economy can influence ideas and see the many institutions, including art, religion, and politics, as "codeterminate," or equally capable of influencing one another. For instance, Max Weber argued that religious beliefs influence the economic life of a society as much as the other way around. It was ascetic, rationalistic seventeenth-century Protestantism, he said, that stimulated industrial capitalism—a case of ideas generating material conditions rather than the reverse. The Industrial Revolution could not have emerged in a society dominated by religions such as Hinduism and Buddhism, because they denied rationality and the central importance of the material world.

As we've seen, Max Weber wrote of the *elective affinity* people have for certain ideas and beliefs (1946, pp. 62–63, 284–285)—that is, the social and material conditions in which they live influence the likelihood that they would be receptive to certain ideas. They do not directly choose (or "elect") their beliefs—they do so indirectly, through their social and material conditions. The privileged classes tend to be attracted to religions that assure them that their status is justified and legitimate. For the poorer strata, religious beliefs (or, alternatively, political beliefs) will be appealing to the extent that these beliefs offer a salvation of compensation—that is, righting the wrongs they feel have been inflicted upon them, whether in this world or the next. The prophecy of seventh-century Islam was especially appealing to warriors. The religious expression that middle-class urban-dwellers during early Protestantism found compatible with their way of life was practical, rational, based on a mastery of nature and relations with others. Members of the bureaucratic class—whether in ancient Rome or in the contemporary West—have found irrational, ecstatic, or completely otherworldly religious expression unappealing, but were comfortable with a religion that offered ways of controlling the masses (Weber, 1922/1963, pp. 89, 107, 108, 265). Weber sees much more diversity in the ideas of the many social classes in the society than did Marx—who only pictured two social classes. Weber neither sees the ruling class so overwhelmingly dominant that their ideas are the "ruling" ideas of the era, nor does he see liberation as the only function of the ideas of oppressed peoples. Ideas and beliefs may serve many functions aside from their economic interests.

In other words, unlike Marx, Max Weber saw a *two-way street* between the ideational world—the world of beliefs and ideas—and the material conditions of people's lives. People are attracted to beliefs because they are compatible with the way they live. But "the way they live" is much more than economic circumstances alone. It includes the many and myriad facets of our existence. And ideas and beliefs, in turn, can act back on material conditions. For instance, a religion can generate ideas that either stimulate or inhibit a certain kind of economic system. Buddhism, practiced in Tibet and Bhutan, rejects materialism—and therefore the very basis of industrial capitalism. In contrast, as we saw, according to Weber the beliefs of seventeenth-century Protestantism actively encouraged the Industrial Revolution. So, to Weber, there is reciprocity here. In contrast, to Marx, it was more of a one-way relationship—economic circumstances cause beliefs. On this issue, most contemporary theorists prefer Weber's way of thinking to that of Marx.

The functions that deviant belief systems serve can be looked at from two different approaches—one, the functions they serve for the believer and two, the functions that *opposing* unconventional beliefs, and the *condemnation* of their believers serve, for the society at large or, more specifically, their condemners.

Each of the belief systems discussed in this chapter functions in one way or another for certain strata or social circles or segments of the society. Each affirms the believer's way of life or upholds a certain vision of the way things are. Each is supported by a specific epistemology or "way of knowing" and each points to a way of looking at things, a belief system that it rejects or which rejects theirs. Some are backed up by a *demonology*—the designation of an immoral, fiendish wrongdoer who represents evil in the flesh—while others merely point out the errors perpetrated by persons who fail to see things the way they see them. Beliefs respond or correspond to issues that are a vital part of the way their believers live their lives; all answer questions and provide solutions to problems that make them believable or credible to some of the members of a society rather than others.

Thus, in cognitive deviance there are usually two sets of deviants—to each side of the controversy, the *other* side. To Martin Luther, Catholicism was deviant—indeed, evil. To the pope, Martin Luther and his Protestant followers were deviant, a representative of the devil. To the person who believes that UFOs are spaceships from another planet, anyone who denies that belief is wrong, cognitively in error—or part of the cover-up to hide the fact that aliens are all around us. Looked at from the other end of the controversy, the parties who are wedded to the mainstream institutions, UFO believers are wrong, silly, irrational, and most decidedly deviant. To the fundamentalist Christian, proponents of evolution are secular humanists and hence the spawn of Satan; to the traditional scientist, creationists are ignorant, closed-minded enemies of reason and enlightenment. The list could be multiplied endlessly. In this sense, we are talking about looking at definitions of deviance in horizontal terms—from one group, category, or social circle to another.

But there's another dimension, the vertical dimension: What is central in any controversy is which side has the influence to legitimate and validate its own special view of right or wrong and true or false. *Whose* notion of right and wrong are we talking about here? It is true that *in* creationist circles and *to* creationist audiences, evolutionists are considered deviant. But it's also true that with respect to power, influence, legitimacy, and credibility, creationists are *marginalized*; their views are *not* mainstream in the society at large. This is what makes creationism a deviant belief system—not because it is empirically wrong. (That is a separate issue.) Evolution, not creationism, is taught in the dominant institutions, promulgated in the dominant media, believed among the most well-educated strata. In the event that the mainstream institutions were to legitimate creationism and stigmatize and marginalize evolutionist thinking, then it would be the other way around, it would be the evolutionist whom the sociologist would designate as the cognitive deviant.

The same applies to the belief that UFOs are real. The belief that unidentified flying objects are alien space ships is held by just under half of all Americans; the belief that they are not is held by roughly the same proportion. So what then makes the belief, "UFOs are real," deviant? It is deviant *societally* because it does not have hierarchical legitimacy. The most influential media (the news divisions of the television networks, *The New York Times*, *The Washington Post*, *Time*, *Newsweek*, etc.), the relevant departments in major universities, and the major, mainstream churches do not accept the belief as true. If a political candidate were to announce the belief in a speech—or to urge that its truth be adopted by educational curricula—he or she would be ridiculed by the media. When John Mack, a Harvard professor, published a book asserting his belief that people had been kidnapped by aliens (1995), a shockwave of horror rumbled through the university community. When Minister Farrakhan announced that he had visited an extraterrestrial spaceship, observers denounced him as a crackpot (Brackman, 1996). Again, charges of deviance can more easily be legitimated by influential representatives of social institutions than by those who are weaker and more marginal. But once again, *within* those weaker, more marginal sectors of the society, the dominant definitions of right and wrong may nonetheless be regarded as deviant. To repeat, as students of deviance, we need to think in terms of *both* the vertical *and* the horizontal dimensions of deviance.

RELIGIOUS SECTS AND CULTS

An "ecumenical" denomination or church is one that promotes cooperation and mutual tolerance among all churches and denominations. The Episcopal, Congregational, Presbyterian, Methodist, Lutheran, and, today, Catholic churches tend to be ecumenical. Most mainstream, old-line American religious denominations tend to be moderate, ecumenical, and comfortable with secular society. But the cost of adapting to secular society is promoting a lukewarm, unemotional, unenthusiastic, and unzealous form of religious expression. In other words, the more tolerant a religious body is toward the faith of other religious bodies, the more cooperative it is toward those other faiths, and the more accepting it is with the compromises the material world has wrought on the faith of its followers, the more reserved, the more tepid, and the less "muscular" its members' faith is likely to be. The 2009 Barna Poll revealed an extremely strong correlation between evangelism and church attendance, and evangelism and orthodoxy of religious belief. ("Evangelism" is a fervent, zealous belief in heavenly salvation through Christian faith, especially in the Gospel—i.e., the first four books of the New Testament, and the impulse to spread the "good news" of the Gospel to others.) All religious bodies, including the mainline ecumenical churches, harbor members with evangelical tendencies, but the largest religious bodies that are evangelical as a rule include the Southern Baptist, Pentecostalism, and Assemblies of God churches.

Members of the old-line, ecumenical denominations attend church services less frequently than members of the strong evangelical faiths. In the 2009 Barna Poll, a very small minority of the members of mainstream, ecumenical churches (such as Episcopalian) attended weekly, but a strong majority of Baptists, Pentecostalists, Assemblies of God, and other evangelicals did so. Only about one in ten of Episcopalians said they must tell their faith to others, whereas, again, a majority of evangelicals felt this way. Satan is materially real? Only one in five Episcopalians agreed, but a third Baptists, half of Pentecostalists, and almost nine in ten of Assemblies of God did so. In short, mainline denominations offer a *weaker, milder* version of Christianity, while the evangelical sects offer a *stronger and more intense*, more *zealous* version. In contrast with the mainline denominations, members of the more fervent and "muscular" evangelical faiths are much more likely to accept articles of orthodox Christian dogma and to believe that they must vigorously proselytize their faith in the Gospel to others (www.adherents.com/misc/BarnaPoll.html and www.adherents.com/rel_USA.html).

In addition, *social* and *political* ideologies are strongly related to *religious* beliefs and practices. Another Barna Poll, also conducted in 2009, indicates that conservatives are significantly more likely hold more intense religious views; engage in regular religious practices, such as church attendance, prayer, reading the Bible; believe that the Bible is the literally accurate world of God; live a spirituality-centered life; and believe that they have a "personal responsibility to share their religious beliefs with others," than is true of liberals. Liberals, in turn, are more likely to live a secular life, believe that religious faith is not a basic "moral guide" to their lives, and reject the notion that they have a responsibility to share their religious beliefs with others. Liberals are also more likely to have discovered their own religious beliefs instead of embracing those promulgated by an organized church or religion and are more open to "accepting different moral views" than they once held. Conservatives and evangelicals tend to hold and express a "stronger" version of religiosity, while that of liberals is typically "weaker."

Weak denominations do not answer the need of the more fervent parishioners who long for a strong expression of their faith. Hence, they tend to stimulate "new, more vigorous religions to replace them" (Stark and Bainbridge, 1996, p. 103). Two types of religious bodies contrast with established, mainstream bodies. The first is the *sect*, a religious group that breaks off from the mainstream religion and is "within the conventional religious tradition(s) of a society, but one that imposes stricter demands on its adherents than do mainstream groups" (pp. 103–104). Such groups are only "moderately deviant." And what *makes* them deviant is that they are "*too religious*" (p.104).

Even more deviant is the *cult*. As with "deviant," the term "cult" has become such a pejorative word that it seems to connote a religion that is "kooky," "bizarre," "pathological," "creepy," and "strange," in other words, it is an "insult to stir up fear and oppression" (Stark and Bainbridge, 1996, p. 104). In a straightforward definitional sense, however, cults are simply religious groups that are "outside the conventional religious tradition(s) in a society" (p. 104). They differ less with respect to the intensity of their members' religiosity as to their *difference from* the mainstream religious body. They are not a *variation on* the usual theme, they are *outside* the usual theme altogether. Some cults are imported from a cultural tradition foreign to a specific country's religions, while most arise "because someone creates or discovers [a] new religious culture and successfully attracts a group of followers" (p. 104). In the United States, examples of domestic cults include The Church of the Latter Day Saints (the Mormons) in the nineteenth century, Christian Science in the 1920s and, today or in the recent past, the Church of Scientology; imported cults include Hare Krishna, the Divine Light Mission, and the Unification Church (or "Moonies"). Cults "engender far more concern, antagonism, and repressive efforts than do sects" (p. 104). While sects are *moderately* deviant to the mainstream, cults tend to be *very* deviant.

Many conventional religionists adopt the "absolutist" perspective I spelled out earlier; they argue that cults are *not like* traditional or conventional religious bodies, believing them to be evil, sinister, or at the very least, strange. Their leaders are said to engage in "manipulative mind control" to seduce, capture, and "brainwash" their young acolytes. These leaders are up to no good and they must be stopped from engaging in their nefarious practices. "Cults are groups that often exploit members psychologically and/or financially, typically by making members comply with leadership's demands through certain types of psychological manipulation and through the inculcation of deep-seated anxious dependency on the group and its leaders" (Chambers et al., 1994, p. 90).

To the absolutist, the evil nature of cults must have a sinister origin, cause, or dynamic. "No rational or sane person would choose to join a cult.

Given such assumptions, how does one explain cult involvement?" (Perrin, 2008). The absolutist responds by invoking such mechanisms as "brainwashing," by arguing that clever but malicious leaders trap, seduce, manipulate, and hypnotize innocent parties into their spider's web of deceit (Singer and Lalich, 1995). Note that the absolutist perspective demands that a truly anomalous, aberrant phenomenon such as cult membership demands an explanation that invokes anomalous, aberrant causes. The proposition that cult members are recruited in much the same way that members of mainstream churches are is unacceptable. This is what experts who study the logical structure of arguments call the "evil causes evil" fallacy: something the observer doesn't like must have an origin, which the observer also doesn't like. As some researchers have pointed out (Perrin, 2008), the "brainwashing" explanation for cult membership goes back to the 1950s, when the Chinese communists were said to "brainwash" American prisoners of the Korean War into betraying their country.

Perrin (2008) locates four interest groups whose members compete to define the nature of cults: the anticult movement, the media, the cults (or "new religious movements") themselves, and academics, including sociologists of religion, who study them from a social science perspective.

The anticult movement attempts to define cults as deviant and in doing so, to drive them out of business. Most anticult organizations were started by parents who "lost" their children to cults, whose theology and religious practices these parents found puzzling, incomprehensible, troubling, very different from the conventional Christianity or Judaism these young people grew up with. Many parents, says Perrin, "were confused by their child's conversion and fanatical commitment, and were anxious to 'expose' the sinister cults and get their children back." Deprogrammers and "exit counselors," some health professionals, other Christian ministers or committed Christian laypeople, attempt to "unbrainwash" converts and to indoctrinate potential converts into the "evil" nature of cults. Some parents of cult members have even hired deprogrammers to kidnap their children from a cult setting and force deprogramming on them. Many anticult activists have been defectors, former cult members who became disillusioned and now "want the evil practices of the cult exposed" (p. 16). Many Christian clergy and laypeople oppose cults because they "want to win the world for Jesus."

The media don't necessarily attempt to define cults as evil or deviant. "However, faced with time and space restrictions, and obviously drawn to sensationalistic and controversial topics, media accounts sometimes ignore the mundane and non-newsworthy elements of NRM [new religious movements, or cults], and thus contribute to a distorted perception of NRMs" (p. 16). Hence, by making sensationalistic and distorted claims, the media unwittingly serve the interests of the anticult movement in defining cults as deviant.

Jostling on this stage where interest groups attempt to define cults as deviant—or as legitimate religions—are the cults themselves. Clearly it is in the interests of cult participants to define themselves, and to convince others, to define cults as not only legitimate but also as altruistic, as dedicated to saving a corrupt world. Cult leaders also have a material interest as well: As a given cult organization grows, its leadership prospers.

Sociologists and other academics usually provide a more sober and balanced if not necessarily "objective" view of cults. In their effort to produce original, non-trite, and counterintuitive findings and conclusions, academics often find themselves defending cults. Moreover, since sociologists often attempt to understand social phenomena as their participants understand them, they may present cult members' views of reality as one version of acceptable and believable truth. Outsiders, especially those with an anticult agenda, often see such efforts as a defense of cults. However, psychologists, who are more interested in the special means by which cults convince their members of the truth of their vision, are more likely to see the dark side of these new religious movements. For instance, *Cultic Studies Review*, "an internet journal of research, news and opinion," is dedicated to disseminating "information on cults, psychological manipulation, psychological abuse, spiritual abuse, brainwashing, mind control, thought reform, abusive churches, extremism, totalistic groups, authoritarian groups, new religious movements, exit counseling, recovery, and practical suggestions." Clearly, this journal focuses mainly on the negative, deviant side of cults.

Conflicts between cults and mainstream society were depicted prominently in the news in the 1970s and early 1980s. But into the 1980s and the 1990s, cult membership declined and defections increased (Perrin, 2008). Twenty or thirty years ago, Hare Krishna members danced in the street and begged in airports. Since that time, events, media reports, and defectors have exposed many cults as anything but "normal," legitimate, or altruistic. In 1978, Jim Jones, a charismatic but mentally unstable leader of his own self-created new religious movement, exhorted his flock to commit mass suicide. By the end of the day, nearly a thousand of his followers lay dead in the jungle compound. A book entitled *Monkey on a Stick* revealed that a Hare Krishna organization was deeply involved in stealing, rape and beating of members, murder, drug smuggling, and building an arsenal of weapons that would equip a small army (Hubner and Gruson, 1989). These and countless other revelations hurt the cause of the new religious movements, convinced nonmembers that they were right to denounce and attack these movements, and contributed to the movements' demise.

CREATIONISM AND INTELLIGENT DESIGN VERSUS EVOLUTION

In December 2005, a federal district court judge rejected the suit brought by the school board of the Dover, Pennsylvania, school district (by the time of the ruling, already voted out of office) to introduce intelligent design into the science curriculum. Intelligent design does not belong in the science classroom, the judge ruled, because it is a religiously motivated belief that violates the constitutional mandate of separation of church and state. The judge, John Jones III, a conservative and a Republican appointed by President George W. Bush, went further; he lashed out at school board members for lying under oath and for being guilty of "breathtaking inanity" in their attempt to infuse religion into science courses. Intelligent design, declared Judge Jones, "relies on the unprovable existence of a Christian God and therefore is not science" (Powell, 2005, p. A1).

From our point of view, the decision raised the issue of whether and to what extent the struggle between supporters of intelligent design and advocates of evolution to define reality illuminates an aspect of cognitive deviance. Clearly, the position of most scientists is that both creationism and intelligent design are *deviant* explanations for the origin of the universe and the origin of the species. It is their intention to rule these theories invalid and inappropriate for inclusion in the science curriculum. They are not scientific, most scientists argue, and have no more place in the teaching of science than Zulu, Navajo, or Australian aborigine explanations of the origin of the universe and the species. On their behalf, fundamentalist Christians wish to relegate evolution to the nether world of error, untruth, falseness, and Godlessness. In short, the creationism-evolution controversy is a classic case of *mutual deviantization* (Aho, 1994, p. 62).

This controversy is fraught with conceptual and theoretical confusion and misunderstanding, which I'd like to dispel. To begin with, Charles Darwin was not the first to advocate the evolution of the species. Dozens of scientists before him thought of the same thing; Darwin was the first to have thought of the *mechanism* that drove or caused evolution. (More on this momentarily.) Actually, to be more precise, Darwin and Alfred Russel Wallace published a summary of their ideas simultaneously. Moreover, one or another form of evolutionary thinking had been accepted as valid by many scientists and intellectuals for more than a half century before Darwin published *On the Origin of Species* in 1859. In addition, it's not clear why creationists focus specifically on evolutionary theory in biology as subverting Biblical literalism since the findings of astrophysics, paleontology, genetics, and geology also contradict a literal interpretation of the Bible. Biology is just one of a number of fields whose findings contradict Genesis as a scientific tract.

In addition, in spite of their equation in the media, creationism is not the same thing as intelligent design. In fact, these two perspectives disagree on most of their claims and agree on only one point. There are many versions of creationism, but classic, "new Earth" or Biblical creationism holds that the universe, Earth, and all species on Earth, were created by God in six 24-hour days less than 10,000 years ago. In sharp contrast, intelligent design accepts the fact that the universe and the Earth are billions of years old and that the process of evolution produced all the species on Earth. Where intelligent design parts company with the scientific view of evolution is that it argues that the hand of God *guided* the process of evolution and designed and created all species on Earth, including humans. Hence, intelligent design and evolution have a great deal in common, in fact, in many ways, more in common than creationism and intelligent design do.

Much of this confusion is caused by the designation of evolution as a "theory." Most laypeople think that "theory" means "speculation" or "an unproven hypothesis." This is wrong. The scientific definition of theory is an *explanation*, a cause-and-effect account for a general class of phenomena or observations. When people say "evolution is just a theory," what they mean is it hasn't yet been shown to be true. But scientifically, what the phrase really means is that evolution is an *explanation* for something. But what?

People who refer to evolution as a theory confuse *the fact* of evolution—that is, whether the species evolved over millions, even billions, of years—with *the mechanism* of evolution. Intelligent design theorists accept the *fact* of evolution but reject a materialist mechanism or *explanation* of the process. Their theory is that "God did it," the "it" being the actual causal mechanism of evolution itself. In contrast, the scientific explanation of evolution holds that the explanation, cause, or mechanism for the process is *natural selection*—that is, genetic variation, the adaptation of organisms to a particular environment, and differential survival and hence, differential productive success. Hence, the "theory" that is referred to in the phrase "the theory of evolution" is not a theory of evolution at all, but the theory of natural selection—that is, an explanation for *why* evolution occurred. Scientists take evolution as the observation or *fact*, and natural selection as the "theory" or explanation *for* the fact of evolution. Intelligent design advocates accept the fact of evolution but reject the mechanism of natural selection. And most scientists believe that the concept, "guided by the hand of God," is an unprovable, supernatural explanation. It cannot be tested with the tools of natural science, they say.

In spite of the fact that intelligent design and creationism are almost totally contradictory theories on the fact of evolution, the point they agree on is that God plays a causal role in observable material reality. In contrast, the scientific version of evolution, and all natural phenomena, is that material reality has material causes; the observer need not invoke the hand of God in these processes. So important is the role of God here that most observers believe that intelligent design is a "foot in the door" or a "wedge" for creationism to enter into the biology curriculum. Grant intelligent design in the public schools, say its opponents, and creationism will follow. Hence, their strong opposition.

Information on the beliefs of different segments of the population will make this controversy clearer and will situate it more firmly within the topic of cognitive deviance. Polls have been conducted yearly on the public's attitude on creationism, some form of intelligent design, and evolution, and the results are fairly consistent.

In 1987, *Newsweek* magazine estimated that of the nearly half a million life and earth scientists (mainly biologists and geologists) in the world, less than 1 percent believe in some form of creationism. Another estimate has it that 99 percent of scientists take the strictly naturalistic view of evolution (Shermer, 1997, p. 156). In the United States, in poll after poll, in the general public, roughly 45 percent of respondents believe in creationism—that is, the universe and all species on Earth were created by God less than 10,000 years ago. About 40 percent believe in some form of intelligent design—that is, that evolution occurred, but the process was guided by the hand of God. Less than 10 percent of the American population believes in evolution and a materialist cause-and-effect mechanism—that is, "Man has developed over millions of years from less advanced forms of life. God had no part in the process." The level of support for creationism and intelligent design in the United States is unique in the Western world. A British survey of over 100 Catholic priests, Anglican bishops, and Protestant ministers and pastors found that 97 percent did not believe the universe was created in six days, and 80 percent did not believe in the existence of Adam and Eve.

Here we have a belief that 99 percent of scientists hold (depending on the year the question is asked and the wording of the question) but only 9 percent of the general public accepts. Says one observer: "It would be hard to imagine any other belief for which there is such a wide disparity between the person on the street and the expert in the ivory tower" (Shermer, 1997, p. 156). Moreover, nearly all the dominant social institutions affirm that evolution took place: the educational system, especially higher education, and most especially, the most prestigious institutions of higher learning, the most influential media, such as network news, *The New York Times*, *The Washington Post*, all the science magazines, such as *Smithsonian*, *The National Geographic*, *Scientific American*, and *Science*, every major science museum in the country, all its zoos and aquariums, and the mainstream, old-line, ecumenical churches, such as the Catholic, Episcopalian, Presbyterian, Methodist, Congregationalist, and Lutheran churches. For us, as students of deviance, the interesting questions become; first, why does such a discrepancy exist; second, what functions does such a belief serve for the social circles holding them; and third, what does this discrepancy say about definitions of deviance in different audiences?

It might seem strange to refer to beliefs, such as creationism and intelligent design, held by nearly half of the population, as deviant. How could such common beliefs be deviant? The answer is that "deviant" cannot be equated with "different"; "conventional" cannot be equated with "common" or "usual." Many common actions, beliefs, and physical traits are deviant. Most of us—in fact, very possibly, nearly all of us—lie once or more in our lives, but lying is a deviant act; the people we lie to don't like it, resent us for doing it, and would punish us in one way or another if they knew we did it to them. A very high proportion of the population has taken something that's not theirs at least once, but that doesn't mean that stealing isn't deviant. Most American women are not happy with some feature of their bodies, consider their bodies, in one way or another, deviant. Contrapositively, owning a house with five bathrooms, receiving 100 items of mail a day, and taking three showers a day is unusual—but not deviant. As I said in Chapter 1, sociologists do not define conventionality by how common or widespread a belief or act is, nor deviance by its rarity.

What makes creationism and intelligent design deviant? What makes evolution deviant? Deviance is something that's "out of place," like a weed. It is that, which is judged invalid or bad or silly or evil or reprehensible *by* a particular audience *in* a particular context. Deviance is defined or *constituted by* the negative reactions it generates in certain audiences, in certain contexts. Evolutionists are emphatic in insisting that creationism, creation science, and intelligent design are *out of place*, and therefore deviant, in any science context. Anyone who believes in them is, by definition, not a scientist, and has no place in that context. Any attempt to teach science to students, whether at the elementary or the graduate school level, *cannot* include Biblical teachings on the subject. In contrast, among creationists, believing in evolution is evil, contrary to God's teachings, certain to bring forth divine retribution; their attacks on proponents of evolution are powerful, denunciatory, and savage.

Make no mistake about it: The struggle between creationists and intelligent design advocates on one side and materialist evolutionists on the other is a battle to define a particular body of knowledge as valid and another as *deviant*.

Michael Dini, associate professor of biology at Texas Tech University, has a strict policy of never giving a recommendation to a student who does not accept what he refers to as "the most important theory in biology," that is, evolution. Michael Spradling, a senior at Texas Tech who needed a recommendation to medical school, enrolled in, then dropped Dini's course when he found out about the professor's policy. Spradling transferred to Lubbock Christian University and enrolled in that same course so that he could obtain a recommendation from its instructor. Dini feels that believing in creationism is a simple case of looking at rock-solid evidence and being incapable of reaching conclusions, in a phrase, being incapable of reasoning scientifically. Denying evolution is no different from denying that gravity exists, he says. Most, although not all, of Dini's colleagues agree. Spradling appealed to the Department of Justice, arguing that Dini's policy is a case of discriminating against a student's religious beliefs (Brulliard, 2003; Madigan, 2003).

Commenting on one creationist's claim that evolutionary theory can be traced back to the early Greek atomists and before, to Babylonian philosophy—and was, perhaps, revealed by Satan himself—an evolutionist comments that he finds it "hard to believe that anybody . . . accepts this shaggy-dog story" (Kitcher, 1982, p. 193). After a scientific meeting, commenting on the efforts of creationists, one scientist declared *we've got to stop the bastards* (my italics). This, comments a historian of creationism, is the "prevailing attitude" among scientists (Numbers, 1992, p. xvii). Says the guidebook of the Museum of the Earth in Ithaca, NY: "Essentially all available data and observations from the natural world support the hypothesis of evolution. No serious biologist or geologist today doubts whether evolution occurred" (Kates, 2005, p. A22). Clearly scientists wish to define creationism as intellectually and cognitively unacceptable—in a word, deviant.

After the citizens of Dover, Pennsylvania, voted for a school board whose members opposed intelligent design (and voted out of office a board whose members supported it), Pat Robertson, a religious broadcaster, announced that the "good citizens of Dover . . . voted God out of your city. . . . If there is a disaster in your area, don't turn to God. You just rejected Him from your city. . . . If they have future problems in Dover, I recommend they call Charles Darwin. Maybe hc can help them." Robertson also called for the assassination of President Hugo Chavez, a radical; recommended that the State Department be blown up with a nuclear device; and that feminists encourage women to "kill their children, practice witchcraft, destroy capitalism, and become lesbians" (Associated Press release, November 11, 2005).

In his well-known antievolutionist tract, *The Icons of Evolution*, Jonathan Wells writes that his prayers convinced him that he should devote his life to "destroying Darwinism." When the Rev. Sun Myung Moon "chose" him to enter a PhD program, he said, he "welcomed the opportunity to prepare" himself for battle (Wells, 2000). Indeed, "battle" is an excellent metaphor for the debate between creationists and evolutionists since many of its participants believe that it is a struggle between good and evil, right and wrong, light and darkness.

During one Louisiana case, *Edwards v. Aguillard*, intended to bring "creation science"

into the educational curriculum, creationists sent letters to the scientists testifying on behalf of evolution. One letter sent to Murray Gell-Mann, a Nobel Prize winner, read: "The blood of Jesus Christ cleanses us from all sin. Whosoever is not found written in the book of life will be cast into the lake of fire. The wages of sin is death, but the gift of God is eternal life through Jesus Christ our Lord. Ask Jesus Christ to save you now! The second law of thermodynamics proves evolution is impossible. [Actually, the Second Law of Thermodynamics states that energy cannot be increased in a closed energy system. Since the Earth receives energy from the Sun, it does not constitute a closed energy system.] Why are you so afraid of the truth of creation-science?" (Shermer, 1997, pp. 169–170). Says Henry M. Morris, a prolific creationist: "Evolution is the root of atheism, of communism, nazism, behaviorism, racism, economic imperialism, militarism, libertinism, anarchism, and all manner of anti-Christian systems of belief and practice" (1972, p. 75).

The elementary school superintendent of Marshall County, Kentucky, Kenneth Shadowen, glued together two pages of his fifth and sixth graders' science textbooks dealing with the "big bang"—according to scientific theory, the origin of the universe 15 billion years ago—so that his students could not read them. Shadowen claimed he had done it because the text didn't present "alternatives" to the big bang theory (Shermer, 1997, p. 138). Governor Fob James of Alabama used taxpayers' money to purchase and send a copy of a book supporting intelligent design and critical of evolutionary theory to all high school instructors of science courses (p. 139).

To repeat: It is the goal of creationists to depict evolutionary theory as cognitively, intellectually, theologically, and morally bankrupt, in error, and hence, deviant; it is the goal of evolutionists to do the same for creationism—except they leave morality and theology out of the picture.

What makes the conflict between creationists and evolutionists so particularly bitter and protracted? Why are the differences between them so quickly and readily translated into denunciation and reproach? And why is this conflict such an ideal example of cognitive deviance labeling?

Belief in creationism versus evolution is very strongly correlated with several key and basic factors, including education, urban-rural residence, and blue state-red state, or "metro" versus "retro" residence. (Liberal or "blue" states are located in the northeast and mid-Atlantic, from Maryland to Maine, the upper Midwest, and the west coast; conservative or "red" states are in the South, much of the Midwest, and the Rocky Mountains.) Creationists are more likely to be uneducated, politically conservative, and reside in a less-populated area of a red or "retro" state. Believers in some form of evolution are more likely to be better educated, politically liberal, and live in a more metropolitan area of a blue or "metro" state. (We can find many exceptions, of course, as we can for every valid generalization.) Hence, this controversy expresses not merely the merits of one or the other side, but also entire worldviews, indeed, ways of life as well. Both sides have a substantial investment in their positions as well as a great deal invested in discrediting the other side. "Live and let live" is an impossibility for many adherents of both positions. While homosexuality does not necessarily discredit heterosexuality and vice versa, in contrast, creationism and evolution *automatically* contradict one another. Each, inherently and by its very nature, provides a critique of the other. If one is right, the other *must* be wrong, and vice versa. (There's another logical possibility: In theory, both could be wrong.) Hence, the special vehemence of the adherents of these two positions.

For creationists, the dominance of evolution in the educational curriculum represents the triumph of secular materialism. If we descended from animals, we must have a kinship *with* animals; if what brought humanity out of the slime is a random, Godless power, it follows that humanity itself is guided *by* a Godless power; if apes are our ancestors, we must *be* apes. Clearly, the propositions on which evolutionary theory is based must be false, reasons the creationist, otherwise we live in a society dominated by bestiality, not Christianity. Humans stand next to angels; they are touched by the hand of God; they share no kinship with beasts of the forest. To the creationists, the implications of evolution are terrifying: They seem to undermine the very foundation of Christianity; indeed, their very notion of their intimate bond with God. Evolution implies that forces that created humanity were accidental,

indifferent, unguided, capricious, purposeless. If certain events had turned out differently, humans would not have evolved at all. Humans were not fated or destined to appear on Earth, as Christianity decrees; we appeared at a particular time and place by a roll of the bio-geological dice. Evolution seems to deny every particular of the Christian cosmology. To the unsophisticated Christian who reasons in Manichean, black-or-white, either-or terms, evolutionary theory is a conspiracy to subvert Christian faith and weaken Christian world altogether. It should come as no surprise that evolution has become a lightning rod for creationists everywhere, and that evolutionists have become labeled as deviants.

For their part, evolutionists regard the belief in creationism as a failure in the scientific program. Like Professor Dini, scientists believe it is their task to draw reasonable conclusions from the available evidence, and the task of science educators to teach their students to reason likewise. The fact that some of their students, not to mention nearly half of the American public, hold a belief that contradicts the very foundation of modern biology indicates that scientists have failed at their task. In a sense, creationist belief represents an *indictment* of science education, a failure of one of the central missions of science itself. Evolutionists rarely bother to address the creationist challenge, which they find frustrating and puzzling; rather, most ignore it. To the extent they do address that challenge, creationists are depicted as ignoramuses, country bumpkins—or charlatans who hoodwink the masses into believing bogus assertions about how nature works.

Rationalistic nineteenth century thinkers such as Karl Marx (1818–1883), Auguste Comte (1798–1857), and Herbert Spencer (1820–1903) argued that as societies became increasingly educated, and as scientific knowledge became widely disseminated, mystical, occult, superstitious beliefs, including Christian and other religious dogma, would disappear. These writers would have been astounded by the persistence of religion in the modern age, in particular, the belief in Biblical creation. In a conversation, a prominent evolutionist predicted that when the implications of the relevance of DNA research for evolutionary theory sinks in to the public at large, creationists will be convinced of the error of their ways; they'll pack up their road show and slink off into the night. I disagreed; I said there is no conceivable accumulation of evidence that will change minds on either side of this issue. Clearly the belief that the account of the origin of the universe described in Genesis plays a major role in the lives of fundamentalist Christians. It is not going to go away any time soon. Clearly, the evolution-creation debate provides a major source of defining cognitive deviance—on both sides of the debate.

PARANORMAL BELIEFS AS DEVIANT

What makes paranormal beliefs—those that contradict what scientists believe to be the laws of nature—a form of cognitive deviance? As with creationism, how can beliefs held by half, or more than half, of the population be regarded as *deviant*? Gallup and Harris polls show that nearly half the American public believes in ghosts, a third in astrology, three-quarters in miracles, and six in ten in the devil. How can beliefs with such widespread support be unconventional or non-normative? It's simple: *In* certain contexts, these beliefs are derided, scorned, not permitted a serious hearing. These beliefs are not valorized in the dominant institutions; they are non-hegemonic, not validated by the dominant educational, media, and religious institutions. The higher we move on the ladder of prestige and power, the less and less acceptable—and the more deviant—they are.

Sociologically, we look at paranormal beliefs by focusing on how they are generated and sustained. The routes through which this takes place are many and varied. Perhaps five are most likely to be interesting to the sociologist. For each, we should ask the basic question: "Who is the paranormalist's social constituency?" And for each belief, the answer is significantly different.

First, there are paranormal beliefs that originate from the mind of a social isolate, a single person with an unusual, highly implausible vision of how nature works. The isolate's message is presumably directed mainly at scientists, although any connection with the scientific community is tenuous or non-existent. Scientists refer to these people as *cranks*. Here, the social constituency of the crank usually does not extend beyond himself (most cranks are men). It is deceptive to think that cranks address their message to the scientific community, since they do not engage in science-like activities or associate with other scientists; their goal is to *overturn* or *annihilate* conventional science, not contribute to it. Not enough attention has been paid to the crank, but it is a sociologically revealing subject nonetheless. Donna Kossy devotes an entire book, entitled *Kooks*, to the topic (1994).

Second, there are paranormal belief systems that begin within a religious tradition that existed long before there was such a thing as a scientist. Such beliefs sustain, and continue to be sustained by, an identifiable religious organization. Creationism is a prime example. The social constituency of the creationist is the like-minded religious community.

Third, there are beliefs that depend on a client-practitioner relationship. In other words, the key fact of certain belief systems is that they are validated by professionals who possess special expertise that is sought by laypersons in need of personal assistance, guidance, an occult interpretation of reality of their lives, or a demonstration of paranormal proficiency. Astrologers and other psychics exemplify this type of paranormalism. The social constituency of the astrologer and the psychic is made up primarily of the client and secondarily, of other astrologers and psychics.

Fourth, another form of paranormalism is kept alive by a core of researchers who practice what seems to be the *form* but not the *content* of science. Many adherents are trained as scientists; they conduct experiments, publish their findings in professional journals, and maintain something of a scientific community of believers, but most traditional scientists reject their conclusions. As we've seen, parapsychology offers the best example here. Unlike astrologers and psychics, parapsychologists do not have clients. They are researchers and theorists, not hired for a fee. While a substantial number of laypersons may share the beliefs paranormalists claim to validate in the laboratory, these paranormal scientists or "protoscientists" form the sociological core of this system of thinking. For the *professional* parapsychologist—that is, the parapsychological *researcher*, the social constituency is that tiny band of other professional parapsychologists and, ultimately, the mainstream scientific community.

Fifth, there are paranormal belief systems that can be characterized as "grass roots" in nature. They are sustained less by individual theorists, a religious tradition or organization, a client-practitioner relationship, or a core of researchers, than by a broad-based public. In spite of the fact that it is strongly influenced by media reports and the fact that there are numerous UFO organizations and journals, the belief that unidentified flying objects (UFOs) are "something real" has owed its existence primarily to a more-or-less spontaneous feeling among the population at large. The ufologists' social constituency is primarily other ufologists, secondarily the society as a whole.

The assertions of the scientific "crank" represent one of the most interesting of all paranormal belief systems. He is a self-styled scientist or (from most scientists' point of view) a *pseudoscientist* who persists in advancing views of how nature works that are regarded as either nonsensical or contradicted by the available evidence (Gardner, 1957, pp. 7ff). While many legitimate scientists have advanced theories that were later overturned, falsified, or refuted by evidence, most of their peers regarded their theories as plausible, even though they were ultimately proven false. Moreover, many of the legitimate scientists who propose erroneous theories are able to recognize the error of their ways once the evidence against their hypotheses begins piling up. (To the extent that a real scientist continues to advance an incorrect theory, even after it has been disproven, he or she is more likely to be called a *curmudgeon* than a crank.) In contrast, the crank usually advances theories that are completely implausible to most scientists, or irrelevant or contrary to the way the world operates, or simply impervious to empirical test.

Have proponents of novel theories that were eventually validated and accepted regarded as cranks? Why aren't Albert Einstein (whose theory of relativity subsumed Newton's laws of physics), Alfred Wegener (who proposed the theory of continental drift), Karl Jansky and Grote Reber (who discovered radio waves), and Ignaz Semmelweis (who discovered that germs could infect mothers who were delivering babies)—all of whose theories were initially either rejected or considered controversial (Ben-Yehuda, 1985, pp. 106–167)—cranks?

For instance, did any physicist in 1905 regard Albert Einstein a crank for proposing his theory of relativity? One physicist says no, that Einstein's contemporaries did not and would not have branded him a crank (Bernstein, 1978). To begin with, Einstein published his ideas in a recognized journal of physics. Second, his theory of relativity passed the test of the "correspondence" principle—that is, it proposed exactly *how* it fit into or extended existing and established theory. In other words, Einstein's theory was very clear on just where Newton's principles ended and where his own theory began. In contrast, crank theories "usually start and end in midair. They do not connect in any way with things that are known" (p. 12). Third, most crank theories "aren't even wrong."Says physicist Jeremy Bernstein, "I have never yet seen a crank physics theory that offered a novel quantitative prediction that could be either verified or falsified." Instead, they are "awash in a garble of verbiage . . . , all festooned like Christmas decorations." Einstein's paper was very clear about its predictions; it virtually cried out to be empirically tested (p.13).

Cranks tend to have at least two basic characteristics. First, they usually work in almost total isolation from orthodox scientists. They have few, if any, fruitful contacts with genuine researchers and are unaware of, or choose to ignore, the traditional canons of science, such as falsifiability and reproducibility. Cranks tend not to send their work to the recognized journals; if they do, it is rejected for what scientists regard as obvious, fundamental flaws. They tend not to be members of scientific academies, organizations, or societies. And they tend not to receive grants or fellowships or awards from scientific organizations. In short, they are not members of the scientific *community*.

Second, cranks have a tendency toward *paranoia*, usually accompanied by *delusions of grandeur* (Gardner, 1957, pp. 12–14). I am not using these terms in the clinical or psychiatric sense, but descriptively. That is, they believe they are unjustly persecuted and discriminated against because they are geniuses, because their ideas are so important and revolutionary they would threaten the scientific establishment. Cranks argue that practitioners of entire fields are ignorant blockheads; they are wrong blinded by pigheaded stubbornness and stupidity. Only they themselves, the true visionaries, are able to see the light. Consequently, they have to continue to fight to expose the truth. If the scientific establishment ignores them, that only demonstrates their arguments are unanswerable. If scientists challenge their charges and attempt to answer their arguments, that only shows they are out to destroy them. It is all part of a plot. It never occurs to cranks that this opposition is, in all probability, generated by basic flaws to their work (Gardner, 1957, pp. 8ff). As a consequence, cranks are usually *driven*, compelled to spell out their theories, and get them recognized as valid. Like many other paranormalists, they are seized with a messianic zeal (Kossey, 1994, p. 56).

The central concept in the field of sociology is the group. In fact, it can be said that sociology is the *study* of group life. Sociologists are very interested in the social "glue" that binds the members of a society—the networks of relations and associations, both formal and informal, which make interaction an ongoing enterprise. It is the shared expectations people have of who we are and what we should be doing, as well as the sanctions we apply to transgressors, that bring most disruptive and destructive behavior under control. In the absence of such communal links, mutual obligations, and shared meanings, social life as we know it would be impossible. It is the sociologist's job to understand exactly how social life operates.

Social isolates choose to live apart—or have been driven—from the bosom of the conventional group and hence, from these social influences. (Although, even before their isolation, all of them have already been influenced by the groups that have shaped them and will manifest that influence to their dying day.) As a result of this social isolation, sociologists have not paid much attention to cranks.

In my estimation, this is a mistake. Cranks and their theories are worth examining, even by sociologists. In fact, I'll state this even more strongly: Sociologists ought to be *especially* interested in

cranks. They seem to defy the sociologist's insistence that the group is the measure of all things. In a way, the crank offers an example of the limiting or negative case: someone who pursues a line of action that is not validated by any relevant social groupings. How did the crank come to generate ideas that practically everyone else considers crackpot? Where did these ideas come from in the first place? What motivates the crank? What keeps him (again, they are usually male) at the task of churning out missive after elaborate, detailed missive, spelling out theories or interpretations of reality that only he grasps? Where does the crank fit into the sociologist's relentless pursuit of understanding group dynamics?

All crank theories take scientists to task for the error of their ways, their inability to see what is clearly and plainly in front of their noses. Nearly all deride or demean the existing scientific hierarchy of power, prestige, and influence. All argue that the "crank" creators and proponents are vastly wiser and more intelligent than the scientific establishment. Nearly all assert the wisdom of good common sense and challenge the warping, distorting perspective of encrusted scientific dogma. Many challenge the narrow specialization of practicing scientists and respond with their own broad, sweeping view of things. Most offer a critique of the dehumanizing tendency of science, especially its emphasis on rationality (Kossey, 1994, p. 58). It might be said that cranks possess much the same hubris, arrogance, and self-righteous audacity manifested by biblical prophets. They offer a kind of apocalyptic vision of how we ought to view reality and, hence, to reorder our lives, reform our behavior, and transform the society. Cranks are a cultural phenomenon; rather than debunking or dismissing them, we should attempt to understand them.

In a way, then, cranks want it both ways.

On the one hand, they want to *annihilate* the prevailing theories of established science. Scientists are wrong, I am right, they are ignorant, I am well-informed, seems to be the prevailing position of the crank. The hubris or *arrogance* of the person possessed of superior wisdom and knowledge seems to suffuse the crank's self-presentation.

But on the other hand, the crank also lusts to be *accepted* by the scientific fraternity as well.

Otherwise, why do they send established scientists their writings? Cranks deeply and sincerely believe that, through the presentation of their evidence and the sheer power of their argument, they will convince the scientific powers that they are right.

What they want is contradictory, of course; it can be said that cranks have a *love-hate* relationship with established science. On the one hand, they do not play by the rules of conventional science. But on the other, they are sufficiently removed from social contact with those who set those rules that they are either unaware of what those rules are or are deluded into thinking that such rules are mere technicalities that can be swept away by the tidal wave of truth. And it is they alone who are possessed of that truth.

SUMMARY

The processes by which some members of the society come to hold beliefs thought in mainstream social circles to be unacceptable, is interesting and significant. Sociologically, we can refer to such beliefs as *cognitive* or intellectual deviance. Yet few sociologists of deviance discuss or deal with the topic. Atheism is a prime example of cognitive deviance; many Americans, for example, believe that an atheist cannot be trusted, and less than half of the public would even consider voting for an atheist for president. As with deviant behavior, unacceptable beliefs elicit negative reactions from audiences, including stigma, social rejection and isolation, criticism, even punishment. Different audiences "deviantize" different beliefs. Indeed, different audiences deviantize *one another*: Liberals deviantize conservatives and vice versa; evolutionists deviantize creationists, and vice versa; atheists deviantize theists and vice versa. At the same time, it's not a matter of a random hodgepodge of different, separate, and independent belief systems: Some audiences have more power to define what's cognitively acceptable and what's deviant.

Some conceptual distinctions are in order here. Not all deviant beliefs lead to deviant behavior; many beliefs remain in the cognitive realm.

Hence, the topic is important in and of itself; it is not a simple extension of the fear that deviant beliefs will translate into deviant behavior. Deviant beliefs should be distinguished from mental disorder. While nearly all mental disorders have a cognitive manifestation—just about all mental disorders entails deviant beliefs—most holders of deviant beliefs are psychologically normal. Beliefs are deviant not because they are "wrong" in some empirical sense, but because they are *regarded as* wrong by specific audiences. Galileo was *right* about the Earth revolving around the Sun, but in the 1600s, that belief ran afoul of the Catholic Church hierarchy and hence, Galileo was defined *by* the Church at that time as a deviant. The fact that Galileo made empirically correct observations has no bearing on his deviant status. Some beliefs become dominant (and therefore conventional) at a later point in time. In the 100s, Christians were persecuted for their beliefs; by the medieval era, Christianity was the dominant religion in Europe and it was non-Christians who were persecuted.

Belief systems are never "just" beliefs; beliefs are never a simple matter of what one individual believes. Human consciousness is a product of social existence. Marxism argued that our beliefs are a product of our economic life. Scholars no longer accept a simple Marxist theory of social and ideological beliefs. Max Weber, an early twentieth-century sociologist, held a more sophisticated view of the origin of belief systems, arguing that people tend to have an *affinity* for certain beliefs, based on their social circumstances and their position in the society's system of ranking. In addition, Weber argued that ideas could influence social position as much as social position influences ideas.

Religion is a major source of differing definitions of true and false; hence, religion spawns a substantial sector of cognitive deviance. People "know" religious truths to be valid in the same way that they know that the Sun sets every night. Religion and deviance intersect in a variety of ways. Religion influences and hence, correlates with acts the society defines as deviant; this is a case of religion *and* deviance. Mainstream religions define certain religious sects and cults as unorthodox and heterodox, that is to say, deviant; this is a case of religion *as* deviance. In addition, religious bodies define certain secular practices as deviant; this is deviance *according to* religion. Theological disputes among practitioners of a particular religion and wrongdoing by religious functionaries, may be referred as deviance *within* a religious organization. And religious bodies attempt to define other religious beliefs and bodies as deviant; this might be referred to as deviance *between and among* religious organizations.

One of the interesting instances of religious deviance is how a mainstream body defines and reacts to sects and cults. A "sect" is a religious body that breaks off from an established, mainstream body. A "cult" is a religious body that is radically different from an established, mainstream body; some cults stem from within the same society, while others stem from outside the same society, as the established body. In the United States at this time, sects that offer a stronger, more evangelical, more zealous, and more dogmatic version of Christianity are growing faster than the old-line, established, mainstream ecumenical denominations. In a sense, sects are deviant—albeit only moderately deviant—because they are "too religious." In contrast, cults are deviant because they contrast too sharply with the established denomination. In the nineteenth century, the Church of the Latter Day Saints (the Mormons) was an example of a cult. Their difference with established denominations has declined over the years.

The struggle to define creationism as deviant and evolutionary theory as intellectually acceptable, and vice versa, is one of the more interesting examples of cognitive deviance we might examine. The controversy is fraught with conceptual confusion. In the past two decades or so, "intelligent design," the view that evolution occurred but it was guided by the hand of God, has been added to the struggle. Nearly half of the American public believes that the earth is less than 10,000 years old and that all species on the planet were created in six days, as spelled out in the Genesis account. Less than 10 percent accepts a materialistic version of evolution—that is, that evolution occurred but God had nothing to do with it; in contrast, roughly 99 percent of biological and geological scientists accept this belief. In addition, representatives at the pinnacle of society's major institutions accept the evolutionary account. Perhaps for no other major belief is there such a yawning gulf between what the public believes and what scientists believe. Since both creationism and evolution are tied in to a larger world view, this controversy is unlikely to disappear any time soon.

Paranormal beliefs, those that scientists argue contradict the laws of nature, are extremely widespread. Some paranormal beliefs originate with a "crank," someone disconnected from the scientific establishment who attempts to overturn conventional science by proposing a "theory" that challenges what scientists believe to be true. Observers argue that cranks are completely different from legitimate scientists, like Einstein, who propose a revolutionary theory that challenges conventional paradigms. The theories of cranks usually cannot be empirically tested, falsified, or verified. Other paranormal beliefs originate from a religious community; examples include creationism and the belief that angels and the devil exist as material beings that influence worldly events and behavior. Still other paranormal beliefs are sustained in a client-practitioner relationship; here, astrology is a prime example. And some paranormal beliefs are sustained through the activities of a body of researchers whose work, in the estimation of scientists, is deviant because it lacks the form but not the content of science. Here, parapsychologists offer the prime example, since, in the judgment of the vast majority of scientists, its practitioners are unable to offer a satisfactory, testable, cause-and-effect model for how the mind can influence material phenomena. Finally, many paranormal beliefs have "grass roots" or popular origin; they are an aspect of the traditional culture. Examples include beliefs that UFOs, ghosts, and witches are "real."

Account: One Man's Theory about 9/11

Dan Gordon is in his sixties, very smart, and a former newspaper writer; over the past decade or so, he has supported himself by betting on sporting events as well as consulting bettors and line-makers on how to bet and set prices on NFL and NBA games. Dan has a higher won-lost ratio than anyone else in the business, higher even than sports analysts. Until a recent illness, Dan supplemented his income by playing blackjack in a number of casinos around the country. Dan considers himself an anarchist, a strong advocate of individual freedom, and he is an amateur analyst of politics. His beliefs on current events—what has happened in the political realm and why—would be considered unconventional, even deviant, to the majority of Americans. His views are not endorsed by the media, the educational curriculum, or in speeches or writings by any mainstream political figures. Dan is ill and believes he will not live out the year; he considers the following statement to represent a statement of his political "last will and testament."

I don't and never have believed in conspiracies. What I do believe is that people tend to act in a way that supports THEIR OWN PERCEIVED SELF-INTERESTS. Often, this means involve coordinating acts with others. If two people are in a room and decide they'd be more comfortable in another room and they move, is that a conspiracy? The term "conspiracy" has gotten a bad name; people do a lot of things in coordination with one another to maximize their own self-interests, and most of their actions do not qualify as conspiracies.

As two examples of activities or events that some observers might call conspiracy theories that are simply groups of people acting in their self-perceived interests, consider Facebook and the recent killings in Arizona, Colorado, and Newtown, Connecticut. To me, it is evident that Facebook, which charges its users not a penny, is a CIA-funded operation. It is readily available to the masses so that the government can gather information from its users who rather stupidly

make it available to the world. ALL governments love gathering information on people in order to control them.

Likewise, the recent spate of seemingly senseless killings from Arizona to Connecticut—the type of which virtually NEVER used to happen in days in which the purchase of firearms was far easier than it is now—has taken place in order to con the populace into supporting gun control, a key element of any totalitarian society. In the United States, giving up the right to own various types of firearms cedes ownership to the clearly sick psychopaths who run the only government in history to drop nuclear weapons as an act of war—in this case, the defenseless Japanese population that had clearly been ready to surrender by late 1944. It seems quite obvious that these mass killers (along with Timothy McVeigh of Oklahoma City fame being the best-known example) are all CIA drug zombies. Such zombies were created in CIA drug tanks in Langley, Virginia, during the Vietnam War, when many tons of heroin were documented to have been imported to the United States from Vietnam in the bodies of dead GIs. The original reason for doing this was for then-President Richard Nixon and his cronies to create a law-and-order issue. It was also the same time when marijuana was prevented from reaching the United States from a number of foreign sources as a result of U.S. government operations such as Operation Intercept, which stopped the drug at the Mexican border.

I am 3,000 percent positive that the shootings in Arizona, Colorado, and Newtown, Connecticut were conducted by CIA drug zombies—setups supported by the American tax dollar to prepare us for the ultimate murder. Did you notice that the shooters had the EXACT same gleam in their eyes when their mug shots were taken? This is because they had been given their reward for their deeds: a shot of heroin, which the CIA had addicted them to. The shot of heroin is the CIA's way of telling these zombies: "Good job!" The Newtown killer said that he had no emotion and never felt any sort of pain. These are the EXACT qualities the CIA insists that EVERYONE applying for a job with them should possess. The CIA operates more on Nazi principles than the Gestapo did. They are TOLD WHAT EMOTIONS TO FEEL and to OBEY ORDERS AND NEVER QUESTION THEM!!

Throughout history, certain people have tried to get power over the lives of others. When power is at stake, people often go to great lengths to achieve that end. At times this includes killing others who are in their way. Is the belief that some folks plan mass exterminations so incredible? Some people might say so. I wouldn't believe it if the evidence weren't there. I believe it is. Let's look at a few events in recent world history. Consider the mass buildups of nuclear arsenals—the deployment of only a SMALL PERCENTAGE of which could destroy life on Earth. Even if one side "wins" and the other "loses," we'd all lose because we'll all be dead. Is this unbelievable? Yes. Has it happened? Absolutely. Consider the current buildups of nuclear power plants. Their power source is toxic, leakages are inevitable, long-term safe storage of waste fuel is impossible, and these plants are the LEAST efficient of power sources. The chief executive officers of power companies certainly know how unsafe nuclear is, and they've gone at great lengths to cover up any problems that have arisen. At the very least, they KNOWINGLY risk mass extermination of humanity by running their plants.

9/11 was perhaps the most important event that has happened in the past fifty years. When I heard that Muslim terrorists hijacked airplanes and flew them into the World Trade Towers, I realized that the explanation that was being fed to the masses was a complete lie. I felt then and I still feel that this official version of the events of 9/11 is a government fable. ANYONE who believes it is a total fool; their brain has been destroyed; is living in a land of total denial; or is a shill or confederate for the powers that are pulling off this confidence game. I base my view on the events of 9/11 on hundreds of facts I'm aware of and experiences I've had.

Just a few of these experiences and known facts are the following. Two months BEFORE 9/11, at an airport check, security confiscated from me a simple pair of scissors. How could four groups of men bring box-cutters and knives onto four planes without a peep from the metal detectors? How could these so-called terrorist pilots be totally incapable of flying, and yet two of them performed the difficult maneuver of flying the planes into office buildings, and one into the Pentagon? Why was it that the plane manifests showed no Arab passenger names? Why was it that airline stocks went through the floor starting several days BEFORE 9/11? Why did many top-level, important CEOs somehow have the foresight to call in sick that day and did NOT show up for work? How was it possible that the bin Laden family—a fictional character created by the CIA in the same way that the FBI creates lives for people living in witness protection programs—was able to take hundreds of millions of dollars out of the U.S. days AFTER the government froze the assets of all Arabs doing business in America?

As I said, I have long felt that Osama bin Laden was a fictional character, with no corporeal existence, created long ago by the CIA. Why? In order to generate patriotic hysteria from the doped American populace. This was done in the same manner in which Emanuel Goldstein, enemy of the state, was created by the rulers of Oceana in George Orwell's book, *1984*, and, as I said, in the same manner that the FBI creates entire past lives for people they put into their witness protection programs. Bin Laden supposedly escaped SWAT teams in the Pakistan and Afghan deserts despite being on dialysis, and, after he was supposedly assassinated, the fact that his dead body was NEVER shown to the public, are strong pieces of evidence that indicate his reality is fictional. And all of these facts, taken together, provide strong evidence that my theory about 9/11 is correct.

I feel that there were two principle reasons why the fable of 9/11 was created to con the masses. The first and shorter-term one was to end whatever small amount of freedom and privacy that still existed at the time; the goal, in short, was to set up a police state. The second and far more important reason was to conceal from the world populace the total and inevitable world-ending slaughter that soon awaits them. Both of these insane aims are facilitated by the increasing stupidity of people on

(*Continued*)

Account: One Man's Theory about 9/11   Continued

this planet, which is being accomplished in various ways I'll detail momentarily.

Let's see how the fable of 9/11 has been used to help set up a worldwide police state.

I believe that 3,000 lives were sacrificed by the American government and the super-rich who control the government to create a worldwide police state in which every person would eventually have a microchip installed in their body which would forever end our freedom and privacy. The increasingly forced use of governmentally approved IDs for the population since 9/11 is one way in which this ultimate scam is being set up.

One key method of making the human cows docile is to con them into thinking that their governments exist to protect them. A great way of accomplishing this is to create a threatening situation where the government is needed to come to the rescue. The creation of fake terrorist incidents generates the fear of more to come, which manipulates the masses into docilely accepting the government's "protection," serves this purpose VERY WELL! Anyone with a brain can see this clearly during the tenth anniversary of 9/11, which led to Gestapo-like cops stopping people all over the world and violating their privacy and checking their cars. Many people in the United States SUPPPORTED this invasion of their privacy. Of course, no acts of terrorism occurred.

I should also mention the recent invasion of the Nazi-like census-takers into the lives of the American people. And the bank credit and debit cards, that are strongly encouraged by banking companies. Anyone who believes that census-taking is done to benefit the people is a TOTAL FOOL whose brain has been destroyed in the ways I've just described. NOTHING that ANY government HAS EVER DONE is done to give any sort of benefits to ANYONE who is not super-rich. The most that ANY government has done for the population as a whole is to throw an occasional bone to the masses to con them into thinking that the system works for them. And in every case, the sucker getting this bone is made to pay a huge interest on it. The reason why the United States takes the census of the population is to GATHER MORE

INFORMATION ON PEOPLE. Same reason that bank debit and credit card use is so strongly encouraged.

Some present accompaniments of the police state will help the government accomplish their insane aims. Concentration camps have been in existence since the 1950s and are maintained by your tax, pension, and retirement monies. Any people who are defined as dangerous will be sent to them. Knowing as much as possible about the population is the way that the super-rich have of controlling the masses, and the keys to this knowledge are the U.S. Census and the information gathered as a result of bank and debit cards. The more that the super-rich and the government know about people—where they live, where they do business, what transactions they take part in, and so on—the easier it is to relocate and control them. Since so many people are already brain-dead, it is far easier to control them.

The biggest motive of selling the fable of 9/11 is to set up the world population to go to their deaths as docilely as cows do when they are slaughtered. To me this seems certain to happen soon due to the long-term financial realities that are taking place today. The world tries to live on money that does not really exist. In the United States this reality was shown quite clearly in the financial crash of 2008. In this crash or melt-down, OVER ONE TRILLION DOLLARS THAT millions of people thought they had suddenly DISAPPEARED. Many long-planned retirements vanished from people's retirement portfolios. The U.S. government did not punish the perpetrators of this theft (big banks, companies, and CEOs) but in fact, it gave these crooks trillions of dollars in bail out money!! To anyone with a brain, this proved that the U.S. government is a front for a few thousand rich people.

As reality reveals and as the masses will soon discover, all government programs, nearly all pensions, and all accounts in banks as well as cons like mutual funds and money in the stock market also operate on the "money that does not really exist" principle. The FDIC only guarantees money up to the reserve requirement of the bank—usually under 2 percent—which gives as much protection as used toilet paper. The sad fact is that the super-rich control all of these monies and supposed wealth for the average person. It can ALL disappear, with the support of the guns of the government, who are there ONLY to serve the super-rich. The sad fact is that the super-rich NEVER INTENDED these monies to exist for the baby boomers on their retirement.

The inescapable financial problems of the world likewise risk humanity's lives by risking its economic support. The money that's being used to pay for things does not exist. And at some point, the bills have to be paid. When the poor realize that they've been ripped off, what will the response of the super-rich be? Will they say, "Oh, we are so sorry. We've been bad, bad little boys, and we promise not to do it again. We'll even pay you back"? Who do you think will pay the bills? Will these high-level thieves stick around for the Nuremberg-type trials that people will demand to punish these CEOs for their crimes? The super-rich will never be brought to trial and will never be held accountable for their crimes against humanity.

The problem is that this money will not exist and, in fact, was never intended to be there when the baby boomer retirements take place. That money, supposedly kept safely in retirement funds in banks and other respected financial institutions, was used for other purposes, the main one being a spaceship that has been planned to take a few thousand super-rich to The New World—the same one that the Challenger astronauts have lived on since the fake explosion that was supposed to have occurred in 1986. (Think about it: Metal contracts in cold weather and the astronauts were sent off on the coldest day of the year. And Ronald Reagan, that embryonic moron of a president, was told to write a speech eulogizing the astronauts days BEFORE the ship took off and supposedly exploded.)

Thus, to me, the only solution for the super-rich and the only way in which they can pull off the massive financial theft they have perpetrated is for them to leave this planet and kill everybody left behind. The super-rich of the world control all governments and use them as vehicles to carry out their orders by means of violence when it is needed. The

fact that governments have used no nuclear weapons, despite all the supposed near-misses of the 1970s from Soviet and American silos, shows that governments probably have NO access to nuclear weapons. In reality, ALL NUCLEAR WEAPONS are owned by the super-rich and will be used by them when it is in THEIR INTEREST TO DO SO. Again, this is not a conspiracy; it is the coordinated actions of people doing what they perceive as their own best interests.

The "final solution" for the economic problems of the world is to destroy it completely. This will be done by the super-rich when they leave on their spaceship. Bill Gates has long had two cobalt bombs stored in his basement. What a joke it is that he has been made to seem such a benevolent super-philanthropist! These bombs will do the "honors" when the space ship leaves the earth's atmosphere.

What helped the fable of 9/11 to be sold to the populace and helped to hide THE REAL WHYS OF IT from the people is the fact that the governments and the super-rich who control them have long gone to great lengths to make people into idiots. In effect, the world has been "dummified."

People have long been made stupid enough to accept obvious lies like 9/11 in some of the following ways. For instance, the microwave beaming that began in the early 1970s, which is accomplished off of telephone and other lines, has destroyed the ability of most people to think for themselves, which, in turn, has made all of these cover-ups easier to pull off. The world-wide use of computers has destroyed the brain power by replacing the brain power of humans with the brain power of computers. Today, most people can't perform even the simplest mathematical calculations. The poisons that are put into most foods and water systems likewise are brain-destroyers. The fluoride that is put into most big city water systems was first used in Nazi concentration camps—whose gasses were supplied by major U.S. businesses, which "made a killing" off of the Holocaust—which made prisoners much more docile and obedient, right up to when they took their final "shower." The huge number of chemicals that are put into processed foods—remember, the companies that make these poisons receive

(Continued)

Account: One Man's Theory about 9/11   Continued

hundreds of billions of dollars a year in subsidies, or WELFARE, from YOUR pension—work to make the population lethargic; these chemicals destroy our brains, thereby stopping the simplest forms of thinking ability. The huge government subsidies that large disco businesses received in the late 1970s represent another way we are being turned into cows. (I avoided those places like the plague, not because I knew their real purpose back then but because I wanted to have a real dialogue with people.) The LOUD, blasting music that discos played ended up destroying the hearing ability of BILLIONS of people the world over. And the super-rich, soon-to-be killers of seven billion-plus people know that if you take away people's ability to listen, it stops dialogue and makes it easier to lead them to slaughter. These days, when people talk, they need to have what's said repeated three times before they really hear it. Most of the time, people truly hear nothing you're really saying. This wasn't true in the pre-disco days.

I feel that my purpose in life is to make people aware of matters that are important to us all. I hope that anyone who reads this will have LEARNED something from it. Due to serious health problems, my own life will not be much longer. I've been ready to die for at least ten years; I have no FEAR OF DEATH. I fully know that the next phase of existence is far saner than the madness and insanity that exists on this planet. One of the things that keeps me going is to see that I mete out some forms of justice. I also know that I am marked for death both by the super-rich and their governmental puppets due to my sports-based winnings. And I have full knowledge of the TRUTH of the whys of 9/11, which also makes me marked for death. The only question for me is exactly how I will meet my end. Will it happen as a result of a bullet to the head or a health-related malady? By the way, I am convinced that the government created my life-threatening condition of neuropathy late in 2006. But now, today, all of this has little importance for me. Most people, however, have far stronger reasons

for living than I do, which is why I shared my insights with you about the whys and the TRUE REASONS for 9/11.

QUESTIONS

Everyone has an opinion on what happened on 9/11, 2001. In the Western world, the most widely-believed explanation for the attack is that a coordinated anti-American conspiracy, conducted by nineteen Muslims and financed by Osama bin Laden, a wealthy Saudi business-man, resulted in the hijacking of four airliners, of which one landed in a field near Shanksville, Pennsylvania, one crashed into the Pentagon, and two hit and brought down the north and south towers of the World Trade Center in lower Manhattan; nearly 3,000 people, mostly Americans, died in the crashes. Not everyone believes this narrative, however. Dan Gordon, who wrote the account, has a different theory. Are you convinced that he is right? If not, why? Do you believe that the government has targeted him for death? How do you think most Americans would react to his assertion of these beliefs? React to him personally? Do you believe that his theory is a form of cognitive deviance? Can you think of some related beliefs that are consistent with his theory? Do such beliefs comprise a "package" or assemblage of cognitive constructs about how the world works? Are Americans being turned into "cows"? What evidence supports your view rather than Dan's? Do you find the evidence he presents for his theories convincing? Do you find it plausible that Bill Gates has nuclear bombs in his base-ment? Again, are Dan's beliefs conventional or non-normative? What if he is right? If they were, would you feel different about him and the society in which you live? And what kind of society—what kind of world—do we live in if he is right? On the other hand, what impli-cations does his being wrong have for whether and to what extent we can refer to his assertions as deviant?

Mental Disorder

Learning Objectives:

After reading this chapter, you will be able to:

- answer the question "What is mental disorder?";
- identify essentialism approaches to mental disorder;
- understand constructionism as a model to discuss mental disorder;

- discuss labeling theory;
- understand the arguments surrounding the modified labeling approach;
- comprehend the epidemiology of mental disorder;
- discuss chemical treatment of mental disorder;
- discuss mental disorder as deviance.

We all know someone who seems odd, bizarre; who acts in a totally inappropriate fashion. A stroll down many streets in the nation's larger cities will reveal men and women who look disheveled and mutter incomprehensible phrases to no one in particular. Some people are so fearful of lurking, unmentionable forces that they are literally incapable of walking out of their front door. Others are unable to hold a conversation that anyone else would regard as intelligible. Some people are convinced that their dentist has implanted an electronic receiver in a filling in their teeth that is sending bizarre messages into their brain. Some people wear a perpetual, peculiar smile, and seem to exist in "their own little world."

In everyday language, we have terms for such persons. "He's whacko," we say. "She's out of her mind,""He's a nut,""She's completely cracked,""He's a weirdo,""She's a sicko," or "He's off his rocker," we declare, pointing to the people who display what we regard as manifestations of a mind that's "not right." More formally, the condition such people suffer from is referred to as *mental illness* or, more broadly, *mental disorder*.

What is mental disorder? In what way can a mind be said to be "disordered"? What is a mental "illness"? How can a mind be said to be "ill"? Is disorder an instance of deviance? If so, in what specific ways?

WHAT IS MENTAL DISORDER?

At first glance, defining mental disorder is not as easy or as straightforward a task as might appear. Even explaining specific non-disordered deviant behaviors such as murder, homosexuality, drug use, and prostitution, proves to be an extremely thorny matter. But mental disorder presents a much more formidable definitional problem because it is not a type of behavior as such; instead, it is regarded as a mental condition that presumably *manifests* itself in certain behaviors, thought patterns, and verbal utterances. And, as we just saw, even the behavior supposedly associated with it cannot be pinned down to any one type

of action with much precision. (Of course, certain specific *categories* of mental disorder have more clear-cut symptoms than others, but mental disorder *as a whole* does not.) Rather, mental disorder is a set of conditions that exhibits itself in a *wide range* of behaviors. Hence, no general definition of the phenomenon can be completely satisfactory.

The term "mental illness" does not appear in the table of contents or the index of the latest edition of the American Psychiatric Association's *Diagnostic and Statistical Manual*, its fifth edition, known as *DSM-V* (2014), nor is it in the leading textbook on abnormal psychology (Kring et al., 2010). Psychiatry and clinical psychology, the "healing professions" that deal with and attempt to treat persons who are emotionally troubled, prefer the term "mental disorder" to "mental illness." The term "mental illness" has been used until fairly recently among some sociologists; witness the titles of two textbooks in the field—*A Sociology of Mental Illness* (Tausig, Michello, and Subedi, 2004) and *The Sociology of Mental Illness* (Gallagher, 2011), but such a practice is decreasingly common. And clearly there is a world of difference between the classic mental "illnesses" (mainly schizophrenia and clinical depression) and the grab-bag category that is covered by mental "disorder," including impotence, "transient tic disorder," "mathematics disorder," "reading disorder," and "disorder of written expression." Sociologists study *epidemiology*—the distribution of mental disorders in the population—and hence, are acutely aware of the fact that the broader the category, the lower the likelihood that any single generalization can cover all disorders. Clearly, no single factor or variable could possibly correlate consistently with or be caused by all mental disorders. On the other hand, a number of social characteristics are statistically related to mental "illness," which is a narrower and more specific phenomenon. When I refer to mental disorder here, I'll be referring *mainly* to schizophrenia and clinical depression, and secondarily to cognate phenomena, such as autism.

The American Psychiatric Association issues a standard reference work, the *Diagnostic and Statistical Manual of Mental Disorders*. Its first edition (referred to as *DSM-I*) appeared in 1952 and its fifth edition in 2014 (*DSM-V*). We might expect *DSM-V* to be a good place to find a coherent framework for understanding mental disorder. In this expectation we would be disappointed. *DSM-V* does not so much *define* mental disorder as *enumerate* a range of mental disorders. In fact, this "manual" of mental disorders is descriptive, atheoretical, and lacking in any explanatory framework. It provides a long list of symptoms the clinician is likely to encounter in therapeutic practice, and leaves matters at that.

With all its shortcomings, *DSM-V* offers a sketchy definition of mental disorder. Each of the disorders enumerated in the manual is conceptualized as a clinically significant behavioral and/or psychological syndrome, or pattern, that is associated with distress or disability or impairment and/or with an important loss of freedom. The manual emphasizes that such suffering is not the manifestation of a mental disorder if it is in response to a temporary event, such as the loss of a loved one. Moreover, mere *deviant behavior*—for example, political, religious, or sexual activities or beliefs that run counter to the norms—is *not* to be included as a mental disorder *unless* such behavior is a symptom of a dysfunction in the individual. *By itself*, political radicalism, religious heterodoxy (such as atheism), or homosexuality does *not* indicate a mental disorder. In addition, the manual states, different cultures, subcultures, and ethnic groups have somewhat different customs. Hence, the clinician must make sure to avoid making judgments of psychopathology that ignore the complexities of the individual's cultural perspective.

The original edition of *DSM* listed 100 disorders. There are hundreds disorders listed in *DSM-V*. There are those that are initially diagnosed in infancy, childhood, or adolescence, such as mental retardation, learning disorders, autism, attention deficit disorders, and Tourette's syndrome. There are delirium, dementia, and amnesiac and other cognitive disorders, including Alzheimer's and Parkinson's syndromes. The list includes all the substance-related disorders—that is, abuse of and intoxication and dependence on, a variety of psychoactive substances (including caffeine and nicotine). Schizophrenia and other psychotic disorders are listed, as are mood disorders, both simple depression and bipolar disorders

(manic-depression). A variety of other syndromes follow, including anxiety disorders (panic disorder, agoraphobia, obsessive-compulsion, etc.); sexual and gender identity disorders, including sexual dysfunctions (a lack of sexual desire, male impotence, an inability to achieve orgasm), "paraphilias" (exhibitionism, fetishism, masochism, sadism, voyeurism); eating disorders, sleeping disorders, impulse-control disorders, personality disorders. This represents a remarkably diverse and miscellaneous grab-bag of mental disorders. This grab-bag has no internal logic, and the categorization of its contents is, as I said, atheoretical; it *sidesteps* the issue of causality—what generates disorders in general, or each disorder in particular.

The public recognizes that there are *degrees* of mental disorder. This dimension is commonsensically captured in the distinction between *neurosis* and *psychosis*. We tend to reserve the concept of the psychosis for those cases that are considerably more serious, and vastly less common, than the neurosis. Without medication, the psychotic's condition, unlike the neurotic's, is almost always a barrier to academic and occupational achievement and social relationships, including marriage and the family. And, although the outbreak of a psychosis is frequently grounds for institutionalization in a mental hospital, that of a neurosis almost never is. *DSM-V* does not mention psychosis or the psychotic, and the term "neurosis" does not appear anywhere in its index. Still, the neurosis-psychosis distinction captures most laypeople's thinking about the dimensional quality of mental disorders.

There is no assumption among experts that mental disorders can be clearly separated from the condition of mental health. Mental disorder is not a specific, concrete, discrete entity with a sharp, clean, bright boundary dividing it from other mental disorders or from normalcy. In reality, most experts argue, extreme or "textbook" cases can be detected by encountering the most florid or stereotypical symptoms such as those enumerated in the *DSM*. Clinicians are emphatic in insisting the fact that mental disorder is a continuum does *not* mean these disorders cannot be diagnosed or do not exist. One critic (Rimland, 1969) has argued that this fuzziness does *not* mean disordered conditions cannot be diagnosed.

"While I will agree that some patients in mental hospitals are saner than nonpatients, and that it is sometimes hard to distinguish between deep unhappiness and psychotic depression, I do *not* agree that the difficulty sometimes encountered in making the distinction between normal and abnormal necessarily invalidates all such distinctions" (p. 717). Clinicians feel that because some distinctions are difficult to make—for example, deciding whether sundown is day or night—does not mean that it is impossible to distinguish grosser distinctions, such as that between noon and midnight (Kring et al., 2010).

We have to answer two questions in order to characterize the various approaches to or models of mental disorder. The first is: *How is the reality of mental disorder defined?* And the second is: *What causes mental disorder?* In asking the first question, what I mean is: *Wherein does its reality lie?* We can divide psychiatric researchers into two camps on this issue, the same two that look at all the phenomena we've discussed so far: *essentialists* and *constructionists*.

ESSENTIALISM APPROACHES MENTAL DISORDER

The essentialist approach defines mental disorder as an objectivistic condition that can be located in the real world, in the concrete behavior or verbalizations of persons who are disordered. Such behaviors or verbalizations are outward signs or manifestations of a disordered mind, in much the same way as the height of a column of mercury on a thermometer indicates or measures temperature. To this perspective, we can locate mental disorder much as we can locate a specific geological formation or a biological organism. True, defining and locating mental disorder is a bit more complicated, difficult, and intellectually challenging than identifying entities in the physical world, but the essential reality of mental disorder is an objective fact, identifiable by behavior and speech that persons with the conditions manifest. Of course, mental disorder appears in somewhat different ways in different societies, but there is a *common core* to mental disorder everywhere.

A severe schizophrenic in Zambia would be a severe schizophrenic in Thailand, Panama, or Norway. What counts are not the social definitions or constructs of the condition but *the nature of the condition itself* (Murphy, 1976).

The "hardest" or most extreme version of the essentialistic approach is often referred to as the *medical* model. It argues that mental disorder is very much like a medical disease; a disease of the mind is very much like a disease of the body. The bizarre and inappropriate behaviors exhibited by mentally disordered persons are symptoms of an underlying or internal pathology of some kind. Mental patients present *symptoms*, those symptoms can be *categorized*, and, contrary to what some have argued (Rosenhan, 1973, p. 250), the sane *are* clearly distinguishable from the insane. More colloquially: "Some people *are* more crazy than others; we can tell the difference; and calling lunacy a name does not *cause* it" (Nettler, 1974, p. 894). The medical mode stresses the *intrapsychic* forces in mental disorder; it is an internal *condition* within the psyche of the disordered person. Much as a physical disease is internal to the sufferer, a mental disorder is a disease that is "in" the insane.

Essentialists are interested in, and study, the *epidemiology* and the *etiology* of mental disorder. "Epidemiology" refers to how mental disorders are distributed in categories in the population; "etiology" refers to explanations of the *causes* of mental disorder. Essentialists would argue that there is a "true" rate or incidence of mental disorder in a given population and a given society. They investigate whether men or women have higher rates of mental disorders, and more specifically, *which* disorders. Are married or unmarried men and women more likely to become mentally disordered? Blacks or whites? Urban or rural dwellers? How is socioeconomic status or social class related to mental disorder—and to *which* disorders? Are lower-class people more mentally dysfunctional because lower-class life is more stressful than middle-class life? Or because, if one is disordered, is it more difficult to become successful? These and other questions are asked by epidemiologists who regard mental disorder as a concretely real phenomenon with essentialistic qualities. Essentialists hold that there exists a pregiven entity or syndrome that researchers can define, identify, locate, lay their hands on, and eventually explain or account for. Mental disorder is not merely a label or a social construction. *It does not matter* how the disorder is socially defined—the reality exists *independently* of that definition. The application of the label and the treatment of persons so labeled are not the most interesting things about it. The most interesting thing about mental disorder is what it is, its dynamics, how it works, what causes it—and how we may cure it and restore the mentally disordered to mental health.

Epidemiology is usually seen as being in the service of etiology. The goal of studying how diseases are distributed in the population, many experts feel, is that an explanation of illness can be devised and tested. Someone with an essentialistic orientation sees the primary task of anyone who studies mental disorder as devising a valid theory or account of etiology:*What causes it?* Again, whether this theory is sociological, psychological, or biological does not determine the essentialist's model. The sociologist of mental disorder would argue that it is caused, at least in large part, by social factors: stress, for instance, brought on by lower-class status, gender membership, or racial and ethnic prejudice. Most sociologists agree that social factors combine with genetic, neurological, hormonal, and/or psychological factors. Certain persons who are *genetically predisposed* could experience socially induced stressful conditions, which push them over the edge into mental disorder. Still, these sociological etiologists would say, social factors are *crucial* in the causal dynamics leading to mental illness. Again, simply because a theory is sociological does not mean that it is any less essentialistic: Even sociological theories of mental disorder hold that mental disorder is an identifiable clinical entity. What counts is how the condition is caused, how it came about, what brought it on. And what does not count, what is not interesting or problematic—or at least is of secondary significance—is the creation and application of the label. The enterprise of mental health diagnosis and treatment is crucial only insofar as it relates specifically to the success of treatment outcomes. It is important to know which treatments work and which ones don't, but it isn't important to study treatment as an intellectually or theoretically problematic dynamic in its own right, as a phenomenon to be explained and understood for its own sake.

The strict medical model argues that mental disorder is largely or always a manifestation of abnormal biophysical functioning—brain damage, a chemical imbalance, pathological genes, neurological malfunction, and so on (Torrey et al., 1994). This school suggests that certain environmental factors, such as stress or early childhood experiences, have little independent etiological significance. Of course, they may act as "triggering" mechanisms that exacerbate an already established susceptibility to mental disorder. Consequently, any legitimate and effective therapy for psychic disorder must be physical in nature, such as drugs, electroshock therapy, or surgical intervention. The strict medical model has been gaining adherents in recent years. Electroshock therapy has been making a comeback in the past decade, while the use of psychoactive drugs has almost literally overtaken all other forms of therapy since their introduction in the 1950s. (In contrast, surgery, such as prefrontal lobotomies, has been almost completely abandoned as treatment for mental disorder.) At the other end of the spectrum, psychoanalysis, the "talk" therapy introduced by Sigmund Freud, has plummeted in popularity since the 1950s; in some professional circles, it has been completely discredited (Gruenbaum, 1993; Torrey et al., 1994; Crews, 1995).

Just as biological and genetic theories of mental disorder, which hold that sociological factors are of secondary importance, could be seen as "hard" essentialistic theories, psychological and sociological theories could be seen as "soft" essentialistic theories; they are emphases or varieties of the same approach rather than radically different approaches. Both agree that the clinical entity, mental illness, or mental disorder, is concretely real, that diagnoses tap or measure something in the real world. Both agree that mental disorder represents a genuine malfunction or dysfunction, a true or objectively real disorder above and beyond the mere label or diagnosis itself. But these approaches—the biological on the one hand and the psychological and the sociological on the other—part company on the *cause* of mental disorders. Psychological and sociological theories emphasize that they are caused by the patient's experiences, not by an inherent or inner biological or chemical condition. That is, they stress *nurture*, or environment, rather than *nature*. A mentally disordered person may have nothing physically wrong, yet, as a result of his or her experiences, still have a dysfunctional mind. Since physical, biological, or congenital theories posit causes that are more indwelling, more inherent, the only way that mental disorders can be cured or treated is changing the very physical factors that caused them. This means surgical, chemical, hormonal, genetic, or electrical treatment. Merely changing the conditions of the patient's life, or attempting to cure by means of "talk" therapies, will not change the pathological mental patient's condition. Still, these approaches or theories agree that, because the condition is concretely real, researchers can identify and explain it and, possibly, eventually, treat and cure it. The sociological and psychological theories of mental disorder argue that certain experiences exist in some persons' lives that cause or influence them to "go crazy." And being disordered can be measured by means of certain concretely real objective criteria or indicators. So the psychological and sociological essentialists don't differ on this particular point with the biological essentialists: Mental disorder is concretely real; it is not simply a label.

Earlier, I introduced the term, the "medical" model. The medical model sees mental disorder as a condition that is internal to, or "in," the mental patient, just as cancer, say, is "in" a medical patient. Once a person "has" a mental disorder, it manifests itself under any and all conditions. The medical model is the most *extreme* version of essentialism. Not all essentialistic models of mental disorder conform strictly to the medical model, however. Many sociologists and some psychologists believe that mental disorder will manifest itself more under certain conditions than others. For example, some persons who are vulnerable or susceptible to mental disorder may be perfectly normal or healthy under certain conditions—for instance, those that are less stressful, or when they have a social support network. Essentialists who adhere to the non-medical model stress that mental disorder may be a *temporary* condition, one that is not solely "in" the individual, one that is as much dependent on the social environment in which the individual interacts

as on the individual's internal condition. Again, non-medical essentialists retain the idea of mental disorder as a real "thing" in the material world as well as a disorder. But they see its appearance as much more heavily dependent on external factors than do proponents of the strict medical model. Biogenetic and biochemical theories of mental disorder most definitely adopt a medical model; mental disorder is a condition "in" the individual; again, that manifests itself pretty much everywhere. Psychoanalysis, too, adopts a medical model, although it could be seen as a "softer" version, since mental disorder can be treated by means of a form of therapy that does not entail physical or strictly medical intervention. Once someone has gone through certain pathological childhood experiences, again, one will remain mentally disordered until treatment intervenes.

CONSTRUCTIONISM

A social constructionist model would argue that locating the "common thread" or "common core" to mental disorder is not the most theoretically challenging, interesting, or problematic issue. What counts is the *enterprise* of mental disorder, again, what is *said* and *done* about persons who are *defined* as mentally disordered. One major reason why this is such a crucial question is that diagnoses differ in societies around the world; hence, the reality of mental disorder varies along with them. Definitions of mental disorder are culture-bound; what is labeled dysfunctional in one society or social context may be seen as perfectly normal in another—or possessed, extraordinary, saintly, inspired by the holy spirit.

The constructionists regard mental disorder as socially defined, both by the general public and the psychiatric profession. In other words, as with deviance, constructionists do not think that mental disorder can be defined "objectively" by focusing on the common thread that all disorders share. Instead, they argue, what mental disorder "is" is how it is seen, judged, reacted to, treated, and evaluated in a given society. There exists a mental illness *enterprise* or, in the words of Michel Foucault, a mental illness *discourse*: the psychiatric, legal, and social machinery designed to deal with persons designated as mentally disordered, the writing, the research, the diagnostic manuals, the mental health industry and the drug industry built around administering medication to the mentally disordered, not to mention public attitudes focusing on mental disordered, the popular beliefs, stereotypes, prejudices, legend and folklore, media attention, and so on (1967, 2003). Thus, to the constructionist, what mental disorder *is* is what we *say* and *do* about it, what we say and do about persons designated as mentally disordered. Mental disorder has no "essential" reality beyond these social constructions, this "discourse," these reactions, the social enterprise surrounding it.

The constructionist model of mental disorder argues the following points: (1) *it is a form of deviance*; (2) its reality is *called into being* by the labeling process; and (3) the application of the label is influenced at least in part by a variety of *extrapsychiatric* factors or variables. The mentally ill are derogated and stigmatized, excluded from full social acceptance; the process of judging persons *to be* mentally ill makes their behavior or mental states sociologically relevant (although, of course, such judgments do not *create* the condition in the first place); and these judgments are influenced by a number of factors *in addition to* the severity of their condition. In a nutshell, these are the basic assumptions of the constructionist approach to mental disorder. It is not a theory that attempts to explain *why* some people are or become mentally ill; instead, it is an approach or framework, or set of "sensitizing concepts" that help to understand one major aspect of the phenomenon.

Consider the fact that, in the first edition of the *Diagnostic and Statistical Manual of Mental Disorders* (1952), homosexuality was deemed an instance of a "sociopathic personality disturbance." In the second, it was listed as belonging under the category "sexual deviance." In 1973, under pressure from movement activists and militants, the American Psychiatric Association (APA) decided that, in and of itself, homosexuality was not a disturbance; it represented a disorder only if it created conflict and generated the wish to change one's sexual orientation. In the third edition (1980) this was further modified to apply only to persons for whom such a wish was a "persistent concern"; the APA referred to this condition as "ego-dystonic homosexuality." In the revised third edition (1987, p. 426), an explanation as to why this condition was dropped was offered ("it suggests to some that homosexuality was considered a disorder"). In the fifth edition (2014), there is no mention of homosexuality whatsoever as a disorder of any kind. It is difficult to imagine such contortions taking place, in the era we're discussing (i.e., after 1950 or so), for a physical state or condition; though between 1952 and today, the medical profession has changed on its explanations for the causes of cancer, it has *not* deemed that cancer, once thought to be a disease, is now regarded as of no medical consequence.

The influence of extrapsychiatric factors is in large part due to the vagueness of psychiatric diagnosis. Although certainly more precise and reliable today than in the past, diagnoses of mental disorder are considerably less so than are strictly medical diagnoses—that is, those concerning strictly physical conditions. It is clear that agreement among psychiatrists as to patients' conditions is high only when they present "classic" or "archetypical" symptoms. In contrast, agreement is low for patients who present symptoms that are less clear-cut and more ambiguous. In fact, the majority of cases psychiatrists see are less classic and more ambiguous in their symptomatology (Townsend, 1980, pp. 270–272). A summary of the reliability of psychiatric diagnoses found it to be high only when the categories were extremely broad or the symptoms extreme and clear-cut; where the categories were specific or detailed or the symptoms less than clear-cut, disagreement between and among psychiatrists was high (Edgerton, 1969, pp. 68–69). Two commentators conclude that "art far outweighs science" in psychiatric judgments (Stoller and Geertsma, 1963, p. 65). An author of a textbook on psychiatric methodology states that expert judgments on mental disorder "are of a social, cultural, economic and sometimes legal nature" (Loftus, 1960, p. 13).

In one study (Kendall et al., 1971), videotapes of diagnostic interviews with patients were shown to a large number of psychiatrists in the United States and Great Britain. Those patients presenting "classic, textbook" symptoms generated almost unanimous agreement as to psychiatric condition. However, patients manifesting less than clear-cut symptoms touched off less than unanimity in diagnosis. One patient was deemed schizophrenic by 85 percent of the American psychiatrists, but only 7 percent of the British; another was judged to be schizophrenic by 69 percent of the Americans, but only 2 percent of the British. Clearly, the American concept of schizophrenia is much broader than is the British. Again, it is difficult to imagine such disparities in the diagnosis of a strictly medical disease, such as cancer or tuberculosis, even decades ago.

Examining *informal* mental disorder labeling around the world, even greater variation prevails. Cross-culturally, certain terms or labels are applied everywhere to persons "who are thought to be conducting themselves in a manner that is inappropriate, abnormal, or unreasonable for persons in that culture who occupy a similar social position; that is, to persons who can provide no otherwise acceptable explanation for their conduct" (Edgerton, 1969, p. 50). Every culture has a label that indicates some version of mental disorder or illness. How are these labels applied? A summary of the available anthropological literature points to two conclusions. First, the recognition and labeling of persons "who are both severely and chronically psychotic" typically occurs with a high degree of consensus "because persons such as these are typically so dramatically, and enduringly, far beyond the pale of everyday rationality" (p. 51). And second, most people who act strangely or "crazily" do not do so in an extreme or chronic fashion; consequently, being labeled for these persons is a complex matter, influenced by a wide range of contingencies. As to whether someone is or is not regarded socially and publicly as psychotic is open to *negotiation* (pp. 51, 65)—that is decided in a give-and-take interaction between two or more parties on the basis of factors unrelated to objective psychiatric condition.

Thus, the constructionist is vastly more likely to be concerned with the dynamics of mental disorder labeling than etiological issues. What factors are related to being labeled as mentally disordered? Is it psychiatric condition alone? Or do extrapsychiatric factors play a role in this process? And how prominent is this role? The medical model would hold that psychiatric diagnoses (although not popular or public labels) are an accurate reflection of the patient's "objective" condition. The constructionist and labeling approach argues that this process of mental disorder labeling is considerably less rational than

the medical model holds, that factors other than severity of psychiatric symptoms influence diagnoses and the decision to admit and discharge patients. (However, labeling theorists do *not* claim that this process is random, that persons are singled out randomly or capriciously, that patients do not differ in any appreciable way from the population at large.) This process is guided by a number of contingencies, they argue. There is, in other words, "a clear tendency for admission and discharge of mental patients to be related more to social than to psychiatric variables" (Krohn and Akers, 1977, p. 341). Sociocultural factors, such as family desires and living arrangements, adequate patient resources outside the mental hospital, cultural conceptions, region of the country, and the danger the patient represents to others can be determinants of psychiatric case outcomes (Krohn and Akers, 1977; Townsend, 1978).

Thus, constructionism argues that, *independent of etiology*, independent of the *consequences* of labeling, and independent of the *validity* of psychiatric diagnoses, the sociologist is obliged to study *the social organization of the labeling process* that leads to a judgment or diagnosis of mental disorder. Over a half century ago, Edwin Lemert, an important precursor of labeling theory, stated: "One of the more important sociological questions here is not what causes human beings to develop such symptoms as hallucinations and delusions, but, instead, what is done about their behavior which leads the community to reject them, segregate them, and otherwise treat them as . . . insane" (1951, p. 387). As a qualification: "Hard" or strict constructionists see *all* views of mental disorder, including those held by psychiatrists, as constructions, and sidestep the issue of whether any of them is more valid than the other. In contrast, "soft" or moderate constructionists argue that the reality of mental disorder is not *solely* a construction, and would grant that some constructions strike closer to the empirical reality of mental disorder than others.

LABELING THEORY

A theory that has always been treated as a variant of the constructionist model, but which in fact harbors a strong essentialistic component, is the labeling theory of mental disorder. It may sound confusing to stress the essentialistic strains in labeling theory, since I discussed labeling theory as a constructionist approach in Chapter 3. But, as with Lemert's theory of secondary deviation, the labeling theory of mental illness emphasizes the causal dynamics or etiological factors underlying mental illness, *not* the nature and dynamics of the social construction of mental illness. To be more specific, it argues that mental disorder *is* concretely real, a material phenomenon in the physical world. (Remember, Lemert's theory of secondary deviation emphasizes that it is *being labeled* that often strengthens one's commitment to a deviant role and further deviant behavior.) Thomas Scheff, the primary proponent of the labeling theory of mental illness takes this mechanism several steps further. Being labeled as crazy for engaging in mildly eccentric, slightly bizarre behavior results in *really*, *actually*, and *concretely going crazy*. The definition becomes a *self-fulfilling prophecy*. One learns to act out the symptomatology of mental illness as a result of being exposed to the definitions that are prevalent in a given society; behaving like a crazy person is how one is supposed to act if one has been defined *as* a crazy person. Hence, engaging in odd, eccentric, unconventional behavior for which there is no ready label—"residual deviance"—results in being *labeled* crazy which, in turn, results in acting the way a crazy person is *supposed* to act, which eventually results in actually *going* crazy. But note: The labeling theory argues that there really *is* such a thing as being crazy; although the label creates the condition, *the condition becomes concretely real* (Scheff, 1984, 1999).

It should be emphasized that, although the two approaches have often been confused, Scheff's labeling theory of mental illness and the more general interactionist theory of Becker and his associates are substantially different approaches. Although for Scheff the *initial* process of labeling *is* a social construction, the process of labeling actually *produces* an identifiable condition all can point to and identify as "true" mental illness. In other words, Scheff is not quite a true constructionist, since his primary concern is etiological. In contrast, labelists' concerns are much more heavily concentrated on constructionist matters and far less on issues of causality. Becker

and the other labeling theorists never *intended* their theory to be an explanation of deviance in the sense of accounting for its origin or etiology (Kitsuse, 1972, p. 235; Becker, 1973, pp. 178–179). Nor did it insist that the process of labeling always and inevitably results in an intensification of a commitment to deviance, the deviant role, or deviant behavior; this is an empirical question and must be studied in individual cases (Becker, 1963, pp. 34–35, 1973, p. 179). For Scheff, in contrast, the whole point is to devise a theory accounting for the origin of mental illness. Note that Walter Gove, a critic of Scheff's "harder" version of labeling theory of mental illness, *supports* "a softer" version of labeling theory "that is not concerned with specific predictions [of causality] but is concerned with how social institutions function and how such functioning is related to our understanding of mental illness as a social category and as a social career" (1989).

For Scheff, then, the *initial* process of labeling *is* a social construction; "normal" will often label eccentricity or "residual deviance" *as* mental illness. To the extent that this process is arbitrary and not based on scientific or real-world criteria, Scheff adopts a constructionist approach. Why are eccentrics being labeled as crazy? Is it because of their condition? Clearly not; a variety of extra-psychiatric social and cultural factors rule this process. However, *once the labeling process has been launched* and the person who is labeled as crazy begins to take on a crazy role, a very real condition of mental illness begins to take over. What was *defined* as real *becomes* real. Thus, Scheff has one foot in constructionism and the other foot in essentialism, more specifically, in etiology.

Scheff emphatically states that he is *not* a constructionist (personal communication). His theory is *etiological*; it is an attempt to explain the origin of mental illness (1966, 1984). To Scheff, the *how* and *why* of the social construction of mental illness is secondary; what counts is its power to generate behavior and a condition the psychiatric profession knows as mental illness. Hence, he must be regarded at least as much an essentialist as a constructionist. It must be said that labeling theory, in the form stated by Thomas Scheff, has very few followers among clinicians; it is of interest almost exclusively to a very small circle of sociologists. Today, the overwhelming majority of psychiatrists adopt some version of the bio-medical model. But Scheff's theory has received, and continues to receive, a great deal of attention in the sociological study of deviance.

THE MODIFIED LABELING APPROACH

Gove (1975a, 1975b, 1979a, 1980, 1982) argues that Scheff's labeling theory of mental illness is empirically wrong. Gove argues that mental patients are unable to function in the real world not because they have been stigmatized but because they are mentally ill; the mentally disordered have a debilitating disease that cripples their capacity to function normally and effectively. Moreover, Gove argues, the process by which the psychiatric profession singles out someone as mentally ill is not significantly influenced by sociological or other extra-psychiatric variables. Instead, this process is almost exclusively determined by the nature and severity of the illness. Labeling, the medical model argues, is neither capricious or arbitrary, nor is it based on such hierarchical factors as race, sex, socioeconomic status, or power. Persons who are sick tend to be labeled as such; in turn, those who are well are extremely unlikely to be labeled as sick.

With respect to *informal*, as opposed to professional, far from being eager to label someone as mentally ill, the general public is extremely reluctant to do so and, moreover, does not hold particularly strong, negative, or stigmatizing feelings about the mentally ill. This is especially true for intimates—spouses, children, parents, close friends—of the mentally ill, who avoid labeling until the disturbed person's behavior becomes intolerable. Lastly, hospitalization and other treatment intervention, far from making the patient's condition worse, as the labeling approach claims, most often results in an amelioration of his or her symptoms. In short, a genuine healing process does seem to take place. Gove, the most outspoken and persistent of the critics of the labeling theory of mental illness, argues that these generalizations are so empirically well-founded that he flatly states: "For all practical purposes,

the labeling explanation of mental illness is of historical interest only" (1979a, p. 301).

Which model is correct? Which one approximates empirical reality most closely? To begin with, we need not be forced into an either-or, black-or-white position. It is possible that there is some middle ground here; labeling theory may be correct on some points, while its critics may be right with respect to some others. In my opinion, what has come to be referred to as a "soft" or *modified* labeling theory approach seems to fit the facts of mental illness most faithfully (Link et al., 1989). The modified labeling approach both accepts certain aspects of the medical model and stresses the importance of the labeling process.

Mentally disordered persons, while they do have difficulty in their everyday lives because of their psychiatric condition, also suffer serious debilitation and demoralization as a consequence of stigma and labeling. Everyone who grows up in this society, including the disordered, is aware of the negative image of the mentally ill. Persons who suffer from a mental disorder anticipate negative treatment from others, and these beliefs taint their interaction with "normal" and with mental health professionals (Thoits, 1985; Link, 1987; Link et al., 1989).

As we've seen, constructionism is concerned with how judgments of reality and imputations of deviance are made and put into practice; but labeling theory is, in addition, concerned with the *consequences* of such judgments and imputations. Constructionism also argues that there exists a certain measure of arbitrariness when applying psychiatric labels to psychiatric conditions. As we saw, American psychiatrists are far more likely to apply the label of schizophrenia to patients than British psychiatrists are (Kendall et al., 1971); in a civil case which centered around psychic damages to plaintiffs, psychiatrists for the defense found no psychic damage, while psychiatrists for the plaintiffs found considerable psychic damage (Simon and Zussman, 1983); in fact, a wide range of extra-psychiatric factors influence psychiatric judgments (Krohn and Akers, 1977; Townsend, 1978, 1980). While this must be tempered by the qualification that, as seriousness of the condition increases, the uniformity of the psychiatric judgment increases correspondingly, *most* of the judgments that psychiatrists make are of patients with a less rather than more serious condition. It is clear that extra-psychiatric contingencies do play a major role in psychiatric labeling.

The labeling approach is clearly wrong when it comes to treatment outcomes, however. Enough valid, reliable studies have been conducted on treatment outcomes to demonstrate that psychiatric intervention is more likely to be beneficial than harmful to the patient. Far from entrenching the mental patient more deeply in the mentally ill role, treatment does appear to have some positive effects (Smith, Glass, and Miller, 1980; Landman and Dawes, 1982). Some of these effects are not profound, and many do not persist over time; nonetheless, "it would be difficult for societal reaction theorists to argue that the effects of [psychiatric] labeling are uniformly negative" (Link and Cullen, 1989). Psychiatric intervention

is more likely to move the patient out of rather than more deeply into disordered behavior and undetected, untreated mentally disordered conditions often persist over long periods of time, refuting "the labeling theory notion that symptoms are transient in the absence of labeling" (Link and Cullen, 1989).

Although it is difficult to deny the impact of the objective nature of mental disorder, stigma, labeling, and societal reaction remain potent and crucial sociological factors to be taken into account in influencing the condition of the mentally disordered. Proving or disproving the strict labeling or the strict medical model *in toto* seems a futile exercise. Both have a great deal to offer; in short, a "modified" labeling theory approach seems to be the most productive model in understanding mental disorder (Link et al., 1989).

On Being Sane in Insane Places

"If sanity and insanity exist, how shall we know them?" Psychologist and law professor David Rosenhan decided to answer the question by having eight normal or "sane" persons, including himself, take part in an experiment. A "varied group" of people, they included three psychologists, a psychiatrist, a pediatrician, a painter, a full-time homemaker, and a graduate student; three were women, five were men. They "gained secret admission" to twelve different mental hospitals around the country by complaining of hearing hallucinatory voices, which said "empty," "hollow," and "thud." All but one were admitted with a diagnosis of schizophrenia. (That one was diagnosed as a manic-depressive.) Once admitted, the pseudopatients acted normally—that is, did not simulate any symptoms of mental illness or abnormality. No psychiatric staff detected that these pseudopatients were normal; they were hospitalized for an average of nineteen days, and were released with a diagnosis of schizophrenia "in remission," that is, without signs of mental illness. Rosenhan's conclusion is that psychiatry "cannot distinguish the sane from the insane" (1973). His view is extremely critical of the medical and psychiatric approaches toward mental illness and it supports some version of the constructionist or labeling theory.

Rosenhan's study has received a great deal of attention, the bulk of it favorable. A review of thirty-one psychology textbooks published three years after the experiment found that fifteen cited the article, twelve of them favorably (Spitzer, 1976). And most of the articles that appeared in mental health and psychology journals commenting on the experiment had positive things to say. The media, too, gave the Rosenhan study a great deal of attention and overwhelmingly favorable coverage, in large part, said one critic, because "it said something that many were delighted to hear." This single study, this critic stated, "is probably better known to the lay public than any other study in the area of psychiatry in the last decade" (Spitzer, 1976, p. 459).

Not all the attention paid to "On Being Sane in Insane Places" has been favorable, however. The Journal of Abnormal Psychology devoted its volume 33, April 1976, issue to comments on

(Continued)

Rosenhan's piece; most were critical. Robert Spitzer (1975, 1976), a psychiatrist and co-pre-parer of and consultant to several editions of the American Psychiatric Association's *Diagnostic and Statistical Manual of Mental Disorders*, is perhaps the most articulate and outspoken of Rosenhan's critics. He sees the experiment and the article, which summarized it as "pseudoscience presented as science"—prompting a diagnosis of "logic, in remission" (1975, p. 442). Why?

"One hardly knows where to begin," says Spitzer (1975, p. 443). The study "immediately becomes confused" on terminology. As Rosenhan should know (he is a professor of both psychology and the law), the terms "sane" and "insane" are legal, not psychiatric concepts. The central issue for the law (inability to distinguish right from wrong) "is totally irrelevant" to the study, which is concerned with whether psychiatrists can detect a psychiatric condition. But let's assume that Rosenhan is referring to mental disorder, not "insanity." The pseudopatients simulated mental illness in gaining admission to a mental hospital. Said another critic, "If I were to drink a quart of blood and . . . come to the emergency room of any hospital vomiting blood," the chances are, he would be labeled and treated as having a bleeding peptic ulcer. But "I doubt that I could argue convincingly that medical science does not know how to diagnose that condition (Kety, 1974, p. 959). These pseudopatients claimed to present symptoms of schizophrenia, and that is how they were diagnosed. What reason did the admitting psychiatrists have to doubt the genuineness of the stated symptoms?

For Rosenhan, the fact that no one detected the pseudopatients as "sane" and they were re-leased with a diagnosis of "in remission" was significant; this means, he said, in the judgment of the hospital, they were neither sane, nor had they been sane at any time. Spitzer argues exactly the reverse: The fact that these patients were discharged "in remission" indicates that the psychiatric profession is able to detect mental disorder. The diagnosis "in remission" indicates that patients are free from any signs of mental illness, which characterizes these cases in a nutshell. It is an extremely rare diagnosis, appearing, in one hospital, only once in 100 discharges; in a check of twelve hospitals, eleven never used the diagnosis, and in the remaining hospital, in only 7 percent of its discharges. Says Spitzer, "we must marvel" at the fact that, in Rosenhan's study, the eleven psychiatrists who discharged the pseudopatients"all acted so rationally as to use at discharge . . . a category that is so rarely used with real schizophrenic patients" (1975, p. 445). Not one used any of the descriptions that were available to them that would have demonstrated Rosenhan's point far more effectively: "still psychotic,""probably still hallucinating but denies it now,""loose associations," or "inappropriate affect" (p. 445).

Spitzer admits that "there are serious problems with psychiatric diagnosis, as there are with other medical diagnosis" (p. 451). However, diagnosis is not so poor "that it cannot be an aid in the treatment of the seriously disturbed psychiatric patient" (p. 451). But, this critic of Rosenhan's experiment says, a correct interpretation of "On Being Sane in Insane Places" contradicts the author's conclusions. "In the setting of a psychiatric hospital," argues Spitzer, "psychiatrists are remarkably able to distinguish the 'sane' from the 'insane'" (p. 451).

THE EPIDEMIOLOGY OF MENTAL DISORDER

Epidemiology is the study of the distribution of diseases in the population. One absolutely crucial fact to keep in mind about the distribution of mental disorder in the population is that many people who are mentally disordered receive no diagnosis and no treatment whatsoever (Kessler, Merikangas, and Wang, 2010, p. 192). Psychiatry makes the assumption that the distribution of mental disorders can be determined in much the same way the distribution of physical diseases can be determined. The field of psychiatric epidemiology is based on the idea that there is, or can be, a "true" rate or prevalence of mental disorder, just as there is a "true" rate of cancer or AIDS. Clearly, this is an essentialist assumption—that is, that mental disorder is a concrete entity on whose reality all reasonable and informed observers can agree. The constructionist, in contrast, seeing mental disorder as a socially determined judgment, does not make the assumption that a "true" rate or prevalence of mental disorder can be determined. Instead, constructionists are interested in how mental disorder is conceptualized and defined, how certain categories in the population come to be *designated* as having higher, or lower, rates of mental disorder, and what extra-psychiatric factors influence rates of institutionalization.

All epidemiologists agree that measuring mental disorder in the population, or in certain segments of the population, is problematic. The issue of how mental disorder is diagnosed and determined for the purposes of an epidemiological study has filled a substantial number of very fat tomes. The rate of admissions to mental hospitals has been used as one measure or index of mental disorder in the population and categories in the population. However, we all recognize that there are many factors that make it likelier that some persons, and persons in certain categories, will end up in a mental hospital than others, holding mental condition constant. Some conditions cause a great deal of trouble for others, while for other conditions, the mentally disordered person suffers in isolation; clearly, the first is more likely to be hospitalized than the second. Some people live among groups and categories who consider mental hospitalization a viable option only under extreme circumstances; others look to institutionalization much more quickly and readily, upon signs of relatively minor abnormality or dysfunction. The point is, there is a huge noninstitutionalized segment of the population who *would be* diagnosed as mentally disordered were they to be evaluated by a psychiatrist. Because of problems such as these, another measure of mental disorder has been developed: a diagnostic interview schedule, which, presumably, can determine mental condition in a sample of respondents. Over the years, different interview schedules have been used, and

somewhat different findings have been obtained. Still, many experts believe that, over time, these research instruments are becoming increasingly accurate. Currently, a huge ongoing study, the Epidemiological Catchment Area Program survey, is measuring mental health and disorder in a random sample of the noninstitutionalized population at large (Kessler et al., 1994).

A large number of studies have been conducted that have reached conclusions concerning the differential proneness of the groups and categories in the population to mental illness or disorder. Recently, a team of psychiatrists, psychologists, statisticians, and epidemiologists summarized dozens of studies of the distribution of diagnosed mental disorders in the American population (Reeves et al., 2011). The team focused mainly on diagnosis of clinical depression and answers to questions about "psychological distress" and "mentally unhealthy days." They emphasized that mental disorder is strongly related to *comorbidity*—that is, it tended to be associated with other illnesses, such heart disease, diabetes, asthma, obesity, and cancer. Most sociologists believe that specific social processes are related to mental disorder and that these processes are characteristic of certain groups than others. What characteristics are most important? How do members of these social categories fare with respect to mental health and disorder? Perhaps the most basic and often-studied characteristics studied by psychiatric epidemiologists have been *sex* or *gender*, *marital status*, and *socioeconomic status*.

Gender: Men versus Women

It is not clear that there is a consistent relationship between sex or gender and a crude, unidimensional, undifferentiated measure of mental disorder. Reviews of the literature (for instance, Dohrenwend and Dohrenwend, 1976) have revealed that some studies find that women have higher rates of mental disorder than men, while others show men to have higher rates. This is the case for two reasons.

When it comes to *surveys* of the general population, women have somewhat higher rates of mental disorder. One nationally representative study of households across the United States conducted jointly by the National Institutes of Health and the National Center for Health Statistics identified 1.94 million females and 1.32 million males as having a serious mental disorder; rates of mental disorder were 20.6 for females and 15.5 for males. The Epidemiological Catchment Area Project study mentioned earlier, which was focused on five urban centers, found rates of mental disorder of 16.6 for females and 14.0 for males (Reiger et al., 1988). A later study using the same research instrument, based on a more nationally representative sample, reached the same conclusion (Kessler et al., 1994). A major textbook sums up the recent evidence and concludes that women have greater tendencies toward mental disorder, mainly depression, than men (Cockerham, 2011).

On the other hand, males are significantly more likely to be *admitted to mental hospitals* than females (p. 164). Moreover, during much of this country's history, the ratio of males to females was increasing over time. For instance, in 1900, there were 106 males admitted to state mental hospitals for every 100 females; by 1975, this had risen to 193, and in 1985, it reached a high of 199. Since then, the ratio has somewhat subsided. In 1997, there were 162 male admissions per 100,000 males in the population, and 89 males versus 54.9 female admissions per 100,000 females in the population (Cockerham, 2003, p. 165, 2011). It is entirely possible that both essentialists and constructionists would have something to say on the subject. In fact, experts believe that this disparity is due to the conjunction of the specific *type* of mental disorder males are more likely to suffer from (an essentialistic phenomenon) and professional stereotyping (a constructionist phenomenon). While men are strikingly more likely to fall victim to antisocial personality disorders, women are far more likely to suffer from a mood disorder, especially depression. Each of these disorders manifests itself in a strikingly different way. More specifically, the antisocial personality is highly likely to cause havoc in the lives of others—for instance, in the form of aggressiveness and violence—while depressive mood disorders are more likely to result in withdrawal and isolation. Someone who causes disruptive social and interpersonal trouble is more likely to be institutionalized than someone who withdraws.

The mental disorder of men, even holding severity of disorder constant, is regarded as more disabling, threatening, and dangerous to the society than is that of women (Gove, 1972; Rushing, 1979a, 1979b). Women are regarded as more cooperative and compliant and more readily influenced by the hospital staff and, therefore, are more likely to be released (Doherty, 1978). Some researchers also feel that the social roles men and women and boys and girls are forced to play impact on their mental health—or lack of it. Males are expected to be more aggressive, independent, and adventurous; consequently, the disorders they manifest (again, antisocial tendencies, especially toward violence) reflect that role expectation. Females are socialized to be passive, dependent, and lacking in confidence; they, too, exhibit this tendency in extreme form in their characteristic disorder, depression (Gove and Herb, 1974, p. 259).

There is something of a "double standard" among clinicians in the diagnosis, hospitalization, and release of mental patients with respect to gender (Cockerham, 2003, pp. 174–176, 2011). Psychiatrists and clinical psychologists seem to have a lower standard of mental health for women than for men. They are more likely to diagnose mental disorder for men, other things being equal; a woman's condition would have to be more severe to warrant hospitalization, and a man's less severe, to warrant release. In addition to the nature of the symptoms (disruption and violence versus withdrawal and isolation), one hypothesis that has been put forth to explain this observed regularity is that in a sexist or patriarchal society, males are expected to perform in a society to more exacting standards. Being a man in a very achievement-oriented society is incompatible with being mentally disordered; the penalties for stepping out of line are swift and strong. On the other hand, where women are relegated to an inferior and dependent role, their performance in that role is met with more indulgence and leeway. Clinicians and the general public, both male and female, feel that a mildly psychically impaired woman can perform in an imperfect fashion and still "get by." Ironically, these sexist values result in a higher rate of mental disorder labeling for men, supposedly the more powerful social category, and less for women, who are generally less powerful. As sex roles become more equalitarian, one would expect these gender disparities in diagnosis, hospitalization, and release, to diminish and eventually disappear.

When all is said and done, it seems clear that women are significantly more like to suffer from clinical depression (Reeves et al., 2011), while men are more likely to suffer from schizophrenia. A recent systematic survey of hundreds of studies of mental disorder in countries around the world verified that the incidence of schizophrenia is significantly and substantially higher among men than women, on the order of a 1.4 to 1 ratio (Saha et al., 2005). Hence, their overall rates tend to obscure the differences between them with respect to *type* of diagnosis far more than overall incidence.

Marital Status

Among men, a very consistent finding emerges from the many studies that have been conducted: Single, never-married men are strikingly more likely to score high on every available measure of mental disorder than are married men; separated and divorced men rank somewhere in between (Reeves et al., 2011). Two hypotheses have been advanced to account for the observed relationship. The first is that men who are married and stay married are more stable, psychologically healthy, and conventional than men who never marry—and therefore, they are less mentally disordered. The experience of marriage itself, these observers argue, has little or nothing to do with this regularity: It is only that *the kind of man* who marries is also the kind of man who exhibits relatively few personality problems, while the man who does *not* marry is far *more likely* to exhibit those same problems. Getting married entails a certain degree of social competence to attract a spouse; men with severe mental problems are not considered desirable partners and thus, will be socially avoided by women (Rushing, 1979b). "The more symptomatic and/or ineffective an individual, the less likely [it is that] he will find a marital partner . . . , and the more likely [it is that] he will spend extended periods in the hospital" (Turner and Gartrell, 1978, p. 378). It is, some say, "the inadequate man who is left over after the pairing has taken place" (Gallagher, 2002, p. 203, 2011).

A second hypothesis is that marriage confers a kind of immunity on a man: Married men have fewer mental problems than do bachelors because the experience of being married is conducive to a man's mental health, security, and well-being. "Marriage does not prevent economic and social problems from invading life," two researchers argue, "but apparently can help fend off the psychological assaults that such problems otherwise create" (Pearlin and Johnson, 1977, p. 714). Bachelors are more socially isolated from others; they lack the social supports and resources that married men have at their disposal. Hence, they are more likely to be psychologically vulnerable and fall victim to mental disorders. Again, whether this is a question of social selection or differential experiences, the tendency for single men to exhibit strikingly more, and serious, symptoms of mental disorder is well documented in the literature (Gallagher, 2002, pp. 203–204, 2011; Cockerham, 2003, pp. 177–179; 2011).

This generalization does not hold in the same way for women. Some studies show single women to have the same rates of mental disorder as married women (Warheit et al., 1976), while other studies show married women to have *higher* rates of disorders (Gove, 1979b). In short, the special protection that supposedly extends to men seems to offer no special protection for women. It is even possible that the opposite is the case: Some observers argue that marriage is a stressful, anxiety-provoking, oppressive, exploitative institution, incompatible with the mental health of women (Bernard, 1982). Men have all the advantages in marriage, they feel, and thus profit from the experience; in contrast, women suffer as a result of being married because marriage is more demanding on women. It is frustrating, unsatisfying, and lacking in gratification for them (Gove, 1972). It is also possible that the social selection process that operates so strongly for men does so far less for women. That is, sexual stereotyping rejects mentally impaired men far more strongly than women (Phillips, 1964); a man who is mentally ill is seen by all women as an undesirable partner, while a woman who displays certain mental disorders may still be considered marriageable. In any case, the differences are far less strong among women than men. The evidence seems to favor few differences between married and unmarried women in mental health and disorder (Warheit et al., 1976), yet the remarkable difference in the impact of marriage between men and women should strike the observer forcefully. While it is probably a bit too rash to state that, in terms of mental health, marriage is good for men and bad for women, the evidence does at least suggest it may be good for men and of considerably less consequence for women. In a less patriarchal society, marriage will become more equalitarian and, possibly, equally good for both sexes.

Socioeconomic Status

Of all sociological variables, the relationship between social class or socioeconomic status (SES) and mental disorder has probably been the most frequently studied. And the most commonly used indicators measuring socioeconomic status are income, occupational prestige, and education. The higher someone ranks on any one or all three of these dimensions, the higher is his or her socioeconomic status or social "class," sociologists hold. Mental disorder is very closely related to socioeconomic status: The higher the SES, the lower the rate of mental disorder; the lower the SES, the higher the rate of mental disorder (Kessler et al., 1994; Gallagher, 2002, pp. 168–190, 2011; Cockerham, 2003, pp. 138–155, 2011). This holds regardless of the specific measure or indicator of SES that is used—occupational prestige, income, or education. People at the bottom of the class ladder are far more likely to suffer from psychiatric distress, especially schizophrenia, than those at the top. There are a few mental disorders that are more common toward the top of the class structure, such as obsessive-compulsive neuroses and some mood disorders, but the most serious illnesses, especially schizophrenia, are most common toward the bottom of the class structure. In dozens of studies, conducted in countries on three continents, the relationship between mental disorder and SES has been studied; almost without exception, these studies find schizophrenia significantly and strikingly more likely in the lower socioeconomic strata. This generalization has been verified empirically by studies stretching back two-thirds of a century (Hollingshead and Redlich, 1958; Srole et al., 1962; Leighton et al., 1963).

Why should this strong inverse relationship between psychopathology and SES exist? There are at least four possible explanations.

The first stresses *types* of disorder. The kinds of disorder exhibited by lower-status persons are more likely to come to the authorities than the kinds of disorders exhibited by middle- and upper-status persons. Lower-status persons are less likely to attribute their problems to a psychiatric condition, since they are more likely to feel that some stigma adheres to consultation with a "shrink" or being committed to a mental hospital. Hence, they are less likely to seek out psychiatric assistance voluntarily. Lower status persons are most likely to come to the attention of psychiatric authorities as a result of referral by the police or a social worker. In contrast, upper- and middle-status persons are more likely to be referred by relatives or a private physician. A great deal of lower-status mental disorders, especially among men, manifests itself in the form of "antisocial" behavior, particularly violence, which is likely to attract the attention of agents of formal social control, the police. This explanation does not say that lower-SES persons are more mentally disordered than middle- and upper-SES persons overall so much as it focuses on how certain conditions, differentially distributed by social class, intersect with the social structure.

The second is the constructionist explanation. Some observers have argued that this strong inverse relationship between SES and mental disorder may be due to class bias and the labeling process. Middle-class psychiatrists find lower-class behavior troublesome and are more likely to label it disordered than the behavior of middle-class persons (Wilkinson, 1975). There is something of a built-in bias in psychiatric diagnosis against lower-class subculture and lower-class persons. Mental health is judged by a middle-class yardstick; lower-class values and behavior are more likely to be regarded as disordered by the psychiatric profession, composed, as it is, of persons who are toward the middle or near the top of the social class ladder. It seems almost unarguable that class bias plays a role in psychiatric diagnosis. Nonetheless, this explanation cannot be the whole story, since much of the behavior of the psychiatrically disordered is deemed undesirable by members of *all* social classes. Characteristically, the lower-class person comes to psychiatric attention as a result of being troublesome to, and being reported by, other lower-class persons.

A third hypothesis attempting to explain why mental disorder is more heavily located at the bottom reaches of the SES continuum focuses on the greater *stress* experienced by persons located there. Economic deprivation, poverty, occupational instability, and unemployment are strongly related to psychological impairment (Liem and Liem, 1978). As a result of having to deal with living in an economically deprived existence and coping with this deprivation, the lower-status person suffers a higher level of emotional stress and consequently is more vulnerable to a psychiatric breakdown (Kessler, 1979). The pressure of daily living under deprived circumstances becomes overwhelming; problems that cannot be solved mount, become unmanageable, and force the person into a break with reality (Cockerham, 2003, p. 149–150, 2011).

A fourth hypothesis attempting to explain the strong inverse relationship between SES and mental disorder is the *social selection* or the *drift* hypothesis. This theory argues that social class is a *consequence* rather than a *cause* of mental disorder. The mentally disordered are incapable of achieving a higher position on the SES hierarchy *because* they are mentally disordered (Dunham, 1965). Members of the lower class who are mentally disordered are either stuck there or have drifted there because their mental disorder prevents them from achieving a higher position. Their disorder retards their social mobility (Harkey, Miles, and Rushing, 1976).

CHEMICAL TREATMENT OF MENTAL DISORDER

By the 1950s, it had become clear to psychiatrists who worked with mental patients that conventional therapy was not working; in the treatment of the most serious mental disorders, especially schizophrenia, psychiatrists "functioned mainly as administrators and custodians" (Berger, Hamberg, and Hamberg, 1977, p. 264). In 1952 in France, and in the United States in 1954, a drug was first used that seemed to show some promise in reducing the most blatant, florid, and troublesome symptoms of institutionalized schizophrenic mental patients. Bearing the chemical name chlorpromazine and the trade name Thorazine, it belonged to a major type of psychoactive drugs that are regarded as having an *antipsychotic* effect. Antipsychotics do not produce a high or intoxication, they are not used recreationally, and are not sold illegally on the street. Nearly all the use of the antipsychotics is legal, licit prescription use for the purpose of controlling mental illness. Antipsychotics in addition to Thorazine include Mellaril, Compazine, Stelazine, and Haldol.

It is likely that experts would say that the two most dramatic changes that have taken place in the United States since the 1950s with respect to mental illness are the degree to which antipsychotics are administered to the mentally disordered and, correlatively, the number of patients who are in residence in mental hospitals. There is some controversy concerning the role that antipsychotics have played in depopulating the mental hospitals; some observers argue that the antipsychotics were less a cause than an opportunity (Gronfein, 1985), while others hold to a more directly pharmacological explanation (Pollack and Taube, 1975, p. 49). Regardless of the exact mechanism, the fact is, in 1955, there were nearly 560,000 patients in residence in public mental hospitals; this figure dropped almost every year until, by the 1990s, it was roughly 80,000. This figure increased slightly during the twenty-first century, and now stands at roughly 100,000. The overall decline is not due to the number of *admissions* to mental hospitals, which actually increased from 178,000 in 1955 to 385,000 in 1970, and then declined to about 255,000 in 1992, but increased again in the late 1990s and early 2000s (Blader, 2011). The fact is, length of stay was roughly six months in 1955; for the past decade or so, it has leveled off at two weeks. (Data are supplied by the National Institute of Mental Health.) As a result of much quicker discharges, mental hospitals are emptying out. Regardless of the precise timing and the causal mechanism of this change, it is impossible to argue that it could have come about in the absence of the administration of antipsychotics to schizophrenic mental patients. Roughly 85 percent of all patients in public mental hospitals are being administered some form of antipsychotic medication.

When the drug was initially introduced, Thorazine was described as having the following effects on agitated, manic, schizophrenic patients: The drug, an observer wrote, "produces marked quieting of the motor manifestations, patients cease to be loud and profane, the tendency to hyperbolic [that is, exaggerated] association is diminished, and the patient can sit still long enough to eat and take care of normal physiological needs" (Goldman, 1955). The emotional withdrawal, hallucinations, delusions, and other patterns of disturbed thinking, paranoia, belligerence, hostility, and "blunted affect" of patients are significantly reduced. As a result of the use of the antipsychotics, patients exhibit fewer and less dramatic symptoms of psychosis, become more manageable, and, as a result, have permitted hospitals to discontinue or reduce such ineffective or dangerous practices as hydrotherapy and lobotomies. And, as a result of the administration of these drugs, hospitals have, in the words of one observer, been transformed from "zoo-smelling, dangerous bedlams into places fit for human beings to live and, at times, recover from psychosis" (Callaway, 1958, p. 82). By inducing a more "normal" psychological condition in patients, it has been possible to release them into the community as outpatients, with only minimal treatment and care in aftercare facilities. This process is referred to as *deinstitutionalization*; unfortunately, what this has produced is a huge population of mentally ill homeless people who are subject to virtually no supervision or treatment whatsoever. (See the boxed insert on deinstitutionalization.)

Studies have shown that roughly three-quarters of all acute schizophrenics demonstrate significant improvement following the administration of antipsychotic drugs, and between 75 to 95 percent of patients relapse if their medication is discontinued (Hart and Ksir, 2013). The use of the antipsychotic drugs is regarded as not only effective for most mental patients, but it is also the least expensive of all treatment modalities. However, it should be added that although these drugs do reduce the most bizarre symptoms of schizophrenia, they are not a "cure" for mental illness. They calm the agitated, disturbed patient; the symptoms of mental illness are reduced, and patients are no longer as troublesome to others as they once were: They do not manifest their former signs of craziness. Antipsychotics permit the patient to behave in a more socially acceptable fashion; the patient's problems do not surface so painfully or disturbingly. Surely that represents progress of a sort. However, it is a stopgap measure rather than a genuine cure; no mental health specialist can be satisfied until a more substantial and more permanent treatment modality has been developed. Unfortunately, there is no prospect of this for the foreseeable future.

It is not known just why the antipsychotic drugs have this calming effect on mental patients. In any case, psychiatry has not been successful in treating seriously ill patients by means of any of its more conventional "talking" cures, such as psychoanalysis. Using the antipsychotics keeps patients out of trouble and out of the way of "normals," and enables some to function in important social roles, such as education, marriage, and occupation. Some observers see the use of antipsychotics as a "revolution" in the field of psychiatry (Gove, 1975a, p. 245). Others (Townsend, 1980, p. 272) are more cautious and see the change not as a genuine treatment but merely as the suppression of troublesome, disruptive behavior.

The antipsychotics are not addictive and very rarely result in lethal overdoses. However, there are some serious side effects that are experienced by many patients with the administration of these drugs, including abnormal, involuntary, and sometimes bizarre movements of the tongue, lips, and cheeks, facial tremors, rigidity, and a shuffling gait. These symptoms can be treated with a separate type of drug, the anti-Parkinsonian drugs. Patients also complain of feeling "doped up." At higher, often therapeutic, doses, their responses are often sluggish, they tend to be less acute mentally than usual, display less interest in external stimuli, including other people, and slower in arousal and response. Thus, the reduction of the socially and culturally bizarre and unacceptable behavior and thinking of mental patients is bought at a not inconsiderable price. Many patients realize this and, if unmonitored by mental health professionals, stop taking their medications.

Deinstitutionalization

In 1961, the Joint Commission on Mental Illness submitted a report that criticized warehousing mental patients in huge, dehumanizing, impersonal, and ineffective publicly funded asylums. Smaller facilities should be maintained in local communities that care for the mentally ill on a more personal and humane basis. In 1963, President John F. Kennedy signed federal legislation into law mandating local community care facilities for the mentally ill (Mechanic, 1989). Any complex and large-scale change is likely to be a product of many actors and a variety of motives. Still, the desire to improve the lives of mental patients must be counted among the original reasons for deinstitutionalization—releasing the mentally ill from large hospitals into the community. In addition, some politicians reasoned, these asylums were extremely expensive to maintain (not to mention ineffective). Thus, community care facilities will save the taxpayer a great deal of money. And thirdly, as we saw, starting in the mid-1950s, psychiatric medicine possessed an inexpensive and seemingly effective treatment modality at its disposal: psychotropic drugs. Thus, as we've seen, within a few short years, the mental hospitals were practically emptied of patients. By the mid-1970s, only the most untreatable patients remained in public mental hospitals.

Unfortunately, things did not go as these early idealists planned. The war in Vietnam (which United States troops entered in 1961 and departed from in 1975) drained an almost unimaginably huge proportion of resources from the public coffer. President Richard Nixon (1969–1974) proved to be hostile to the idea of community mental health; in 1972 he announced plans to phase out federal support for its programs. Though partially restored, Presidents Ronald Reagan (1981–1989) and George H.W. Bush (1989–1993) continued to put the axe to federal support for local halfway houses and treatment centers.

The upshot of these cuts was that the mentally ill were often released into the community with little more than a vial of pills and a prescription for more. Some lived with relatives (many of these were eventually ejected), while others were simply on their own. A high proportion gravitated to low-income areas in the community where disorganization and violence are common. Hundreds of thousands became homeless. (Experts estimate that roughly a third of America's homeless are released former mental patients.) Half of all mental patients released into the community are reinstitutionalized within a year. While the majority of released mental patients prefer living in the community, even under adverse conditions, to life in a mental ward, the fact is, most do not receive the kind of care they need—the kind of care that was envisioned in the idealistic 1960s. Meanwhile, city streets have become "open mental wards" (Goleman, 1986). We see the mentally ill on the streets of our cities—and even in smaller communities— wandering into traffic, looking wild-eyed and disheveled, screaming incomprehensible phrases to no one in particular. They have been dumped there, transferred from the asylum to the streets, the victims of massive budget cuts. The system has failed to help them; they are "a silent witness to the heartlessness and befuddlement that has created no better alternative for them" than the street (Goleman, 1986, p. C1).

Perhaps just as important, according to a report issued in 2010 by the Treatment Advocacy Center, there are more mentally disordered individuals who are in jails and prisons than are being treated in mental hospitals. That is, the process of deinstitutionalization has not merely released the mentally ill into the community, onto the streets, but, in doing so, many of them stop taking their medications, commit crimes, including some serious ones, get into trouble with law enforcement, and end up incarcerated. E. Fuller Torrey and others at the Center estimate that

(Continued)

16 percent of prisoners in the United States are "seriously ill" and that the ratio of disordered persons who are incarcerated versus those who are being treated in a mental hospital is roughly three to one (Torrey et al., 2010). "Emptying America's mental hospitals without ensuring that the discharged patients received appropriate treatment in the community has been an egregious mistake," state Torrey and his colleagues. "Although deinstitutionalization was well intended, the failure to provide for the treatment needs of patients has turned this policy into one of the greatest disasters of the twentieth and the twenty-first centuries. . . . *America's jails and prisons have become our new mental hospitals*" (pp. 1, 11; emphasis in original).

MENTAL DISORDER AS DEVIANCE: AN OVERVIEW

Mental disorder has both parallels and dissimilarities with the other forms of deviant behavior we encountered in earlier chapters, such as drug use, crime, and unconventional beliefs and sexual behavior. Both deviance and mental disorder represent a departure from the normative order. Being regarded as mentally abnormal by others is usually a result of breaking the rules of the society; one behaves in a way that is considered odd, eccentric, bizarre, and/or troublesome. One says things that others regard as "crazy," one interacts with others in ways that make them feel uncomfortable. To the extent that manifestations of mental illness result in normative violations, the disruption of smooth social relations, and attracting a socially undesirable label, it represents a form or type of deviance.

In addition, deviance is nearly always located in specific actions—that is, in clearly locatable behavioral and attitudinal spheres. One is not *a* deviant generally; few people even use the term. One is a deviant in specific areas of life—sex, drug use, politics, harming others, and so on. The label of mentally disordered is almost unique in that it is free-floating, eminently generalizable. One is considered mentally disordered not because of having done anything in a delimited area of life, but because one has done many things in many areas that are supposedly manifestations of a psychiatric disorder, dysfunction, or disorganization. This is true of practically no other form of deviant behavior.

The major thrust of psychiatric writings published in past decades has been in the direction of adopting the medical model of mental disorder—that is, regarding it as perfectly analogous to, or literally and concretely, a manifestation of a physical pathology. The implication of this model is that the mental patient should be treated in much the same way as the sufferer of a physical disease, both by clinicians and the lay public. The social stigma that adhered to the mental patient in the past is regarded in some quarters as an archaic remnant of the past. Being regarded as crazy, this view holds, does not cause others to view the person as deviant but instead will "redefine the deviance in a fairly positive way." Commitment to a mental hospital "tends to shift the person's label from that of being obnoxious and intolerable to that of being mentally ill and in need of help" (Gove, 1975a, p. 245). Insofar as this is true, *mental disorder is not a form of deviance.* To the extent that the public sees mental disorder on par with physical disorder, qualitatively no different from, and attracting no more stigma than, contracting cancer, and regards the mentally disordered as not responsible for their actions, it is not a form of deviance. But remember, earlier in this century the cancer patient suffered some degree of stigma, and even today certain diseases, such as AIDS and leprosy are considered loathsome, so physical disease is not always exclusively physical. Even for some physical diseases, the sufferer is seen in some social circles as a deviant.

But consider this: Being physically disordered in our society does harbor a dimension of deviance. By that I mean that it represents a departure from being self-reliant, taking care of one's obligations; it is a failure to be healthy, productive, and "normal" (Freidson, 1970, pp. 205–223;

Parsons, 1951a, pp. 428–479). Illness, then, is a violation of a number of strongly held values. To a degree, being mentally disordered will always be regarded as a form of deviance in the *same* sense that physical illness is. Falling down on the job, being unable to cope, failing to meet one's obligations, and disrupting interpersonal relations will always be despised in a society that values performance and achievement. Being mentally ill emphasizes one's incapacity and incompetence. As such, it will always be looked down upon.

SUMMARY

Of all deviant phenomena, mental disorder comprises the most diverse and miscellaneous category. Mental disorder is a set of conditions that characteristically manifests itself in actions, mental patterns, or speech utterances that are deemed bizarre and deranged by both clinicians and the lay public. Even the behaviors associated with this condition are vastly more diverse than any other deviant behavioral category, however broad it may be, we have discussed so far.

In the fifth edition of its *Diagnostic and Statistical Manual of Mental Disorders*, the American Psychiatric Association (2014) defines mental disorder as a syndrome or condition that is associated with distress, disability, or an increased risk of suffering, death, pain, disability, or an important loss of freedom. Over 300 disorders are listed; however, as we saw, *DSM-V* does not provide a framework or a theoretical model for disorders, but a listing of them and a description for each of the symptoms the clinician is likely to encounter in practice. Schizophrenia (a thought disorder entailing hallucinations, delusions, and disorganized speech) and mood disorders (particularly depression) are two of the most commonly encountered and most often studied mental disorders.

Experts approach the subject of mental disorder through the lens of several different perspectives.

Essentialism is the view that mental disorder is a real, concrete "thing" the observer can identify, locate, and explicate, much as one can pick an apple off a tree. Essentialists examine issues such as etiology (a study of the causes of mental disorder), epidemiology (a study of how mental disorder is distributed in the population), and the effectiveness of treatment. "Strict," "hard," or "radical" essentialism sees mental disorder as the manifestation of a disease, much like cancer; in its most extreme form, essentialism regards the condition as an actual, literal disease—that is, a product of biophysical pathology.

Constructionism, in contrast, focuses not on the condition but on how it is regarded, thought about, talked about, and dealt with. Here, treatment is looked at not as a means to a cure, but as a social enterprise, which is itself to be explained and understood. The "hard," "strict," or "radical" constructionists deny the existence of mental disorder in the real or concrete world and focus exclusively on judgments of and reactions to a "putative" or so-called condition. Softer or more moderate constructionists either set aside the question of the reality of mental disorder, or agree that it exists and make comparisons between such judgments and reactions and the condition itself. Constructionists emphasize contingency (factors other than condition influence judgments about mental disorder), stigma (judgments of mental disorder are stigmatizing), and the creation of mental disorder through labels.

Labeling theory is a distinct perspective from constructionism. While constructionism focuses on the *conceptual* creation of mental disorder through judgments and reactions, labeling theory focuses on its *literal* creation through these processes. It is a perspective that argues that being labeled and treated *as* mentally ill is the primary *cause* of mental disorder. Labeling theory straddles essentialism and constructionism, in that the *initial* or *primary* judgments about mental condition are made to some degree independent of "true" mental condition, they act to *create* a true mental disorder. In the past decade or so, a "modified" labeling perspective has arisen, which adopts bits and pieces of the approach but not all of its particulars. It emphasizes the stigma of being labeled as mentally ill, the contingency involved in applying such labels, and the fact that treatment is often effective.

Some sociologists study the epidemiology of mental disorder. Three of the most often studied characteristics that correlate with mental disorder are gender, marital status, and socioeconomic status.

While women are more likely to be diagnosed as mentally disordered in surveys, men are much more likely to be institutionalized. The conditions that men are more likely to manifest (for instance, character or personality disorder, which often leads to violence) often cause more trouble for others and result in more official intervention and hence, psychiatric labeling and commitment. In contrast, the conditions that are more prevalent among women (for instance, depression) often result in withdrawal and isolation and hence, no official notice.

Married men are significantly less likely to be disordered than single men. This may be because marriage offers a kind of immunity or psychological protection for them; they receive support in times of trouble. It may also be because men who are mentally disordered can't get married, since they make undesirable marital partners. With women, the picture is not so clear-cut. Many studies show no differences in mental disorder between married and single women, and some studies actually show married women to have higher rates of disorder than single women. It could be that marriage is more stressful for women than for men, or it could be that disordered women are deemed not nearly as undesirable as marital partners by men as disordered men are by women.

Socioeconomic status (SES) is the single social characteristic that correlates most strongly with mental disorder. Studies conducted in the past and studies conducted today, and studies around the world as well as in the United States, agree: The lower the SES, the higher the rate of mental disorder, most specifically, schizophrenia, regarded as one of the most common, and perhaps the most serious, of all the disorders.

Why? At least four explanations come to mind. Personality disorder, which is common among lower-SES men, frequently results, as we saw, in official and therapeutic intervention, whereas the disorders most characteristic of middle- and upper-middle-status persons are less troublesome and intrusive to the society. Second, labeling may play a role: Middle-class psychiatrists may be quicker to judge pathology in lower-class persons, particularly males. Third, lower-class life is more stressful than middle-class life and hence, more likely to lead to a psychiatric breakdown. And fourth, the mental condition of the mentally disordered *precedes* achievement in the social class ladder and inhibits that achievement; hence, they "drift" into the lower class.

In 1954, psychoactive chemicals began to be used on a widespread basis to treat the mentally ill. That year, there were over half a million patients in publicly funded mental hospitals, and their average length of stay was six months. While the use of drugs was not the only cause, it was certainly instrumental in emptying out insane asylums. Today, there are roughly 80,000 patients, and their average length of stay is two weeks. Antipsychotic drugs make schizophrenic patients less agitated, more manageable, and their symptoms less bizarre. They also produce a number of undesirable side effects. The "deinstitutionalization" of these patients has resulted in relatively little medical care for many of them, and a very high proportion of those who lack family or social supports become homeless and live on the street, often neglecting to take their medication. They have been "dumped" there in large part because the society is unwilling to pay for their shelter and an adequate system of halfway houses or treatment facilities that would alleviate the problem of the huge numbers of mentally ill homeless street people. Many of these former mental patients engage in behavior that attracts law enforcement, and they are arrested and incarcerated.

Account: On Being a Paranoid Schizophrenic

The author, "Nicole," is in her sixties and lives in New York City.

There's a saying, the more creative you are, the more trouble you have with your mind. I must be very, very, very creative as my mind has taken me to hell on earth and back a thousand or more times during its reign of terror against me, for practically my whole life. I was afraid to know I had a mind in my body, let alone fight it or master it. The best I could do was distract it. I've been terrified of my mind ever since, at age five, one Sunday morning as I was sitting in church listening to a sermon, when I suddenly heard the preacher bellow the words, "burn in hell for eternity." Seconds later, my mind began burning me in hell. Terror engulfed me. I was in shock, I was petrified and perplexed; I had perceptions of myself burning in hell for all eternity. Or so I believed. I was burning in hell. After this feeling passed, I remained stunned, mystified. I had many questions. What happened to me? How could it be that I was forced to feel this unexpected, unbearable fear? Why had I experienced this sheer terror, this paralyzing shock? Why do I have no control over what happens to me?

After that experience, I was hypervigilant. I left the church tensed, feeling unsafe in my body, unsafe on earth, certain I was in mortal danger. My mind was in turmoil, in a state of panic. I had no one to talk to or share my feelings and experience with. I felt sorry for myself and at a complete loss to explain how this could have happened to me, baffled and dumbfounded. It took years and many efforts to reach back to the day when I had that experience before I became capable and strong enough to face the terror again, realizing that I was simply imagining it. Over the years, my mind has had its way with me. I had no clue as to how to focus it. From the age of 25 on, it dragged me down to the level of insanity aka a nervous breakdown—indeed, several or more.

One day, my beautiful, intelligent mother asked me if I saw the butterflies. What butterflies? There were no butterflies in the dimension where I was at; I didn't know where Mama was at. I knew

Mama was hallucinating. I must have learned about what hallucinating was watching television. I looked into my mother's eyes and I saw sheer terror staring back at me. I still don't know what was in her mind, why her thoughts were scaring her so. Somehow, I managed to remain calm. I rubbed Mama's arm and told her everything was OK. Then I called my aunt and told her Mama was seeing things; she and her son came to the house right away. But when they came through the door, Mama took one look at them and said, "You're not taking me anywhere. I am not crazy." She decided not to be crazy. She willed away insanity. She kept herself sane by deciding to be sane and willing it so. Having the conviction that she was choosing sanity made her sane. I'm thrilled that she chose to save herself from a lifetime of insanity. But she had to medicate herself for depression. First she drank beer, then hard liquor. She died at the age of 54. Her doctor told me that her organs looked twenty years older than her actual age. I recall another incident when she lost her bearings. I was sitting in a car in front of my house with a boy I liked. Mama came out, paranoid and suspicious, and asked if we took her bottle. It was clear there was something wrong with her and that filled me with shame. The boy was from a well-to-do family and I'm sure he had never seen a family as poor and crazy as mine. I decided I could not bring boys from well-to-do families home with me, and I never did.

When I was six, my aunt had me stand on a chair at the sink and wash dishes. I began but in the middle of washing a plate, I decided to stop washing. I refused to continue. My refusal to wash the dishes made no sense to Mama so she grabbed a broom handle to force me to continue. I snatched the broom handle from her and it seemed as if there was about to be a confrontation between us. My sister pulled Mama from the kitchen and said to her, "You know she's crazy." *What?* I thought. *Crazy?* Mama knew, and my sister knew, that I was *crazy?* How could this be true? How long have they known? I became paranoid because people knew things about me that I didn't know about myself. *Am* I crazy?

(Continued)

Account: On Being a Paranoid Schizophrenic   Continued

For years, I desperately longed for a father. I felt having a father would give me admiration, love, respect; for me, it was a matter of survival. It would make me feel worthwhile. With a father, I'd be OK, I'd have a full refrigerator and enough to eat; we'd be safe, protected, taken care of, approved, provided for, accepted. I'd be happy, I was sure of it. Not having this, I couldn't be at peace knowing that something was wrong. I lived with a constant feeling of butterflies in my stomach, on the verge of tears, in a state of agitation, puzzled as to how this could have happened, waiting for relief, always on the edge, desperately needing my father to take care of me. I prayed every night, sobbed, begged, pleaded with God to send my father back to me to rescue me. Then I prayed to Him to send someone, anyone, to rescue me. It didn't happen. I knew I was screwed. Fucked. I stopped caring about anything or anyone—including myself—when I discovered my father didn't care about me, and there was no hope he ever would. I lived in a reality where there was no love for me. As I grew up, into my teens, I began seeking father substitutes, first boys, then men. When one of my specimens disappointed me, I sought out another; there were many to choose from, so I went from one to another, seeking daddy substitutes. But I knew they weren't going to love me because my Daddy hadn't loved me, and that was the script. But if they stopped acting as if they loved me, they were out of my life as fast as Christmas is over for a child, and I was on to the next one. The need to be loved by a daddy has never left me. I felt sorry for myself, but I had no choice; I felt bitter but I had to do what I had to do to survive. My mother didn't like me, I couldn't bear my life, knowing my father didn't love me or even like me or even notice that I existed.

One day, when I was six, when I came home from school, I saw a man, a stranger, sitting on our love seat. I was shocked. Before I could get my bearings, Mama nudged me toward him saying, "This is your father." He sat, staring at me, expressionless, waiting, I suppose, for me to impress him. Did Mama want me to impress him? I hadn't a clue. What was I supposed to do? I must have failed to do whatever it was I was supposed to do

because the next day, his ass was out of there. That encounter didn't work out for me. I had met my father for all of fifteen minutes and I could see he didn't particularly like me. My father's love and approval was as important to me as food and drink—and I didn't get them from him. But one thing did kind of work to keep me from panicking. At some point, he told me that he'd send me a dollar for every letter I wrote him. At least we'd stay connected, I presumed. I wrote one letter—my aunt offered to help, but I decided I could do it myself—and I received the dollar as promised. Immediately, I wrote him another. But I never heard from him again. From then on, I waited for the mailman to hand me a letter and money from Daddy; I never got one.

I adored Mama but I also blamed her for sending Daddy away again, believing that he would have gotten used to me and I would have adjusted to him and we would have started loving each other. This was my "we woulda" fantasy—we woulda been happy and normal. But years later, Mama speculated about whether Daddy would have been alive if she hadn't left him. I hated her at that moment. Mama said that Daddy couldn't stand small-town life. He had been an officer in the military. He had gotten a job as a milkman. Later, he got fired for giving away milk to poor people. He worked for the Campbell Soup company; he must have hated that job because he never talked about it and he wouldn't eat soup after that. He went to law school and quit two weeks before graduation. He studied to become a mortician, and he never did.

I remember the moment I decided, half-consciously, that there was no way I could bear the truth of the awareness that my father didn't love me, didn't accept me, wasn't impressed with me, didn't value me, couldn't connect with me. NO! I will never accept or know this truth! I cannot know this. Having made this decision, my mind automatically decided to alter my consciousness, my level of awareness. It blurred the truth, became unfocused, off and on moved to another dimension. Tentatively, after many hospitalizations, I chose to remain sane, especially after my last one. The truth was that both my Mama and my Daddy couldn't stand me. In my Mama's case, it went

(Continued)

back to the day of my birth. When I was four, she admitted that she had tried to abort me. Neither Mama nor Daddy loved me or wanted me. They rejected me and so I rejected myself.

When I was twelve, I got pregnant. Mama managed to find $100 and money for transportation to send me to the biggest nearby city, to a doctor who stuck a thin rubber hose up in me. What were my feelings about what was going on? I was at that stage where my consciousness had not yet seen the light.

When I was 17, I moved to a big city far away. I was raped by a man who reminded me of my father. At some point, I just stopped trying to resist him, suppressing my disgust and rage. I didn't throw up all over him; I hid my revulsion and utter contempt for him. When he was finished emptying himself in me, I didn't make a big deal of it. I never told anyone—not the authorities, not his wife, not any of my relatives. I didn't tell my Mama. Besides, I had been seduced at age three and again at age nine. So I went on as though nothing had happened. Who cared? I just went on living, taking it in stride. Later, repressing my feelings about the matter to guys and to myself, I was surprised by what a big deal the society began making about rape and its victims. I marched in a SlutWalk protest—so-called because someone made a comment that if a woman hadn't been dressed like a slut, she wouldn't have gotten raped. (By the way, I wore a waitress uniform the day I was raped.) During the protest, a half-dozen teenage girls joined us, walking and chanting, "Don't be a wussy, ask for that pussy." I thought that was the funniest thing I'd ever heard. Great advice, right?

When I was locked up in Bellevue, I hallucinated that I was alone in the actual Creation; that felt really scary. No mom, no dad to trust. It's enough to make anyone go crazy. But I liked rich and powerful and creative men and they liked me. I put a lot of work into my relationships—just as I was willing and eager to do with my Daddy, had I had the chance. The game was to get him to love or at least like me, knowing that was impossible, because my father never did. I've managed to cure myself of phobias, hallucinations, delusions, and shyness; I don't need to drink, and I have enough confidence to interact with people. Still, when I feel some mutual love developing, I panic. I don't have a script for that. I think what scares me about really falling in love is the fact that it must end. Don't give your heart to a man because he'll break it in death or in life. Love just doesn't last. I haven't resolved this issue; I'll get back to you when I grow up a little more.

Questions

Is schizophrenia a form of deviance? Why? How does its "deviantness" manifest itself? How can we reconcile the currently dominant psychiatric view that mental illness is caused by a chemical imbalance with the earlier view, spelled out by sociologist Ned Polsky (1998), that conditions, which are "not the individual's fault" are not forms of deviance. Do you believe that it is possible to *decide* not to be schizophrenic and have it happen? This chapter summarizes the epidemiology of mental illness—that is, its distribution in the population. From what Nicole tells us about her life, is her schizophrenia predictable, or not? Are her experiences the cause of her condition, or her condition the cause of her experiences? Or is it one or the other—is it possible that it's both? Does Nicole's account give you special insight into schizophrenia? How?

Deviant Physical Characteristics

Learning Objectives:

After reading this chapter, you will be able to:

- understand the history of thought on "abominations of the body";
- define "physical disability";
- discuss the concepts of conformity to and violations of esthetic standards;
- recognize how extreme body modifications can be a form of physical deviance;
- discuss obesity as a prime example of "abomination of the body";
- understand the use of the word "freaks" as a way to describe the physically different;
- recognize and define the concept of "tertiary deviance."

Whoever he be . . . that hath any blemish, let him not approach to offer the bread of his God. For whatsoever man he be that hath a blemish, he shall not approach [the altar]: a blind man, a lame, or he that hath a flat nose, or any thing superfluous, or a man that is brokenfooted or brokenhanded, or crookbacked, or a dwarf, or that hath a blemish in his eye, or be scurvy, or scabbed. . . . No man that hath a blemish. . . . shall come nigh to offer the bread of his God. . . . [He] shall not go unto the veil, nor come nigh unto the altar, because he hath a blemish; that he profane not my sanctuaries: for I the Lord do sanctify them (Leviticus 21:17–23).

Judge not according to the appearance (John 7:24).

What is considered "normal," constructionist sociologists say, is a matter of definition, a cultural product, dependent on which sectors of the society wield power. Moreover, persons who fall under the penumbra of normalcy tend to be treated positively and favorably and those who do not are denied certain rights and privileges typically extended to "normals." In the case of physical traits and characteristics, it is the human *body* that, and its possessor who, experience such outcomes, positive or negative. Undesirable and negatively valued physical traits are not universally regarded as a form of deviance, even within the field of sociology. But it seems undeniable that persons who depart from a socially constructed notion of normalcy are viewed by "normals" as morally inferior. For several decades, cultural and literary studies scholars have "interrogated" society's definition and treatment of *deviant bodies* (Terry and Urla, 1995; Garland Thomson, 1997), and dozens of universities in the United States have offered courses in "deviant bodies" and "disability in American culture" (www.journalofliterarydisability.com/exepmplarycourses.html). I'm arguing that this territory should be no less the domain of the sociologist. In this chapter, we'll look at the consequences of four types of bodies that are judged wanting—abnormal, deficient, repugnant, defective, unaesthetic, unappealing: First, the physically disabled; second, the esthetically wanting or ugly; third, the radically altered; and fourth, the obese. We'll also consider the matter of *tertiary deviance*—the political demands made by the physically deviant, different, and disabled to enjoy their right to equality.

In her memoir, *Poster Child*, Emily Rapp describes the experience of becoming, and living as, a girl with one leg. Because she was born with a birth defect, an orthopedic specialist recommended the amputation of her left foot. "After this procedure and other operations to modify my body, he believed I could be fitted with an artificial limb and have hope for a normal life. . . . I regained consciousness in the recovery room with my head over a plastic bowl, vomiting. . . . I looked down at my body. My left leg looked like a rounded, bat-like object, covered in plaster. The foot was gone" (Rapp, 2007, pp. 14, 22, 23). After the operation, Emily was fitted with a prosthetic leg, which she learned to use effectively. Her mom and dad taught her not to feel handicapped. "I saw myself as strong, able, and special." The idea that she was "disabled" rarely crossed her mind (p. 60). She became a "poster child" for a local March of Dimes campaign. When she was twelve, she began skiing. But in school one day during recess, a girl began limping and dragging her arms like a monkey; Emily realized that the girl was making fun of her. "*Do I look like that? Like an animal?*" she thought. "The strength of my shame confused me because it felt like a physical force—it was overwhelming. . . . I thought, *I'm ugly; I'm a bad person.* . . . Is that what people think about me?" (p. 77). She began thinking of herself as a circus freak, like "the people who used to tour in carnivals. *The bearded lady. The four-hundred-pound man. The legless girl*" (p. 78). Her shame deepened.

The possession of undesirable physical characteristics is stigmatizing; hence, sociologists define it as a form of deviance. As we've seen, Erving Goffman's *Stigma* (1963) focuses on the *grading system* of stigma based on behavior, belief, and physical characteristics. Stigma is the manifestation or outward appearance of an inner deficiency, one that either *has been* or *may be* noticed, which results, or would result, in *infamy* and *dishonor*. Deviance and stigma are closely related concepts; the parallels are so strong it is difficult to distinguish them. A stigmatized person, Goffman writes, is "a blemished person," a person who is "disqualified from full social acceptance" (p. 1). Such a person is considered "different from others . . . , reduced in our minds from a whole and usual person to a tainted, discounted one" (p. 3). In sum, "the person with a stigma is not quite human" (p. 5).

To be stigmatized is to possess a *contaminated* or *discredited* identity. Interaction with "normals" will be strained, tainted, awkward, inhibited. While "normals" may, because of the dictates of polite sociability, attempt to hide their negative feelings toward the stigmatized trait or person, they remain, nonetheless, acutely aware of the other's blemish. Likewise, the stigmatized person remains self-conscious about his or her relations with "normals," believing (often correctly) that the stigma is the exclusive focus of the interaction. "I am always worried about how Jane judges me because she is a real beauty queen and the main gang leader," explains a girl who considers herself—and would be widely considered—overweight. "When I am with her, I hold my breath hard so my tummy doesn't bulge and I pull my skirt down so my fat thighs don't show. I tuck in my rear end. I try to look as thin as possible for her. I get so preoccupied with looking good enough to get into her gang that I forget what she's talking to me about. . . . I am so worried about how my body is going over that I can hardly concentrate on what she's saying. She asks me about math and all I am thinking about is how fat I am" (Allon, 1976, p. 18).

Highly stigmatized persons walk along one of two possible paths.

One is to *resist* or *reject* their stigmatized status by forming subcultures or collectivities of persons who share their characteristic and to treat their difference from the majority as a badge of honor—or at least, no cause for shame. The homosexual subculture provides an example of this path: Most homosexuals feel that mainstream society is wrong in denigrating homosexuality, that its judgment of them as tainted is invalid, illegitimate, just plain wrong. Homosexuals typically reject the very legitimacy of the stigma—the basis or foundation for the judgment. At some point, many homosexuals *come out*, joining the gay community, *announcing* that they belong to the rest of humanity.

The second path the stigmatized may take is *internalization*. Here, the stigmatized person holds the same negative feelings toward themselves and their disvalued trait as the majority does. Such a person is dominated by feelings of self-hatred and self-derogation. In these cases, persons who put others down make them feel they deserve it; the stigmatized person comes to accept the negative treatment as just; they feel that the majority has a *right* to stigmatize them for what they are or do. They hold themselves off from the tribe to which others would assign them if they knew who they were and what they do. They reject their personal affiliation with the derogated community to which they fear they belong.

Goffman (1963) discusses stigmata that manifest themselves in physical characteristics as distinct from the stigma that represent violations of what's considered proper behavior and belief. He refers to physical stigma as "abominations of the body—the various physical deformities" (p. 4). Goffman refers to behavior and belief as "blemishes of individual character perceived as weak will, domineering or unnatural passions, treacherous and rigid beliefs, and dishonesty, these being inferred from a known record of, for example, mental disorder, imprisonment, addiction, alcoholism, homosexuality, unemployment, suicidal attempts, and radical political behavior" (p. 4). Goffman also delineated a third type of stigma, "tribal stigma of race, nation, and religion," which is rarely discussed as a form of deviance; they will be the subject of the next chapter.

In distinguishing his own perspective on deviance from that of Goffman's, Ned Polsky argues that Goffman missed the fact that he and some other sociologists excluded from their definition of deviance "people who were not *morally* stigmatized; that is, that excluded from our definition (and our courses on the sociology of deviance) various kinds of people, such as those unusually ugly (according to society's current standards of physical attractiveness) who might indeed be stigmatized (by for example being avoided socially or joked about and discriminated against in employment) but whose condition is recognized to be 'not their fault'" (1998, pp. 202–203).

Polsky is wrong about this. *Many* negative definitions of statuses are entirely unearned. At one time, and in many societies of the world, children born out of wedlock were referred to as "bastards" and were stigmatized—considered deviants—but were not responsible for their status. The moral infamy from which they suffered did not reside in behavior they willfully enacted; we have to look to the parents, not the child, for that behavior.

More broadly, I do *not* exclude from my definition of deviance any feature, behavior, affliction, belief, or experience that is not the individual's "fault." Recently, in India, a sixteen-year-old girl was raped; as a result of the intense stigma the rape brought on the family, her father committed suicide, and she dropped out of school. In India, especially in small villages, "a rape victim is usually regarded as a shamed woman, unfit for marriage. . . . Even sympathizers of the teenage victim doubt she can assimilate back" into the village's life (Yardley, 2012, pp. 1, 12). The same applies people to who possess traits or characteristics, which are not the "fault" of their possessors, and yet they *are* stigmatized and *are* treated differently—in a pejorative, derogatory, or down-putting fashion—by persons who are not similarly blemished, who, as we saw, Goffman refers to as "normals." In fact, the very concept, "not their fault," is not as simple as Polsky implies.

As Lutz Kaelber, whose University of Vermont course on "Disability as Deviance" demonstrates, the Nazi regime accused the mentally and physically disabled—feebleminded, schizophrenic, epileptic, deaf, "criminally insane," persons suffering from dementia, encephalitis, and other chronic neurological disorders—of *euthanasia-worthy crimes*, and exterminated them without mercy. It is possible that the Nazi extermination of the physically and mentally "unfit" paved the way for the Holocaust. To the Third Reich, the involuntary disabled were *deviants*, even though their disability was "not their fault."

Closer to home, in the first half of the twentieth century, as a result of the eugenics movement, all states of the United States passed a law that mandated that people with an unacceptable appearance, low IQ, mental disability, criminal "tendencies," and moral "degeneracy" be involuntarily sterilized so that they could not produce defective children and place an undue burden on "normals." This policy was supported by "progressive" luminaries, including two American presidents, Theodore Roosevelt and Woodrow Wilson, an early feminist, Margaret Sanger, who argued that birth control and contraception would weed out the physically and mentally unfit, a physical anthropologist and professor at Harvard named Earnest Hooton, who believed blacks were closer to apes than whites, a socialist and

novelist, H.G. Wells, and a supposedly progressive playwright, George Bernard Shaw. In all likelihood, the Third Reich's advocacy of eugenics discredited the program. In the United States, between 1907 and 1941, 60,000 disabled people were involuntary sterilized; the laws mandating such sterilization were not repealed until the 1960s. (An eugenics program was continued in Sweden until 1975.) Again, supporters of eugenics regarded the mentally and physically defective as deviants, even though their condition was "not their fault." And again, we see all the manifestations of deviance and stigma directed specifically at persons who were considered less than abled. As children, they are teased and taunted, and as adults, they are denied full social acceptance.

Moreover, as we'll see, many condemners of possessors of unacceptable physical traits believe that these traits *are* "their fault." In addition to categorizing physical characteristics as deviant or undesirable, we also have to consider whether these traits are acquired voluntarily or involuntarily. The acquisition of certain unconventional physical traits or characteristics that are widely regarded as undesirable is not always entirely involuntary. Some are chosen outright: tattoos, nose rings, various kinds of piercing, for example. And some are the result of engaging in risky—including deviant—behavior, for example, sexually transmitted diseases. But whether observers make this connection between risky behavior and injury or illness is partly a matter of interpretation—a social construction. Someone may have become paralyzed as a result of a skiing or a motorcycle accident—that is, as a result of engaging in behavior that entails a certain measure of risk—but very few of us will say the people this happens to *should be blamed* for their condition. Critics will charge those who make such an attribution with "blaming the victim." But the fact is, engaging in risky behavior *is* causally related to the possession of certain undesirable physical conditions. However, "cause" and "blame" are distinct and separate notions (Felson, 1991); causality is an empirical and scientific notion while blame is a *moral* one. And it is blame, not cause, that's intricately intertwined with condemnation, deviance, and stigma.

For instance, most (although far from all) persons infected with HIV/AIDS received the virus as a result of unprotected, high-risk sex, often anal intercourse, or through intravenous illicit drug use. Many observers believe it is unfair to blame AIDS sufferers for their plight—and I agree with this assessment—but the fact is, much of the public *does* hold a condemnatory attitude toward them. (This negative sentiment has declined over the years, thankfully.) Somehow, some people feel, AIDS sufferers *are* responsible for their plight. Early in the AIDS epidemic, fundamental Christian spokespersons claimed that the disease was God's retribution for engaging in wicked behavior. The point is, seeing a connection between "deliberate" behavior and possessing a physical trait is a cultural and constructed phenomenon, not a simple factual or empirical matter. Many people deem that some physical conditions are more or less entirely a product of the possessor's own behavior. Here we have the example of obesity. Much of the non-obese public holds negative attitudes toward the obese because they believe fat people are gluttonous and self-indulgent and "could control their weight if they really wanted to" (Katz, 1981, p. 4). On the other side of the spectrum, we find persons who are heavily tattooed from one's bald, shaved skull to one's toes, and are thus totally responsible for their physical condition—which is, to many members of this society, a case of *extreme* deviance (Goode and Vail, 2008).

Here are a few possible routes to how a person came by certain physical traits or characteristics. *First*, a person can be born with them as a result of the genetic roll of the dice; here we have dwarfism and albinism. *Second*, someone can get into an accident or suffer from a disease, whether in the womb or after birth, for instance, most forms of blindness. *Third*, the actor can engage in risky, harmful behavior, for instance, the smoker's lung cancer, the addict's or homosexual's AIDS, the skydiver's broken neck. *Fourth*, cultural norms may mandate that the person acquire them, for instance, the Maori's tattoos. And *fifth*, a person individually may choose to acquire them, for instance, tattoos in Western culture, various forms of body-piercing or alteration, and shaving, clipping, or dyeing one's hair into unconventional forms, patterns, or colors.

ABOMINATIONS OF THE BODY

In earlier eras, babies born with serious deformities were referred to as "monsters." Their appearance was regarded as an evil omen, a sign of divine retribution, a prediction of disasters and epidemics to come. In fact, the word "monster" is derived from the Latin verb, *monere*, which means "to warn," "to predict" or "to foretell." Throughout ancient times, in certain societies, many deformed children were killed or exposed to the elements and left to die. A number of Roman authors, including Cicero and Tacitus, describe the drowning or burning of deformed children, an effort to propitiate the gods. The ancient Greeks, likewise, usually put to death children with undesirable characteristics, less out of fear of the wrath of the gods than being ruled by an ethic that was strongly oriented to physical perfection. Aristotle opposed the feeding of handicapped children, believing that their appropriate end would be to starve to death. Plato wrote: "Deformed and infirm children should be hidden away in a secret place." The ancient Assyrians believed that if a woman gave birth to a disabled child, her house would be destroyed; if a woman gives birth to twins joined at the spine, "the gods will forsake the people and the king will abdicate his throne" (Monestier, 1987, p. 13).

In the European Middle Ages, for the most part, Christianity attributed all "unexplained natural phenomena" either to God or the devil. Medieval theologians reasoned that if God created man in His own image, monsters—who were clearly *not* in God's image—were therefore created by the hand of Satan. Hence, the hunchback "bore the weight of a horrible curse on his back," the blind baby's eyes "had surely been seared by the red-hot coals of Hell," the "mute baby's tongue had doubtless been wrenched from his head by infernal tongs," deaf child "was thought to be receptive only to the murmurings of the Beast, and unable to hear the teachings of men of God" (Monestier, 1987, p. 13). During the medieval era, the deformed and disabled suffered most distinctly from Goffman's "abominations of the body." Today, although far less severely, and less specifically because of satanic intervention, they do so as well.

"Abominations of the body": What does Goffman mean by this term? Two distinctly different types of physical deviance come to mind: *violations of aesthetic norms* and *physical incapacity*.

Aesthetic norms represent standards that dictate how people ought to *look*: their height, weight, attractiveness, coloration, the possession of the requisite limbs and organs (no more, no less), the absence of disfigurement, the absence or presence of specific more or less permanent body adornment or alteration (scarification, tattoos, lip plugs, elongation of the ear lobes, etc.). For instance, the skin and hair of albinos lack pigmentation. In virtually all societies, albinos are stigmatized, treated as "blemished," "tainted," "spoiled"; they are "disqualified from full social acceptance." Likewise, dwarfs and midgets, hermaphrodites (people born with sexual characteristics of both males and females), and persons who are extremely ugly by society's standards— all are treated as less than fully human.

The second category of bodily "abomination," physical incapacity, is made up of bodily impairments that limit one's ability to perform certain activities considered important, such as walking, seeing, and hearing. Of course, all of us are limited in our ability to perform a number of activities. Most of us are too short, or simply can't jump high enough, to slam-dunk a basketball, or too slow to run a four-minute mile. But walking, seeing, and hearing are regarded as so crucial to everyday life that persons who lack the ability to perform them at all are treated differently, and distinctly negatively, from those who possess it.

Numerous explanations have been offered for why the physically different are assigned to a deviant status. Many of us suspect that we could be afflicted by the same random, terrorizing forces that have afflicted the possessors of negatively evaluated physical characteristics. By interacting with them, we could, we fear, be contaminated with whatever struck them down. Hence we suspect we might very well be vulnerable to such forces and want to keep their possessors as far away from us as possible.

In his analysis of stigma, Katz (1981, pp. 1, 5–11) introduces the notion of *ambivalence*. Admittedly, most of us temper our negative feelings toward the disabled and the unaesthetic with positive ones. In addition to stigmatizing them, Katz claims, most people feel sympathy for the underdog, distress over their suffering, and respect for persons who are able to triumph over adversity. So why stigmatize them in the first place? The reasons are diverse, Katz argues, but they may be traced to a half-dozen widespread dynamics that are difficult to ignore; two of them are the "just world" hypothesis and the sense of vulnerability.

Interaction with persons who possess a socially undesirable trait or characteristic that is strictly involuntary (it's "not their fault") may "cast doubt" on the widely held belief that the world is a just place where the innocent do not suffer (Lerner, 1980). Many of us believe that we get pretty much what we deserve. The disabled remind us that there are many people out there for whom that is not true. Justice does not triumph, the wicked may not be punished, and extreme misfortune may befall the virtuous and the innocent. This is a painful lesson, one of which "normals" are reminded nearly every time they come face to face with someone who possesses a disability or a disfigurement.

If undesirable physical traits are inflicted on people who did nothing to deserve them, the conclusion is obvious, says Katz: We are all *vulnerable* to sudden, catastrophic, and undeserved misfortune. The disabled and the disfigured do not merely overturn one of our ideological and moral apple-carts, they also hit home with the message that we, ourselves, could be victims of the same misfortune that befell them. This is an extremely uncomfortable message, one that most "normals" do not want to be reminded of. Hence, we avoid the disabled and the disfigured, we put social distance between ourselves and them, we treat them in a pitying and condescending fashion, and the cruelest of us stigmatize them. If such a misfortune were to befall someone else simply as a result of happenstance, it could also happen to us. Coming face to face with the handicapped reminds us of *our own* vulnerability, and many of us find that experience painful. Hence, we want to banish the possessors of these traits from our presence.

PHYSICAL DISABILITY

According to Eliot Freidson (1966), the possession of a physical disability or handicap is a form of deviance. This is so because it represents an imputation of undesirable difference as judged by Goffman's "normals." A person so designated departs or deviates from what others *believe to be normal or appropriate*. It is "normal" or "appropriate" to be able to see, walk, and hear. Not to be able to do so represents an undesirable departure from what is regarded as "normal." Put another way, deviance is not merely statistical variation or difference from the average, the mode, or the statistical norm. Rather, it is that which "violates institutional expectations" (Cohen, 1959, p. 462). We are *expected* to be able to see, walk, and hear. When we are not able to do so, we violate the norms—the "institutional expectations"—that others have of our performance. In recent years, a variety of euphemistic and politically correct terms have been applied to the physically handicapped, such as the "differently abled," the reason being that plain, straightforward, descriptive terms stigmatize persons to whom the terms apply. Simi Linton (1998, p. 14), a disabled spokesperson, refers to such terms as "nice words," "well-meaning attempts to inflate the value of people with disabilities," which are "rarely used by disabled activists and scholars (except with palpable irony)." Many deaf militants reject the label "disabled" and claim membership in the deaf culture. But the fact is, the norms in this society do call for certain kinds of performance, and persons who are unable to meet those norms are looked down upon in one way or another.

When such violations are in a significant and important sphere of life and are "persistent," persons guilty of them are "assigned a special negatively deviant role" (Freidson, 1966, p. 73) and are "generally thought to require the attention of social control agencies" (Erikson, 1964, pp. 10–11). Social agencies that work with the physically disabled and handicapped distinguish between those who cooperate and work at ameliorating their condition—who, for instance, play the role of the "good" amputee—as opposed to those who are uncooperative and do not work toward rehabilitation (Freidson, 1966, p. 81). What these agencies hold out is not an exit from the disabled role—indeed, even after their intervention, those who are rehabilitated by them will still occupy the status and play the role of handicapped person—but an *accommodation to* that role. In other words, the "handicapped *remain* deviant, and the task of rehabilitation is to shape the form of their deviance, which is quite a different task than that of healing the sick or punishing or salvaging the delinquent" (p. 95). In the words of Erving Goffman: "The stigmatized individual is asked to act so as to imply neither that his [or her] burden is heavy nor that bearing it has made him [or her] different from us. . . . A *phantom acceptance* is thus allowed to provide the base for a *phantomnormalcy*" (1963, p. 122).

Disability, like behavioral deviance, is socially constructed, "produced," or "created" (Freidson, 1966, p. 83). This does not mean that the *physical conditions* on which judgments of disability are based are "created" by the society. Rather, it means the definition demarcating a given condition *as* a disablement, and judgment that a specific case or person *belongs* to the general category of disablement, are to some degree arbitrary and based on social and cultural criteria. Agencies that deal with the disabled as well as the general public create such definitions. They "objectify" or "reify" (p. 83) disability—much the same way all social entities do with deviance in general—in that they assume every member they so classify by a given category possesses all of the characteristics the category refers to. But as it turns out, *most* people who are legally classified as physically "handicapped" can walk, even though the assumption is that they cannot; most people who are legally "blind" can see, even though the assumption is that they cannot. The stereotype "normals" hold is that persons defined as handicapped will fit the most severely impaired end of the impairment continuum, even though most are in fact at the less impaired end of that spectrum (p. 84).

One of the central tasks of the person who possesses a physical handicap, and who is widely regarded as disabled, is dealing with the nondisabled—that is, with persons Goffman refers to as "normals." Rehabilitation agencies usually encourage the fiction that the population at large does not stigmatize the disabled, since this fiction furthers their rehabilitative goals. But the fact is, most "normals" do hold a stigmatizing attitude of one kind or another toward the disabled. True, as we saw, most also feel *ambivalence* toward the handicapped—that is, compassion is mingled with the stigma (Katz, 1981, pp. 5–11). But stigma is there nonetheless. "Normals" generally reject and avoid the handicapped socially. A "social distance" scale reveals this rejection with crystal clarity. When samples of respondents are asked if they would "accept" persons who belong to various disvalued categories in a range of relationships—as neighbors, as coworkers, as friends—members of *none* of those categories are accepted, on average, as readily as persons who are normally abled. For instance, one study asked respondents if they would "accept" members of twenty-two categories, "every one was rejected to some extent"; cerebral palsy sufferers, epileptics, and paraplegics (along with dwarfs and hunchbacks) were rejected even as next door neighbors (p. 18). Anecdotal evidence backs up these systematic surveys. "In a host of written and oral accounts [by the handicapped], the theme of being pitied, subordinated, and ignored is expressed again and again" (p. 18). Content analyses of cultural materials, such as jokes, indicate the inferior status of the handicapped. In one study of jokes, the handicapped were made fun of 80 percent of the time, whereas jokes about farmers, dentists, and judges were vastly less likely to be insulting (p. 18). There is a measure of *aversion* toward the disabled, just as there is toward disfigurements, in part because they provoke anxiety in "normals," reminding them that they, too, could fall victim to the same misfortune (p. 20). In other words, "normals" fear the handicapped as much as they pity them.

Times are changing. In 1990, the Americans with Disabilities Act, which guaranteed prohibition against job discrimination and physical access to public spaces, was passed with bipartisan support. In the late 1990s, new style activist researchers—most of whom are disabled persons themselves—published a substantial spate of books that argue for changing the way things are rather than adapting to existing circumstances (Hockenberry, 1995; Thomson, 1996, 1997; Davis, 1997; Mairs, 1997; Mitchell and Snyder, 1997; Linton, 1998; Fiffer, 1999; Charlton, 1999). In 1997, Mattel introduced a "Barbie" doll

friend in a wheelchair. In 1991, Dayton Hudson, an advertising firm, introduced ads using disabled models. In 1992, critics protested the muscular dystrophy telethon hosted by comedian Jerry Lewis; these protesters included some who were themselves disabled former poster children for the cause. They objected to the telethon fostering an image of the disabled as pitiable and childlike. Given these beginnings, the disability rights movement gained momentum during the course of the twenty-first century, and has gone global. According to Thomas Cook, Professor of Public Health at the University of Iowa, the Americans with Disabilities Act, signed into law by President George Bush in 1990, has generated an international grassroots movement. In May 2012, the World Health Organization and the World Bank jointly published the first World Report on Disability. Worldwide, roughly a billion people suffer with a disability, many of whom are discriminated against and victimized, less likely to attend and complete school, and suffer from a higher rate of premature mortality; women are frequently victims of sexual violence. Nearly eight out of ten live in lower-income countries. The movement supports national legislation everywhere to protect the disabled and an international treaty that recognizes their right to access to the same resources that the conventionally abled enjoy; this movement "promises to improve the quality of people everywhere" (Cook, 2011). Disability rights movement activists abroad have experienced both successes and resistance, says Suzanne Richard, a movement activist; she seeks ratification of the Convention on the Rights of Persons with Disabilities (CRPD) around the world—for instance, in Macedonia and Myanmar (Burma), in 2011. Currently, in the Asia-Pacific region, twenty-three out of fifty countries have ratified the Convention; but in Bolivia, riot police prevented activists from delivering their petition to the legislature. The Zambian Deaf Women and Youth plan "Hungry Walk Campaign" that will culminate in presenting the legislature with the demand that it implement the CRPD it has already ratified (http://usicd.worldpress.com/2012/04/04/the-disability-rights-movement.org). "Tertiary" deviance—when people who are judged nonnormative by the rest of society fight for equal rights—is a crucial element in the physical deviance equation. It is effective, however, only to the extent that Goffman's "normals" share the view that a category of deviants *are* oppressed and that their oppression *does* need to be redressed. Some other categories, such as the obese, possess less moral capital than the disabled, in the eyes of the general public.

CONFORMITY TO AND VIOLATIONS OF ESTHETIC STANDARDS

"I'm too ugly to get a job," declared a Miami bank robber after the police apprehended him (Morin, 2006). This felon's rationalization may have some basis in fact. One of the more remarkable pieces of evidence suggesting that ugliness is a form of deviance comes from a study indicating that, among young adults (age eighteen to twenty-six), ugliness is statistically associated with criminal behavior (Mocan and Tekin, 2006). The uglier the person, the greater the likelihood he or she will have difficulty in high school and, seven to eight years later, will engage in a range of criminal activities, including burglary and drug selling; this is especially true of females. One possibility: Judgments of deviance close off legitimate avenues of success and make illegitimate avenues seem more attractive. Violations of esthetic standards offer one major type of "abominations of the body." All societies hold their members to certain standards of physical attractiveness. Says Nancy Etcoff, a neuroscientist conducting research on the role of looks in human attraction and author of *Survival of the Prettiest* (1999): "Every culture is a beauty culture. . . . I defy anyone to point to a society anytime in history or any place in the world that wasn't preoccupied with beauty" (Cowley, 1996, p. 62). Moreover, in all societies, there are negative consequences for not measuring up to these standards of beauty; ugly people everywhere are treated as deviants. Naturally, these consequences vary from society to society and from one period of history to another; they vary from being an object of teasing to being put to death. In one way or another, all societies reward the attractive and punish the ugly.

At one time, most anthropologists believed that aesthetic standards were completely arbitrary, that looks judged attractive in one society may be regarded as ugly in another. Most contemporary researchers and scholars reject this radically relativistic view. In fact, the valuation of looks is considerably less variable and relativistic than was once believed. It turns out there is a fairly substantial measure of agreement in aesthetic standards from one society to another. There is some variability, of course, and it is interesting and significant. The crucial point to keep in mind is that the variation is much less substantial than was believed in the past, and the consensus is probably a great deal more significant than the variation. For the most part, looks that are considered beautiful in one society are regarded as beautiful in societies all over the world; looks that are considered ugly in one society tend to be regarded as ugly in societies the world over. When researchers show photographs of faces of people from all racial categories to subjects from backgrounds as diverse as Greece, China, India, and England, they find a remarkably high level of agreement as to which ones are attractive and which ones are unattractive. In the judgment of the evaluators in this study, the ethnic background of the subjects in these studies makes little or no difference.

Skeptics might argue that, as a result of the influence of Western, mainly American, movies, television programs, and magazines, the aesthetic standards that rule here have spread to the inhabitants of all societies. But when Judith Langlois projected images of the faces of "attractive" and "unattractive" persons—males and females, adults and babies, whites and persons of African descent—before three- and six-month-old babies, the same pattern prevailed. These babies "gazed significantly longer" at the "attractive" than at the "unattractive" faces. Says Langlois: "These kids don't read *Vogue* or watch TV. . . . They haven't been touched by the media. Yet they make the same judgments as adults" (Cowley, 1996, p. 63; Langlois et al., 2000; Lemley, 2000).

What's behind these judgments? Is there something about a face or a body that dictates why we find it attractive? Does the same process take place in reverse for the "unattractive" face? Some psychobiologists think they have the answer: evolution. They believe that many clues point to the possibility that humans are biologically "hardwired" to make specific, distinct, and universal aesthetic judgments.

Some of the rules of aesthetic judgment are commonsensical and not especially mysterious. In nearly all persons, physical good heath is more attractive than illness. "As far as anyone knows," according to Helen Fisher, an anthropologist who studies love, mating, and physical attractiveness, "there isn't a village on earth where skin lesions [sores], head lice, and rotting teeth count as beauty aids" (Cowley, 1996, p. 63). Surprisingly, *symmetry* turns out to be a major factor in determining the physical attractiveness of human faces and bodies—a balance of each side with the other, in equal proportion. (Interestingly, the same principle holds for animals, some of them as lowly as scorpion flies. Females of many species refuse to mate with males who do not display the requisite symmetry.) Other features include, for human males, slightly above average height, a broad forehead, prominent brow and cheekbones, a large jaw and strong chin, slightly above-average body musculature, and a waist that is 90 percent the measurement of the hips. For females, these features include youth as well as large eyes, a small nose, delicate jaw, small chin, full lips, firm, symmetrical breasts, smooth, unblemished skin, and a waist-hip ratio of 70 percent (Cowley, 1996, p. 63).

Most evolutionary psychologists believe that these judgments are genetic in origin, that, without realizing it, our bodies are telling us to seek partners who offer the maximum potential to reproduce our own genes in our children and in subsequent generations. Each of these traits, from age to smooth, unblemished skin to the flair of a woman's hips and the jut of a man's jaw, evolutionary psychologists argue are maximally related to fertility and hence, according to their theory, maximum attractiveness. We find in a potential partner that which tells us that if we mate with him or her, our genetic material stands the highest likelihood of being propagated to later generations. Genes are "selfish"; they seek to reproduce themselves. Seeking out the most attractive available partner is a way of doing that. Our esthetic judgments are ruled by our "selfish" genes.

In contrast, most sociologists, anthropologists, and other social scientists argue that culture—not genes—explains judgments of attractiveness. If judgments of beauty were biologically "hardwired" and designed to perpetuate the judge's genes, how do we explain homosexuality? Why do same-sex partners find many of the same physical traits attractive that opposite-sex partners do? Says Micaela di Leonardo, an anthropologist who studies human attractiveness: "People make decisions about sexual and marital partners inside complex networks of friends and relatives. . . . Human beings cannot be reduced to DNA packets" (Cowley, 1996, p. 66).

Regardless of the source or cause of the consistency of aesthetic judgments about human appearance, they are a fact of life. And studies have shown that, just as *conforming* to a society's aesthetic standards is likely to bring forth rewards, *violating* those standards is likely to result in punishment. We "set narrow standards of beauty and then insult and hurt those who fall outside those standards" (Beuf, 1990, p. 1). The possession of an unaesthetic appearance is not the possessor's "fault," and this punishment is decidedly unfair. Yet, such punishment is a reality in the lives of many people who fail to attain the aesthetic ideal.

In a classic study by social psychologist Karen Dion (1972), a sample of college women was asked to read over a teacher's notes describing the behavior of the children in her class. Attached to the notes was a photograph of the child. The notes did not describe a real child or actual behavior; in fact, they were manipulated to describe a fictional incident in which the child hurt a dog or another child in a trivial or a serious way. The photographs, likewise, were varied so that they depicted one attractive girl, one unattractive girl, one attractive boy, and one unattractive boy. The researchers asked members of the sample to evaluate the behavior and the child. Dion hypothesized that physical appearance would make a difference in these evaluations—and they did.

If the child's misbehavior was mild (stepping on a dog's tail), the women in the sample were not influenced by the children's looks. But when the misbehavior was more serious (throwing stones at a dog, causing it to yelp and limp away), for the unattractive children, members of the sample regarded this as a serious character flaw; for the attractive children, the sample of college students tended to be more lenient and indulgent, to give them the benefit of the doubt, passing off their misbehavior as trivial. One student who read the notes and saw the photograph of an attractive girl made these comments about an attractive girl who had thrown rocks at the dog: "She appears to be a perfectly charming little girl, well-mannered, basically unselfish. It seems that she can adapt well among children her age and make a good impression. . . . She plays well with everyone, but, like everyone else, a bad day can occur. Her cruelty . . . need not be taken too seriously" (Berscheid and Walster, 1972, p. 45).

In contrast, here are the remarks another student made, commenting on an unattractive girl who committed exactly the same act: "I think the child would be quite bratty and would be a problem to teachers. . . . She would probably try to pick a fight with other children. . . . She would be a brat at home. . . . All in all, she would be a real problem" (p. 45). In addition to evaluating attractive and unattractive children and their behavior differently, these respondents expressed expectations that the unattractive ones would be likelier to commit similar transgressions in the future. In short, the attribution of deviance is closely tied to looks: Other things being equal, unattractive people are more likely to be suspected of engaging in wrongdoing, more likely to be evaluated negatively, and more likely to be punished.

Standards of beauty are crucial to defining its absence—ugliness—as deviant. The fact is, "uglier people are assigned all kinds of undesirable qualities. They are expected to do evil things, and their misdeeds are judged as more wicked than if the same thing was done by a better looking wrongdoer" (Jones et al., 1984, p. 53). An enormous number of studies have confirmed the impact of looks on how we are treated by others. After they have met them, people are more likely to forget about less attractive people than those who are more attractive; they evaluate work done by less attractive people more negatively than work done by more attractive people; people tend to work less hard for more unattractive people than for attractive people; and they are less likely to return something that is lost if the owner is physically unappealing (p. 53). As a result of this differential treatment, less attractive people tend to have a lower sense of self-esteem and to have less satisfactory relations with peers (p. 54). In sum, "ugly or physically deviant people are clearly disadvantaged both by the immediate negative effect they elicit and by the longer term cumulative consequences of coping with the avoidant and rejecting behavior of others" (p. 56).

At the age of nine, Lucy Grealy was diagnosed with cancer. To save her life, surgeons removed a third of her jaw. After the operation, when she looked in the mirror, Lucy realized she was different. She endured thirty separate operations, most of them to reconstruct her jaw so that she would look normal. The boys in her school taunted her cruelly. "Hey, girl, take off that monster mask—oops, she's not wearing a monster mask," shouted one (Grealy, 1995, p. 118). "*What* on earth is *that*?" yelled another (p. 124). "*That* is the ugliest girl I have *ever* seen" declared a third (p. 124). The taunts, which were especially frequent during lunch period, became so painful for Lucy that, in the seventh grade, she went to her guidance counselor to complain. Rather than reprimand the children who hurled them, he asked if she wanted to eat lunch in his office, an offer she decided to accept. Sadly, in 2002, at the age of 39, Lucy Grealy, a talented writer, sensitive poet, and perceptive observer of unconventional human identities, succumbed to an overdose of heroin.

All societies value beauty. Hence, "the person whose appearance is impaired, who stands out because of obvious flaws and disfigurements, is perceived as a deviant." Such a person is deviant in two ways—one, by failing to live up to an ideal cultural standard of beauty and two, by failing to live up to what is regarded as a "normal" or *unexceptional* appearance (Beuf, 1990, p. 7). Ugly or extremely unattractive persons are often stared at, teased, taunted ("How did your face *get* like that, anyhow?"), humiliated; people with average or "normal" appearance often feel disgusted, repelled, even *tainted* to be in their presence. The cruelty of children toward the appearance-impaired "seems limitless" (p. 51). It is clear that, in spite of the fact that such people did not *do* anything to deserve their appearance, many audiences regard—and treat—them as deviants.

Should ugliness be against the law? Is it fair to criminalize someone for their appearance? Every one of us would say that such a thing is grossly unfair and unjust, that how one looks should most emphatically not be against the law. Today, no such laws remain on the books, but consider the fact that, in 1881, the city of Chicago passed a municipal ordinance that read: "Any person who is diseased, maimed, mutilated, or in any way deformed, so as to be an unsightly or disgusting object, or an improper person to be allowed in or on the streets, highways, thoroughfares, or public places in this city, should not therein expose himself to public views." The penalty was a fine of a dollar, or about $20–25 today. As it turns out, a similar law had been passed in San Francisco fourteen years earlier, and similar versions were soon enacted in Portland, Oregon; Denver, Colorado; Lincoln, Nebraska. The law attempted to outlaw the "unsightly beggar," the mendicant who displays his deformities so as to generate more sympathy and collect more money from a disgusted public. The issue for the law is whether and to what extent the law can mandate *sequestration*, or hiding the unsightly beggar from the citizenry. And what was the intention of the local lawmakers—to prohibit people with noticeable physical disabilities from visiting public spaces (Schweik, 2009, p. 4). These so-called "ugly laws" remained on the books until well into the 1970s. The last recorded arrest on the basis of the unsightly beggar statute took place in 1974, in Omaha; the arresting officer, who had been trying to get the mendicant off the streets for some time, reasoned that the suspect had "marks and scars across his body" and hence, was fair game (p. 6). No such laws exist today (p. 18). Nonetheless, all of us are still judged, informally, according to our looks, and looks deemed unusually unsightly are considered *deviant*—beyond the pale—and their bearer tends to be shunned, humiliated, and punished. Even in organizational settings, deviant features attract negative judgments. Schewik (p. 284) describes a court case, *Robichaud v. RPH Management*, involving an employee of MacDonald's whose superiors informed her that she would never become a member of management because she had an "unsightly" birthmark on her face. Why

are looks so important? The "ugly" laws may be off the books, but *informal* judgments of deviance remain in force. This is unjust in the extreme, but it's a seemingly ineradicable feature of conventional norms.

Most forms of deviance entail judgments and actions made by the general public. In the case of the "unsightly beggar" ordinance, it is the police, not the public at large, who initiates agency, although most arrests on minor charges begin with a complaint by a citizen. In the case of the ugly law, residents of local neighborhoods or small merchants took the initiative to remove the unaesthetic mendicant from their midst. Another parallel: With most forms of behavioral deviance, we find that contingencies (age, sex, status, characteristics of the observer or the victim, if there is one) play a role in judgments of deviance; in the case of the "ugly law," the police ignored most instances of its violation, when a complainant stepped forward, often, action was taken. What has happened is an "astonishingly rapid transformation in American attitudes toward disabled people" (Imrey, 1996, p. 61). While ugliness and physical disability are still forms of physical deviance, public attitudes toward the disabled and the ugly have softened, and virtually no one wants to invoke the might of the law against poor people who are unsightly and, in all probability, unable to support themselves. The dynamism of what's considered deviance is one of its most remarkable features. While some aspects of physical deviance have stayed the same, others have undergone an impressive turnaround. To the extent that esthetic standards are applied to desirability, ugliness will remain a form of deviance. By dominant cultural standards, attractive marital partners still gravitated toward one another, since the rewards and punishments on the basis of the desirability of the looks of one's partner likewise remain. But the virulence of esthetic judgments—how much the ugly are punished—has diminished over the centuries, and is likely to be even more tempered as alternate values are weighed against the sledgehammer of looksism. In an achievement-oriented society, persons who are deemed wanting in the esthetic department lose out less than in one where looks are everything.

EXTREME BODY MODIFICATION AS PHYSICAL DEVIANCE

Some people modify their bodies in ways that elicit suspicion, stigma, and condemnation. Erik Sprague, 27, is a "performance artist" and a PhD student in philosophy at the State University of New York at Albany. Mr. Sprague "is slowly transforming himself into a reptile." Not literally, of course, but his appearance is becoming increasingly reptilian. Scale-like tattoos appear on his body from head to foot. He's having the scales filled in, one by one, with green. He convinced surgeons to implant a bony ridge on his forehead and shape his tongue into a reptile's proverbial forked tongue. His fingernails are in the form of claws, and several of his teeth are filed down to look like "crocodile-like chompers."

Sprague calls his transformation an "experiment." The idea isn't to shock, he says, but to "stimulate dialogue, to get people thinking, to make people wonder." He wants to test the limits of what it means to be human. After his metamorphosis, he wonders, can others still regard him as a full-fledged human being? He says he knows who his real friends are by their willingness to remain friends with him, even after taking on his dramatically altered appearance. "I learn a lot more about a person by their reaction to me than they could ever learn about me by just looking at my physical appearance."

Sprague works as a performer with the traveling Jim Rose Circus. He swallows swords, eats live insects, breathes fire, and sticks metal skewers through his cheeks. His ongoing bodily transformation, he says, has been great for his show business career (Anonymous, 2000).

Aside from ear-piercing, which, for women, is considered conventional and normative, tattooing is probably the most widely practiced form of voluntary body alteration. No statistics are kept on the number of people who receive a permanent tattoo, but in the United States the number certainly runs into the millions. Is tattooing a form of physical deviance?

In many societies of the world, of course, getting a tattoo is not only accepted, it is also normatively demanded. In Western society generally and in the United States specifically, people who "choose to modify their bodies" by getting a tattoo "violate appearance norms" and hence "risk being defined as socially and morally inferior. Choosing to be a physical deviant symbolically demonstrates one's disregard for the prevailing norms" (Sanders, 1989, p. 2). In many ways, persons who choose to be tattooed play on that unconventionality by demonstrating their "disaffection from the mainstream." For many people who are unconventional, tattooing is a symbolic affirmation—indeed, a public proclamation—of the tattooee's "special attachments to deviant groups" (p. 2). It is an "effective social mechanism for separating 'us' from 'them'" (p. 3). This separation may be partial, as exemplified by the Wall Street lawyer who receives a single, small, inconspicuous tattoo to affirm his or her *mild* unconventionality, or it may range up to *total* unconventionality, as with the person who is tattooed from head to toe in wild designs and who therefore cannot move in any social circle whatsoever without being regarded as an out-and-out deviant—and wants it that way (Goode and Vail, 2008).

Tattooing is deviant both for its direct symbolic value and for it being symbolically connected with deviant groups and categories. Here we have "voluntary guilt by association." Tattooing is common among convicts, prostitutes, bikers, drunken sailors, and other disreputable types. Therefore wearing a tattoo symbolizes the "general deviance and untrustworthiness of the wearer" (Sanders, 1989, p. 126). Wearing a tattoo announces to the world, "I am a great deal like these other disreputable people who are known for wearing a tattoo." Hence, wearing "a stigmatizing mark by most members of mainstream society," one became aware of "the potential negative social consequences of being tattooed" from employers, relatives, one's spouse, and other representatives of "straight" society (p. 126). Many tattooed persons do belong to deviant groups for whom the tattoo is a badge of honor rather than shame.

In addition, tattooing represents a major commitment. Before the advent of lasers, tattoos could be removed only through conventional surgery, which was expensive and produced scarification. Hence, until recently, a tattoo, once on the body, remained there for life. In a phrase, the wearer was "indelibly marked" (p. 126). Although vastly more common than a decade or two ago, even today, getting a tattoo is considered a "big deal." As a result, most receivers of a tattoo "start small." Getting a small, inexpensive, and readily concealable tattoo is the usual way of limiting one's commitment (p. 126). By testing the waters in this fashion, one can determine whether, in one's group or circle, social reactions to the tattoo are sufficiently negative as to call a halt to further body alterations. If these reactions are mild among their peers, more accepting than rejecting, many recipients will escalate the process, receiving larger and more conspicuous tattoos.

In short, there is a "certain level of risk" in receiving a tattoo. One may not choose an artful or reputable tattooist, the process is somewhat painful, one risks infection, the final product may not be quite what one had hoped for, one may later have a change of heart, one may be criticized or condemned for bearing a tattoo on one's body by one's peers, or one may take up with new friends or lovers who will find the connection with tattooing repugnant, one's employers may react more harshly than one had anticipated, and so on. In short, yes, tattooing is a form of physical deviance, albeit a relatively mild form. In contrast, more complete or full-body tattooing may be regarded as more "extreme" deviance. To put the matter another way, the degree of deviance of tattooing runs the gamut from mildly deviant (a small, inconspicuous tattoo) to strongly deviant (being tattooed over one's entire body, including one's face). What makes it especially interesting is that, unlike many forms of physical deviance, it is voluntary. Many tattooees *choose* to receive tattoos on their body specifically because of its association with deviant social categories and groups (Sanders, 1989).

One among a number of indications that tattooing is an instance of deviance is that the National Longitudinal Study of Adolescent Health included a question about tattooing in its survey, as well as, in a later survey wave, whether the respondents later matriculated into college. High school students who had tattoos were significantly less likely to go to college than students without them, and the difference was substantial as more traditional factors such as educational attainment and socioeconomic status of the respondent's family of origin. Having tattoos was also associated with a variety of deviant activities, such as smoking, participation in delinquency and gang membership, drinking, marijuana smoking, and infrequent use of birth control. Clearly, tattooing did not cause but *tapped into, symbolized,* or indirectly *indicated* a deviant, non–college oriented lifestyle that accompanied later lack of success in a variety of ways (Silver et al., 2011).

Alicia Horton (2010) argues that "extreme body practices" such as the insertion of cheek skewers, flesh hook pulling, inserting and sewing objects under one's skin onto one's body, and radical branding make claims that critique prevailing standards of normalcy and attractiveness, challenge body-changing practitioners to negotiate and manage a stigmatized identity and conventional audiences to defend their practices, and reorients the notion of what's blameworthy and what's praiseworthy. These represent a bold, even outrageous "in your face" challenge to notions of deviance and conventionality. Manifestations of the practice of extreme body alteration, in Goffman's terms, are not only blatantly visible and evident to the "normal" but they are *obtrusive*—difficult to ignore and "disattend to." They remind the "normal" that one stigmatized trait spreads to others, and to other parties in the interaction, and these close connections tell conventional people that such relations should be avoided or, if initiated, terminated. They question such assumptions—whether and to what extent they are based on prejudice or wisdom (Goffman, 1963, p. 30).

OBESITY

Obesity represents a prime example of an "abomination of the body" that violates aesthetic standards. What makes it even more interesting than most of the characteristics with which it shares this quality is that, in addition to being physical in nature, most people mistakenly believe it to be the product of immorality, or deviant behavior. The majority of people who are not fat feel that the obese became fat because they are gluttonous and lazy—that is, because they eat too much and don't exercise enough. Hence, obesity partakes of both of Goffman's forms of stigma: It is both an "abomination of the body" and a "blemish of individual character." Some stigmatizing traits, Goffman says, are highly visible or *self-evident* to others in a social interaction, and obesity is one such extremely evident trait. However, the capacity of audiences to "disattend" to or "decode" stigmatizing characteristics depends on the audience. Some traits are very obtrusive; they are noted because they interfere with the flow of social interaction. Most audiences of average size find it difficult to ignore the fact that the person they are face to face with is extremely large; it remains the center of attention and, though they may try to ignore that fact, it intrudes into relations between "normals" and the obese.

In this society, extreme fatness is itself looked upon with repugnance because most Americans consider it unsightly and unaesthetic, and, in addition, fatness is a sign or manifestation that the person who carries the weight got that way because of a weak, self-indulgent nature. In other words, not only does the thin majority regard obesity as unfashionable and unaesthetic, they also consider it "morally reprehensible," a "social disgrace" (Cahnman, 1968, p. 283). They set apart fat people from themselves, men and women of average size. They socially isolate the obese from "normal" society (Millman, 1980). Today, being obese bears something of a stigma.

"Generally speaking," declares an anthropologist who studied body ideals in an Arab area of Niger, an African country, "fat bodies are appreciated where food is hard to come by, and thin ones are admired in places where food is abundant." Worldwide, she says, roughly 80 percent of human societies "have had a preference for plumper bodies" (Popenoe, 2005, p. 18). But as Western ideals of beauty spread to societies everywhere, and as societies begin having an abundant food supply, female bodies come to be seen "in a new way" that "make new kinds of bodies desirable" (p. 18). "Fat Stigma," reads a *New York Times* headline, "Is Fast Becoming a Global Epidemic" (Parker-Pope, 2011). And in contemporary America, the obese are more decidedly stigmatized. Fat people are considered less worthy human beings than thin or average-sized people are. They receive less of the good things that life has to offer and

more of the bad. Men and women of average weight tend to look down on the obese, feel sorry for them, pity them, feel superior to them, reward them less, punish them, and make fun of them. The obese are often an object of derision and harassment for their weight. What is more, average-sized persons tend to feel that this treatment is just, that the obese deserve it, indeed, that it is even something of a humanitarian gesture, since such humiliation will supposedly inspire them to lose weight. The stigma of obesity is so intense and pervasive that many, perhaps most, fat people come to see themselves as deserving of it, too.

The obese, in the words of one observer, "are a genuine minority, with all the attributes that a corrosive social atmosphere lends to such groups: poor self-image, heightened sensitivity, passivity, withdrawal, a sense of isolation and rejection." They are subject to relentless discrimination, they are the butt of denigrating jokes, they suffer from persecution; it would not be an exaggeration to say that they attract cruelty from the average-sized majority. Moreover, their friends and family rarely give the kind of understanding they need in order to deal with this cruelty. In fact, it is often friends and family who mete out the cruel treatment. The social climate has become "so completely permeated with anti-fat prejudice that the fat themselves have been infected by it. They hate other fat people, hate themselves when they are fat, and will risk anything—even their lives—in an attempt to get thin. . . . Anti-fat bigotry . . . is a psychic net in which the overweight are entangled every moment of their lives" (Louderback, 1970, pp. v, vi, vii).

Negative feelings toward being overweight are a matter of degree, of course. If the grossly obese are persecuted mightily for their weight, the slightly overweight are persecuted proportionally less—they are not exempt. In spite of the fact that Americans are gaining weight over time (or perhaps because of it), we remain a weight-obsessed society. It is impossible to escape reminders of what our ideal weight should be. Standing at the checkout counter in our local supermarket, we are confronted by an array of magazines, each with its own special diet designed to shed those flabby pounds. Television programs and advertising display actresses and models who are considerably slimmer than average, setting up an almost impossibly thin ideal for the public. If we were to gain ten pounds, our friends would notice it, would view the gain with negative feelings, and only the most tactful would not comment on it.

Obesity is sociologically interesting, among other reasons, because the thin or average-sized majority consider it as both a physical characteristic, like blindness and paraplegia, and a form of behavioral deviance, like prostitution and alcoholism. They hold the obese, unlike the physically disabled, responsible for their condition. The non-obese majority view fatness both as a physical deformity as well as a behavioral aberration (Cahnman, 1968, p. 293; Allon, 1982, p. 130). They regard being fat as a matter of *choice*. The obese have gotten that way because of something they have done, many feel, as a result of a major character flaw.

Overweight persons "are stigmatized because they are held responsible for their deviant status, presumably lacking self-control and will-power. They are not merely physically deviant as are physically disabled or disfigured persons, but they [also] seem to possess characterological stigma. Fat people are viewed as 'bad' or 'immoral'; supposedly, they do not want to change the error of their ways" (Allon, 1982, p. 131). Contrary to the strictly and involuntarily disabled, "the obese are presumed to hold their fate in their own hands; if they were only a little less greedy or lazy or yielding to impulse or oblivious of advice, they would restrict excessive food intake, resort to strenuous exercise, and as a consequence of such deliberate action, they would reduce." In contrast, Cahnman argues, while blindness "is considered a misfortune, obesity is branded as a defect. . . . A blind girl will be helped by her agemates, but a heavy girl will be derided. A paraplegic boy will be supported by other boys, but a fat boy will be pushed around. The embarrassing and not infrequently harassing treatment which is meted out to obese teenagers by those around them will not elicit sympathy from onlookers but a sense of gratification; the idea is that they have got what was coming to them" (Cahnman, 1968, p. 294).

The obese are overweight, according to the popular view, because they eat immodestly and to excess. They have succumbed to temptation and hedonistic pleasure-seeking, where other, more virtuous and less self-indulgent persons have

resisted. As with all forms of behavioral deviance, getting fat represents a struggle between vice and virtue. Most of us are virtuous—witness the fact that we are not fat. Some of us are consumed with vice—and the proof of the pudding, so to speak, is in the eating. Therefore, the obese must pay for their sin of overindulgence by attracting well-deserved stigma (Cahnman, 1968; Maddox, Back and Liederman, 1968). The obese suffer from what the public sees as "self-inflicted damnation" (Allon, 1973; Allon, 1982). In one study of the public's rejection of persons with an array of behavioral and physical traits and characteristics, researchers found that the degree of the stigma of obesity was somewhere in between that of physical handicaps, such as blindness, and behavioral deviance, such as homosexuality (Hiller, 1981, 1982). In other words, the public stigmatizes the obese significantly *more* than they do the possessors of involuntarily acquired undesirable characteristics, but somewhat less than persons who engage in unconventional, despised behavior.

This introduces a *moral* dimension to obesity that is largely lacking in most other physical characteristics. The stigma of obesity entails three elements or aspects. (1) The obese attract public scorn. (2) They are told that this scorn is deserved. (3) They come to accept this negative treatment as just (Cahnman, 1968, p. 293). A clear-cut indication that the obese are put down because of their presumed character defects is seen in the fact that when respondents were informed that a person's obesity was caused by a hormonal disorder—in other words, it was not his or her "fault"—they stigmatized him or her far less than if their condition is left unexplained (DeJong, 1980). Unless otherwise informed, most of us assume that obesity is the fat person's "fault." A trait that is seen as beyond the person's control, for which he or she is held not to be responsible, is seen as a misfortune. In contrast, character flaws are regarded in a much harsher light. Obesity tends to be seen as the outward manifestation of an undesirable character. It therefore invites retribution in much of the public's eyes.

In an editorial in *The New York Times*, one observer (Rosenthal, 1981) argues that obesity has replaced sex and death as our "contemporary pornography." We attach some measure of shame and guilt to eating well. Our society is made up of "modern puritans" who tell one another "how *repugnant* it is to be fat"; "what's really disgusting," we feel, "is not sex, but fat." We are all so humorless, "so relentless, so determined to punish the overweight. . . . Not only are the overweight the most stigmatized group in the United States, but fat people are expected to participate in their own degradation by agreeing with others who taunt them."

The Female Ideal

These exacting weight standards fall, not surprisingly, more severely on the shoulders of women than on men's. In a survey of the 33,000 readers of *Glamour* magazine placed in the August 1983 issue, 75 percent said they were "too fat," eventhough only one-quarter were overweight according to the Metropolitan Life Insurance Company's 1959 height–weight tables, and even fewer of them were deemed overweight by the current standards. Still more surprising, 45 percent who were *underweight* according to Metropolitan Life's figures felt that they were too fat. Only 6 percent of the respondents felt "very happy" about their bodies; only 15 percent described their bodies as "just right." When looking at their nude bodies in the mirror, 32 percent said that they felt "anxious," 12 percent felt "depressed," and 5 percent felt "repulsed." Commenting on the *Glamour* survey, one of the researchers who analyzed the survey, Susan Wooley, a psychiatrist, commented: "What we see is a steadily growing cultural bias—almost no woman of whatever size feels she's thin enough."

Evidence suggests that the standards for the ideal female form have gotten even slimmer over the years. Women whose figures would have been comfortably embraced by the norm a generation or more ago are now deemed unacceptably overweight, even fat. In 1894, the model for the White Rock Girl, inspired by the ancient Greek goddess Psyche, was 5'4" tall and she weighed 140 pounds; her measurements were 37"-27"-38". Over the years, the women who have been selected to depict the White Rock Girl have gotten taller, slimmer, and have weighed less and less. Today, she's 5'8", weighs 118 pounds, and measures 35"-24"-34". Commenting on this trend in an advertising flyer, the executives of White Rock explain: "Over the years the Psyche image has become longer-legged, slimmer-hipped,

and streamlined. Today—when purity is so important—she continues to symbolize the purity of all White Rock products." Since 1893, White Rock has regularly held contests encouraging the public to vote for their favorite Psyche, out of a series of pictures; twelve have been held, the last in 2004, and, again, the winner becomes increasingly slimmer. The equation of slenderness with purity is a revealing comment on today's obsession with thinness: Weighing a few pounds over a mythical ideal is to live in an "impure" condition. In the 1980s, American woman averaged 5'4" in height and weighed 140 pounds, the same size as White Rock's model in 1894; in the 2000s, according to Gallup polls, she weighs 160 pounds. During the past quarter century, Americans, male and female, have put on about 20 pounds.

Advertising models represent one kind of ideal; they tend to be extremely thin. They are not, however, the only representation of the ideal female form as depicted by the media. There are, it may be said, several ideals rather than just one. Photographs appear to add between five and ten pounds to the subject; clothes add a few more in seeming bulk. (White Rock's Psyche wears very little in the way of clothes, however.) Consequently, fashion models typically border on the anorexic, and women who take them as role models to be emulated are subjecting themselves to an almost unattainable—and unhealthy—standard. It would be inaccurate to argue that all—or even most—American women aspire to look like a fashion model, and moreover, it would be inaccurate to assert that women in all media are emaciated. Still, it is entirely accurate to say that the ideal woman's figure as depicted in the media has become slimmer over the years. And that many women are influenced by that ideal, even if it only manifests itself in how they feel about themselves.

Aside from advertising, another ideal is depicted in Miss America pageants. Prior to 1970, Miss America contestants weighed 88 percent of the average for American women their age. After 1970, this declined slightly to 85 percent. Even more significant, before 1970 pageant *winners* weighed the same as the other contestants; after that date, however, they weighed significantly less than the contestants who didn't win—82.5 percent of the average weight for American women as a whole. Similarly, the weight of women who posed for *Playboy* declined between 1959 and 1979. Centerfolds for 1959 were 91 percent of the average weight for American women in their twenties; by 1978, this had declined to 84 percent. In addition, these models grew *decreasingly* voluptuous and curvaceous and *increasingly* thin, tubular, and angular over time. Interestingly, during this same period of time, American women under the age of 30, gained an average of five pounds, which was entirely attributable to a gain in height, not body mass (Garner et al., 1980). The tendency toward even thinner *Playboy* models and Miss America contestants to be thinner than young American women as a whole has continued unabated into the twenty-first century. Kelly Beth Smith, a graduate of Meredith College, wrote her senior thesis, entitled "Cultural Expectations of Thinness in Women: From the 1920s to the 2000s," under the guidance of faculty member Jack Huber, a psychology professor. The two researchers recorded the height and weight of Miss America contestants beginning in 1921, the first year of the pageant, and those of *Playboy* centerfolds. They broke the time frames into three eras, 1959–1978, 1979–1988, and 1989–2000, and found that the BMI (body mass index, or degree of heaviness by height) for both sets of women have decreased over time; the contestants and models have gotten thinner, lighter, and taller, with a declining BMI. Katharine Gammon reported in the February 2009 issue of *Wired*, that, likewise, while the average weight of the American woman increased between the 1950s and the first decade of the 2000s by twenty pounds, women who posed for *Playboy* centerfolds *declined* by a roughly equal amount, in spite of the fact that they were more roughly three inches taller.

The increasingly slim standards of feminine beauty represent the most desirable point on a scale. The opposite end of the scale represents undesirable territory—obesity. If American women have been evaluated by standards of physical desirability that have shifted from slim to slimmer over the years, it is reasonable to assume that during that same period, it has become less and less socially acceptable to be fat. In tribal and peasant societies, corpulence was associated with affluence. An abundant body represented a corresponding material abundance. In a society in which having plenty to eat is a mark of distinction, heaviness draws a measure of respect. This tended to be true not only for oneself, but also for one's spouse (or spouses) and one's children as well. With the arrival of mature industrialization, however, nutritional adequacy becomes sufficiently widespread as to cease being a sign of distinction. Slenderness rather than corpulence comes to be adopted as the prevailing aesthetic standard among the affluent (Powdermaker, 1960; Cahnman, 1968, pp. 287–288). Over time, all social classes adopt the slim standard; while more firmly entrenched in the upper socioeconomic strata, the slim ideal permeates all levels of Western society.

Fat Admirers

Goffman describes a process of "guilt by association"—because of their relationship with persons who bear "abomination of the body," so-called normals experience a "courtesy stigma." These are "persons who are normal but whose special situation has made them privy to the secret life of the stigmatized individual and sympathetic with it, and who find themselves accorded a measure of acceptance, a measure of courtesy membership in the clan" (1963, p. 28). Such associations, he adds, "tend either to be avoided or to be terminated" because there is a "tendency for a stigma to spread from the stigmatized individual to his [or her] close connections" (p. 30). Still, some people without the stigmatizing trait are willing to nurture such relationships; either they feel that the rewards accrued as a result are worth the denigration or they "hide in the closet," keeping the whole thing a secret. Two such denizens—one more extreme than the other—are the fat admirer (Goode and Preissler, 1983) and the feeder (Bestard, 2008).

There are perhaps millions of men in the United States who have a specific sexual preference, and engage in certain sexual practices, that run so sharply against the grain of conventional taste and behavior that most Americans would either refuse to believe that they exist or would regard their behavior as "sick," a kind of "fetish." (Wikipedia defines "fat fetishism" as "the strong or exclusive sexual attraction to overweight or obese people." It does *not* define as a fetish the "strong" or "exclusive" sexual attraction to a person of average weight or with a slim or slender figure.)

Further, the predilections and experiences of such men are so well concealed that they have largely escaped serious study or scrutiny by sociologists and psychologists. The men to which I refer have a strong erotic desire for obese women. Within the circles of men with this preference, and among the women who attract the sexual attention of these men, they are referred to as *fat admirers*, or FAs.

To be plain about it, these men prefer their sexual partners to be fat—and for some, the fatter the better. They do not date fat women in spite of their size, but in part because of it. The vast majority of all men, FAs and non-FAs alike, choose their partners partly—and at first, mainly—because of how pleasing their looks are to them. "It's a matter of chemistry," one FA explained to me. "I simply can't start a relationship unless the woman turns me on physically." However, the features that "turn on" the FA are quite different from those that excite his non-FA counterpart. The FA is aroused by the softness, the roundness, and the weight of women, their curves and bulges, how much their flesh "jiggles" when it is shaken. "After all," a man I interviewed asked rhetorically, "who wants to impale himself on a bag of bones?" FAs emphasize the sexual desirability of qualities that fat women possess as they contrast with those of most men—softness versus firmness, fatness versus muscularity, an ample versus a narrow posterior, a voluptuous versus a lean shape, a round versus an angular form, fleshy versus "washboard" abs.

Feederism

Fat admirers are stigmatized partly by virtue of the fact that they intimately associate with an already-stigmatized category of humanity—that is, obese women—and partly by virtue of the fact that they *enable* that category's stigmatizing characteristic—that is, they encourage their obesity. But in the case of feederism, these men enable the obesity not merely by tacit endorsement and approval, that is, through dating and sexual reinforcement, but by actively, overtly, and vigorously aiding and abetting that obesity—that is, by feeding obese women themselves. It is difficult to avoid the analogy of French farmers stuffing geese to make an incredibly tasty but fatty and unhealthful *pâté de foiegras*. (Tasty for humans but lethal for the geese.) All of

Bestard's interviewees are "out" with respect to their sexual preference for fat women, but only three are "fully out" about their interest in feederism. All her respondents seem to be less comfortable with admitting their feederism than with being a fat admirer. Said Derek, "I'm openly an FA and privately a feeder." Another interviewee, Stewart, stated, "I found out that I must use discretion in discussing feederism." And a third, Jeffrey, admitted that no one in his everyday life knows about his being a feeder. "*That would be suicidal,*" he told Bestard; "*the harassment and abuse would be unbearable*" (her emphasis). Feederism is a form of deviance in the extreme; it severely limits the conventional activities of the woman, the object of the man's lust, and, if it is known about, limits the man's potential for conventional sociability to a substantial degree. Hence, the secrecy.

Are Things Changing?

The astute observer can notice micro-changes here and there. A major clothing manufacturer creating a line of supersize dresses. A department store creating a section devoted to selling clothing for the larger woman. An advertising agency hiring plus-size models. Articles in magazines, newspapers, on the Web, on Twitter, statements by major spokespersons, that proclaim fat pride, the right of fat people to look the way they want, the cruelty and sadism of fat jokes, the insanity of the thin ideal, the desirability of a wide range of standards of appearance. In October 2012 (10/19/2012), Stella Boonshoft posted a photograph of herself on *Humans of New York*, a photo blog. The picture depicts an attractive, chubby, young woman dressed in nothing but a black bra and brief black panties, exposing her full belly and plump arms. Stella pridefully tells the reader: "This picture is for the boy at the party who told me I looked like a beached whale. This picture is for Emily from middle school who bullied me incessantly, made mocking videos about me, sent me nasty emails, and called me 'lard.' She made me feel like I didn't deserve to exist. . . . MOST OF ALL, this picture is for me. For the girl who hated her body so much she took extreme measures to try to change it. Who cried for hours over the fact she would never be thin. Who was teased and tormented and hurt just for being who she was.

I'm so over that. THIS IS MY BODY. DEAL WITH IT." Stella is trying to educate the American public in a neutral or polyvalent aesthetic: To the people who judge others on the basis of size, she says: shame on you. "No one is the authority on beauty, and everyone has a different road to trudge to happy destiny." Her picture—and her cause—became, according to a reporter writing for *People* magazine, "a cyberspace hit, with more than 2.4 million views on Facebook; 80,000 shared her photograph." Later she appeared with a photographer on the *Today* show, creating even greater media attention. After years of soul-searching, she explained, "I finally came to a place where I was really happy with the way that I looked." Explaining her posting of the bikini shot on the Web, she said, "I wanted to leave a message to the bullies who tormented me" (Billups, 2012).

FREAKS

When writing his book on the physically different, literary critic Leslie Fiedler floundered around for a more appropriate and less demeaning term than *Freaks* (1978), the title he eventually chose. "I should be searching for some other term, less tarnished and offensive," he wrote, introducing his subject. All those that came to mind—anomalies, human "oddities," monsters, "very special people," "sports," mistakes of nature, deformities—seemed inadequate and improperly descriptive, he decided. Society's hostility toward freaks, Fiedler writes, has typically been less than a "total genocidal onslaught" (p. 21). True, in the name of eugenics, the Nazis killed dwarfs and the ancient Spartans left infants with birth defects to die on a rocky mountain ledge. But most societies, Fiedler wrote, cultivated a measure of compassion and pity toward the physically different that was mixed with scorn; they manifested a kind of ambivalence that prevented an unrelieved hostility from taking root. Freaks elicited as much amusement as contempt, Fiedler argues.

For at least a hundred years, freaks were displayed in circus sideshows. But according to sociologist Robert Bogdan, author of *Freak Show* (1988), until well into the twentieth century, these human oddities were presented as awesome and amazing prodigies of nature, to be marveled at rather than ridiculed. These "prodigies" had a special niche in the society; their differences were accepted as a tolerable form of physical eccentricity rather than a source of contempt. It was not until modern medicine gained a stranglehold on definitions of normal and pathological that "freaks" were no longer exhibited. Medicine had developed the arrogance—the Greek term for it is *hubris*—that all such deformities could be cured rather than tolerated; any exhibition of persons who possessed such traits was exploitative and degrading, a "pornography of disability" (p. 2). Instead of correcting such anomalies, however, modern society has relegated their possessors to the "contemptible fringe," no longer marveled at but regarded as distressing, distasteful, and repulsive.

What is it about freaks that causes such a shudder of fear among "normals"? Fiedler asks (1978). While eliciting some sympathy, freaks stir up "supernatural terror" in us for a variety of reasons, he argues. Most freaks are the children of normal parents. By what strange and mysterious chemistry—"forces we do not understand"—is the budding child in the womb transformed into a mythic beast, a creature no one of us wants to be, of being apart from the rest of us? The freak challenges the boundaries that separate male from female (the hermaphrodite, the bearded woman), large from small (giants and fat ladies, midgets and dwarfs), animals from humans (the hairy "wolf-man," humans with an apelike appearance), and the physical integrity of one human being as distinct from that of another (Siamese or "conjoined" twins). Consequently, Fiedler argues, freaks tear down the barrier between reality and illusion, experience and fantasy, and fact and myth. Quite literally, he says, they are a threat "to those desperately maintained boundaries on which any definition of sanity ultimately depends" (p. 24).

The "myth of monsters" originates "in the deep fears of childhood" (p. 31). The need to create and maintain firm boundaries separating these cosmic categories, Fiedler writes, stems from childhood struggles with matters of size, sexuality and gender, humanness, and togetherness/apartness.

After all, children are midgets in relation to adults, and adults are giants in relation to children.

Moreover, various organs, those relating specifically to sexual functioning, change enormously in size, transforming themselves from midget-sized (those belonging to children) to giant-sized (those belonging to adults); for instance, from preadolescence to adulthood, and from flaccid to aroused, the penis changes from small to large. Moreover, boys compare penis size with one another. (Are you a midget? Or a giant?) And the preadolescent girl simultaneously fears that her breasts will never grow—that is, will be midget-sized—or will grow much too large (will become giant-sized).

Fears and insecurities around sexuality and gender are fundamental and eternal: the little boy who is chastised for toying with his penis; the girl who is told not to kiss the little girl next door on the lips; the children who are caught playing "doctor"; the tomboy; the too-effeminate boy; the boy who catches sight of his dad's vastly larger penis; the trauma of the girl's first menstruation.

Many children are obsessed by the fear of being attacked and devoured by wild beasts, yet, at some point, they become aware that humans eat animal flesh. Hair grows in the vicinity of the genitals and in the armpits—which, in girls, is expected to be removed—and, Fiedler writes, hairiness represents our animalistic side. Perhaps the very first intellectual realization children have is the awareness of being an entity separate from the mother whose breast they suck on. As they grow older, they fear separation from their parents, yet they desperately have the need to make that separation to maintain their own personal sense of integrity. Boys, upon understanding the nature of the female anatomy, try simultaneously to imagine emerging from and at the same time entering the vagina.

In other words, says Fiedler, the freak projects our "infantile or adolescent traumas." They manifest or dramatize our "primordial fears . . . about scale, sexuality, our status as more than beasts, and our tenuous individuality" (p. 34). Fiedler's argument seems to be that both our negative and our tempered reactions to people who are different from ourselves are likely to respond to some sort of universal, transcultural appeal. Instead, they are based on who we are as human beings, where we stand in the scheme of things, and what we had to struggle with when we were growing up. They

are not simply learned as a result of the accident of arbitrary cultural norms, he seems to be saying. There are limits to the capacity of social constructionism to "normalize" or routenize the extreme whimsy, caprice, and folly of nature. Our rootedness in childhood, adolescence, sex and sexuality, humanness, and our need to be a personal entity separate from all others, transcends and overwhelms any and all local customs dictating who and what should be stigmatized. They dictate our interactions with and posture and attitudes toward the persons who were once designated as *freaks*.

DISABILITY AND TERTIARY DEVIANCE

John Kitsuse (1980) introduces the concept of "tertiary" deviance—the notion of socially disvalued people standing up, fighting for their rights, demanding equality with "normals." Edward Sagarin disapprovingly refers to this phenomenon as *Odd Man In* (1969)—or "societies of deviants." Over the past few years, a growing number of militant disabled spokespersons have stepped forward and confronted the abled, demanding that the blind, the deaf, the wheelchair-bound be accorded justice and the respect and dignity they deserve. Central among their demands is that the *image* or *public presentation* of the handicapped recognizes their essential humanity.

Abigail Saguy and Anna Ward (2011) are interested in the political implications of "coming out" which, as they argue, "may have travelled" from queer to fat politics. The "coming out" narrative has become "increasingly available for appropriation" in a diversity of settings. Its ubiquity renders it appropriatable with little effort by actors in settings other than and in addition to those of its original context. And such migration may be facilitated by the fact actors in multiple contexts possess overlapping memberships, thereby diffusing such narratives—more specifically, from a queer to a fat political identification. A Lexis-Nexis search for the phrase, "coming out," yields news stories not only for gays and lesbians but also for categories whose members announce themselves as belonging to a particular politically-charged category (p. 62). Goffman's assumption that being fat is a status whose evidentness is visible for all to see is not as straightforward as he assumed. It is also a narrative that affirms a visible stigma. It is an announcement that embraces fatness and borders on "flaunting" an identity that is widely stigmatized. Yet, the contemporary fat acceptance movement is "pre-Stonewall," teetering uneasily between "a strategy of assimilation" and a flaunting identity for critique or embracing differentness. In other words, the fat-pride culture "remains largely virtual" (p. 70). Almost everywhere fat people turn there are "social costs." Their body size "makes them a second-class citizen" (p. 71). Physical deviants are "fighting back"—engaging, that is, in tertiary deviance— but their efforts are limited in scope and impact.

In *Nothing About Us Without Us*, James Charlton (1999) writes of "disability oppression," alienation, raising the consciousness of the disabled, and organizing "empowerment."

In *Creatures That Time Forgot*, David Hevey (1992) gives us an "in your face" political argument about disability, demanding "rights, not charity."

In *Freakery*, Rosemarie Garland Thomson (1996) offers an anthology of analyses by two dozen writers who argue that, over the centuries, western society has presented "cultural spectacles of the extraordinary body."

In *Claiming Disability*, Simi Linton (1998) engages her readers, demanding that they put themselves emotionally into everyday issues and situations involving decisions about disability. "You are an architect," she says, and takes us through the decisions and emotional identifications a designer of a community center has to go through to build a facility that can accommodate the handicapped. "You are the parent of a nondisabled young woman away at college," Linton writes, and describes the experience of that parent dealing with the fact that her daughter is bringing a disabled male friend home to visit. "You are the new personnel director for a mid-sized company," she conjectures, taking us through the demands made by a disability action group to accommodate the employment disabled personnel. "Hidden and disregarded for too long," Linton says, "we are demanding not only rights and equal opportunity but are demanding that the academy take on the nettlesome question

of why we've been sequestered in the first place" (p. 185). Academics have been "complicit" in the confinement of the disabled; it's time for that confinement to end, she argues.

In many ways, the disabled represent an example of an oppressed minority group. There are many parallels between the civil rights movement and the new and most decidedly militant field of disability studies. Where this new militancy will take persons with a disability is anyone's guess. But its central message is clear: The disabled do not wish to be treated as deviants. Currently, the clout of the physically different is limited; culturally, they can no longer be held in derision, but silently, secretly, the majority does not wish to be *like* the disabled, and do not want those who are close to them to be like them either. To the extent that the disabled cannot perform conventional tasks and activities, they will always be treated as deviants, but the stigma that embraces them will fade as "normals" become more enlightened and more flexible. Perhaps, one day, disability will no longer be discussed as a form of deviance.

SUMMARY

Undesirable or non-normative physical characteristics represent a form of deviance. They tend to attract stigma and generate a contaminated identity for their possessors. Although some sociologists insist that involuntarily acquired traits cannot be a form of deviance because they are not the possessor's fault, the fact that their possessors *do* attract stigma and condemnation is specifically what defines deviance; hence, they are, according to this definition, deviants. In fact, there is a *continuum* of personal causality or responsibility for possessors of deviant characteristics—yet all are stigmatized. Personal responsibility is only weakly related to the dimension of deviance. Responsibility (or "fault") for one's physical characteristics is not only a matter of degree, it is also a social construct. Many eras and cultures have claimed divine retribution for past sins as the cause for a range of disabilities and esthetic violations.

Why do "normal" fear and avoid physical deviants? Katz argues that, though we feel ambivalence toward them, our repugnance is based on a nonconscious faith in "the just world hypothesis," that is, we believe that we all get what we deserve; if someone is disabled, maybe they deserve their faith. To deny the just world hypothesis opens up the possibility that we are vulnerable to the possibility that we, too, could end up like the disabled.

Erving Goffman referred to a form of stigma as "abominations of the body." For our purposes, two such "abominations" stand out: violations of esthetic norms and physical incapacity.

Esthetic norms refer to the way we look; our appearance is judged by audiences and found normal or unacceptable. The latter, if extremely so, is deemed worthy of punishment, condemnation, social isolation. Persons who fail to meet an acceptable standard are seen as possessing a "spoiled" identity, "disqualified from full social acceptance."

Physical incapacity is made up of the inability to perform at life's various essential tasks, such as walking, seeing, hearing, and so on. Given the achievement norms in our society, persons unable to perform everyday functions or tasks are deemed unworthy on certain dimensions—even deviants.

Attractiveness is obviously the flip side of ugliness; in fact, a violation of esthetic standards is the extreme absence of beauty. Standards of attractiveness are not nearly as relative as has been assumed in the past. In fact, from society to society, from culture to culture, many of the same standards prevail. Most of the traits or characteristics that are found attractive in one place are likewise found attractive in others. In fact, beauty is *not* in "the eye of the beholder," at least, not entirely. Very likely, some universal causal force or dynamic influence determines what humans (and other creatures) find attractive and desirable in a mating partner. Some researchers with an evolutionary orientation believe that it is the impulse to pass on one's genetic material to later generations that explains this panhuman tendency to judge physical attractiveness. Many culturally oriented researchers are skeptical of this explanation. Whatever the tendency or explanation, children deemed unattractive tend to bear the brunt of the negative side of evaluations of attractiveness. That is, their actions are deemed more deviant and more worthy of punishment than the same actions engaged in by more attractive actors. In a phrase, unattractiveness is a form of deviance; it attracts stigma and condemnation.

Some forms of physical deviance are voluntary, for instance, body modification, especially extreme tattooing. Tattooing indicates identity, namely that one belongs to a category that is alienated from the mainstream. But the mainstream also "reads" a message in sporting tattoos: Such a person is an untrustworthy, reprehensible person—a deviant. In the past couple of decades, many more or less conventional people have been getting small tattoos on inconspicuous places on their bodies as a mild form of rebellion.

Obesity is a prime example of a deviant or undesirable physical characteristic. What makes obesity more interesting than most other forms of physical deviance is that it is regarded as both physical and behavioral. That is, the obese are denigrated for being fat *and* for behaving in such a shamelessly self-indulgent fashion—usually overeating and not being sufficiently active—that *caused* their obesity. Most non-obese persons feel superior to the obese, and the obese, in turn, tend to internalize stigma—that is, they usually think they are *worthy* of the condemnation that average-sized persons visit upon them. The condemnation of the obese operates, in scale, on people who are only somewhat above average—that is, the hugely obese receive the harshest condemnation for their weight while the somewhat overweight receive condemnation in proportion to their more moderate degree of overweight. Standards of weight fall unequally on the shoulders of women: Women tend to be condemned more harshly for every degree of overweight than is true of men. Over the years, the ideal standard of female beauty has gotten slimmer and slimmer; hence, the downside of being obese has correspondingly steeper and deeper, the stigma and condemnation, more intense and pervasive.

Freaks are both fascinating and fearful to the majority, in part because they challenge the separation between categories we regard so solid and unbridgeable: normal versus pathological, male versus female, tiny versus averaged-sized versus huge, human versus beast. At one time, freaks were exhibited in circus sideshows. Now, such a practice is regarded as inhumane, exploitative, and politically incorrect, although some claim that, as sideshow performers, freaks had a legitimate place in the society; today, through genetic and surgical intervention, medical science attempts to correct these "mistakes of nature."

Physical deviants have challenged their demeaned status through political movements and demands for equal rights. This militancy of a previously oppressed minority may lead to the end of their categorization as deviants, although some sociologists would argue that, as with alcoholism, an inability to fully perform conventional roles will always be disvalued and regarded as a form of deviance.

Account: Interviews with Three NAAFA Members

The National Association to Advance Fat Acceptance is a civil rights organization founded in 1969, dedicated to improving the lives of fat people. It works to eliminate size discrimination, aims to self-empower fat people, and to eliminate the stigma and humiliation of large people in the media, the culture, and the educational system, believing that everyone deserves to be treated with dignity and respect regardless of size. NAAFA is opposed to weight loss surgery, takes the position that dieting for the purpose of losing weight is likely to be futile and may be harmful, and that the terms "obese" and "overweight" are pejorative, while the term "fat" is simply descriptive of a substance that fat people have a great deal of. NAAFA is also a social club that sponsors dances, parties, and other social occasions to foster the socializing of fat women with men (called "FAs" or "fat admirers") who are attracted to fat women. At the time of this interview, Suzanne weighs 300 pounds; she's in her 30s and she's been a member of NAAFA for eight years. Sandra is not a member of NAAFA, but attends a number of its functions; she weighs 250 pounds, and is in her 30s. Mary has been a member for four years and weighs over 350 pounds; she's in her late 20s. I am the interviewer.

ERICH: Do you feel more comfortable at NAAFA activities than at those that are not sponsored by NAAFA.

SUZANNE: Definitely. In NAAFA I'm with my own kind. I'm not the only fat girl in the room.

ERICH: As you know, there are men who are referred to as FAs, Fat Admirers, who are attracted to fat women specifically because of their weight. What's your overall assessment or opinion of these men?

SUZANNE: I feel uncomfortable with them. They all seem to have what I'd call a "guilty-closet" attitude toward going out with fat women. They're very much into fat women's bodies specifically because they are fat. I've never met an FA who was comfortable with a fat woman in public. It's as if they have a sign on them that says, "I love being in bed with this woman but I hate being seen with her in public." Many FAs are so uncomfortable with fat woman that they make us feel uncomfortable with them. There's a lot of physical attraction there—it's a kind of lust—but not much emotion, not much love. There's a lot of jiggling and squeezing and fondling—a *lot* of foreplay. When they're in bed with you, you can feel their reverence, but the action is heavily physical. They're amazed that they are with you, this sexy, gorgeous, fuck-doll woman. I like the fact that FAs are attracted to me, but I hate it that they don't feel I'm worthy of a real relationship. They don't want to *associate* with you. They don't want anybody to *know* you're with them. It's *sneaky* with them. I've just about given up. I can't seem to get a serious relationship going. I can't stand society's pressures on me for being fat—family, friends, the people I work with, and especially men who go out with me.

ERICH: Have you ever gone to a bar to meet a man?

SUZANNE: Yes. About twenty times. Not one has produced a date.

ERICH: Have you ever been fixed up with a date by a friend or a relative?

SUZANNE: Yes—about twenty–twenty-five times. Those times resulted in a second date only twice, but those two were hot.

ERICH: Are there activities you would feel uncomfortable attending because of your weight?

(Continued)

Account: Interviews with Three NAAFA Members   Continued

SUZANNE: Yes. Bar-b-ques. Picnics. Swimming—anything having to do with a pool or a beach. People stare at me if I'm in a bathing suit. They act like I have leprosy, they move away from me. I see it in their faces. They think you have some nerve getting into the pool at your weight. Boating. Restaurants. Bars. In fact, most events in the mainstream of society. High school reunions. Cocktail parties. Any outside summer-type activity where seating is provided—I'd be afraid I wouldn't fit into the seats. I don't like going to clothing stores—nothing fits me.

ERICH: Have you ever experienced a stranger remarking on your size or weight in public?

SUZANNE: Yes—thousands of times. It's happened so many times I can hardly come up with just one example. "Hey, look at the size of that one!" is a pretty common reaction—I must have heard that a hundred times. Hardly a week goes by when I don't hear something. "There goes a big one!" "Look at the fat lady, mommy." Big fat slob, pig, that sort of thing. People in a supermarket elbow one another out of the way to get a good look at you.

ERICH: Have there been situations in which you felt that you were ignored or left out because of your weight?

SUZANNE: It happens all the time. Weddings. Parties. Any kind of outdoor activity. They've told me to my face that they're ashamed to be with me, they leave me out of parties and family functions. Girlfriends don't invite me along if they go somewhere to meet men—you just don't get asked. Sports. Lots of activities.

ERICH: Have you ever had any direct, personal experiences with job discrimination?

SUZANNE: I know that I didn't get certain jobs because of my weight. People have told me that right to my face.

ERICH: What else?

SUZANNE: Airline seats. I have a hard time fitting in. People sitting next to you hate your guts. Airplanes are too small. Doctors. It doesn't matter what you have, doctors will tell you it's because you're fat. I've experienced times when doctors wouldn't even look at me. They said, "You're too obese." They just turned me away, refused to give me medical attention. In every single aspect of your life, if you're obese, life is more difficult. Everything would be easier and more pleasant if I weighed less. I'd feel less stress, less pressure, less discomfort. I'd be more active. I'd be more sexual. If you're fat, people don't love you. Your health, fitting into clothing, shoes, sitting in chairs. Every relationship I have is strained because I'm fat. I'm just not accepted. The constant horror of dieting. As a teenager, even when I had a boyfriend, they were usually below me—dumb and not that good-looking. Other kids called you bad names, they left you out of games.

ERICH: What's your feeling about NAAFA?

SUZANNE: Too much of NAAFA can be harmful. When you're in NAAFA, the men there make you feel beautiful and desirable and sexy and wonderful, and then you go out into a public place and you discover that none of that is true. That experience can be devastating.

ERICH: What do you think your ideal weight is?

SUZANNE: I'd feel satisfied if I lost 100 pounds. I'd be OK at 200.

* * * * *

ERICH: Why did you quit your membership in NAAFA?

SANDRA: I didn't agree with some of its policies, like its stand on weight and health. I'm a nurse, I know being fat isn't healthy. And the scene is often boring. A lot of the men are boring. In the past couple of years, I've attended maybe twenty NAAFA-sponsored activities, and of those, four have resulted in a date with a man.

ERICH: Do you feel more comfortable, maybe less self-conscious, at NAAFA activities?

SANDRA: Usually, because I know, at my weight, I'm not being judged solely by my appearance.

ERICH: Have you been helped by NAAFA?

SANDRA: Yes, definitely! It's really helped my self-esteem by allowing me to like myself the way I am. I approve of its social aspect, getting fat women and FAs together, but it was originally founded to fight size discrimination, and I think more attention ought to be paid to that.

ERICH: What's your assessment of the FAs who attend the parties and functions and dances?

SANDRA: The majority are "momma's boys" who are looking for a certain kind of image that is associated with heavier women. Only a few are self-confident and secure enough for my taste. Most of them are like kids in a candy store, so they're more obnoxious than the men you'd meet in other settings. When they come over to you, they talk right away about you, your looks, your weight. Actually, in many ways, FAs treat women better. They're always flattering you, they offer a real ego-boost. But it's always about your physical appearance, how cute you are, how you'd feel in their hands. They're more into the sexual side right away, they think we're "easier" sexually. Maybe they're more considerate lovers, though—they just can't get enough of you.

ERICH: Have you ever gone to a singles or "pick-up" bar to meet a man?

SANDRA: Yes, maybe fifty times.

ERICH: How many times did it result in a date?

SANDRA: Maybe forty times, and a long-term relationship, more than a few dates, maybe thirty times. I've never answered a personals ad, never met a man on the street that I had a date with. I've been fixed up with a date by friends only once—and that once was enough; he turned out to be a creep—he was married.

ERICH: Are there activities you would be reluctant to engage in or attend because of your weight?

SANDRA: No. Only at a swimming pool or a beach.

ERICH: Have there been situations when you felt that you were ignored or left out because of your weight?

SANDRA: Only when I was younger—a teenager. I was left out of groups or parties.

ERICH: Have members of your family or friends ever expressed shame toward you because of your weight?

SANDRA: Nope.

ERICH: Do you feel your life would change if you were of average weight?

SANDRA: Yes. I wouldn't get depressed as much. But being overweight gives me a neurotic payoff. I'm different, so I stand out in a crowd by being fat. I guess that's good, in a way. But being fat is also unhealthy, I don't care what NAAFA says. And it also influences my self-esteem. I don't feel as good about myself.

ERICH: Have you experienced any form of size discrimination?

SANDRA: Here's something that never ceases to amaze me. I've never been discriminated against on the job, in my education, I can sit into most seats, I have good relations with friends, family, men seem to like me, whatever. But strangers—this is one aspect of being over-weight. I mean, think about it. People don't go up to strangers and remark about any other physical attributes. They don't say, "Gee, you're short." Or, "Gee, you have a really big nose." Even the most crass and obnoxious people in this society don't do that. But it seems that a lot of people don't even think twice about making a remark about my size. It's not that it's always cruel or spiteful, but just the fact that they feel free to say, "Goodness—you're fat." Something like that. And I'm not even that fat! What's wrong with them? I don't get it.

ERICH: Have you lost weight and put it back on? Has this influenced the way people, especially men, react to you?

SANDRA: In dating situations, my partners have for the most part been fairly supportive of me when I've been dieting. Their reaction has usually been positive, and I don't feel they've been any different when I've lost weight then gained it back. But the one true FA I dated didn't see me as attractive when I lost a lot of weight.

(Continued)

Account: Interviews with Three NAAFA Members   Continued

Most of the men I've gone out with have liked me for who I am and not just what I look like. But this one man didn't want to have anything to do with me when I was thinner—he couldn't see past the size thing. Other people, friends, acquaintances, whatever, if I lost a lot of weight and hadn't seen them for a while, and they saw me, they made such a big deal of it. "Oh, you're so slim, you're really beautiful!" This, that, and the other thing. But then, when I put it back on, conversely, "What happened to you? I thought you were on a diet!" That's when I want to say, "Oh, go fuck yourself!" But I'm a diplomatic person and I don't say that.

ERICH: If you could swallow a magic pill and wake up tomorrow weighing 125 pounds, would you take it?

SANDRA: No—it would be too much of a shock. My ideal weight is probably 135, and I'd like to take that off gradually.

ERICH: Why do you think you weigh more than average?

SANDRA: Because I consume more calories than I can burn off. I do have a slow metabolism, which doesn't help. It's not the main reason. I think the reason is psychological. I usually binge when something upsets me. I've been on a lot of diets, and I'd lose weight and put it right back on. The only healthy, balanced diet is Weight Watchers. That's been my only long-term success.

* * * * *

MARY: In the past year, I've attended about a dozen NAAFA-sponsored activities. I feel more comfortable and less self-conscious at a NAAFA function because all the women are fat, and you can just relax and not have to worry about anyone criticizing or making fun of you because of your weight. The people there are more accepting about the weight business. It's almost like a family thing. There are positive support groups, a friendly atmosphere, a warmth about NAAFA people that you don't feel anywhere else. There's nothing to compare it with, really.

ERICH: In NAAFA, have you dated FAs?

MARY: All of the men I've dated in the past two years I met through NAAFA, they were all FAs. FAs treat fat women better. They can make fat women feel better and help them with their inhibitions. I don't want to say that all of them are nice, but at least they go out with fat women, they give them a dating experience, a sexual experience—they don't hurt anyone. Some of them are shy and awkward about their preference. Maybe what they like is the way we feel in bed—you know, we have a hard time liking ourselves because no one likes us. So FAs feel uncomfortable about their preference, and at a NAAFA function, there's a lot of difficulty getting the mixing and mingling going—there's a lot of staring going on at first. But then, I haven't had much experience with men who weren't FAs. I haven't really done much dating outside of NAAFA to compare with my experiences in NAAFA, though. I have no idea how non-FA men treat me or any other fat woman because the only dates I've had have been in NAAFA—100 percent. With FAs, you don't have to worry about them liking you with your clothes off—you already know they'll like you with your clothes off! With a man who's not an FA, you have to worry that he won't like you with your clothes off. I've never been to a singles bar, I don't like bars. I answered one personal ad, which didn't result in a date. I met one man on the street who sort of picked me up, but that didn't result in a date. My family fixed me up with one date, which did *not* result in a second date, thank God. Other than NAAFA, I've never joined an organization of any kind to meet men. I don't go out and look for men. I worry about meeting a man because of my weight. I feel insecure because I feel he won't like me because I'm fat.

ERICH: What are your parents like?

MARY: They're very fat and have extremely low IQs. They can barely converse. I still live with them. We have no pictures of us in the house. Because I'm fat, I can't keep pictures of myself. The only one I have is one from a friend; it's on my desk at work.

ERICH: Do you feel uncomfortable or self-conscious about your weight in different kinds of settings?

MARY: Restaurants, movies, anyplace seating is provided. Yes, definitely—I worry about fitting in the seats. Swimming pool or beach? Yes. I'm self-conscious in a bathing suit. In a public place, like a shopping mall? Yes; people laugh at me. Sports? I can't play them.

ERICH: If you look at a model advertising some product, do you wish you looked like that?

MARY: Not really. I don't hate her, I just don't want to look like that. Most of them look sick. They are too boney.

ERICH: Have you ever experienced a stranger remarking on your size or weight in public?

MARY: I've heard things. Like, "Oh, you have such a beautiful face, you should lose weight." Things like that.

ERICH: Have you ever been in a situation where you felt you were ignored or left out because of your weight?

MARY: Yes. I've been with other girls where they didn't want me to be with them because they were afraid that if guys came over to them, they wouldn't want to come over to them and be with them because they're with a fat girl.

ERICH: What about your family?

MARY: My father doesn't want my sister's husband to see me. My legs are too fat, he says. I think he's worried that my brother-in-law will think my sister will get as fat as I am.

ERICH: If you could wave a magic wand, what aspects of your life would be different?

MARY: I'd like to weigh 210. I'd be teaching math, married to a sweet guy, have kids of all ages, have a nice house, a couple of cars.

ERICH: If you could swallow a magic pill and wake up weighing 125 pounds, would you take it?

MARY: I couldn't handle it. My ideal weight is 210.

ERICH: Why do you think you weigh more than average?

MARY: I eat too much. It has to be glandular or physiological. I was in Weight Watchers and lost 60 pounds, and gained 80 back. Overeaters Anonymous—I went to one meeting, it was all bullshit.

QUESTIONS

Should we regard physical characteristics as a form of deviance? Can we consider characteristics or traits that are "not the individual's fault" *deviant* in any meaningful sense of the word? Should all deviance be *motivated behavior*? What is the most important quality or feature of deviance—why it's caused or how it is regarded by others? In certain respects obesity possesses two qualities that researchers of deviance look at: it is a physical attribute, and it is widely regarded as *caused* by the individual. In the latter respect—or so says this claim—the individual overeats, fails to exercise, and gets fat as a result. Do you agree with this judgment? Is it the "individual's fault"? What's your theory explaining obesity? Should the obese be stigmatized for being fat? Do they *deserve* our rebuke and condemnation? What's your reaction to these interviews? Do you have compassion for these women? Disgust? Are you neutral about their weight? They told me that they are often made fun of in public—is this fair? If it's not, should they not be regarded as examples of physical deviants? Isn't derision and condemnation what the sociologist *means* by the term "deviance"? And if so, shouldn't Suzanne, Sandra, and Mary be studied sociologically as deviants? If we do so, are we colluding in their condemnation? Or is it our obligation to understand both obesity and the reactions to obesity?

Tribal Stigma
Labeling Race and Ethnicity

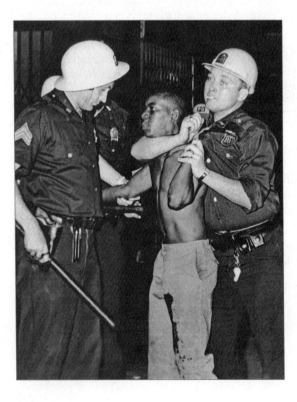

Learning Objectives:

After reading this chapter, you will be able to:

- identify ethnic images and ethnic stigma;
- discuss racism and discrimination;
- define "Islamophobia" and discuss its effects;
- understand ethnic, religious, and national attitudes in Muslim nations;
- discuss discrimination against Palestinians;
- define and discuss anti-Semitism.

During the nineteenth century, Americans and Europeans frequently referred to Africans and persons of African descent as apes and gorillas—subhumans that deserved enslavement. Allied propaganda during World War II often depicted Japanese soldiers and politicians as buck-toothed monkeys, bats, or vultures who wore glasses with black, round frames and thick lenses. In turn, Japanese propaganda depicted Americans and British as freakishly narrow-headed, thin-nosed, and thin-lipped, "the ugly enemy," "hairy, twisted-nosed savages," "panting heavily, menacingly" approaching "the Land of the Gods." One poster portrayed President Roosevelt as a rapacious beast with fangs and outsized hands, reaching toward Japanese lettering (Brcak and Pavia, 1994). On September 11, 2012, Egyptian Muslim Brotherhood party member Mahmoud Khalil stated on Al-Nas television that the American "has a huge body. Eats like a pig. He is like a raging bull" (source: MEMRI TV). Nazi propaganda depicted Jews as octopuses, spiders, snakes, vultures, and so on—and, given that they were beasts and vermin, the better to persecute and murder them since they were not human and possessed no admirable qualities whatsoever. These images and metaphors represented efforts by some members of one ethnic or national category to stigmatize, inferiorize, and verminize the members of another category of humanity, to invite members of their own "kind" to treat the "others" *as if* they were animals fit only for slaughter. Such language and representations are often born during times of conflict, such as warfare and extreme international tension, much of which was generated by the regime in power that produced and endorsed these despicable images in an attempt to influence the popular mind to think along the same lines.

Such verminization or "othering" of tribal, racial, or ethnic categories have continued, in some societies, to the contemporary era. In his 1998 *fatwa* (or edict) urging Muslims to kill Americans and "plunder their money wherever and whenever they find it," Osama bin Laden referred to "Crusaders" (Christians) as "locusts." Abd al-Jalil al-Karuri, a Sudanese preacher, referred to Jews as "mosquitoes" and "malarial microbes." Palestinian preacher Ibrahim Mudeiris portrayed Americans as dogs, and Jews as "serpents." And Abd al-Aziz al-Rantisi, a Gazan leader and Hamas spokesperson, referred to Jews as "despicable monkeys" (www.tau.ac.il /Anti-Semitism/asw2004/arab.htm and YouTube). Verminization need not entail animal imagery to represent a species of "othering" by casting members of another ethnicity outside the pale of respectability. In 2010, as the leader of the Egyptian Muslim Brotherhood, Mohamed Morsi, then ousted President of the country, delivered a speech, preserved on video, in which he declared that the Egyptians should "nurse our children and our grandchildren on hatred" for Jews and Zionists. On television two months later, he called Zionists "bloodsuckers who attack Palestinians, these warmongers, the descendants of apes and pigs" (*The New York Times*, January 16, 2013, p. A22). No doubt *most* Egyptians do not endorse these words, but Morsi was the leader of the largest, most important country in the Middle East, and many there do.

Often, toxic sentiments are reciprocal. In August of 2012, seven Israeli youths beat then attempted to lynch several Palestinian teenagers—the youngest, a thirteen-year-old girl—leaving one boy, seventeen years old, wounded and unconscious. Bystanders did not attempt to intervene, but the police arrested the Israelis. Referring to one of the victims, a fifteen-year-old Israeli boy said, "If it was up to me, I would have murdered him. . . . He cursed my mother." Another said, "For my part, he can die, he's an Arab." The Israeli press agonized over the inability of some Israelis to make a distinction between legitimate acts aimed to protect Israel from lethal attack and "pointless, immoral acts of violence" against a disparaged, stigmatized "Other." A relative of the hospitalized boy said a mob of fifty Israelis chased the victims, shouting "Death to Arabs" (Kershner, 2012, pp. A1, A3). Observers in the Western world typically stress negative images and sentiments conveyed and held by Palestinians and other Arabs about Israelis and Jews. In fact, recent research indicates that not only does this formula work both ways, but the hatred in Palestinian educational texts tends to be exaggerated; "extreme examples of dehumanization and demonization" are "very rare" on both sides

(Bar-Tal et al., 2009; Adwan et al., 2012; Kershner, 2013). The most extreme stereotypes stand out as distinctly quotable, but they are not necessarily characteristic of the entire curriculum. Still, both Israeli and Palestinian texts offer "unilateral national narratives" that present the other side as the enemy, and fail to provide detail about the lives of their people (Kershner, 2013).

At the same time, looking at the big picture, the history of relations between and among peoples of diverse racial, ethnic, religious, and national backgrounds is saturated with hatred, invidious distinctions, stereotypes, and hostile acts—even mass murder. The most extreme instances of ethnic relations lead us to conclude that, over the centuries, what some of us have said about and done to members of an ethnicity other than our own vividly and painfully expresses the hostility and contempt that we feel for our fellow human beings. And, at certain times and in certainly places, racial and ethnic hatred is toxic and extreme. "The only good Indian is a dead Indian" (Gen. Philip Sheridan, 1869, in Wallechensky and Wallace, 1975). "Ragheads Go Home!" (Marvasti, 2008, p. 664). "Say what you will, the American Negro is still a primitive human being" (United States Army War College, 1936). "[The] personification of all evil assumes the living shape of the Jew. . . . How many diseases have their origin in the Jewish virus! We shall regain our health only by eliminating the Jew" (Adolph Hitler, *Mein Kampf*, "Racial State"). "If fans want to know the trouble with American baseball they have it in three words—too much Jew" (Henry Ford, in Reiss, 1988). "Look at the Negro. Is he shaped like any white person? Is the anatomy of his frame, his muscles, or organs, like ours? Does he walk like us, think like us, act like us? Not in the least. . . . Can the black races become civilized? I should say not" (Knox, 1850, pp. 161, 162). It is true that not all, or most, of us feel such hostility toward members of different ethnicities, but such extreme statements express the sentiment that some feel or have felt that "other" ethnicities *are not our kind*. And when members of the dominant ethnicity wield enormous power over another whom they treat brutally and with detestation, the result can be toxic and lethal.

ETHNIC IMAGES, ETHNIC STIGMA

These ugly, hateful quotes communicate the contempt that their speakers or authors hold or held—and have encouraged others to hold—about a particular category of humanity. And they justify ill-treatment of members of the referred-to category and inspire audiences and other ethnic peers to mistreat those putatively inferiorized members as well. True, from where we stand today, these messages mainly morally stain their sources, but they also manifest the stigma that members of certain racial and ethnic categories cast at their targets; they crystallize hostile sentiments that the audiences they represent felt or feel toward members of specific human collectivities. (The word "stigma" is indefinite as to plural.) Racism, discrimination, prejudice, tribal stereotypes, and hostility. Anti-Semitism and Islamophobia. Xenophobia—the hatred of foreigners. Ethnic hostility, ethnic cleansing. Genocide, the deliberate attempt to wipe an entire category of humanity off the planet—the most extreme possible expression of tribal stigma. These sentiments and actions are the subject of this chapter. What *defines* tribal stigmata, according to Goffman, is that they are "*transmitted through lineages*" and they "*equally contaminate all members of a family*" (1963, p. 4; my emphasis).

Ethnic stigma is a prejudice conveyed and expressed by political, cultural, educational, and media institutions, and felt and expressed *by* members of one category *against* another; the sender enacts, conveys, and communicates it, and, if its message is successful, the target thereby is thought to possess it. Both a sentiment and a form of behavior, this prejudice is a matter of degree and kind; the prejudicial sentiment *energizes* discriminatory behavior, running the gamut from mild prejudice, which results in no overt behavior except avoidance, all the way over to wild hostility and blind hatred whose overt manifestation is extermination. While the variability among specific historical expressions of stigma and prejudice are more important than the similarities, a *common thread* nonetheless runs through all of them that enables us to discuss their totality as a family of social phenomena. Millions of North American Indians died when Europeans migrated to and occupied the New World, killed them in battle, infected them with previously unknown diseases, drove them off their tribal lands, and introduced them to alcoholic spirits; Americans enslaved persons of African ancestry and exploited their labor, brutally punishing—branding, torturing, even killing—any who resisted; the agents of King Leopold II of Belgium mercilessly terrorized the population of Congo by ordering them beaten, starved, tortured, and worked them to death—even having their hands chopped off—if they did not meet ivory and rubber quotas; the Ottoman Empire systematically starved or exterminated a million Armenians, along with tens of thousands of Greeks and Assyrians; Imperial Japan conquered a huge swath of Asia and killed between one and two million Chinese and Koreans; the Third Reich exterminated 5.7 million Jews, along with over 26 million Russians (half military, half civilians), and tens of millions of Poles, Hungarians, Czechoslovakians, Bulgarians, Ukrainians, and Belarusians who resisted its army's invasion and occupation, or simply lived in areas Nazi Germany coveted and lusted to occupy as its own "*Lebensraum.*" All these cases represent instances of genocide or "ethnic cleansing," the attempt to remove a people from their ancestral lands, or annihilate them altogether. In each case, regimes and their representatives justified this brutal behavior with an ideology that proclaimed the superiority of the dominant group and the alien, unassimilable, or inferior character of the conquered or annihilated people. In all these cases, the dominant category attempted not only to subordinate the people it vanquished, but also to disgrace, discredit, stigmatize, and *verminize* them—to stamp "the Other" on its members' brow.

When members of two recognizable or presumed ethnicities or races interact in a context of conflict and hostility, as we've seen, there's always a possibility of *reciprocal denunciation*, in which members of each side stigmatize, deviantize, and anathematize *one another* (Aho, 1994, p. 62). But in any investigation of ethnic hostility, it is necessary to introduce the dimension of *power*. Some instances of inter-ethnic hostility take place where the groups in question are balanced or nearly equal in power, while other instances occur under extremely imbalanced circumstances; in the latter cases, the attempt by the weaker group to demonize the stronger is to no avail—such an attempt has no traction and produces no meaningful action or reaction. During the period of slavery in the United States, blacks were exploited and oppressed, and white landowners were their exploiters. It is misleading under such circumstances to refer to "inter-ethnic hostility" since power relations were so one sided. In Rwanda, Hutus were in the numerical majority but for generations, Tutsis held the effective power, a state of affairs that radically reversed itself. Everywhere we look, power lends a foundation, a context, a structure to the picture. In processes of conflict, ethnicities become imagized in a certain way, and powerful categories possess the resources to disseminate their images more effectively than those who are powerless and unable to control the image-making institutions, such as the media and the educational system. The more powerful ethnicity is capable of creating a cultural and social "center" that dispenses and withholds values and resources, dispenses and withholds punishment and condemnation, rendering the powerless marginal, ineffectual—as outsiders, the "other." But interpersonally, whether power relations are more balanced or more one sided, in micro-relations among one's own collectivities, the "otherness" of each ethnicity is often accomplished; limited as those resources are, members of the less powerful category create micro-niches wherein they are able to control their destiny. And when these processes are activated, the scholar and researcher wants to know how and why.

As we saw, bias against the members of a racial, national, religious, or tribal category runs the gamut from mild to homicidal. At one end, we have what's called a "polite" or "gentleman's" prejudice—snobbery and social avoidance, the subdued forms of discrimination and bigotry—at the other, the deliberate annihilation of an entire swath of the human species. The more poisonous forms of racism, tribal stigma, anti-Semitism, and Islamophobia represent prejudice and bias on steroids; the persons who express them intend to stigmatize and deviantize a segment of the population, and with a bloodthirsty vengeance. Mind you: *Most* of what the diverse peoples of the planet do with and to one another is at least superficially free of rancor and discord, but at its worst, ethnic hatred and hostility are sad commentaries on humanity, as well as an opportunity for the deviance specialist to take a closer look at social interaction.

Erving Goffman identified "tribal stigma of race, nation, and religion" (1963, pp. 4, 5)—the subject of this chapter. In traditional or "proper" company a person with a racial difference "possesses a stigma, an undesired differentness from what we had anticipated" (p. 5). Goffman argued that such stigmata stick out like a sore thumb; the stigmatized person "possesses a trait that can obtrude itself." The people *without* stigmatizing characteristics expect those with whom they interact to be equally free of stigma; for them, encountering the tribally stigmatized person violates that expectation, making social interaction strained, awkward, and difficult. A Jew in an exclusive WASP Boston social club in the 1930s, an upwardly mobile Italian-American student in a genteel prep school in the 1940s, an African American family in a lily-white, upper-middle-class suburb in the 1950s—these and other representatives of certain ethnic categories in specific social circles were, by Goffman's lights, stigmatized, intruding into settings in which they were made to feel outside their element, somehow *staining* their surroundings.

Goffman was a man of his time. In the late fifties and early sixties, when he wrote *Stigma*, what he said about discrediting tribal—or ethnic, racial, national, and religious—characteristics was largely true. Racism (and its many conceptual brothers and sisters) was an ugly, intrusive element of the social landscape. Civil rights legislation, not yet passed in 1963, the publication date of his book, has since rendered overt discrimination against minorities more difficult than in the past. Today, in the United States, largely as a result of the upheaval of the politics of the sixties, American society, though politically still contentious, has become vastly more diverse, cosmopolitan, less ethnically judgmental, and less overt in its forms of discrimination. For example, most persons who belong to majority ethnicities no longer *feel* open contempt toward members of racial, national, or religious minorities. Moreover,

today, *even if they did*, the chances are, among most of the people they know, they would be chastised for openly ventilating—and hence, in anticipation, would become inhibited from expressing—those contemptuous feelings. Over the past five or six decades, in the United States at least, and for the most part, in the Western world, the undisguised, blatant, and florid expressions of racism and anti-Semitism that once virulently stigmatized members of minority ethnicities—and could be encountered in everyday talk, in the media, in advertising, the church pulpit, on the job, throughout the educational system—have been driven to the corners of society, to small, private gatherings of like-minded bigoted friends and acquaintances and fellow members of exclusive associations and organizations. The social exclusion of minority ethnicities cannot be practiced as publicly or as brazenly as before; it must be done deviously, subtly, with qualifiers, codicils, rationalizations, and ratiocinations. Today, in America, we live in an ambience in which race, tribe, and national origin have substantially different consequences than those explicated in Erving Goffman's *Stigma*. Comparing then versus now, we clearly see the decline in the expressions and manifestations of racism and inter-ethnic hostility. One major exception: Islamophobia, or prejudice against Muslims, which has substantially increased since 2001. We'll take a look at this form of tribal stigma momentarily.

In spite of this decline, "tribal" discrimination remains alive and well in the United States—and it is even stronger in some other places on the globe—and today, it exerts enough influence to stigmatize persons on the receiving end. Even though we must seriously qualify Goffman's observations, his discussion of tribal stigma truly belongs in any thorough and systematic examination of deviance.

It's important to keep in mind that stigma of tribe, races, ethnicities, nationalities, and religions are branded *collectively*. Members of the ethnic majority demean members of the designated minority *as a whole*—that is, categorically. They may make room for individual exceptions, but to the bigoted person, *all* members of the entire grouping are demonized, dehumanized, verminized—each and every individual member is looked down upon because of his or her membership in a grouping of humanity that has its origins in ancestral roots. Once again, it's important for us to understand that such stigma is a matter of degree; and moreover, what is most important is the expression of stigma in overt behavior: As I explained above, negative treatment of an ethnic group ranges from milder forms of discrimination, through persecution, to genocide. Levels of prejudice and discrimination that vary from one society to another are inflicted on specific ethnicities; hence, in discussing tribal stigma, we must be both historically and societally specific. And yet let's keep our eyes on the prize: In every chapter of this book, the key ingredient is the *audience*. That is, locating specific individuals who *designate* an act, a belief, and a category of humanity, *as deviant*, is central; a given audience may be scattered all over the society or it may be the society generally, but if a significant number feels that way and are primed to act on the basis of their bigoted opinion, we have a case of ethnic stigma on our hands—and hence, a case of deviance. Sociologists do not claim that this designation is essentialistically correct. In fact, most of us almost disagree with it. But the designation exists, it is a reality in the social world, and it has consequences for the lives of people so designated; it is a *constructed* definition that *becomes* real when it is *regarded* and *acted upon* as real. And *that* is what makes such designations manifestations of deviance. But keep in mind that among certain audiences, *racism* may be stigmatized and hence deviant; but at the same time, among *completely different* audiences, *race itself* is stigmatized. When we think of racial and ethnic stigma, we cannot rule out the role that *mutual vilification* plays in designating who is deviant—*to* specific audiences, *with* specific quanta of power.

Here, we'll be looking at members of certain ethnic groups *as* deviants—that is, the way they are regarded and treated *by* other, usually majority, ethnicities. To anti-Semites, Jews are deviants; to the Islamophobe, Muslims are deviants; to the white racist, anyone of African descent is a deviant. In tribal stigma, members of human categories *are designated as deviants*. As enlightened human beings, *we*—you, the reader, I, the author—do *not* share in this judgment. We don't agree with it, but as observers of social reality, we take note of its existence, acknowledge its

consequences, and contemplate on what could transform it, what would wipe it off the face of the planet. Racial stigma has no status in the cosmic world—such prejudice is invented, a product of historical competition and conflict that cannot be wished or washed away, though, in the distant future, human society may eventually abandon such stigmatizing. Ethnic status has hardly ever been discussed in textbooks as a form of deviance. (Though, for an exception, in a book of readings, see Marvasti, 2008. In addition, in *Social Deviation*, James Ford's one-page discussion of "Race Conflicts," p. 481, is surprisingly enlightened for its time, 1939.)

In my opinion, not regarding ethnicity as a form of deviance is a serious mistake. Ethnicity contains all the essential elements of deviance: an audience who condemns a people and their supposed sins, and the retribution or punishment audiences inflict on others for those supposed sins. In nearly all cases of ethnic bias, as I said, these sins are imaginary, invented. The ethnic groups whose members have been viewed negatively and stereotypically are nonetheless persecuted—not for anything they have done but for their ethnicity alone. This persecution is real; the beliefs regarding their supposed sins are real. But the negative traits and behavior that are *attributed* to them by the majority or by other minorities are typically *not* real. If we want to understand racism, anti-Semitism, and Islamophobia, we have to look to the characteristics of the *audiences* who persecute blacks, Jews, Muslims, and other ethnicities—not to the targets of the stigma. For the bigot, the designated ethnic group is *a representation of evil*, the repository of a *demonology* that varies with respect to local particulars. In its most extreme cases, ethnic prejudice is a process of *dehumanization*; members of the designated category are defined as less than human—in fact, as we saw, *sub*-human. It is the process of dehumanization that allows members of a majority group to inflict humiliating, demeaning, degrading, harmful—and even lethal—acts upon an ethnic minority. And this behavior comes about only as a result of specific and identifiable sociological forces. Tribal stigma exists among all categories of humanity, but it takes a virulent, overtly hostile form only under certain circumstances, and those circumstances have to be understood.

RACISM AND DISCRIMINATION

Human beings vary biologically, both genetically and in appearance, but clear-cut, discrete racial categories do not exist. Instead, there is "continuous variation" across the entire world, "with no sharp boundaries" delineating one supposed racial category from another (Lewontin, 2006). In other words, the traits that we use to signify "races" shade off into one another gradually and imperceptibly; moreover, the traits or characteristics that supposedly *define* or identify racial categories subjectively represent a jumble rather than a cluster of attributes—skin color, nasal shape, hair texture, height, jaw protrusion, lip thickness, and so on—and can vary independent of one another. Which one of these traits is the signifier of race? Is it one or several indicators? What determines whether someone is black, white, Asian, Asian Indian, or Native American? What if a person is dark-skinned but has wavy or straight hair? Fair skin and frizzy hair? A narrow nose but thick lips? And how much of a difference delineates racial distinctiveness? Which groups of people make up races? Where are the boundaries between the supposed races? And what group of characteristics, taken together, constitutes the quality of "racialness"? These are cultural, not scientific, issues.

Virtually all scientists agree that there is no such thing as "pure" races; scientists agree that races cannot be clearly separated from one another. Yet scientists also agree that there is *some* connection, however loose, between DNA and what most commonsensically refer to as "races." Most scientists agree that races are for the most part socially and culturally constructed. At the extreme ends, anyone can make distinctions among humans based on specific physical or phenotypical characteristics; that is, we all can tell the difference between dark skin and light, between straight and frizzy or kinky hair, a sharp, thin nose and a broad, flat one. But where do we draw the line? And we do see, as Lewontin says, "microsatellites" of physical characteristics—for instance, hair form, skin color, and so on, which are often, but not always, and perhaps not even typically, found together (1995, 2006). What

humans see as "races" have no iron-clad predictability with respect to distinguishable genetic differences. But, as I've said, these characteristics do not automatically group themselves into coherent "packages" of traits. There is no clear basis to racial groupings. While some genes are more common in certain populations, there are no genes that *all* members of one population possess and that *no* member of another possesses (Morning, 2005, 2007). To reiterate, *humans* decide what races are—not nature.

All of this is to say that race is *socially constructed*; who is considered white and who's black depends on culture, not biology. This view was not always accepted. In fact, the very concept of race is a historical artifact. Prior to the 1920s, in the United States, ethnic, national, and religious groups such as Slavs (mainly Russians and Poles), Italians (mainly Sicilians and Southern Italians), Jews (mainly from Eastern Europe), and Celts (mainly from Ireland) were considered *races*, and divisions among them were as crucial as the major racial divisions between white, black, and Asians that we perceive today. These European immigrants were clearly not Anglo-Saxon or Nordic, yet they weren't quite "black"; hence, in the minds of established Yankee Americans, they belonged to the category of the "other," which was then occupied by persons of African ancestry. Particularly nasty anti-Italian riots broke out in New Orleans in 1891 (eleven Italians were lynched) after a murder trial had been "fixed" by the local Mafia. *The New York Times* referred to the lynch mob as being composed of the city's "best element," using the incident for suggesting that Italian immigrants' behavior was racially determined and questioning their "fitness" for citizenship. One *Times* editorial referred to "sneaking and cowardly Sicilians" who are ruled by "lawless passions" and "cutthroat practices." Rattlesnakes, the editorial concluded, "are as good citizens as they." In the 1890s, a journalist asked a West Coast construction worker if Italians were white: "No, sir," he replied, "an Italian is a Dago" (Jacobson, 1998, p. 56). Political cartoons published in the nineteenth century depicted Irish immigrants as hot-tempered, savage, and threatening, and looking distinctly swarthy and Negroid in countenance. In *How the Irish Became White*, historian Noel Ignatiev (1995) argues that the

Irish, arriving on American shores as a "lowly" and oppressed category of humanity, rose in the economic structure and "became" white only as a result of treating persons of color the way Anglo-Saxons treated them—as a lowly race of humanity, exploiting and oppressing them. It wasn't until well into the twentieth century that white Anglo-Saxon Protestants accepted white ethnics as fully—or at least as marginally—white. Today, most Americans regard the tripartite division of the races as manifesting natural or biological categories, but in past centuries, we saw "race" in a very different light, regarding many persons of European origin as sharing more racial characteristics with blacks than with Anglo-Saxons. To repeat, race is socially constructed, historically and culturally unstable.

The ideology of racism holds that humanity can be divided into biological entities, or "races," and that their representatives are superior or inferior as a result of their lineage. Racism *justifies* unequal treatment of members of different races, that members of a certain race should have specific privileges, including the mandate to rule over or dominate those of another. Racism justifies a policy of supremacy of one category of people over another, that this supremacy is dictated by ancestry. It was racism that fueled slavery, racial segregation, discrimination, and South African apartheid. Racism manifests itself in individual attitudes and behavior, as well as in the institutions of society. And institutional racism can exist even without individual racism—through sheer inertia, the absence of a will to overcome ingrained privileges. Arthur (2007) delineates two principal types of institutional racism. The first is direct, which takes place when policies "are consciously designed to have discriminatory effects" (p. 3766); and the second, which is indirect, are those policies that inadvertently have a racialist impact, even though they were not designed to do so. In the first category we find "redlining," steering, or guiding African American homebuyers away from lily-white neighborhoods. In the second category we have many union membership practices that are based on kinship and friendship networks, which effectively, though not necessarily intentionally, keep out members of racial and ethnic categories that are not well connected, which generally includes African Americans. In the

second category we also find racial profiling by the police, which entails the more intense focusing of criminal justice surveillance and proactive behavior in high-crime communities and hence, those that are most likely to be African American. High housing prices can also keep members of certain races and ethnicities out of a neighborhood—even though that is not necessarily the specific or direct intent of expensive housing, which is to own a big, comfortable house in an attractive, safe community among rich, agreeable neighbors.

During the past generation or so, individual racist attitudes have sharply declined in intensity, but indirect institutional racism is decaying only by inches—not yards or miles. In fact, in most contexts, expressing blatantly *racist* attitudes is a form of deviance. In November 2012, Denise Helms, a 22-year-old California resident and an employee at Stone Cold Creamery, referred to President Obama by the N-word on Facebook, and expressed the hope that he would be assassinated. In response, her employer fired her, her Facebook account was deactivated, and she received a mountain of criticism and derision. Ms. Helms denies being a racist (Bennett-Smith, 2012). Clearly, expressing overtly racist views is a deviant act. Still, a substantial gap remains with respect to differences in attitudes between whites and African Americans concerning race and equality. On the matter of whether racism and discrimination have declined over time, we still have very much of an "on the one hand, but on the other" type of situation. Enormous changes have taken place in some areas of life, while others seem stagnant, seemingly resistant to change. Anyone who has lived through the segregationist South notices the absence of "whites" and "coloreds" signs on toilets, drinking fountains, and public transportation. African Americans have made enormous occupational strides—as supervisors and executives, television actors and spokespersons, physicians, students and faculty at major colleges and universities, lawyers, athletes, entertainers; the list is long and, and the change has been impressive. Says an Air Force medic about the military, "All the segregation is gone; race is not allowed to matter. We have a zero-tolerance policy" (Page and Mallenbaum, 2011). And yet differences remain, as do attitudes about the degree of change.

The Economic Gap. A *USA Today*/Gallup Poll conducted in 2011 found that nine out of ten respondents nationwide say that civil rights for African Americans have substantially improved during their lifetimes. But friction perseveres; blacks are more likely to see discrimination in areas where whites say that equality has been achieved. "When it comes to getting a job, whites see a level playing field; blacks say discrimination persists," the poll summed up. In 1963, only 41 percent of whites said that blacks had as good a chance to get a job they were qualified for as whites did; in 2011, that nearly doubled, to 78 percent. But in 1963, only 23 percent of blacks said they were treated equally in the job market; today, only 39 percent say that's true. In other words, *most* whites think that blacks now get a fair shake in employment, whereas most backs think that they *don't* receive equality in hiring. In 2011, a memorial to Martin Luther King was dedicated near the National Mall, which prompted pollsters to ask respondents whether Dr. King's dream of equality had been achieved. Just over half said that it had, including 49 percent of whites and 54 percent of blacks. One respondent said he didn't think King's dream has been realized, "but I don't think he'd be unhappy, either." A country that is currently represented by a twice-elected African American president seems surprisingly ambivalent about the decline of racism and discrimination (Page and Mallenbaum, 2011).

The 2011 U.S. Census verifies a bleaker rather than a more optimistic picture. Median family income for the American population at large fell 1.7 percent from the previous year in real dollars, and 8.9 percent since 1999; income was the lowest since 1999. More than two-and-a half-million Americans moved into poverty; they now total 15 percent of the population. In spite of—or perhaps *because* of—the economic stagnation, the racial gap in income between black and while families not only persists, it seems to be growing. Income among black households fell during the 2010–2011 period by 2.7 percent, to $33,137; among whites, the decline was 2.1 percent, to $53,340. The overall economy is declining slightly, and the racial gap in earnings is increasing slightly. While white families are becoming slightly poorer over time, black families are a little *more* likely to be growing even poorer. Interestingly enough, among intact, married couples, the economic position of African Americans is improving relative to that of whites; it is mainly among nonintact male households and single or divorced female households with children that the position of blacks is declining most steeply.

Residential Segregation

During 2011 and 2012, four different research teams conducted their own major analyses of racial segregation based on the 2010 Census data. Though their findings back up one another, the conclusions of their authors are somewhat divergent. Has racial segregation disappeared? No, all of these studies say; racial segregation still persists. Is the separation of the races as great today as it was four or more decades ago? No, they all agree; Americans are more likely to live in racially mixed neighborhoods today in comparison with the past. Granted, much of the national desegregation has taken place as a result of a substantial number of African Americans moving to Sun Belt cities of the Southwest. Nonetheless, concludes Reynolds Farley, who is at the University of Michigan's Population Studies Center, today, there is much more black-white neighborhood integration than there was four decades ago. Vastly more African Americans are no longer living in predominantly or exclusively black neighborhoods. Edward Glaeser and Jacob Vigdor, authors of one of these four reports, concluded that currently, only 20 percent of African Americans live in "ghetto" neighborhoods (where 80 percent or more are black), whereas a half century ago, 50 percent of blacks did (2012). The authors entitle their report, published by The Manhattan Institute, "The End of the Segregated Century." Their critics say that claims of the death of segregation are "greatly exaggerated" (Rothwell, 2012). But the desegregation that is taking place is inconsistent; it is happening in bits and pieces, more in some places than in others. Says Douglas Massey, a Princeton sociologist, "we really see two trends: in metro areas with small black populations, we indeed observe sharp decreases in segregation; but in those with large black populations, the declines are much slower and at times nonexistent. Although all-white neighborhoods have largely disappeared, this is more due to the entry of Latinos and Asians into formerly all-white neighborhoods" rather than to the movement of African Americans into them. Adds William Frey, chief demographer at the Brookings Institution, these studies indicate that "the average black resident still lives in a neighborhood that is 45 percent black and 36 percent white. At the same time, the average white lives in a neighborhood that is 78 percent white and 7 percent black" (Roberts, 2012).

John Logan, director of another of the major recent studies on changes in residential segregation (Logan and Stults, 2011), commented on one of the reasons for the disparities between white and black communities—reasons not mentioned in the reports themselves: desirable amenities such as schools, libraries, and grocery stores, as well as numerous other features of neighborhoods that residents find attractive. "We know affluent white neighborhoods have more supermarkets," Logan explains. "They have more private doctors. They have much lower crime rates. Home values have increased at a higher rate, and the rate of foreclosure is lower" (p. 21). The differences are quite striking; a substantial proportion of relatively affluent African Americans are living in segregated areas wracked by relatively low family incomes, high poverty rates, low levels of education, and higher rates of housing vacancies. In two mainly black neighborhoods, Prince George's County, near Washington, D.C., and DeKalb County, outside Atlanta, blacks (and Hispanics) who earn more than $70,000 live in communities that measure the same on these indexes (income, poverty, education, and foreclosures) as those which whites who earn only $40,000 live in. In other words, segregation is more than simply racial separation; for African Americans, it entails being denied access to community amenities *even at the same or at a higher income* as their white counterparts. Again, what we see is the process of deviantization of the residence of members of minorities, even if they attain middle-class incomes.

Police Profiling

On the night of July 16, 2009, James Crowley, a police sergeant employed with the Cambridge Police Department, received a call to the effect that two black men were on the porch of a residence located in a predominantly middle-class, white neighborhood, one of whom was attempting to force open the front door with his shoulder. When Crowley arrived at the house, the men were inside; the officer asked for ID and requested that the two step out onto the porch. The man who had forced the door open, Henry Louis Gates, Jr., refused to leave the house but did produce two sets of identification that announced that he was a licensed driver of the state of Massachusetts and a professor at Harvard University. The officer informed him that he was there to investigate a possible break-in, to which Gates loudly asked, "Why— because I am a black man in America?" Gates then accused Crowley of being a racist and demanded that he contact his chief. "You don't know who you are messing with!" Gates proclaimed. After a second officer arrived, Gates added, "This is what happens to black men in America!" (Ogletree, 2010, pp. 22, 23, 26; Bolton, 2011, pp. 791–792). Crowley then arrested Gates on the charge of disorderly conduct. Charles Ogletree, chronicler of this event, argues that Crowley's treatment of Gates was influenced by race—that, in effect, the professor was *profiled*, treated as a suspect and a deviant because he was black—and that the police should not have the right to arrest when they receive what they interpret as offensive verbal abuse.

We all profile one another, and have since the dawn of humanity; we all use shorthand methods by means of appearance and cues to determine what others are likely to do. Presumably, at some point, the evidence of what people actually do modifies our expectations of what they are likely to do based solely on their appearance and characteristics. In particular, the police operate in a threatening environment, and the people with whom they deal day to day are, in all likelihood, vastly more threatening than the people most of us face. In his classic work, *Justice Without Trial* (1966, 1994), Jerome Skolnick explains that the police construct a profile of a "symbolic assailant," picturing themselves as vulnerable to the threat of "sudden death through violent means." Danger "typically yields self-defensive conduct," and to protect themselves, they develop "a personalized perceptual shorthand that allows them to quickly detect persons possessing weapons or the propensity to unleash physical violence." Though this police profile is based on suspicions, hunches, and intuition," what is paramount on the cop's mind is "arriving home safely at the end of the shift" (Bolton, 2011, p. 793). A healthy police attitude "is one that constantly scans for the person who seems fidgety, unusual, odd, or extraordinary, or is somewhere he does not belong." Skolnick includes African American males among the cop's candidates for potentially dangerous parties, as are perceived loiterers and known thieves, prostitutes, pimps, drug dealers, and ex-cons—all of whom receive extra scrutiny (Skolnick, 1994, pp. 44, 47; Bolton, 2011, p. 793).

Is this practice racist? On the face of it, it is; it represents the denial of equal rights before the law. Clearly, the members of one category of humanity (blacks) are being treated differently by the police than another (whites). By being black, they are automatically suspicious, much more closely scrutinized as a potential deviant and criminal. All of this is true, but the police characteristically deny being racist, though some of the more insightful ones might admit to being "pragmatic racists"—making judgments on the basis of race for practical, empirical reasons. Yes, it's true, they say, I suspect that this particular African American male walking along the sidewalk is more to have committed this particular reported crime than a random white male because African American males *are* more likely to commit crimes. And I'm protecting the community—their own community—by engaging in that practice. Says sociologist Amitai Etzioni, "all racial profiling is not necessarily racist, and ending the practice would penalize those African American communities with high incidences of violent crimes because they would lose the levels of policing they need to be relatively secure" (2007, p. 313).

Where does this leave the black man? In a phrase, at the receiving end of institutional racism. Caught in the vice of a dilemma, an unfair practice in an unfair, far-from-ideal world—mistreated for supposedly hardheaded, utilitarian reasons. A study found that African Americans are more likely to oppose police profiling, and that they believe that they, themselves, as well as their children, could become the target of unwarranted police harassment (67%) than is true of whites (22%); Latinos are closer to blacks (59%) in this respect (Schuck, Rosenbaum, and Hawkins,

2008, p. 512; Higgins, Gabbidon, and Vito, 2010). In 2009, the New York Police Department (NYPD) conducted 575,000 pedestrian stop-and-frisks. Of that total, 55 percent involved blacks, even though blacks are only 23 percent of the city's population. Non-Latino whites were caught up in only 10 percent of all stops, even though they are 35 percent of New York's residents. Civil rights and civil liberties organizations expressed outrage at the disparities, criticizing the NYPD for racial imbalance; some threatened to sue the department to put an end to such practices (MacDonald, 2010).

But the cops have a tool at their disposal, an argument to back up what they see as commonsensical profiling: CompStat—a methodology that tabulates crime, not populations. CompStat reports daily, and deploys police personnel where crime is happening and where it is increasing, the intent being to locate "hot spots" of crime, thus stopping the most serious criminal acts before they happen. In New York in 2009, the NYPD reported that African Americans committed 66 percent of all violent crime in New York, including 80 percent of gun assaults and 70 percent of robberies; blacks and Latinos combined committed 98 percent of all gun assaults. Moreover, the vast majority of the victims of these crimes were of the same racial and ethnic group as the perpetrators. In contrast, non-Hispanic whites committed less than 5 percent of the robberies and 1.4 percent of the reported shootings. It makes no sense, the police say, to deploy police manpower to places where crime is rare to non-existent. Hence, the stop-and-frisk practice is racist *in theory* but it is color-blind *in practice*. Supporters of the policy believe that no police practice has done as much for the poor and minority residents as CompStat policing has. "More than 10,000 black and Hispanic males are alive today who would have been killed had homicide rates remained at the levels of the early 1990s." A Quinnipiac University poll indicated that two-thirds of the city's black residents (68%) approve of the job Ray Kelly, NYPD's police commissioner, is doing, implicitly endorsing CompStat (MacDonald, 2010). In 2010, the city's stop-and-frisks totaled 600,000. On the opposite side of the fence, in 2008, the Center for Constitutional Rights launched a lawsuit against the city to stop the practice, but in August of 2011, a federal judge threw the case out of court (Baker, 2011). A poll conducted by *The New York Times* in August of 2012 revealed that a majority of the sample said that the police "favored whites over blacks" in stopping, questioning, and frisking suspects. In 2011, the police stopped 700,000 suspects; 85 percent were black or Latino. Over half the whites (55%) approved of the practice, saying that it made the city safer, while only a third of the African Americans (35%) approved and 55 percent opposed it (Grynbaum and Connelly, 2012).

Incarceration

As we know, the crime rate in the United States sharply declined in the 1970s, 1980s, and 1990s, as measured by victimization surveys, self-report surveys, and official police statistics (the Uniform Crime Reports). Between 1973 and 2011, according to the National Crime Victimization Survey, the total property crime for American households declined by three-quarters; and in the past two decades, as tabulated by the FBI's Uniform Crime Reports, violent crime in the United States has declined by roughly 40 percent. Common sense would dictate that as the crime rate declines, with the appropriate time lag, the rate of imprisonment would correspondingly decline. In this case, common sense would be wrong. According to the Bureau of Justice Statistics, in 1980, the incarcerated population in the United States, including those held in local and county jails as well as in state and federal prisons (but not including those on probation and parole), was just over half a million—501,886. In 2010, the total was just over 2.2 million, or 2,266,832—more than a *quadrupling*. Why do we have less crime but more prisoners?

The reason is that the same crimes today are more likely to result in incarceration than was true in the past; in addition, more prisoners are being denied parole, or are having parole delayed, and so are spending longer sentences in prison. And over the past three decades, the number of people who are currently imprisoned for substance abuse has increased by ten times—from 50,000 to half a million. And more than half of persons behind bars—roughly 1.3 million—are there for committing a non-violent offense. With 5 percent of the world's population, the U.S. incarcerates a quarter of prisoners in the world (Tierney,

2012, p. A29). All of these factors add up to the reasons why, in spite of the decline in violent crimes, there's a larger jail and prison population. (Actually, between 2009 and 2010, the total number of prisoners in the United States declined for the first time since 1972.) The *rate* of incarceration has remained stable over the past decade, at just under, and just over, 500 per 100,000 in the population—in 2010, for men, 943; for women, 67. Many criminologists believe that the country's excessively high rate of incarceration is "criminogenic"; that is, it generates more crime than it prevents, by tearing at the social fabric of communities and damaging the economic prospects of prisoners and their families (Tierney, 2012, p. A28).

What does the racial composition of penal institutions tell us about institutional racism? One child out of forty in the United States has a parent who is incarcerated; for African American children, this figure is one out of fifteen (p. A28). As Katheryn Russell-Brown has pointed out, for decades, the rate of black-versus-white arrests has remained at about the same level: 28 percent of arrests are of African Americans and 70 percent are whites—numerically, two and a half times as many whites as blacks; and in terms of representation in the population, blacks are about twice as likely to be arrested as their numbers (2009, pp. 28–48). Only the naïve observer would assume therefore that black-white incarceration rates would reflect the same proportion as for arrests. According to Department of Justice figures, in 2010, the rate of incarceration for African American males was just over 3,000 per 100,000 in the population (or 3,074), based on imprisonment with a sentence of a year or more—a figure that is 6.7 times that of whites (459) and 2.4 times that of Latinos (1,258). To put these ratios in absolute numbers, on any given day, roughly 840,000 African American males, 700,000 white males, and 440,000 Latino males are behind bars; for women, the comparable figures are 65,000 blacks, 92,000 whites, and 32,500 Latinas.

To interpret these figures, we have to think about the economic position of blacks in American society, especially their lower income and substantially lower wealth; the "selective" or increasingly bifurcating employment structure (skilled versus unskilled) in our twenty-first century global economy; the "splintering" of the black community; the demographic distribution of African Americans, including their higher residence in large cities, their relative youth compared with whites, and their higher proportion of single, unattached males and the number of single or once-married black women with children and the proportion of these children who grow up without a father; and, for the society at large, a shift from a rehabilitative ethic to relying on more punitive measures and the tendency to "quarantine" miscreants away from mainstream society (Seidman, 2010; Alexander, 2012). There is practically no sphere in American society where the gap between whites and blacks is as enormous as it is with incarceration. Unemployment among African Americans is roughly twice the figure for whites, not an astronomical difference but still a substantial one. And recreational drug use may even be a little more common among whites than blacks. But blacks are *hugely* more likely to be encompassed in deviant or "outsider" roles with respect to two crimes—robbery and homicide— and they are incarcerated at *stupendously* higher rates in comparison with whites. According to the figures tallied by the Department of Justice, African Americans are six times as likely to be victims of criminal homicide as whites, and almost eight times as likely to commit homicide (Cooper and Smith, 2011, p. 3), but murder is a minuscule proportion of all offenses—seven-one-hundredths of 1 percent. That African Americans are incarcerated at a rate almost seven times that of whites is a fact of enormous significance. It is as if African Americans were caught up in a "perfect storm" of history, biography, culture, racism, and

social and economic structure, all of which have conspired to isolate, deviantize, and "other" them from the American mainstream. And of all such outcomes, their higher incarceration rates are the most disruptive and marginalizing (Roberts, 2004; Wacquant, 2008). Even if no personal or individual racism were involved, we would still have a manifestation of *institutional* racism—an instance of "punishing race" (Tonry, 2011).

Racial Intermarriage

Surprisingly, the *biggest* change in attitudes that has come about over time concerns interracial marriage—which is mainly manifested in attitudes and only secondarily in behavior itself. In 1958, Gallup asked the question: "Do you approve or disapprove of marriage between white and colored people?" The very wording of the question is significant; today, the term "colored people" is considered archaic and racist. (Consider the cultural grounding out of which the account that follows this chapter grew; the author's very use of the word "colored" indicates its racist origin.) In addition, in 1958, the question did not ask whites and blacks the question separately but rather resorted to the "default" category, assuming that all the respondents were white. At that time, only 4 percent of respondents said that they approved of interracial marriage. In 2011, 83 percent of whites and 96 of blacks approved, while only 11 percent of whites and 2 percent of blacks disapproved— an increase in positive attitudes, among whites, of *twenty times*. Table 13.1 charts the gradual erosion

TABLE 13.1   ATTITUDES TOWARD INTERMARRIAGE, 1958–2011

	APPROVE	*DISAPPROVE*
1958	4	94
1968	20	73
1972	29	60
1978	36	54
1983	43	50
1994	48	37
2007	77	17
2011 (whites)	83	14
2011 (blacks)	96	2

Source: Data from Gallup Polls, Poll respondents chart racial progress since MLK.

of negative attitudes toward intermarriage among whites over time. Virtually no other opinion has shifted in the past half century from virtually completely opposed to almost completely in favor. At the same time, racial intermarriage remains low in the United States, although it is substantially higher than it once was. In 1967, it was not even legal in many states for members of different races to marry; that year, the Supreme Court ruled that laws against "miscegenation" were unconstitutional. In 2001, among married black women, 3.8 percent had a husband who was not black, and 7.6 percent of married black men had a wife who was not black. In 2010, these numbers had increased to 5.1 and 12.5 percent, respectively (Kellogg, 2011; tabulations supplied by Roderick Harrison). However, some stigma remains: Asians and Latinos are more likely to marry whites than to marry blacks, even when accounting for their numbers in the population. "It reflects status hierarchy," says Harrison, an African American demographer at Howard University. "If you're trying to marry up, clearly whites are it. If you're trying to avoid marrying down, it would still look like blacks might be the least preferred." But the data do make one thing clear—"all racial and ethnic groups are marrying each other more often than they did in the past" (Kellogg, 2011).

ISLAMOPHOBIA

In 2012, Sam Bacile, a 52-year-old Israeli American real estate developer, released a four-teen-minute trailer for a video, entitled "Innocence of Muslims," in which he invested $5 million. "Islam is a cancer," Bacile declared. Terry Jones, an American pastor who has publicly burned the Koran and threatened repeatedly to tear pages from it, opined that the film was not designed to attack Muslims but "to show the destructive ideology of Islam." The film was posted on YouTube by a third party, also anti-Muslim, an Egyptian Coptic Christian, Morris Sadek. The aftermath of the posting was immediate and fierce. In Benghazi, Libya, an attack, presumably instigated by al-Qaeda, and presumably pre-planned, on the U.S. consulate killed the Ambassador to Libya and three other consulate officials. In Cairo, demonstrators stormed and climbed the walls of the

U.S. embassy after learning of the film, and gun battles exploded between guards and protesters. In Egypt, the first elected president, Mohamed Morsi, urged U.S. officials to prosecute the "mad-man" who made the film. In response, representatives of the government declared that the United States "[condemn] the continuing efforts by misguided individuals to hurt the religious feelings of Muslims—as we condemn efforts to offend believers of all religions" (Kirkpatrick, 2012, pp. A1, A12). While most Americans would regard the sentiment the film unleashed as offensive—and, in all likelihood, most Libyans disapproved of the attack—it did express Islamophobia on the part of an extremely loud minority.

In the United States, beginning in 2010, a loud, vociferous interest group, the American Freedom Defense Initiative, has been paying for ads in busses and subways designed to heighten public awareness about what it calls the "Islamicization of nations." When charged with Islamophobia, its supporters claim, "It's not Islamophobia. It's Islamorealism." Islam is the enemy of freedom and democracy, the organization argues; the West is too tolerant toward Islam. In these ads, the organization quotes prominent Muslims, including Muhammad, to the effect that the goal of Islam is nothing less than world domination. "Killing Jews is worship that draws us close to Allah," a quote supposedly uttered on Hamas MTV. "Soon shall We cast terror into the hearts of the Unbelievers" (Quran 3:151). "Jihad, holy fighting in Allah's cause, with full force of numbers and weaponry, is . . . an obligation and duty in Islam on every Muslim," a quote supposedly uttered by failed Times Square car bomber Faisal Shazad. All Muslims are urged to practice jihad, or holy war, emphasizes the Initiative; Islam as a whole wants to convert all unbelievers and strengthen the faith of all Muslims. Islam wants nothing less than to accomplish the complete domination of the world, to wipe out all non-Muslims by sword or conversion, it stresses. True or false? It should be clear that the American Freedom Defense Initiative is taking the more radical and extreme Islamic view and presenting it as if it were characteristic of the entire swath of the faith; it is also clear that the organization aims to frighten non-Muslims enough to act against any and all initiatives launched by the faith—in effect, to shut Islam down. Despite its protestations, the initiative is practicing *Islamophobia.*

Intolerance toward, and discrimination against, Arabs and other immigrants from the Middle East has existed in the West for generations, but the attacks on the Twin Towers and the Pentagon on September 11, 2001, stimulated hostility in the Western world toward Islam and Muslims—the assumption being that 9/11 alerted non-Muslims to the religion's agenda to conquer or annihilate the West. Anti-Muslim sentiment in the United States has risen consistently since 9/11. According to an ABC News/*Washington Post* poll, only 37 percent of Americans hold a favorable opinion of Muslims, the lowest such rating since September 11, 2001. A *Time* magazine poll revealed that 28 percent of American voters believe that Muslims should not be allowed to sit on the Supreme Court, and a third think they should be barred from running for President; over a fifth (22%) say that they don't want a Muslim as their neighbor, and four out of ten (39%) believe that Muslims—even those who are American citizens—should be required to carry a special ID (Mujahid, 2011).

The term "Islamophobia" immediately generates opposite reactions—contrary claims that negate one another. On one side, at the extreme, we encounter the reaction: "Islamophobia—*what* Islamophobia?" Daniel Pipes (2005) argues that Westerners do not fear Islam so much as they fear *radical* Islam. It is entirely appropriate, he asserts, to fear that which intends to destroy us; hence, the fear of Islam is not "undue." Likewise, in an op-ed in the Australian newspaper, the *Sydney Morning Herald*, columnist Paul Sheehan asserts that "Islamophobia is a fabrication" (2009). Muslims have been doing terrible things in his country, he asserts, including targeting and sexually assaulting non-Muslim women. There is no "undue" fear of Islam, this argument goes; this fear is entirely rational and well-grounded. In *Marked for Death*, Dutch anti-Islamist Geert Wilders (2012) claims that Islam is waging a "war against the West"—as well as a war against one Geert Wilders. There is no such thing as "Islamophobia," he insists. And though there may be moderate Muslims, there is no such thing as a moderate *Islam*; by its very nature, Islam is *mandated* to destroy the West and conquer the planet—hence, it should be rightfully feared. Or so one side of the controversy claims.

The other side condemns Islamophobia and the Islamophobe, arguing that hostility toward Islam is inappropriate. In 1996, the Runnymede Trust, a British organization devoted to fighting racial and ethnic discrimination in Britain, formed the Commission on British Muslims and Islamophobia; after a year-long investigation, the Commission produced a report entitled "Islamophobia: A Challenge for Us All." The report reached the conclusion that anti-Muslim attitudes and discrimination create problems both for Muslim communities and for British society as a whole. More specifically, the Commission highlighted discrimination against Muslims in health and education, the social exclusion of Muslims from the mainstream of British society in employment and government, the bias against Muslims in the media and in everyday conversation, and the vulnerability of Muslims to physical and verbal violence and harassment.

Runnymede Trust's report spelled out two "views" of Islam—one discriminatory and "closed," the second, more enlightened, accepting, and "open." The "closed" view is the Islamophobic view, regarding Islam as monolithic, static, unchanging; regarding Islam as divergent and distinctly different from the West, having little in common with European culture; regarding Islam as inferior to the West—barbaric, primitive, and backward; aggressive, terroristic, violently anti-Western; carrying an explicit political, ideological, and military anti-Western message and agenda; hostile to any and all critiques of the West by supporters of Islam; supportive of discrimination against Muslim assimilation into Western society; and supportive of anti-Muslim hostility, viewing it as normal, natural, and inevitable. In contrast, the "open" conception is based on respect for Islam and its beliefs and traditions. Teachers, lawyers, journalists, and religious and community leaders, and the government, the report urged, should adopt a more enlightened and more just approach in their relations with their Muslim fellow subjects.

Beyond the reach of the Runnymede Trust, beyond the Western world, beyond 9/11 and the charge of terrorism, in Myanmar (the former Burma), Buddhists have been attempting to drive Muslims out of their western provinces, branding them "unwanted guests," "invaders," "vipers in our laps." Human rights organizations regard the treatment of Muslims in the region by the local Buddhist population as "ethnic cleansing." A teacher in a monastery in Rkhine State greets the reporter with a rant. "According to Buddhist teachings," he declares, "we should not kill. But when we feel threatened we cannot be saints" (Fuller, 2012, p. A1). Recent violence has left well over 150 dead and a hundred thousand homeless; the violence, designed to drive the presence of Islam from the area, has touched off an exodus consisting nearly entirely of Muslims. Monks have begun making demands that anyone unable to prove three generations of legal residence in the country must be shipped off to camps, there to await deportation to any society willing to accept them. Five decades of authoritarian rule have kept the tension between ethnic groups in check, but the transition to democracy has unleashed populist Buddhist rage against Muslims in this fragile, newly born country. "We are very fearful of Islamicization," says a representative of the largest party in the state. "This is our native land; it's the land of our ancestors" (p. A16). In some villages, residents are armed with clubs, swords, and sharpened bicycle spokes. Muslims have fought back—some huts and monasteries have been burned—and so the violence continues. Many Muslims do not "practice human morals," a monk declares; they should be sent to Muslim lands to be with "their own kind" (p. A16).

In its Global Attitudes Project, the Pew Research Center conducted a survey on the attitudes of the populations of twenty-four countries toward Jews, Muslims, and Christians, as measured by agreement with whether the respondent had an "unfavorable opinion" of each category. The *least unfavorable* opinion of Muslims—outside of countries with a substantial Muslim population—was expressed in the United States (23%) and the United Kingdom (23%). A *majority* holding an *un*favorable opinion was expressed in Germany (50%), South Korea (50%), Spain (52%), Brazil (53%), China (55%), India (56%), and Japan (61%)—some of these nations have had virtually no Muslim residents. In other words, there is substantial country-by-country variation with respect to the "deviantization" of Islam.

Interestingly enough, we observe a fairly strong correlation between Islamophobia and anti-Semitism. The nations with the most tolerant attitudes toward Muslims—again, aside from Islamic countries—are also those with the lowest levels of anti-Semitism, that is, the United States and the United Kingdom. In Europe, the Spanish sample expressed the highest level of *in*tolerance toward both Muslims and Jews (52% and 46%, respectively); likewise, residents of East Asia (China, Japan, and South Korea) exhibited high levels of intolerance toward both groups, as did those from Brazil, Mexico, and South Africa. All the other countries were in-between on both counts. Japan, a country with virtually no Jews or Muslims, registered high levels of unfavorable attitudes toward both, very likely due to its xenophobia—the dislike of foreigners. Edward Said, author of the extremely influential book *Orientalism* (1978), takes note of the Islamophobia/anti-Semitism irony, arguing that, oddly enough, hostility to Islam, in the modern Christian West, "has gone hand in hand with, has stemmed from the same source, and has been nourished at the same stream, as anti-Semitism," finding that, almost contrarily, defenders of Zionism have typically expressed Orientalism in its fullest flower (1985, p. 9), that is, they viewed Islam as a strange, exotic, and lascivious fruit, very much, in relation to Europe, as the "other"—inferior, backward, irrational, barbaric, unruly, effete, dishonest, fatalistic, despotic, and *conquerable*. (Although many Orientalists *love* the Orient, they do not love it as an equal partner in world affairs or as a cultural equal with respect to the West; they love it because of its exoticism and difference from the West.) In contrast, Western Orientalists regard the West as rugged, authoritative, intelligent, and superior—hence, deserving of launching an imperialist program against the Orient.

Is the linkage between Islamophobia and anti-Semitism ironic? A parallel ideological structure drives evangelical Christian opposition to both Islam and Judaism as religions—and Jews as a people—but it remains staunchly supportive of the Zionist program, Israel being the locus of the manifestation of the Second Coming of Christ. More specifically, the most conservative and religiously fundamentalist sectors in the West, and specifically in the United States, tend to hold the most negative attitudes toward both Muslims and Jews—that is, are most likely to be

Islamophobic *and* anti-Semitic. According to a recent Gallup poll, respondents who said that they felt "a great deal of prejudice" toward Muslims also reported feeling a bias toward Jews, and vice versa (Boorstein, 2010). Clearly, ethnic biases come in clusters or "packages." And such biases tend to be strongest at the extreme right wing of the American political spectrum, which tends to harbor the most xenophobic and hyper-patriotic views. It is this ideological position that most strongly views both Muslims and Jews as "outsiders" or deviants.

In addition to religious and political conservatism, the variables that most powerfully explain Islamophobia in the West are education, age, knowledge of Islam, and acquaintance with a Muslim. The older the person, the higher the likelihood of holding an unfavorable opinion of Muslims; the younger the person, the greater the likelihood of holding a favorable opinion. The lower the level of education, the greater the likelihood that someone will hold an unfavorable opinion of Muslims; the higher the level of education, the more likely it is that the person will hold a favorable opinion. The Pew Research Center conducted a survey that asked respondents several questions about Islam; the less respondents knew about Islam, the more unfavorable their opinion was about it. And respondents who knew no one who was a Muslim had a less favorable opinion of Islam; those who knew someone who was Muslim had a more favorable opinion. Perhaps these factors could be summed up into a single variable: cosmopolitanism. The most cosmopolitan person is least likely to characterize the actions of a small minority of extremists as typical and emblematic of the religion of Islam, taken as a whole. The less cosmopolitan individual is more likely to regard terrorism as the work of the few and as paradigmatic of Muslims in general. Though most American Protestants have discarded the majority of their "historical suspicions" of Catholics and Jews, says the Pew Research Center, Muslims have not yet been "fully accepted" by a substantial sector of the American public. And yet, the report suggests, greater education, acquaintance with Muslims, and knowledge of Islam reduce these suspicions and "might lead to more favorable views." Still, "the news is not entirely positive." The more conventional, anti-foreign, and

religiously fundamentalist the person, the more Islamophobic—and anti-Semitic—he or she is. It is possible that strongly conservative and fundamentalist Christian views are incompatible with ecumenical tolerance toward non-Christian faiths and compatible with a suspicion that their members are up to no good. Religious discord persists and poses "a challenge for inter-religious understanding," concludes the Pew Research Center's report.

Remember, however, that deviantization can work both ways. While many individuals in the non-Islamic world hold negative attitudes toward Islam and prejudices toward Muslims, the same works in the opposite direction. For the most part, the Western world generally, and the United States specifically, tends to be stigmatized in the Muslim world. In 2012, the Pew Global Attitudes Project asked, among other questions, how non-Americans felt about the United States. While a majority of the residents of many countries held positive views of the United States, the same was not true of those living in Muslim nations. For instance, only 12 percent of Pakistanis said that they had favorable views of the United States, and the figure was 15 percent for Turks, and 19 percent for Egyptians. Only in Lebanon (48%) did the proportion approach even a bare majority. In effect, in the Muslim world, Americans are regarded as *deviants*; they are stigmatized and, in the most extreme cases, *anathematized*. As I've said, the process of "mutual deviantization" is crucial in understanding how deviance labeling works.

ETHNIC, RELIGIOUS, AND NATIONAL ATTITUDES IN MUSLIM NATIONS

On September 30, 2005, a Danish newspaper the *Jyllands-Posten* published twelve editorial cartoons depicting Muhammad in an unflattering light. The paper accompanied the cartoons with an editorial that stated that Muslims are just like any other people and, along with the rest of us, have to endure satire, insult, and ridicule. The cartoons touched off a conflagration of reactions in more than a dozen Muslim countries, including protests, demonstrations, the recall of ambassadors, apologies, riots, boycotts, death threats, at least one murder attempt, several jailings, a suicide, political resignations, several failed lawsuits, the cancellation of diplomatic visits, fines, the shooting and wounding of a Somali intruder in Denmark, who was armed with an axe and a knife—and everywhere, endless controversy and commentary. Did the cartoons demean and "demonize" Islam, as numerous critics claimed? Most Muslims viewed the cartoons as guilty of demonizing Islam; most Westerners saw the cartoons as part and parcel of the rough-and-tumble of political commentary that is regarded as acceptable in the West.

The Pew Global Attitudes Project refers to "how Westerners and Muslims view each other" as *The Great Divide.* The survey asks Muslims and Westerners whether relations between their respective nations are "generally good" or "generally bad." The median figure responding to this question in five European countries plus the United States was 65 percent "generally bad." For Muslims living in four Western countries, it is 62 percent "generally bad." For residents of seven Muslim countries, the median saying "generally bad" is 54 percent. Clearly, where both Muslims and Westerners live, the majority say that relations between them are bad. To quote Pew's report, many Westerners see Muslims as "fanatical, violent, and as lacking tolerance," while Muslims in the Middle East and Asia regard Westerners as "selfish, immoral and greedy—as well as violent and fanatical." For the most part, according to this report, Muslims feel "embittered" toward the West and its people. In general, Muslims blame Westerners for their plight. Westerns blame the difficulty between Islam and the West as residing within Islam itself, the source of the conflict caused by the contradiction between being a devout Muslim and living in the modern world. Islam, in its most fervent form, cannot be reconciled with the practice of democracy or the equality of women—or so most Westerners say. Muslims do not think that the contradiction exists and see no tension between religious tradition and Western values. Moreover, residents of the West remain perplexed by the high percentage of Muslims who say they do not believe that Muslims committed the September

11, 2001, terrorist attacks—well over 50 percent, even among those living in the United Kingdom. (Oddly enough, this view is held by the same persons who believe that such an attack was *justified.*) And, while a strong plurality or even a majority of the populations of Muslim nations say that democracy can "take root" in their country, a *minority* of non-Muslims in Western countries believe that democracy can work in Muslim countries (http://pewglobal.org/reports/display .php?ReportID=253). Perhaps it is an exaggeration to refer to the gaze and treatment of Islam and the West toward one another as "a clash of civilizations," but it is not a mutually empathetic judgment, either. In these typifications, we see great deal of reciprocal vilification and demonization and, unfortunately, they are likely to remain with us for some time to come. For the most part, substantial segments of the population of both the West and Islam see one another as "the other"— as deviants.

DISCRIMINATION AGAINST PALESTINIANS

Israel discriminates against Palestinians. (It is true that the Arab states do as well—for the most part, Palestinians are not admitted as candidates for citizenship by any Arab nation—but that is a separate issue.) With the loss of Arab-owned land to the Israelis, the 1948 residents of the British Mandate who left or were expelled, as well as those living in the West Bank, Gaza, and East Jerusalem as of 1967, were stateless; currently, there is no fully fledged, internationally recognized, official state of Palestine. In addition, the Israelis expelled roughly 150,000 Syrians from the Golan Heights, which was conquered in the 1973 tank war. Today, only about 15,000 Druze (non-Muslim, non-Christian, Arabic-speaking people) remain in Golan; about 15,000 Israelis have moved in and are engaged mainly in agriculture—principally viticulture. The Golan is not considered part of Palestine.

A geographic and cultural entity of Palestine has existed for thousands of years. Egyptian hieroglyphics dating to 1150 B.C.E. mention a region and a people near and around the Dead Sea as "Pereset." Assyrians at the time called them Pilistu. The Hebrew Bible mentions "Peleshet," which scholars have translated as "Philistia." The Old Testament mentions the place or its people 250 times; they are the historical "Philistines." Herodotus and Aristotle mention "Palaistine; the Romans used the same name. In short, the cultural and historical provenance of Palestine is unimpeachable.

The area was conquered and Islamicized by Muslims in 636. The Crusader invasion in the eleventh and twelfth centuries brought more Christians, whether the knights themselves or Crusader converts, into the area. Saladin's Islamic forces in the 1100s drove some Christians out, and essentially stabilized the demographic equation. Muhammad Ali, an Egyptian, seized the territory in 1840, and the British took it over in 1920, just after World War I. Following a war against the Arabs, Israel carved out a state in 1948, which was ratified by the United Nations. Currently, not quite 20 percent of seven million Israeli citizens are Arabs (1.2 million), of whom 80 percent are Muslim, 10 percent are Christian, and 10 percent are Druze. Roughly 2.6 million Muslims live in the West Bank (excluding Israeli settlers), 1.7 million in Gaza, and 200,000 in East Jerusalem. While Israeli Arabs are often referred to as Palestinians, the world unambiguously considers the 4.5 million residents of the West Bank and Gaza to be *Palestinians*. Virtually all of them want their own autonomous, self-governing country. Hence, there are two categories of "Palestinians" against whom Israel and Israelis discriminate: Arabs who are Israeli citizens, and stateless Palestinians, that is, Arabs living within the pre-1967 borders—the occupied territories of the West Bank and Gaza.

On November 30, 2012, the United Nations voted to upgrade Palestine from, essentially, a nonentity territory to a nonmember observer state of the UN—very possibly the first step toward full statehood. Everyone regards the move as a blow to the position of Israel and the United States, which oppose statehood; only nine nations voted against the change in the status of Palestine. Israeli society applies numerous formal and informal restrictions on the rights of its citizens of Arab descent. (See Katie Hesketh, *The Inequality Report: The Palestinian Arab Minority in Israel*, Haifa, 2011.)

Arab-Israeli citizens were not granted the right to vote until 1966. An Arab resident of the occupied territories may not become an Israeli citizen by marrying an Arab-Israeli citizen. More than seventy Palestinian villages are unrecognized by the Israeli state, receive no government services, and are not on any official map; they are considered "illegally constructed villages." No new Arab town or community has been established since 1948; in contrast, over 600 predominantly Jewish municipalities have been established during this time. In October 2010, the Knesset (Parliament) permitted certain smaller Israeli communities to reject residents who do not fit their "fundamental outlook"—an obvious attempt to keep Arabs and other non-Jews out. The Acquisition for Public Purposes Ordinance permits the Finance Minister to confiscate land for "public purposes"; in practice, this land is nearly always Arab-owned land. An amendment was passed in 2010 that confirms state ownership of land confiscated under this ordinance. The Law of Return and the Citizenship Law of 1950 and 1952 permit any Jew emigrating from any country to become an Israeli citizen, but the same is not true of non-Jews, including Arabs from the occupied territories. Certain jobs, especially in the government, are open only to persons who have served in the Israeli military (the IDF, or the Israeli Defense Force), service in which is mandatory for all Jewish citizens but not for non-Jewish citizens. (Note that the ultra-Orthodox or *haredi* Jews also do not serve in the military.) Only 6 percent of public sector jobs go to Arabs, who represent 20 percent of the Israeli population—in spite of the government's declarations to address the problem of inequality. Arab-Israeli incomes are less than two-thirds of Jewish-Israeli incomes. Poverty among Arabs is twice as high as that among Jews, as is unemployment. Arab schools receive only a third of the government funding that schools in predominantly Jewish neighborhoods receive; Arab schools are "overcrowded, understaffed, and sometimes unavailable" (Coursen-Neff, 2005, p. 749). Arab schoolchildren drop out of school at three times the rate of Jewish children. The representation of Arabs among university students and faculty is a quarter that of Jews.

Israeli discrimination against Arabs in the occupied territories is vastly harsher than against its own Arab citizens. Restrictions that apply to Palestinians, says the Human Rights Watch report "Separate but Unequal," do not apply to Jewish Israelis. Building permits denied; Arab villages demolished; access roads blocked off; water, sewage, electricity rejected and unavailable; land seized and turned over to Jewish settlers; applications turned down—all resulting in the restriction of Palestinian habitation in the West Bank and the expansion of Israeli settlements. In many cases, because of Israeli checkpoints and roadblocks, Palestinians cannot get to medical facilities in adequate time to receive adequate medical care, workers cannot get to their jobs in time, and relatives cannot visit one another. The discriminatory policies that Israel has imposed on its Palestinian territories has effectively disenfranchised and displaced its Arab-Muslim inhabitants. The Palestinian people are not only stateless, they have effectively and increasingly become landless—they cannot make use of the little land they do have.

Such restrictions do not apply to the Jewish settlements in these territories. In cases where Israel acknowledges differential treatment of the Jewish settlements, the official justification for it is that its purpose is to protect the Jewish settlements, which have expanded in size in the past three decades from a quarter of a million to half a million. (Most West Bank Palestinians live in areas under the jurisdiction of the Palestinian Authority, and Gaza is under Hamas rule.) Jewish settlements continue to receive government subsidies for housing, education, roadways, and wells and other such infrastructure necessities. In contrast, the Human Rights Watch argues, the differential treatment of Arabs in Palestine cannot be justified by a security rationale when it comes to such mundane rights such as permits allowing the repair or building of homes, schools, roadways, and wells. All Muslims living in Israel's territories do not represent the security threat the government seems to assume they are—or treats them as if they were.

Some observers note that there is a *hardening* mood on the part of Jewish Israelis, an increase in intolerance against a range of non-mainstream groups and practices. A recent Israel Democracy Institute poll found that nearly half of Jewish Israelis expressed a desire not to live next to an

Arab family. "But the list of unwanted neighbors didn't stop there," explained a reporter commenting on the survey's findings. "More than a third didn't want to live next to foreigners or the mentally ill, and nearly one in four said they wouldn't want to share a street with gays or the ultra-Orthodox" (Sanders, 2011). The country's leading newspaper, *Ha'aretz*, summarized the poll with the headline, "A Time to Hate." In spite of the broad front of intolerance, the reporter emphasized that Arab Israelis (and foreigners) "have borne the brunt" of the agenda of the right-wing sector of the political spectrum. In 2011, dozens of rabbis issued an edict banning the sale of real estate to non-Jews, particularly Arab citizens. A warning from rabbis' wives accompanied the edict that warned Jewish women to avoid contact with Arab men.

On the occasion of a declaration issued by the Israeli Education Minister Gideon Sa'ar to the effect that the school system should take action against racism, teachers expressed their concern to Ynetnews.com (released January 19, 2011). One teacher said that a twelfth grader wrote "Death to Arabs" on a test in a civics class. Another high school student stood up in a class in Tel Aviv and, to the horror of his teacher, said that his dream was to become a border guard "so that I can spray Arabs to death." His fellow students applauded his view. Minister Sa'ar blamed Israeli politicians for inciting hate. It is the responsibility of the educational system, he said, "to raise a generation free of racist attitudes [and] which is able to manage social tension and disagreement in a manner that respects the values of Judaism and democracy, on which our state is founded."

ANTI-SEMITISM

In a December 2012 interview conducted by Iranian Press TV, Michael Harris, the financial editor of a Web site Veterans Today and a former Republican candidate for Governor of Arizona, declared that Israeli death squads had committed a number of recent attacks in the United States and elsewhere, including those that took place in a Colorado movie theater, an Arizona mall, an elementary school in Connecticut, and a small island off the coast of Norway. "Zionist-controlled Hollywood" and the "Zionist-controlled news media" serve as a "conduit to all this violence," Harris stated. "Let's connect the dots here," he said. The "Zionist-occupied" American government has covered up the evidence that would reveal this conspiracy. Ironically, he added, while Hollywood Jews supported a culture of violence, Jewish politicians are trying to take away law-abiding citizens' guns. "They've been trying to destroy this country and destroy the Constitution for 70 years," he alleged. "I want Israel off the face of the Earth; they're the source of all the problems in the Middle East," he concluded (Ben Zion, 2012). It's not clear how many people agree with the conspiracy theory Harris advocates, but his opinion that Jews control the media, hold liberal views, and foster Zionism are widely held views.

All the elements of deviance are blatantly evident in anti-Semitism: defilement, ritual pollution, isolation, social exclusion, denunciation, and inferiorization. To the virulent anti-Semite, the sins of the Jews are legion: They killed Jesus; they "stick together" more than other ethnicities; they care only about their own kind; they are crafty, scheming, and dishonest, engage in shady practices, and have gotten rich by cheating and exploiting gentiles; they have "too much power" in business; they have too much control over Wall Street; they intend to undermine society's institutions and control and dominate the world; contemporaneously, they are more loyal to Israel than America; and they engineered 9/11. Not one of these claims is true, but, together, they embody the ideology and the stereotypes that constitute anti-Semitism.

A History of Anti-Semitism

The Jews constitute an "ethnoreligious" group or category; they possess both *peoplehood* and a *theological origin*. The ancient Israelites formed a nomadic, tribal, Middle Eastern, Hebrew-speaking desert-dwelling society; the Bible has it that beginning with Abraham's covenant with God (roughly 1800 BCE) and culminating in the Ten Commandments of Moses (roughly 1400 BCE), these tribes and bands acquired, and united on the basis of, a common bond drawn from

religion, language, and heritage. Throughout their early history, the Israelites were surrounded by vastly more powerful enemies, who conquered, captured, and scattered them to diverse lands while their homeland was carved up by succeeding imperialistic powers. Throughout this 4,000-year history, most of the population in the area circumscribed by the Mediterranean Sea, the Jordan River, the Sinai Peninsula, and the Golan Heights, were not Jewish; the majority were Arabic speaking and eventually, in the seventh century, most of them became Muslims. At the end of World War I (1914–1918), when the Jewish population of present-day Israel stood at only 65,000, Zionists began calling for Jews to "return" to their ancestral homeland—what is referred to in Hebrew as "alyiah" (or "ascent"). Historians estimate that during the Holocaust (the killing began in earnest in 1941 and ended with the termination of World War II in Europe, in May 1945) roughly a third of the Jews in the world were murdered by the Nazis and their allies. By 1947, demographers estimate, roughly two million people lived in the non-Jordanian or western side of the Palestine Mandate—the British colony that comprised much of the present-day state of Israel—of whom nearly 60 percent were Muslims; just over a third (350,000) were Jews, and 150,000 were Arab Christians. Today, there are 13.3 million Jews worldwide, over 40 percent of whom live in Israel (5.7 million) and about 40 percent in the United States (5.3 million). The remaining 20 percent are scattered around the globe. With a few exceptions, one of them being Iran, only a tiny handful of Jews live in predominantly Muslim countries. And in most societies in which Jews live, a substantial but varying proportion of the population consider them as deviants—outsiders, suspicious characters, wrongdoers, persons who possess malicious intent. In some societies, anti-Semites—persons who hate Jews as a category and hold stereotypical, prejudicial, derogatory feelings and beliefs about them—make up more than half of the population. In the United States, Canada, the United Kingdom, Italy, and France, staunch anti-Semites represent a fairly small minority, and are themselves considered deviants.

The history of the Jews is drenched in anti-Semitism; relatively few periods of Jewish history are free from significant, overt episodes of discrimination, hostility, and violence. The word "pogrom" refers to the organized attacks of and even massacres of Jewish people, typically in Eastern Europe, especially Russia—which occurred episodically, even routinely, and were encouraged by the authorities, mainly the Tsars and their minions. Interestingly, according to the Bible, the ancient pagan tribes spoke approvingly of Jews. But hostility toward the Jews began in earnest with the ancient Greeks—probably because of anti-Greek xenophobia, because Jews tended to cluster into tightly knit communities with high solidarity, and because they refused to worship the Greek gods; there was nothing specifically anti-Semitic about this hostility. In the fourth century, Rome adopted Christianity as the state religion, and passed a series of harsh anti-Jewish laws, which resulted in the destruction of synagogues and the passage of statutes designed to restrict the rights of Jews, including the barring of Jews from military service and careers in the state bureaucracy (Cohn-Sherbok, 2006).

During the Middle Ages, many Christians came to believe that, collectively, all Jews were guilty of the murder of Jesus and of God as well as having made a pact with the devil and being in possession of his diabolical powers. A particularly pernicious belief that took hold among uneducated, rural Europeans during the Middle Ages was that, to celebrate the Passover ceremony, Jews murdered Christian children, ate their flesh for matzos, and drank their blood for wine; this came to be called the "blood libel" accusation, and, over the stretch of perhaps a millennium, has resulted in the torture and massacre of many thousands of Jews. During the First Crusade of the eleventh century, knights routinely slaughtered the Jews (along with the Muslims) they encountered. Jews were expelled from Paris in the 1100s, and from all of France in the 1200s and 1300s. In the fourteenth century, when the Black Plague infected and killed roughly a third of the population of Europe, Jews were routinely accused of fomenting the disease, and were murdered in numerous and hideous ways. In 1492, a year famous for the "discovery" of the Americas by Christopher Columbus, King Ferdinand and Queen Isabella expelled all the Jews (along with the Moors) from Spain; Jews in Spain had constituted the largest and most cultured and distinguished Jewish community in Europe. During the majority of Europe's history, Jews were excluded from most professions and forced to practice usury—moneylending, for a profit, enjoined by the Bible—which earned them the enmity of the gentiles who had difficulty repaying them. Martin Luther, a religious reformer, wrote a pamphlet entitled "On the Jews and their Lies," in which he claimed "we are not at fault for slaying them." Contemporary observers feel that Luther was the forerunner of twentieth-century anti-Semitism and the historical inspiration for the Holocaust (Johnson, 1997).

In 1921, Adolph Hitler (1889–1945), an Austrian and a World War I veteran, became the head of the Nazi Party, which late in 1923 attempted a failed overthrow or *Putsch* of the government in Munich, Germany. Hitler was sentenced to a five-year prison sentence, during which he wrote his memoir, *Mein Kampf* ("my struggle"), a screed based on extreme German nationalism, the superiority of the Nordic "race," seething resentment concerning Germany's defeat in World War I, and, most notably, virulent anti-Semitism. Following his release from prison, Hitler reorganized his party, eventually becoming Chancellor of Germany in 1933; six years later, on September 1, 1939, seeking *Lebensraum*—living space for the Germans to live in land they considered rightfully theirs—his army launched an assault on Poland, igniting World War II. Concentration camps were set up at the beginning of the Third Reich, but they did not begin their explicitly lethal operations until 1941. Although a number of categories or groups were also targeted for extermination—notably, the Gypsies or Roma people, homosexuals, communists, the mentally disordered and physically handicapped, and Jehovah's witnesses—Jews were the primary targets: Two-thirds of Europe's Jews lost their lives in the Holocaust, and, in the final solution to the Jewish question, Nazi ideology most explicitly and clearly targeted Jews for extermination. The horror of the Holocaust cannot be exaggerated; it was the most catastrophic event in Jewish history, and perhaps the most catastrophic willful event in the history of humanity. Narratives of the violence and slaughter inflicted on its victims fill entire libraries and chill, shock, and disgust the contemporary reader. Perhaps it is sufficient to say that nearly six million Jews lost their lives in the Final Solution, specifically and solely *because* they were Jewish; the Nazis had dehumanized and verminized them—which gave them license to murder their victims. It is possible that as many non-Jews were also exterminated for not conforming to the racial, physical, mental, and ideological demands of the Third Reich. To the fanatical Nazi, Jews were the ultimate deviants, and they deserved to die.

Anti-Semitism Today

Fortunately, sociologists need not wait until overt anti-Semitic behavior breaks out to understand the causes and dynamics of anti-Semitism; we already know a thing or two about the origins of anti-Jewish tendencies. Over the years, the ADL (Anti-Defamation League) has conducted surveys of anti-Semitic "propensities" of sectors of the American population. The surveys use agreement with statements hostile to Jews as an index or measure of anti-Semitism. If respondents agree with none, or one, of these statements, according to the index, the study considers them "free of prejudicial attitudes toward Jews"; if they agree with two to five of them, they are "neither prejudiced nor unprejudiced"; if they agree with six or more, they belong in "the most anti-Semitic" category. Since 1992, the first year the ADL asked about all eleven statements, the percentage of 6s in the population has wobbled somewhat. In the latest survey (2011), just over half of the sample (54%) scored as 0s or 1s, that is, were "free" of prejudice against Jews, while 15 percent were 6s, highest on the anti-Semitic scale. The ADL survey found that anti-Semitism is not randomly distributed throughout the American population—although in all categories, the virulent or "most" anti-Semitic respondents are in the minority. The less educated the respondent, the greater the likelihood of prejudice toward Jews: in 2011,

22 percent of the "high school only" category were 6s; 13 percent of the "some college" group were; and 9 percent of the college graduates were. Hispanic Americans who are born outside the United States hold more anti-Semitic views (42%) than Hispanics born in the United States (20%). And African Americans tend to have a more negative view of Jews (29%) than the general population (15%). Internationally, the Pew Global Attitudes Project drew samples in two dozen countries, then asked respondents if they agreed with the statement, "I have an unfavorable opinion" of Jews. Americans were least likely to agree with this anti-Jewish statement (7%), and the British (9%) and Australians (11%) were almost as unlikely to do so. In Europe, we find France (20%), Germany (25%), Russia (34%), Poland (36%), and Spain (46%) all further along the scale.

I should emphasize that *in most Western countries* (and in Israel, of course) it is anti-Semitism that is considered deviant, and anti-Semites, the deviants. These public opinion polls, especially those conducted in Anglophone countries, indicate that the majority of the population *opposes* anti-Semitism, considering it, and its expression, a form of deviance. A recent incident reflects this mirror image sentiment—that is, that anti-Semitism is freely expressed and endorsed in some countries and opposed and punished in others. On the evening of February 24, 2011, in a Paris café, Dior fashion designer John Galliano reportedly made an anti-Semitic remark to a female patron, who is Jewish—and an anti-Asian insult to her companion, who is Asian. "Dirty Jewish face, you should be dead," he shouted to the woman, and "Fucking Asian bastard, I will kill you," he yelled at the man. The police report that the couple and the designer exchanged slaps. Four days after the incident, Christian Dior, Galliano's employer, suspended him, a ban that remained in effect two years later. On the same day of his suspension, a video publicly appeared on the Internet of Galliano praising Hitler. Later during that day, Natalie Portman, a spokesperson for Dior and herself Jewish, denounced and disassociated herself from Galliano and his insults. (In 2013, Oscar de la Renta, a high-end fashion firm, hired John Galliano as a "temporary employee," very probably ending his period of exile.) In specific societies of the world, among most social circles, the *expression* of anti-Semitic sentiments is a form of deviance, usually followed by condemnation and punishment. Hence, racial and ethnic hostility is *socially constructed and relative to time and place.*

Anti-Semitism in Muslim Countries

Polls also indicate that substantially higher levels of anti-Semitism prevail in Muslim countries as compared with the West. The Pew Global Poll (and numerous others as well) indicate that in Muslim countries, the percentage of respondents who say that they have an "unfavorable" opinion of Jews is very nearly ubiquitous—for instance, in Egypt (95%), Jordan (96%), and Lebanon (97%). As I said, with only four exceptions (one being Iran), virtually no Jews live in predominantly Muslim lands, nearly everywhere having been pressured to leave. Perhaps one of the strangest manifestations of the insidious trail of anti-Semitism is the contemporary credibility and popularity of the scurrilous *The Protocols of the Elders of Zion* in much of the Muslim world. The Protocols, a forgery concocted by the Russian secret police in 1903, purports to be the minutes of a meeting held by Jewish leaders (or "elders") who are discussing their plans for global domination by subverting gentile morality and taking over and dominating the world's media and the economy. The Protocols lay out a conspiracy by Jews against the world and, have been reinterpreted or retrofitted from its European origin to be relevant to events in the Middle East, against Muslims specifically (Webman, 2011). Rumors have circulated, and have been widely accepted as fact, in all the Arab Muslim countries that thousands of Jews employed in the World Trade Center were warned about, and stayed away from work during, the attacks on September 11, 2001. In a poll conducted by the Pew Research Center, in every country in the Middle East, less than 30 percent of the Muslim respondents believed that Muslims carried out the 9/11 attacks; most claimed it was an American, an Israeli, or a joint-American-Israeli operation. "The Jews and the Zionist lobby" are responsible for 9/11, said SobhiSaleh, an Egyptian Muslim Brotherhood legal theoretician; referring to a Lebanese Christian volume making this assertion, he stated that "this study is well known in America and it's on the Internet. . . . It was scientific research" (Trager, 2011). In an article entitled "The Empires of Zion," which appeared in the November 12, 2012, issue of *Al-Yawm*, a Saudi government daily newspaper, columnist Anisa Al-Sharif Makki stated that the Protocols are the "source that the Zionists use today, and from which they derive their ideology and satanic plans." They boast, the column continued, that they can best achieve world domination through "terrorism and violence." Another of their methods is to ensure that Jews take "an iron grip on global banking and the media." The Jews are engaged in "a war of extermination," which would "destroy their enemies to the very last one" (www.memri.org/report/en/print6884.htm). These bizarre beliefs and assertions are widespread within the Muslim world; they manifest an anti-Semitism not previously seen in Islamic lands, and not seen in the Western world since the defeat of Nazi Germany in 1945 (Trager, 2011). The question is, why?

Observers who support such views argue that these statements are not anti-Jewish as much as anti-Israel. But the most virulent Arab anti-Semites do not distinguish between Jews and Zionists or Israelis and Jews; to them, all three are interchangeable. This seething hatred is not historical or traditional. Prior to the twentieth century, Arabs felt tolerance toward their Jewish compatriots, typically holding enlightened views toward them, treating them and their religion with respect, conducting relations with Jews in a non-conflictual manner. Until the twentieth century, for the most part, Jews in Muslim lands were not persecuted, nor, with only a few exceptions, were they expelled or forced to convert. But with the rise of colonialism and the infusion of European anti-Semitism into Arab lands, Muslims began to see the Jews through Western eyes and treat them accordingly. In addition, ironically, Western secularism caused devout Muslims to seek out a scapegoat for the decline of Islamic religiosity and authority; the foreign agent of corruption they settled on was the Jews. Zionism—the call for Jews to return to the Holy Land—increasingly took root during the 1900s, and in 1948, as a result of a bloody war, led to the establishment of a Jewish state in the heart of the Middle East, a region populated mainly by Arabs. Repeated attempts to retake Palestine from Israel, in 1953, 1967, and 1973, led to humiliating defeats and theories of a conspiracy between Zionists and the West generally and the United States specifically. (How could such a tiny, struggling nation defeat our mighty Arab powers? It must have been because Israel was backed by the "Great Satan," the United States.) Moreover, struggles by Palestinians over water rights, grazing lands, freedom of mobility to cross borders, and constant police surveillance and harassment, not to mention the intermittent, ongoing confiscation of land, has caused many Muslims to feel rage against Jews, Israelis, and Zionists, and any and all of their supposed allies. The resilience of such a tiny number of Jews to maintain a nation in the midst of a region that, traditionally, Muslims have considered their rightful holy land represents a galling reminder of Arab Muslim impotence and fuel for any number of conspiracy theories. The result: public opinion polls that affirm demonic plots involving an international Jewish conspiracy; stereotypes about Jewish craftiness; disbelief in the Holocaust—the very basis of Israeli legitimacy in the Middle East; newspaper cartoons depicting Jews as octopuses, spiders, vultures, snakes, scorpions, ravens, wolves, worms; the sale of *The Protocols of the Elders of Zion* in mosques and on the street; the belief that the claims in the Protocols are historically and contemporaneously true; phony scholarship based on the Protocols or explaining 9/11 conspiracies against Arabs; and comparatively high levels of anti-Semitism, and designations of the Jew, the Israeli, the Zionist as "the other," the enemy—a truly evil *deviant* (Greenberg, 2001; Trager, 2011).

SUMMARY

Ethnic prejudice defines one or another category of humanity as outsiders or "the other." Tribal stigma defines members of categories as deviants. In his original discussion in *Outsiders*, Howard Becker laid down the groundwork for, but did not explicitly spell out, ethnicity as a form of deviance; in contrast, Erving Goffman specifically stipulated that stigma applies to condemned ethnicities as much as to condemned behaviors (1963). Tribal stigma defines members of the disfavored categories as deviants. Most of us have been taught to regard racism, prejudice, and discrimination as wrong—as a form of deviance. This is a decent, honorable sentiment, but the fact is bigoted sentiments and acts are sociologically real, and they do turn the equation around, transmogrifying members of the stigmatized category into deviants. Tribal stigma is transmitted through ancestry of lineage. Persons so designated haven't done anything wrong, but those who are prejudiced against them persist in their prejudices anyway. It is this sociological reality that we, as students of society, have to struggle to understand and, in the best of all possible worlds, overthrow.

Why do racism, prejudice, and discrimination exist? Sociologists argue that inter-ethnic hostility arises from conflict between and among human categories for scarce resources. A dominant group intends to gain an advantage by exploiting a less powerful group, earning a profit from their sweat and exclusion. Over time, less powerful groups fight back and struggles sort out power relations, tilting toward more equality; consequently, exploitation becomes less blatant, less overt, and less permissible, and thus, exploitation retreats into the shadows. Occasionally, political claims *verminize* a category of the population, and genocide is the result—the mass slaughter of enormous numbers of the members of an ethnic category of humanity simply because of their membership in a particular group. Genocide is the most extreme form of deviantization; it translates contempt and hostility into a death warrant. Racism against African Americans in the United States, hatred in the Western world post-9/11 of Islam and of Muslims, the hatred of Jews almost everywhere, and prejudice against Palestinians in Israel illustrate how tribal stigma transforms the "other" into a deviant and why we can regard the deviance perspective as a fruitful way of looking at ethnic conflicts.

Account: Growing Up Colored in the South during the 1950s

Michelle Birdsong

The author has written and published a children's book, several commercially released and publicly performed songs, and a number of Kindle-edition essays; she lives in San Francisco.

I attended a school in the 1950s that was located in a community in Tennessee near the Kentucky border. When I was in the 7th grade, one of my teachers often came to class with a hangover. He'd tell me to take over the class while he went to the back of the room and slept for the duration of the class. Another teacher told me that his friend, also a teacher, liked me. I didn't like him and said so. Otherwise, I would have had an affair with him. I was 13. My colored school—as it was called then—used outdated textbooks. One day, I saw a box on the floor of the lobby of our school, addressed to Clarksville High School, the white high school. It had been opened, so I peeked in; it contained books, so I reached in and picked up one and looked inside. The date of publication was from years back. I realized that our colored school was receiving and adopting the white school's used, old, discarded, outdated textbooks!

I had problems growing up in the Jim Crow South. One of my friends was killed by a car bomb. It was outside the area, but it was the racist anti-civil rights people who killed him. When I was in high school I borrowed clothes from Joan, a girl who was the out-of-wedlock daughter of a rich man who could afford to buy her expensive, quality clothes. One day, a friend of hers came into the bathroom where I was washing my hands in the sink. She saw me wearing Joan's plaid skirt, and asked me with a sly grin on her face, "What do you and Joan have in common?" I didn't say anything, but I was so humiliated that I never again borrowed Joan's clothes. Once, the local tire store repossessed the tires on my mother's car. She was behind in her payments. Mama had to drive to get to her job—there were no busses or subways. She

seemed pathetic, begging them not to take her tires. As the men were removing the tires, Mama went into the house and fainted in the living room. One of the men who were taking the tires said matter-of-factly, "She's as dead as a doornail." In a panic I ran down the alleyway to a neighbor's house, who was eight months pregnant. The neighbor picked up Mama as if she were a baby and put her in her bed. I thought she was dead. My sister, Mama, and I always had to be quiet when the insurance man and bill collectors knocked on our door because Mama didn't want to have to face them because she didn't have the money to pay them. Doorbells were unheard of then. Even to this day, I refuse to buy life insurance. The water company turned off the water regularly. Fortunately, the old man who lived with my Mama—we called him Papa— would go into our front yard and stick a metal pole in the ground where the water meter buttons were and turn the water right back on. When they turned off the electricity, we'd bathe in our neighbor's bathtub. Credit and layaway were a way of life. Our poverty caused us to feel constant humiliation. Mama never complained. I didn't know how poor we were until one day, Mama had me go to the laundry, when she worked there, and get her paycheck. She was too sick to pick it up herself. The check was for $23. One night, I heard the poverty levels in the country announced on the radio. I asked Mama how much money we had each year. She laughed. I knew that meant we were poor; a joke—we were poorer than poor.

My Daddy grew up in the North. He always felt uncomfortable living in a segregated community. The daily humiliation, the signs telling coloreds to sit in the back of the bus, to use separate toilets and water fountains, rules about not being allowed to eat here and there because of your skin color. Getting off the train in Clarksville, some white locals said to my Daddy, "Where you going, yellow nigger?" Constant disrespect. He had to leave, go back North. Who can blame him?

My Mama told me that women around here are poor because they have too many babies. Southern black people at that time couldn't think of anything

(Continued)

Account: Growing Up Colored in the South during the 1950s   Continued

positive to do; we fight, fuck, and kill, and stay drunk on weekends. And talk shit. It was madness. People were crazy down there then, everywhere I turned. On Sunday mornings, somebody would stop by the house and give us reports of Saturday night fights, that so-and-so knifed somebody, and blah-blah-blah's wife shot somebody in the head. I knew by the first grade that I would be leaving ASAP. I had to get out of here, I thought, I must leave this dumb-ass town. I hated it. My Mama reminded me in case I forgot; don't get too comfortable down here, she said, when you can, get out of here.

She often showed me her scrapbook which she collected when she lived in Chicago. I looked at all the fun my parents had in Chicago. She told about the high times she and Daddy had, night-clubbing, going to Joe Louis fights—they whetted my appetite for the city lights. I saw that the Jim Crow laws and inferior schools held people back and lessened my chances of finding happiness in life. Plus it was so boring down there. She wanted me to have self-respect. She wanted me to have a better life and escape the crushing humiliation of a Jim Crow existence and crappy schools. I lived in a world of evil and I pushed it out of my consciousness. What could I do about it? I knew nothing I felt. It was a world in which white people simply did not see blacks. They only saw your skin color.

If it weren't for my big sister, I would have been even lonelier than I was. I was a light-skinned colored girl. Just as today, some black people expect whites to mistreat them because they don't like the color of their skin, I was on the lookout for black people who would mistreat me because they didn't like the fact that I was not dark enough— I was too light. In that little southern hometown community, there was always jealousy and envy, and a lot of it among girls was based on skin color and hair texture.

I'll call one girl I knew Frances. She had fallen for the propaganda she saw on TV and in the movies and magazines that said the only beautiful girl is one with light skin and long, straight hair. My skin was lighter than most of the colored

children's. Skin and hair were hugely important in the hearts and minds of the colored community in the South at that time. Even today, people aren't sure what my racial background is; am I Hispanic, Indian, white, black? When I say, light-skinned black, they say, "What's that?" In Frances' belief system, my skin color and almost-straight hair meant that I was beautiful. She thought I was more beautiful than she was—and better than her—and she presumed *I* thought so, too. So she punished me. Once, when I wanted to join a group of girls, including Frances, playing ball, Frances immediately said, "No—you think you're better than us." I was flabbergasted. I couldn't imagine where she got that idea from. I didn't think it, I didn't believe it. She wasn't talking about me. It was many years later that I realized Frances was talking about how *she* felt. She thought I was better than her, and she hated me for what she believed to be the truth. Eventually, after I hung around long enough watching them play each day, Frances' older sister said, "Aw, let her play," and I got to play softball. Still, Frances never liked me. She'd come up behind me in the crowded hallways between classes and shove me hard into the kid in front of me. I ignored her, acted like she hadn't pushed me. Eventually, she left me alone. But I didn't have any friends to share the experience with. So I went a little crazy—distorted perceptions arose in my psychological makeup.

Because my mother and my teachers thought I was pretty, my teachers entered me the Queen of the High School contests. "Pretty is as pretty does," my mother used to say, although enough boys said so. I was runner-up three times. I once lost to a light-skinned girl who was the daughter of a teacher in my school. When I had campaigned for votes, a teacher promised me that her class's votes would go to me. She was dating my ex-stepfather, who I called "Daddy Frank." At school football and basketball games, I'd see him and go up to him and say, "Hi, Daddy Frank." He'd say hi and ask for my wallet, which he called a "bill-fold," and slip in a dollar bill. But the teacher broke her promise, maybe because she was jealous of my being close to my stepfather, or maybe the teachers stuck together and elected the teacher's daughter. I just knew that the teacher had lied to me. She had told me that the class was going to vote for me for Queen. I felt wronged, ganged-up on. I lost respect for the teachers. I saw they were no better than everyone else; if they lie to a little girl, maybe they're even worse.

Another girl who beat me out for Queen of the High School (it was like a homecoming-type celebration) was a light-skinned daughter of one of the town's two colored doctors. This girl deserved to be Queen. She outclassed us all. My mother spent hours twirling my hair around the handle of a toy shovel to make a crop of Shirley Temple curls. After looking the chic hair style she had created, I hated it. I was a 13-year-old wearing a five-year-old's Shirley Temple curls. I was shocked and depressed by how current and up-to-date the other girl looked. She looked as good as any model in a magazine. Her dress was sophisticated. It was strapless; it was apparent that mine had been made by an amateur seamstress. I was so unhappy with the way I looked that Homecoming Day, I judged myself to be a country bumpkin in comparison to her. And I had to sit in the back of a convertible and wave to the crowd lining the streets, acting as though I was happy with the world when just the opposite was true.

I never bought into the colored community's concept of good and bad hair. Hair can't study for a test or obey parents. Hair can't be bad. Calling hair "bad" was a shorthand way of saying it had to be straightened with a hot comb. I thought the emphasis on hair was ridiculous and boring—unimportant—and I never thought light skin made a person beautiful. Frances was wrong about me; I thought she was beautiful, and I liked her hair. It was very short, like a boy's, but it fit her face. I didn't see the problem. I hated the fact that she didn't know that I thought she was cute.

Living in the South during Jim Crow was all you've read and heard about. The colored people were Democrats. Before every election, the Dems held a rally at the fair-grounds. They gave each colored family a chicken or a ham. This generosity was to show the coloreds that the Democrats were our friends. But as coloreds, we were supposed to sit at the back of the bus. One time, my sister and I didn't; we sat in the front seat. No driver with a heart could ask two cute little girls to go sit in the back of a half-empty bus.

I ran away from home—and left the South—at the age of sixteen. They spoke a different language in Chicago. I had to learn new words, a new pronunciation. That's why I say that standard English isn't my native language. In the fifties, most colored females wore their hair pressed—straightened and curled with a hot curling iron. Even some teen-aged boys and men wore their hair straightened, or "conked." It had been fried, and it was kind of wavy. Nat King Cole's hair was conked.

Afros didn't become fashionable until the sixties. One day, a black musician came up to me and before I knew what he was doing, he put his hand at the nape of my neck and quickly examined my hair there. (When I was growing up, we called that place the "kitchens.") He was trying to find out if my roots were nappy—whether I had "good" hair or "bad" hair, down to the roots. In the late sixties a male friend from the South came to visit me when I was living in New York. His hair was conked. I was about to say, "Aren't you a little behind the times?" But he stopped me by saying, "You don't do that," meaning, I don't criticize or shame other colored people. Meaning that, as a light-skinned person, I don't get to criticize people who are darker than me. I felt that that placed me as a kind of underdog with fewer rights because others believed that I had much more going for me because of my skin and hair than most colored people. To their way of thinking, I was ahead in the game. And the game was: The female who looks most like she's white, wins; she's the best. That was the message of race in our culture at the time. I resented it, but I shut up. Ironic, wasn't it? I believed that God made all of us, and all of us were beautiful in our own way. If we'll just be who we truly are.

I never understood the obsession with skin and hair. I figured that it's all good. A lot of people didn't. The person I loved most (outside of my Dad, who I loved symbolically and who I hardly ever saw), was an uncle by marriage. This uncle, Brother Wright, had nappy hair, thick lips, chocolate skin, and a wide nose. I wrote this in a song: "Brother Wright, a giant among less loving men.

(Continued)

Account: Growing Up Colored in the South during the 1950s   Continued

He gave whatever he could to whomever he saw needed help." Brother Wright was always kind to me. So I associate dark-skinned men with being decent and kind.

In the sixties, I went through a Black Power phase—I even dated Stokley Carmichael—even though I had been rejected by both races; I was too white for blacks, and too black for whites. Still, I love some people in both races. I value qualities in people that have nothing to do with race—being honest, fair-minded, color-blind, and having honor, integrity, courage, and decency. Skin color just tells us where your ancestors lived, it says nothing about a person's character. Being rejected by both races made me feel alone in the world—alone in all of God's creation. And the good of it was, this makes it impossible to play favorites. I look at people objectively. Not with bias. I see what you are, not what your skin color is.

QUESTIONS

Do you think that it is pejorative for a sociologist to refer to race and ethnicity as "deviant"? Is it "blaming the victim"? If we believe that this is true, why are we still using an archaic, essentialistic definition of deviance? Or is looking at race and ethnicity as deviance an effort to understand what the target of racism experiences? If racism is condemned in certain social circles, isn't racism *itself* a form of deviance? If it's wrong to stigmatize someone for his or her racial status, then why do some people do it? If sociologists attempt to understand or empathize with the drug abuser, shouldn't they also attempt to understand or empathize with the racially stigmatized person as well? And if so, should they attempt the same process with the racist—the person who discriminates? Why or why not? Judging from Michelle Birdsong's account, describing her experiences in the 1950s, do you believe that racist behavior has changed in the past five or six decades? Has tribal and racial stigmatizing and deviantizing disappeared in the United States? Or does it still exist in more subtle forms? Consider her experiences; as she said, she was "deviantized" by both whites and blacks. Growing up today, would a person of her appearance suffer the same racial reproach? Is it legitimate to consider racial prejudice and genocide and "ethnic cleansing" as part of the same spectrum—tribal stigma? Knowing that representatives or members of the dominant ethnic group killed millions of people belonging to non-dominant ethnicities in Rwanda, Congo, Armenia, Nazi-occupied Europe, Imperial Japan–occupied China and Korea, and North America, we encounter a tormenting dilemma: Which is deviant—*persecuting* members of a non-dominant ethnic group or *belonging* to a non-dominant ethnic group? If it is the former, then how do we account for the marginalization and the persecution? If it is the latter, then how do we account for the fact that monstrous, horrendous acts can be condoned, legitimated, even encouraged, by the powerful? And if such acts have been perpetrated by powerful ethnicities against less powerful ones, going back to Chapter 1, doesn't this stress the historical *relativity* of what's defined as deviance? Or are some acts so horrendous that situational, societal, and historical relativity don't apply? Doesn't looking at ethnicity as deviance take a giant step away from the charge, made by Alexander Liazos (1972) decades ago, that sociologists tend to focus on "nuts, sluts, and deviated preverts"?

Summary and Conclusions

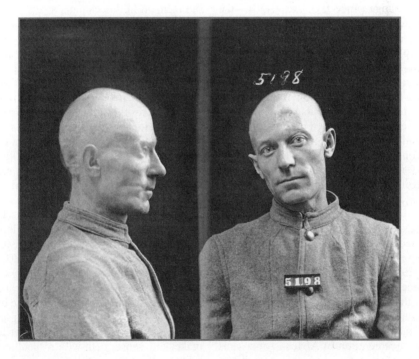

Learning Objective:

After reading this chapter, you will be able to:

- synthesize and analyze the information presented in the text on deviant behavior.

The first edition of this book was published in 1978. The changes in deviance and crime that have taken place in American society specifically, and the Western world more generally, have been remarkable and, in their confluence, unprecedented. Here, I have attempted to document and explicate them. Perhaps most notably among these changes is the fact that the rate of criminal behavior—to focus for the moment exclusively on the Index Crimes—has declined to a degree unknown since such records have been kept. Crimes such as robbery and motor vehicle theft have declined by more than half, and murder, rape, and serious assault, by roughly 40 percent.

At the same time, and seemingly contradictorily—and this is another consequential and remarkable change since the late 1970s—the rate of incarceration, as measured by the jail and prison population, has skyrocketed, tripling, even quadrupling, since 1980. In, again, a seemingly contradictory fashion, thirdly, tolerance and acceptance for a range of unconventional, even deviant behaviors, have grown to the point where activities that were illegal, considered serious normative violations, which once drew strong criticism and condemnation, are now ignored, accepted, considered variations on a mainstream theme, as for example, premarital intercourse, birth control, abortion, interracial marriage, homosexual relations, gay marriage, small-quantity marijuana possession, and marijuana as medicine. Racial prejudice and ethnic intolerance have declined, diversity has grown and almost inevitably will continue to grow, and residential segregation of racial and ethnic groups has declined. According to the U.S. Census Bureau, even before the middle of the twenty-first century, no single racial or ethnic group will constitute a majority of the population.

And yet, incarceration of African Americans continues to grow relative to that of whites. Today, blacks are arrested twice as frequently as their numbers would predict and are incarcerated at a rate nearly seven times that of whites. (And they are six times as likely to become a victim of criminal homicide.) And even though the use of illicit psychoactive substances is lower and more moderated than it was at its peak in the late seventies and early eighties, half a million people are currently incarcerated for drug offenses—*ten*

times the number as was true in 1980. More generally, as we saw, more than half of the jail and prison population was imprisoned for a non-violent offense. We live, it seems, in an era of "mass incarceration," an age in which a mother of three can receive a *mandatory* sentence of life in prison for (presumptively) unknowingly keeping a quantity of cocaine for a former boyfriend (Tierney, 2012). Moreover, economic distribution in the United States has become more unequal, with the rich monopolizing an ever-greater proportion of the gross domestic product, and the economic gap increasing between the rich and the poor. Since 2008, the economy has stagnated and, adjusting for standard dollars, the poor earn less than they did in the late 1960s. And deviance is a substantial element in this change, since, in many ways, poverty activates disrepute. Hence, while in some ways, matters are improving over time—we certainly live in a more cosmopolitan era than was true in the past—in other ways, the situation of the modal American is worsening.

Poverty is *strongly* related to imprisonment. Relative to other industrialized societies, the United States incarcerates convicted felons for significantly longer sentences, and for many more non-violent crimes (principally drug possession and sale). Today, prisoners serve longer sentences than ever before in the history of this country, remaining inmates "into middle age and old age, well beyond the peak age for crime," which is the late teenage years (Tierney, 2013, p. D6). According to the latest statistics (p. D6), black men in their 20s and early 30s without a high school diploma are more likely to be incarcerated (40%) than they are to have a job (30%). The problem is not that these men are being incarcerated—some men deserve a prison sentence—it is that they are being imprisoned far longer than makes any sense, both with respect to their rehabilitation and the cost of long-term incarceration on their neighborhoods, that is, keeping their families' poor and a segment of their residents off the employment rolls and not earning money and not contributing to their communities' economy. And disproportionally high rates of imprisonment fall unevenly on the shoulders of poor people, and African Americans, and hence, these negative consequences *further entrench* poor, black people in poverty, and make them even more vulnerable to reincarceration (Tierney, 2013). For instance, incarceration has a catastrophic impact on the convict's family, and the longer he is imprisoned, the more devastating this impact will be: higher rates of illness, including mental disorder, behavioral problems, and mortality of his children and even of his spouse or partner. Our society must decide whether it wishes to pursue a policy of excessive and counter-productive punishment of offenders, or simply punish and deviantize offenders simply for the sake of retribution and revenge.

We live, it seems, in an era in which two visions struggle for hegemony: a liberal, tolerant vision, in which peccadillos and legal blunders are granted some leeway, where minor forms of deviance are tolerated, even incorporated into the mainstream, where "the culture of civility" (Becker, 1971) has become the norm, alongside a different vision, a vision that is more repressive, more punitive, more protective, where the interpretation of the rules is stricter and punishment is more likely and harsher. On some issues and in some geographical areas, the more liberal, cosmopolitan, more progressive vision wins out; on others, the more conservative, protective, and traditional vision triumphs.

In the United States over time, as I said, incomes are becoming more maldistributed; the rich are becoming richer and the income of the poor, is (in adjusted dollars) stagnating, even declining relative to the past. The *percentage* of the total Gross Domestic Product is becoming more unequal, and this growing inequality is having a significant impact on deviance, crime, and criminalization. The poor are substantially more likely to become ill and die prematurely, and here, the sick are treated with condescension, pity, and an emotion that borders on disdain. Poverty is itself a form of deviance, and several theories of deviance argue that poverty is strongly related to a number of deviant behaviors, the Index Crimes most notable among them. It is possible that, in an economically polarized society, the affluent are more likely to feel scorn for the poor than the rich do in a more economically equitable society, and are more likely to engage in a range of deviant activities.

* * *

In 2012, the American voters defeated a Republican candidate and temporarily checkmated conservative ideology, at least in the matter of *social* issues. (Over the past several decades, *economic* ideology in the United States has moved substantially to the right, a separate but related matter.) It's possible that the shrinking percentage of white males in the American population will force conservatives to re-think how to fashion the planks on which the Republicanism platform is built. Social conservatism is based on a religious and quasi-religious moralism that may be shrinking in influence and adherence among the American population to the point where it cannot sustain the election of a national candidate. Several of those planks include strong opposition to gay rights, a rigidly anti-abortion stance, strong support for a traditional women's role, staunch anti-secularism, and an uncompromising position on the criminalization of illicit drugs, including opposition to medical marijuana and the decriminalization of marijuana. The 2012 election exposed the ideological cracks and splinters in those planks.

Currently, seven jurisdictions—six states and the District of Columbia—sanction gay or same-sex marriage, and all of them have come by this legal status legislatively or judicially; in contrast, 32 straight elections have voted down such a proposal. But in the 2012 contest, that changed; three states—Maine, Washington, and Maryland—voted to legalize same-sex marriage; Minnesota voted to end the ban against gay marriage. A sign of things to come? Perhaps. In any case, in 2013, the Supreme Court's decision to permit same-sex marriage in Utah, an extremely conservative state, indicates future legal acceptance in all states of the Union; supporters of gay marriage are overjoyed and pundits predict a nullification of the "defense of marriage" laws that prevail in conservative states. On election night, discussing the development of the vote, political commentator George Will stated that the issue of being gay "is boring—it's like being left-handed." Not all Americans feel that way, but the election, and Will's comment, add further evidence to the disappearing stigma of being gay. In addition, seven-term congresswoman Tammy Baldwin became the first openly gay U.S. Senator, and the only openly gay *non-incumbent* ever to have been elected to Congress. (Seven gay Representatives of the House had previously announced their sexual orientation *during* their term of office—two were involuntarily ousted—and some were reelected, some weren't.) Baldwin is also Wisconsin's only female senator in the state's history; the 2012 election likewise voted into the House of Representatives Kyrsten Sinesma, an openly bisexual Democrat from Arizona. The respectability and hence, political electability, of gay candidates, as reflected by the election of 2012, once again indicates that in many areas of the country, homosexuality is "exiting from deviance." At this writing, the Boy Scouts of America, one of the country's most venerable and mainstream institutions, is debating whether to drop the ban on gay scouts—which, if the step is taken, would represent a truly momentous step in the direction of acceptance of homosexuality.

The progress of women's rights was likewise advanced by the fact that two senators who made statements that were widely interpreted as belittling the appalling experience of women becoming pregnant after having been raped were voted out of office. In the months before the election, Richard Murdock of Indiana said: "Life is a gift from God. And, I think, even when life begins in that horrible situation of rape, it is something that God intended to happen." Joe Donnelly, a Democrat, decisively defeated Murdock, and the incumbent's comment may have played a role in his defeat. Likewise, only months before the 2012 election, Senator Todd Aiken stated, with reference to a woman's pregnancy and the possibility of her having to seek an abortion: "If it's a legitimate rape, the female body has ways of shutting that whole thing down," a statement that was widely denounced not only as grossly insensitive but shockingly unscientific. Claire McCaskill, the incumbent—who in 2006 became the first U.S. Senator from Missouri—trounced Aiken to the tune of a 54 to 39 percent vote. Again, the election may presage a growing tendency toward women's rights, a woman's right to choose, and a more sophisticated tendency on the part of the American public to distinguish between once-illegal, *non-victim* unconventional acts (such as having an abortion) and crimes that entail a victim (such as rape). Anti-abortionists or pro-lifers believe that abortion is murder, and they base this belief on the assumption that *at the moment of the penetration of the human egg* by the sperm, the

resulting zygote is a full-fledged human being. Persons who are pro-choice are not so much pro-abortion as in favor of *the woman's right to choose*. The pro-choice position argues that a zygote is not a full-fledged human being, adopting the position that the exact moment when the process of the human soul or "spirit" enters the fetus cannot be determined scientifically. Hence, they do not consider aborting the fetus as murder. For the voters in Indiana and Missouri, the candidate's position on victim's rights outweighed his or her position on fetal rights.

Two other votes cast during the 2012 election bear mentioning. While 18 states have legalized medical marijuana (the possession and sale of the drug at the federal level remains a crime) and a dozen states have decriminalized the possession of small quantities of the drug, until this election, no state (and no jurisdiction in the world) has *voted* to legalize recreational marijuana—until now. In 2012, the voters of Colorado and Washington State elected to legalize the sale of marijuana specifically for the purpose of getting high. (Oregon defeated a similar bill.) According to the provisions of Colorado's bill, a resident can grow up to six marijuana plants; by the lights of Washington's bill, users will be able to purchase the substance from state-licensed providers. At this writing, it is too early to know whether and how authorities will implement these voting decisions. Some observers foresee a federal crackdown on the dispensation of marijuana. But as we know from the chapter on drug use as deviance, a Gallup poll indicated that roughly half of the American population believes in some form of marijuana legalization, and these elections may give us a clue to the likelihood of that belief's legal institutionalization. Still, politicians don't want to seem as if they are "soft on drugs" and hence, typically avoid mentioning the issue.

In short, the election of 2012 may have presaged a growing *de-deviantization* of several activities, beliefs, and conditions that were once condemned. Edwin Schur's classic, *Crimes without Victims* (1965), which argued in favor of the decriminalization of three then-illegal actions or conditions—abortion, homosexuality, and drug addiction—was prescient. In the United States, homosexual acts were decriminalized in the 1960s, abortion in the 1970s, and, though the possession of most psychoactive substances remains illicit, hundreds of thousands of addicts are now treated in a range of facilities across the countries rather than imprisoned, and small-quantity marijuana possession is increasingly becoming semi-decriminalized. What is happening today, and what may have been manifested in the 2012 election, could represent changes as momentous as those that began in the 1960s. American evangelical and conservative Christians were "absolutely shocked" by the "avalanche" of the electoral results of 2012, says Albert Mohler, Jr., President of the Southern Baptist Theological Seminary. The "entire moral landscape" of the country has changed, he said. "An increasingly secularized America understands our positions, and rejects them" (Goodstein, 2012b, p. A3).

Consider some of the changes in social attitudes the election revealed. About a fifth of American adults say they have no religious affiliation; a third of eighteen to twenty-two-year-olds say they are atheists, agnostics or "nothing in particular" with respect to religion. And "nones" are more likely to vote for liberal candidates and support same-sex marriage and other gay rights issues. Conservative churches such as the Southern Baptist Convention and Assemblies of God are losing members and their membership is aging. Catholic bishops have been railing against gay rights and especially gay marriage and tolerance for abortion, policies that President Obama supports, yet Obama retained the Catholic vote (by a narrow margin), 50 to 48 percent. And he overwhelmingly won the Latino vote—71 percent of Hispanics voted for Obama—in spite of the fact that the vast majority are Catholics. Clearly, Obama's more liberal stand on immigration was more important to them than the abortion issue (Goodstein, 2012b).

This is far from saying that deviance is dying. Humans will always react negatively to actions, beliefs, and conditions they consider wrong. But exactly what is considered wrong changes over time. Consider the fact that the first substantive chapter of a deviance textbook published more than forty years ago (Bell, 1971) discussed premarital sex as a form of deviance, which was followed by a chapter on birth control, then one on abortion. These behaviors will continue to be considered deviant—but not to the majority, though to

a dwindling minority. Moreover, in an increasingly tolerant society, in which the majority accepts or tolerates a growing number of once-condemned activities, intolerance will increasingly be regarded as deviance. In a society that, increasingly, adopts a "live and let live" attitude, peers who denounce unconventionality may themselves become increasingly denounced. Consider race. At one time, many white Americans considered being black as stigmatizing—a "stain," a form of deviance. Today, someone who expresses racist views is condemned. What won't change is that no society, including ours, can relinquish its punishment of crimes that entail true victimization—larceny, rape, robbery, and murder—though a more secular, less condemnatory society may very well stress less harsh punishment and treatment or rehabilitation. And of course, the cornerstone of all of this change is secularization—the decline of a strong, muscular, punitive Christianity, and the strengthening of an attitude that religious traditionalism should not wield control over the lives of *nonbelievers* or adherents of a different faith. "Blue laws" (bans on selling during the Sabbath) used to keep stores closed on Sunday; today, shopping at the local mall on Sundays has become a kind of family custom. What is likely to come out of all this is that over time, a more liberal stance for mainstream Christianity will take hold, and the conservative, Bible-based, evangelical "Tea Party" right will decline in influence. None of this discussion should be interpreted to mean that I endorse these changes. Here, I am describing, analyzing, and noting what the changes mean for the future of the social construction of deviance. In the future, who and what is condemned is changing, and it is likely to change dramatically over the course of the coming generation.

* * *

Sociologists do not regard deviance as a hard, definite, and concrete "thing" like a Monarch butterfly, a sycamore tree, or a gold nugget, but a socially constructed category whose reality is subject to debate, argument, struggle, relativity, and change, the outcome of the exercise of power by one sector of the society over another, or the fluctuating or changing will of the majority. What's deviant is what the social definitions and judgments say it is; certain judgments of deviance may be widely shared—for instance, whether a given killing by Person A of Person B is a murder. But our job as sociologists is not to justify one definition of deviance over another but to understand how certain dominant definitions came into being and how they work, and what consequences they have. In the realm we're exploring here, when it comes to definitions of deviance, there isn't any clear-cut right or wrong, though there may be victims, and there are greater, or lesser, degrees of agreement in the population with regard to wrongness and victimhood. All definitions of right or wrong are social constructions of reality that sectors of the society *assert* are right or wrong, and take steps to affirm the correctness of that definition.

Deviance entails wrongdoing from the perspective of the members of one or more collectivities in a given society. Acts defined as deviant are not necessarily harmful, though they may be. The prohibitions that ban them are not always religious in origin, though they may be. Actions regarded as deviant are not necessarily against the law, though they may be. What is judged as deviant is not usually a manifestation of a mental disorder, but it very, very occasionally is. The efforts of certain parties to define acts, beliefs, or characteristics as deviant may or may not be widely practiced, but the greater the number of people or institutions that define something as deviant, the more likely it is to exemplify what sociologists *mean* by deviance. The sentiment that supports condemnation need not be widespread—there's no exact line that the sociological observer can draw and declare, *here* we have an instance of deviance on our hands, *there* we don't—but, once again, the more widespread a given judgment is, the more certain sociologists are that they have a case of deviance on their hands.

And sociologists need not agree with public judgments that condemn deviance; all that is necessary to define deviance is that, somewhere, at some time, we can observe that negative sentiment expressed in real-world condemnation and punishment. No value judgment whatsoever is expressed by the concept of deviance. No one is condemned *when the sociologist uses the terms* "deviant" or "deviance." But when members of the society condemn certain actions, beliefs, and conditions—when they use words and engage in actions virtually everyone agrees are negative, hostile, punishing, and denunciatory—they regard them as deviant. It is the condemnation that expresses and *manifests* the sentiment, the state of social being. The sociologist is not the conveyor of that sentiment; it is the members of the society, whose reactions the sociologists describe and analyze, who convey that sentiment.

Deviance, like nearly everything in the social world, is a matter of degree, not an either-or proposition. Some normative violations are regarded as so heinous, so seriously deviant, that the members of some societies in which such violations occur put such offenders to death; other violations shame, humiliate, and stigmatize the offender for life; still others engender a "slap on the wrist" punishment that the offender shrugs off, their consequences, neither very serious nor long-lasting. Though all of us commit normative violations, not all of us commit violations that corrupt and taint our identities in significant ways.

Moreover, as I've emphasized, deviance is relative to time and place; it is an elastic concept. What is considered and reacted to as wrong or bad changes over time and varies from one society and social context to another. Acts for which people were once burned at the stake—religious heresy, apostasy, nonconformity, and dissent— now produce no outcry, no serious condemnation or punishment. On the other hand, what's considered "politically incorrect" behavior and utterances—for instance, those now seen as insulting to women, persons of African descent, the physically disabled, that once went unpunished, uncommented on, even encouraged— are likely to draw punishment and condemnation today. At one time, smoking was allowed in most indoor places; now, mostly, it is banned. In other words, for some acts and expressed beliefs, the line designating what's considered deviant, is now drawn "up" rather than "down" (Krauthammer, 1993; Moynihan, 1993). A century ago, married politicians often engaged in extramarital affairs. Such behavior touched off a wink and a nod; it was considered the privilege of the male members of a certain class and power stratum. Presidents who carried on extramarital affairs include Warren Harding, Franklin Delano Roosevelt, John F. Kennedy, and Lyndon Baines Johnson. But times have changed, and now, the careers of political figures who engage in such behavior, once discovered and made public, crash and burn or become seriously tainted by the scandal and spectacle that results. The authority of President Bill Clinton's presidency was seriously undermined as a result of his lying about his sexual dalliance with white House aide Monica Lewinsky in 1995–1996. In 2012, David Petraeus resigned as Director of the Central Intelligence Agency (CIA) because of the revelation of his long-time affair with his biographer Paula Broadwell. Times change, the norms change, and public reactions to the norms likewise change. It is an axiom of this book that *the social construction of deviance* is relative to time and place.

"Is America dead"? That question is on the July 30, 2012 cover of *New York* magazine, and the theme of its lead story. Its answer, "Um, no," tells the reader that the United States has declined in certain respects but it's still very much alive. That's how I feel about the field of the sociology of deviance: It's not in its glory days, but it's still a vigorous and important area of investigation. The study of deviance has undergone a *renaissance*, according to a team of sociologists (Dellwing, Katarba, and Pino, 2014). It's difficult to disagree with them.

Nonetheless, in the past decade or two, some critics have put forth the charge that "the sociology of deviance is dead," or even more generally, "deviance is dead," that the study of deviant behavior is outmoded, passé, no longer applicable to contemporary society (Sumner, 1994; Hendershott, 2002). Oddly enough, the two sides to this argument are contradictory. The radical, liberal, and humanistic supporters of the "deviance is dead" argument claim that the term, "deviance," insults and demeans the participants of the behaviors, beliefs, and conditions it examines (Liazos, 1972; Sumner, 1994)—in a phrase, that the study of deviance is a conservative or reactionary enterprise. In contrast, the *conservative* or *reactionary* "deviance is dead-ers" argue that the course, the subjects, and the books on the subject has spawned tolerance and acceptance of deviance, which is a very bad thing. Instead, we should be reminded that deviance is wrongful, harmful behavior—that which is "contrary to natural law" (Hendershott, 2002, p. 163)—clearly, charging the study of deviance with a *liberal* or

radical bias. Of course, both can't be true, and both miss the point completely, which is whether or not the study of deviance is "dead" has nothing to do with whether students walk out of a deviance course with *less* or *more* respect toward the unconventional members of our society. My experience with teaching the course inclines me to agree more with Hendershott than Liazos on this question, that is, students who take this course tend to emerge with more rather than less tolerance toward putative deviants.

But on either side, the "deviance is dead" argument may be one of the silliest claims ever made by more than one sociologist. Deviance is an analytic concept; it is relevant to social life everywhere, and it will be relevant for as long as humans exist and possess analytic powers to reflect on their own behavior. No society has ever existed without having created and enforced social norms, and none has existed without their violation. Some of us in every society will be unable or unwilling to abide by all the rules society sets; some of us will resort to cutting corners, lying, cheating, stealing, scheming, philandering, and even engaging in violence to get what we want. It is in the nature of being human that we engage in deviance—some of us more frequently and in more serious ways than others. Moreover, since deviance is also about condemnation, the reactions that certain actions and expressed beliefs touch off—even unjust accusations—will always be with us. Without any measure of social control, or the effort to bring violators into line and ensure the conventional social order, society will collapse into chaos and disintegration. And in all societies, some injustice prevails; sometimes, one party will lodge a false accusation against another, and the second will suffer an unjust conviction for a crime he or she didn't commit. It is true that *the angle of vision* that the sociology of deviance perspective offers is not as productive for some matters as for others, and—who knows?—such an inquiry may fall out of fashion. But *deviance* is one of the most generic and ubiquitous social phenomena in existence, relevant for practically everything in which the sociologists might be interested. To my mind, the "the sociology of deviance is dead" position was stillborn the moment it was conceived, and the "the sociology of deviance is experiencing a renaissance" position (Dellwing, Katarba, and Pino, 2014) reflects the view that the study of non-normative behavior is unlikely to disappear any time soon.

At the 2011 York Deviancy Conference, presenters gave 175 papers on multiple aspects of deviance; their abstracts filled 70 pages of 11-point type. The conference was truly international, with presenters from, and teaching at universities in, locales all over the globe—Canada and the West Indies; Mexico and Argentina; Oslo, Stockholm, Copenhagen, and Helsinki; Barcelona and Lisbon;and Armenia, Poland, Cyprus, South Africa, India, Tasmania, Queensland, and Melbourne. This conference, and the background of its speakers, gives pie-in-the-face testimony to the fact that, rather than being "dead," the sociology of deviance is very much alive and well—indeed, is flourishing—and is studied by sociologists literally all over the world. Moreover, the papers tell us that the deviance concept has become extremely diverse, having transmogrified into something far broader than the narrow notion that its critics stereotypically imagined it to be. The conference also reminds us that what is practiced in the United States under the banner of the sociology of deviance may be more uniform than its cousins elsewhere in the world—the former, perhaps reflected by the articles published in the American journal, *Deviant Behavior*, and the latter, very likely, by the conference papers. The American version of the sociology of deviance is more pragmatic, more policy-oriented, and perhaps more aligned with criminology and the field of criminal justice, while the international version is more theoretical, free-wheeling, open, diverse, and politically attuned.

It is true that some sociologists of deviance define their mission in a positivistic, essentialistic fashion. They define deviance as an objectivistic and concrete phenomenon, a reality in the material world whose enactment demands deterministic, cause-and-effect explanations. Certain measurable conditions—such as anomie, the failure of parents to appropriately sanction and socialize children, the effectiveness of communities and neighborhoods to control the behavior of their residents—cause or encourage deviance *in general*. To the sociologists who devise such explanations, the study of deviance represents a scientific or positivistic mission. How do we explain or account for deviant behavior? Why do some people engage in deviance? What is it about certain people that causes them to engage in this identifiable behavior? In what types of societies is deviance more common? In what types of societies is it rarer? Such a mission hardly ever encompasses deviant *beliefs*, and it never addresses deviant *traits*. Even though all explanatory sociologists agree that deviance is relative to time and place and would reject the label of essentialists, some argue that we can devise theories that account for its enactment. Contemporary versions of causal theories of deviance have argued that an array of factors—including psychological disorder, a rationalistic calculation of pleasure and pain, social disorganization, anomie or social strain, differentially associating with peers who define wrongdoing in positive terms, a lack of social control, a lack of self-control—causes untoward behavior. If one or more of these factors cause "deviant" behavior, then by definition, all deviance must have something in common, must have some common thread or "essence" that connects the cause with the consequence. Or so the positivistic approach reasons. There is no doubt that this is true in a general sense, but deviance is a constructed phenomenon, and hence, *some* forms of deviance are not connected in any way to the factors these positivistic explanations presuppose.

In contrast to the positivistic approach, other sociologists define their mission primarily in constructionist terms. What needs to be explained, they say, is how and why certain rules come to be made and enforced, and what happens to offenders who violate them. How are acts, beliefs, and traits organized into a coherent framework or set of rules, the violation of which results in scorn, stigma, ridicule, pity, scorn, and/or hostility toward the violator? Is condemnation a simple product of real and present threat or danger to the society, or is threat and danger more symbolic, abstract, spiritual, and emblematic of a realm of meaning that exists to some extent independent of threats to society's material survival? Constructionist theories include labeling theory, conflict theory, feminist theory, and controlology, or the new sociology of social control. In addition, constructionism pays close attention to the inner world of the deviant: how persons defined and labeled as deviant experience stigma and social condemnation.

Any sociologist contemplating a description of the extent and scope of deviance must consider the realms in which normative violations occur. Such a consideration inevitably runs into the issue of numbers as well as seriousness. How many people are judged to be on the wrong side of the norms, and how serious are these violations? In other words, as a criterion that enables us to select topics on specific forms of deviance, we have to consider how many people we are talking about and how much of a violation has taken place. Textbooks that discuss deviance in general are likely to include chapters on alcohol and drug abuse, sexual violations, criminal behavior, economic malfeasances, deviant beliefs, deviant physical characteristics, and mental disorder. The inclusion of these topics for discussion, again, makes sense by virtue of the fact that they are relatively common and are regarded as relatively serious normative violations. Critics who call for a discussion of very different topics usually fail to consider one or the other or both of these topics. An instructor or author who complains that sociologists of deviance typically trot out a "freak of the week" for discussion—and offers alternative candidates (Liazos, 1972; Lauderdale, 2011, p. xi)—must contend with these two considerations.

The subject of deviance is foundational for sociology. It spells out processes, issues, and subjects that are essential for any consideration of how society works. Deviance is neither marginal nor trivial for an understanding of the social order. It is central to everything we see and experience in the social world, from the economic to the religious realm, from birth to death, and from the intimacy of a love affair to the public proclamations made on the soap box and the drama of the television and movie screen. Without an understanding of deviance, we cannot comprehend social relations, social interaction, the workings of the community, or, indeed, what we call the human spark. To simplify the matter, "Deviance is us," and it will remain "us" forever. Every thinking person has an obligation to understand it—and hence, the field of the sociology of deviance, and hence, the appearance of this book.

* * *

In 2012, Andrew Solomon, author of The *Noonday Demon: An Atlas of Depression* (2001), a memoir about the author's own experience with clinical depression, published *Far From the Tree*, a study of how parents deal with the deviancies—dwarfism, Down Syndrome, autism, schizophrenia, children conceived in rape, those who become transgendered or criminal, and, oddly, those who are prodigies—of their children. Except for the prodigies, any of these categories could fit comfortably in the chapters of this book. Solomon interviewed 300 parents of children with one of the conditions listed in the table of contents. A physician told the parents of a newborn: "You have given birth to a circus dwarf." The father of a disabled daughter told the author: "You go to Central Park with a special-needs child, and the other parents look straight through you. They would never think to come over and suggest that their child could play with your child." Until his daughter was born, he said, "I was one of those people" (2012, p. 75). It is true that, for the conventionals or "normal" who interact with their children, compassion is sometimes mingled with contempt and rejection, but these parents are never free from the fear that someone, at some time, will do something terrible to their children because of their condition.

Solomon is a "*lumper*," that is, he works with a very broad conceptualization of his subject; what do, say, dwarfism and being a criminal have in common? Even the people Solomon interviewed for his book "were put off by the broadness of his book" (p. 76). Deaf people, he said, didn't want to be compared with schizophrenics, who in turn didn't want to be put into the same category as dwarfs; criminals couldn't stand the idea that they had anything meaningful in common with transgendered individuals. Certainly from a *moralistic* point of view, this is true; most of us regard crime as an individual choice and dwarfism as a genetic condition that no one chooses. But what they have in common is the stigma (again, with the peculiar exception of bring a prodigy) that their possessors attract from the conventional or, in Goffman's term, "normal" public. And what they have in common is, as Solomon stresses, the unusual emotional and logistical demands they all place on the parents of such children. As the parent of an autistic son, I have no difficulty assigning my experiences to the same category as those that a parent of a schizophrenic, disabled, deaf, or Down Syndrome child is forced to struggle with. Yes, as *all* of the parents Solomon interviewed agreed, such experiences brought about in them a greater sense of compassion. But virtually none of the parents would have *chosen* such conditions for their children, nor would they have wanted their children to have suffered the taunts and ridicule they had to endure. And in that sense, these conditions *do* belong to the same category; all are deviant, all are stigmatized, and all are a fit subject for this book.

My wife, Barbara, and I are the sorts of parents Solomon describes. We have a son, Danny, who fell "far from the tree." He is not like us in that he is autistic, and yes, his behavior, regarded as odd, eccentric, annoying, and peculiar by many of the people he encounters, creates problems for us—as it does for him. Hence, I have chosen our son, through me as his interlocutor, to offer the last account in this book.

Account: Autism

Autism is typically diagnosed in early childhood. Parents usually become aware of the condition when the child exhibits what is euphemistically referred to as "speech delay"—an inability to verbally communicate at the appropriate age, usually by two or three. Most children whose speech is delayed are not autistic. At one time, experts estimated that perhaps two out of every 1,000 children in the general population were autistic. Now, according to the Centers for Disease Control and Prevention, the estimate is one out of 88. Autism is a "spectrum disorder," which means that it manifests itself throughout a broad range of seriousness, from nearly normal to severe. The hallmark of Autism Spectrum Disorder (ASD) is impaired social interaction. "As early as infancy, a baby with ASD may be unresponsive to people or focus intently on one item to the exclusion of others for long periods of time." Early indicators include: no babbling or pointing by age one; no single words by 16 months or two-word phrases by age two; no response to name; poor eye contact; no smiling or social responsiveness. Later indicators include an inability to sustain a conversation; stereotyped, repetitive, or unusual use of language; restricted patterns of interest; preoccupation with certain objects or subjects; inflexible adherence to specific routines or rituals. The theory that parental practices are responsible for ASD "has long been disproven." There "is no cure for autism." (See the pamphlet issued by the National Institute of Neurological Disorders and Stroke,

10/22/2012). The unusual behaviors and speech patterns of autistic individuals cause difficulties for them in interacting with others, which frequently draws attention to them, sometimes attracting derision and conflict. At one time, supposed experts such as Bruno Bettelheim (the toxic and tyrannous monster of many an autistic parent) regarded autism as characterized by the child's withdrawal from social interaction and an inability to speak. One of Danny's oddities of speech is that his daily volume of words is enormous—a virtual Niagara of speaking; he speaks, it sometimes seems, almost nonstop, and most of the time, it is to himself, frequently while he is alone, and frequently when he is in a public setting. Sociologically, it is the derision and conflict that Danny attracts from what Goffman refers to as "normals" that defines the autistic as deviant.

Danny, our autistic son, is now 24 years old.

"Aloysius O'Hare [from Dr. Seuss' *The Lorax*] is *such* an odious villain," Danny announced at lunch with an emotion that bordered on vehemence. "I hate him so much!"

"But Danny," my wife Barbara replied, "Aloysius O'Hare is a fictional villain. He doesn't exist in the real world. Why are you getting so worked up about this?"

"To me, fiction is more real than what you call the real world," he replied.

"I'm a little distressed," his mom replied, "that you're getting so angry about the fictional world. There are lots of things that are far more important in the real world. The fictional world just *feels* real to you."

"Not to me," Danny replied. "It *is* real."

"I'm just trying to get you to pay attention to things you have to take care of in the here and now. We are trying to prepare you for independent living," she said. "It's not that far off, you know."

"I don't want you to cramp my style. I am what I am, and that's all there is to it."

"I'm your parent, Danny, and I have a responsibility to teach you how to live on your own."

"You're my parent and I'm your son. You should understand me."

Danny decided to go out and buy a Coke Zero. A moment later, we could hear a loud monologue on the sidewalk, two floors below our terrace. Barbara stepped out onto the terrace and yelled down to Danny that he was talking too loudly.

"OK Mom," he replied, "I'll try to be a little quieter."

On Saturday and Sunday mornings, when we're sitting at our breakfast counter quietly having a copy of coffee, Danny comes in and, with his big, loud, booming voice, offers a rendition of what he's being reading or watching lately. "In *A Bad Case of Stripes*, Camilla turns all kinds of funny colors. She doesn't care what other kids think of her after she eats lima beans."

"Danny, can you please lower your voice. We're trying to drink our coffee and read the paper in peace."

"Lima is an anagram of 'Male.'"

"Could you lower your voice, Danny, we'd like some peace and quiet."

We see a sour look on Danny's face; he stalks out of the room, unable to understand that our interests are different from his.

Autism, a spectrum disorder, manifests itself in a myriad of ways. One of them, presumably, is in a "withdrawal" from reality. This doesn't apply at all to Danny; he is firmly in touch with what we refer to as the real or material world—but he isn't always that interested in it. To him, the fantasy world is vastly more real, vibrant, and captivating.

"I once tried to interest Miyazaki and Studio Ghibli to do a sequel or a prequel of *Spirited Away* with mice and elephants using its characters in the *Kingdom Hearts* series, once known as Square, but my plan ended in failure." Danny means that he wrote and mailed off several letters to the famed Japanese filmmaker suggesting his idea, but received no reply. *Kingdom Hearts* is an immensely successful interactive role-playing series of videogames, many involving Disney characters; it is produced jointly by Square Enix, a Japanese studio, and Disney Interactive. Danny is a huge fan of Disney and Japanese animated cartoons, especially those produced by Studio Ghibli. A few of his favorite movies include Disney's *The Princess and the Frog, Fantasia* (specifically the dinosaur sequence, which he has watched literally hundreds of times), *The Wind in the Willows, Legend of Sleepy Hollow,* and *The Simpsons Movie, Who Framed Roger Rabbit,* Hayao Miyazaki's *Princess Mononoke, Spirited Away,* and *Kiki's Delivery Service*— though he is fascinated by and discusses at length the complex moral dilemmas posed by *Pinocchio and Castle in the Sky* or those faced by Sora of the *Kingdom Hearts* series, and he fumes at the outrage of the evil deeds committed by the likes of Filcher in *Black Beauty,* Mansley of *The Iron Giant,* and the doings of Master Xehanort and the personnel of the True Organization XIII in *Kingdom Hearts.*

Danny has a rich fantasy life and relatively little understanding of how the world of practical affairs works. Most of the time, he is capable of negotiating physical cause-and-effect (when you cross the street, look for oncoming traffic, when you drop something, it's going to fall), enacting routine, day-to-day commerce (buying items in the deli and the supermarket), and navigating the streets of New York and its subway system— but most ordinary human relations frequently flummox and frustrate him. He is very articulate and talkative, though most of what he says is a monologue directed to no one in particular. He frequently walks around the apartment, and even in public, babbling to himself. He speaks of many themes, but those that are most persistent are centered on two subjects: his

(Continued)

Account: Autism   Continued

resentments concerning past injustices, and recitations of story lines, or possible alternative story lines, in animated cartoons.

Danny is extremely, almost savantishly, knowledgeable about his particular sub-universe of movies and certain on-line videogames that interest him. With great frequency, at almost any time—though not usually after 11:30 or so at night—we hear a sharp rap on our bedroom door. (Barbara's study is in an alcove in our bedroom; mine is down the hallway, five or six feet away.) Entering, standing straight and looking serious, Danny begins with a pregnant, expectant, emphatic, "Mom." Then there is his announcement; typically, he announces one statement per visit. "The original story of *Peter Pan* was called *Peter and Wendy*." Mom admits that she didn't know that. Usually he waits for a response, and each of Barbara's answers is followed by a look on Danny's face that indicates he's seriously considering the implications of her response; her answers are usually followed by his hasty departure. Some of them require more commentary from us than others. "You know that Dumbo makes the most significant appearance of any Disney character in *Who Framed Roger Rabbit*?" Mom says she did know that. "*Cinderella II* doesn't violate the rules of the original *Cinderella* because it narrates her future life in a new home, but *Cinderella III* definitely violates the rules of the original *Cinderella* because it involves time travel." Mom says that's an interesting point. "The Adam Zelinski of *Honey, I Shrunk Ourselves* is the Drisella of his time." Or: "*The Fox and the Hound* is the *Bambi* of its generation." Analogies frequently populate Danny's monologues. "Mom, what do you think of the scene when a doctor was about to operate on Roger Rabbit by cutting him open with a chain saw?" We had to explain that doctors do not operate with a chain saw and Roger Rabbit is, after all, a "toon" who can't be hurt. "*Gumby* is more age-appropriate than *Care Bears*. *Gumby* is a series of surreal cartoons, and it appeals to grown-ups as well as children, whereas *Care Bears* only appeals to children because it's childish and syrupy." Barbara has received thousands of such announcements, although I'm often

close enough to be in earshot. When she's not around, he delivers them to me; I have received hundreds of them.

One feature of Danny's communication is to present us with complaints from the past, often the distant past—four, five, eight, or even ten or more years ago. He usually asks the question accompanied by an emotion bordering on righteous indignation. "Dad," he'll begin, "how come you told me that in non-fantasy movies and films, things change? In fantasy movies and TV programs, things change, but in non-fantasy drama, nothing really changes. Why did you say that it did?" I try to meet his challenges head-on, but with tact.

"Danny," I explain, "in drama that depicts real life, a lot of change is depicted. In prison movies, someone is a criminal, he robs banks, he's a thief, he gets into fights, he's a bad guy, he hurts people. Then he gets arrested, he's put in prison, a priest or a good guy who's inside turns him around, and then, when he gets out, he's a good guy, he doesn't steal, he isn't violent—he's reformed. That's a big change, isn't it? *Most* prison movies are like that. And a *lot* of movies about real life show change. A geek becomes a brave hero. A kid who's a bad student works hard, applies himself, succeeds in school, and gets a scholarship to college. A boy who's afraid to ask girls out for a date gets an inspirational speech from a friend, and so he asks a girl he has a crush on for a date and she accepts. I don't see how you can say there's no change in real-life dramas in movies. There's a *lot* of them."

Danny wasn't satisfied with my answer. "That's not what I'm talking about," he tells me. "*The Goonies* is not a fantasy movie, and the characters are the same at the end as they are at the beginning. There's no real change." My mind fumbles around for the flaw in his logic.

"Danny, I'm not talking about *The Goonies*. You asked me about non-fantasy movies, and I mentioned several kinds of movies, which represent *hundreds* of movies, and involve no fantasy, and *most* of them—hundreds and hundreds of them—show *major* change in the characters."

"I'm sorry, Dad," he replies. "I don't want to talk about it anymore."

"I never got any of the crafts I made at Ramapo Anchorage Camp," he said to us recently, with a strong measure of resentment. The last time he went to summer camp was over twelve years ago—for him, more than a half a lifetime in the past. Barbara was stunned. "Danny, that was— what? Twelve and a half years ago. It was so far in the past, why don't you think more about the hear-and-now? Why get worked up about something that happened to long ago that you can't do anything about?"

"I can't help it, Mom. That's the way I am," he replied with some finality.

"We have to get you into a recreational program, Danny. You have to take you mind off things that cause you to stew."

Recently, Danny slipped a note (in 36-point font) under our bedroom door that read:

"To Mom:

Why did you betray me by being originally on *my* side over the way Sarah [his sister] treated me about Clover [a pet rabbit we had over ten years ago] and then turning to her side when I said I would never forgive her for the way she treated me about Clover?"

On day, not long ago, Danny disappeared into the bathroom and, presumably, sat on the toilet. The sound of "Duck and Cover," a song taught to schoolchildren during the Cold War and with which Danny had no direct familiarity, began wafting through the door. He must have learned it from an old black-and-white training film he stumbled across in his Internet browsing. I decided not to ask him about it. Yes, a recreational program, I thought. That's the ticket. With other young people his age. And condition.

Danny loves to recite lengthy lines of dialogue from animated cartoons, sometimes word-for-word, sometimes in revised form to suit a particular interpretation of the text—the latter of which he usually delivers with an ironic and sly smile on his face. He loves "intertextuality," whereby he'll transpose lines, characters, music, or action from one cartoon into that of another. He transforms Goofy into Popeye's role as Olive Oyl's husband because both Goofy and Olive are tall and thin and Popeye isn't. Often his transposition is literal in that he does a great deal of editing of material,

usually the soundtrack, from one film into the images of another. One day Danny integrated the song, "Time is a Gift," from *The Phantom Tollbooth* into an action sequence of *The Yellow Submarine*. It was perfectly coordinated in such a way that the viewer imagined that the lyrics and music might have been written for the Beatle's movie, down to the movement of the figures to the beat of the action. At one point, when clocks were a subject of the song, clocks appeared on the screen, and in time to the beat. It's sad that the boy's condition prevents him from practicing a profession for which he is clearly gifted.

Normally, the interested observer would suggest that Danny has the capacity to work in a film library, or perhaps even at editing film, at which he is remarkably talented, but, autism being closely related to obsessive-compulsive disorder (OCD), our son is only interested in what he is interested in; it is virtually impossible to move him off his dime. Moreover, though once he gets past his first sentence or two, he can be very articulate, his ability to communicate with others in a conventional conversation is rudimentary at best; he displays no interest in what his interlocutor might want to talk about. And he does not work well with authority figures. Currently, Danny attends a kind of work rehab program which should prepare him for a menial job—stacking boxes for supermarkets, removing the plastic protective cover from dry-cleaned clothes, walking dogs, delivering products to clients and customers, that sort of thing. He recently worked at a U.S. Open tennis tournament restaurant, clearing and cleaning tables. But because of various incidents—mostly walking off his job when he grew tired of working—one of Danny's instructors told us that he will be unable to engage in unsupervised employment.

At home, Danny spends a great deal of time making up extensive lists on lined paper; mostly they refer to animated films. He prints his words in an elaborate, archaic-looking script of his own invention—recently, an artist used some of his writing in her sculpture, which was exhibited in a gallery in Cambridge, Massachusetts—and he sometimes places a dot between each word. He recently made up a list that was numbered from 1 to 43; the numbers were accompanied by years,

(Continued)

Account: Autism   Continued

which ran from 1937 to 1992, and were followed by a colon, after which there was the title of a feature-length animated cartoon. It turns out, he just sat down and wrote out the list, from beginning to end, off the top of his head, without having to consult a single reference guide. A few years are missing, and some years are followed by two titles rather than one. I picked up the list from our dining table and couldn't make sense of it: What was their common thread? For instance, some were Disney movies, some weren't. Some were serious, esthetically appealing films (*Snow White and the Seven Dwarfs*; *Pinocchio*; *Bambi*), while some lacked artistic value and seemed to have been made mainly for juveniles and strictly for laughs (*Hey There, It's Yogi Bear; The Man Called Flintstone; The Bugs Bunny/Road Runner Movie*). I asked Danny what these films had in common.

"These are the most significant, feature-length, animated cartoons for each year," he replied. I asked him why the list ended with 1992. "I got too tired. It would take too much time and energy to finish it," he said. I asked why some years were missing—1938, for instance, 1944, 1952, and so on. "Those were years when no significant, feature-length, animated film was made." I asked why some years listed two movies. "In some years, *two* significant, feature-length, animated cartoons were made."

I opened my mouth to formulate another question but decided against it. Danny's list made more sense than I realized; he had his logic and I had mine. A week later, I asked him about another list he had drawn up, but he was unable to explain its logic to me and when I pursued the matter, he became exasperated. "Let's drop it," he finally said, and I agreed.

Danny also obsesses about issues that seem trivial to us, and he'll stir up arguments over them—over the period of years, six or eight or a dozen times. He'll approach both of us with a sour, annoyed face and ask a rhetorical question about something my wife or I did or that he didn't agree with. He won't like our answer, and an angry, seemingly interminable exchange will ensue that ends only with one or the other of us exclaiming,

"Danny, I don't know why you're arguing about this. That's enough! *Stop* it!" For instance, several times, he's approached my wife and asked, "Mom, why didn't we drive to Cambridge instead of taking a bus?" None of our answers satisfy him, and he'll rigidly stick to his objections to our answers to the bitter end. Sometimes we can't even recall the incident to which he refers; sometimes the formulation of the question will be so complex and convoluted that we can't even understand what's on his mind. Clearly, he wants to right a presumably dastardly wrong that cannot be righted, or perhaps he simply enjoys stirring up trouble.

Danny is also obsessive about having his say when he wants to say it. He knows his Mom engages in activities that compete for his attention. He knows she works at a paying job and can't be in the apartment all the time, he knows she enjoys her crossword puzzle in the morning, but if his Mom is busy discussing an important matter with someone else (it's usually me) and he's not allowed to interrupt, he becomes annoyed and shows it. Once, over our breakfast coffee, in the middle of a serious discussion, Danny urgently wanted to make some announcement—about Snow White, as I recall—and was told he'd have to wait his turn. He stalked away, returned several minutes later, and handed Barbara a sheet of paper, on which he had printed, in 48-point font, this message: "All I want is a mother who still works very hard for the family but doesn't go around drinking stupid coffee and doing stupid crossword puzzles."

At the age of three, after experiencing a protracted speech delay, Danny was diagnosed with a possible pervasive developmental disorder (PDD)—a grab-bag category that psychologists use when no other disorder seems to stand out. Between the ages of three and four, Danny attended a pre-school educational center; there, he received a recommendation that he be placed in a program for children with special needs, a BOCES (Board of Cooperative Educational Services) school. When Danny was nine, Michael Eberlein, his school psychologist, gave him the following evaluation: "Danny is an adorable boy with blonde hair and brown eyes [actually, his hair is light brown and his eyes are hazel] who appears to be of average height and weight for his age. He used his left hand to write and evidenced a normal gait, with normal coordination. Speech was usually in good phrases . . . as well as with good articulation, but with a lack of varied tonality. Delayed echolalia [the repetition of words spoken by another person] . . . was noted intermittently. Eye contact and interpersonal relatedness were adequate but somewhat deviant. Activity level was somewhat above average and attention was variable and seemed dependent on his interest in the task and the incentive used to motivate him to perform. . . . Danny displays idiosyncratic interests in [certain things, for example] making puppets of Pinocchio, [collecting] images of past US presidents, collecting coins, and writing out the words to songs. . . . He also has excellent calendar calculation skills [which is common among autistic children]. His interests . . . change, and he sometimes gets very upset if his routines are changed or of his idiosyncrasies are not addressed. For instance, at times, he becomes upset if adults use certain verbal phrases [like 'I don't care,' or 'Why, I oughtta . . .']. No self-injurious behaviors were noted, but when [he gets] upset, he sometimes becomes mildly aggressive or verbally belligerent. Danny sleeps well. He eats fairly well but again, idiosyncratically. Specifically, he will eat sausage pizza (after removing the sausages and cheese), chicken nuggets, with occasional hot dogs, strawberries, and corn on the cob" (7/14/97).

After four years in BOCES schools, my wife and I arranged to mainstream him into the regular curriculum in his local public school, with the assistance of a full-time aide. To that end, a psychologist from the New York Autism Network observed his BOCES classroom behavior. In this class, there were six students, one teacher, and one aide. The following is a paraphrase from his report, dated 6/9/98, written by Christopher E. Smith:

"When the psychologist arrived, Danny was participating in a math game that involved going up to the board to solve a problem. In front of the class, Danny began untying then retying his sneakers. When he was redirected to the task at hand, he was able to answer the question. Then he took his seat. When the teacher read a story, Danny began fiddling with his shoelaces. He began humming and looking around the classroom. The teacher redirected his focus by asking him to read from the book. Toward the end of his selection, he began writing in the air with his left finger. When she asked him to stop, he said, 'Don't be mean. I can write in the air.' During an exercise with workbooks, Danny sharpened his pencils several times, repeatedly asked other students for an eraser, and played with his shoelaces. However, when the teacher called on him, he was able to give the correct answer. While waiting for the next activity to begin, Danny took off his sneakers. When his teacher told him to put them back on, Danny announced, 'You're a witch. It's a plot.' The teacher allowed him to leave his sneakers on his desk and to go on to the next activity, making shirts for Father's Day. He watched attentively and patiently as two other students made shirts. During this time he did not fidget or engage in self-stimulatory behavior."

When Danny was 19, we moved to New York. The move from a suburb, in Silver Spring, Maryland, to the City, has made him vastly more independent, enabling him to go out on expeditions on his own; in addition, he has access to the New York subway system. But he doesn't always communicate sufficiently effectively or smoothly with service personnel, and hence, sometimes has "incidents." One day, he decided to see *The Princess and the Frog*, which was playing in a limited engagement only at the Clearview Cinema at 54th Street, over fifty blocks from where we live, which meant he had to take a subway to get there. The woman at the theater booth asked Danny: "Are you here to pick up tickets?" Danny said yes. She asked for ID; Danny said he didn't have any. He took the subway back to the apartment, got an ID, and took a subway back to the theater and handed the ID to her. She said she didn't have any tickets for him. He said he wanted to *buy* tickets to see the movie. She said they cost $30 and $50. Danny screamed, "That's too much!" and stormed off, taking the subway home. Two trips, four subway rides, no tickets, no movie.

Danny likes going to Central Park, where he has room to walk around, talk to himself, and enjoy nature. His embarkation point is now

(Continued)

Account: Autism   Continued

59th Street. (I had to explain that 110th Street is not the best location to enter the Park, and he had to do it just once to discover that for himself.) After visiting the Park, he walked into a restaurant near the Plaza (he didn't tell us, or know, its name) and sat down, expecting the waiter to approach him and hand him a menu so that he could order. But while waiting, he began talking to himself. While he was talking to himself, a waiter approached him and said to him, "Sir, if you are going to talk to yourself, I'm going to have to ask you to leave." Danny bolted from the restaurant.

For weeks, after his mother told him he was getting a little chubby (at 5'7", he weighs over 190), Danny continues to use our bathroom scale to weigh himself, but he leaves it in the middle of our bathroom, where we sometimes trip over it. So I gave him our scale and I told him I was going to buy Mom and Dad a scale and put it in our bathroom; he can keep ours, but to help him understand the process of what it means to buy something you want, I said he'd have to come with me to buy it at K-Mart, which is at Broadway and 9th Street. He objected but agreed to come along. On the street, Danny complained about a crowd of young people, maybe 13–14 years old, boys and girls together, who, a few months ago, made fun of him ("they screamed insults at me," he claimed). I said, yes, the kids were bad and they shouldn't have done that, but if you talk to yourself on the street, people are going to stare at you and you'll attract attention to yourself, and some bad kids will do things to you that you won't like. He said no, no, he hadn't talked to himself, they didn't yell at him because he was doing anything wrong, he said that they did that because they thought he was following them. He said he wanted to "get a baseball bat and smash them on their butts." I explained that is illegal and he could get arrested. "Do you want to go jail?" He said he didn't. Then he said he was going to bring a cell phone and when the kids yell at him, he would call the police (sounding very emotional, practically screaming) "and I'd tell the police come and arrest these bad kids, they're screaming at me." I said that unless screaming carries with it a threat of violence, I didn't think

it's illegal. Well, he said, they should be arrested anyway. I was tried to explain what's illegal and what's not, and he accused me of "badgering" him. I said, OK, Danny, let's drop this, but he insisted that they should be arrested. I let him get the last word in, and then we were quiet for a while. At K-Mart, I picked up the scale and while standing at the cashier's counter, I looked over at Danny. He had his left hand across his mouth. The cashier stared at him, but she completed the transaction. After I paid, as we were walking away, I asked what he had been doing. He said he was making sure he wasn't talking to himself. I said, Danny, "Even that gesture calls attention to yourself. The cashier was staring at you." Every public interaction with Danny involves inappropriate behavior and reactions indicating that Danny has acted in a peculiar fashion. There is no way of relaxing around that boy.

As I explained, most individuals on the autism spectrum disorder suffer from OCD. Danny spends a substantial portion of his day alone, staring into space, pacing the apartment, or babbling aloud. Most of the content of his one-sided monologic conversations entail reciting the dialogue of certain movies he has seen—either as it appears or in his alternate form—or explaining the motivations for the actions of specific cartoon characters, or offering alternative plots of these films. He also describes perceived unjust acts—some of which took place years ago—committed against him, and the retribution he plans to take against their perpetrators; his descriptions are often accompanied by an emotional, self-righteous voice that indicates that he might actually carry out such vengeance. He never has. My wife and I try to talk Danny down and away from such tirades, but it's an often fruitless and unrewarding effort.

Recently, Danny told me about the following incident, which happened at a local restaurant. "I was paying for a meal I just ate. The cashier grabbed my hand because he claimed that I should have given him a dime that I tried to put back in my pocket. I began yelling at the man. I was considering eliminating his existence by throwing *chakrams* [weapons supposedly used in India and featured in *Tron* and *Kingdom Hearts*] through him and causing him to explode into ashes. As I was yelling at the man, a boy who is a little younger than me but taller than me, said: 'I'll punch you in the mouth—I'll break your arm' or 'I'll break your neck,' something like that. I poured a Coke Zero on him, and he squirted sauce out of one of those plastic squeeze bottles all over my shirt. He made my clothes a mess. Then he tried to block my exit from leaving the restaurant, with his arms outstretched, but I ran out anyway, and when I got to Third Street, he was still pursuing me. I ran into the lobby of our building, and he barged in. I told Hajji [the doorman who was in service at the desk in our building at that time] to kick the boy out of the lobby. I got into the elevator and pressed the button for the third floor, but the boy stopped the elevator door from closing. I hit him with my bottle of Coke Zero and it got knocked to the floor of the lobby. I yelled at him to leave me alone, and he kept saying, 'Or what? Or what?' Hajji dragged the boy out of the elevator, but he tried one more time to stop the elevator door from closing. No one's ever chased me on my way back to the apartment before." I'm certain Danny described the action accurately—he never makes up that sort of thing—but why it all happened is often a complete mystery.

Whether he was in the right or not, Danny continues getting entangled in such incidents. I fear that one day he will encounter someone who commits serious violence against him. After all, we're concerned about him and, whatever his faults, we love him.

QUESTIONS

As we saw before, in his "classic study of deviance," *Hustlers, Beats, and Others*, Ned Polsky argues that conditions that are "not the person's fault," are not instances of deviance. What about autism? The autism spectrum disorder prevents individuals from doing what is socially expected, and creates difficulties in relating to others. What about stigma—is exhibiting autistic behavior stigmatizing? Is it deviant? What about causation? If a cause for autism cannot be explicated, what does this say about theories of deviant behavior? Does that make them invalid? What about social constructions of deviance? If autism exhibits a specific form everywhere, does that mean that the social construction of autism is not relative to time, place, and culture? Does this weaken the social constructionist argument? If autism is a spectrum disorder, does this mean that some autistic individuals are able to interact among some social circles under certain circumstances without being detected as abnormal? Does this mean that it's not a "disorder" at all? Does this fact weaken the whole notion of abnormality or pathology— or strengthen it?

Credits

Photo Credits

Chapter 1. **1:** Igor Korionov/Fotolia.
Chapter 2. **23:** Shannon J. Hager/Getty Images.
Chapter 3. **49:** Chase Jarvis/Getty Images.
Chapter 4. **74:** Tomasz Zajda/Alamy.
Chapter 5. **97:** Comstock/Getty Images.
Chapter 6. **129:** David J. Phillip/AP Images.
Chapter 7. **154:** Véronique Burger/Photo Researchers, Inc./Science Source.

Chapter 8. **184:** David J. Green – lifestyle themes/Alamy.
Chapter 9. **200:** Nisian Hughes/Photodisc/Getty Images.
Chapter 10. **225:** Halfpoint/Fotolia.
Chapter 11. **251:** es/Michele Constantini /PhotoAlto/Alamy.
Chapter 12. **276:** outsiderzone/iStock/Getty Images.
Chapter 13. **304:** Everett Collection Historical/Alamy.
Chapter 14. **333:** Thinkstock Images/Stockbyte/Getty Images.

Text Credits

Chapter 1. **2:** Dao, James. 2012. "For Soldier Disfigured in War, A Way to Return to the World." *The New York Times*, January 31, pp. A1, A16; Barstow, David. 2012. "Vast Mexico Bribery Case Hushed Up by Wal-Mart After Top Level Struggle." *The New York Times*, April 22, pp. 1, 8–10. **3:** Greenhouse, Steven, and Jim Yardley. 2012. "As Walmart Makes Safety Vows, It's Seen as Obstacle to Change," *The New York Times*, December 29, pp. A1, A6. **7:** Adler, Patricia A., and Peter Adler (eds.). 2009. *Constructions of Deviance: Social Power, Context, and Interaction*. Belmont, CA: Thompson Wadsworth. **8:** Reprinted with permission of Scribner Publishing Group from the Touchstone edition of *STIGMA: Notes on Management of Spoiled Identity* by Erving Goffman. Copyright © 1963 Prentice Hall. Copyright © renewed 1991 by Simon & Schuster, Inc. All rights reserved; St. Augustine. 400/1963. *The Confessions of St. Augustine*. New York: Mentor/Penguin Books. **9:** Pew Global Attitude Survey (taken in 2011). **11:** Reprinted with permission of Scribner Publishing Group from the Touchstone edition of *STIGMA: Notes on Management of Spoiled Identity* by Erving Goffman. Copyright © 1963 Prentice Hall. Copyright © renewed 1991 by Simon & Schuster, Inc. All rights reserved. **12:** Krauthammer, Charles. 1993. "Defining Deviancy Up." *The New York Republic*, November 22, pp. 20–25. **14:** Pascale, Richard, Jerry Sternin, and Monique Sternin. 2010. *The Power of Positive Deviance: How Unlikely Innovators Can Solve the World's Toughest Problems*. Cambridge, MA: Harvard Business Press; Robinson, Bryan E., and Nell H. Fields. 1983. "Casework with Invulnerable Children," *Social Work*, 28 (1): 63–65; Jones, Angela Lewellyn. 1998. "Random Acts of Kindness: A Teaching Tool for Positive Deviance." *Teaching Sociology*, 26 (3): 179–189; Hughes, Robert, and Jay Coakley. 1991. "Positive Deviance among Athletes: The Implications of Overconformity to the Sports Ethic," *Sociology of Sports Journal*, 8 (4): 307–325. **19:** Dolnick, Sam, and Danny Hakim. 2012. "Women Employed by Lawmaker Describe Sexually Hostile Office." *The New York Times*, August 30, pp. A1, A24.

Chapter 2. 24: Nettler, Gwynn. 1984. *Explaining Crime* (3rd ed.). New York: McGraw-Hill. **26:** Nettler, Gwynn. 1974. "On Telling Who's Crazy." *American Sociological Review*, 39 (December): 893–894. **27:** (1939, p. 309) Hooton, Ernest A. 1939. *The American Criminal*. Cambridge, MA: Harvard University Press. **28:** Brunner, H.G., et al. 1993. "Abnormal Behavior Associated with a Point Mutation in the Structural Gene for Monoamine Oxidase A," *Science*, 262 (22 October): 578–580; Robert C. Green, as quoted in Kolata, Gina. 2012. "Seeking Answers in Genome of Gunman," *The New York Times*, December 25, pp. D5, D6; Kolata, Gina. 2012. "Seeking Answers in Genome of Gunman," *The New York Times*, December 25, pp. D5, D6. **31:** Bursik, Robert J., and Harold G. Grasmick. 1993. *Neighborhoods and Crime: The Dimensions of Effective Community Control*. New York: Lexington Books. **32:** Unnever, James D. 1987. Review of James M. Byrne and Robert J. Sampson (eds.), *The Social Ecology of Crime*. New York: Springer-Verlag, 1986, in *Contemporary Sociology*, 16 (November): 845–846; Pfohl, Stephen. 1994. *Images of Deviance and Social Control: A Sociological History* (2nd ed.). New York: McGraw-Hill. **33–37, 41, 43:** Reprinted with permission of Simon & Schuster Publishing Group from the Free Press edition of *Social Theory and Social Structure*, Revised & Enlarged Edition by Robert K. Merton. Copyright © 1967,1968 by the Free Press; Copyright renewed 1985 by Robert K. Merton. All rights reserved. **33:** Brezina, Timothy. 2011. "Anomie-Strain Theory." In Clifton D. Bryant (ed.), *The Routledge Handbook of Deviant Behavior*. London & New York: Routledge, pp. 99–105. Clinard, Marshall B. 1964b. "The Theoretical Implications of Anomie and Deviant Behavior." In Marshall B. Clinard (ed.), Anomie and Deviant Behavior: A discussion and Critique. New York: Free Press, pp. 1–56; Kornhauser, Ruth. 1978. *Social Sources of Delinquency: An Appraisal of Analytic Models*. Chicago: University of Chicago Press; Bourgeois, Philippe. 1995, 2003. *In Search of Respect: Selling Crack in the Barrio* (1st & 2nd eds.). Cambridge, UK & New York: Cambridge

University Press. **37:** Duneier, Mitchell. 1999. *Sidewalk.* New York: Farrar, Straus & Giroux. **38:** Cressey, Donald R. 1960. "Epidemiology and Individual Conduct." *Pacific Sociological Review,* 3 (Fall): 47–58. **39:** Sampson, Robert J., and John H. Laub. 1993. *Crime in the Making: Pathways and Turning Points Through Life.* Cambridge, MA: Harvard University Press. **40–41:** Gottfredson, Michael R., and Travis Hirschi. 1990. A General Theory of Crime. Stanford, CA: Stanford University Press. **38, 40–42, 44:** Excerpts from A General Theory of Crime, Michael Gottfredson and Travis Hirschi. Copyright © 1990 by the Board of Trustees of the Leland Stanford Jr. University.

Chapter 3. **51:** Black, Donald J. (ed.). 1984. *Toward a General Theory of Social Control.* Orlando, FL: Academic Press. **54:** Hawkins, Richard, and Gary Tiedeman. 1975. *The Creation of Deviance: Interpersonal and Organization Determinants.* Columbus, OH: Charles E. Merrill. **55:** Traub, Stuart H., and Craig B. Little (eds.). 1999. *Theories of Deviance* (5th ed.). Itasca, IL.: Peacock. **56:** Lemert, Edwin M. 1972. *Human Deviance, Social Problems, and Social Control* (2nd ed.). Englewood Cliffs, NJ: Prentice Hall. **57:** Grattet, Ryken. 2011a. "Societal Reactions to Deviance." *Annual Review of Sociology,* 37: 185–204; Akers, Ronald L. 1968. "Problems in the Sociology of Deviance: Social Definitions and Behavior." *Social Forces,* 46 (June): 455–465; **57, 59:** Reprinted with permission of Simon & Schuster Publishing Group from the Free Press Edition of *The Other Side: Perspectives on Deviance* by Howard S. Becker. Copyright © 1964 by the Free Press, a Division of Simon & Schuster, Inc. All rights reserved; Glassner, Barry. 1982. "Labeling Theory." In M. Michael Rosenberg, Robert A. Stebbins, and Allan Turowitz (eds.), *The Sociology of Deviance.* New York: St. Martin's Press, pp. 71–89. **60:** Becker, Howard S. 1963. *Outsiders: Studies in the Sociology of Deviance.* New York: Free Press; Grattet, Ryken. 2011a. "Societal Reactions to Deviance." *Annual Review of Sociology,* 37:185–204; Sampson, Robert J., and John H. Laub. 1997. "A Life-Course Theory of Cumulative Disadvantage and the Stability of Delinquency." In T. P. Thornberry (ed.), *Developmental Theories of Crime and Delinquency.* New Brunswick, NJ: Transaction, pp. 133–161. **61:** Pager, Devah. 2007. *Marked: Race, Crime, and Finding Work in an Era of Mass Incarceration.* Chicago: University of Chicago Press. **62:** White, Rob. 2011. "Marxist and Critical Theory." In Clifton D. Bryant (ed.), *The Routledge Handbook of Deviance.* London & New York: Routledge, pp. 150–156; Conyers, Addrain. 2011. "Conflict Theory." In Clifton D. Bryant (ed.), *The Routledge Handbook of Deviant Behavior.* London & New York: Routledge, pp. 135–142; Friedman, Wolfgang. 1964. *Law in a Changing Society.* Harmondsworth, UK: Penguin Books. **63:** Bailey, Carol A. 2011. "Feminist Theory." In Clifton D. Bryant (ed.), *The Routledge Handbook of Deviant Behavior.* London & New York: Routledge, pp. 164–170; Tong, Rosemarie. 2009. *Feminist Thought: A More Comprehensive Introduction.* Boulder, CO: Westview Press. **64:** Gelsthorpe, Loraine, and Alison Morris. 1988. "Feminism and Criminology in Britain." *British Journal of Criminology,* 28 (Spring): 223–240; Heidensohn, Frances. 1968. "The Deviance of Women: A Critique and an Enquiry." *British Journal of Sociology,* 12 (2): 160–175; Leonard,

Eileen B. 1982. *Women, Crime, and Society: A Critique of Theoretical Criminology.* New York: Longman; Quinney, Richard. 1970. *The Social Reality of Crime.* Boston: Little, Brown. **65:** Millman, Marcia. 1975. "She Did It All for Love: A Feminist View of the Sociology of Deviance." In Marcia Millman and Rosabeth Moss Kantor (eds.), *Another Voice: Feminist Perspectives on Social Life and Social Science.* Garden City, NY: Doubleday-Anchor, pp. 251–279; Reckless, Walter C. 1950. *The Crime Problem.* New York: Appleton-Century-Crofts; Jones, Trevor, Brian MacLean, and Jock Young. 1986. *The Islington Crime Survey: Crime, Victimization, and Policing in Inner City London.* Aldershot, UK: Gower. November 22, pp. 20–25; Matthews, Roger, and Jock Young (eds.). 1986. *Confronting Crime.* Thousand Oaks, CA: Sage; Burgess-Proctor, Amanda. 2006. "Intersections of Race, Class, Gender, and Crime," *Feminist Criminology,* 1 (1): 27–47. **66:** Cohen, Stanley. 1985. *Visions of Social Control.* Cambridge, UK: Polity Press. **66:** Marshall, Helen, Kathy Douglass, and Desmond McDonnell. 2007. *Deviance and Social Control: Who Rules?* South Melbourne, Australia: Oxford University Press. **67:** Scull, Andrew. 1988. "Deviance and Social Control." In Neil J. Smelser (ed.), *Handbook of Sociology.* Thousand Oaks, CA: Sage, pp. 667–693. **68:** Foucault, Michel. 1979. *Discipline and Punish: The Birth of the Prison* (trans. Alan Sheridan). New York: Vintage Books; Lowman, John, Robert J. Menzies, and T. S. Palys (eds.). 1987. *Transcarceration: Essays in the Sociology of Social Control.* Gower, UK: Aldershot.

Chapter 4. **75:** Merton, Robert K. 1957. *Social Theory and Social Structure.* (rev. & expanded ed.).Glencoe, IL: Free Press. **75, 76:** Anleu, Sharyn L. Roach. 1991. *Deviance, Conformity and Control* (1/e). Melbourne, Australia: Longman Cheshire; Reprinted with permission of Simon & Schuster Publishing Group, from the Free Press edition of *Outsiders: Studies in the Sociology of Deviance* by Howard S. Becker. Copyright © 1963 by the Free Press. Copyright © renewed 1991 by Howard S. Becker. All rights reserved. **77:** Weber, Max. 1963. *The Sociology of Religion* (trans. Ephraim Fischoff). Boston: Beacon Press (orig. pub. 1922). **78:** Matza, David. 1966b. "Poverty and Disrepute." In Robert K. Merton and Robert A. Nisbet (eds.), *Contemporary Social Problems* (2/e). New York: Harcourt, Brace & World, pp. 619–669; Matza, David. 1966a. "The Disreputable Poor." In Reinhard Bendix and Seymour Martin Lipset (eds.), *Class, Status, and Power: Social Stratification in Comparative Perspective.* New York: Free Press, pp. 289–302. **79:** Sen, Amartya. 2000. "Social Exclusion: Concept, Application, and Scrutiny," Social Development Papers, no. 1. Manila: Asian Development Bank; Reyles, Diego Zavaleta. 2007. "The Ability to Go About without Shame." *Oxford Development Studies,* 35 (December): 405–430. **80:** Wacquant, Loïc. 2008. *Urban Outcasts: A Comparative Sociology of Advanced Marginality.* New York: Polity Press. **83:** Starrin, Bengt. 2002. "Unemployment, Poverty and Shame— Exploring the Field." Norway: Lillehamer University College, unpublished paper. **84:** Mollman, Marianne. 2011. "Americans Demonstrate Changed Attitude towards Poverty Since the 2008 Crisis." *Huff Post Politics,* December 26; Zawadski, Bohan, and Paul Lazarsfeld. 1935. "The

Psychological Consequences of Unemployment." *Journal of Social Psychology*, 6 (May): 224–251. **85:** Wanberg, Connie R. 2012. "The Individual Experience of Unemployment." *Annual Review of Psychology*, 63 (January): 369–396; Rose, Hilary. 1975. "Who Can Delabel the Claimant?" In M. Adler and A. Bradley (eds.), *Justice, Discretion, and Poverty*. London: Professional Books, pp. 143–154; Rogers-Dillon, Robin. 1995. "The Dynamics of Welfare Stigma." *Qualitative Sociology*, 18 (Winter): 439–456. **86:** Rogers-Dillon, Robin. 1995. "The Dynamics of Welfare Stigma." *Qualitative Sociology*, 18 (Winter): 439–456; Stuber, Jennifer, and Mark Schlesinger. 2006. "Sources of Stigma for Means-Tested Government Programs." *Social Science and Medicine*, 63 (August): 933–945; Jütte, Robert. 1994. *Poverty and Deviance in Early Modern Europe*. Cambridge, UK, and New York: Cambridge University Press; Lankenau, Stephen E. 1999. "Stronger Than Dirt: Public Humiliation and Status Enhancement among Panhandlers." *Journal of Contemporary Ethnography*, 28 (June): 288–318. **87:** O'Riordan, Alison. 2010. "The Humiliation of Begging for a Day on Dublin's Mean Streets." *National News* (Dublin, Ireland), May 30; Shalay, Anne B., and Peter H. Rossi. 1992. "Social Science Research and Contemporary Studies of Homelessness," *Annual Review of Sociology*, 18: 129–160; Phelen, Jo C., and Bruce G. Link. 1999. Who Are 'the Homeless'? Reconsidering the Stability and Composition of the Homeless Population." *American Journal of Public Health*, 89 (9): 1334–1338. **88:** Phelen, Jo. C., Bruce G. Link, Robert E. Moore, and Ann Stueve. 1997. *Social Psychology Quarterly*, 60 (4): 323–337; Reprinted with permission of Scribner Publishing Group from Touchstone edition of *STIGMA: Notes on Management of Spoiled Identity* by Erving Goffman. Copyright © 1963 by Prentice Hall. Copyright © 1991 renewed by Simon & Schuster, Inc. All rights reserved; McDonough, Peggy, Greg J.Duncan, David Williams, and James S. House. 2001. "Income Dynamics and Adult Mortality in the United States, 1972–1989." American Journal of Public Health, 87 (September): 1476–1483. DeNavas-Walt, Carmen, Bernadette D. Proctor, Jessica C. Smith. 2012. *Income, Poverty, and Health Insurance Coverage in the United States: 2011*, U.S. Census Bureau, Current Population Reports, P60–243. Washington, DC: U.S. Government Printing Office; Scambler, Graham, Miriam Heijnders, and Wim H. van Brakel. 2006. "Understanding and Tackling Health-Related Stigma." *Psychology, Health & Medicine*, 11 (August): 269–270; Twaddle, Andrew. 1973. "Illness and Deviance." *Social Science and Medicine*, 7 (October): 751–762. **90:** DeNavas-Walt, Proctor, and Smith, 2012, p. 24. Pearson Education, Upper Saddle River, NJ. **92:** Gans, Herbert J. 2005. "Race as Class." *Contexts*, 4 (Fall): 17–21; Gans, Herbert J. 2005. "Race as Class." Contexts, 4 (Fall): 17–22.

Chapter 5. Archibold, Randal C., and Damien Cave. 2012. "Numb to Carnage, Mexicans Find Diversions, and Life Goes On." The New York Times, May 16, pp. A1, A3. Walsh, Declan, and Salman Masood. 2012. "Christian Girl's Blasphemy Arrest Incites a Furor in Pakistan." The New York Times, August 21, p. A4; FBI, Uniform Crime Reports, Crime in the United States 2011 (2012); rate is number per 100,000 in the population. **107:** The Ten Commandments, King James Bible "Authorized Version," Cambridge Edition, 1769. **110:** Katz, Jack. 1988. *Seductions of Crime: Moral and Sensual Attractions of Doing Evil*. New York: Basic Books. **112:** Balko, Radley. 2009. "The El Paso Miracle." www.Reason.com, July 6. **113:** Givens, James B. 1977. *Society and Homicide in Thirteenth-Century England*. Stanford, CA: Stanford University Press. **114:** Ruderman, Wendy. 2012. "414 Homicides a Record Low for New York," *The New York Times*, December 29, pp. A1, A3; For 1992, Rand, Lynch, and Cantor, 1997, and Taylor, 1997; for 2002 and 2011, Truman and Planty, 2012. Rand, Michael R., James P. Lynch, and David Cantor. 1997. "Criminal Victimization,1973–95," Bureau of Justice Statistics National Crime Victimization Survey, April, pp. 1–8.; Truman, Jennifer L. and Michael Planty. 2012. "Criminal Victimization, 2011." BJS Bulletin, October, pp.1–19.; Taylor, Bruce M. 1997. "Changes in Criminal Victimization, 1994–95," Bureau of Justice Statistics, National Crime Victimization Survey, April, pp. 1–14. **116:** Abdulali, Solaila. 2013. "I Was Wounded; My Honor Wasn't." *The New York Times*, January 8, p. A23). **117:** Griffin, Susan. 1971. "Rape: The All-American Crime." *Ramparts*, September, pp. 26–35. Grinspoon, Lester, and James B. Bakalar. 1976. *Cocaine: A Drug and Its Social Evolution*. New York: Basic Books. **118:** Scully, Diana. 1990. *Understanding Sexual Violence: A Study of Convicted Rapists*. Boston: Unwin Hyman. **119:** Williams, Joyce E., and Willard A. Nielson, Jr. 1979. "The Rapist Looks at His Crime." *Free Inquiry in Creative Sociology*, 7 (November): 128–132; Scully, Diana, and Joseph Marolla. 1984. Convicted Rapists' Vocabulary of Motive: Excuses and Justifications." *Social Problems*, 31 (June): 530–544. **121:** Tjaden, Patricia, and Nancy Toennes. 2006. *Extent, Nature, and Consequences of Rape Victimization: Findings from the National Violence against Women Survey*. Washington, DC: U.S. Office of Justice Programs. **122:** The Ten Commandments, King James Bible "Authorized Version", Cambridge Edition, 1769; McCaghy, 2006. *Deviant Behavior: Crime, Conflict, and Interest Groups*. Boston: Allyn & Bacon; Messner, Steven F., and Richard Rosenfeld. 1997. *Crime and the American Dream* (2nd ed.). Belmont, CA: Wadsworth.

Chapter 6. **130:** Fishman, Steve. 2010. "Bernie Madoff, Free at Last." *New York*, June 14–21, pp. 30–37; Fishman, Steve. 2011. "The Madoff Tapes," *New York*, April 7, pp. 22–27, 91–93. **131:** Mayne, Jerome. 2010. *Diary of a White Collage Criminal*. Minneapolis, MN: Jerome Mayne/Fraudcon. **132:** David Friedrichs 2010, Chapter 1. David Friedrichs "Trusted Criminals" 2010, Chapter 1. **136:** Ross, Edward Alsworth. 1907. *Sin and Society: An Analysis of Latter-Day Iniquity*. Boston & New York: Houghton Mifflin; Sutherland, Edwin H. 1949. *White Collar Crime*. New York: Dryden Press. Sutherland, Edwin H. 1961. *White Collar Crime*. New York: Holt, Rinehart, & Winston. Sutherland, Edwin H. 1983. *White Collar Crime: The Uncut Version*. New Haven, CN: Yale University Press. **137:** Newman, Donald J. 1958. "White-Collar Crime." *Law and Contemporary Problems*, 23.(Autumn): 735–753; Mannheim, Karl. 1965. *Comparative Criminology*. London: Routledge & Kegan Paul; Egan, Timothy. 1989. "Putting a Face on Corporate Crime." *The New York Times*, July 14, p. B8. **137, 138:** Geis, Gilbert.

1962. "Toward a Delineation of White-Collar Offenses," *Sociological Inquiry*, 32 (Spring): 160–171. **139:** Weisburd, David, Stanton Wheeler, Elin Warning, and Nancy Bode. 1991. *Crimes of the Middle Classes: White-Collar Offenders in the Federal Courts*. New Haven, CN: Yale University Press. **141:** Braithwaite, John. 1985. "White Collar Crime," *Annual Review of Sociology*, 11: 1–21; Gross, Edward. 1978. "Organizational Crime: A Theoretical Perspective." In Norman Denzin (ed.), *Studies in Symbolic Interaction*. Greenwich, CT: JAI Press, pp. 55–88. **143:** Benson, Michael L. 1985. "Denying the Guilty Mind: Accounting for Involvement in a White Collar Crime." *Criminology*, 23 (November): 589–599. **145:** Punch, Maurice. 2008. "The Organization Did It: Individuals, Corporations and Crime." In John Minkes and Leonard Minkes (eds.), *Corporate and White Collar Crime*. Los Angeles: Sage, pp. 102–121.

Chapter 7.   156, 159: ADAM II, 2011 Annual Report, 2012. **156–158:** "The DAWN Report," ED visits, July 2, 2012. **165:** Goldstein, Avram. 2001. *Addiction: From Biology to Drug Policy*. New York: Oxford University Press. **168:** Testa, Maria. 2004. "The Role of Substance Use in Male-to-Female Physical and Sexual Violence." *Journal of Interpersonal Violence*, 19 (December): 1494–1505; Muehlenhard, Charlene L, and Melaney A. Linton. 1987. "Date Rape and Sexual Aggression in Dating Situations: Incident and Risk Factors." *Journal of Counseling Psychology*, 34 (2): 186–196. **168:** Ullman, Sarah E, George Karabatsos, and Mary P. Koss. 1999. "Alcohol and Sexual Assault in a National Sample of College Women." *Journal of Interpersonal Violence*, 16 (June): 603–625. **169:** Finch, Emily, and Vanessa E. Munro. 2007. "The Demon Drink and the Demonized Woman: Socio-Sexual Stereotypes and Responsibility Attribution in Rape Trials Involving Intoxicants." *Social and Legal Studies*, 16 (4): 591–614. SAMHSA, 2007, "Detailed Tables" (not in SAMHSA, 2008). **178:** April 2009, *The Washington Post* and ABC News.

Chapter 8.   187: Davison, Bill. 1967. "The Hidden Evils of LSD." *The Saturday Evening Post*, August 12, pp. 19–23; Brecher, Edward M., et al. 1972. *Licit and Illicit Drugs*. Boston: Little, Brown. **188:** Ashley, Richard. 1975. *Cocaine: Its History, Uses, and Effects*. New York: St. Martin's Press; Colonel J. W. Watson of Georgia, New York Tribune, June, 1903; Dr. Christopher Koch, *Literary Digest*, 1914. **191:** Inciardi, James A. 1987. "Beyond Cocaine: Basuco, Crack, and Other Coca Products." *Contemporary Drug Problems*, 14 (Fall): 461–492; Cohen, Stanley. 1972, 2002. *Folk Devils and Moral Panics* (1st ed.), London: MacGibbon & Kee; 3rd ed., London: Routledge. **192:** Toufexis, 1991, p. 56. Toufexis, Anastasia. 1991. "Innocent Victims." *Time*, May 13, pp. 56–60. **196:** ADAM, 2011, p. xii. ADAM (Arrestee Drug Abuse Monitoring). 2011. *ADAM II 2010 Annual Report*. Washington: Office of Drug Control Policy; "'Meth' Moves East" www.usatoday.com/news/nation/2003-07-29-meth-cover_x.htm; Shafer 2007. Shafer, Jack. 2007. "Meth Madness at Newsweek," *Slate Magazine*, January 31.

Chapter 9.   209: Pearson Education, Upper Saddle River, NJ. **211:** Lane, Charles. 2003. "Justices Overturn Texas Sodomy Ban." *The Washington Post*, June 27, pp. A1, A16. **211, 215:** Minton, Henry L. 2002. *Departing From Deviance: A History of Homosexual Rights and Emancipatory Science in America*. Chicago: University of Chicago Press. **212–213:** Copyright © Gallup, Inc. All rights reserved. The content is used with permission; however, Gallup retains all right of republication. **214:** Gilbert Herdt, January 2, 2006 *The Washington Post*; Broadway, Bill. 2003. "Homosexuality in the Biblical Sense." *The Washington Post*, August 9, pp. B8, B9. **215:** Pat Robertson, March 27, 2012. Christian Broadcasting Network; Pastor Charles Worsley May 13, 2012, in Maiden, NC, CNN, quote from speech given by Worsley on YouTube video. **216:** Konigsberg, Eric. 1998. "The Cheating Kind." *The New York Times Magazine*, March 8, p. 65. **217:** Roiphe, Katie. 1997. "Adultery's Double Standard." *The New York Times Magazine*, October 7, pp. 54–55. **218:** Begley, Sharon. 1996/1997. "Infidelity and the Science of Cheating." *Newsweek*, December 30, 1996/January 6, 1997, pp. 57–59; Richardson, Diane. 1996. "Heterosexuality and Social Theory." In Diane Richardson (ed.), *Theorizing Heterosexuality*. Buckingham, UK: Open University Press, pp. 1–20. **218–219:** Weitzer, Ronald (ed.). 2000. *Sex for Sale: Prostitution, Pornography, and the Sex Industry*. New York & London: Routledge. **219:** Clark Russell D., III, and Elaine Hatfield. 1989. "Gender Differences in Receptivity to Sexual Offers." *Journal of Psychology and Human Sexuality*, 2 (1): 39–55.

Chapter 10.   227: Markoff, John. 2009. "With Sensitive Software, Iranians And Others Outwit Net Censors." *The New York Times*, May 1, pp. A1, A3; Schwartz, John. 2009. "Vocal Minority Insists It Was All Smoke and Mirrors." *The New York Times*, July 14, p. D8. **228:** Douglas, Jack D., and Frances C. Waksler. 1982. *The Sociology of Deviance: An Introduction*. Boston: Little, Brown. **229:** Kring, Ann M., Sheri L. Johnson, Gerald C. Davison, and John M. Neale. 2010. *Abnormal Psychology* (11th ed.). New York: John Wiley & Sons. **231:** Charon, Joel M. 1995. *Ten Questions: A Sociological Perspective* (2nd ed.), Belmont, CA: Wadsworth; Marx, Karl, and Friedrich Engels. 1947. *The German Ideology, Parts I and III*. New York: International Publishers (orig. written 1846). **234:** Stark, Rodney, and William Sims Bainbridge. 1996. *Religion, Deviance, and Social Control*. New York and London: Routledge; Chambers, W.V., et al. 1994. "The Group Psychological Abuse Scale: A Measure of the Varieties of Cultic Abuse." *Cultic Studies Journal*, 11 (1): 88–17. **235–236:** Perrin, Robin. 2008. "When Religion Becomes Deviance: Introducing Religion in Deviance and Social Problems Courses." In Bruce Hoffman and Ashley Demyan (eds.), *Teaching and Learning About Deviance: A Resource Guide*. Washington, DC: American Sociological Association, pp. 53–65. **235:** *Cultic Studies Review*. Vol. 1, 2002. **236:** Powell, Michael. 2005; "Judge Rules against Intelligent Design." *The Washington Post*, December 21, pp. A1f. **238–239:** "Two (2) Quotes" from the book *Why People Believe Weird Things* by Michael Shermer. Copyright © 1997, 2002 by Michael Shermer. Used by permission of Henry Holt Company, LLC. **239:** Kitcher, Philip. 1982. *Abusing Science: The Case Against Creationism*. Boston: MIT Press; Kates, William. 2005. "Museums Answer Critics of Evolution." *The Washington Post*, December 26, pp. A22, A23; Pat Robertson, Associated Press release, November 11, 2005; Morris, Henry M. 1972. *The Remarkable Birth of Planet Earth*. San Diego: Creation-Life Publishers. **242:** Bernstein, Jeremy.

1978. "Scientific Cranks: How to Recognize One and What to Do Until the Doctor Arrives," *The American Scholar*, 47 (March): 8–14.

Chapter 11.   253: Rimland, Bernard. 1969. "Psychogenesis versus Biogenesis: The Issue and the Evidence." In Stanley C. Plog and Robert B. Edgerton (eds.), *Changing Perspectives in Mental Health*. New York: Holt, Rinehart & Winston, pp. 702–735; Nettler, Gwynn. 1974. "On Telling Who's Crazy." *American Sociological Review*, 39 (December): 893–894. **257:** Loftus, T.A. 1960. *Meaning and Methods of Diagnosis in Clinical Psychiatry*. Philadelphia: Lea & Febinger. **258:** Edgerton, Robert B. 1969. "On the Recognition of Mental Illness." In Robert B. Edgerton (ed.), *Perspectives in Mental Illness*. New York: Holt, Rinehart, & Winston, pp. 49–72; Krohn, Marvin D., and Ronald L. Akers. 1977. "An Alternative View of the Labeling Versus Psychiatric Perspectives on Societal Reaction to Mental Illness." *Social Forces*, 56 (December): 341–361; Lemert, Edwin M. 1951. *Social Pathology: A Systematic Approach to the Theory of Sociopathic Behavior*. New York: McGraw-Hill. **260:** Gove, Walter R. 1979a. "The Labelling Versus the Psychiatric Explanation of Mental Illness: A Debate That Has Become Substantially Irrelevant (Reply to Horwitz)," *Journal of Health and Social Behavior*, 20 (September): 89–93. **261:** Link, Bruce G., and Frances T. Cullen. 1989. "The Labeling Theory of Mental Disorder: A Review of the Evidence." In James Greenly (ed.), *Mental Illness in Social Context*. Detroit: Wayne State University Press; Rosenhan, David L. 1973. "On Being Sane in Insane Places." *Science*, 179 (January 19): 250–258; Spitzer, Robert L. 1976. "More on Pseudoscience in Science and the Case for Psychiatric Diagnosis: A Critique of D.L. Rosenhan's 'On Being Sane in Insane Places' and 'The Contextual Nature of Psychiatric Diagnosis.'" *Archives of General Psychiatry*, 33 (April): 459–470. **262:** Spitzer, Robert L. 1975. "On Pseudoscience in Science, Logic in Remission, and Psychiatric Diagnosis: A Critique of Rosenhan's 'On Being Sane in Insane Places.'" *Journal of Abnormal Psychology*, 84 (5): 442–452. **265:** Turner, R. Jay, and John W. Gartrell. 1978. "Social Factors in Psychiatric Outcome: Toward a Resolution of Interpretive Controversies." *American Sociological Review*, 43 (June): 368–382; Gallagher, Bernard J., III. 2002, 2011. *The Sociology of Mental Illness* (4/e & 5/e). Upper Saddle River, NJ: Pearson Prentice Hall; Pearlin, Leonard I., and Joyce S. Johnson. 1977. "Marital Status, Life Strains, and Depression." *American Sociological Review*, 42 (October): 704–715. **267:** Berger, Philip B., and Beatrix Hamberg, and David Hamberg. 1977. "Mental Health: Progress and Problems." In John H. Knowles (ed.), *Doing Better and Feeling Worse: Health in the United States*. New York: W.W. Norton., pp. 261–276. **268:** Goldman, Douglas. 1955. "Treatment of Psychotic States with Chlorpromazine." *Journal of the American Medical Association*, 157 (April 19): 1274–1278; Callaway, Enoch, III. 1958. "Institutional Use of Ataractic Drugs." *Modern Medicine*, 1958 Annual, Part I (January 1-June 15): 26–29. **270:** Torrey, E. Fuller, et al. 2010. *More Mentally Ill Persons Are in Jails and Prisons Than Hospitals: A Survey of the States*. Arlington, VA: Treatment Advocacy Center; Arlington, VA: National Sherriffs' Association; Gove, Walter R. 1975a. "The Labelling Theory of Mental Illness: A Reply to Scheff." *American Sociological Review*, 40 (April): 242–248.

Chapter 12.   277: Leviticus 21:17–23, King James Bible. "Authorized Version," Cambridge Edition, 1769; John 7:24 King James Bible. "Authorized Version," Cambridge Edition, 1769; Rapp, Emily. 2007. *Poster Child: A Memoir*. New York: Bloomsbury. Reprinted by permission from ICM Partners, Inc. **277, 278, 282, 293:** Reprinted with Permission of Scribner Publishing Group from Touchstone edition of *STIGMA: Notes on Management of Spoiled Identity* by Erving Goffman. Copyright © 1963 by Prentice Hall. Copyright © 1991 renewed by Simon & Schuster, Inc. All rights reserved. **278:** Allon, Natalie. 1976. *Urban Life Styles*. Dubuque, IA: W. C. Brown; Polsky, Ned. 1998. *Hustlers, Beats, and Others* (exp. ed.). New York: Lyons Press. **279:** Yardley, Jim. 2012. "A Village Rape Shatters a Family, and India's Traditional Silence." *The New York Times*, October 28, pp. 1, 12. **280:** Katz, Irwin. 1981. *Stigma: A Social Psychological Analysis*. Hillsdale, NJ: Lawrence Erlbaum; Monestier, Martin. 1978. *Human Oddities: A Book of Nature's Anomalies*. Secaucus, NJ: Citadel Press. **282:** Erikson, Kai T. 1964. "Notes on the Sociology of Deviance." In Howard S. Becker (ed.), *The Other Side: Perspectives on Deviance*. New York: Free Press, pp. 307–314; Freidson, Eliot. 1966. "Disability as Deviance." In Marvin B. Sussman (ed.), *Sociology and Rehabilitation*. Washington, DC: American Sociological Association, pp. 71–99. **283:** Cook, Thomas. 2011. "Disability Rights: A Global Grass-Roots Movement." *The Gazette*, 28 July. **284–285:** Cowley, Geoffrey. 1996. "The Biology of Beauty." *Newsweek*, June 3, pp. 61–66.535–550. **284:** Lemley, Brad. 2000. "Isn't She Lovely?" *Scover*, January, pp. 43–49. Cowley, Geoffrey. 1996. "The Biology of Beauty." *Newsweek*, June 3, pp. 61–66.535–550. Langlois, Judith, et al. 2000. "Maxims or Myth of Beauty: A Meta-Analytic and Theoretical Review." *Psychological Bulletin*, 126 (3): 390–423; Beuf, Ann Hill. 1990. *Beauty Is the Beast*. Philadelphia: University of Pennsylvania Press. **286:** Berscheid, Ellen, and Elaine Walster. 1972. "Beauty and the Best," *Psychology Today*, March 1972, pp. 42–46, 74. www.psychologytoday.com; Jones, Edward E., et al. 1984. *Social Stigma: The Psychology of Marked Relationships*. New York: W.H. Freeman; Grealy, Lucy. 1995. *Autobiography of a Face*. New York: HarperCollins. **287:** Imrey, Rob. 1996. *Disability and the City: International Perspectives*. New York: St. Martin's Press. **288:** Sanders, Clinton R. 1989. *Customizing the Body: The Art and Culture of Tattooing*. Philadelphia: Temple University Press. **290:** Louderback, Llewellyn. 1970. *Fat Power: Whatever You Weigh Is Right*. New York: Hawthorn Books. **291:** Allon, Natalie. 1982. "The Stigma of Overweight in Everyday Life." In Benjamin B.Wolman (ed.), *Psychological Aspects of Obesity: A Handbook*. New York: Van Nostrand Reinhold, pp. 130–174; Cahnman, Werner J. 1968. "The Stigma of Obesity." *Sociological Quarterly*, 9 (Summer): 283–299" John Wiley & Sons, Inc. Reprinted with permission of the Scribner Publishing Group from the Touchstone edition of STIGMA: Notes on Management of Spoiled Identity by Erving Goffman. Copyright © 1963 by Prentice Hall. Copyright © renewed 1991 by Simon & Schuster, Inc. All Rights Reserved. **294:** Stella Boonshoft, October 2012 (10/19/2012), http://thebodyloveblog.tumblr.com/post/32881501880/warning-picture-might-be-considered-obscene. **295:** Billups, Andrea. 2012. "Stella Boonshoft Becomes Body-Image Hero After Posting Bikini Picture on

Her Blog," *People*, October 23; Bogdan, Robert. 1988. *Freak Show: Presenting Human Oddities for Amusement and Profit.* Chicago: University of Chicago Press. **297:** Linton, Simi. 1998. *Claiming Disability: Knowledge and Identity.* New York: New York University Press.

Chapter 13.   305: MEMRI TV, September 11, 2012; *The New York Times*, January 16, 2013, p. A22. **306:** Wallechensky, David, and Irving Wallace. 1975. *The People's Almanac.* Garden City, NY: Doubleday; United States Army War College, 1936; Hitler, Adolph. 1925/1971. *Mein Kampf.* Munich: Eher-Verlag/Boston: Houghton Mifflin; Reiss, Stephen A. 1988. *Sports and the American Jew.* Syracuse: Syracuse University Press; Knox, Robert. 1850. *The Races of Men: A Fragment.* Philadelphia: Lea & Blanchard. **308, 328:** Reprinted with permission of the Scribner Publishing Group from the Touchstone edition of *STIGMA: Notes on Management of Spoiled Identity* by Erving Goffman. Copyright © 1963 by Prentice Hall. Copyright © renewed 1991 by Simon & Schuster, Inc. All Rights Reserved. **311:** Arthur, Makaila Mariel Lemonik. 2007. "Racism, Structural and Institutional." In George Ritzer (ed.), *The Blackwell Encyclopedia of Sociology.* New York & Oxford, UK: Blackwell, pp. 3765–3767. **311–312:** Page, Susan, and Carly Mallenbaum. 2011. "Poll Respondents Chart Racial Progress Since MLK." www.usatoday.com/news/nation/2011–08–17-race-poll-inside_n.htm. **312–313:** Douglas Massey, Roberts, Sam. 2012. "Segregation Curtained in U.S. Cities, Study Finds." *The New York Times*, January 30; Logan, John R., and Brian J. Stults. 2011. "The Persistence of Segregation in the Metropolis: New Findings from the 2010

Census." Census Brief prepared for Project US2010. http://www.s4.brown.edu/us2010. **313–314:** Bolton, Michael J. 2011. "Premature Exuberance, Police, Profiling, and African Americans in a Postracial Society." *Public Administration Review*, 71 (September/October): 791–795. **314:** Etzioni, Amitai. 2007. "Another Side of Racial Profiling." In Frank Schmalleger (ed.), *Criminal Justice Today: An Introductory Text for the Twenty-First Century.* Upper Saddle River, NJ: Pearson Prentice Hall, pp. 313–314. **316:** Gallup, 1958. **317:** Kellogg, Alex. 2011. "The Changing Face of Seeing Race." *NPR Broadcast*, October 14; Kirkpatrick, David D. 2012. "Anger Over a Film Fuels Anti-American Attacks in Libya and Egypt." *The New York Times*, September 12, p. A4; Quran 3:151, Yusuf Ali. Muhummad Ashraf Publisher, Lahore, India (later Pakistan), 1934. **319:** Fuller, Thomas. 2012. "Ethnic Hatred Tears Apart a Region of Myanmar." *The New York Times*, November 30, pp. A1, A16. **322:** Coursen-Neff, Zama. 2005. "Discrimination Against Palestinian Arab Children in the Israeli Educational System," *New York University Journal of International Law and Politics*, 36 (May): 749–816. **323:** Sanders, Edmund. 2011. "Israeli Intolerance Shows up on Internet, in Knesset, on the Street." *The Los Angeles Times*, January 23. **327–328:** Trager, Eric. 2011. "Why the Middle East Is Still in Thrall to 9/11 Conspiracy Theories." *The New Republic*, September 3.

Chapter 14.   336: Richard Murdock, U.S. Senate Debate, October 23, 2012. **337:** Goodstein, Laurie. 2012b. "Christian Right Failed to Sway Voters on Issues." *The New York Times*, November 10, pp. A1, A3. **341–342:** Solomon, Andrew. 2012. *Far From the Tree.* New York: Scribner.

References

Abdulali, Solaila. 2013. "I Was Wounded; My Honor Wasn't." *The New York Times*, January 8, p. A23.

ADAM (Arrestee Drug Abuse Monitoring). 2011. *ADAM II 2010 Annual Report*. Washington, DC: Office of Drug Control Policy.

Adler, Freda, and William S. Laufer (eds.). 1995. *The Legacy of Anomie Theory*. New Brunswick, NJ: Transaction.

Adler, Jerry. 1996. "Adultery: A New Furor over an Old Sin." *Newsweek*, September 30, pp. 54–60.

Adler, Patricia A., and Peter Adler (eds.). 2009. *Constructions of Deviance: Social Power, Context, and Interaction*. Belmont, CA: Thompson Wadsworth.

Adwan, Sami, et al. (eds.). 2012. *Side By Side: Parallel Histories of Israel-Palestine*. New York: New Press.

Agnew, Robert. 1995. "The Contribution of Social-Psychological Strain Theory to the Explanation of Crime and Delinquency." In Freda Adler and William S. Laufer (eds.), *The Legacy of Anomie Theory*. New Brunswick, NJ: Transaction, pp. 113–137.

Agnew, Robert. 2006. *Pressured into Crime: An Overview of General Strain Theory*. Los Angeles: Roxbury.

Agnew, Robert. 2011. "Control and Social Disorganization Theory." In Clifton D. Bryant (ed.), *The Routledge Handbook of Deviant Behavior*. London & New York: Routledge, pp. 114–120.

Ahern, Jennifer, Jennifer Stuber, and Sandro Galea. 2007. "Stigma, Discrimination, and the Health of Illicit Drug Users." *Drug and Alcohol Dependence*, 88 (2–3): 188–196.

Aho, James A. 1994. *This Thing of Darkness: A Sociology of the Enemy*. Seattle: University of Washington Press.

Akers, Ronald L. 1968. "Problems in the Sociology of Deviance: Social Definitions and Behavior." *Social Forces*, 46 (June): 455–465.

Akers, Ronald L. 1991. "Self-Control as a General Theory of Crime." *Journal of Quantitative Criminology*, 7 (2): 201–211.

Akers, Ronald L. 1998. *Social Learning and Social Structure: A General Theory of Crime and Deviance*. Boston: Northeastern University Press.

Alexander, Michelle. 2012. *The New Jim Crow: Mass Incarceration in the Age of Colorblindedness* (rev. ed.). New York: The New Press.

Allon, Natalie. 1973. "The Stigma of Overweight in Everyday Life." In G. A. Bray (ed.), *Obesity in Perspective*. Washington, DC: U. S. Government Printing Office, pp. 83–102.

Allon, Natalie. 1976. *Urban Life Styles*. Dubuque, IA: W. C. Brown.

Allon, Natalie. 1982. "The Stigma of Overweight in Everyday Life." In Benjamin B. Wolman (ed.), *Psychological Aspects of Obesity: A Handbook*. New York: Van Nostrand Reinhold, pp. 130–174.

Altman, Alex. 2010. "Majority Oppose Mosque, Many Distrust Muslims." *Time*, August 19.

Anderson, Jenny. 2012. "Retired Horace Mann Teacher Admits to Sex with Students." *The New York Times*, June 23, pp. 1ff.

Andrews, George, and David Solomon (eds.). 1975. *The Cocoa Leaf and Cocaine Papers*. New York: Harcourt Brace Jovanovich.

Anleu, Sharyn L. Roach. 1991. *Deviance, Conformity and Control* (1st ed.). Melbourne, Australia: Longman Cheshire.

Anleu, Sharyn L. Roach. 2006. *Deviance, Conformity and Control* (4th ed.). Sydney, Australia: Pearson.

Anonymous. 2000. "He's Shedding His Human Skin." *The Chronicle of Higher Education*, January 28, p. A12.

Archibold, Randal C., and Damien Cave. 2012. "Numb to Carnage, Mexicans Find Diversions, and Life Goes On." *The New York Times*, May 16, pp. A1, A3.

Ariely, Dan, and George Lowenstein. 2006. "In the Heat of the Moment: The Effect of Sexual Arousal on Sexual Decision Making." *Journal of Behavioral Decision Making*, 19 (1): 87–98.

Armstrong, Edward G. 2007. "Moral Panic Over Meth." *Contemporary Justice Review*, 10 (December): 427–442.

Arthur, Mikaila Mariel Lemonik. 2007. "Racism, Structural and Institutional." In George Ritzer (ed.), *The Blackwell Encyclopedia of Sociology*. New York & Oxford, UK: Blackwell, pp. 3765–3767.

Ashley, Richard. 1975. *Cocaine: Its History, Uses, and Effects*. New York: St. Martin's Press.

Atwater, Lynn. 1982. *The Extramarital Connection: Sex, Intimacy, and Identity*. New York: Irvington.

St. Augustine. 1963. *The Confessions of St. Augustine*. New York: Mentor/Penguin Books.

Bailey, Carol A. 2011. "Feminist Theory." In Clifton D. Bryant (ed.), *The Routledge Handbook of Deviant Behavior*. London & New York: Routledge, pp. 164–170.

Baker, A. L. 2011. "Judge Declines to Dismiss Case Alleging Racial Profiling by City Police in Street Stops." *The New York Times*, August 31.

Baker, Dean, and Kevin Hassett. 2012. "The Human Disaster of Unemployment." *The New York Times*, May 13, p. SR9.

Balko, Radley. 2009. "The El Paso Miracle." www.Reason. com, July 6.

Ball, Richard A. 2011. "Biological and Biosocial Theory." In Clifton D. Bryant (ed.), *The Routledge Handbook of Deviant Behavior*. London & New York: Routledge, pp. 157–163.

Barron, James. 2012. "Gunman Massacres 20 Children at School in Connecticut." *The New York Times*, December 15, pp. A1, A16.

Barstow, David. 2012. "Vast Mexico Bribery Case Hushed Up by Wal-Mart After Top-Level Struggle." *The New York Times*, April 22, pp. 1, 8–10.

Bar-Tal, Daniel, Lily Chernyak-Hal, Noa Schori, and Ayelet Gundar. 2009. "A Sense of Self-Perceicev Collective Victimhood in Intractable Conflicts," *International Review of the Red Cross,* 91 (June): 229–258.

Bastian, Lisa. 1993. "Criminal Victimization 1992." *Bureau of Justice Statistics Bulletin*, October, pp. 1–8.

Beck, Allen J. 2010. *Sexual Victimization in Prison and Jails Reported by Inmates, 2008-09*. Washington, DC: U.S. Department of Justice, Bureau of Justice Statistics.

Becker, Howard S. 1963. *Outsiders: Studies in the Sociology of Deviance*. New York: Free Press.

Becker, Howard S. (ed.). 1971. *Culture and Civility in San Francisco*. Chicago & New Brunswick, NJ: Aldine/Transaction.

Becker, Howard S. 1973. "Labelling Theory Revisited." In *Outsiders: Studies in the Sociology of Deviance* (exp. ed.). New York: Free Press, pp. 177–212.

Beeghley, Leonard. 2003. *Homicide: A Sociological Explanation*. Lanham, MD: Rowman & Littlefield.

Begley, Sharon. 1996/1997. "Infidelity and the Science of Cheating." *Newsweek*, December 30, 1996/January 6, 1997, pp. 57–59.

Bell, Robert R. 1971. *Social Deviance: A Substantive Analysis*. Homewood, IL: Dorsey Press.

Ben Zion, Ilan. 2012. "Iranian News Site Pins Newtown Shooting on 'Israeli Death Squad.'" *The Times of Israel*, December 18.

Bennett-Smith, Meredith. 2012. "Denise Helms, California Woman, Fired After Calling Obama N-Word, Hoping He's Assassinated." *The Huffington Post*, November 11.

Benson, Michael L. 1985. "Denying the Guilty Mind: Accounting for Involvement in a White Collar Crime." *Criminology*, 23 (November): 589–599.

Benson, Michael L., and Sally S. Simpson. 2009. *White-Collar Crime: An Opportunity Perspective*. New York & London: Routledge.

Ben-Yehuda, Nachman. 1980. "The European Witch Craze of the 14th to 17th Centuries: A Sociologist's Perspective." *American Journal of Sociology*, 86 (July): 1–31.

Ben-Yehuda, Nachman. 1985. *Deviance and Moral Boundaries*. Chicago: University of Chicago Press.

Ben-Yehuda, Nachman. 1990. "Positive and Negative Deviance: More Fuel for a Controversy." *Deviant Behavior*, 11 (3): 221–243.

Berger, Peter L., and Thomas Luckmann. 1966. *The Social Construction of Reality: A Treatise on the Sociology of Knowledge*. Garden City, NY: Doubleday.

Berger, Philip B., Beatrix Hamberg, and David Hamberg. 1977. "Mental Health: Progress and Problems." In John H. Knowles (ed.), *Doing Better and Feeling Worse: Health in the United States*. New York: W.W. Norton, pp. 261–276.

Bergler, Edmund. 1956. *Homosexuality: Disease or Way of Life?* New York: Hill & Wang.

Bernard, Jesse. 1982. *The Future of Marriage* (2nd ed.). New Haven, CT: Yale University Press.

Bernstein, Jeremy. 1978. "Scientific Cranks: How to Recognize One and What to Do Until the Doctor Arrives." *The American Scholar*, 47 (March): 8–14.

Berscheid, Ellen, and Elaine Walster. 1972. "Beauty and the Best." *Psychology Today*, March, pp. 43–46, 74.

Best, Joel. 2001. *Damned Lies and Statistics: Untangling Numbers from the Media, Politicians, and Activists*. Berkeley: University of California Press.

Best, Joel. 2011. "Constructing Deviance." In Clifton D. Bryant (ed.), *The Routledge Handbook of Deviant Behavior*. London & New York: Routledge, pp. 17–23.

Bestard, Alyshia D. 2008. *Feederism: An Exploratory Study into the Stigma of Erotic Weight Gain*. M.A. Thesis, Department of Sociology, University of Waterloo, Waterloo, Ontario, Canada.

Beuf, Ann Hill. 1990. *Beauty Is the Beast*. Philadelphia: University of Pennsylvania Press.

Bieber, Irving, et al. 1962. *Homosexuality: A Psychoanalytic Study of Male Homosexuals*. New York: Basic Books.

Billups, Andrea. 2012. "Stella Boonshoft Becomes Body-Image Hero After Posting Bikini Picture on Her Blog." *People*, October 23.

Black, Donald J. (ed.). 1984. *Toward a General Theory of Social Control*. Orlando, FL: Academic Press.

Black, Donald W. 1999. *Bad Boys, Bad Men: Confronting Antisocial Personality Disorder*. New York: Oxford University Press.

Black, Michelle C., et al. 2011. *The National Intimate Partner and Sexual Violence Survey: 2010 Summary Report*. Atlanta, GA: National Center for Injury Prevention and Control Centers for Disease Control and Prevention (CDC).

Blader, Joseph C. 2011. "Acute Inpatient Care for Psychiatric Disorders in the United States, 1966 Through 2007." *Archives of General Psychiatry*, 68 (December): 1276–1283.

Blumer, Herbert. 1969. *Symbolic Interactionism*. Englewood Cliffs, NJ: Prentice Hall.

Blumstein, Alfred, and Joel Wallman (eds.). 2000. *The Crime Drop in America*. Cambridge, UK: Cambridge University Press.

Bogdan, Robert. 1988. *Freak Show: Presenting Human Oddities for Amusement and Profit*. Chicago: University of Chicago Press.

Bolton, Michael J. 2011. "Premature Exuberance, Police, Profiling, and African Americans in a Postracial Society." *Public Administration Review*, 71 (September/October): 791–795.

Bonger, Willem A. 1916. *Criminality and Economic Conditions* (trans. Henry P. Horton). Boston: Little, Brown.

Boorstein, Michelle. 2010. "Americans' Bias Against Jews, Muslims Linked, Poll Says." *The Washington Post*, January 21.

Bourgois, Philippe. 1995, 2003. *In Search of Respect: Selling Crack in the Barrio* (1st & 2nd eds.). Cambridge, UK & New York: Cambridge University Press.

Bourque, Linda Brookover. 1989. *Defining Rape*. Durham, NC: Duke University Press.

Brackman, Harold. 1996. "Farrakhan Conspiracy: Louis Farrakhan and the Paranoid Style in African-American Politics." *Skeptic*, 4 (3): 36–43.

Braithwaite, John. 1985. "White Collar Crime." *Annual Review of Sociology*, 11: 1–21.

Brcak, Nancy, and John R. Pavia. 1994. "Racism in Japanese and U.S. Wartime Propaganda." *The Historian*, 56 (Summer): 671–684.

Brecher, Edward M., et al. 1972. *Licit and Illicit Drugs*. Boston: Little, Brown.

Brezina, Timothy. 2011. "Anomie-Strain Theory." In Clifton D. Bryant (ed.), *The Routledge Handbook of Deviant Behavior*. London & New York: Routledge, pp. 99–105.

Briar, Scott, and Irving Piliavin. 1965. "Delinquency, Situational Inducements, and Commitments to Conformity." *Social Problems*, 13 (1): 35–45.

Broadway, Bill. 2003. "Homosexuality in the Biblical Sense." *The Washington Post*, August 9, pp. B8, B9.

Brody, Jane E. 2003. "Gay Families Flourish as Acceptance Grows." *The New York Times*, July 1, p. D7.

Bronner, Ethan. 2012. "Adultery, an Ancient Crime That Remains on Many Books." *The New York Times*, November 15, p. A12.

Broude, Gwenn J., and Sarah J. Greene. 1976. "Cross-Cultural Codes on Twenty Sexual Attitudes and Practices." *Ethnology*, 15 (October): 409–429.

Brownmiller, Susan. 1975. *Against Our Will: Women, Men, and Rape*. New York: Simon & Schuster.

Brulliard, Karin. 2003. "In Texas, a Darwinian Debate." *The Washington Post*, February 16, p. A7.

Brunner, H. G., et al. 1993. "Abnormal Behavior Associated with a Point Mutation in the Structural Gene for Monoamine Oxidase A." *Science*, 262 (October 22): 578–580.

Buettner, Russ. 2012. "Selling Prostitution, and the Book and Film Rights, Too." *The New York Times*, April 11, pp. A17, A21.

Bull, Chris. 1999. "His Public Domain, His Private Pain." *The Washington Post Magazine*, July 11.

Burgess, Robert L., and Ronald L. Akers. 1966. "A Differential Reinforcement Theory of Criminal Behavior." *Social Problems*, 14 (Fall): 128–147.

Burgess-Proctor, Amanda. 2006. "Intersections of Race, Class, Gender, and Crime." *Feminist Criminology*, 1 (1): 27–47.

Bursik, Robert J., and Harold G. Grasmick. 1993. *Neighborhoods and Crime: The Dimensions of Effective Community Control*. New York: Lexington Books.

Buss, David, et al. 1994. *The Evolution of Desire: Strategies of Human Mating*. New York: Basic Books.

Byck, Robert (ed.). 1974. *Cocaine Papers by Sigmund Freud*. New York: Stonehill.

Cahnman, Werner J. 1968. "The Stigma of Obesity." *Sociological Quarterly*, 9 (Summer): 283–299.

Callaway, Enoch, III. 1958. "Institutional Use of Antarctic Drugs." *Modern Medicine, 1958 Annual*, Part I (January 1–June 15): 26–29.

Cameron, Mary Owen. 1964. *The Booster and the Snitch*. New York: Free Press.

Carnes, Patrick. 1983. *Out of the Shadows: Understanding Sexual Addiction*. Minneapolis, MN: CompCare.

Chambliss, William J. 1964. "A Sociological Analysis of the Law of Vagrancy." *Social Problems*, 12 (Summer): 67–77.

Chambliss, William J. 1973. "The Saints and the Roughnecks." *Society*, 11 (December): 24–31.

Chambers, W. V., et al. 1994. "The Group Psychological Abuse Scale: A Measure of the Varieties of Cultic Abuse." *Cultic Studies Journal*, 11 (1): 88–17.

Charlton, James I. 1999. *Nothing About Us Without Us: Disability, Oppression, and Empowerment*. Berkeley: University of California Press.

Charon, Joel M. 1995. *Ten Questions: A Sociological Perspective* (2nd ed.). Belmont, CA: Wadsworth.

Chasnoff, Ira J., et al. 1989. "Temporary Patterns of Cocaine Use in Pregnancy." *Journal of the American Medical Association*, 261 (March 24–31): 1741–1744.

Chesney-Lind, Meda. 2006. "Patriarchy, Crime, and Justice: Feminist Criminology in an Era of Backlash." *Feminist Criminology*, 1 (1): 6–26.

Clark, Russell D., III. 1990. "The Impact of AIDS on Gender Differences in Willingness to Engage in Casual Sex." *Journal of Applied Social Psychology*, 20 (9): 771–782.

Clark, Russell D., III, and Elaine Hatfield. 1989. "Gender Differences in Receptivity to Sexual Offers." *Journal of Psychology and Human Sexuality*, 2 (1): 39–55.

Clarke, Ronald V., and Marcus Felson (eds.). 1993. *Routine Activities Theory and Rational Choice*. New Brunswick, NJ: Transaction.

Clinard, Marshall B. 1952. *The Black Market: A Study White Collar Crime*. New York: Rinehart.

Clinard, Marshall B. 1957. *Sociology of Deviant Behavior*. New York: Rinehart.

Clinard, Marshall B. 1964. "The Theoretical Implications of Anomie and Deviant Behavior." In Marshall B. Clinard (ed.), *Anomie and Deviant Behavior: A Discussion and Critique*. New York: Free Press, pp. 1–56.

Clinard, Marshall B., and Robert F. Meier. 2011. *Sociology of Deviant Behavior* (14th ed.). Belmont, CA: Wadsworth/Thompson.

Cockerham, William C. 2003. *Sociology of Mental Disorder* (6th ed.). Upper Saddle River, NJ: Pearson Prentice Hall.

Cockerham, William C. 2011. *Sociology of Mental Disorder* (8th ed.). Upper Saddle River, NJ: Pearson Prentice Hall.

Cohen, Albert K. 1955. *Delinquent Boys: The Subculture of the Gang*. New York: Free Press.

Cohen, Albert K. 1959. "The Study of Social Disorganization and Deviant Behavior." In Robert K. Merton, Leonard Broom, and Leonard S. Cottrell, Jr. (eds.), *Sociology Today: Problems and Prospects*. New York: Basic Books, pp. 461–484.

Cohen, Lawrence E., and Marcus Felson. 1979. "Social Change and Crime Rate Trends: A Routine Activity Approach." *American Sociological Review*, 44 (August): 588–608.

Cohen, Maimon M., Michelle J. Marinello, and Nathan Back. 1967. "Chromosomal Damage in Human Leukocytes Induced by Lysergic Acid Diethylamide." *Science*, 155 (March 17): 1417–1419.

Cohen, Stanley. 1972. *Folk Devils and Moral Panics* (1st ed.). London: MacGibbon & Kee.

Cohen, Stanley. 1985. *Visions of Social Control*. Cambridge, UK: Polity Press.

Cohen, Stanley. 2002. *Folk Devils and Moral Panics* (3rd ed.). London: London: Routledge.

Cohn-Sherbok, Dan. 2006. *The Paradox of Anti-Semitism*. New York: Continuum.

Cole, Stephen. 1975. "The Growth of Scientific Knowledge: Theories of Deviance as a Case Study." In Lewis A. Coser (ed.), *The Idea of Social Structure: Papers in Honor of Robert K. Merton*. New York: Harcourt Brace Jovanovich, pp. 175–220.

Coles, Claire D. 1992. "Effects of Cocaine and Alcohol Use in Pregnancy on Neonatal Growth and Neurobehavioral Status." *Neurotoxicology and Teratology*, 14 (January–February): 1–11.

Connor, John M., and Gustav Helmers. 2007. "Statistics on Modern Private International Cartels, 1990-2005," AAI Working Paper No. 07-01. Washington, DC: American Antitrust Institute.

Conyers, Addrain. 2011. "Conflict Theory." In Clifton D. Bryant (ed.), *The Routledge Handbook of Deviant Behavior*. London & New York: Routledge, pp. 135–142.

Cook, Thomas. 2011. "Disability Rights: A Global Grass-Roots Movement." *The Gazette*, July 28.

Cooley, Charles Horton. 1902. *Human Nature and the Social Order*. New York: Scribner.

Cooper, Alexa, and Eric L. Smith. 2011. "Homicide Trends in the United States, 1980-2008." *Bureau of Justice Statistics*, November, pp. 1–35.

Cooper, Helene, and Jeremy W. Peters. 2012. "For Some, Same Sex Marriage Is Not Politics, It's Personal." *The New York Times*, May 15, p. A17.

Coser, Lewis. 1956. *The Functions of Social Conflict*. New York: Free Press.

Costello, Barbara J. 2006. "Cultural Relativism and the Study of Deviance." *Sociological Spectrum*, 26 (November–December): 581–594.

Coursen-Neff, Zama. 2005. "Discrimination Against Palestinian Arab Children in the Israeli Educational System." *New York University Journal of International Law and Politics*, 36 (May): 749–816.

Cowley, Geoffrey. 1996. "The Biology of Beauty." *Newsweek*, June 3, pp. 61–66, 535–550.

Cozzarelli, Catherine, Anna V. Wilksinson, and Michael J. Tagler. 2001. "Attitudes Toward the Poor and Attributions for Poverty."*Journal of Social Issues*, 57 (2): 207–227.

Cressey, Donald R. 1953. *Other People's Money*. Glencoe, IL: Free Press.

Cressey, Donald R. 1960. "Epidemiology and Individual Conduct." *Pacific Sociological Review*, 3 (Fall): 47–58.

Crews, Frederick. 1995. *The Memory Wars: Freud's Legacy in Dispute*. New York: New York Review of Books.

Cross, Hugh. 2006. "Interventions to Address the Stigma Associated with Leprosy: A Perspective on the Issue." *Psychology, Health & Medicine*, 11 (August): 367–373.

Curra, John. 2000. *The Relativity of Deviance*. Thousand Oaks, CA: Sage.

Currie, Elliott P. 1993. *Reckoning: Drugs, the Cities, and the American Future*. New York: Hill & Wang.

Dalal, Ajit. 2006. "Social Interventions to Moderate Discriminatory Attitudes: The Case of the Physically Challenged in India." *Psychology, Health & Medicine*, 11 (August): 374–382.

Daly, Kathleen, and Meda Chesney-Lind. 1988. "Feminism and Criminology." *Justice Quarterly*, 5 (December): 497–538.

Dao, James. 2012. "For Soldier Disfigured in War, A Way to Return to the World." *The New York Times*, January 31, pp. A1, A16.

Davey, Monica. 2013. "A Soaring Homicide Rate, A Divide in Chicago." *The New York Times*, January 3, pp. A1, A14.

Davis, Kingsley. 1937. "The Sociology of Prostitution." *American Sociological Review*, 2 (October): 744–755.

Davis, Kingsley, and Wilbert E. Moore. 1945. "Some Principles of Stratification." *American Sociological Review*, 10 (April): 242–249.

Davis, Lennard J. (ed.). 1997. *The Disability Studies Reader*. New York: Routledge.

Davison, Bill. 1967. "The Hidden Evils of LSD." *The Saturday Evening Post*, August 12, pp. 19–23.

Deaton, Angus. 2003. "Health, Inequality, and Economic Development." *Journal of Economic Literature*, 41 (2): 113–158.

DeJong, William. 1980. "The Stigma of Obesity: The Consequences of Naive Assumptions Concerning the Causes of Physical Deviance." *Journal of Health and Social Behavior*, 21 (March): 75–87.

Delacoste, Frédérique, and Pricilla Alexander (eds.). 1998. *Sex Work: Writings by Women in the Industry*. San Francisco: Cleis Press.

Dellwing, Michael, Joe Katarba, and Nathan Pino (eds.). 2014. *The Death and Resurrection of Deviance*. London & New York: Palgrave Macmillan.

DeNavas-Wald, Carmen, Bernadette D. Proctor, and Jessica C. Smith. 2013. "Income, Poverty, and Health Insurance Coverage in the United States. 2012." U.S. Census Bureau, Current Population Reports, No. P60-245. Washington, DC: U.S. Government Printing Office.

DeParle, Jason, and Robert Gebeloff. 2009. "Across U.S., Food Stamp Use Soars and Stigma Fades." *The New York Times*, November 29, pp. 1, 26.

Dingeman, M. Kathleen, and Rubén Rumbaut. 2010. "The Immigration-Crime Nexus and Post-Deportation Experiences: En/Countering Stereotypes in California and El Salvador." *University of La Verne Law Review*, 31 (2): 363–402.

Dion, Karen K. 1972. "Physical Attractiveness and Evaluation of Children's Transgressions." *Journal of Personal and Social Psychology*, 24: 207–213.

Disha, Ilir, James C. Cavendish, and Ryan D. King. 2011. "Historical Events and Spaces of Hate: Hate Crimes Against Arabs and Muslims in Post-9/11 America." *Social Problems*, 58 (February): 21–46.

Dishotsky, Norman, William D. Loughman, Robert F. Mogar, and Wendell R. Lipscomb. 1971. "LSD and Genetic Damage." *Science*, 172 (April 30): 431–440.

Dodge, David. 1985. "The Over-Negativized Conceptualization of Deviance: A Programmatic Exploration." *Deviant Behavior*, 6 (1): 17–37.

Doherty, Edmund G. 1978. "Are Different Discharge Criteria Used for Men and Women Psychiatric Inpatients? *Journal of Health and Social Behavior*, 19 (March): 107–116.

Dohrenwend, Bruce P., and Barbara Snell Dohrenwend. 1976. "Sex Differences and Psychiatric Disorder." *American Journal of Sociology*, 81 (May): 1447–1454.

Dokoupil, Tony. 2012. "High Times in America." *Newsweek*, October 20, pp. 27–31.

Dolnick, Sam, and Danny Hakim. 2012. "Women Employed by Lawmaker Describe Sexually Hostile Office." *The New York Times*, August 30, pp. A1, A24.

Donadio, Claudia. 2009. "Bishop Offers Apology for Holocaust Remarks," *The New York Times*, February 22, p. A6.

Douglas, Jack D., and Frances C. Waksler. 1982. *The Sociology of Deviance: An Introduction*. Boston: Little, Brown.

Duneier, Mitchell. 1999. *Sidewalk*. New York: Farrar, Straus & Giroux.

Dunham, H. Warren. 1965. *Community and Schizophrenia: An Epidemiological Analysis*. Detroit: Wayne State University Press.

DuPont, Robert L. 1997. *The Selfish Brain: Learning from Addiction*. Center City, MN: Hazelden.

Durkheim, Émile. 1933/1960. *The Division of Labor in Society* (trans. George Simpson). New York: Macmillan (orig. pub. 1893); Glencoe, IL: Free Press.

Durkheim, Émile. 1938/1958. *The Rules of the Sociological Method* (trans. Sarah A. Soloway and John Mueller; ed. George E. G. Catlin). Chicago: University of Chicago Press (orig. pub. 1895); Glencoe, IL: Free Press.

Durkheim, Émile. 1951. *Suicide: A Study in Sociology* (trans. John A. Spaulding and George Simpson; ed. George Simpson). New York: Free Press (orig. pub. 1897).

Duster, Troy. 1970. *The Legislation of Morality: Law, Drugs, and Moral Judgment*. New York: Free Press.

Dworkin, Andrea. 1981. *Pornography: Men Possessing Women*. New York: Perigee.

Dworkin, Andrea. 1987. *Intercourse*. New York: Free Press.

Eagleman, David. 2011. "The Brain on Trial," *The Atlantic*, July/August, pp. 112–122.

Eckholm, Erik. 2012. "Somalis in Twin Cities Shaken by Charges of Sex Trafficking." *The New York Times*, November 20, pp. A16, A18.

Edgerton, Robert B. 1969. "On the Recognition of Mental Illness." In Robert B. Edgerton (ed.), *Perspectives in Mental Illness*. New York: Holt, Rinehart & Winston, pp. 49–72.

Egan, Timothy. 1989. "Putting a Face on Corporate Crime." *The New York Times*, July 14, p. B8.

Eiserer, Tanya, and Christina Rosales. 2011. "Dallas Police Change Policy on Shoplifting Complaints Under $50." *Dallas Morning News*, December 30.

Elias, Norbert. 1994. *The Civilizing Process* (trans. Edmund Jephcott). Oxford, UK & Cambridge, MA: Blackwell Publishers (orig. pub. 1939).

Ericson, Richard V., Patricia M. Baranek, and Janet B. L. Chan. 1991. *Representing Order: Crime, Law, and Justice in the News Media*. Toronto: University of Toronto Press.

Erikson, Kai T. 1964. "Notes on the Sociology of Deviance." In Howard S. Becker (ed.), *The Other Side: Perspectives on Deviance*. New York: Free Press, pp. 307–314.

Erikson, Kai T. 1966. *Wayward Puritans: A Study in the Sociology of Deviance*. New York: John Wiley & Sons.

Erikson, Kai T. 1990. "Toxic Reckoning: Business Faces a New Kind of Fear." *Harvard Business Review*, 68 (January–February): 118–126.

Estrich, Susan. 1987. *Real Rape*. Cambridge, MA: Harvard University Press.

Etcoff, Nancy L. 1999. *Survival of the Prettiest: The Science of Beauty*. Garden City, NY: Doubleday.

Etzioni, Amitai. 2007. "Another Side of Racial Profiling." In Frank Schmalleger (ed.), *Criminal Justice Today: An Introductory Text for the Twenty-First Century*. Upper Saddle River, NJ: Pearson Prentice Hall, pp. 313–314.

Feagin, Joe R., and Robert Parker. 1990. *Building American Cities: The Urban Real Estate Game* (2nd ed.). Englewood Cliffs, NJ: Prentice Hall.

Felson, Richard B. 1991. "Blame Analysis: Accounting for the Behavior of Protected Groups." *The American Sociologist*, 22 (Spring): 5–23.

Fiedler, Leslie. 1978. *Freaks: Myths and Images of the Secret Self*. New York: Simon & Schuster.

Fiffer, Steve. 1999. *Three Quarters, Two Dimes, and a Nickel: A Memoir of Becoming Whole*. New York: Free Press.

Finch, Emily, and Vanessa E. Munro. 2007. "The Demon Drink and the Demonized Woman: Socio-Sexual Stereotypes and Responsibility Attribution in Rape Trials Involving Intoxicants." *Social and Legal Studies*, 16 (4): 591–614.

Fishbein, Diana. 2002. "Biocriminology." In David Levinson (ed.), *Encyclopedia of Crime and Punishment*. Thousand Oaks, CA: Sage, pp. 109–118.

Fishman, Steve. 2010. "Bernie Madoff, Free at Last." *New York Magazine*, June 14–21, pp. 30–37.

Fishman, Steve. 2011. "The Madoff Tapes." *New York Magazine*, April 7, pp. 22–27, 91–93.

Ford, James. 1939. *Social Deviation*. New York: Macmillan.

Foucault, Michel. 1967. *Madness and Civilization: A History of Insanity in the Age of Reason* (trans. Richard Howard). New York: New American Library/Mentor Books.

Foucault, Michel. 1979. *Discipline and Punish: The Birth of the Prison* (trans. Alan Sheridan). New York: Vintage Books.

Foucault, Michel. 2003. *Abnormal* (trans. Graham Burchell; ed. Valerio Marchelli and Antonella Salomoni). New York: Picador.

Freidson, Eliot. 1966. "Disability as Deviance." In Marvin B. Sussman (ed.), *Sociology and Rehabilitation*. Washington, DC: American Sociological Association, pp. 71–99.

Freidson, Eliot. 1970. *Profession of Medicine: A Study of the Sociology of Applied Knowledge*. New York: Dodd, Mead.

Friedman, Wolfgang. 1964. *Law in a Changing Society*. Harmondsworth, UK: Penguin Books.

Friedrichs, David O. 2010. *Trusted Criminals: White Collar Crime in Contemporary Society* (4th ed.). Belmont, CA: Wadsworth.

Fuller, Thomas. 2012. "Ethnic Hatred Tears Apart a Region of Myanmar." *The New York Times*, November 30, pp. A1, A16.

Furnham, Adrian, and Barrie Gunter. 1984. "Just World Beliefs and Attitudes Towards the Poor." *Journal of Social Psychology*, 23 (September): 265–269.

Gagnon, John H., and William Simon. 1973. *Sexual Conduct: The Social Sources of Human Sexuality* (1st ed.). Chicago: Aldine.

Gagnon, John H., and William Simon. 2005. *Sexual Conduct: The Social Sources of Human Sexuality* (2nd ed.). New Brunswick, NJ: Transaction Aldine.

Gallagher, Bernard J., III. 2002. *The Sociology of Mental Illness* (4th ed.). Upper Saddle River, NJ: Pearson Prentice Hall.

Gallagher, Bernard J., III. 2011. *The Sociology of Mental Illness* (5th ed.). Upper Saddle River, NJ: Pearson Prentice Hall.

Gans, Herbert J. 2005. "Race as Class." *Contexts*, 4 (Fall): 17–21.

Gardner, Martin. 1957. *Fads and Fallacies in the Name of Science* (2nd rev. ed.). New York: Dover.

Garland, David. 1990. *Punishment and Modern Society: A Study in Social Theory*. Chicago: University of Chicago Press.

Garland Thomson, Rosemarie (ed.). 1996. *Freakery: Cultural Spectacles of the Extraordinary Body*. New York: New York University Press.

Garland Thomson, Rosemarie (ed.). 1997. *Extraordinary Bodies*. New York: Columbia University Press.

Garner, David M., et al. 1980. "Cultural Expectations of Thinness in Women." *Psychological Reports*, 47: 483–491.

Geis, Gilbert. 1962. "Toward a Delineation of White-Collar Offenses." *Sociological Inquiry*, 32 (Spring): 160–171.

Gelsthorpe, Loraine, and Alison Morris. 1988. "Feminism and Criminology in Britain." *British Journal of Criminology*, 28 (Spring): 223–240.

George, William H., and Jeannette Norris. 1991. "Alcohol, Disinhibition, Sexual Arousal, and Deviant Sexual Behavior." *Alcohol Health and Research World*, 15 (Spring): 133–138.

Gibbs, Jack P. 1966. "Conceptions of Deviant Behavior: The Old and the New." *Pacific Sociological Review*, 9 (Spring): 9–14.

Gieringer, Dale. 1990. "How Many Crack Babies?" *The Drug Policy Letter*, 11 (March/April): 4–6.

Gilbert, Neil. 1991. "The Phantom Epidemic of Sexual Assault." *The Public Interest*, 103 (Spring): 54–65.

Gilbert, Neil. 1992. "Realities and Mythologies of Rape." *Society*, May/June, pp. 4–10.

Givens, James B. 1977. *Society and Homicide in Thirteenth-Century England*. Stanford, CA: Stanford University Press.

Glaeser, Edward, and Jacob Vigdor. 2012. "The End of the Segregated Century: Racial Separation in America's Neighborhoods, 1890-2010." www.manhattan-institute.org/html/cr_66.htm

Glassner, Barry. 1982. "Labeling Theory." In M. Michael Rosenberg, Robert A. Stebbins, and Allan Turowitz (eds.), *The Sociology of Deviance*. New York: St. Martin's Press, pp. 71–89.

Goffman, Erving. 1963. *Stigma: Notes on the Management of Spoiled Identity*. Englewood Cliffs, NJ: Prentice Hall/Spectrum.

Goldberg, Carey. 1997. "On Adultery Issue, Many Aren't Ready to Cast the First Stone." *The New York Times*, June 9, pp. A1, A18.

Goldman, Douglas. 1955. "Treatment of Psychotic States with Chlorpromazine." *Journal of the American Medical Association*, 157 (April 19): 1274–1278.

Goldstein, Avram. 2001. *Addiction: From Biology to Drug Policy*. New York: Oxford University Press.

Goleman, Daniel. 1986. "To Expert Eyes, Streets Are Open Mental Wards." *The New York Times*, November 4, pp. C1, C3.

Goode, Erich. 2002. "Does the Death of the Sociology of Deviance Claim Make Sense?" *The American Sociologist*, 33 (Fall): 107–118.

Goode, Erich (ed.). 2008. *Out of Control: Assessing the General Theory of Crime*. Stanford, CA: Stanford University Press.

Goode, Erich, and Joanne Preissler. 1983. "The Fat Admirer." *Deviant Behavior*, 4 (January–March): 175–202.

Goode, Erich, and Angus Vail (eds.). 2008. *Extreme Deviance*. Thousand Oaks, CA: Pine Forge Press/Sage.

Goodstein, Laurie. 2012a. "Popular Priest Fathered a Child and Says He'll Step Aside." *The New York Times*, May 16, p. A15.

Goodstein, Laurie. 2012b. "Christian Right Failed to Sway Voters on Issues." *The New York Times*, November 10, pp. A1, A3.

Goodstein, Laurie, and Rachel Donadio. 2012. "Vatican Scolds Nun for Book on Sexuality." *The New York Times*, June 5, p. A13.

Goring, Charles. 1913. *The English Convict: A Statistical Study*. London: Her Majesty's Stationery Office.

Gottfredson, Michael R., and Travis Hirschi (eds.). 1987. *Positive Criminology.* Newbury Park, CA: Sage.

Gottfredson, Michael R., and Travis Hirschi. 1990. *A General Theory of Crime.* Stanford, CA: Stanford University Press.

Gouldner, Alvin W. 1968. "The Sociologist as Partisan: Sociology and the Welfare State." *The American Sociologist,* 3 (May): 103–116.

Gouldner, Alvin W. 1970. *The Coming Crisis of Western Sociology.* New York: Basic Books.

Gove, Walter R. 1972. "The Relationship between Sex Roles, Marital Status, and Mental Illness." *Social Forces,* 51 (September): 34–44.

Gove, Walter R. 1975a. "The Labelling Perspective: An Overview." In Walter R. Gove (ed.), *The Labelling of Deviance.* New York: John Wiley & Sons/Halstead/Sage, pp. 35–81.

Gove, Walter R. 1975b. "The Labelling Theory of Mental Illness: A Reply to Scheff." *American Sociological Review,* 40 (April): 242–248.

Gove, Walter R. 1979a. "The Labelling Versus the Psychiatric Explanation of Mental Illness: A Debate That Has Become Substantially Irrelevant (Reply to Horwitz)." *Journal of Health and Social Behavior,* 20 (September): 89–93.

Gove, Walter R. 1979b. "Sex, Marital Status, and Psychiatric Treatment: A Research Note." *Social Forces,* 58 (September): 89–93.

Gove, Walter R. (ed.). 1980. *The Labelling of Deviance: Evaluating a Perspective.* Thousand Oaks, CA: Sage.

Gove, Walter R. (ed.). 1982. *Deviance and Mental Illness.* Thousand Oaks, CA: Sage.

Gove, Walter R. 1989. "On Understanding Mental Illness and Some Insights To Be Gained from the Labelling Theory of Mental Illness." Unpublished paper.

Gove, Walter R., and Terry R. Herb. 1974. "Stress and Mental Illness Among the Young: A Comparison of the Sexes." *Social Forces,* 53 (December): 256–265.

Gowan, Teresa. 2010. *Hoboes, Hustlers, and Backsliders: Homeless in San Francisco.* Minneapolis: University of Minnesota Press.

Grattet, Ryken. 2011a. "Labeling Theory." In Clifton D. Bryant (ed.), *The Routledge Handbook of Deviant Behavior.* London & New York: Routledge, pp. 121–128.

Grattet, Ryken. 2011b. "Societal Reactions to Deviance." *Annual Review of Sociology,* 37: 185–204.

Grealy, Lucy. 1995. *Autobiography of a Face.* New York: HarperCollins.

Green, Jesse. 2001. "The New Gay Movement." *New York Magazine,* March 5, pp. 27–28, 82.

Greenberg, David. 2001. "The Roots of Arab Anti-Semitism." *Slate,* October 31.

Greenhouse, Steven, and Jim Yardley. 2012. "As Walmart Makes Safety Vows, It's Seen as Obstacle to Change." *The New York Times,* December 29, pp. A1, A6.

Griffin, Susan. 1971. "Rape: The All-American Crime." *Ramparts,* September, pp. 26–35.

Grinspoon, Lester, and James B. Bakalar. 1976. *Cocaine: A Drug and Its Social Evolution.* New York: Basic Books.

Gronfein, William. 1985. "Psychotropic Drugs and the Origins of Institutionalization." *Social Problems,* 32 (June): 437–454.

Gross, Edward. 1978. "Organizational Crime: A Theoretical Perspective." In Norman Denzin (ed.), *Studies in Symbolic Interaction.* Greenwich, CT: JAI Press, pp. 55–88.

Gruber, Staci A., Kelly A. Sagar, Mary Kathryn Dahlgren, Megan Racine, and Scott E. Lukas. 2012. "Age of Onset of Marijuana Use and Executive Function." *Psychology of Addictive Behaviors,* 26 (3): 496–505.

Gruenbaum, Adolph. 1993. *Validation in the Clinical Theory of Psychoanalysis: A Study in the Philosophy of Psychoanalysis.* Madison, CT: International Universities Press.

Grynbaum, Michael M., and Marjorie Connelly. 2012. "Majority in City See Police Department As Favoring Whites, a Poll Finds." *The New York Times,* August 21, pp. A1, A16.

Gurr, Ted Robert. 1989. "Historical Trends in Violent Crime: Europe and the United States." In Ted Robert Gurr (ed.), *Violence in America,* Vol. I. Newbury Park, CA: Sage, pp. 21–54.

Hall, Jerome. 1952. *Theft, Law, and Society* (2nd ed.). Indianapolis, IN: Bobbs-Merrill.

Hargrove, Thomas. 2012. "Interracial Murder Rate Growing in U.S." *Scripps Howard News Service,* April 23.

Harkey, John, David L. Miles, and William Rushing. 1976. "The Relationship Between Social Class and Functional Status: A New Look at the Drift Hypothesis." *Journal of Health and Social Behavior,* 17 (September): 194–204.

Harman, Leslie D. 1985. "Acceptable Deviance and Social Control: The Cases of Fashion and Slang." *Deviant Behavior,* 6 (1): 1–15.

Harrison, Daniel M. 2008. "Positive Deviance, Edgework, and Wilderness Survival." Unpublished manuscript.

Harrison-Pepper, Sally. 1990. *Drawing a Circle in the Square: Street Performing in New York's Washington Square Park.* Jackson: University Press of Mississippi.

Hart, Carl L., and Charles Ksir. 2013. *Drugs, Society, and Human Behavior* (15th ed.). New York: McGraw-Hill.

Harvey, David L. 2007. "Poverty and Disrepute." In George Ritzer (ed.), *The Blackwell Encyclopedia of Sociology.* Malden, MA & Oxford, UK: Blackwell Publishing, pp. 3589–3594.

Hawkins, Richard, and Gary Tiedeman. 1975. *The Creation of Deviance: Interpersonal and Organization Determinants.* Columbus, OH: Charles E. Merrill.

Heckert, Druann. 1989. "The Relativity of Positive Deviance: The Case of the French Impressionists." *Deviant Behavior,* 10 (2): 131–144.

Heidensohn, Frances. 1968. "The Deviance of Women: A Critique and an Enquiry." *British Journal of Sociology,* 12 (2): 160–175.

Hendershott, Anne. 2002. *The Politics of Deviance.* San Francisco: Encounter Books.

Henshel, Richard L. 1990. *Thinking About Social Problems.* San Diego, CA: Harcourt Brace Jovanovich.

Hesketh and Katie. The Inequality Report: The Palestinian Arab Minority in Israel, Haifa, 2011

Hevey, David. 1992. *The Creatures Time Forgot: Photography and Disability Imagery.* London: Routledge.

Higgins, Heorge, Shaun Gabbidon, and Gennaro Vito. 2010. "Exploring the Influence of Race Relations and Public Safety Concerns on Public Support for Racial Profiling During Traffic Stops." *International Journal of Police Science & Management,* 12 (Spring): 12–22.

Hiller, Dana V. 1981. "The Salience of Overweight in Personality Characterization." *Journal of Psychology,* 108: 233–240.

Hiller, Dana V. 1982. "Overweight as a Master Status: A Replication." *Journal of Psychology,* 110: 107–113.

Hindelang, Michael J. 1974. "Decisions of Shoplifting Victims to Invoke the Criminal Justice Process." *Social Problems,* 21 (Spring): 58–593.

Hirschi, Travis. 1969. *Causes of Delinquency.* Berkeley: University of California Press.

Hirschi, Travis, and Michael R. Gottfredson (eds.). 1994. *The Generality of Deviance.* New Brunswick, NJ: Transaction.

Hitler, Adolph. 1925/1971. *Mein Kampf.* Munich: Eher-Verlag/Boston: Houghton Mifflin.

Hockenberry, John. 1995. *Moving Violations: War Zones, Wheelchairs, and Declarations of Independence.* New York: Hyperion.

Hollingshead, August B., and Frederick C. Redlich. 1958. *Social Class and Mental Illness.* New York: John Wiley.

Hooton, Ernest A. 1939. *The American Criminal.* Cambridge, MA: Harvard University Press.

Horton, Alicia. 2010. *Making Meaning of Extreme Flesh Practices.* M.A. thesis, Department of Sociology, Queen's University, Kingston, Ontario, Canada, April.

Horwitz, Allan V. 1990. *The Logic of Social Control.* New York: Plenum Press.

Hough, Michael. 1987. "Offenders' Choice of Target: Findings from Victim Surveys." *Journal of Quantitative Criminology,* 3 (3): 355–369.

Hubner, John, and Lindsey Gruson. 1989. *Monkey on a Stick.* New York: Harcourt, Brace, Jovanovich.

Hughes, Robert, and Jay Coakley. 1991. "Positive Deviance Among Athletes: The Implications of Overconformity to the Sports Ethic." *Sociology of Sports Journal,* 8 (4): 307–325.

Human Rights Watch. 2006. *World Report.* Washington, DC: Human Rights Watch.

Human Rights Watch. 2010. *Separate and Unequal: Israel's Discriminatory Treatment of Palestinians in the Occupied Palestinian Territories.* New York: Human Rights Watch.

Hunt, Morton. 1971. *The Affair: A Portrait of Extra-Marital Love in Contemporary America.* New York: New American Library/Signet.

Ignatiev, Noel. 1995. *How the Irish Became White.* London: Routledge & Kegan Paul.

Imrey, Rob. 1996. *Disability and the City: International Perspectives.* New York: St. Martin's Press.

Inciardi, James A. 1987. "Beyond Cocaine: Basuco, Crack, and Other Coca Products." *Contemporary Drug Problems,* 14 (Fall): 461–492.

Inderbitzen, Michelle, Kristen Bates, and Randy Gainey. 2013. *Deviance and Social Control: A Sociological Interpretation.* Los Angeles: Sage.

Irwin, Katherine. 2003. "Saints and Sinners: Elite Tattoo Collectors and Tattooists as Positive and Negative Deviants." *Sociological Spectrum,* 23 (2): 27–57.

Jacobs, Patricia, et al. 1965. "Aggressive Behavior, Mental Sub-Normality, and the XYY Chromosome." *Science,* 208 (December 25): 1351–1352.

Jacobson, Matthew Frye. 1998. *Whiteness of a Different Color: European Immigrants and the Alchemy of Race.* Cambridge, MA: Harvard University Press.

Jarrett, Robin L. 1996. "Welfare Stigma among Low-Income, African-American Single Mothers." *Family Relations,* 45 (October): 368–374.

Jefferson, David J. 2005. "America's Most Dangerous Drug." *Newsweek,* August 8.

Jennings, Wesley G., and Ronald L. Akers. 2011. "Social Learning Theory." In Clifton D. Bryant (ed.), *The Routledge Handbook of Deviant Behavior.* London & New York: Routledge, pp. 106–113.

Johnson, Anne, et al. 1994. *Sexual Attitudes and Lifestyles.* Oxford, UK: Oxford Scientific Publications.

Johnson, Eric A., and Eric H. Monkkonen. 1996. *The Civilization of Crime: Violence in Town and Country since the Middle Ages.* Urbana: University of Illinois Press.

Johnson, Paul. 1997. *A History of the Jews.* New York: HarperCollins.

Johnston, Lloyd D., et al. 2005. *National Survey Results on Drug Use, 1974-2004, Vol. I, Secondary School Students.* Bethesda, MD: National Institute on Drug Abuse.

Johnston, Lloyd D., Patrick M. O'Malley, Jerald G. Bachman, and John E. Schulenberg. 2012. *Monitoring the Future: National Results on Adolescent Drug Use, Overview of Key Findings, 2011.* Ann Arbor: Institute for Social Research, The University of Michigan.

Jones, Angela Lewellyn. 1998. "Random Acts of Kindness: A Teaching Tool for Positive Deviance." *Teaching Sociology,* 26 (3): 179–189.

Jones, Edward E. 1986. "Interpreting Interpersonal Behavior: The Effects of Expectancies." *Science,* 234 (October): 41–46.

Jones, Edward E., et al. 1984. *Social Stigma: The Psychology of Marked Relationships.* New York: W.H. Freeman.

Jones, Russell A. 1977. *Self-Fulfilling Prophecies: Social, Psychological, and Physiological Effects of Expectancies.* Hillsdale, NJ: Lawrence Erlbaum.

Jones, Trevor, Brian MacLean, and Jock Young. 1986, November 22. *The Islington Crime Survey: Crime, Victimization, and Policing in Inner City London.* Aldershot, UK: Gower, pp. 20–25.

Jütte, Robert. 1994. *Poverty and Deviance in Early Modern Europe*. Cambridge, UK and New York: Cambridge University Press.

Kates, William. 2005. "Museums Answer Critics of Evolution." *The Washington Post*, December 26, pp. A22, A23.

Katz, Irwin. 1981. *Stigma: A Social Psychological Analysis*. Hillsdale, NJ: Lawrence Erlbaum.

Katz, Jack. 1988. *Seductions of Crime: Moral and Sensual Attractions of Doing Evil*. New York: Basic Books.

Katz, Michael B. 1989. *The Undeserving Poor: From the War on Poverty to the War on Welfare*. New York: Pantheon Books.

Kellogg, Alex. 2011. "The Changing Face of Seeing Race." *NPR Broadcast*, October 14.

Kendall, R. E., et al. 1971. "Diagnostic Criteria of American and British Psychiatrists." *Archives of General Psychiatry*, 25 (August): 123–130.

Kershner, Isabel. 2012. "Young Israelis Held in Attack on Arab Youths." *The New York Times*, August 21, pp. A1, A3.

Kershner, Isabel. 2013. "Academic Study Weakens Israeli Claim That Palestinian School Texts Teach Hate." *The New York Times*, February 4, p. A6.

Kessler, Ronald C. 1979. "Stress, Social Status, and Psychological Distress." *Journal of Health and Social Behavior*, 20 (September): 259–272.

Kessler, Ronald C., et al. 1994. "Lifetime and 12-Month Prevalence of DSM-III Psychiatric Disorders in the United States."*Archives of General Psychiatry*, 51 (1): 8–19.

Kessler, Ronald C., Kathleen Ries Merikangas, and Philip S. Wang. 2010. "Epidemiology of Mental Disorders." In Bruce Lubotsky Levin, Kevin D. Hennessy, and John Petrila (eds.), *Mental Health Services: A Public Health Perspective*. Oxford, UK & New York: Oxford University Press, pp. 169–200.

Kety, S. S. 1974. "From Rationalization to Reason." *American Journal of Psychiatry*, 131 (September): 957–963.

Kilpatrick, Dean G., et al. 2007. *Drug-Facilitated, Incapacitated, and Forcible Rape: A National Study*. Charleston: National Crime Victims Research & Treatment Center, Medical University of South Carolina.

Kinsey, Alfred C., Wardell B. Pomeroy, and Clyde E. Martin. 1948. *Sexual Behavior in the Human Male*. Philadelphia: W.B. Saunders.

Kinsey, Alfred C., Wardell B. Pomeroy, Clyde E. Martin, and Paul H. Gebhard. 1953. *Sexual Behavior in the Human Female*. Philadelphia: W.B. Saunders.

Kirkpatrick, David D. 2012. "Anger Over a Film Fuels Anti-American Attacks in Libya and Egypt." *The New York Times*, September 12, p. A4.

Kirkpatrick, David D., and Steven Lee. 2012. "Libya Attack Brings Challenges for U.S.," *The New York Times*, September 12, pp. A1, A12.

Kitcher, Philip. 1982. *Abusing Science: The Case Against Creationism*. Boston: MIT Press.

Kitsuse, John I. 1972. "Deviance, Deviant Behavior, and Deviants: Some Conceptual Problems." In William J.

Filstead (ed.), *An Introduction to Deviance: Readings in the Process of Making Deviants*. Chicago: Markham, pp. 233–243.

Kitsuse, John I. 1980. "The New Conception of Deviance and Its Critics." In Walter R. Gove (ed.), *The Labelling of Deviance: Evaluating a Perspective*. Thousand Oaks, CA: Sage, pp. 381–392.

Knox, Robert. 1850. *The Races of Men: A Fragment*. Philadelphia: Lea & Blanchard.

Kolata, Gina. 2012. "Seeking Answers in Genome of Gunman." *The New York Times*, December 25, pp. D5, D6.

Konigsberg, Eric. 1998. "The Cheating Kind." *The New York Times Magazine*, March 8, p. 65.

Kornhauser, Ruth. 1978. *Social Sources of Delinquency: An Appraisal of Analytic Models*. Chicago: University of Chicago Press.

Kossey, Donna. 1994. *Kooks: Guide to the Outer Limit of Human Belief*. Venice, CA: Feral House.

Krauthammer, Charles. 1993. "Defining Deviancy Up." *The New York Republic*, November 22, pp. 20–25.

Kring, Ann M., Sheri L. Johnson, Gerald C. Davison, and John M. Neale. 2010. *Abnormal Psychology* (11th ed.). New York: John Wiley & Sons.

Krohn, Marvin D., and Ronald L. Akers. 1977. "An Alternative View of the Labeling Versus Psychiatric Perspectives on Societal Reaction to Mental Illness." *Social Forces*, 56 (December): 341–361.

Landler, Mark, and Jeff Zeleny. 2012. "Obama Campaign Pushes the Issue of Gay Marriage." *The New York Times*, May 11, pp. A1, A20.

Landman, Janet T., and Robyn Dawes. 1982. "Psychotherapy Outcome: Smith and Glass' Conclusions Stand Up Under Scrutiny." *Psychological Bulletin*, 57: 504–516.

Landsman, Janet T., and Robyn Dawes. 1982. "Psychotherapy Outcome: Smith and Glass' Conclusions Stand Up Under Scrutiny." *Psychological Bulletin*, 57: 504–516.

Lane, Charles. 2003. "Justices Overturn Texas Sodomy Ban." *The Washington Post*, June 27, pp. A1, A16.

Langlois, Judith, et al. 2000. "Maxims or Myth of Beauty: A Meta-Analytic and Theoretical Review." *Psychological Bulletin*, 126 (3): 390–423.

Langton, Lynn, Marcus E. Berzofsky, Christopher Krebs, and Shirley McDonald. 2012. "Victimizations not Reported to the Police, 2000-2012: National Crime Victimization Survey." Special Report. NCJ 28536. Washington, DC: U.S. Department of Justice, Bureau of Justice Statistics.

Lankenau, Stephen E. 1999. "Stronger Than Dirt: Public Humiliation and Status Enhancement among Panhandlers." *Journal of Contemporary Ethnography*, 28 (June): 288–318.

Lattman, Peter. 2013. "Forfeiture from Crimes Adds Luster to Enforcers." *The New York Times*, January 2, pp. B1, B7.

Lauderdale, Pat (ed.). 2011. *A Political Analysis of Deviance* (3rd ed.). Whitby, ON: de Sitter.

Laumann, Edward O., John H. Gagnon, Robert T. Michael, and Stuart Michaels. 1994. *The Social Organization of Sexuality: Sexual Practices in the United States*. Chicago: University of Chicago Press.

Lawson, Annette. 1988. *Adultery: An Analysis of Love and Betrayal*. New York: Basic Books.

Leighton, D.C., et al. 1963. *The Character of Danger: Psychiatric Symptoms in Selected Communities*. New York: Basic Books.

Lemert, Edwin M. 1951. *Social Pathology: A Systematic Approach to the Theory of Sociopathic Behavior*. New York: McGraw-Hill.

Lemert, Edwin M. 1972. *Human Deviance, Social Problems, and Social Control* (2nd ed.). Englewood Cliffs, NJ: Prentice Hall.

Lemley, Brad. 2000. "Isn't She Lovely?" *Discover*, January, pp. 43–49.

Leonard, Eileen B. 1982. *Women, Crime, and Society: A Critique of Theoretical Criminology*. New York: Longman.

Leonnig, Carol D., and David Nakamura. 2012. "Secret Service Scandal." *The Washington Post*, May 22.

Lerner, Melvin J. 1980. *The Belief in a Just World: A Fundamental Delusion*. New York: Plenum Press.

Lerner, Michael A. 1989. "The Fire of 'Ice.'" *Newsweek*, November 27, pp. 37, 38, 40.

Levi, Michael. 2009. "White-Collar Crimes and the Fear of Crime: A Review." In Sally S. Simpson and David Weisburd (eds.), *The Criminology of White-Collar Crime*. New York: Springer, pp. 79–109.

Levine, Martin P., and Richard R. Troiden. 1988. "The Myth of Sexual Compulsivity." *Journal of Sex Research*, 25 (August): 347–363.

Levitt, Steven D. 2004. "Understanding Why Crime Fell in the 1990s: Four Factors That Explain the Decline and Six That Do Not." *Journal of Economic Perspectives*, 18 (1): 163–190.

Levitt, Steven D., and Stephen J. Dubner. 2005. *Freakonomics: A Rogue Economist Explores the Hidden Side of Everything*. New York: William Morrow.

Lewontin, Richard C. 1995. "Sex, Lies, and Social Science." *The New York Review of Books*, April 20.

Lewontin, Richard C. 2006. "Confusions About Human Races." http://raceandgeonomics.ssrc.org/Lewontin/printable.html

Liazos, Alexander. 1972. "The Poverty of the Sociology of Deviance: Nuts, Sluts, and Deviated Preverts." *Social Problems*, 20 (Summer): 103–120.

Liem, Ramsay, and Joan Liem. 1978. "Social Class and Mental Health Considered: The Role of Economic Stress and Economic Support." *Journal of Health and Social Behavior*, 19 (June): 139–156.

Link, Bruce G. 1987. "Understanding Labeling Effects in the Area of Mental Disorders: An Assessment of the Effects of Expectations of Rejection." *American Sociological Review*, 52 (February): 96–112.

Link, Bruce G., and Frances T. Cullen. 1989. "The Labeling Theory of Mental Disorder: A Review of the Evidence." In James Greenly (ed.), *Mental Illness in Social Context*. Detroit: Wayne State University Press.

Link, Bruce G., Frances T. Cullen, Elmer Struening, Patrick Shrout, and Bruce P. Dohrenwend. 1989. "A Modified Labeling Theory Approach to Mental Disorders: An Empirical Assessment." *American Sociological Review*, 54 (June): 400–423.

Linton, Simi. 1998. *Claiming Disability: Knowledge and Identity*. New York: New York University Press.

Lofland, John. 1969. *Deviance and Identity*. Englewood Cliffs, NJ: Prentice Hall.

Loftus, T.A. 1960. *Meaning and Methods of Diagnosis in Clinical Psychiatry*. Philadelphia: Lea & Febinger.

Logan, John R., and Brian J. Stults. 2011. "The Persistence of Segregation in the Metropolis: New Findings from the 2010 Census." Census Brief prepared for Project US2010. http://www.s4.brown.edu/us2010

Louderback, Llewellyn. 1970. *Fat Power: Whatever You Weigh Is Right*. New York: Hawthorn Books.

Lowman, John, Robert J. Menzies, and T. S. Palys (eds.). 1987. *Transcarceration: Essays in the Sociology of Social Control*. Gower, UK: Aldershot.

Lynch, Michael J., and W. Byron Groves. 1995. "In Defense of Comparative Criminology: A Critique of General Theory and the Rational Man." In Freda Adler and William S. Laufer (eds.), *The Legacy of Anomie Theory*. New Brunswick, NJ: Transaction, pp. 367–392.

MacDonald, Heather. 2010. "Fighting Crime Where the Criminals Are." *The New York Times*, June 25.

Macdonald, Scott, et al. 2006. "Variations of Alcohol Impairment in Different Types, Causes and Contexts of Injuries: Results of Emergency Room Studies from 16 Countries." *Accident Analysis and Prevention*, 38: 1107–1112.

Mack, John. 1995. *Abductions: Human Encounters with Aliens* (rev. ed.). New York: Bantam Books.

MacKinnon, Catherine A. 1979. *Sexual Harassment of Working Women: A Case of Sex Discrimination*. New Haven, CT: Yale University Press.

Macq, Jean, Alejandro Solis, and Guillermo Martinez. 2006. "Assessing the Stigma of Tuberculosis." *Psychology, Health, and Medicine*, 11 (August): 346–352.

Maddox, George L., Kurt W. Back, and Veronica Liederman. 1968. "Overweight as Social Deviance and Disability." *Journal of Health and Social Behavior*, 9 (December): 287–298.

Madigan, Nick. 2003. "Professor's Snub of Creationists Prompts U. S. Inquiry." *The New York Times*, February 3, p. A11.

Mairs, Nancy. 1997. *Waist-High in the World: A Life Among the Disabled*. Boston: Beacon.

Manchester, Colleen Flaherty, and Kevin Mumford. 2010. "Welfare Stigma Due to Public Disapproval." University of Minnesota and Purdue University, unpublished working paper.

Mannheim, Karl. 1965. *Comparative Criminology*. London: Routledge & Kegan Paul.

Markoff, John. 2009. "With Sensitive Software, Iranians and Others Outwit Net Censors." *The New York Times*, May 1, pp. A1, A3.

Marmot, Michael. 2004. *The Status Syndrome: How Social Standing Affects Our Health and Longevity*. New York: Henry Holt/Times Books.

Marsh, David R., et al. 2004. "The Power of Positive Deviance." *BJM.com*, 328 (November 13).

Marshall, Helen, Kathy Douglass, and Desmond McDonnell. 2007. *Deviance and Social Control: Who Rules?* South Melbourne, Australia: Oxford University Press.

Martin, Dell. 1976. *Battered Wives*. San Francisco: Glide Foundation.

Marvasti, Amir. 2008. "Being Middle Eastern American: Identity Negotiation in the Context of the War on Terror." In Edward J. Clarke (ed.), *Deviant Behavior: A Text-Reader in the Sociology of Deviance* (7th ed.). New York: Worth, pp. 648–671.

Marx, Karl, and Friedrich Engels. 1947. *The German Ideology, Parts I and III*. New York: International Publishers (orig. written 1846).

Masters, William H., and Virginia E. Johnson. 1966. *Human Sexual Response*. Boston: Little, Brown.

Masters, William H., and Virginia E. Johnson. 1970. *Human Sexual Inadequacy*. Boston: Little, Brown.

Masters, William H., and Virginia E. Johnson. 1979. *Homosexuality in Perspective*. Boston: Little, Brown.

Matsueda, Ross L. 1992. "Reflected Appraisals, Parental Labeling, and Delinquency: Specifying a Symbolic Interactionist Theory." *American Journal of Sociology*, 97 (May): 1577–1611.

Matthews, Roger, and Jock Young (eds.). 1986. *Confronting Crime*. Thousand Oaks, CA: Sage.

Matza, David. 1966a. "The Disreputable Poor." In Reinhard Bendix and Seymour Martin Lipset (eds.), *Class, Status, and Power: Social Stratification in Comparative Perspective*. New York: Free Press, pp. 289–302.

Matza, David. 1966b. "Poverty and Disrepute." In Robert K. Merton and Robert A. Nisbet (eds.), *Contemporary Social Problems* (2nd ed.). New York: Harcourt, Brace & World, pp. 619–669.

Matza, David. 1971. "Poverty and Disrepute." In Robert K. Merton and Robert A. Nisbet (eds.), *Contemporary Social Problems* (3rd ed.). New York: Harcourt Brace Jovanovich, pp. 601–656.

Matza, David, and Henry Miller. 1976. "Poverty and Proletariat." In Robert K. Merton and Robert A. Nisbet (eds.), *Contemporary Social Problems*. New Work: Harcourt Brace and Jovanovich, pp. 641–673.

Mayne, Jerome. 2010. *Diary of a White Collar Criminal*. Minneapolis, MN: Jerome Mayne/Fraudcon.

McCaghy, Charles H. 1967. "Child Molesters: A Study of their Career as Deviants." In Marshall B. Clinard and Richard Quinney (eds.), *Criminal Behavior Systems: A Typology*. New York: Holt, Rinehart & Winston, pp. 75–88.

McCaghy, Charles H. 1968. "Drinking and Disavowal: The Case of Child Molesters." *Social Problems*, 16 (Summer): 43–49.

McCaghy, Charles H., et al. 2006. *Deviant Behavior: Crime, Conflict, and Interest Groups*. Boston: Allyn & Bacon.

McDonough, Peggy, Greg J. Duncan, David Williams, and James S. House. 2001. "Income Dynamics and Adult Mortality in the United States, 1972-1989." *American Journal of Public Health*, 87 (September): 1476–1483.

Mechanic, David. 1989. *Mental Health and Social Policy* (3rd ed.). Englewood Cliffs, NJ: Prentice Hall.

Meier, Madeline H., et al. 2012. "Persistent Cannabis Users Show Neurological Decline from Childhood to Midlife." *Proceedings of the National Academy of Sciences of the United States*, 109 (40, October 2): E2657–E2664.

Meier, Robert F. 1982. "Perspectives on the Concept of Social Control." *Annual Review of Sociology*, 8: 35–55.

Merton, Robert K. 1938. "Social Structure and Anomie." *American Sociological Review*, 3 (October): 672–682.

Merton, Robert K. 1948. "The Self-Fulfilling Prophecy." *Antioch Review*, 7 (Summer): 193–210.

Merton, Robert K. 1957. *Social Theory and Social Structure*. (rev. & expanded ed.). Glencoe, IL: Free Press.

Merton, Robert K. 1979. "Foreword." In Eugene Garfield (ed.), *Citation Indexing: Its Theory and Application in Science, Technology and Humanities*. New York: John Wiley & Sons, pp. ix-x.

Messner, Steven F., and Richard Rosenfeld. 1997. *Crime and the American Dream* (2nd ed.). Belmont, CA: Wadsworth.

Michael, Robert T., John Gagnon, Edward O. Laumann, and Gina Kolata. 1994. *Sex in America: A Definitive Survey*. Boston: Little, Brown.

Miller, Judith Droitcour, and Ira H. Cisin. 1980. *Highlights from the National Survey on Drug Abuse: 1979*. Rockville, MD: National Institute on Drug Abuse.

Millman, Marcia. 1975. "She Did It All for Love: A Feminist View of the Sociology of Deviance." In Marcia Millman and Rosabeth Moss Kantor (eds.), *Another Voice: Feminist Perspectives on Social Life and Social Science*. Garden City, NY: Doubleday-Anchor, pp. 251–279.

Millman, Marcia. 1980. *Such a Pretty Face: Being Fat in America*. New York: W.W. Norton.

Mills, C. Wright. 1963. *Power, Politics, and People: The Collected Essays of C. Wright Mills* (ed. Irving Louis Horowitz). New York: Ballantine Books.

Minton, Henry L. 2002. *Departing from Deviance: A History of Homosexual Rights and Emancipatory Science in America*. Chicago: University of Chicago Press.

Mitchell, David T., and Sharon L. Snyder (eds.). 1997. *The Body and Physical Differences: Discourses of Disability*. Ann Arbor: University of Michigan Press.

Mocan, Naci, and Erdal Tekin. 2006. "Ugly Criminals," NBER Working Paper No. 12019, January. Cambridge, MA: NBER.

Mollman, Marianne. 2011. "Americans Demonstrate Changed Attitude towards Poverty Since the 2008 Crisis." *Huff Post Politics*, December 26.

Monestier, Martin. 1987. *Human Oddities* (trans. Robert Campbell). Secaucus, NJ: Citadel Press.

Montada, Leo, and Melvin J. Lerner (eds.). 1998. *Responses to Victimization and Belief in a Just World*. New York: Plenum Press.

Morin, Richard. 2006. "The Ugly Face of Crime." *The Washington Post*, February 17, p.2.

Morning, Ann. 2006. "On Distinction." http://raceandgeonomics.ssrc.org/Morning/printable.html

Morris, Henry M. 1972. *The Remarkable Birth of Planet Earth*. San Diego: Creation- Life Publishers.

Moynihan, Daniel Patrick. 1993. "Defining Deviancy Down." *American Scholar*, 64 (Winter): 25–33.

Muehlenhard, Charlene L., and Melaney A. Linton. 1987. "Date Rape and Sexual Aggression in Dating Situations: Incident and Risk Factors." *Journal of Counseling Psychology*, 34 (2): 186–196.

Mujahid, Abdul Malik. 2011. "Islamophobia Statistics USA." http://www.soundvision.com/info/islamophobia/usastatistics.asp, September 8.

Murphy, Jane M. 1976. "Psychiatric Labeling in Cross-Cultural Perspective." *Science*, 191 (12 March): 1019–1028.

Murray, Charles. 1984. *Losing Ground: American Social Policy, 1950-1980*. New York: Basic Books.

Musto, David F. 1987, 1999. *The American Disease: Origins of Narcotic Control* (3rd & expanded ed.). New York: Oxford University Press.

Nettler, Gwynn. 1974. "On Telling Who's Crazy." *American Sociological Review*, 39 (December): 893–894.

Nettler, Gwynn. 1984. *Explaining Crime* (3rd ed.). New York: McGraw-Hill.

Neuspiel, D. R., et al. 1991. "Maternal Cocaine Use and Infant Behavior." *Neurotoxicology and Teratology*, 13 (March-April): 229–233.

Newman, Donald J. 1958. "White-Collar Crime." *Law and Contemporary Problems*, 23 (Autumn): 735–753.

Newman, Graeme. 1976. *Comparative Deviance: Perception and Law in Six Cultures*. New York: Elsevier.

Newman, William M. 1973. *American Pluralism: A Study of Minority Groups and Social Theory*. New York: Harper & Row.

Nicholas, Peter. 2011. "The Lavender Letter: Appling the Laws of Adultery to Same-Sex Couples and Sam-Sex Conduct." *Florida Law Review*, 63 (1): 97–127.

Norland, Stephen, John R. Hepworth, Duane Monette. 1976. "The Effects of Labeling and Consistent Differentiation in the Construction of Positive Deviance." *Sociology and Social Research*, 6 (1): 83–95.

Numbers, Ronald L. 1992. *The Creationists: The Evolution of Scientific Creationism*. Berkeley: University of California Press.

Nussbaum, Martha. 2004. *Hiding from Humanity: Shame, Disgust, and the Law*. Princeton, NJ: Princeton University Press.

Nyaronga, Dan, Thomas K. Greenfield, and Patricia A. McDonald. 2009. "Drinking Context and Drinking Problems Among Black, White, and Hispanic Men and Women in the 1984, 1995, and 2005 U. S. National Alcohol Surveys." *Journal of Studies on Alcohol*, 70 (January): 16–26.

Nyblade, Laura. 2006. "Measuring HIV Stigma: Existing Knowledge and Gaps." *Psychology, Health & Medicine*, 11 (August): 335–345.

Ogletree, Charles J., Jr. 2010. *The Presumption of Guilt: The Arrest of Henry Louis Gates and Race, Class, and Crime in America*. New York: Palgrave Macmillan.

Oreskes, Michael. 1990. "Drug War Underlines Fickleness of Public." *The New York Times*, September 6, p. A22.

O'Riordan, Alison. 2010. "The Humiliation of Begging for a Day on Dublin's Mean Streets." *National News* (Dublin, Ireland), May 30.

Ovesey, Lionel. 1969. *Homosexuality and Pseudohomosexuality*. New York: Science House.

Page, Susan, and Carly Mallenbaum. 2011. "Poll Respondents Chart Racial Progress Since MLK." www.usatoday.com/news/nation/2011-08-17-race-poll-inside_n.htm

Pager, Devah. 2007 *Marked: Race, Crime, and Finding Work in an Era of Mass Incarceration*. Chicago: University of Chicago Press.

Park, Robert E. 1926. "The Urban Community as a Spatial Pattern and a Moral Order." In Ernest W. Burgess (ed.), *The Urban Community*. Chicago: University of Chicago Press, pp. 3–18.

Parker-Pope, Tara. 2011. "Fat Stigma Is Fast Becoming a Global Epidemic." *The New York Times*, March 31, pp. A1, A3.

Parks, Kathleen A., and William Fals-Stewart. 2004. "The Temporal Relationship Between College Women's Alcohol Consumption and Victimization Experiences." *Alcoholism: Clinical and Experimental Research*, 28 (April): 625–629.

Parsons, Talcott. 1951a. "Illness and the Role of the Physician." *American Journal of Orthopsychiatry*, 21 (July): 452–460.

Parsons, Talcott. 1951b. *The Social System*. Glencoe, IL: Free Press.

Pascale, Richard, Jerry Sternin, and Monique Sternin. 2010. *The Power of Positive Deviance: How Unlikely Innovators Can Solve the World's Toughest Problems*. Cambridge, MA: Harvard Business Press.

Pearlin, Leonard I., and Joyce S. Johnson. 1977. "Marital Status, Life Strains, and Depression." *American Sociological Review*, 42 (October): 704–715.

Perrin, Robin. 2007. "Deviant Beliefs/Cognitive Deviance." In George Ritzer (ed.), *The Blackwell Encyclopedia of Sociology*. Malden, MA & Oxford, UK: Blackwell Publishing, pp. 1140–1142.

Perrin, Robin. 2008. "When Religion Becomes Deviance: Introducing Religion in Deviance and Social Problems Courses." In Bruce Hoffman and Ashley Demyan (eds.), *Teaching and Learning About Deviance: A Resource Guide*. Washington, DC: American Sociological Association, pp. 53–65.

Perrow, Charles. 1984. *Normal Accidents: Living with High-Risk Technologies*. New York: Basic Books.

Petersilia, Joan. 2003. *When Prisoners Come Home: Parole and Prisoner Reentry*. New York: Oxford University Press.

Pfohl, Stephen. 1994. *Images of Deviance and Social Control: A Sociological History* (2nd ed.). New York: McGraw-Hill.

Phelen, Jo C., and Bruce G. Link. 1999. "Who Are 'the Homeless'? Reconsidering the Stability and Composition of the Homeless Population." *American Journal of Public Health*, 89 (9): 1334–1338.

Phelen, Jo. C., Bruce G. Link, Robert E. Moore, and Ann Stueve. 1997. "The Stigma of Homelessness: The Impact of the Label 'Homeless' on Attitudes Toward Poor Persons." *Social Psychology Quarterly*, 60 (4): 323–337.

Phillips, Derek L. 1964. "Rejection of the Mentally Ill: The Influence of Behavior and Sex." *American Sociological Review*, 29 (October): 755–763.

Pinker, Steven. 2009. "Why Is There Peace?" *Greater Good Magazine*, April.

Pipes, Daniel. 2005. "Islamophobia?" *New York Sun*, October 25.

Plummer, Kenneth. 1975. *Sexual Stigma: An Interactionist Account*. London: Routledge & Kegan Paul.

Plummer, Kenneth. 1979. "Misunderstanding Labelling Perspectives." In David Downes and Paul Rock (eds.), *Deviant Interpretations*. London: Martin Robinson, pp. 85–121.

Plummer, Kenneth. 1982. Symbolic Interactionism and Sexual Conduct: An Emergent Perspective." In Mike Brake (ed.), *Human Sexual Relations: Toward a Redefinition of Politics*. New York: Pantheon Books, pp. 223–241.

Polk, Kenneth. 1991. Review of Michael R. Gottfredson and Travis Hirschi, *A General Theory of Crime*, Stanford, CA: Stanford University Press, 1990. *Crime and Delinquency*, 37 (2): 275–279.

Pollack, Earl, and Carol A. Taube. 1975. "Trends and Projections in State Hospital Use." In Jack Zussman and Elmer Bertsch (eds.). *The Future Role of the State Hospital*. Lexington, MA: D.C. Heath, pp. 31–55.

Polsky, Ned. 1998. *Hustlers, Beats, and Others* (exp. ed.). New York: Lyons Press.

Popenoe, Rebecca. 2005. "Ideal." In Don Kulick and Anne Meneley (eds.). *Fat: An Anthropology of an Obsession*. New York: Jeremy P. Tarcher/Penguin, pp. 9–28.

Portes, Alejandro, and William Haller. 2005. "The Informal Economy." In Neal Smelser (ed.), *Economic Sociology* (2nd ed.). Russell Sage, pp. 403–425.

Posner, Jennifer. 1976. "The Stigma of Excellence: On Being Just Right." *Sociological Inquiry*, 46 (2): 141–144.

Powdermaker, Hortense. 1960. "An Anthropological Approach to the Problem of Obesity." *Bulletin of the New York Academy of Medicine*, 36: 286–295.

Powell, Michael. 2005. "Judge Rules Against Intelligent Design." *The Washington Post*, December 21, pp. A1f.

Priest, G.L. 1990. "The New Legal Structure of Risk Control." *Daedalus*, 119: 207–228.

Punch, Maurice. 2008. "The Organization Did It: Individuals, Corporations and Crime." In John Minkes and Leonard Minkes (eds.), *Corporate and White Collar Crime*. Los Angeles: Sage, pp. 102–121.

Quinney, Richard. 1970. *The Social Reality of Crime*. Boston: Little, Brown.

Quinney, Richard. 1977. *Class, State, and Crime: On the Theory and Practice of Criminal Justice*. New York: David McKay.

Rabin, Roni Caryn. 2013. "Legalizing of Marijuana Raises Health Concerns." *The New York Times*, January 8, pp. D1, D6.

Rand, Michael R., James P. Lynch, and David Cantor. 1997. "Criminal Victimization, 1973-95." *Bureau of Justice Statistics National Crime Victimization Survey*, April, pp. 1–8.

Rapp, Emily. 2007. *Poster Child: A Memoir*. New York: Bloomsbury.

Ray, Joel G., et al. 2008. "Alcohol Sales and Risk of Serious Assault." *PLos Medicine*, May, pp. 1–15.

Reckless, Walter C. 1950. *The Crime Problem*. New York: Appleton-Century-Crofts.

Reckless, Walter C. 1961. *The Crime Problem* (3rd ed.). New York: Appleton-Century-Crofts.

Reeves, William C., et al. 2011. "Mental Illness Surveillance Among Adults in the United States." *MMWR (Morbidity and Mortality Weekly Report)*, 60 (September 2): 1–32.

Reiger, Darrel A., et al. 1988. "One-Month Prevalence of Mental Disorders in the United States Based on Five Epidemiological Catchment Areas Sites." *Archives of General Psychiatry*, 45 (November): 977–986.

Reinarman, Craig, and Harry G. Levine (eds.). 1997. *Crack in America: Demon Drugs and Social Justice*. Berkeley: University of California Press.

Reiss, Albert J., Jr. 1951. "Delinquency as the Failure of Personal and Social Controls." *American Sociological Review*, 16 (April): 196–207.

Reiss, Stephen A. 1988. *Sports and the American Jew*. Syracuse: Syracuse University Press.

Reuter, Peter, and Franz Trautmann (eds.). 2009. *A Report on Global Illicit Drugs Markets, 1998-2007*. Amsterdam: European Commission.

Reyles, Diego Zavaleta. 2007. "The Ability to Go About without Shame." *Oxford Development Studies*, 35 (December): 405–430.

Rhodes, William, Mary Layne, Anne-Marie Bruen, Patrick Johnston, and Lisa Becchetti. 2001. *What America's Users Spend on Illegal Drugs*. Washington, DC: Executive Office of the President, Office of National Drug Control Policy.

Richardson, Diane. 1996. "Heterosexuality and Social Theory." In Diane Richardson (ed.), *Theorizing Heterosexuality*. Buckingham, UK: Open University Press, pp. 1–20.

Richardson, Gale A., and Nancy L. Day. 1994. "Detrimental Effects of Prenatal Cocaine Exposure: Illusion or Reality?" *Journal of the American Academy of Child and Adolescent Psychiatry*, 33 (January): 28–34.

Rieger, Gerulf, and Ritch Savin-Williams. 2012. "The Eyes Have It: Sex and Sexual Orientation Differences in Pupil Dilation Patterns." *PLoS ONE*, 7 (8): electronic pagination.

Rimland, Bernard. 1969. "Psychogenesis versus Biogenesis: The Issue and the Evidence." In Stanley C. Plog and Robert B. Edgerton (eds.), *Changing Perspectives in Mental Health*. New York: Holt, Rinehart & Winston, pp. 702–735.

Rittner, Carol, and John K. Roth. 2012. *Rape: Weapon of War and Genocide*. St. Paul, MN: Paragon House.

Roberts, Dorothy E. 2004. "The Social and Moral Cost of Mass Incarceration in African American Communities." *Stanford Law Review*, 56 (5): 1271–1305.

Roberts, Sam. 2012. "Segregation Curtained in U.S. Cities, Study Finds." *The New York Times*, January 30.

Robinson, Bryan E., and Nell H. Fields. 1983. "Casework with Invulnerable Children." *Social Work*, 28 (1): 63–65.

Roche, Bryan, and Dermot Barnes. 1998. "The Experimental Analysis of Human Sexual Arousal: Some Recent Developments." *The Behavioral Analyst*, 21 (Spring): 37–52.

Rogers-Dillon, Robin. 1995. "The Dynamics of Welfare Stigma." *Qualitative Sociology*, 18 (Winter): 439–456.

Roiphe, Katie. 1993. "Date Rape's Other Victim." *The New York Times*, June 13.

Roiphe, Katie. 1997. "Adultery's Double Standard." *The New York Times Magazine*, October 7, pp. 54–55.

Room, Robin. 2005. "Stigma, Social Inequality, and Alcohol and Drug Use." *Drug and Alcohol Review*, 24 (March): 143–155.

Rose, Hilary. 1975. "Who Can Delabel the Claimant?" In M. Adler and A. Bradley (eds.), *Justice, Discretion, and Poverty*. London: Professional Books, pp. 143–154.

Rosenfeld, Richard, and Janet I. Lauritsen. 2008. "The Most Dangerous Ranking." *Contexts*, 7 (Winter): 66–67.

Rosenhan, David L. 1973. "On Being Sane in Insane Places." *Science*, 179 (January 19): 250–258.

Rosenthal, Jack. 1981. "The Pornography of Fat." *The New York Times*, May 29, p. A26.

Ross, Edward Alsworth. 1907. *Sin and Society: An Analysis of Latter-Day Iniquity*. Boston & New York: Houghton Mifflin.

Rothwell, Jonathan. 2012. "Reports of the End of Segregation Greatly Exaggerated." *The New Republic*, January 31.

Ruderman, Wendy. 2012. "414 Homicides a Record Low for New York." *The New York Times*, December 29, pp. A1, A3.

Rushing, William. 1979a. "The Functional Importance of Sex Roles and Sex-Related Behavior in Societal Reactions to Residual Deviants." *Journal of Health and Social Behavior*, 20 (September): 208–217.

Rushing, William. 1979b. "Marital Status and Mental Disorder: Evidence in Favor of a Behavioral Model." *Social Forces*, 58 (December): 540–556.

Russell-Brown, Katheryn, 2009. *The Color of Crime* (2nd ed.). New York: New York University Press.

Ryan, William. 1976. *Blaming the Victim*. New York: Random House.

Sagarin, Edwin. 1969. *Odd Man In: Societies of Deviants in America*. Chicago: Quadrangle Books.

Sagarin, Edward. 1985. "Positive Deviance: An Oxymoron." *Deviant Behavior*, 6 (2): 169–181.

Saguy, Abigail C., and Anna Ward. 2011. "Coming Out as Fat: Rethinking Stigma." *Social Psychology Quarterly*, 74 (1): 53–75.

Saha, Sukanta, David Chant, Joy Welham, and John McGrath. 2005. "A Systematic Review of the Prevalence of Schizophrenia." *PLoS Med*, 2 (5), May, 1–17.

Said, Edward W. 1978, 1979. *Orientalism*. New York: Random House/Vintage Books.

Said, Edward W. 1985. "Orientalism Reconsidered." *Race & Class*, 27 (October): 1–15.

Sampson, Robert J., and John H. Laub. 1992. "Crime and Deviance in the Life Course." *Annual Review of Sociology*, 18: 63–84.

Sampson, Robert J., and John H. Laub. 1993. *Crime in the Making: Pathways and Turning Points Through Life*. Cambridge, MA: Harvard University Press.

Sampson, Robert J., and John H. Laub. 1997. "A Life-Course Theory of Cumulative Disadvantage and the Stability of Delinquency." In T. P. Thornberry (ed.), *Developmental Theories of Crime and Delinquency*. New Brunswick, NJ: Transaction, pp. 133–161.

Sampson, Robert J., and John H. Laub. 2003. *Crime in the Making: Pathways and Turning Points Through Life*. Cambridge, MA: Harvard University Press.

Sampson, Robert J., Stephen W. Raudenbush, and Felton Earls. 1997. "Neighborhoods and Violent Crime: A Multilevel Study of Collective Efficacy." *Science*, 277 (15 August): 918–924.

Sanders, Clinton R. 1989. *Customizing the Body: The Art and Culture of Tattooing*. Philadelphia: Temple University Press.

Sanders, Edmund. 2011. "Israeli Intolerance Shows up on Internet, in Knesset, on the Street." *The Los Angeles Times*, January 23.

Scambler, Graham, Miriam Heijnders, and Wim H. van Brakel. 2006. "Understanding and Tackling Health-Related Stigma." *Psychology, Health & Medicine*, 11 (August): 269–270.

Scheff, Thomas J. 1966, 1984, 1999. *Being Mentally Ill: A Sociological Theory* (1st, 2nd & 3rd eds.). Chicago: Aldine/New York: Aldine de Gruyter.

Scheff, Thomas J. 2003. "Shame in Self and Society." *Symbolic Interaction*, 28 (2): 239–262.

Schmidt, Michael S., and Joseph Goldstein. 2012. "Killing of Police Continues Rising as Violence Falls." *The New York Times*, April 10, pp. A1, A3.

Schneider, Friedrich. 2012. "Size and Development of the Shadow Economy of 31 European Countries and 5 Other OECD Countries from 2003 to 2012: Some New Facts." Linz, Austria, Kepler University.

Schuck, Amie M., Dennis P. Rosenbaum, and Darnell F. Hawkins. 2008. "The Influence of Race/Ethnicity, Social Class, and Neighborhood Context on Residents' Attitudes Towards the Police." *Police Quarterly*, 11 (December): 496–519.

Schultes, Richard Evans, and Albert Hofmann. 1979. *Plants of the Gods: Origins of Hallucinogenic Use*. New York: Alfred van der Mark Editions.

Schulz, Kathryn. 2012. "What Child Is This? *New York Magazine*, November 19, pp. 74–76.

Schur, Edwin M. 1965. *Crimes without Victims, Deviant Behavior and Public Policy: Abortion, Homosexuality, and Drug Addiction*. Englewood Cliffs, NJ: Prentice-Hall/Spectrum.

Schur, Edwin M. 1971. *Labeling Deviant Behavior: Its Sociological Implications*. New York: Harper & Row.

Schur, Edwin M. 1984. *Labeling Women Deviant: Gender, Stigma, and Social Control*. New York: Random House.

Schwartz, John. 2009. "Vocal Minority Insists It Was All Smoke and Mirrors." *The New York Times*, July 14, p. D8.

Schweik, Susan M. 2009. *The Ugly Laws: Disability in Public*. New York: New York University Press.

Scull, Andrew. 1984. *Decarceration: Community Treatment and the Deviant—A Radical View* (2nd ed.). Cambridge, UK: Polity Press.

Scull, Andrew. 1988. "Deviance and Social Control." In Neil J. Smelser (ed.), *Handbook of Sociology*. Thousand Oaks, CA: Sage, pp. 667–693.

Scully, Diana. 1990. *Understanding Sexual Violence: A Study of Convicted Rapists*. Boston: Unwin Hyman.

Scully, Diana, and Joseph Marolla. 1984. Convicted Rapists' Vocabulary of Motive: Excuses and Justifications." *Social Problems*, 31 (June): 530–544.

Seidman, Louis Michael. 2010. "Hyper-Incarceration and Strategies of Disruption: Is There a Way Out?" Georgetown Public Law and Legal Research Paper No. 10-76.

Sen, Amartya. 2000. "Social Exclusion: Concept, Application, and Scrutiny," Social Development Papers No. 1. Manila: Asian Development Bank.

Severson, Kim. 2012. "Edwards Trial Set to Begin, Reopening a Story of a Derailed Political Career." *The New York Times*, April 22, pp. 17, 22.

Shackleford, Todd K., and Avi Besser. 2007. "Predicting Attitudes toward Homosexuality: Insights from Personality Psychology." *Individual Differences Research*, 5 (2): 106–114.

Shafer, Jack. 2007. "Meth Madness at *Newsweek*." *Slate Magazine*, January 31.

Shaffer, Josh. 2011. "Begging Rules Intensify Humiliation." *Raleigh News and Observer*, December 26.

Shalay, Anne B., and Peter H. Rossi. 1992. "Social Science Research and Contemporary Studies of Homelessness." *Annual Review of Sociology*, 18: 129–160.

Shaw, Clifford R., and Henry R. McKay. 1942. *Juvenile Delinquency in Urban Areas*. Chicago: University of Chicago Press.

Sheehan, Paul. 2009. "Islamophobia is a Fabrication." *Sydney Morning Herald*, March 30.

Sheldon, William H. 1949. *Varieties of Delinquent Youth*. New York: Harpers.

Sheleg, Sergey, and Edwin Ehrlich. 2006. *Autoerotic Asphyxiation: Forensic, Medical, and Social Aspects*. Tucson, AZ: Wheatmark.

Shermer, Michael. 1997. *Why People Believe Weird Things: Pseudoscience, Superstition, and Other Confusions of Our Time*. New York: W.H. Freeman.

Short, James F., Jr. 1990. "Hazards, Risk, and Enterprise: Approaches to Law, Science, and Social Policy." *Law and Society Review*, 24 (1): 179–198.

Siegel, Larry. 2011. *Criminology* (11th ed.). Belmont, CA: Wadsworth.

Silver, Eric, Stacy Rogers Silver, Sonja Siennick, and George Farkas. 2011. "Bodily Signs of Academic Success: An Empirical Examination of Tattoos and Grooming." *Social Problems*, 58 (November): 538–564.

Simon, Jesse, and Jack Zussman. 1983. "The Effect of Contextual Factors on Psychiatrists' Perception of Illness: A Case Study." *Journal of Health and Social Behavior*, 24 (2): 186–198.

Singer, Margaret, and Janja Lalich. 1995. *Cults in Our Midst*. San Francisco: Jossey-Bass.

Skolnick, Jerome. 1966. *Justice without Trial: Law Enforcement in a Democratic Society*. 3rd ed. New York: John Wiley & Sons.

Skolnick, Jerome. 1994. *Justice without Trial: Law Enforcement in a Democratic Society*. 3rd ed. New York: Macmillan.

Slovic, Paul, Baruch Fischoff, and Sarah Lichtenstein. 1980. "Risky Assumptions." *Psychology Today*, June, pp. 44–48.

Slovic, Paul, Mark Layman, and James H. Flynn. 1991. "Risk, Perception, Trust, and Nuclear Waste: Lessons from Yucca Mountain."*Environment*, 33 (April): 28–30.

Smith, Adam. 1776, 1976. *An Inquiry into the Nature and Causes of the Wealth of Nations*. Oxford, UK: Clarendon Press.

Smith, Mary Lee, Gene Glass, and Thomas Miller. 1980. *The Benefits of Psychotherapy*. Baltimore: Johns Hopkins University Press.

Socarides, Charles W. 1968. *The Overt Homosexual*. New York: Grune & Stratton.

Socarides, Charles W. 1978. *The Overt Homosexual* (rev. ed.). New York: Jason Aronson.

Solzhenitisyn, Aleksander. 1994. *The Gulag Archipelago, 1918–1956: An Experiment in Literary Investigation*, vol. 1. New York: Harper & Row.

Solomon, Andrew. 2001. *The Noonday Demon: An Atlas of Depression*. New York: Scribner.

Solomon, Andrew. 2012. *Far From the Tree*. New York: Scribner.

Sommers, Christina Hoff. 1995. "Researching the 'Rape Culture' of America: An Investigation of Feminist Claims about Rape." *The Real Issue*, 14 (September/November): 1–13.

Sorkin, Aaron. 2012. "Infamy in Perpetuity? Astor, Madoff, Spitzer, Weiner." *New York Magazine*, April 9, pp. 66–67.

Spillane, Joseph F. 2000. *Cocaine: From Medical Marvel to Modern Menace in the United States, 1884-1920*. Baltimore, MD: Johns Hopkins University Press.

Spira, Alfred, et al. 1992. "AIDS and Sexual Behavior in France." *Nature*, 360 (3 December): 407–409.

Spira, Alfred, et al. 1993. *Les Comportments Sexuels en France*. Paris: La Documentation Francais.

Spitzer, Robert L. 1975. "On Pseudoscience in Science, Logic in Remission, and Psychiatric Diagnosis: A Critique of Rosenhan's 'On Being Sane in Insane Places.'" *Journal of Abnormal Psychology*, 84 (5): 442–452.

Spitzer, Robert L. 1976. "More on Pseudoscience in Science and the Case for Psychiatric Diagnosis: A Critique of D.L. Rosenhan's 'On Being Sane in Insane Places' and 'The Contextual Nature of Psychiatric Diagnosis.'" *Archives of General Psychiatry*, 33 (April): 459–470.

Srole, Leo. et al. 1962. *Mental Health in the Metropolis: The Midtown Manhattan Study*. New York: McGraw-Hill.

Stark, Rodney, and William Sims Bainbridge. 1996. *Religion, Deviance, and Social Control*. New York & London: Routledge.

Starrin, Bengt. 2002. "Unemployment, Poverty and Shame—Exploring the Field." Norway: Lillehamer University College, unpublished paper.

Stebbins, Robert A. 2011. "Tolerable, Acceptable, and Positive Deviance." In Clifton D. Bryant (ed.), *The Routledge Handbook of Deviant Behavior*. London & New York: Routledge, pp. 24–30.

Stelter, Brian. 2010. "One Comment, Two Takes at NPR and Fox." *The New York Times*, October 22, pp. B1, B7.

Stiglitz, Joseph E. 2013. "Inequality Is Holding Back Recovery." *The New York Times*, January 20, pp. 1SR, 8SR.

Stoller, Robert J., and R. H. Geertsma. 1963. "The Consistency of Psychiatrists' Clinical Judgment." *Journal of Nervous and Mental Disease*, 137 (January): 58–66.

Stormo, Karla J., Alan R. Lang, and Werner G. K. Stritzke. 1997. "Attributions about Acquaintance Rape: The Role of Alcohol and Individual Differences." *Journal of Applied Social Psychology*, 24 (4): 279–305.

Stuber, Jennifer, and Mark Schlesinger. 2006. "Sources of Stigma for Means-Tested Government Programs." *Social Science and Medicine*, 63 (August): 933–945.

Substance Abuse and Mental Health Services Administration. 2007. "Results from the 2006 National Survey on Drug Use and Health: Summary of National Findings." Rockville, MD: SAMHSA.

Substance Abuse and Mental Health Services Administration. 2008. "Results from the 2007 National Survey on Drug Use and Health: Summary of National Findings." Rockville, MD: SAMHSA.

Substance Abuse and Mental Health Services Administration. 2011. "Results from the 2010 National Survey on Drug Use and Health: Summary of National Findings," NSDUH Series H-41, HHS Publication No. (SMA) 11-4658. Rockville, MD: SAMHSA. (Including detailed tables.)

Substance Abuse and Mental Health Services Administration. 2012. "Results from the 2011 National Survey on Drug Use and Health: Summary of National Findings." Rockville, MD: SAMHSA.

Summers, Anne. 1981. "Hidden from History: Women Victims of Crime." In Satyanshu K. Mukerjee and Jocelynne A. Scutt (eds.), *Women in Crime*. North Sydney, Australia: George Allen & Unwin, pp. 22–30.

Sumner, Colin. 1994. *The Sociology of Deviance: An Obituary*. Buckingham, UK: Open University Press.

Sutherland, Edwin H. 1939. *Principles of Criminology* (3th ed.). Philadelphia: Lippincott.

Sutherland, Edwin H. 1940. "White-Collar Criminality." *American Sociological Review*, 5 (February): 1–12.

Sutherland, Edwin H. 1949. *White Collar Crime*. New York: Dryden Press.

Sutherland, Edwin H. 1956. "Crimes of Corporations." In Albert K. Cohen, Alfred Lindesmith, and Karl Schuessler (eds.), *The Sutherland Papers*. Bloomington: Indiana University Press.

Sutherland, Edwin H. 1961. *White Collar Crime*. New York: Holt, Rinehart & Winston.

Sutherland, Edwin H. 1983. *White Collar Crime: The Uncut Version*. New Haven, CT: Yale University Press.

Takahashi, Lois M. 1997. "The Socio-Spatial Stigmatization of Homeless and HIV/AIDS: Toward an Explanation of the NIMBY Syndrome." *Social Science and Medicine*, 45 (6): 903–914.

Tannenbaum, Frank. 1938. *Crime and the Community*. New York: Ginn.

Tausig, Mark. 2007. "Mental Disorder." In George Ritzer (ed.), *The Blackwell Encyclopedia of Sociology*. Malden, MA & Oxford, UK: Blackwell, pp. 2951–2954.

Tausig, Mark, Janet Michello, and Sree Subedi. 2004. *A Sociology of Mental Illness* (2nd ed.). Upper Saddle River, NJ: Prentice Hall.

Tavernise, Sabrina. 2011. "Poor Dropping Further Behind Rich in School." *The New York Times*, February 10, pp. A1, A3.

Tavernise, Sabrina. 2012. "Gay Prosecutor Is Denied Virginia Judgeship Despite Bipartisan Support." *The New York Times*, May 16, pp. A15, A16.

Taylor, Bruce M. 1997. "Changes in Criminal Victimization, 1994-95," Bureau of Justice Statistics Publication No. NCJ-162032, National Crime Victimization Survey, April, pp. 1–14.

Taylor, Ian, Paul Walton, and Jock Young. 1973. *The New Criminology: For a Social Theory of Deviance*. London: Routledge & Kegan Paul.

Taylor, Ian, Paul Walton, and Jock Young (eds.). 1975. *Critical Criminology*. London: Routledge & Kegan Paul.

Terry, Jennifer, and Jacqueline Urla (eds.). 1995. *Deviant Bodies: Critical Perspectives on Difference in Science and Popular Culture*. Bloomington: Indiana University Press.

Testa, Maria. 2004. "The Role of Substance Use in Male-to-Female Physical and Sexual Violence." *Journal of Interpersonal Violence*, 19 (December): 1494–1505.

Thoits, Peggy. 1985. "Self-Labeling Processes in Mental Illnesses: The Role of Emotional Distance." *American Journal of Sociology*, 91 (September): 221–249.

Tierney, John. 2012. "For Lesser Crimes, Rethinking Life Behind Bars." *The New York Times*, December 12, pp. A1, A28–A29.

Tierney, John. 2013. "Prison and the Poverty Trap." *The New York Times*, February 19, pp. D1, D6–D7.

Tillyer, Marie Skubak. 2011. "Routine Activities Theory and Rational Choice Theory." In Clifton D. Bryant (ed.), *The Routledge Handbook of Deviant Behavior*. London & New York: Routledge, pp. 143–149.

Tjaden, Patricia, and Nancy Thoennes. 2006. *Extent, Nature, and Consequences of Rape Victimization: Findings from the National Violence Against Women Survey*. Washington, DC: U.S. Government Printing Office.

Toby, Jackson. 1957. "Social Disorganization and Stake in Conformity: Complementary Factors in the Predatory Behavior of Hoodlums." *Journal of Criminal Law, Criminology, and Police Science*, 48 (1): 17–19.

Tong, Rosemarie. 2009. *Feminist Thought: A More Comprehensive Introduction*. Boulder, CO: Westview Press.

Tonry, Michael 2011. *Punishing Race: A Continuing American Dilemma*. New York & Oxford, UK: Oxford University Press.

Torrey, E. Fuller, Anne E. Bowler, Edward H. Taylor, and Irving I. Gottesman. 1994. *Schizophrenia and Manic Depressive Disorder: The Biological Roots of Mental Illness as Revealed by the Landmark Study of Identical Twins*. New York: Basic Books.

Torrey, E. Fuller, et al. 2010. "More Mentally Ill Persons Are in Jails and Prisons Than Hospitals: A Survey of the States." Arlington, VA: Treatment Advocacy Center; Arlington, VA: National Sherriff's Association.

Toufexis, Anastasia. 1991. "Innocent Victims." *Time*, May 13, pp. 56–60.

Townsend, John Marshall. 1978. *Cultural Conceptions of Mental Illness*. Chicago: University of Chicago Press.

Townsend, John Marshall. 1980. "Psychiatry Versus Societal Reaction: A Critical Analysis." *Journal of Health and Social Behavior*, 21 (September): 268–278.

Tracy, Paul E., Marvin E. Wolfgang, and Robert M. Figlio. 1990. *Delinquency in Two Birth Cohorts*. New York: Plenum Press.

Trager, Eric. 2011. "Why the Middle East Is Still in Thrall to 9/11 Conspiracy Theories." *The New Republic*, September 3.

Traub, Stuart H., and Craig B. Little (eds.). 1999. *Theories of Deviance* (5th ed.). Itasca, IL: Peacock.

Truman, Jennifer L., and Michael Planty. 2012. "Criminal Victimization, 2011." *Bureau of Justice Statistics Bulletin*, October, pp. 1–19.

Turk, Austin T. 1969. *Criminality and the Legal Order*. Chicago: Rand McNally.

Turley, Jonathan. 2010. "Adultery, in Many States, Is Still a Crime." *USA Today*, April 20.

Turner, Ronny E., and Charles Edgley. 1983. "From Witchcraft to Drugcraft: Biochemistry as Mythology." *Social Science Journal*, 20 (October): 1–12.

Turner, R. Jay, and John W. Gartrell. 1978. "Social Factors in Psychiatric Outcome: Toward a Resolution of Interpretive Controversies." *American Sociological Review*, 43 (June): 368–382.

Twaddle, Andrew. 1973. "Illness and Deviance." *Social Science and Medicine*, 7 (October): 751–762.

Uggen, Christopher, and Jeff Manza. 2006. *Locked Out: Felon Disenfranchisement and American Democracy*. New York: Oxford University Press.

Ullman, Sarah E., George Karabatsos, and Mary P. Koss. 1999. "Alcohol and Sexual Assault in a National Sample of College Women." *Journal of Interpersonal Violence*, 16 (June): 603–625.

Ungar, Sanford J. 2012. "Leopold's Ghost." *New York Magazine*, July 30, pp. 38–43, 87.

Unnever, James D. 1987. Review of James M. Byrne and Robert J. Sampson (eds.), *The Social Ecology of Crime*. New York: Springer-Verlag, 1986, in *Contemporary Sociology*, 16 (November): 845–846.

Vold, George Bryant, Thomas J. Bernard, and Alexander L. Gerould. 2009. *Theoretical Criminology* (6th ed.). New York: Oxford University Press.

Wacquant, Loïc. 2008. *Urban Outcasts: A Comparative Sociology of Advanced Marginality*. New York: Polity Press.

Wallechensky, David, and Irving Wallace. 1975. *The People's Almanac*. Garden City, NY: Doubleday.

Walsh, Declan, and Salman Masood. 2012. "Christian Girl's Blasphemy Arrest Incites a Furor in Pakistan." *The New York Times*, August 21, p. A4.

Wanberg, Connie R. 2012. "The Individual Experience of Unemployment." *Annual Review of Psychology*, 63 (January): 369–396.

Warheit, George J., Charles E. Holzer III, Roger A. Bell, and Sandra A. Avery. 1976. "Sex, Marital Status, and Mental Health: A Reappraisal." *Social Forces*, 55 (December): 459–470.

Warren, Carol A.B., and John M. Johnson. 1972. "A Critique of Labeling Theory from the Phenomenological Perspective." In Robert A. Scott and Jack D. Douglas (eds.), *Theoretical Perspectives on Deviance*. New York: Basic Books, pp. 69–92.

Weber, Max. 1946. *From Max Weber: Essays in Sociology* (trans. & eds. Hans H. Gerth and C. Wright Mills). New York: Oxford University Press.

Weber, Max. 1963. *The Sociology of Religion* (trans. Ephraim Fischoff). Boston: Beacon Press (orig. pub. 1922).

Webman, Esther. 2011. "Adoption of the Protocols in the Arab Discourse on the Arab- Israeli Conflict, Zionism, and the Jews." In *The Global Impact of The Protocols of the Elders of Zion: A Century-Old Myth.* London & New York: Routledge, pp. 175–195.

Webster, Richard. 1995. *Why Freud Was Wrong: Sin, Science, and Psychoanalysis.* New York: Basic Books.

Weisburd, David, Stanton Wheeler, Elin Warning, and Nancy Bode. 1991. *Crimes of the Middle Classes: White-Collar Offenders in the Federal Courts.* New Haven, CN: Yale University Press.

Weitzer, Ronald (ed.). 2000. *Sex for Sale: Prostitution, Pornography, and the Sex Industry.* New York & London: Routledge.

Wellings, Kaye, Julia Field, Anne Johnson, and Jane Wadsworth. 1994. *Sexual Behavior in Britain: The National Survey of Sexual Attitudes and Lifestyles.* New York: Penguin.

Wells, Jonathan. 2000. *The Icons of Evolution.* Washington, DC: Regnery.

West, Brad. 2003. "Synergies in Deviance: Revisiting the Positive Deviance Debate." *Electronic Journal of Sociology,* 7 (4). http://www.sociology.org/content/vol7.4/west.html

Western, Bruce. 2006. *Punishment and Inequality in America.* New York: Russell Sage Foundation Press.

Wheeler, Stanton. 1960. "Sex Offenses: A Sociological Critique." *Law and Contemporary Society,* 25 (Spring): 258–278.

White, Rob. 2011. "Marxist and Critical Theory." In Clifton D. Bryant (ed.), *The Routledge Handbook of Deviance.* London & New York: Routledge, pp. 150–156.

Wilders, Geert. 2012. *Marked for Death: Islam's War Against the West and Me* (Kindle Edition). Washington, DC: Regnery.

Wilkins, Leslie T. 1964. *Social Deviance: Social Policy, Action, and Research.* London: Tavistock.

Wilkinson, Gregg S. 1975. "Patient-Audience Social Status and the Social Construction of Psychiatric Disorder: Toward a Differential Frame of Referential Hypothesis." *Journal of Health and Social Behavior,* 16 (March): 28–38.

Williams, Joyce E., and Willard A. Nielson, Jr. 1979. "The Rapist Looks at His Crime." *Free Inquiry into Creative Sociology,* 7 (November): 128–132.

Wilper, Andrew P., et al., 2009. "Illness Is Often Undiscovered and Untreated Among the Uninsured." *Physicians for a National Health Program,* October 19.

Wish, Eric D. 1995. "The Drug Use Forecasting (DUF) Program." In Jerome H. Jaffe (ed.), *Encyclopedia of Drugs and Alcohol.* New York: Simon & Schuster/Macmillan, pp. 432–434.

Wolfe, Linda. 1976. *Playing Around: Women and Extramarital Sex.* New York: New American Library/Signet.

Wood, Daniel B. 2012. "Poll Shows Strong Support for Legal Marijuana: Is it Inevitable?" *The Christian Science Monitor,* May 23.

Wright, Charles. 1984. *Constructions of Deviance in Sociological Theory: The Problem of Commensurability.* Lanham, MD: University Press of America.

Wright, Susan E. 1993. "Blaming the Victim, Blaming Society or Blaming the Discipline: Fixing Responsibility for Poverty and Homelessness." *The Sociological Quarterly,* 34 (1): 1–16.

Yacoubian, George S., Jr. 2000. "Assessing ADAM's Domain: Past Problems and Future Prospects." *Contemporary Drug Problems,* 2 (Spring): 121–135.

Yardley, Jim. 2012. "A Village Rape Shatters a Family, and India's Traditional Silence." *The New York Times,* October 28, pp. 1, 12.

Young, Robert, Helen Sweeting, and Patrick West. 2008. "A Longitudinal Study of Alcohol Use and Antisocial Behaviour in Young People." *Alcohol and Alcoholism,* 43 (October): 204–214.

Young, Stanley. 1989. "'Zing!' Speed: The Choice of a New Generation." *Spin Magazine,* July, pp. 83–84, 124–125.

Zawadski, Bohan, and Paul Lazarsfeld. 1935. "The Psychological Consequences of Unemployment." *Journal of Social Psychology,* 6 (May): 224–251.

Zawitz, Marianne W., et al. 1993. *Highlights from 20 Years of Surveying Crime Victims: The National Crime Victimization Survey, 1973-92.* Washington, DC: U.S. Department of Justice, Bureau of Justice Statistics.

Zimring, Franklin E. 2007. *The Great American Crime Decline.* Oxford, UK & New York: Oxford University Press.

Author Index

Subject Index